THE PRICE
OF PARADISE

Praise for *Gun Baby Gun* by Iain Overton

'A brilliantly researched journey, capturing the gun's strangely
accepted place in human life and, far too often, death'
Jon Snow

'Adventurous . . . thoughtful . . . contains
moments of great poignancy'
Financial Times

'A gripping book that's as disturbing as it is enlightening'
GQ

'A shocking book about the realities of war and weapons'
Scotland's *Sunday Mail*

'Relentlessly engrossing'
Spectator

'Shocking . . . Overton has supped full of horrors
and is not reticent about sharing them'
Newsweek

'One of the most thought-provoking books
you'll read this year'
National

THE
PRICE
OF
PARADISE

How the Suicide Bomber
Shaped the Modern Age

IAIN OVERTON

Quercus

First published in Great Britain in 2019 by

Quercus Editions Ltd
Carmelite House
50 Victoria Embankment
London EC4Y 0DZ

An Hachette UK company

A CIP catalogue record for this book is available
from the British Library

HB ISBN 978 1 78747 085 9
TPB ISBN 978 1 78747 086 6
Ebook ISBN 978 1 78747 088 0

10 9 8 7 6 5 4 3 2

Author photo by Iain Overton

Typeset by CC Book Production

Printed and bound in the UK by Clays Ltd, Elcograf S.p.A.

For my parents

Contents

Prologue

We live in the age of the suicide bomber.

Today, their threat looms over our cities and our families, from Brussels to Baghdad, Cairo to Kabul, London to Lahore; whether it was the 9/11 attacks or the crises that continue to engulf the Middle East, bombings in the heart of Europe, or assaults on Muslims the world over, the suicide bomber has become a defining feature of the modern era. A symbol, to some, of unbridled inhumanity, to others of the ultimate sacrifice, it is a form of violence that has changed the world.

Suicide bombers are the real weapons of mass destruction. In total, since the first suicide bomber killed the Tsar of Russia in 1881, this weapon has ended the lives of over 72,000 people and injured at least twice that, many of them in the last decade.[1] Such attacks have proved more harmful than many air strikes, have been able to kill more in one explosion than any gun massacre has ever done, and have triggered military counter-responses that, almost inevitably, have proved more lethal than the threat they set out to defeat.[2]

They are also on the rise. Of the ten worst explosive incidents the world has witnessed between 2011 and 2018, seven were by suicide bombers. Putting it in another way, in 1976 there were no suicide bombs anywhere in the world. Forty years later, 2016 saw twenty-eight countries witnessing 469 attacks.

This 'weapon of the weak' has invoked terror like none other – helping level the field of battle and challenge militaries to their core. Used against civilians and occupying forces alike, suicide attacks have shown themselves to be cheap, brutally effective and terrifyingly unexpected. And they have been profoundly impactful: they, and the inevitable counter-attacks, have fuelled the creation of fortresses Europe and America, helped destabilise entire nations, justified the passing of laws that endanger our civil liberties, while all the time fanning the flames of a seemingly endless 'War on Terror'.

How did this weapon gain such a hold over us? How did it get to the point that teenagers in Manchester or Paris are being targeted at concerts and football matches? How is it that we now read, on a weekly basis, about suicide attacks killing dozens of civilians in this country or that? And why are so many people willing to put on a bomber's vest, convinced their murderous death would usher in a brave new world?

Such questions have led me to write this book. It is an attempt to unpick what has driven the suicide bomber's violent rise, to trace the roots of this terrible weapon and, ultimately, to capture what has been born in the ensuing mayhem. In so doing it aims to chart how, by fighting fire with fire, we have risked setting the whole world ablaze.

It is a search that has led me around the world: to interview failed suicide bombers, to sit with still-grieving families, to listen to victims racked with pain. It is one driven by an ambition, of sorts, to walk in the same footsteps of men and women walking their last steps to 'martyrdom'; to listen to those who would wage holy war; and to speak to those who would stop them. It has found me visiting memorials and sites of massacres, radical mosques and belligerent militaries – all the while trying to remember how this violent epoch of the suicide bomber was born and what can be done – what must be done – to stop it.

The trigger to write this book came in early November 2015. On a Geneva day that was swiftly fading into night, I found myself talking to a room of United Nations diplomats about suicide attacks. In my concluding words I said: 'It is not if but when there will be a suicide strike at the very heart of a European city.' Less than a week later 130 people were killed in Paris as 7 terrorists, armed with guns and suicide vests, wreaked havoc upon stadiums, concerts, cafés and restaurants. And in reading the reams of news that came out about that attack, I realised that I did not fully understand what paths had led these men to kill in such a terrible and random way. This book was a personal journey to find greater illumination to that darkness.

Certainly, there is darkness. When you sit down and look at the raw data, it is easy just to see hard numbers. There have been over 13,500 recorded suicide attacks since their first use.[3] Where known, well over 90 per cent of these attackers were men, and nine-tenths of their victims were men also.[4] Fifty-five countries have suffered from a bombing, with about a quarter of a million people harmed along the way. Iraq has been by far the worst impacted, followed by Afghanistan, Pakistan, Syria and Nigeria. The bombings are perpetrated mainly by those heralding a warped vision of Islam – with ISIS, the Taliban, Al-Qaeda and Boko Haram the most persistent proponents in the modern age.

Patterns emerge from those figures, such as in the ingenious ways the suicide bomb has been deployed. There is always the suicide vest – webbing belts filled with explosives, usually worn by boys or men with either fear in their eyes, or the burning fires of faith, but there are many other ways that death is delivered. There have been underpants stuffed with explosive materials, and shoes designed to be set alight on transatlantic flights. There have been cars laden with explosives, welded with enormous sheets of iron so they look like metal rhinos, driven headlong into checkpoints and markets. Then there are the motorbikes, planes, submarines, even donkeys, that have all borne bombers to their believed nirvana in an explosive flash of flesh and muscle. The most lethal method of delivery of all has been the aeroplane – suicide attacks that have killed, on average, 745 people in each deadly fireball.

Other figures stand out. The youngest suicide bomber has been just four years old – barely strong enough to carry the lethal burden strapped to him.[5] The oldest was a seventy-two-year-old Japanese man.[6] Some bombers have been 'lone wolves' acting without much guidance; others have gone to their deaths as whole families. Some bombers have been profoundly disabled, lifted into the driving seat of a car for their final mission. Some have been high on drugs, babbling incoherently. Others have been terrified, their last moment filmed with them in tears or laughing hysterically. And some seem as steady as the grave.

Their numbers have been made up of Muslims, Buddhists, Christians, Shintoists and Hindus (and one Jewish bomber whose bomb didn't detonate), and they come from all different nations. A recent batch of leaked intelligence data – a cache of recruitment files for ISIS volunteers – showed at least two dozen different nationalities agreeing to join the terror group's 'martyrdom' battalion.

Their motivations have been diverse and complex. A collection of group beliefs has compelled the suicide bomber onwards: utopianism, militarism, nationalism, apocalypticism, to name just some. They all speak of the tyrannies of teleology – their belief that the suicide bomber's act will propel them towards a better place. But suicide attacks have also been driven by a myriad of individual motivations, too – men and women who have blown themselves up with minds full of ideas unique to no faith or creed. Loners seeking meaning, angry men bent on revenge, conspiracy theorists, the sexually frustrated, the mentally ill, the drug addicts – all finding an end to their private, inner hells in one way or another.

What is clearer is that suicide attacks, and our responses to them, have been central to the formation of the modern age. They helped create the conditions that caused the Russian Revolution; they were in the forefront of the minds of men who created a nuclear epoch and, unwittingly, the Cold War that followed; they were there at the beginning of the War on Terror that still dominates our headlines; and they have helped drag the Middle East into the quagmire that it is today. In so doing, they have fuelled fears about migrants and refugees the world over, they have challenged the UN to its very core, and they have fed off conspiracy theories, post-truth propaganda and a view that the world is witnessing a millenarian clash of civilisations that heralds the end of days.

Such influences inspired the title of this book – *The Price of Paradise*. It refers to the acceptance of death as the price of a bombing; how a suicide attack is perceived as the best way – even the only way – to defeat the enemy and to usher in a new, peaceful age on earth; how a suicide attack is seen to offer the martyr access to paradise in their next life as a reward for their actions. But it refers to another price as well. How man's responses to these attacks have been more violent, more destructive, than the deeds themselves; and how in that overstep, we have ended up doubly paying for the martyr's act in many hidden and unexpected ways.

It is the combination of these two prices that I have tried to capture within this book – for such a mixture has proved not just terrifyingly lethal, but transformative too; not just destroying countless lives but shaping the modern world as we know it.

Chapter 1

Utopia's Weapon

The 1st of March 1881 was a Sunday. Snow lay heaped upon St Petersburg's roofs and along the city's streets, muffling the sound of the carriages. Tsar Alexander II – the Emperor of Russia, King of Poland and Grand Duke of Finland – was on his way back from reviewing his Imperial Horse Guards on St Isaac's Square. The mounted troops had been on fine form.

He was in a beautifully decorated, closed, iron-clad carriage – the height of fashion, a gift from Napoleon II. But one thing stood out about this particular fairy-tale transport: it was bulletproof. This was for good reason. In 1870, a revolutionary group called the People's Will (Narodnaya Volya) had ordered their monarch's assassination. By that first day in March, the Tsar had already survived seven assassination bids, but on that morning, as he rode under Russia's pewter clouds, the Tsar was confident the threat against his life was on the wane: a leading figure of the People's Will had been arrested the previous afternoon; he was in a secure coach; and beside him rode six Cossacks, with a seventh sitting beside the coachman. Instead of fear, the sixty-three-year-old Tsar felt only life – he had said to his friends just the day before that he was filled with an energy that surprised even him.

To some degree, he was right to feel luck's hand upon him. The revolutionaries had sought to kill him that day with a massive bomb, hiring out a cheese shop to tunnel their way deep beneath a St Petersburg street, and had filled their excavation with dynamite, designed to blow up the Tsar as he took his usual route home. But Alexander had spontaneously decided to pay his cousin a visit, and his change of plans meant he avoided the seventh attempt on his life.

But, as luck has a habit of doing, his was fast running out. As he was exchanging family gossip, three members of the People's Will were busy preparing their next attempt on the Tsar's life. Altering their plans in line with the Tsar's new route, they arrived at a spot now filled with onlookers and joined the expectant throng lining the pavement. One of the rebels was Nikolai Ivanovich Rysakov, a swarthy twenty-year-old with thick features and dark, deep-set eyes. Under his arm he carried a small white package wrapped in a handkerchief – a home-made bomb. And, as the Tsar's carriage came around the corner, he took a decision that set in motion a chain of events that was to leave five people dead that day.

'After a moment's hesitation,' Rysakov said later, 'I threw the bomb. I sent it under the horses' hooves . . . The explosion knocked me into the fence.' A spray of snow, earth and metal splinters fanned out from where the bomb landed, and blue smoke filled the air. The blast tore into a young boy and one of the Cossacks, fatally wounding them and severely harming the carriage driver and several others.

The floor and rear end of the royal carriage were shattered, the windowpanes reduced to jagged glass, but – incredibly – the Emperor was alive. Eight times lucky, he had suffered just a slight cut on one of his hands. Getting down from the vehicle, he crossed himself and asked if his would-be assassin had been captured. Rysakov was already under arrest, and the Tsar saw one of the soldiers smacking the captive hard across the face. Another officer urged his emperor to leave the area at once, but Alexander, a man whose territories ran from the Arctic Ocean in the north to the Black Sea in the south, from the Baltic Sea to the west to the Pacific Ocean to the east, was not used to being given orders, and chose instead to check on the health of the injured and inspect his carriage. An eyewitness later recalled seeing his Tsar wag a threatening finger at his assailant.

Such dallying was to prove fatal. A second member of the group, Ignaty Grinevitsky, had manoeuvred into place. Seeing the Tsar standing among the smoking ruins, he acted. 'It is too early to thank God,' he shouted and threw a second bomb at the Tsar's feet.

'I was deafened by the new explosion, burned, wounded and thrown to the ground . . .' the Chief of Police, Dvorzhitsky, was to write, 'His Majesty was half-lying, half-sitting, leaning on his right arm. I tried to lift him but the Tsar's legs were shattered, and the blood poured out of them.'

The smoke cleared and there, upon the dirty snow, lay the Tsar; his legs were splintered below the knee, his stomach ripped open, his face mutilated. A loyal subject lay to one side, dying, and on the other side lay Grinevitsky, gravely wounded and unconscious. In a blur of action, Alexander was carried by sleigh to the Winter Palace to his study where, twenty years before almost to the day, he had signed the Emancipation Edict that gave Russia's serfs their freedom. As his family hurried to his side, the dying Tsar was given the last rites. When the attending physician was asked how much time the Emperor had left, his reply was a cold 'fifteen minutes'. At 3.30 in the afternoon, the standard of Alexander II was lowered for the last time.

His murderer, Grinevitsky, who had been carried to the infirmary attached to the Palace, regained consciousness a few hours later. However, he did not live to see midnight, having refused to disclose even his name.

The world's first suicide bomber, and his victim – the most powerful man in all of Russia – were both dead. Terror had taken on a new and deadly form; the suicide bomber was to be born and to die in the same moment and the world, in a sense, was to change for ever.

Tsar Alexander II's shredded coat, now in the Hermitage Museum in St Petersburg

I had been walking for miles.

My journey to St Petersburg was with purpose – to visit the spot where Alexander II was blown up. Why, I wanted to know, had the world's first suicide bomb assassination emerged here? What was it about the Russian spirit of the age that led to that particular form of murder?

As I walked, the city slowly revealed itself. In a sense, this city's skyline helped me comprehend a little bit more Russia's violent past, explaining why such brutality was to visit these streets. Here, in St Petersburg, the stamp of Mother Russia was not on grand display. If anything, I saw the architecture of France on steroids. Peter the Great's fervour to raise a city that would rival Paris was clearly evident, but in her endless streets grace had been replaced with size, as if through magnitude alone the Emperor's point about civilisation could be made. The neoclassical colonnades of this huge palace, the grand arch of that heavy monument – these forms revealed hidden battles of identity and culture. The buildings that were built here were exclamation marks about Russian progress, rendered in stone.

But Russia's monarch did more than just import French architecture to their most European city. The thousands of French perfumers, tailors, hairdressers, actors and restaurateurs who came to live here brought their way of life with them. Traces of these remain; St Petersburg's State Hermitage holds the most extensive collection of French art outside France, while the Russian National Library stores two French collections: the archive of the Bastille,[1] rescued during the French revolution, and Voltaire's library of over 7,000 books.

These buildings and these books, these expats and their expectations, all had impact. The influence of France turned the theories of the French Enlightenment into something more than just ideas in Russia – they became physical. They became revolution. And at the heart of that revolution lay philosophies about the freedom of the individual, one where the imperial shackles of social, political and religious dogma were seen clearly, and where the call for them to be shaken off was heard loudly.[2] In those books were found ideas that set some on a path to that first suicide attack.

When, in 1789, the French Revolution abolished feudalism, established a republic and executed their king, they showed the world the merits, and the horrors, of a Reign of Terror, alongside that of a Reign of Virtue.[3] France became a country where anyone opposing her bright new principles was executed in an 'attempt to close, once and for all, the gap between human nature and human aspirations.'[4] And what was born in the murder of some 40,000 citizens was the notion that a fair society could only be achieved through a brutal shaping of human behaviour.[5]

It was proof to many, including the Russians who set out to kill their Tsar here in 1881, that revolutions demand sacrifice and death.

Over time, terrorism began to be seen by groups such as the People's Will as a 'cost-effective' form of struggle – it was even an ethical choice, given the alternative. Those nineteenth-century Russian revolutionaries had read their history: they knew the terrible depths the French Revolution had sunk to, killing even those that had kindled the flame of revolt. To the People's Will, decapitating the

Russian Bear by killing their Tsar was far better than the carnage of mass insurrection, or the repeated swish of the guillotine. Assassination was, in this sense, limited. Even humane.

Today, the canal-way leading to where that assassination took place is lined with black-sided stalls, where merchants sell their goods to slow-moving lines of tourists. Here are the icons of Russia's heart and soul ready for sale, and they pointed to themes that, to me, clarified why the Tsar had been murdered here over a century ago.[6]

The most popular items were, by far, brightly painted matryoshka dolls – row upon row of them. I stopped and picked one up: it was that typical peasant figurine that separated, top from bottom, revealing a smaller figure of the same sort inside. This gauche doll spoke of the continuity of the Russian peasantry, a nineteenth-century design that seemed to romanticise the rural poor in an unsubtle way. The truth was that those peasants – the muzhiks – were far from smiling and polished. Making up over 85 per cent of the population, under Alexander II they were forced to eke out basic, hard lives in one-room wooden huts with earthen floors. They slept next to pigs and goats, ate bread and cabbage soup, and drank vodka. Theirs was not the easy life suggested by the dolls' benign smile. Overpopulation and economic stagnation, along with ancient farming methods, meant the typical peasant at the time of the Tsar's death was worked hard unto death – forced to supplement their farming work as hired hands, or by selling home-made nails, sacking or cutlery, to whomever they could.[7]

Change, though, was in the wind. Poor, but not poor enough to starve, downtrodden, but not so downtrodden they lacked a voice, these peasants were, by the 1880s, increasingly exposed to the rush of the modern. Railways meant Russia's provinces were opening up to trade and, inevitably, modern political ideas followed in the wake of train engines' vapour. Discontent came close behind.

The wretched condition of the Russian peasantry was matched

only by the lives of the growing number of industrial workers. While their parents were born into serfdom, these men and women found themselves uprooted from villages and crowded into squalid factory dormitories. They were to suffer the most from modernity's progress: brutalised by martinet factory foremen, impoverished by pittance wages, their sense of injustice suffocated by the absence of legal redress, theirs was, ultimately, the tinderbox of revolution.

The stage was set. The spark for revolt, though, came from the educated poor. University students whose lives were marked by dreary lodgings and debt were the ones most embittered by the injustices of the Russian Tsar's regime, and most disheartened by the prospect of a minor post in the bureaucratic machine. The People's Will, then, were neither peasants nor workers, rather a group of middle-class children, often young students who no longer had the assurance of an income and whose heads were filled with ideas from Europe and America.

Those intellectuals' call to overthrow the state was on behalf of those peasants, whose icons now line the tourist shelves. As with so many revolutions, it was the educated elite that had taken it upon themselves to burn down a despotic regime for the benefit, as they saw it, of 'a vast and inert mass of the ignorant and misled common people'.[8]

It would be too much to say I saw all this in such sentimental dolls, but the living history that revealed the cultural foundations of the People's Will seemed present in these stalls. The stand next door mainly sold paintings and photographs, but above a picture of Pushkin doffing his cap to a cat stood a small row of books. There was a copy of Karl Marx's *Das Kapital* – another marker from history. This book had been published in Russia in 1868, and had a far greater influence here 'than in any other country'.[9] It affected radicals enormously in St Petersburg, causing them to embrace Marx's call 'to carry out their terroristic phrases'.[10] Beside it stood a red-backed copy of Dostoyevsky's *Crime and Punishment*, a book that explored the idea Russian society had allowed certain crimes to be admissible, while letting corrupt materialism run rampant.[11]

These books spoke of how the spread of ideas in nineteenth-century Russia was potently impacted by rising levels of literacy. In the middle of the century, about one in five Russian men could read and write; by the turn of the century almost half could.[12] Such literacy was sufficient to fill the heads of young, angry men and women with powerful ideas, but – crucially – was not enough to start a mass insurrection. The realisation that words alone were never going to transform their world led a French anti-parliamentarian, Paul Brousse, to argue that newspapers or pamphlets were of limited use. The ideas in them would be countered by the 'lies' of the bourgeois press and the political classes. The downtrodden masses, he thought, had little time for such intellectual debates. What was required was a thing that could not be ignored, but would awaken the conscious-ness of the masses. Brousse called it 'propaganda by deed', to others it became just 'terrorism'.[13]

Peter Kropotkin, a leading Russian anarchist in the 1870s, took Brousse's theory and ran with it. He argued that 'propaganda by deed' had to take the form of constant agitation by any means, including guns and bombs. Individual terror, he thought, would rouse the spirit of revolt.[14] In all of this, political assassination was the best weapon of all: the future might be for the revolt of the masses, but individual acts of terror had to light the way. It led some of the 'intelligentsia' to believe in terror 'like in God'.[15] One of them was Mikhail Bakunin, the co-author of a book that was to deeply influence the People's Will called *The Revolutionary Catechism*.[16] Published in 1869, it was an angry call for sacrifice and change, stressing the need for revolution-aries to harden their hearts.

'Tyrannical toward himself, [the Revolutionary] must be tyran-nical toward others,' Bakunin entreated, 'Night and day he must have but one thought, one aim – merciless destruction . . .' The hero of the book was a nameless soldier sacrificed at the altar of the political ideal.

Bakunin certainly lived up to the revolutionary cliché. He was a brooding, glass-eyed man, but with a thick beard and even thicker waist. A headstrong revolutionary orator – sepia photographs show him with undone waistcoats, stained jackets and bloated features – he resembled a dishevelled Karl Marx. In Russia, Bakunin said, only a 'revolutionary abyss' could provide 'the liberation and deliverance of our poor martyred people'.[17]

He provided a clarion call for the spirit of the age and, soon enough, Russian terror organisations began sprouting up. One, pre-dating the People's Will, called itself 'Hell'.[18] Its members were committed to assassinating the Tsar and discussed how they would draw lots to choose the martyr who would do the job. That person would forgo partners or friends, take on an assumed name, and, on the morning of the murder, would stand and pour chemicals onto their face to stop people recognising them. Then, once the assassination had been carried out, they would swallow poison.

While 'Hell' never carried out their plans, the notion of suicidal terrorism had been established.[19] In 1876, a group called Land and Liberty was formed. Many of its members shared both Bakunin's and 'Hell's' views and, meeting in private, they formed committees and wrote manifestos demanding that Russia's land be handed over to the peasants and that the state be destroyed. How they were to go about securing such requests though – through violence or peaceful political means – was, ultimately, to split them. By 1879, the majority group, favouring a policy of terrorism, broke away and established the People's Will.

This new group upped the ante. They began to demand universal suffrage and political liberties. They threatened to kill anyone who informed on them.[20] Ostensibly led by Andrei Zhelyabov, a man with a magnetic personality, the People's Will grew bolder, their focus intensified on the assassination of the Tsar, a singular passion that ultimately led to their treacherous attack on Alexander II in 1881.

Passing more stalls, more dolls, more radical books, I reached the spot where the People's Will eventually carried out their strike, and stopped to photograph the scene. Here, on the wet cobblestones where the Tsar had lain dying, now stood a soaring monument to the fallen Emperor. The Church of the Saviour on the Spilled Blood is St Petersburg's most elaborate and nationalistic building. It rises high above the milling crowds and fills the space between the austere five-floored apartment blocks to its left and the Mikhailovsky Gardens to the right. Officially called the Cathedral of the Resurrection of Christ, it took over two decades to build, and went over budget by one million roubles – a fortune at the time.

The Church on Spilled Blood in St Petersburg –
the site of the world's first suicide bombing

It is as Russian as they come: an explicit rejection of French styles with an elaborate exterior, topped by nine onion domes and *kokoshnik* peasant-hat gables in gold and emerald and cerulean, it is a riot of gilding and enamelling. Coats of arms, each representing the provinces, regions and towns of Alexander II's empire, circle the building. Along its front runs a line of red granite plaques that record the main events of Alexander's reign. They were an attempt to portray the Tsar as a forward-thinking, modern monarch, but, walking counter-clockwise, they revealed more the efforts of the Tsar to hold on to his power than a philosophy born from the brother-hood of man.

This was a dictated history lesson in stone. Russia's humiliating defeat in 1851 in the Crimean War had been an immense shock to the royal family; without a strong army they feared that the winds of revolution that had swept Europe in 1848 could easily blow north.[21] Faced with this, and aware that theft and corruption had corroded the seat of empire, Alexander II acted out of self-preservation. The eighth plaque along showed how, in 1861, he had agreed upon the emancipation of Russia's serfs, a ruling that was to change the basic system of property ownership in the country. Other reforms followed – a shakeup of the judiciary, the abolition of branding soldiers as a form of punishment in the military, the relaxation of censorship, the ending of some noble privileges, the funding of university educa-tion – all designed to appease those who would seek a more brutal alternative.

Walking the steps towards the main entrance, you sensed in each plaque the Tsar's desperation to halt a rising tide.

These reforms culminated on 25 February 1880, when the Tsar announced he was considering granting the Russian people their own constitution. Magnanimously, he released a handful of political prisoners, but, true to form, just as one hand gave, the other took. He established a special section in the Russian police department to deal with internal security, a unit that was to become known as the Okhrana and whose undercover agents infiltrated political organisations campaigning for social reform. It was a secretive force that was, over time, to mutate and harden into the Soviet's Cheka, the NKVD, the KGB and, ultimately, the FSB of today – the state's iron fist.

With such a fist, Alexander crushed dissent in Poland, executing hundreds and deporting thousands more to Siberia. He imposed martial law in Lithuania that lasted four decades.[22] He banned numerous regional languages, only letting Polish be spoken in private.[23] None of these acts was inscribed in stone outside this church, but Alexander II's despotic power, alongside the fact he showed that he could, indeed, transform the system virtually overnight with one stroke of his pen, meant the People's Will's anger and hope for reform were roused simultaneously.[24] Reform, for them, simply could not come fast enough – and that meant ending the life of their head of state.

The Tsar narrowly missed death in 1866, 1867 and 1870. His would-be murderers were not experts in the art of killing – one bomb maker lost three fingers making a device. When some of them attempted to blow up his train with nitroglycerine, they miscalculated and destroyed another locomotive instead. Others tried to obliterate a bridge the Tsar was due to cross, but the explosive charge was not up to the job. One radical, finding work as a carpenter in the Winter Palace, smuggled in over a hundred pounds of dynamite that he hid under his bedding, until one freezing day in February he detonated the lot using a timed device – fixing the bomb so that it went off at the precise moment he planned, killing eleven and wounding thirty others. But the Tsar was not one of them; he had been delayed.

With each attempt, and each failure, you can see how Grinevitsky could have looked on and, realising just how hard it was to kill the Tsar, understood what drastic measures were needed to do the job. How something more controlled, more directed was required: a human bomb. After all, the grand, open boulevards of St Petersburg offered no easy way for revolutionaries to win the day by manning barricades. Modern, rapid cannon fire and musket drills would have decimated the People's Will's ranks. Their attack had to be up close and personal, and a new weapon technology offered a potent new opportunity just for that.

The invention by Alfred Nobel of dynamite, then, comes at a crucial point in this story. Today, Alfred Nobel is better known for having his name on annual awards for the great and the good.[25] But when Alfred, trying to treat a cut finger, had his eureka moment in 1864, combining nitroglycerine with silicon, he took the highly volatile and turned it into something stable and predictable. He was to name the substance he created after the Greek word *dynamis*, meaning power, and dynamite was to prove to be about twenty times more powerful than traditional 'black powder'.[26] As a tool to challenge the structures of power, it was a chrysalis of destruction, for not only did it blast the way for railroad tunnels and canals, but it also put into the hands of terrorists a source almost unimaginable in its potential. The balance seemed to swing overnight; the state's monopoly of power, once maintained through lines of men on horseback and rows of field artillery, was challenged to its core over a carefully placed stick of dynamite.

Revolutionaries became infatuated with the idea that an explosion could change the tide of history. One so-called 'apostle of dynamite', the radical Johann Most, said in 1880 that dynamite could 'destroy the capitalist regime'.[27] And to some of the members of the People's Will, the very spectacular nature of the bomb became intrinsic to the drama of the act. Ending the Tsar's life in a hail of bullets, one said, would 'have been seen as an ordinary murder', not 'a new stage in the revolutionary movement'.[28]

In the end, the bomb that killed Alexander weighed only five pounds and had a blast range of one metre. This restricted range was a case of reality not quite living up to the hype. The limitations of the bomb meant that the Tsar's would-be assassins had a choice: either to lob their device from a distance and risk missing, or to detonate it so close it would kill both killer and target. In the case of the suicide bomb, necessity was not the mother of invention, but the invention of dynamite created a new design. Because while dynamite promised a grisly death, it needed a controlled system that could decide the time and the place of the explosion. The assassin's death had to be the price of success.

In this respect, the suicide bomber was an evolution of a phenomenon with a long and painful history: the assassin who accepts death as part of their mission. The most famous practitioners of this – the al-Ḥashāshīn's or Assassins – were extremist members of a sect of Shiite Muslims in the eleventh and twelfth centuries known as the Ismailis, men who operated in the craggy mountains of what is now Iran. These pious devotees saw those that controlled their homelands, the Sunni Seljuk Turks, as being unbelievers, and thought they had a religious duty to resist their heretical masters – even by violence. Reflecting the purity of their ideals, they were scrupulous in their choice of weapon: the dagger alone was their weapon of choice. Eschewing the arrow or poison – either promising death from a distance – meant they would almost certainly be unable to escape, and a tortured death would follow capture, a fate many of their ranks accepted.

The difference between these ancient assassins and Grinevitsky, though, was that the suicide bomber's death was integral to the deed. The Assassin usually had the option, however remote, of escape, and if they were killed, they would not die by their own hand. The suicide bomber, however, made their death and the death of their victim a singular event; strangers up to their final moments, they would share their deaths equally.

The church that rose above me, then, may well have marked the spot of a Tsar's assassination, but it also was the place where the social tensions of modern Russia, the evolution of terrorism and the violent logic of dynamite were to coalesce; where, in the end, the world's first suicide bomber was to be mortally wounded. Inseparable truths, no matter how much you covered them in gold and marble.

It is hard to know the inner workings of anyone's heart, let alone a terrorist's, but those facing death sometimes leave clues that show us something of their thoughts. A few days after Grinevitsky's death, the authorities were to discover a letter he had written; the first suicide bomber had left the first suicide bomb note, and in it I think we can find a further explanation as to why it was St Petersburg, not Paris or Berlin or London, that saw the first suicide bomb emerge.

'Alexander II must die,' Grinevitsky had penned. 'He will die, and with him, we, his enemies, his executioners, shall die too . . . I shall not see our victory, I shall not live one day, one hour in the bright season of our triumph, but I believe that with my death I shall do all that it is my duty to do, and no one in the world can demand more of me.'[29]

At the centre of that note lies that hyperbolic phrase: 'the bright season of our triumph'. It is a literary flourish that is also at the heart of this book: a twenty-five-year-old's fervent belief that, in death, he could usher in a future infused with hope, a utopia of light. It is, indeed, a vision central to almost all suicide bombers – that their violent act will leave the world a better place, albeit one that they will never inhabit. But what compelled Grinevitsky to write such words, to choose to die in such a way?

We know far more about the way that Grinevitsky died than the way he lived. He was born in 1856, in a rough-road village that lies in present-day Belarus. He came from nobility and, true to revolutionary cliché, he was a former student – enrolled in mathematics at the St Petersburg Polytechnic. In short, he fitted the stereotype of the members of the People's Will, but this does not explain why he was so prepared to die for their cause.

Some historians say that he was not that willing, that the existence of other bomb plots meant that Grinevitsky was just a backup plan. Perhaps this is so. Some say that he might have been suicidal, that the devotion to a violent revolution coincided with a fascination in Russian society with suicide. But such arguments only go so far. Grinevitsky was not alone in his willingness to die: the executive committee of the People's Will had called for volunteers, and forty-seven men had signified their 'willingness to sacrifice themselves' in response. It's unlikely they all just wanted to commit suicide.

Some also say that Grinevitsky knew that the long arm of the Russian law – which for him meant torture and death – was just seconds away from grabbing him by the collar: Rysakov had just been arrested in front of him. In this case, he had nothing to lose. Perhaps this is true, too.[30]

But had Grinevitsky not been resigned to dying the way he did, he would not have written about it beforehand. Seeing the plot fail before his eyes, he could have just turned and walked away. He did not; he chose, at that moment, to end the Tsar's life and his with it, and that is a fact. It was also an act of murder entirely in keeping with the creation of that which he wrote about in his final letter: the bright season of triumph.

A bright season. This is the utopian vision of many a revolutionary: one who sees, in the wrecking of empire and the destruction of faiths, arise the 'glittering towers' of their ideal world (as George Woodcock, one of anarchism's leading interpreters, would have it).[31] It is a deeply religious framing. Some historians call the People's Will atheists.[32] But, in reality, they were a group remarkably infused with religious sentiment. For all their claims that they had rejected God, we know the revolutionaries kissed the cross before their deaths on the scaffold; that they took part in séances at their New Year parties, calling up the ghost of Nicholas I; and that they framed the killing of the Tsar in deeply Christian terms. 'Let our blood be shed and flow to redeem humanity,' said one.[33]

In this sense, the first suicide bombing was a continuation of religion by other means: after all, the destruction of one world to create another is a marked hallmark of faith.[34] For the People's Will, they saw their mission as eradicating evil and cleansing the Russian soil, and by focusing on the season of triumph, Grinevitsky articulated a clear timeline. One where the People's Will, like the Marxists that followed them, and the Christian zealots that pre-dated them, saw history as something that had the potential to flow 'forwards' to a universal paradise. Grinevitsky was, in this way, the heir to a Russian mainstream millenarian tradition that continues to this day.

Such a tradition was undoubtedly present in this church, built in memory of the attack. For, if the People's Will had used utopian violence to paint their propaganda, the royal family of Russia had responded here with a palette of sacrifice and selfless suffering. On the outside of the church stood plaques to the life of the Tsar and on the inside murals represented the life of Christ, mirroring the Tsar in virtue. On the exterior, above the spot where the Tsar was mortally wounded, was a mosaic of the crucifixion of Christ. All these spoke towards the purposeful allegory of depicting the Tsar's death as martyrdom.

When I walked inside, the messaging was even starker. Here, Russian babushkas wiped down and kissed tortured icons that lined the crowded church, fervent in their piety, and it was clear the Christian belief in sorrow and salvation was alive and well. But this sense of sacrifice and redemption was apparent to me in two different ways: both here, in the commemoration of the Tsar, and also in the motivations of the suicide bomber who killed him. It is true that many Russians, then and now, framed their world view as having both a catastrophic past and future, and the solemn lamentations heard in this church recalled to me that Christian lament: 'blessed are they that mourn'.

Yet, even if Grinevitsky did believe in this Russian link between suffering and redemption, why would he be willing to go so far as to lay down his own life? The answer to that lies in another thread that runs through nearly all suicide bombers' justifications: that for others to live in this better world to come, a sacrifice is required.

This idea that paradise requires sacrifice is a deep-rooted one indeed. Lyman Tower Sargent's bibliography on *Utopian Literature* has over 3,000 entries, and central to many of them runs the idea that utopia demands a loss. Plato's *Republic* forced its philosopher princes to renounce private property and family. Thomas More's *Utopia* made everyone wear a plain uniform, need a permit to travel, and ordained marriage as 'strict and unsentimental'.[35] Tommaso Campanella's *Solarians* only flourished through eugenics and enforced sexual union, where large men were encouraged to have sex with slim women. Margaret Cavendish's *The Blazing World* was a utopia only made possible by the widespread castration of males.

These visions hold universal truths about the price of paradise. For, whatever our culture, whatever our genetic make-up, we all know that if we overeat, we will become obese. Taking too many drugs can drag us to a personal hell, despite the promise of a transient heaven. No pain, so the bodybuilder's T-shirt tells us, no gain (and the popularity of weightlifting among jihadists today is no coincidence).[36] It is rooted in our psychologies and physiologies that to reap the rewards requires sacrifice, in the forms of work or self-discipline (or just dumb luck).

This must have framed Grinevitsky's beliefs: that for heaven to be reached, a moment of hell had to be realised, and the price – for him at least – of that paradise was his death. As Friedrich Nietzsche had it: 'everyone who has ever built anywhere a new heaven – first found the power thereto in his own hell.'[37]

So it was perhaps apt, then, that here, on the spot of Grinevitsky's and Alexander's own hell, they were to build a church. But in so doing, they had also omitted to state anywhere that this was a site of a suicide bombing. Whereas the cross was evident everywhere as a contemplation of the tortured Christ, a visitor could easily come and go unaware this was the site of the world's first suicide attack.

And with that thought, I walked over to a machine that produced coins imprinted with the head of Alexander II on one side, and an image of the church on the other. For 100 roubles I had one stamped for me and slid it into my pocket, and walked away from this memorial of simultaneous birth and death.

The murder of the Tsar led, swiftly, to the abuse of human rights. One of the bombers arrested, Nikolai Rysakov, was so severely tortured by the Okhrana secret police that he spilt the beans and let his interrogators know where his co-conspirators were hiding. The military was called in; thousands of Cossacks descended on St Petersburg, roadblocks were set up and routes out of the city barred. But when the police raided one of the People's Will's hideouts it was empty, save for a single rouble left to pay the butcher for the meat they had bought for the cat. They hadn't managed to get far enough though, and were soon shackled. Some of the radicals managed to escape, but arrests soon followed for most. One even chose to end his life with a single shot when the police came knocking at the door, but most of his accomplices were led away in chains.

The trials that followed were transparent and public, yet the conclusions were foregone. Count Leo Tolstoy asked Alexander III to spare the murderers, to offer them 'another ideal, higher than theirs, greater and more generous',[38] but for some it was not to be. Death sentences were handed down, and on 3 April 1881, the sleepless night of five of the prisoners ended with the arrival of cups of strong tea and the provision of black execution clothes. Placards were hung round their necks, 'Tsaricide' scrawled upon them. A pale spring sun shone down as the condemned moved through the streets. Despite the early hour, the route was already crowded, onlookers waving and shouting.

Twelve thousand troops were said to have lined the execution square, the crowd estimated at a hundred thousand strong.

Russia's only executioner, a drunk called Frolov, was at the end of the journey, there seen fiddling with the nooses. The condemned – four men and one woman – were not granted the quick death of the trapdoor, but faced the slower one of strangulation. They were, in a sense, lucky: previous Russian state executions had involved pouring molten metal down the prisoner's throat. Three of the men kissed the woman, Sophia Perovskaya. The hangman took off his blue peasant coat, revealing a red shirt beneath, and the time had come.

One by one the prisoners were led to the gallows. Twice the rope broke under the weight of one of them and some in the crowd began to call out that this was a sign from heaven, but the staggering executioner tied another noose and this time it worked. Then it was Perovskaya's turn. She turned to her executioner and complained the rope was too tight. Perhaps she was lucky in this: she died quickly. Zhelyabov, following her, had a knot that was too loose: he died in agony. Since the first bomb that had been thrown on 1 March, eleven people were now dead.

Those not condemned to death – partly down to protests led by the author of *Les Misérables*, Victor Hugo – faced lengthy sentences in Russia's infamous prisons. Few were to survive: rape and torture were commonplace, deep in the dark of soundproofed dungeons. They died one by one; childbirth took one, dysentery another. Two conspirators were forced to travel to the Kara Prison Mines – a two-year journey on foot to the north – a virtual death sentence. One had to give her baby away, knowing that to bring it along would have been a slow murder in itself, and by the time those two reached the frozen mines, their health was so broken that death would soon follow anyway.

Their victory was a false one: all it produced was a more determined repression.[39] Confronted by the murder of their Tsar, the authorities launched massive crackdowns. Alexander II's son and grandson were haunted by the assassins' threat, and the Okhrana became the violent expression of their fears. From 1883, the country descended into a 'state of reinforced security'; thousands of suspects were arrested, hundreds tortured. Repressive legislation limiting the freedoms of the press, of association, of assembly was passed, the justification given being to stop anarchist propaganda from spreading.[40] In the short term, the assassination also caused a significant setback for the reform movement. One of Alexander II's final ambitions was for an elected parliament, or Duma; these plans were completed the day before he died but had not yet been announced to the Russian people. The first action his son, Alexander III, took after his unexpected coronation was to tear them up.

As has so often happened when public anger has flared up in European countries facing the tumult of change, anti-Semitism followed. In the months following the Tsar's death, an ugly rash of attacks on Jewish communities spread to over one hundred districts in the south-western provinces. The authorities looked the other way and, in some cases, even encouraged the persecution.[41] Jewish doctors and lawyers suddenly found getting work harder. At the bottom of his 1887 order to restrict the number of Jews at universities, Alexander III wrote: 'Let us never forget that it was the Jews who crucified Jesus.'[42] Other erosions of civil liberties followed. New property requirements for voting were introduced, causing the numbers of permitted voters in St Petersburg to drop from 21,000 to 8,000, and in Moscow from 20,000 to 7,000.[43] Women found access to higher education harder and harder. Universities lost all autonomy.

The invention of suicide bomb terrorism in this way led to counterterrorism techniques that, once created, spread into everyday use – and abuse. For just as the 1860s and 1870s brought technical innovations that strengthened underground movements, the 1880s and 1890s saw technology aid police counter-surveillance operations.

The tsarist secret police became pioneers in the use of fingerprinting, photofits, codebreaking, bugging and phone tapping. They began using bulletproof vests, tear gas and 'tranquilising guns'.[44]

From the revolutionaries' point of view, though, this heavy-handedness served only to embolden their resolve. Repression led to further revolt. In 1886, a new group that followed the tradition of the People's Will was created in Russia. A year later, after an unsuccessful attempt on Alexander III's life, the group's leaders were – perhaps inevitably – rounded up and executed. There were only three gallows, so the authorities had to hang them in batches. A sack was thrown over their heads and stools kicked from under them. When the St Petersburg newspaper report on the execution reached the family members of one of the executed, his seventeen-year-old brother was reported as saying: 'I'll make them pay for this! I swear it.' His name was Vladimir Ilyich Ulyanov, better known by the alias Lenin. And in this tale of attack and counter-attack, it is hard not to see how the murders by the People's Will led, in some way, straight to the Russian Revolution itself.

Crucially, suicide bombers helped further pave the way, too. By 1902, a new group – the Party of Socialist Revolutionaries – had set up a terror cell. The ghost of Grinevitsky was very present in their midst. When they discussed the murder of the incoming minister of internal affairs, one of the band – Russian poet Ivan Kalyayev – suggested he throw himself under the minister's carriage and detonate a bomb to halt the entourage and allow the others to murder the politician. This plan never went ahead, but in 1905, Kalyayev was recruited in another assassination attempt: the murder of Grand Duke Sergei Alexandrovich. It was a risky operation, and the only reason it was considered at all was because Kalyayev said he'd gladly die in the process.

Kalyayev became the world's first failed suicide bomber. He threw the bomb at the Grand Duke from about four paces away and succeeded in killing Alexander II's fifth son. But Kalyayev himself survived, something that, before his execution, he said diminished the mission's impact. 'To die for one's convictions,' he wrote, is 'but a summons to battle.' Unlike today's suicide-belt bombs, the Russians' bombs were not strapped to the attackers, still allowing for the possibility of the attackers' survival.

Other Russian suicide attacks followed. In 1906, in an attempt to kill Vice Admiral Dubasov, Boris Vnorovsky blew himself up, along with one of the Vice Admiral's aides. The same year, three members of the Maximalists, an extreme revolutionary group, tried to kill the Russian Prime Minister in his villa. Guards stopped them and, instead of being taken alive, the assassins screamed out 'Long Live freedom! Long live anarchy!' and triggered the sixteen-pound bombs they were carrying, killing themselves and twenty-eight others. By now, thirty-five people – four attackers and thirty-one victims – had died as a direct consequence of suicide bombing in Russia: far more than many historians allow. The indirect toll, in arrests and executions, was far higher.

It would have continued, too, had the momentum of the 1917 Russian Revolution not taken hold and men and women sought to create their utopia through mass uprisings. But the origins of such a terror had been firmly laid down in the snow of a Russian winter thirty-six years before.

One postscript: the curious case of Nikolai Ivanovich Kibalchich.

Kibalchich's involvement in the plot on Alexander II's life was fundamental. The son of an Orthodox priest, the twenty-eight-year-old Ukrainian had a long history of clashing with the authorities. In 1875, he spent three years in prison after giving a peasant a banned book. He was also highly educated, a seminarian who went to college to study medicine and engineering. This mix of religious fervour, scientific logic and revolutionary sentiment led Kibalchich to become the chief explosive expert for the People's Will. It was he who, carefully mixing the right amount of chlorate of potash, oil of vitriol and fulminate of silver, was to make the first bomb to be used in a suicide attack.

Like many of his co-conspirators, Kibalchich was seized by the authorities after the Tsar's murder. His sentence was the same as theirs: death by hanging. While in his prison cell, the condemned man began to sketch. Perhaps knowing that his time on earth was ending, the imagination of this 'dead man walking' reached for the stars. A design for a solid-fuel rocket engine began to emerge: a primitive version of the 'gimballed engine' that is a mainstay of modern rocketry.[45] One prosecutor was to note his surprise that the prisoner's mind was not upon his own imminent death, but instead he seemed 'to be immersed in research on some aeronautic missile'.

In a letter to the Minister of Internal Affairs, Kibalchich sketched out an early jet engine, a powder rocket engine that controlled the flight by changing the engine's angle. He requested a meeting with government officials to discuss his ideas. Such a meeting was agreed upon, but only on 26 March 1882, a year after the inventor had been executed.

Kibalchich's proposals would have gone to the grave with him had Bolshevik researchers not unearthed them in August 1917 from a dusty governmental archive. And although his gunpowder-filled engine would have likely killed all those on board, the basis of his idea was to fuel the imagination of Konstantin Tsiolkovsky, the leading Soviet rocket scientist. Such death-row proposals helped illuminate the way to the exploration of the stars.

So great was his influence, that – despite it being among the coldest years of the Cold War – this Russian terrorist was inducted into the International Space Hall of Fame in 1976. On a clear night, if you look upwards, you can imagine the memory of Nikolai Ivanovich

Kibalchich, and his ingenious use and abuse of explosives, etched into the heavens for eternity. Because there, on the far side of the moon, a crater has been named after the inventor of that weapon used by Grinevitsky: the world's first suicide bomb.

Chapter 2

Divine Winds

The way to the shrine reminded me of a runway. The Japanese love of concrete was more than evident here and resonated with a comment I had once read that 'Japan has drastically altered its natural environment in ways that are almost unimaginable'.[1] The avenue, devoid of cars, could have as easily fitted a six-lane motorway. On each side rose mature camphor trees and sweet gums, but the grey tarmacked line, and the looming *ichi no torii* gate, two thick pillars topped with an enormous lintel, drew your eyes forward between the space it created.

There, beyond another *torii*, marking the divide between the physical world of Tokyo and the spiritual world of Shintoism, lay the imposing entrance to the Yasukuni shrine, arguably Japan's most controversial building.

A memorial to Japan's war dead, it commemorates all those who have died in service of their country since 1868, irrespective of how they died or the manner in which they fought their war. Among the list of the names, origins, dates of birth and places of death of the 2,466,532 men, women and children (and some pet animals) remembered, there are 1,068 convicted Second World War criminals, a state of affairs that still angers today. In 2015, a

Korean man was even arrested after being accused of setting off a bomb here in protest.[2]

The shrine itself was filled mainly with elderly Japanese, and they walked beneath four looming white *noren*, huge fluttering swathes of fabric decorated with a simple black flower that acted as dividers between the outside world and the temple. The men were dressed in sombre suits and the women in black mourning kimonos and they entered the main sanctuary, there to pay their respects to long-dead ancestors. It was orderly and peaceful, a far cry from the chaos of war. But what interested me more lay beyond: a small bronze statue that stood a short walk away in the temple grounds.

It was of a kamikaze pilot, raised high upon a plinth. He was young and relaxed, his hands upon his hips, his eyes to the skies. It is just one of a procession of statues here, each commemorating the victims of war: a mother with her children, a horse, a dog, even

A statue to the kamikaze stands in Tokyo's controversial shrine to their war dead

a carrier pigeon. But this statue was different. This man's death was not the tragedy of animals or civilians killed in conflict, but one that remembered the men who had died in suicide attacks in the final days of the Second World War.

The statue stood beside a sizeable glass-fronted museum, and inside that was a section dedicated to the phenomenon of the kamikaze. In the entrance lobby stood a Zero fighter plane found abandoned on an airfield at Rabaul, Papua New Guinea, after the war. This plane, a type often converted into kamikaze planes in the final years of the war, had been restored to remarkable condition. Next to it was another suicide attack vehicle: a Kaiten Type 4 manned torpedo, a thick black cigar that had been designed to be rammed by a sailor-pilot into the hull of an enemy ship. Further back was a reconstruction of an Ohka Model 11 aircraft, a white three-rocket engine that was used exclusively by kamikaze pilots. It was decorated with the red 'circle of the sun' found on the Japanese flag, alongside a white cherry blossom, denoting the fleeting nature of life. Suspended from the ceiling, it looked as if it were in permanent attack mode.

Visitors milled around, captivated by the display of photographs of successful suicide attacks on naval vessels, reading the poems and letters written by men before they died, ones that imbue the suicide bombers with humanity. It was a display that unnerved many who had come here before. 'The museum is a celebration of wasted lives,' said a *Time* magazine report, 'a blatant celebration of the most extreme expression of [an imperial] ideology, the kamikaze.'[3]

'In this looking-glass world,' said another critic, 'suicide bombers are heroes, America is the enemy and the Emperor, supposedly reduced to mortal status after Second World War, is still a deity.'[4]

Outside a group of tourists stopped and had their photographs taken before the statute: the suicide bomber transformed into a holiday snap. Unlike in Russia, the bomber was front and centre of memory. Even with the separation of all those years, the Japanese kamikaze still can anger and fascinate in equal measure. Perhaps this is, in part, because of the sheer number of those who went to their certain deaths in the service of their country. Between October 1944 and August 1945, over 3,000 Japanese army and navy pilots died in their attempts to sink the Allied fleet. Yet more died below the sea and on land, as the Japanese used submarines and bomber vests to attack the enemy wherever they could. In the battle for Okinawa alone, 1,465 kamikaze attacks damaged 157 Allied ships, causing hundreds of deaths.

This museum was an attempt to commemorate the kamikaze fighters. Still noble martyrs in the eyes of many visitors, these were men who died unsullied by the accusations of torture and rape that afflicted some of the Japanese dead also remembered here. To me, the statue, the lovingly preserved weapons, the neat rows of photographs and the encased letters all spoke about a deep need for order and reconciliation. The kamikaze had lost the war, after all; their sacrifices were entirely in vain. This was an attempt to redress those sacrifices, but in so doing it failed to acknowledge that the subjects of these museum pieces had taken more than just their own lives. To some, they had been seen to overstep the boundaries of civilised warfare and, in so doing, had created American widows and forced American girls and boys to grow up without a father. And they had transformed the icon of the suicide bomber from that of a revolutionary with a bomb to an entire culture, one rooted in a terrifying ideology of empire, death, sacrifice and honour.

Above the Philippine seas, five Zero planes were fast approaching their target. Seeking to evade the enemy's radar, their lieutenant, Yukio Seki, had directed his men to stay above 1,000 feet, and, as the Allied fleet came into sight on the shimmering seas below, they began their rapid, deadly descent. Hearing the planes' engines, the sailors and marines of the US fleet rushed to man their guns, but then

A Japanese Zero plane – a plane adapted for use by many kamikaze pilots

quickly realised that something was amiss: the incoming aircraft were not levelling up. They were targeting the ships not with their guns, but with their own planes.

As American veterans described with rheumy eyes decades later, the air was soon filled with fire and screams. In the sound and the fury of what followed, three of the approaching Japanese planes were hit by gunners on the USS *Fanshaw Bay* – they went down in a plume of smoke and spray. A fourth misjudged its aim and clipped the edge of the USS *Kitun Bay*, before exploding, spiralling into the sea. But the fifth careered through the deck of the USS *St. Lo*.[5]

It exploded on the port side of the hangar deck, just where aircraft were in the process of being refuelled and rearmed. A gasoline fireball appeared, followed by the sharp sound of the ship's torpedo and bomb magazine detonating. In seeming terrible slow motion, the *St. Lo* was consumed by flames. Half an hour later, it disappeared, sinking beneath the oil-covered waves. Of the 889 men aboard, 143 died, many trapped below decks.[6]

At 10.47 on 25 October 1944, the age of the kamikaze had officially arrived.

It was not new for planes, especially in the Pacific War, to deliberately crash into enemy ships.[7] There are numerous stories of crippled planes doing so, while reports of planes crashing into enemy aircraft mark the pages of many a war journal. But such suicidal acts were individual decisions carried out in the heat of battle; they were not under express orders. The attack on that Wednesday morning was carried out with official sanction: a strategic decision to stop the Allied advance at whatever cost.

Such orders were the result of a gradual evolution of thinking in the Japanese military. Five months before that October day, Captain Eiichiro Jyo had asked to deploy 'Special Attack Units' after witnessing the crushing defeat of Japan's naval air power at the Battle of the Philippine Sea. Around the same time, a general called Jun Ushiroku, frustrated by Japan's inability to produce enough effective anti-tank weapons, had proposed using backpack bombs in Papua New Guinea and the Solomon Islands. General Yasuda of the army air force was also to include ramming techniques as a secret component of pilot training. While Admiral Takijirō Ōnishi, kept awake at night by an acute lack of supplies and skilled pilots, had burst into a war council meeting and declared: 'If we are prepared to sacrifice 20 million Japanese lives in a kamikaze effort, victory will be ours.'[8]

Such suggestions were all met with resistance, though more for reasons of expedience than humanity. It was felt that the suicide mission, particularly an airborne one, was not cost-effective: the price of losing a trained pilot and his aircraft was too much to bear. But the situation was stark. A few years before, Japan had had some of the best pilots in the world, yet by the autumn months of 1944, almost all of them were dead. The new wave of airmen that took their places had had practically no training in combat or navigation, and they were to prove easy prey for the Allies, their casualty rate so high it was virtually a suicide mission just to get into a cockpit. By that October, over 5,000 pilots had died since the start of the year.

One man decided to take matters into his own hands. Masafumi Arima, an admiral in the Imperial Japanese Navy, concluded that suicide attacks would be the only thing to turn the tide of the war. Despite his rank, he chose personally to lead an air attack against the American fleet. Arima needed a name for his mission and looked back to history for inspiration. There, in the final years of the thirteenth century, he recalled how the shores of Japan had twice been threatened by the forces of the great Mongol warrior Kubla Khan; how twice his great armadas had reached Japan's shores and twice the wind god had sent hurricanes to wreck the Mongol's fleet. Japan was spared from invasion, and so grateful were its people to their god for this deliverance, that they called those storm winds 'heaven-sent' or 'divine wind'. Arima chose the classical Japanese phrase – *Shinpū* – to describe his team, but his mission became better known by the more popular phrase for 'divine wind' – the kamikaze.

In mid-October 1944, after removing his rank and other insignia, he climbed into the cockpit of a twin-engine bomber, not intending to return alive. What happened next is uncertain. Some say that Arima did succeed in the mission, damaging the USS *Franklin*. Others say that Arima's formation never reached their targets. There are even claims that the first of such attacks was not by Arima at all, but by a group of army pilots located on Negros Island who had independently decided to launch a suicide attack on 13 September.[9] But the impetus for more such kamikaze strikes was created. News of the mission was relayed to the Emperor, and after expressing initial shock, he sent a message of congratulations. The kamikaze had received the imperial seal of approval for future attacks.

With that, the propaganda merit of these attacks was firmly

understood. From the outset, Japanese strike units were accompanied by observers, sent out to report back upon the glorious achievements of each attack. But the observers were reluctant to report that their comrades had made their sacrifice in vain, so their debriefing notes were usually over-hyped. These exaggerations about the strategic impact of the missions added to the sense that the kamikaze was the only ray of light for the high command; the wind gods had brought hope.

The propaganda worked. The strike on the USS *St. Lo* happened shortly after, and within weeks at least 1,000 army flying graduates had signed up to become kamikaze pilots. By November 1944, the order came that all air offensives were now to be carried out by such units. For the first time in military history the use of suicide bombing had become a fundamental pillar of a national war strategy.

At first, it was decided to target US transport ships using heavy bombers. Later, swarms of kamikaze in smaller aircraft were deployed, accompanied by escorts to give covering fire. These pilots were trained to fly between Allied navy ships to draw the enemy guns, hoping the Americans would strike their own vessels in doing so. Such tactics sound like they would have been devastating on the enemy, but it was soon apparent that Japan's kamikaze planes – the Mitsubishi A6M Zeros or Zekes – tended to burst into flames when hit by machine-gun fire and could only fly at a maximum speed of 230kph, and even slower when loaded with two 250-kilogram bombs, making them easy targets. What's more, the planes were often so short on fuel they failed to explode.

To address these shortcomings, the Japanese developed a plane specifically for the missions called the Yokosuka MXY7 Ohka, or 'Cherry Blossom'. It was essentially a steerable missile: 20 feet long with stumpy wings, it could only glide 20 miles, so each had to be carried close to the target by a bomber. Once their pilots saw the enemy ship, they would ignite three rocket boosters, generating enough speed to penetrate the ship's armour. They called such pilots 'thunder gods'. And yet, despite such a name, they only sank three Allied ships.

Other strategies followed. There was the development of the Ki-115, a plane designed to drop its landing gear upon take-off so that it could be reused by other aircraft, thereby saving resources.[10] A host of new planes were created, all given names imbued with naturalistic nostalgia: 'Ume Blossom', 'Autumn Water' and 'Wisteria Blossom' among them. On 6 April 1945, waves of such aircraft attacked in an operation called *Kikusui* or 'floating chrysanthemums'. And indeed there was a blossoming – in the end, in preparation for a feared US invasion, as many as 12,700 different aircraft and tens of thousands of volunteers were harnessed for suicide missions.

In addition to the kamikaze, the Japanese navy also invented suicide submarines or *kaiten*, along with suicide boats they called *Shinyo* ('Sea Quake'). The *nikaku* was the name given to Imperial Japanese Army soldiers who strapped explosives to their bodies, allowed tanks to drive over them, and then exploded the charge. When that method was shown to fail, others simply ran at their enemy with a hand grenade. Then there were the *fukuryu* or 'crouching dragons', suicide divers who, weighed down with lead and equipped with a landmine and bottles of compressed air, volunteered to walk along the sea floor for up to six hours, towards the enemy ships. Armed with a long bamboo pole, they would position themselves under a vessel and slam the mine upwards, hard onto the ship's hull, and blow themselves up in the process.[11]

Behind these orchestrated and ordered attacks stood a hard-nosed military strategy: the Japanese (as well as Chinese, Korean,[12] Taiwanese[13] and Filipino) suicide attackers did so because it was seen as the best tactic at the time. To overcome the Americans' technological supremacy, they needed to conduct targeted strikes, and yet by 1944, so-called 'precision-guided missiles' had not yet been developed. The simple fact was this: the Japanese decision to use suicide bombers was because they had not invented a practical alternative.

Ever since warfare began, there have been situations where sacrifice has been deemed necessary to accomplish the military objective. This is perhaps most famously enshrined in the soldier's firm resolve of going 'over the top' in the First World War to face a hail of bullets, but there have been countless moments when soldiers have decided to risk their lives against overwhelming odds, choosing to die rather than surrender.[14] Such actions, however, have mainly been spur-of-the-moment decisions. The soldier who allowed his body to become a weapon was one that only began to fully emerge in Asia in the 1930s. During that time, hidden away in often forgotten narratives of war, there are many instances where soldiers chose to use their bodies as explosive weapons in attacks that laid the ground for the age of the kamikaze.

In the Second Sino-Japanese War, between 1937 and 1945, for example, there were a considerable number of incidents where Chinese forces turned themselves into human bombs. These attacks have been relatively undocumented, at least outside China. Wang Runlan, for instance, a soldier who boxed in the 1936 Olympic Games, blew himself up while attempting to stop a Japanese tank advance in 1937, and in doing so became possibly the first named suicide bomber in military history.[15] Others followed his lead, and suicide attacks were recorded in Nanjing,[16] Shanghai,[17] Guangzhou[18] and Yunnan.[19] Most notable was the 1938 Battle of Taierzhuang, when 'Dare to Die' Chinese corps charged Japanese units while armed with swords and suicide vests stuffed with grenades (an early record of the use of the suicide vest, even though many claim that the Tamil Tigers in Sri Lanka invented it).[20]

Why were such suicide attacks to emerge in China? Before this, China had seen, as in Russia, suicide bombings being used in political assassinations. In 1905, Wu Yue, a member of a nascent revolutionary party, had attempted to assassinate five ministers of the Qing Dynasty during a train journey. His attempt failed because the bomb was triggered by the train's vibration, causing the bomb to explode prematurely, killing him. But it raises the question: had the precedent set by the People's Will carried on along the train tracks from St Petersburg to Beijing, spreading the appeal of suicidal terror?

Perhaps so, because in 1911 another revolutionary called Peng Jiazhen, a Sichuan native, was also to use a suicide bomb in an attempt to kill the Chinese warlord Yuan Shikai. The warlord survived, but Jiazhen did manage to kill Liang Bi, a prominent figure in the anti-revolution faction of the Qing Dynasty. This political assassination was considered such a pivotal act in the lurch towards revolution that Sun Yat-Sen, the first president and founding father of the Republic of China, was later posthumously to bestow on Jiazhen the title of 'General' and build a shrine to his memory.[21]

Certainly, the Japanese used suicide bombers well before the kamikaze onslaughts of 1944. In the 1939 Battles of Khalkhyn Gol – a border conflict fought between the Soviet Union, Mongolia, Japan and Manchukuo – such attacks appear to have been used extensively by an ill-equipped and outnumbered Japanese force. Their first line of defence was a charge by petrol-laden, Type 94 Japanese six-wheeled trucks, designed to blow up the Soviet tanks. The second was a line of men throwing themselves under those oncoming tanks, detonating their suicide vests as they did so.[22] On 28 May 1939, a 220-man reconnaissance team launched 'human bullet' attacks against Soviet tanks armed with just gasoline and charges, and as many as 45,000 Japanese troops died in that border skirmish.[23]

Perhaps to save face, that massacre was still presented as a victory, of sorts, back in Japan, with one officer being honoured for bravery for attacking a tank just with his sword. Meanwhile many of his surviving fellow officers, who had demonstrated neither competence nor common sense, found themselves transferred back to central command in Tokyo, perhaps taking the logic of the suicide bomber with them.

By the Battle of Changsha in 1942 – the first major offensive in China by the Imperial Japanese Army – suicide bombings seem to have become an established feature on the Asian battlefield. Indeed, Changsha also appears to be the first – possibly the only – battle in history where both armies, Chinese and Japanese, deployed suicide bombers against each other.[24] The idea had entered not only the Chinese military mindset, but the Japanese one too.

Such mad sacrifice in war, though, was to infect not just the Chinese and Japanese. Other combatant nations were also to engage in suicide missions throughout the Second World War. In Germany, for instance, on 28 February 1944, Hanna Reitsch, the Nazis' most famous female aviator and test pilot, presented an idea to Hitler at Berchtesgaden called Operation Suicide. She argued that it would 'require men who were ready to sacrifice themselves in the conviction that only by this means could their country be saved.'[25] Despite believing it 'was not the right psychological moment', Hitler gave the project the green light, with the proviso that it would not be used in combat without his on-the-day approval.

Despite this specific order, the Nazis did use suicide bombers. In the final days of the war the idea of defeat loomed so heavily that thirty-five Nazis volunteered to fly into Soviet-controlled bridges over the Oder River near Berlin. Their leaders claimed to have destroyed seventeen bridges with these so-called 'self-sacrifice' sorties between 17 and 20 April 1945, but there appears to be credible evidence of only one successful strike. These last-ditch efforts involved the pilot signing a statement testifying they were 'clear that the mission will end in my death'.[26]

Less well known, perhaps, is the fact that some Allied troops also undertook suicide missions during the Second World War. In June 1941, the German invasion of Russia in Operation Barbarossa wrong-footed the Soviet commanders. In their desperate bid to stem the surging tide of German troops deep into Soviet territory, Russian commanders instructed their fighter pilots to crash their planes into those of the enemy. One of those was a female pilot named Yekaterina Zelenko, who brought down a Messerschmitt fighter with her plane, the only woman to have performed a ramming mission in the war (and arguably making her the first female suicide bomber in history). In total, as many as 270 Soviet pilots are said to have intentionally struck enemy planes between 1941 and 1945.[27]

Other Allied forces also occasionally died in their attacks on the enemy, turning themselves into human bombs. In the Pacific War, the first suicide pilot was possibly a British airman, who appeared to have deliberately crashed his damaged plane into a Japanese troop transport at Kota Bharu in Northern Malaya on 8 December 1941.[28] Nonetheless, it seems that – like the Italians, who only had one suicide bomber (a man who had agreed to sacrifice himself as he had a heart condition anyway) – Western European and American Allied Forces very rarely, if at all, set out on premeditated suicide missions. This observation, though, should not detract from the fact that countless men and women of the Allied Forces undertook incredibly dangerous operations, and many died in so doing.

But whether it was the Japanese, Soviets, Chinese or Germans, at the heart of this history of fighters purposefully dying in the line of duty lay one fundamental challenge: how can you attack the enemy with a semblance of precision from a distance?

It was a question that had fascinated military engineers for a long time. In the late 1870s, an Irish-born Australian inventor called Louis Brennan devised the first wire-guided torpedo, and it became a standard harbour defence throughout the British Empire for more than fifteen years.[29] Other tracked weapons were designed for land. The First World War descended so rapidly into quagmire that the Allies invented machines that could cut through barbed wire and travel through no man's land. The Aubriot-Gabet and Schneider Crocodile land torpedoes of 1915 did this job: looking like miniature tanks, they were able to carry up to 200kg of explosives while being guided by wire.[30]

Towards the end of the Great War, American scientists also invented what many claim is the first air-guided missile, the Kettering Bug. An experimental, unmanned aerial torpedo, it was capable of striking ground targets up to 75 miles away. Technicians determined the distance the bomb had to go by taking into account wind speed and flight path. The total number of engine revolutions was then calculated for the Bug to reach its destination so that, when a revolution counter reached this value, the engine would be shut off and the bolts attaching the wings would detach, causing the bomb to plummet earthwards. Despite some successes during initial testing, the Bug was never used in combat – there was a justifiable concern about flying such a weapon above friendly troops below.

During the Second World War enormous resources were piled into German systems such as the Henschel Hs 293 or the Fritz X – guided missiles that used a radio control link operated by an electrical two-axis joystick invented for the purpose. They posed such a threat that the Allies had to invest heavily in electronic counter-measures to defeat them.

On the side of the Allies, the United States also developed guided missile projects. One – called Operation Aphrodite – involved taking B-17 bombers that had been removed from operational service and adapting them so they could be loaded to capacity with explosives and then flown by radio control into heavy German fortifications. This operation was not a success: it relied on pilots to be in the cockpit as the planes took off and then to parachute from the plane once it was put on 'autopilot'. Out of fourteen missions, none resulted in destroying a target. Many crashed or were brought down by flak, and some pilots even died arming the bombs. One notable loss was that of Lieutenant Joseph P. Kennedy, the elder brother of the future US president, who died priming his plane. A hard irony, perhaps – a brother of an American president dying in the early development of US unmanned drone technology.

What these failures and false starts meant was that, at least in 1944, humans were still the best guided missiles. It is important to stress the word 'humans', because in modern warfare, numerous animals had been and continue to be exploited to this end. Dolphins,[31] donkeys,[32] dogs[33] and chickens[34] have all been loaded up with explosives and sent off in the direction of the enemy – but they often have a habit of veering off target, or running back to their handlers.

The use of birds, though, might not seem as ludicrous as it first sounds. Possibly the most viable project that looked at using animals as 'suicide attack weapons' in the Second World War was one that involved pigeons. The person behind this was B.F. Skinner, a man considered the leading psychologist of the twentieth century. In trials, Skinner placed an image of a ship's target onto a screen, projected as in a camera obscura. The pigeon, fixed in place inside the head of a missile, was trained to peck at the image, guiding the missile according to where the pigeon's beak landed. As Skinner found, 'a pigeon could hold the missile on a particular street intersection in an aerial map of a city'.[35] The experiments also tested the effects of energising narcotics on the birds, meaning that drug-crazed birds were once tested as bombers.

Defending his project, Skinner asserted that pigeons were superior to any of the radio-controlled missiles under development at the time because the domestic pigeon was resistant to jamming. They had exceptional eyesight, were able to process visual information three times faster than a human, and – most importantly – they could be trained using positive reinforcement (like getting a reward of hemp seed when pecking the target that it is told to). Skinner even taught his pigeons to play ping-pong.[36] Yet, despite putting three pigeons in each missile to ensure the 'majority' vote won the day, and the pigeons showing a very successful rate at striking the enemy, the US military pulled the plug, not trusting the idea.

It did not end there; cats were also experimented with. The belief that cats always land on their feet and the fact that they do not like getting wet, led the US high command to consider putting tabbies inside missiles. If, the theory went, they released that missile over a vast ocean with just a single, dry boat in sight, the cat would move its legs, struggling to head for the ship, and would guide the bomb in so doing. It even went as far as being tested, but then it was found the cats passed out halfway through the drop.[37]

In another experiment, thousands of bats were also captured, with the intention of placing tiny incendiary bombs upon them, causing them to fly into the rafters of wooden Japanese homes and burn entire cities to the ground. Predictably, perhaps, testing didn't go as planned. A general's car was destroyed and $30 million was spent until the experiments were dropped and the high command focused on the development of the atomic bomb instead.[38]

Humans, then, appeared to be the most practical option when it came to undertaking directed missile strikes. Suicide bombers are capable of timing and positioning the point of explosion to maximise death and destruction, making them 'perhaps the smartest bombs ever invented'.[39]

But why was there such widespread and often enthusiastic acceptance for suicide missions in Japan? With the possible exception of the Soviets and Chinese, the Germans and the Allied powers never embraced this tactic with a dedicated fervour, so why did it emerge as it did in Japan in 1944 with such mechanised dedication?

If you seek, through the layers and layers of history, to unravel the tricky tangle that explains Japan's embrace of the suicide bomber, you will inevitably pull on a thread that will lead you back to an event that unfolded seven decades before the Second World War. Because then, in 1868, the leaders of Japan's four major domains overthrew the Tokugawa Shogunate in a bid to restore the Meiji Emperor. This was not a liberal revolution but more a return to traditionalism. The conservative takeover was to put the army and the navy at the heart of Japan's constitution and to promote the Emperor to the rank of Supreme Commander. It effectively made the Emperor 'sacred and inviolable' and by 1882, new military recruits were reciting a poem in homage to him. It contained the line: 'duty is heavier than a mountain; death is lighter than a feather'.[40]

A feverish loyalty to the Emperor blossomed in the next decades and this sentiment, combined with a widespread social-Darwinian belief that Japan's manifest destiny was to dominate Asia, created a deep-rooted nationalism. Such ideologies led to a march of conquest that began in 1931 when the Japanese sought to occupy Chinese Manchuria. This act was condemned internationally and caused Japan to withdraw from the League of Nations, but back home a series of political assassinations created a government run by the Japanese military, strengthening their belief that the future was theirs to take.

Jingoistic expansion followed, and within a few years, Nanking in China had been sacked and the Imperial Army had cut a tranche of sorrow through Indochina, driving the British from Shanghai and the Dutch from the East Indies. Then, as so often happens with empires, they overreached themselves and decided – against some of their advisers – to attack the Americans head-on. The attack on Pearl Harbor on 7 December 1941 led the United States into four years of terrible conflict.

At the centre of this Japanese expansionism lay a philosophy: the warrior spirit of Bushido. It emphasised honour in death, and thrust the samurai into the age of mechanised mass warfare, where fighters in planes and armoured ships were supplicant to an emperor godhead.[41] Indeed, just as devout Muslims turn to Mecca, so too did many a Japanese commander offer daily prayers facing their Imperial Palace, and the Emperor's troops all too often died with the battle cry '*Tenno Heika Banzai!*' ('Long Live the Emperor!') on their lips.

Such an acceptance of death for a cause unnerved their enemies. When General Montgomery defeated the German and Italian troops in North Africa in the Second Battle of El Alamein in 1942, about 9,000 Axis troops were killed. When General Slim faced a similar-strength Japanese army at the Battles of Imphal and Kohima in 1944, an estimated 60,000 Japanese soldiers were killed. As General Slim noted: 'Everyone talks about fighting to the last man and last round, but only the Japanese actually do it.'[42]

It was an acceptance of death born from a dark and complex history whose roots lie even further back in Japanese society. If you pull these threads some more, you will find yourself in secluded Shinto temples throughout Japan where age-worn documents can be read that speak of a colourful legend that has left a deep imprint upon the Japanese psyche. It is a story of the first 'God of all' – Ninigi – who descended from the heavens to earth. His gift to the new world was rice seeds and, upon arriving, he built a wedding palace. But a question remained: who, exactly, would be his bride? His choice was between an ugly rock and a flowering cherry tree. So he married a tree that annually, ceaselessly, sprouts beautiful blossoms. These, though, are flowers that within days fall and die. It is a myth filled with the tragedies of impermanence and, with the spread of Buddhism in Japan – a religion that urges people to contemplate the ephemeral nature of life – such pathos came to dominate.[43]

In the early years of the twentieth century, though, the meaning of that story changed. The cherry blossom was appropriated as an icon by a profoundly nationalistic government that said dying for their Emperor was a huge honour. Cherry blossoms were no longer petals: they were the souls of soldiers and sailors, their falling a beautiful, glorious death. Nationwide plantings of cherry trees broke out. A new word was even used for teenage pilots: black-edged cherry blossoms – flowers destined to fall long before their time.

This cultivation of the symbol of the fleeting nature of existence aligned with a revival of the ideal of the samurai. The famous *Book of the Samurai* – the practical and spiritual guide for a warrior – opens with the thought: 'The Way of the Samurai is found in death. When it comes to either/or, there is only the quick choice of death.' It goes on to say: 'The nobler the death, the better the life it was.'[44]

In Japanese culture, the type of death you had was for hundreds of years carefully observed and categorised. *Junshi* refers to the warrior's death in the service of lord and master. *Shinju* is the heart-broken suicide of a lover. *Karōshi* is death from overwork. *Ubasute* is a type of euthanasia that translates roughly to 'abandoning the old woman' – an elderly relative carried to a mountain and left there to die. *Roshi* is death from old age. *Senshi* is a death in the grisly maul of war. The actual word 'death' about an individual's demise is rarely used.

In battle, suicide was chosen above capture. At the Battle of Tarawa in November 1943, shocked American soldiers found lines of dead Imperial Army troops with their heads blown off: they had triggered their Arisaka rifles with their toes. Of the 2,700 Japanese combatants there, just 17 were taken alive: a 99.4 per cent kill ratio. As for the Japanese navy, reports proliferated of sailors found in the water after naval battles refusing to be rescued, swimming out towards a blue horizon so as not to suffer dishonour. Others just begged to be shot. Indeed, in the closing days of the war, the Japanese navy launched what was effectively the largest suicide mission of all time when the super-battleship *Yamato* plotted to sail to Okinawa and, in concert with kamikaze units, attack the Allied forces. The plan was to deliberately beach the 65,000 tonne ship, making it an unsinkable gun emplacement, and those aboard would then fight until all hands were lost. The plan, as with so many Japanese suicide missions, did not succeed. After being riddled with torpedoes and bombs, the *Yamato* sank before it reached the shore; only a handful of sailors lived to see the day out.

It was not just Japanese combatants who opted for suicide. Wives of kamikaze pilots were known to kill themselves on hearing of their husbands' deaths. On 9 July 1944, hundreds of Saipan islanders, mainly women and children – even pregnant women, some of them in labour – threw themselves off the Morubi Cliffs, which rise 800 feet from the sea.[45] An imperial rescript had been sent a week before, urging them to take their lives and promising them a status in death the equivalent of a military one.[46] There is even the story of the kamikaze pilot whose wife killed herself and their two children so her husband might feel liberated to fly to his own death;[47] or of the newlyweds carrying out suicide missions together, the wife sharing the cockpit with her beloved.[48]

But there was also intense peer pressure that pushed the kamikaze and others into these suicides and sacrifices. If a superior officer asked a fledgling pilot if he would die for his country, saying 'no' would have brought shame not just to him, but to his entire family. Those who volunteered to die were, on the other hand, automatically promoted two ranks. When newly graduating pilots filed into the room and were given a form that asked if they wanted to be kamikaze, there were just three answers: 'I passionately wish to join', 'I wish to join' and 'I don't wish to join'. They did not know if anyone had dared refuse, and the few who did were merely told later to pick the right answer.[49] Eldest sons were allowed to live to continue their family lines, but the rest were expected to offer their lives to the Emperor.[50]

Within all this the vulnerability and susceptibility of youth played a part. After all, the majority of navy and army kamikaze pilots were young – between seventeen and twenty-four years old.[51] Their youth shines through in their final letters. A twenty-three-year-old wrote: 'I cannot help crying when I think of you, Mum.' A twenty-year-old wrote the lines: 'I am going but I am not feeling lonely because I have the *haramaki* [belly warmer] which mother made to protect me.'[52] Others trimmed their fingernails and cut their hair, and posted these ephemeral clippings back to parents, in place of words.

Perhaps this is because, sometimes, words were unable to express the fact that to some, suicide missions were, as the Japanese scholar Rumi Sakamoto has put it, 'shocking and unacceptable and extreme.'[53] It is an under-reported hesitation that can be glimpsed, fleetingly, in some of those pilots' final letters home. 'To speak frankly,' wrote Otsuka Akio, a twenty-three-year-old, to his brother and sister, 'I am not dying voluntarily; I am not dying without regrets.' Another wrote, with despair, 'in this war there is no longer any question about righteousness, it is nothing more than an explosion of hate between races.'[54] One pilot was even found chained to his cockpit, while another was shot for baulking at his task nine times.

These stories serve as a useful reminder for us today: the kamikaze are too far away to hurt us now with their violence, but they can educate us about their vulnerabilities and humanity, reminding us that while the suicide attack itself is rarely nuanced, the person undertaking it might be.

Those who did commit their final thoughts to paper may have done so with self-consciousness, hiding the fear in their hearts. Reading these letters, the nobility of their sacrifice or their love for the Emperor sometimes sound like catchphrases, not heartfelt desire. They wrote these letters knowing that their grieving relatives would read them, after all. Nationalism, militarism and fatalism combined created an ideology that seems best summed up by one kamikaze's final letter: 'A man will die sooner or later. The value of being a man is given at the time of his death.'[55] Raised on tales of the ancient samurai, it was deemed virtuous to choose death with firm resolve if the situation called for 'decisive action'.[56]

Another primary motivation throughout the letters appears to be a belief that they were saving their families from a fate worse than their own. That if the Americans were to land, Japan would be turned into a nation of slaves and raped women.

'We were taught that since we were such a small island nation and because we were one country fighting against many, great sacrifices were required,' one kamikaze who lived to see the war out was to tell the US Army years later. 'If one kamikaze pilot could blow up a vessel carrying hundreds of sailors, he would be a hero, and more importantly, Japan could win the war.'[57]

Despite the fire and the fear, the kamikaze did not turn the tide of war.

Overall, the kamikaze managed to sink 47 navy ships, damage 368 more, kill about 4,900 US sailors, and wound over 4,800, but they did not win.[58] As a successful strategy, the kamikaze left a lot to be desired. Lack of training, fuel and planes meant that new pilots were barely capable of flying; one attack led to fifty-two planes being shot down without one ship being sunk. Less than 20 per cent of kamikaze attacks even managed to hit a ship.[59]

The impact of thousands of suicidal fighters hurling themselves to their deaths was, however, undeniable. It caused the US fleet to implement significant changes: more destroyers had to be made available to protect carrier fleets, while the carriers themselves doubled the number of fighters aboard to strengthen their combat air patrols. This was, in part, because US carriers were more susceptible to damage than the British ones, as they had wooden, not steel decks, and a direct strike could put a carrier out of action for over six months. Morale also needed to be as carefully protected: servicemen on leave were ordered not to discuss the suicidal onslaught.

On an individual level, while some Americans responded by calling them *Baka* bombs (the Japanese for fool), the reality was that they instilled a deep fear in many an American fighter. As one veteran recalled: 'If there's ever anything that was going to crack a person's psyche and crack his ability to carry on, it was a kamikaze.'[60] The memories certainly lingered: long-term studies showed that just one attack could have 'lifelong, adverse psychological effects'.[61] As one US naval lieutenant said: 'I never saw the pilot's face but half a century later he lingers in my mind.'[62]

It was this huge psychological impact that brought about the greatest legacy of the kamikaze: the role they played in ushering in the most apocalyptic weapon ever employed by man.

The atom bomb that exploded above Hiroshima in August 1945 was devastating. Thousands of buildings disintegrated; flying birds ignited as ground zero temperatures reached 4,000 degrees Celsius; people were roasted alive, vaporised in an instant, or hideously injured. Thousands of bloated bodies were later seen floating in the river, and 90 per cent of Hiroshima's buildings were reduced to splinters and smouldering rubble. Black rain fell upon the city.

When the first Western journalist, Australian Wilfred Burchett, arrived in Hiroshima, he wrote how 'there is just nothing standing except about 20 factory chimneys . . . A group of half a dozen gutted buildings. And then again, nothing.' He visited a hospital where people who at first had no injuries were now dying. They had lost their appetites, their hair was coming out in clumps, and blood was seeping from their ears and noses and mouths. He pounded out his reports while perched upon a mound of rubble, and described how the doctors gave their patients vitamin A injections. 'The results were horrible,' he said. 'The flesh started rotting away from the hole caused by the injection of the needle. And in every case the victim died.'[63] That day, 130,000 died. Three days later, the United States dropped a second atomic bomb, killing as many as 40,000 people in Nagasaki.

How was the use of such bombs justified? President Truman summed it up when he said that 'we had perfected this devastating weapon for employment against an enemy who started the war and has told us she would rather be destroyed than surrender.'[64] He was later to expand on this in a letter written after the war: 'The Japanese in their conduct of the war had been vicious and cruel savages and I came to the conclusion that if two hundred and fifty thousand young Americans could be saved from slaughter the bomb should be dropped, and it was.'[65]

These three reasons – Japan's refusal to accept an unconditional surrender, the saving of American lives, and the framing of the Japanese as cruel and savage – were what the kamikaze represented: an enemy who would not surrender, were set upon killing as many Americans as possible, and were uncompromising in their cruelty.

Moreover, America was tired of the war and wanted it over quickly. American soldiers celebrating victory in Europe didn't want to be reassigned to the Pacific, and their families concurred. Soldiers in the Pacific were also acutely aware that some of their fighting countrymen were enjoying peace in some far-flung European field.[66]

On 26 July 1945, President Truman and the Allies issued their final ultimatum to Japan – the Potsdam Declaration (Truman was in Potsdam, Germany at the time). The government responsible for the war would be dismantled, it stated; there would be a military occupation of Japan, and the nation would be reduced in size to its pre-war borders. Assurance was given that the Allies had no desire to enslave or destroy the Japanese people, but that there would be war crimes trials. The demand ended with the words: 'The alternative for Japan is prompt and utter destruction.'

The Japanese did not respond. Some say they believed they could get a better deal if they stalled, others that they would rather die than surrender. As the Japanese General Anami said at one war council meeting: 'Would it not be wondrous for the whole nation to be destroyed like a beautiful flower'?[67]

Tokyo's diplomatic obstinacy and the seeming willingness of the Japanese to accept some sort of 'national suicide' must have haunted

Truman.[68] It forced him into a corner: he had to win an unconditional surrender from the Japanese; anything less would have made
him appear weak and embolden those Japanese who wanted to fight
to the death.

Such a realisation caused President Truman to be uncompromising. 'If they do not now accept our terms,' he said in a radio
broadcast, 'they will face a rain of ruin the like of which has never
been seen on this earth.'[69]

But what if the imperial command said no? A drawn-out land war
to take the Japanese mainland would have been costly and bitter. The
worst-case scenario for a full-scale invasion was put as high as 1.7
million Allied casualties, including 800,000 deaths.[70] This was on top
of the 292,000 American military deaths suffered up to that point.

A Japanese army of 4 million and a citizen reserve force of 25
million lay in wait. The Americans faced, too, the densely forested
mountains that cover over 80 per cent of Japan, along with a maze of
rice fields that would have proved a watery death for many a driver
of a Sherman tank. There were thousands of kamikaze aircraft on the
mainland, along with untold numbers of *kaitens*.

The spectre of the kamikaze was undoubtedly in the room when
the Americans made the strategic decision to go nuclear. As Charles
Maier, a professor of history at Harvard University, has written: 'The
Japanese use of suicidal kamikaze attacks had a strong psychological
impact on US military decision-makers who reckoned the whole
country would be mobilized to defend the home islands.'[71] When
confronted with the ferocity of the suicide bomber, the idea of an
atomic bomb as being a necessary evil was accepted by the American
high command without much hesitation.

It was an idea that was also supported by many a US soldier. As
the literary historian Paul Fussell, then a combat soldier expecting
to take part in the anticipated invasion, would later recall after the
bombs had been dropped: 'We learned to our astonishment that we

would not be obliged in a few months to rush up the beaches near Tokyo assault-firing while being machine-gunned, mortared, and shelled, and for all the practiced phlegm of our tough façades we broke down and cried with relief and joy. We were going to live.'[72]

But could the US 'sell' the idea of a nuclear strike to the American people at large, and not just the troops? This was crucial because the atom bomb was dropped on both occasions – the second even more so – with the full knowledge that it would devastate a city. There were, after all, limits to warfare: President Roosevelt had said in 1943 that America would not use poison gas weapons, for instance, on the Japanese people, 'unless they are first used by our enemies'.[73]

In the end, the American people were overwhelmingly supportive. In 1945, immediately after the bombing, a Gallup poll found that 85 per cent of Americans approved the use of the atomic weapons.[74] But they had not seen the flesh stripped off the backs of children, or looked upon the blind white eyes of those who had been under the glare of the bomb. Nonetheless, for many an American – steeped in a national tradition of hard, retributive justice – the strikes on Nagasaki and Hiroshima were a long time coming. The American public was well aware of the atrocities committed by the Imperial Japanese Army – such as the Rape of Nanking, where an untold number of Chinese civilians and disarmed combatants were murdered. The Japanese treatment of prisoners was also known: experimentally exposing them to diseases, such as the bubonic plague, or testing poison gases on them.[75] As President Truman noted: 'When you have to deal with a beast you have to treat him as a beast. It is most regrettable but nevertheless true.'[76]

Besides, a Rubicon had also already been crossed. The first large-scale air raid on Tokyo, on the windy night of 9 March 1945, had set ablaze a hugely densely populated area, and an estimated 86,000 people were incinerated. By August 1945, over sixty city centres across Japan had been gutted. But such fire bombings did not sway

American hearts. Japanese atrocities, combined with their suicide bombers, had hardened them long ago.

The kamikaze, in this sense, led the Americans to using the most murderous weapon of war ever invented. The suicide bomber had created the very conditions in which an act of mass violence against civilians – both through carpet bombing cities and dropping the atomic bomb – was justified and almost universally accepted.

From a Japanese perspective, it was an atrocity beyond reckoning. Despite their nation's cruel treatment of civilians, a Tokyo English-language broadcast to North America asked: 'How will the United States war leaders justify their degradation, not only in the eyes of the other peoples but also in the eyes of the American people? International law lays down the principle that belligerent nations are not entitled to unlimited choice in the means by which to destroy their opponents. This is made clear by Article 22 of the Hague Convention.'[77]

They were right. The atomic bombs were in breach of the Hague Convention. And in many ways, the United States could be said to have lost the moral high ground by engaging in indiscriminate mass bombing of civilians. 'When you kill 100,000 people, civilians, you cross some sort of moral divide,' wrote the historian Edward Drea. 'Yet at the time, it was generally accepted that this was fair treatment, that the Japanese deserved this, that they had brought this on themselves.'[78] This is what the suicide bombers had done. They had helped alter the Allied perspective as to what was an acceptable use of violence.

Today, the percentage of Americans who believe the use of nuclear weapons was justified has fallen to 56 per cent.[79] Distanced from reports of suicide strikes, the public's view of the murderous mushroom cloud has changed. But the problem was that even an atomic bomb could not kill the idea of the suicide bomber.

On 30 May 1972, three members of a group called the Japanese Red Army – founded in 1971 by communist militants – launched an attack on Lod airport (now Ben Gurion International) near Tel Aviv. Armed with guns and grenades they killed 26 people and injured 80 more.

Airport security had been so focused on the possibility of a Palestinian attack that the fact their enemy was Japanese took the guards by surprise. The three men – Kōzō Okamoto, Tsuyoshi Okudaira, and Yasuyuki Yasuda – had been trained in Baalbek, Lebanon and were funded, it transpired, partly from a $5 million ransom that had been paid by the West German government in exchange for the hostages of a hijacked Lufthansa flight in 1972.

The attackers arrived late at night aboard an Air France flight from Rome. Dressed conservatively and carrying slim violin cases, they attracted little attention. As they entered the waiting area, they pulled out Czech vz. 58 assault rifles, the buttstocks removed, and began firing indiscriminately at airport staff and visitors, tossing grenades as they did so. Yasuda was accidentally shot dead by one of the other attackers. Okamoto ran out of ammunition and was overpowered and captured. Okudaira, however, ran away from the terminal out onto the tarmac, firing at passengers disembarking from an El Al aircraft, before pulling out the pin of his grenade. It exploded and he died instantly.

There is some debate as to whether this was an accidental premature explosion or a suicide bomb, but Okamoto, the sole attacker who had been captured, later said that they 'wanted to die a beautiful death for a great cause'.[80] The fact that one died from his own grenade in a terror attack was also noted by the world looking on, aghast. The words 'kamikaze attack' were quickly conjured up from the past because – despite the fact that twenty-six years, eight months and twenty-eight days had passed since the end of the Second World War – the suicide bomber was back.[81]

Perhaps that war had been so devastating and, for many, so point-less in its waging, that the notion of sacrificing your life for a country, or an ideal, had faded into the shadows for a generation. It is telling that the Japanese terrorists who carried out the attack were in their mid-twenties – too young to remember the war and too old to know the futility of terrorism.

But it was an attack that seemed to insert a meme – an idea that spreads from person to person within a culture – of suicide attacks into the Holy Lands at a crucial time. A meme that seems to have started in St Petersburg, spread to revolutionary fighters in China and from there into the Chinese army, then to have been picked up by the Japanese military in China and taken back to Japan. An idea that is elusive to track but that reveals itself in deadly missions with a terrible ferocity. And an idea that seemed, now, to have leapt from north-east Asia right into the heart of the Middle East.

Chapter 3

The Rise of the Martyr

On 30 October 1980, a thirteen-year-old boy was caught in the thick of battle in the Iranian port of Khorramshahr, a trading city that rests along the border with Iraq.[1] Around him lay his dead and dying comrades, Iranian men twice his age and more. Before him approached the enemy: Iraqi troops loyal to the fifth President of Iraq, Saddam Hussein.

The boy, Mohammad Hossein Fahmideh, was not even a teenager when he left his Iranian home town of Qom to travel to the front to defend his country against the invading Iraqi forces, but he had seen things no boy should ever see. Caught in fierce house-to-house skirmishes through the town, it was clear the tide of battle was turning, and not in his favour. The Iraqi soldiers were crushing their opposition with vastly superior firepower, and they had taken a strategically important canal close to where the boy was fighting. The day was almost lost.

Faced with defeat, Fahmideh chose a path that would have a profound and global impact, even if he did not know it at the time. Perhaps driven part mad by the din of battle, or perhaps part desperate that the day would end with his own death, he grabbed a hand grenade off one of the nearby bodies and ran towards the nearest Iraqi tank, pulling the pin as he did. He dived underneath the tracks and the explosive went off with a muffled flash. The tank was disabled; Fahmideh died instantly.

The immediate effect of his death was to slow down the Iraqis. Their commanders, unaware it had been a suicide attack, assumed a minefield had been laid, and halted the advance to clear the way. The long-term impact, though, was far more significant. To his nation, Fahmideh had committed an act of unparalleled heroism, a selfless act that earnt the thirteen-year-old renown throughout Iran. His flawless face, framed by a dark thicket of hair, was to become a symbol of ultimate bravery and honour, and in that face a new icon in the Islamic world was created: the suicidal martyr.

As the war with neighbouring Iraq descended into a terrible stale-mate, memorials to the boy's sacrifice sprang up throughout the Shia nation. A golden monument was erected on the outskirts of Tehran, showing the boy clutching a belt of five hand grenades. Streets began to be named after him, and hospitals, schools and a sports stadium followed.[2] His final moments were turned into an animated film, as well as the focus of an episode of the TV series *Children of Paradise*. There were stamps issued with his face printed upon them.[3] Such was his impact that, if you hold an old 500 or 1,000 Iranian rial bill up to the sun, it is his face you can see imprinted on the watermark.[4]

His death, in this way, fast became political capital. The Ayatollah Khomeini, the Shiite Muslim and Iranian revolutionary leader who made Iran the world's first Islamic republic (from the perspective of the Shias) in 1979, proclaimed: 'There are events that being so astonishing, might sound as unbelievable as fables and legends; but they are real. One of the most beautiful ones is the martyrdom of Basij volunteer teenager Hossein Fahmideh. He was thirteen . . . His memory will last forever; he has turned into legend.'[5]

Such words fertilised a growing veneration of martyrdom: the Basij, of whom Khomeini spoke so glowingly, were martyr brigades that turned self-sacrifice into a fervent passion.[6] These ranks of Iranian youth – reportedly 'modest', 'self-restrained' and 'self-possessed' teenagers – were presented as eager to die for Islam and for the revolution, flying banners that read: 'The Nation for whom Martyrdom means happiness will always be Victorious.' Some 52,000 men were said to join their ranks, a 'martyrdom unit' in every Iranian province.

Like the kamikaze, these youths were responding to a personal sense that their nation and families were under threat. The invasion by the Iraqis had quickly escalated into war; since the mountainous terrain made a speedy ground invasion impossible, the Iraqi forces had begun to launch Scud missiles at Iranian cities to terrorise the population, hoping to bring down their support for their regime. The strategy backfired, and the newly founded Basij militia saw a dramatic increase in volunteers.

Like the kamikaze, the need for martyrs was a strategic necessity born from the Iranians being poorly equipped to wage such a war. By the mid-1980s, the conflict had descended into a stalemate of the sort seen in the Great War: the slaughter of vicious trench warfare, marked by little territorial gain and tremendous human cost, with the use of over-the-top advances, chemical warfare and the bombing of civilians. Since described as the twentieth-century's 'longest conventional war', it bled Iran dry and cost over a million lives, and the Basij were at the forefront of that slaughter.[7] Arriving at the front lines, these volunteers found themselves hopelessly under-resourced, without rifles or proper clothes. One mythical tale leaps out: an elderly woman who travelled a full day to the front lines to give her only remaining piece of food to the troops – an apple.

And, like the kamikaze, the sacrifices of the Basij were marked by ritual and symbolism. Some soldiers were issued colourful identification tags, while others were given a prayer book called *Mafatih al-Janan* ('The Keys to Paradise'). One story often told is how the Basij boys were handed out plastic keys, ordered en masse from Taiwan, to be placed around their necks before they were sent into an Iraqi barrage.[8] The keys, it was said, would open the gates of paradise for them but, like much in Iran, the veracity of such a story is hard to establish.[9]

Keys or no keys, there were human sacrificial waves. The semi-official Iranian daily newspaper *Ettela'at* described 'child volunteers: 14, 15, and 16-year-olds. They went into the minefields . . . [a] few moments later, one saw clouds of dust. When the dust had settled again, there was nothing more to be seen of them. Somewhere, widely scattered in the landscape, there lay scraps of burnt flesh and pieces of bone.' As the article went on to note, the children reportedly found a solution to this problem: 'Before entering the minefields, the children [now] wrap themselves in blankets . . . so that their body parts stay together after the explosion of the mines and one can carry them to the graves.'[10] Children were to clear a path through the minefields for the soldiers that followed them, doing so 'because donkeys (were) too stubborn to do it'. As one survivor later described: 'We fought by throwing ourselves in front of the tanks, by leaping on the mines.'[11]

Such claims of sacrifice need to be read with a cynical eye, as part of the theatrical bombast of war. Was a nine-year-old allowed to join the Basiji's ranks? Did mothers embroider their sons' shirts with the words: 'Imam Khomeini has given me special permission to enter Heaven'? Did veterans mean it when they claimed the rush to martyrdom was 'sometimes like a race. Even without the commander's orders, everyone wanted to be first'?[12]

The point is not so much that the Basij were prepared to die for their country, just like the soldiers of the Great War who surfaced from their trenches despite knowing their chances of being shot. Such sacrifices have long been demanded by modern warfare. It is more that, with Mohammad Hossein Fahmideh's death and veneration the icon of the contemporary Islamic martyr was born in the Middle

East. An acceptance of sacrifice that was first forged in the furnace of the Iranian front lines.

This ideal of the martyr was to be encouraged by the state; all fatalities of the war, Ayatollah Khomeini said, were considered martyrs. A campaign was launched called 'Sacrifice a Child for the Imam' – every family that lost a child upon the battlefield was offered interest-free credit and generous state benefits. Enrolment in the Basij also gave Iran's impoverished a real chance for social advancement, for even those just wounded in battle were called 'living martyrs'.[13]

It led to mass death. In 1982, during the retaking of the city of Khorramshahr, 10,000 died. In February 1984, the corpses of some 20,000 Iranians were left on the battlefield during Operation Kheiber. The 'Karbala IV' offensive, in 1986, cost – again – more than 10,000 lives. In total, some 100,000 Iranian men and boys were said to have died during Basij operations.

With mass death came mass memorial. Pictures of young women and men who had died in the fighting were displayed everywhere, and graveyards became centres of commemoration. A fountain was erected in the middle of the 'Paradise of Zahara' (Behesht-e Zahra), the cemetery that stands south of Tehran, and it flowed with scarlet water. According to officials, the scarlet represented the blood of Iran's martyrs 'irrigating the revolutionary seed'. There were over 40 square kilometres of freshly dug graves.[14]

Rituals followed. Professional flagellators offered their services to the grieving, prepared to whip sharp chains across their backs for a price; military bands were on standby to play sombre dirges; and mullahs were paid to tell stories to make the assembled weep.[15] One grave was said to smell of freshly cut flowers, even though no flowers were there. Another was reported to be visited by the ghost of the Prophet's daughter, Fatimah. A grieving mother built a small hut on top of her son's grave so she might lie upon him. Iranian wedding tables were placed on the graves of virgins. The theatre of mourning served to legitimise the sacrifice, and so it went on.

Streets once called after pomegranates, or angels, or nightingales began to be given new names, shrouded in heartache: Martyr Akbar Sherafat, Martyr Soufian, Martyr Mohsenian, Martyr Khoshbakth . . . The concept of sacrifice stained everything – cityscapes, conversations and politics. It was a transformation of death that was to change Iran and the region for ever.

Since that first suicide on 30 October 1980, up to the end of 2017, twelve countries of the seventeen that make up the Middle East have witnessed suicide bombings. What started off with a child's death in Iran infected an entire territory, as the idea of suicidal martyrdom travelled to the Levant, the Arabian Peninsula, Asia Minor and Egypt. In total, at least 3,000 suicide attacks have taken place throughout the

A poster of Khomeini in Lebanon's Baalbeck Valley

region, with over 32,000 deaths and 76,000 wounded recorded.[16] In total, those twelve Middle Eastern nations have witnessed over half of all suicide attacks globally.

How was it that what began in Iran fuelled such a crucible of violence? Why was it this nation that saw the birth of the modern-day Islamic martyr? And how did it spread from the borders of Iran and Iraq throughout the Middle East and beyond? To answer such questions required digging into the rich soils of history, to uncover layers of Iran's complex relationship with its then spiritual leader, Ayatollah Khomeini, and all that drove him onwards; to find what has long moulded the Shia view of sacrifice; and, deep beneath the surface, to unearth the dualistic thought that penetrates the Iranian psyche in the very dominant roles of Good and Evil, Heaven and Hell.

To do so means turning first to theology and the turbulent years of early Islam. To some degree, all religions have to contend with different interpretations of the faith, but few have divisions so intensely sown into their roots as Islam. This is because, from the very beginning, two branches of this Abrahamic monotheistic faith split during the great *fitna*, or strife, that played out over who would be the successor to the Prophet Muhammad.[17]

On the one side were the Sunnis. When their leader died on 8 June 632 aged sixty-two, they claimed the mantle of leadership had to be passed down the line of the four 'perfect' caliphs, the Prophet's beloved companions: Abu Bakr, Omar, Uthman and (only then) Ali, the Prophet's cousin and son-in-law. After that, most Sunnis believe, the command was to pass to the Umayyads in Damascus, followed by the Abbasids in Baghdad.

Shias disagreed. They said the succession should have passed through the family of the Prophet, for blood, not companionship, confers authority. They asserted the leadership must go first to Ali and then to his son, Hussein. Such a lineage was, however, cut short. Within years of the Prophet's death, Ali was murdered in Kufa and buried in nearby Najaf; Hussein was killed in Karbala, in a battle against the Umayyads, and lies there to this day. After the death of Hussein, Shia leadership was then said to have passed down a chain of imams – a complex interplay of politics that opened up the line of succession to further debate. This is why, today, Shias are fragmented into the Zaydi 'Fivers', the Ismaili 'Seveners' and the 'Twelvers'. This last, majority group of Shias became the state religion of the Persian Safavid Empire – a reason why some Sunni Arabs view Shias, especially Iranians, as foreigners upon their land.

What is incontestable is that a sense of loss pervades the Shia tradition, and the martyrs that blossomed during the Iran–Iraq War were part of that long tradition of Shia suffering. There was the Prophet's uncle, Hamza, the 'Prince of Martyrs' who died fighting the battle of Uhud. Hamza had not wished to die, but he was committed to victory, even if it meant his death in the process.

Then there was Hussein, son of Ali, who, having lost the battle of Karbala in 680, refused to go home in defeat and returned to the field of battle, knowing he too would die. Shia tradition praises his actions, rooting in their rituals the idea of a small force of true believers standing up against an overwhelming enemy army.

The martyrdoms of other Shias – Fatima, Imam Ali, Imam Sadeq, Imam Hassan, Imam Reza – are Iranian public holidays. Eight out of twenty-five holidays in Iran are related to martyrdom, whereas the Sunni nations of Jordan, Egypt, Saudi Arabia and Morocco do not celebrate any sacrificial death.[18] Martyrdom is even part of Iran's official national anthem: 'Oh martyrs, the time of your cries of pain rings in our ears.'

Of all the martyrs, though, Hussein's death has been the most defining – a sacrificial commitment to an Islamic cause that enabled the Shia to present themselves as the opposition, 'to denounce the usurpers so as to re-establish the true religion of the Prophet'.[19] Just as early Christian saints were venerated for accepting the painful 'crown of martyrdom', fervent in the belief their deaths would feed the life of the Church, so too did Shiites come to revere Hussein's martyrdom in their rituals and dramas.[20] Every year, they mourn his sacrifice in the Ashura festival and whip themselves, symbolically re-enacting his suffering. The cold water offered from large containers in the heat of an Iranian summer is meant to recall the urgent thirst suffered by Hussein's troops in the desert. And the Iranian phrase that ends a letter – *qorban-e shoma* – does not mean 'best wishes', but rather 'your sacrifice'.

In the Iran–Iraq War of 1980–88, this Shia sacrificial tradition became woven into the very fabric of the conflict. Saddam Hussein was portrayed as Yazid – the much-loathed general who was involved in the killing of Hussein, the grandson of the Prophet Muhammad, at the Battle of Karbala. The number of casualties in an Iraqi attack was recorded, invariably, as seventy-two – the number who once died alongside the Prophet's grandson. Battles were named 'Karbala II' and 'Karbala III',[21] while posters of the soldiers who fell in them showed their corpses transforming into tulips, because tulips had once sprung from Hussein's spilt blood.[22] Actors were even hired to play the role of Hussein, calling out to soldiers to participate in suicide missions; a horseman on a black steed would appear on the front line, his face shining with painted phosphorus, wearing the clothes of a medieval prince. 'Charge into battle against the infidels!' he would shout. 'Revenge the death of our Imam Hussein!'[23] And they did.

A pivotal player in this development of military religious symbolism was Iran's spiritual leader, Ayatollah Khomeini. For him, the ultimate act of penance was not just to whip yourself, but to kill yourself – provided it was for the greater good of the revolution. Khomeini took the principles of Shiism and gave them a popular jihadist interpretation: he raised the ideal of self-sacrifice, reinforced the concept of salvation, and stressed the imminence of the return of the Mahdi, the 'hidden 12th Imam' who had disappeared in about

940 and who would one day return, alongside Jesus, to fill the world with justice.

Rejecting the doctrines of non-violence, Khomeini used passages from the Quran and the Hadiths (the reports describing the actions of the prophet Muhammad) to legitimise the use of suicide attacks and martyrdom. He downgraded the *taqiya*, the right to be freed from religious duties in times of crisis to avoid danger to life and limb, in favour of one's duty to jihad.[24]

'Happy are those who have departed through martyrdom', he said, 'Happy are those who have lost their lives in this convoy of light. Unhappy am I that I still survive and have drunk the poisoned chalice.'[25]

Such a statement should not be underestimated; Khomeini's considerable praise for the suicide bombing of Mohammad Fahmideh constituted a substantial break with Quranic teachings. Sura 2, verse 195, for instance, reads: 'Cast not yourselves to destruction with your own hands'; while Sura 4, verses 29–30, takes it even further: 'Do not kill yourselves . . . whosoever does so in enmity and wrong, verily, / We shall let him burn in Fire.'

It was a marked divergence. Admittedly, ever since the 1930s the Egyptian Muslim Brotherhood had been calling for 'Victory or Martyrdom', but their aim seemed more towards giving hope to Muslims faced with a hopeless situation than willing their followers onwards to their certain death.[26] Khomeini, however, implored the Basij to die without infusing it with the sentiment of hope. 'It is not so much the outcome of the conflict,' he said, 'as the mere participation in it that provides fulfilment and gratification.'[27] This was new. In his eyes, you did not have to win victory to gain access to paradise; all that was required was dying in the attempt.

According to Khomeini, life was insignificant and death was just the beginning of genuine existence. To him 'the natural world [was] the lowest element, the scum of creation . . . the divine world, that is eternal.'[28] He saw modernity as creating even more scum: where individual self-determination had replaced divine providence, scientific doubt had corrupted faith, and the pleasures of the flesh usurped the stern morality of the sharia – Islam's legal system, derived from the Quran, the Hadiths, and the consensus of Islamic scholars.

America, Israel and Iraq were, in this way, seen as evil incarnate, against whom battle must be waged, for the vanquishing of such malevolent modernism was a precondition for the return of the beloved Twelfth Imam.[29]

This world view was not just Khomeini's. Other Shia theologians and intellectuals had said the same: Ayatollah Mahmoud Taleqani, during a period of marked civil unrest in June 1963, gave a speech in Tehran where he quoted a poem: 'From head to toe, God's light you'll radiate / If in His cause, you self-annihilate!'[30]

In Iraq, the holy city of Najaf became a crucible for such thought, and here, alongside the city of Basra and western Iran in the 1960s, the idea of an 'Islamic revolution' was born.[31] It was pious anger that radiated from the desks of scholars. In 1968, Ni'matollah Salihi Naja-adabi, one of Khomeini's students in Najaf, published a pamphlet stating that Hussein's martyrdom was a political uprising that should be emulated by all Muslims. Another, Dr Ali Shariati, wrote: 'Imam Hussein said "I am going to my death", not "I am going to conquer"; death is an ornament for mankind.'

By the late 1970s, such voices had merged to create a political and religious movement of considerable influence, one that – like the nineteenth-century Russians – referred to itself as 'the fountain-head of rebellion in the struggle for the downtrodden and oppressed masses.'[32] It was an outpouring that gained support, fuelled by widespread economic disenfranchisement, a spreading of communist and post-colonial idealism, and a rise in religious fervour.[33] At the forefront of it all was Khomeini's dominant personality, unleashing the revolutionary potential that had been accumulating for over half a century of Iranian political turmoil.

When Khomeini finally returned to Iran from his exile on 1 February 1979, millions took to the streets to greet him.[34] Four days after his return he went on state television where he unveiled the world's first modern theocracy: no ordinary government, he announced, but 'God's government'. Opposition to that was opposition to God, and by December 1979, a new constitution had been passed by referendum that placed him as the head of a new Islamic Republic.

Yet this story – however compelling a rise of a hero (or a devil, depending on your viewpoint) can be – only explains part of the puzzle. Why did Iranians heed the Ayatollah's plea? Why did they flock to his side, and to their deaths? Was it something more rooted in the Iranian psyche that he was speaking to?[35]

To me, there exists a concealed cultural setting upon which much of the martyrdom narratives of Iran rest. Deep within the Shia-held view that sacrifice is necessary to combat evil, lie traces of an even older religion – Zoroastrianism. Such a suggestion to a Shia would not be well received. As with most faiths, many Shias see their religion as directly mandated by their God; to them, any similarity with another religion just proves God's divine plan is at work. But the deep roots of non-Islamic faiths in Iran should not be ignored.

In the sixth century BCE, Zoroastrianism became the religion of the first Persian Empire. This makes it one of the oldest surviving religions and the oldest monotheistic one. At the heart of this empire's faith was a sense that a cosmic war was being waged, one where two spiritual powers were locked in an eternal battle. Good, seeking to let life blossom in a world of order, and evil, attempting to drag the world into chaos. It was a religion of dualism, akin to that other Persian dualistic religion, Manichaeism.

The historian Norman Cohn was fascinated by this deep history in Iran. He saw, at the very centre of Zoroastrianism, the idea that free choice comes at a price. In Iran, he argued, sacrifice had a 'rich significance': the ancient Persians had 'been allotted the part of a collective saviour . . . meant to prepare the world for its salvation.'[36] To Cohn, the prophet Zoroaster was the first known example of a 'millenarian' and the 'first apocalypt',[37] a man who promised a 'total perfecting of the world'.[38]

Such prophecies set the Zoroastrians as a people apart, where even the lowest of the low could achieve paradise. In short, the possibility that access to heaven was granted to all was sown deep in the Iranian cultural psyche. To dismiss these ancient roots is to ignore the legacy of Zoroastrianism still felt in modern-day Iran. The government has tried, without success, to ban the Chaharshanbe Suri – the fire festival. Every year, people, chanting an ancient Zoroastrian mantra designed to burn away bad luck and ill health for the year to come, jump over bonfires. It is a remnant 'as culturally important to Iranians as the Islamic festivals'.[39] Those bonfires were seen by the early Zoroastrians to be symbolic of the fire of the final days – when flames would melt the metal in the hills to cover the earth in a spreading molten stream. For the righteous, this magma would be like warm milk; for the wicked it would burn like hell. Such symbolism was, over time, transformed into purgation. Fire would cleanse the spirit, and perhaps something equally symbolic is seen by some within the explosive flash of the suicide bomb, where the detonation cleanses the soul, spiriting the martyr to paradise.

The ancient struggle between the forces of good and evil was to find physical form in the Iran–Iraq War. There it intertwined with a theological acceptance of martyrdom deep in the Shia faith, alongside an urging towards sacrifice by the Ayatollah. It was under these conditions that the self-sacrificing warrior was to find meaning and, while it was in Iran that it spread first, it did not stop there. It was a romantic ideal that, like a virus, was to erupt again and again and, soon enough, the rationale of the martyr was to cross borders to Lebanon, where it would reveal itself in the deadliest of fashions.

Chapter 4

Back to Barbarism

On 15 December 1981, a car filled with 100 kilograms of explosives smashed into Iraq's seven-storey embassy building in the Lebanese capital of Beirut; the driver was reportedly a young Iraqi called Abou Maryam.[1] When he detonated his payload, the explosion demolished the embassy, taking with it sixty-one lives, including the Iraqi ambassador, and injuring more than a hundred others. So powerful was the blast that Lebanese security sources initially said the bombs had been strategically placed around the pillars supporting the building.[2] So unexpected, that news outlets had to reach back in history to find words to describe it. Predictably, they lighted upon the Second World War: 'Iraqi Embassy in Beirut racked in "kamikaze" hit' ran one headline.[3]

Today, the Iraqi embassy has been rebuilt into a fortress. The high concrete walls that surround its perimeter have long obliterated any view of the Mediterranean Sea, and Lebanese guards nervously watch the four-lane motorway that runs before it. The day I visited, seagulls filled the cloud-thick air, calling noisily, but the guards, after telling me to delete the photo that I had taken, were monosyllabic. 'Why so much concrete?' I asked. 'Terrorists,' came the reply. Trucks had long ago taken away all the debris from the bomb and replaced it with high walls, obscuring the Assyrian statues that now flanked the fortified gate. The armed men were suspicious – most people I met in Lebanon seemed, at first anyway, suspicious – and the guards quickly retreated into silence.

But years before, on the day the embassy fell, chaos ruled here. Ambulances and reporters swarmed to the devastation, Syrian and Iraqi troops firing their automatic weapons into the air to keep the crowds away. Bulldozers were used to uncover the mangled bodies of the victims. Soon Iraqi, Palestinian and Lebanese sympathisers poured into the Syrian-controlled areas of West Beirut, screaming with fury. Other embassies had been attacked in this beleaguered city, but this was the first time a suicide bomber had been used.

One life lost in the attack here was that of Balqis al-Rawi, a schoolteacher and wife of the Syrian poet, Nizar Qabbani. That grieving poet did not see the path of violence that took his wife from him as leading to any martyrs' paradise, but rather back to the age of Islamic ignorance: 'to insanity, monstrousness and hideousness', he was to write in his poem 'Balqis', 'back again to barbarism.'[4]

Such words, today, seem more than prescient: they sound like a death knell. Throughout the 1980s, except for attacks in Kuwait (1983 and 1985) and Iran (1985), almost all suicide bombings in the Middle East happened here, within Lebanon's borders; at least forty strikes that claimed 934 lives and injured 891 more.[5]

The people behind this particular attack at the Iraqi embassy were an Iranian-funded Islamist group from Iraq called al-Dawa ('the Mission').[6] This Shiite group, men deeply opposed to Saddam Hussein's Baathist party, had already murdered government officials in Iraq, railing against Saddam Hussein's pan-Arab and socialist dreams.[7] But Hussein was not a man to respond meekly; when al-Dawa failed in their bid to assassinate the Iraqi Deputy Prime Minister Tariq Aziz in April 1980, the full might of state retribution kicked in. Al-Dawa's spiritual leader, Grand Ayatollah Muḥammad Bāqir al-Ṣadr was executed, along with his sister. The remaining al-Dawa leadership fled to Iran.

It was a natural homeland for the group. Once the reality sank in that Shia uprisings across the Islamic world would not spontaneously erupt to follow the Iranian Revolution, Tehran had begun doling out money and assistance to help spread their call for an Islamic utopia. From Pakistan to Egypt, Iran encouraged the challenging of secular rule and the denouncing of support for America by whatever means necessary: armed conflict, street protests, even acts of terror. Iran saw the Shia world as a vanguard for an even bigger pan-Islamic revolution; by mobilising them, Khomeini hoped, Sunni support would soon follow.

The bombing on the embassy in Beirut, then, served a dual purpose: for al-Dawa to avenge their persecution by the Iraqi regime, and to act as a message to Muslims the world over to rise against oppressive dictators.

Lebanon was the perfect place for such a bold statement. At the time, it was a country where the logic and language of violence could find root. Torn apart by years of civil war, its Shiite community was increasingly open to a militant interpretation of the faith. Traditionally at the bottom of the pile of Lebanon's confessional politics, Shia Lebanese were to find in Khomeini's concept of martyrdom a potent symbol of empowerment. So, when remnants of al-Dawa also fled to Lebanon, they were to arrive at a point in Lebanon's history where martyrdom was to align with an urgent demand for revolution, and with predictably explosive results.

Such thoughts had already seeped into the Lebanese Shia consciousness through the words of the Iranian-born cleric Musa al-Sadr, who had arrived in Lebanon at the age of thirty-one. Like Khomeini, al-Sadr – also a former student from Najaf – used the image of Hussein-the-martyr as a clarion call for sacrifice. The impoverished Shiite population in Southern Lebanon and the suburbs of Beirut

became a hotbed for his recruitment. By 1975, another militia movement called Amal – the Battalions of the Lebanese Resistance – had
been established, the beginnings of a crowded field of militant bodies
that seemed to sprout up almost overnight.

Amal were emboldened by the entry of another actor onto the
scene: the Syrians, who also chose to fund them.[8] This was out of
Syrian self-interest – they wanted to keep the Palestinian Liberation
Organisation (PLO) in check in Lebanon. By the early 1980s, Lebanese Shiites – fighters for Amal – were travelling over to Syria to be
trained in the art of war.[9] So it was that Amal, emboldened by Syrian
training and fortified by Iranian funding, were to find their voice,
just as Lebanon found itself in the midst of tumult.

In the summer of 1982, Israel invaded this small, mountainous
country. Intent on stamping out the forces of the PLO on the borders,
the Israelis swooped like a hawk. The Syrian air force was quickly
repelled, and within less than a week, Israeli forces had reached the
edge of Beirut. Terror followed; the PLO hid among civilians but the
Israelis did not let that deter their advance. Israeli bombs reportedly
killed thousands of Lebanese civilians. As such violence continued,
'an unfamiliar symbiosis of political demands and theocratic conviction' emerged among the Shiites.[10] As one expert on suicidal terror
has written: 'If Iran's encouragement of a culture of martyrdom created the possibility for suicide attacks, the Israeli invasion created
the perceived need.'[11]

Every Israeli blow at the Shias in Southern Lebanon was seen as
a re-enactment of Hussein's suffering; every killing of Muslims seen
as a massacre of the innocents; and every Western and Israeli soldier
on the ground in Lebanon seen to be the soldiers of Satan. Under the
weight of such anger, Amal split. While many of its members preferred conducting defensive war, a smaller group resolved to attack
the enemy directly. It was this smaller group, along with revolutionary
guards sent from Iran and some Iraqi clerics, that would take action.

Operating as 'Islamic Amal' or 'Islamic Jihad', a group of Lebanese Shiites and 2,000 Iranian Revolutionary Guards seized some army barracks in Lebanon's Bekaa Valley, and it was there that the notion of martyrdom for a Shia cause was to take root: to leap from an Iranian idea into something far more Lebanese.

I had determined to head there, seeking out memories of the Ayatollah's reach. I wanted to trace how this transmission of an idea occurred, and to see where it led. So my fixer – a *Guardian* journalist and real-life Syrian princess called Nadia Al Faour – and I began the slow and unrelenting ascent from the embassy to the Lebanese mountain valley of Bekaa, heading for the ancient city of Baalbek. And as we did so, a morning mist covered the road, blocking the view. It was exhilarating: cars rushed out of the thick fog, and the land seemed to dissolve, becoming liquid. It felt, for a moment, as if I was driving back into history.

The Bekaa Valley has always drawn outsiders. Today, tour buses disgorge sightseers eager to touch the remnants of the ancient past here. Other outsiders are also seen, their presence lightly felt. Syrian refugee camps, faded tents flapping in the wind, line the arterial roads; they hunch like white pilgrims at prayer. These displaced come from beyond the mountains that circle the valley, from beyond the scudding clouds. In the distance, marked by snow, a range of peaks disappears into a horizon of deepening layers of blue and turquoise; the beauty of the place is both striking and painful.

The famous red-rust ruins of Baalbek speak of the appeal of this fertile land. Once people prayed to the sun here, but that worship was diluted by the successive waves of Greeks, Romans, early Christians, Byzantines, Muslims, Damascenes, Crusaders, Mongols, Ottomans and Egyptians who came in turn. Each heralded a fresh usurpation that led to massacres and murders and, sometimes, even alleged cannibalism. Legacies of these conquests can be seen in ancient temple

Roadside memorials to the dead in Baalbeck, Lebanon

ruins, the cobwebbed trinkets of trader stalls and, on the roads out
of the town, in the more recent paintings of Ayatollah Khomeini that
hang, slowly fading, on crumbling walls.

Between olive groves and fields of green, we drove looking for
evidence that the Iranian Revolutionary Guard had come here, and
how they brought their ideas of martyrdom with them.

At the time it was reported that these elite troops had stuck
notices on the doors of army huts in this valley, proclaiming themselves 'lovers of martyrdom' and producing placards and banners
denouncing Israeli and American 'imperialism'.[12] In these banners
lay the dream of transforming Lebanon into an Iranian-style Islamic
state, and that meant sacrifice.

The problem was that many people I had spoken to denied that the
Iranians had ever had such a pivotal role in spreading the notion of

martyrdom here. Lebanon is a country that has been so long divided by sectarianism and conflict that getting a straight answer about anything seemed, on occasion, to be an exercise in futility.

Earlier, in Beirut, I had attempted to take a picture of a man who had been blown off his feet by a suicide bomber. An old tradesman, he had been selling strawberries in Beirut's streets for almost two decades; the bomber's blast cost him ninety stitches and nearly $25,000 on treatment alone, he said. Just as I was about to ask him a few questions, two men with rifles appeared at our sides and demanded to see our papers, permissions, passports. They were the armed guards of Hezbollah, the infamous 'Party of God' that dominates Lebanese politics – Shia Islamists accused of a string of bombings against Jewish and Israeli targets and designated a terrorist organisation by many Western nations, Gulf Arab countries, the Arab League and Israel. In Lebanon they are a formidable influence – a 'state within a state'. So we were escorted away and detained, questions were asked and then more questions were asked until a small nervousness began to creep up on me. Even now the name Hezbollah conjures up to many the kidnapping of the journalist John McCarthy, along with Brian Keenan and, later, Terry Waite. These fighters may have smiled at us and offered us water, but they did so with semi-automatic machine guns slung around their necks.

To these men suspicion was a second language, and it was the same with the people of Baalbek. Where, we asked the Baalbeckers, were the Iranians based? We received obscure, fluid answers that sent us in one direction and then the next. Hostile questions were asked in return for our own: 'Why do you want to know? Who are you with? Why are you asking questions?' Someone said that there had been a Khomeini hospital here once, but in the place where it was said to have stood we just found the Al Quds pharmacy. 'They were never here,' said another man. One old woman just screamed at us: 'Get out, get out, get out.'

Roadside signs proved less elusive, though. 'Imam Khomeini said Musa al-Sadr is one of my sons', read one, linking Iran's spiritual leader with the leader of Lebanon's Shia Muslims. Another advertised a recruitment programme to train up jihadists: 'We thank you for your contribution', it read, beside an image of a soldier in full combats beneath the Lebanese flag and the flag of the 'Hezb'.

Like the Beirut suburb where we had been detained, this area was also a Hezbollah stronghold; along the road fluttered hundreds of its yellow flags, each displaying an AK-47 raised aloft. In between them stood images of the dead. Here was the photo of a martyr who had fallen in Palestine less than a month ago, a rifle held above his head. There was a dedication to two brothers killed. Martyr memorials were everywhere, some commemorated in solid plaques and on round-about shrines, others just peeling posters on front doors. Black flags hung over market streets that read, simply, 'Oh Hussain'.

But despite these haunting reminders of history, no one would testify that the Iranians were ever here. The huts that they once occupied had been torn down years ago, the presence of Iran long since subsumed into the body of Lebanese politics. Perhaps this is what Lebanon does – it takes an outside influence and makes it peculiarly its own.

In Lebanon in the 1980s, a change took hold again. The Shiites were to move from being the poorest and weakest faction of Lebanese society to one armed with Iranian money, weapons and men. And, most importantly of all, the one equipped with a new and explosive idea for a weapon: the suicide bomber. Here Hezbollah were to find their real roots.[13]

Nobody, though, would admit this, as if the presence of the Iranians – like the Greeks, the English and the Egyptians – was best left in the soup of the past. And as the hours ticked away, and as we were met with fingers pointed in the direction that we had just travelled, I turned to Nadia and said we would try one last place before calling it a day. We pulled over in front of an antique store on the edge of town. A few metres away stood a blue sign on the road – an official-looking one. 'The Iranian public is at the service of the Lebanese public', it read.

We walked into the shop, a dusty room filled with brass pots and candlesticks, the redundant luxuries of the dead. At the back sat three men drinking coffee around a table and one of them – a heavyset man with a red shirt, greying hair and a goatee – asked what we were doing. Nadia explained and he looked at me and joked: 'How much money would we get if we kidnapped you?'

Nadia and I laughed weakly. Then he grew serious. 'You should be careful asking those sorts of questions,' he said. 'They'll come after you. Stop asking people left and right.'

'But were the Iranians here?' I asked.

'I'll tell you one name: Khoram,' he said, elliptically. There used to be a hotel nearby, next to a hospital, which had housed the Revolutionary Guard, he said, but everything had been torn down and replaced with new villas. I noted the name down and he began to open up. Someone brought yet more coffee and as he drank his he twirled a line of black prayer beads in his hands, clicking them in the dim light of the shop. His words were languid, voluble. He was sixty-nine now, but back then he had trained with the Revolutionary Guards, and yes, they brought the idea of martyrdom with them.

'This is a game of nations,' he said, 'Lebanon was and still is a field of struggle – for the British, for the Russians, for the Iranians, the Persians, the Romans, Syrians, Israelis . . .' He kept on coming back to the present, to the looming violence in Syria, the Russian air strikes, the nearby crisis that had engulfed the attention of everyone here. He could not understand why I wanted to look over his shoulder into the past. But I pushed him on the point. Above him was a poster of Khomeini etched on bronze plate. What impact did he have here, I wanted to know.

'Khomeini's ghost is not just here in Lebanon,' he said, 'it impacts all the Islamic world. His belief in the martyr led to what we have today – Taliban, Al-Qaeda, ISIS . . .'

This was what I had suspected. This was the strand that I was trying to find – how what started in Iran spread, like an uncontrollable virus, throughout the Middle East and then throughout the world. The contagious idea of the valiant martyr that, within a few years of the Revolutionary Guard stepping on Lebanese soil, was to mutate and expand in a terrible way.

Abdallah was fifteen years old when he saw the suicide bomber explode but can remember it like it was yesterday. It was a Thursday morning, 11 November 1982, and he was opening up his father's car repair workshop for the day. Early in the morning, the street was quiet apart from one car on that almost empty road. Back and forth it went, back and forth. A white Peugeot 504. Back and forth.

It made him nervous: 'Why is this idiot driving around like this?' he said. 'He's going to get us, and himself, in trouble.' On 6 June 1982, the Israel Defence Forces had invaded Southern Lebanon, after repeated attacks and counter-attacks between them and the PLO operating there, and the locals were finding the new status quo strained indeed.

Part inspired by the attack on the Iraqi embassy, part taking advice from the Revolutionary Guard in Baalbek, the group that would one day become Hezbollah had decided upon their target: the Israeli military governor's eight-floor compound in the southern Lebanese town of Tyre. As in Iran, the bomber was a child, a fifteen-year-old called Ahmad Qassir. And, like many in Iran, he was inspired by the ideal of the martyr. Abdallah was the last person to see his face before he died, watching as the driver turned the car and languidly drove into that fortified and occupied compound.

'It wasn't a huge explosion,' he said. 'But a few seconds later the building came crashing down. It began shaking and it just went like this on the floor.' He spread his hands out, mimicking the collapse of the building to the earth. The explosion killed seventy-five Israeli soldiers, border police and agents of Shin Bet, the feared Israel Security Agency. About fourteen Lebanese and Palestinian prisoners that were being held captive on the roof there were also killed.

One of those captives was Abdallah's future father-in-law. 'But he got out alive. Five years later, I married his daughter,' Abdallah said.

It was immediately apparent how much of a propaganda coup the attack was. The Israeli government was quick to announce that the explosion was the result of a gas leak,[14] something they insist on to this day. This would contradict not only Abdallah's claim that he saw the car enter the building, but also an alleged Shin Bet report that detailed the Hezbollah preparations for the bombing.[15]

Either way, the dominant belief here in Lebanon and in Iran was that Ahmad Qassir carried out the attack. The Ayatollah Khomeini personally consecrated the bombing with a fatwa – the ruling of Islamic scholars – and had a memorial built for the boy in Tehran;[16] another was erected near Baalbek.[17] They also put up a plaque here, outside the glass-fronted medical building that now stands on the site of the bombing, its words testifying to the virtue of the horror.

'Martyrs create life', reads the inscription's salvationist message, stamped above a picture of the bomber, a boy whose moustache barely covered his lip, whose face was still soft.

'He created the reign of martyrs', it proclaimed, in 'a hurricane.'

It indeed unleashed a storm: a year later, almost to the day, a nearly identical bombing struck just up the road here, in Tyre – a port once home to the mighty seafaring Phoenician Empire. A pickup truck filled with explosives was driven into a Shin Bet building this time, killing twenty-eight Israelis and thirty-two Lebanese prisoners in the process.

A tribute to the first Lebanese suicide bomber to target Israeli troops

It was not just Israel that was under attack, either. On 18 April 1983, another foreign power was targeted. This time it was the United States who was to pay for supporting Israel, for upholding the Lebanese political system, and for backing Saddam Hussein's Iraq.[18] The United States had intervened in the Lebanese civil war following inter-ethnic massacres in the towns of Sabra and Shatila, and they did so seeking to restore order and central government authority, but to some it was the Great Satan meddling with affairs it should not have. A Texas-bought pickup truck, packed with almost 1,000 kilograms of explosives, was driven into the US embassy in Beirut, killing 63 and wounding 120. Seventeen Americans died, including the CIA's chief intelligence officer for the Middle East, Robert Ames. The explosion broke windows over a mile away.

At the time it was meant to force the US out of Lebanon, but the Americans' initial response was resolution. 'This criminal act on a diplomatic establishment will not deter us from our goals of peace in the region,' said President Reagan.[19] The following day the House

Foreign Affairs Committee approved $251 million in additional economic and military aid for Lebanon.[20]

Such refusal to back down had consequences. On 23 October 1983, the then 'largest non-nuclear explosion ever detonated on the face of the Earth' happened.[21] Two truck bombs targeted separate buildings in Beirut housing the Multinational Force in Lebanon (MNF) peacekeepers – one of them driven by an Iranian national called Ismail Ascari. In total 305 people were killed: 241 American peacekeepers, 58 French and 6 civilians. It was the worst military loss for France since the Battle for Algiers.[22] It took five hours to pull the last survivor from the American rubble – a Lutheran chaplain with the marines called Danny G. Wheeler.

'We had a deep sense that something was going to happen – that it was going to get grim,' he told me. 'We were a juicy target – we were trying to be neutral, with a British and French and American and UN flag – trying to stop a civil war happening. It was an Iranian that did it. And it was very similar to what is happening today . . . I have heard that it was a precursor to those days ahead. And yes, I think there is a relationship with 9/11 in it all.'

Now a seventy-year-old with seven grandsons, he recalls how, when lying in the ruins, he was convinced he was going to die. He was angry at his God and not prepared to go willingly. 'I have to go through that all again when I get to that point,' he said, talking about his own age and the looming shadow of mortality, 'but I do have that memory of touching God.'

He has long ago forgiven the youth who had almost consigned him to an early grave. 'It takes a desperate young person who is promised a paradise – a better world beyond – who believes that his death is for a good cause, a just cause. Fanaticism of any sort can make people do the craziest things.'

Despite his forgiveness, the thirty-four-year-old memory is still fresh: 'I could feel the souls that were being taken. That hurts the most to this day – we all suffered together. It leaves you empty; a part of your life is empty forever. No one can fill that void. It is hard to explain.'

To this day a conclusive finger has yet to be pointed as to who was behind the attacks.[23] We do know that the vehicle and explosives were prepared in the Bekaa Valley.[24] And some claim the attack was authorised by Khomeini himself,[25] a monument to commemorate the bombings and its 'martyrs' being erected in a cemetery in Tehran in 2004.[26] But the response is far better known. France launched an air strike in the Bekaa Valley against the Iranian positions. The Americans planned a counter-strike, too, but did not carry it through: proving Iranian involvement was hard. Using a proxy militant group afforded Khomeini plausible deniability.

Perhaps sensing weakness in this, groups like Islamic Jihad began to phone in new threats. 'The earth would tremble,' they said, unless the MNF left. It worked. On 7 February 1984, President Reagan ordered his marines to begin their withdrawal. Perhaps with the memory of Vietnam still fresh in the American consciousness, there was little congressional appetite to risk more American lives overseas.[27] The suicide bomber had won.

It marked a pivotal point. Shiite Muslims had won a battle against Western nations, further fuelling the idea that an Islamic revival was fast underway. It was for this reason that, in 2017, US Vice-President Mike Pence referred to the bombings as 'the opening salvo in a war that we have waged ever since – the global war on terror.'[28]

With the Americans and others gone, the militant groups concentrated their focus on the other occupiers of their land – the Israelis. Between 1982 and 2000, Hezbollah carried out over 6,000 operations against the Israeli Defence Forces and their proxy, the South Lebanon Army.[29] On occasions the groups mimicked the sacrifice of the Basij, human waves running up hills against a wall of machine-gun fire.[30] On others they deployed suicide bombings, seventeen in all, killing 565 and injuring 979.[31] These were by pre-dominantly Shia groups: Hezbollah, Aisha Umm-al Mouemeneen, Believing Youth Group, Amal and Islamic Amal.[32] They used cars packed with explosives, occasionally suicide belts,[33] and even sent out donkeys and boats to deliver their deadly payloads. These attacks were designed to make their enemy insecure, bridging a significant gap in the imbalance of military power between the Israelis and their enemies.

As in Iran, those who undertook the attacks were venerated – in loud public funerals, in adorned cemeteries and in videos and songs. Today you can see their faces peering out from posters at the sides of motorways, some so bleached by the sun that they take on the appearance of ghosts. The wall that separates the south with Israeli-occupied territories is covered with such images. 'Way to Jerusalem' appears

Faded memorials to martyrs line Lebanon's highways

a common cry, evoking a millenarian hope that the Holy City will once again be regained by the Muslim majority in this region. And, as in Iran, groups like Hezbollah supported the families of suicide bombers with a 'martyrs" fund.[34] Such things worked: in the 1980s a Lebanese sociologist called Waajih Kourani wrote that 'among Lebanese youngsters we can trace a permanent willingness to die for the sake of the greater social group.'[35]

These attacks were also to be, in the main, meticulously planned and ruthlessly carried out. Since they first appeared in the Middle East, four of the five most lethal users of suicide bombers in the world happen to be Lebanese Shia groups – at least in terms of numbers of people killed in each attack. Only one of these five, Al-Qaeda, is Sunni, its average numbers pushed up by its attack on 9/11. On average, fifty-two people have been killed with every Shia suicide attack, five times the average number of fatalities for suicide attacks in the modern world.

Perhaps this is to be expected. The Shias had the advantage of shock on their side – militaries had yet to adapt to the suicide bombers' headlong rush to their deaths. But what such murderous efficiency meant was that other groups, both in and outside Lebanon, began to see a certain appeal in the power of the suicide bomber. So, while the idea of the suicide attack arrived in Lebanon wrapped in an Iranian interpretation of Shia Islam, once there it was transformed.

In part this is because there were limits to how much the Lebanese would accept the deeply orthodox interpretation of Iranian theology. Attempts by Hezbollah to impose a strict Islamic code rankled with locals – the chador didn't take on, and the closure of coffee shops upset many. When the tourist beaches cleared and businesses began closing due to the Islamic restrictions, a backlash followed. It forced Hezbollah to choose pragmatism above proselytisation and instead they offered up a deal: 'Support our resistance against Israel, and we will stop talking about an Islamic republic and stop telling you how to live your lives'.[36] In other words – nationalism and politics had become as important as faith to the martyr.

So successful was the tactic that, over time, secular groups also began to adopt the suicide bomber's mantle. In all, about fifty suicide bombings in Lebanon were undertaken by secular communist and nationalist organisations. These included the Lebanese Communist Party, the Socialist-Nasserist Organization, the Syrian Ba'ath Party, and the Syrian Social Nationalist Party. Their approach was not that different from Hezbollah – the bombers filmed their final testimonies, they gave their lives up for a higher calling, and their God was a form of utopian nationalism (not dissimilar to the Russians').

When, on 30 October 1989, a group called the Popular Front for the Liberation of Palestine (PFLP) launched a suicide boat attack on an Israeli attack craft, it was done with that utopia in mind – the destruction of Israel was integral to ridding the Middle East of Western capitalism. Formed after the occupation of the West Bank by Israel in 1967 by a Palestinian Christian, George Habash, the PFLP combined Arab nationalism with Marxism–Leninism. The sea attack itself was botched – the first terrorist suicide attack carried out against an Israeli boat served only to wound one sailor lightly – but it showed the appeal of the suicidal martyr was spreading, away from fighters for God to fighters for nation, freedom and revenge.

One of those fighters was Lola Elias Abboud, a middle-class Christian who was born in Qara'oun Al-Hunobi, in the southern region of the Bekaa Valley in 1966. The daughter of a journalist, from a family they said had given up many martyrs, she died in a suicide attack on 21 April 1985, not far from where she was born.[37] She detonated in front of an Israeli Defence Forces outpost, the day after Easter – a fact some see as symbolic of her death being 'a resurrection to her people'.[38]

She died as a member of the Lebanese National Resistance Front (Jammoul), the armed wing of the Lebanese Communist Party, which was to fight the Israeli occupation and its proxy force in the region, the South Lebanese Army (SLA). How many people Lola killed is a matter of debate. CNN reported four soldiers died, though her bombing is absent from the Chicago Suicide Attack Database.[39] I tracked down the person who had walked her to her death, her final companion, to ask how it was that a Christian communist could die for a cause, without any promise of paradise offered up to those who kill themselves in an attack. A promise that had been so pivotal in the Shia framing of the act.

At first the conversation was filled with suspicion and he only gave up his nickname: Nassur Abu. He runs a car repair shop now and there is nothing of the revolutionary militant to him today. A charcoal stubble, a dirty denim shirt – he is almost sixty and his hands show a lifetime of working with spanners and bolts and nuts. He didn't talk much, but did provide me with critical insight.

'Our group was very secular,' he said, cleaning his hands with a rag, 'it involved both men and women. Ours was a battle for the Lebanese nation, and involved communists, socialists; everybody fighting as one.' In total, at least eleven of its members have been credited with undertaking suicide attacks for the group, killing at least 157 in so doing; four of these were women.

The first of these was Sana'a Mehaidli, who had died and killed a few weeks before Lola, blowing herself up in a Peugeot filled with explosives next to an Israeli convoy in Jezzine on 9 April 1985. Mehaidli was to be called the 'Bride of the South', and Lola Abboud the 'Flower of the Bekaa Valley'. Religion, though, played no part in their actions – as a leader of the Syrian Socialist Party said in an interview, for the thirty men and women who conducted suicide missions, 'Their country is their paradise.'[40]

Sana'a Mehaidli said this herself: 'I choose to do this because I am fulfilling my duty towards my land and my people . . . Now I am loving my country, sacrificing my life and respecting the people of the south.'[41]

The use of female suicide bombers who were dying neither for God nor faith was to have an intense impact. Photographs of them were seen on the covers of Middle Eastern magazines. The French weekly *Paris Match* ran a double-page article entitled '*La Kamikaze*' – that reference again. Such deaths, the *Washington Post* reported, were 'part of an effort to wrest the banner of successful opposition to Israel and the United States away from the fanatically religious Hezbollah, or Party of God, and other groups believed operating behind the shadowy cover of "Islamic Jihad".'[42] They put a new sense of nationalism front and centre into the Middle East: suicide bombings that spoke as much about the power plays of Lebanon's permanently labyrinthine internal politics as they did about freedom from occupation.

Such suicide attacks, based on patriotism, not just on Shiite forms of fundamentalism, appealed to other fighters around the world. Shop-keepers on Saladin Street in East Jerusalem in Israel put up displays of these female suicide bombers in their windows. And the Israelis, perhaps fearing how this might spread, returned with propaganda of their own. They interviewed a sixteen-year-old called Mohammed Mahoud Burro, whose suicide mission, they said, had failed. Burro, challenging the martyr's message, claimed he was forced into his mission by Syrian-allied intelligence operatives to free his father from debt.

The truth, though, was more complicated than Israeli propaganda: many were now willing to die for a cause. When the leader of the Lebanese Baath Party travelled to Damascus in 1985, he carried with him dozens of letters from party members signed with their blood. The urge for people to show they would die for their country was gaining momentum.

Personal acts were instrumental in this. Because Lola Abboud was a Christian, 'it had an impact even on the national level in Lebanon.' It challenged the stereotype, the mechanic Nassur told me, 'that only Muslims get martyred this way'.

The long-term consequence of her sacrifice, though, was not what she would have wanted. 'I'm proud of her for what she's done and it was the right way to go about it, but unfortunately the outcome we were expecting – change – did not happen,' he said, stretching out his arms, a subtle signal that the conversation was drawing to a close. But what else could he say? Communism did not spread through Lebanon. The utopia that haunted Lola's mind never materialised.

Despite the appearance of secular militant suicide bombers in Lebanon, this does not mean that religion lost its role. The Shia cleric and Hezbollah's 'spiritual guide', Grand Ayatollah Mohammad Hussain Fadlallah, a man also born in Najaf, went from a position of disavowing attacks to accepting them; he compared suicide attacks to a soldier fighting a battle that he cannot win, yet he fights nevertheless.[43] Suicide attacks, to him, were a military necessity in an uphill battle against troops with far superior technology.[44] The fatwas he issued were among the first to justify the use of suicide attacks, and others were to follow. In 1993, Hassan Nasrallah, the current secretary general of Hezbollah, defended suicide attacks with his words: 'Death is not oblivion. It is not the end. It is the beginning of a true life.'[45]

New phrases to condone the suicide bomber emerged. Some words existed: *Istishhad* referred to the act of martyrdom, while *shahada* referred to any incidental death during jihad (such as a soldier falling in battle). But the phrase 'suicide bomber' did not. So Hezbollah coined the term *al-amalyiat al-istishhaadiya* when referring to their martyrdom operations.[46] Suicide bombers themselves were *shahid as-said* or 'happy martyrs'.[47] When the Israelis ordered there to be a minimum of two people travelling in every car in the territories they occupied – believing getting two people to take part in a suicide attack would be so hard that it would stop such bombings – Hezbollah responded. They used the phrase *shahid al-mazlum* – someone who neither planned nor wanted to die, but became a martyr none-theless. It was for the extra passenger.

Such focus on titles and names suggest something else that Hez-bollah was concerned with – the legitimacy of using bombers. While today we are increasingly exposed to the news of random civilians being killed by suicide attacks, in Lebanon targets were carefully chosen. There, in the two decades up until 2000 when the Israelis left, 95 per cent of all attacks were either military or political.

In part because of this targeted use of suicide bombings, they did not flourish in Lebanon for long. Despite their rapid rise in the 1980s, suicide attacks by Hezbollah had dropped off entirely by the 1990s, with only four suicide bombings by them in that decade. There is even anecdotal evidence of Hezbollah trying to prevent a skilled senior military operative called Salah Ghandour from launching his own suicide mission in 1995, though he was ultimately successful.[48]

Over time, Hezbollah preferred instead to use roadside bombs and other forms of explosive attack. In 1998, such attacks were behind sixteen of twenty-four Israeli military fatalities.[49] Fadlallah issued a new fatwa authorising the practice of suicide bombing 'only on special occasions' to prevent 'exaggerated use (by) overzealous youth'.[50]

Why was there this change? Years after he issued this fatwa, I interviewed Fadlallah's son, Sayyid Ali Fadlallah, to ask about his father's reticence. Ushered into his offices in Beirut, it was clear from the formal tone of the meeting the son had stepped into his father's shoes. I would have just fifteen minutes, and when the man himself came in, dressed in the orthodox black and white robes of an imam, his answers were soft-spoken and measured. Over the tiniest cups of tea I have ever drunk, he navigated this dangerous theological territory with soft steps, just as his father had done.

'In Islam,' he began, his hands folded in his lap, a Quran placed open next to him in a presentation case, 'it is a sin to kill yourself;

your soul is not yours to take. There are some who see suicide bombing as a means to fight when there's no other way to respond militarily. On this matter you have three separate opinions: it should never be done; it can only be done if it is the only means to fight back; and, to some, it is an acceptable military means.'

'Civilians must not be killed,' he said. 'But I cannot evaluate if a suicide bomber is in Heaven – it depends on his case and his cause. For Shias, death is not destined or written; I get to choose or at least control the setting of my death, it's not fate. One can choose how one dies.' And with that the time was up, some of his statements posing more theological questions than they answered.

Perhaps the more straightforward answer as to why there had been a spiritual change over suicide attacks was because by then, here in Lebanon, the suicide bombers had done their job. Israeli soldiers, conscripts with barely any stubble on their chins, were terrified of the fanatical attacks. Morale plummeted, and appetite in Israel for the occupation fell with it. In 1995, a paratrooper unit had to be disbanded after asking for an alternative mission when told they were being sent to Lebanon. As many as a quarter of Israeli personnel serving in Lebanon experienced psychological problems, compared to only 5 per cent during the 1973 war.[51] By 2000, following an election campaign promise, Israeli Prime Minister Ehud Barak withdrew Israeli forces, ending fifteen years of fighting there. Like the withdrawal of the US and France, the suicide bomber had played a pivotal role in pushing out another, far stronger nation.

The job done, that same year Ayatollah Fadlallah issued a statement acknowledging the importance of suicide attacks for Hezbollah's victory, but emphasised that they were not necessary any more.[52] Hezbollah was no longer a small organisation needing to use the 'propaganda of the deed' to assert its power – it was in power. Besides, few organisations, when they are in control, commit their ranks to suicidal missions.

Public support for suicide bombings fell, too. In 2007, just 34 per cent of Lebanese Muslims said suicide bombings in defence of Islam were justified; in 2002, 74 per cent had said they were.[53] And with such religious pronunciations, the Shia use of the suicide bomber ended. I can only find two exceptions since: one Shia attack in 2013 in Syria (Iran's supreme leader, Ali Khamenei, had said that Syria's conflict was the second Karbala),[54] and a 2017 strike of three Houthi suicide bombers against a Saudi ship off the western coast of Yemen.[55]

You could argue that Shiite suicide attacks stopped because there was no active threat to Shiite-dominated countries after the end of the Iran–Iraq War or the withdrawal of Israeli forces from Lebanon, but this conclusion would simplify the role ideology and religion played in the creation – and disbanding – of suicide operations. Shiite groups were constantly fighting in Afghanistan and are still actively combating the Saudi Arabian coalition in Yemen, yet neither Afghan Shiites nor Houthi rebels have routinely deployed suicide attackers.

Instead, the notion of the suicide bomber began to spread further afield. The fact that Lebanon's suicide bombings worked – forcing the French, the Americans and the Israelis to leave – lionised the use of suicide attacks in Arab lore, and created a model for others. And so the dark logic of the suicide bomber travelled, away from the Middle East and south to the island of Sri Lanka in the Indian Ocean, there to find new devotees among men and women seeking to win a civil war. Here were people who embraced this devastating weapon with ferocity, in a bid to build a glorious new country from its ashes.

Chapter 5

Death in Paradise

There is a road in Sri Lanka known as the 'Highway of Death'. Officially, it is designated the A9, but its darker title sticks because on
its tarmac, on a daily basis, three-wheel taxi drivers are spun out of
control by careering buses, while ancient Austins, Fords and Morris
Minors – gently rusting memories of a time when the north of the
country had money to buy cars – all too often collide, killing those
inside. The nickname, though, came from a previous age. Because
during the civil war that raged on the island between 1983 and 2009,
this 321-kilometre-long highway, which runs from Jaffna up to the
northern tip of the island, was renowned for being the main arterial
road for both the government's military and the Tamil Tigers they
were fighting. It was a haematic artery, indeed.

Once pitted with potholes and shell holes, it is now perhaps the best
road surface in Sri Lanka. This is by design: the military needs a clear
route to the north in case civil war flares up again. But as we sped down
it, I saw that the broken houses that lined it, hundreds of them, had been
left unrepaired. Empty windows, crumbling red-tile roofs, once-white
walls speckled with the scars of conflict: these were the deserted homes
of war. And each vacant building bore a question mark. I asked my
driver to pull over and jumped out of the van to look at the dereliction.

Everywhere the jungle was trying to reclaim the space the war had emptied. Prickly lantana, with bunches of scarlet blossoms, emerged through gaps in the concrete. Fragrant frangipani clustered below shattered window frames. Stepping over the threshold of one dwelling felt momentarily like a violation; once somebody's front room, it was now a skeleton. Although it was a mere carapace of a home, I still felt like an unwanted intruder.

Walking to the rear of the house, past small mounds of rubble, I saw a simple hole-in-the-floor toilet. Weeds were pushing up from the latrine, and beside it lay a decomposing pile of army fatigues. I looked closer and saw a smear of crusted blood across a flak jacket. I hurried out and headed over to an advertising sign pockmarked with bullet holes, and stepped off the mud track to get a closer look.

'Iain, Iain!' My guide Arun, a Tamil journalist who had agreed to take me to the killing fields of the north, was shouting from the van. 'Please – don't go off the path. This is why nobody is here.' He didn't need to say the word landmines, but it was as if a snake lay in the shrubs.

This land was still shrouded in secrets and threats. It had been a conflict fought far from the world's gaze, where journalists were refused entry and where atrocities on both sides descended into a vicious cycle of tit for tat. On the one side was the Sri Lankan government, predominantly Singhalese, who had littered this ground with landmines. On the other was the separatist Tamil movement led by a fighting force that had, among other tactics, laid down improvised booby traps across this tract of land, seeking to separate the Tamil north from the rest of the mostly Buddhist island.

I walked carefully back to the van. This area had been witness to some of the fiercest fighting in the whole war, and above the car leant a coconut tree shattered from a flying shell, its bark exploded outwards like a black rose. We were a few miles from Elephant Pass – the so-called gateway to the Jaffna peninsula and a narrow causeway that, bound on either side by the Indian Ocean, formed a strategic bottleneck to the north. A military base had been here since 1760, when the Portuguese first built a fort. Dutch and British forces came later, planting their flags into this sea-salt earth. Three battles had marked this land during the civil war: the territory being controlled by the government, then being taken by the rebelling Tamils, and back again. We drove on.

A few minutes later the car pulled over again. Arun had not mentioned it, but here, with the cresting waves of the sea visible on either side, was a memorial to a suicide bomber. In the centre of the square stood a huge, rusting bulldozer, pitted with bullet holes; packed with explosives and two Tamils set upon dying, it had once been driven at the Sinhalese government lines.

In fact, this was a memorial to a suicide bomber stopping a suicide bomber – possibly a unique global monument – for it was not this Tamil-made truck being memorialised, but the Sinhalese soldier who, on 10 July 1991, had laid down his life to stop it: an army lance corporal called Gamini Kularatne. Here, in this place now filled with the caw of crows and the smell of sea air, Kularatne had seen the lumbering hulk of the bulldozer storming towards his lines. It threatened to overrun his military base, so he had chosen to charge at the truck and die a martyr's death. Despite being hit numerous times by machine-gun bullets, he managed to grab hold of the vehicle's ladder and, dragging himself upwards, fling two grenades down the hatch. The blast killed him and the occupants, but saved the base. For a war made famous by the Tamil Tigers' use of suicide bombers, here was a monument to counter that narrative – a man who died for the Sri Lankan state.

The little museum that had been erected next to the monument was lacklustre, as if those who sought to celebrate the man's gallantry had struggled to find things worthy to exhibit. In the government's desire to pad out the slim offerings, they had placed in cabinets a

The improvised suicide truck that was stopped by Corporal Gamini Kularatne when he blew himself up in Northern Sri Lanka

faded payslip, a folded bed sheet and a pink plate all used by the 'legendary hero'. A small display, labelled a 'Souvenir Gallery', had been built to commemorate this man's death, and a video offered a breathless recounting of his sacrifice on a loop, with stirring military music playing in the background. It was hard to gauge from these everyday items what might have motivated Kularatne to give his life in the way he did, but songs were still sung in his name and statues in his image had been erected across the land.[1]

Only later did I learn that Kularatne had been a one-time Buddhist monk who had seen the Tamil Tiger slaughter of thirty-seven passengers on a bus near the village of Aranthalawa, in the east of the country. Witnessing the massacre, one that included thirty-three of his fellow monks, Kularatne had forsaken his robes to put on combat uniform to fight the Tigers.

A mural depicting the corporal's final moments was on a wall behind the souvenir stall. It showed a man who looked nothing like those bleached encased photographs of the stick-thin Kularatne, but that is how memorials go.

Walking back to the bulldozer, I took photographs from all angles and tried to picture the ferocity of the fighting, to get a sense of why people within and without its metal hulk both died for their respective causes. But nothing came. It was just a lump of rusting metal under an unforgiving sun. Suicide bombings may have been a defining feature of the war here, but now, like the empty houses that surrounded this macabre memorial, their backstory was frustratingly elusive.

Even the number of suicide attacks in the civil conflict is still a matter of fierce debate. The fog of war and a bitter propaganda tussle have turned facts into the stuff of high politics. A study by the Sri Lankan Armed Forces claimed 239 Black Tigers (the name given to the Tamil suicide attackers) died in strikes. The University of Chicago database on suicide bombings in Sri Lanka has lower figures. They list some 115 attacks, killing and injuring over 5,500 people.[2] It was an era of bombings that stretched from 5 July 1987 to 5 May 2009, almost two decades of suicide violence.[3]

Certainly, the Tamil Tigers were once world leaders in this use of force: between 1987 and 2001, the group was responsible for between a third and a half of the suicide attacks carried out around the world, and for a time – at least until 11 September 2001 – they were the deadliest terror organisation in existence.[4]

Theirs was a potent weapon. The Tamil Tigers deployed suicide bombers with deadly accuracy to destroy the Joint Operations Command, the nerve centre of the Sri Lankan security forces; the World Trade Centre in Colombo; the Temple of the Tooth Relic, the most hallowed Buddhist shrine; and the oil storage installations in Kolonnawa.[5] They were also the only terrorist organisation in modern history to have killed two world leaders: the former Prime Minister of India, Rajiv Gandhi (1991),[6] and the President of Sri Lanka, Ranasinghe Premadasa (1993). In addition, their suicide bombers killed nine ministers, twenty-six members of parliament and countless civil servants.[7]

As the *New York Times* said, the Tamil guerrillas became 'masters of suicide bombing'.[8] Even so, from a distance, such facts and figures failed to explain why suicide bombings had had such a defining role in this internecine struggle, and this monument offered little more in the way of explanation. But unlike the kamikazes and the Russian anarchists, the people who witnessed these suicide attacks were generally still alive, and that was why I had come to Sri Lanka – to search for Tamil Tigers who had survived the war, and the internment camps that followed, and to ask them about what led so many of their comrades to sacrifice their lives to a cause.

Nirupan had not seen his wife since April 2009, the final days of the war. He did not know if she was alive or dead, he said, his eyes pained. But then, his whole body seemed to exist in the pain of the past, as if mourning had left a permanent mark on him.

His real name was not Nirupan. That was the one the Liberation Tigers of Tamil Eelam (LTTE) had given him when he joined their ranks; he would not tell me his real name, fearing the army would come for him if he did. I was able to come and go, he said, but he would be stuck here to live, and to die, with the consequences. He said that sometimes his knee gives way to unbearable spasms, so much so that he can barely fold into his three-wheel taxi in which he now is forced to earn a living on the streets. I looked down and realised, ten minutes into the conversation, that he did not have a left foot. He had painted his prosthetic limb the colour of his skin and the illusion worked: without proper scrutiny you would never have known he had trodden on a landmine and lost his leg below the knee.

A wife, a foot, a livelihood: his list of loss was mounting. But every one of the former-LTTE fighters that I had spoken to over the past few days had such a toll to tell. To meet some we had to travel deep into the Tamil-dominated countryside, down unmarked roads and past fields of earth so red it looked like the soil was bleeding. Others agreed to meet us under the cloak of darkness, speaking in low voices beneath bare light bulbs. They would only talk in a safe place, at a friend's house, and never under their real names.

'Why did you join to fight?' I asked them all, one after the other over that time, and they looked back at me as if they had never been asked that before. Wasn't it obvious?

'When I joined,' Nirupan said, 'it was out of exuberance. We thought we could change the world and we joined to wreak vengeance. It was only later, after we had met the leader, when we heard his speeches, his way of talking, that we evolved. We began to see it as a fight for our human rights, for the development of our nation.'

Rights and nationhood – these formed the roots of violence that permeated Sri Lanka's recent past. At the end of the British dominion over Ceylon (now Sri Lanka) in 1948, the Sinhalese majority represented 70 per cent of the country's population, with the Tamils a sizeable minority. Under British rule, colonial policy chose to rule by the logic of divide and conquer, and in so doing favoured this Tamil minority, giving it a disproportionate share of power. The fathers of men like Nirupan had had jobs, and good ones at that. But independence from the British just after the Second World War changed everything – it was another group's 'turn to eat'. The political backlash was swift and hard: shortly after they secured power, the new Sri Lankan government adopted Sinhala to be its official language, rather than English, and in so doing effectively disqualified large numbers of Tamils from public service who were unable to speak in that tongue. From 1949 to 1963, Tamil participation in public sector jobs plummeted from 41 per cent to just 7 per cent.[9]

A process of ethnic polarisation ensued that benefited the Sinhalese over Tamils in government positions, university admissions and even their fundamental civil rights.[10]

The tensions created by this division bore fruit. In July 1983, following a strike in Jaffna that left thirteen Sri Lankan soldiers dead, over 3,000 Tamils were murdered in frenzied rioting, many burned alive in their homes. The 'Black Riots', as they came to be known, left more than 150,000 Tamils homeless, with attacks and counter-attacks inflicting a deep cultural wound. As Asoka Bandarage, an associate professor at Georgetown University, wrote later, the Tamil minority was 'traumatized by the experience of utter helplessness and victimization following Sinhala mob attacks. Tamils' sense of insecurity, anger and distrust of the Sinhalese generated by the terrible events of 1983 still remain.'[11]

All the ex-LTTE fighters I spoke to said such attacks had directly led them to take up arms. Nirupan was no different. He had been in the town of Arajampathu in 1990 when he saw security service troops attack two teenagers with wooden clubs, around which they had wrapped coils of barbed wire. Then, as the teenagers lay bleeding upon the ground, he claimed that one of the Sinhalese soldiers had wrapped more barbed wire around their necks, poured oil over the screaming men and thrown a match. The veteran recounted how he saw one of the two trying to run away, until the flames licked up his face and he fell, bubbles coming out of his mouth as his lungs burst with the heat. I could not verify that this happened, but there were many other stories like it.

'Those who suffered at first hand,' he said, leaning forward, 'and those who wanted liberation, they volunteered. It was on our own volition, no one pushed us to this.'

Theirs was a vision of paradise, too, and they called that vision Eelam, the name derived from the ancient Tamil name for Sri Lanka. It was a utopian dream led by a passionate young man: Thiruvenkadam

Velupillai Prabhakaran, a man referred to by most of those I met as, simply, 'the leader'.

'After training for battle,' Nirupan said, 'we would meet the leader. He would explain the strategy of winning Eelam, the history, the context. We won battles with that thought.'

In 1972, to win Eelam, Prabhakaran had founded the Tamil New Tigers (TNT), just one of a long list of organisations that protested the post-colonial changes in the country. He started small. On a remote road that runs along the Jaffna coast, he and a band of brothers stopped a state bus and forced its passengers to stand by the shore. Then they poured diesel along its length. In the flickers of the following flame, an insurgency was born.

By 1975, Prabhakaran had carried out the first major political assassination by a Tamil group, killing the mayor of Jaffna as he was entering a Hindu temple. The victim, Alfred Duraiappah, had backed the then ruling Sri Lanka Freedom Party, a move that had signed his death warrant.[12] The violence began to spread – on both sides. Young men, suspected of being Tigers, were forced by the army to dig their own earth tombs, before getting a bullet in the back of their heads for the effort. Mass graves were found from time to time, as if the carmine earth in this land was unable to hold down her secrets.

In response, the LTTE began to develop and expand. Two wings were set up: a military wing and a subordinate political wing, governed by a central committee. The military section was divided into five units: the Sea Tigers; an elite fighting wing known as the Charles Anthony Regiment; a highly secretive intelligence group; the Leopard Brigade (Sirasu Puli), made up of children; and, most famous of all, the suicide bombers of the *karumpuligal*, better known as the Black Tigers (the female suicide sub-unit was called the 'Birds of Freedom').[13]

The creation of this last group was a decision made by Prabhakaran himself. He believed that the best way to attack the government was through targeted and sensational suicide strikes at its heart.

To achieve this, he asked if any of his cadres was willing to travel to Hezbollah camps to be instructed in the suicide bomber's art.[14] Volunteers stepped up and that year he sent a couple of Tamil Tiger fighters to train in Lebanon, during the time when the suicide truck bombing of the US marines in Beirut killed 241 marines.[15]

Prabhakaran modelled the Black Tigers' first suicide attack on the Shia militant group's Beirut attack. On 5 July 1987 – a date celebrated thereafter as the Day of the Black Tiger – a man called Vallipuram Vasanthan detonated a vehicle loaded with explosives at a former Tamil university taken over by the Sri Lankan army; about forty people died. To the Tamils, the bomber became an instant martyr, celebrated with the *nom de guerre* 'Captain Millar', the founding icon of the Black Tiger movement. A golden statue – now pulled down – was erected on the spot where he died. To others, the strike branded the LTTE as a terrorist organisation.

Among the Tamil Tigers, the murderous success of their first mission led many to volunteer to undertake more. I suspected Nirupan was one of them. He would not say he was, but he had often been to camps specifically formed to train up the suicide bombers. To most, the Black Tigers were a thing feared or admired from the distance. Nirupan, though, had been up close.

'The Black Tigers had separate camps,' he said. 'I was at one of them – Thiruvaiyaru camp – and the thing that struck me when there was that life was . . . well . . . normal. The only thing different was that people knew the date of their mission. They knew the date of their deaths.'

He described how the Black Tigers were ladled out the same food as the other fighters; there were no special privileges for those about to die. And how relaxed the all-male camp – made up of thirteen men, between twenty and thirty years old – seemed to be. Even though they knew their days were numbered, they did not seem to hold on to time in a precious way. They still played carom billiards and chess, still watched films. 'They believed they would succeed. And in that success they thought that the price for a Tamil nation was worth paying,' he said.

I asked if he thought it was a price worth paying, and he said yes, he would have died for the cause. For him, a Tamil nation was itself a paradise. Even now he believed there was a point to the Black Tigers' sacrifices, creating a mentality among the Tamils still defined by dignity and honour.

'So was the suicide bomber an effective weapon for the Tamil Tigers?' I asked, conscious that I was talking to a man who was still suffering the wounds of loss, for whom perspective had been one of the earliest casualties.

His response was quick – almost too quick, as if learnt by heart: 'By minimising the deaths on our side, we could maximise the deaths of our opposition, so we achieved a great deal from the strategy. ISIS's mission is to target civilians, to cause civilian casualties. Our aim was to harm the military; it was rare that we killed innocent people.'

The claim the Black Tigers did not harm innocents was one I heard repeated again and again. Prabhakaran, I was told, forbade the targeting of civilians; he would punish those who punished the innocent. It was a seductive line from the mouths of those who saw themselves as the oppressed and the beaten, but the truth was that atrocities were perpetrated by both sides in this war. Of the 115 attacks in Sri Lanka listed by Chicago University, 15 per cent of the victims were civilians. Grainy CCTV films do indeed show Black Tigers pulling the triggers of their suicide bomb vests in places packed with unwitting passers-by. The 1996 Dehiwala rush hour train bombing killed 64 commuters and wounded 400 others; attempted assassinations of political leaders often murdered dozens of bystanders.

Nevertheless, it does seem that – on the whole – the overall intentions of the Black Tigers were not to cause the same level of civilian deaths seen with today's Islamist extremists: even if civilians died in the process, 92 per cent of their targets were political or members of the security forces.

Like Hezbollah, the Black Tigers did not send their martyrs to their deaths lightly. They invested in scale models of their targets to scope out the pitfalls beforehand. They supported their volunteer bombers with accommodation, transport, food and clothing until the attack date was reached. One of the most meticulous suicide missions was an attempt on the life of a Sri Lankan military commander called Sarath Fonseka. An LTTE volunteer had been sent to southern Sri Lanka six full years before, her fake ID stating that she was Sinhalese. Her task was to marry a soldier, get pregnant and then, on visiting the Sri Lankan army maternity clinic, detonate her vest as Fonseka drove past. She was three months pregnant when she died.[16]

It was not just planning, there was ingenuity, too. Like the Japanese, the LTTE diversified their weapon tactics. Six different types of suicide bomb methods were developed: vest, car, motorcycle, ship, scuba and attacks from the air – using microlights, gliders and mini-helicopters.[17] Not since the Japanese faced an imminent American invasion in 1944 had so many different forms of suicide attack been harnessed by one fighting force.

For the most part, the Black Tigers used suicide belts – so much so that some claim they even invented them, despite their being used by the Chinese Dare to Die battalions. But, unlike an open charge in a war zone as carried out by the Chinese and Japanese, these compact belts adopted by the Black Tigers were mainly used in acts of subterfuge. Hard to detect, the belts enabled bombers to access top-security locations, while the inevitable death of their users prevented the insurgents from surviving and being interrogated. Some inveigled their way close to their targets by pretending to be mad. Some walked to their death dressed in loose saris, the bombs hidden under the cloth. Others painstakingly coated the shrapnel in their vests with cyanide, hoping to ensure all around them died.

Their approach was certainly thorough. In 1991, the Black Tigers sent one of their troops on a mission: to kill President Premadasa, the third leader of Sri Lanka since independence. It took the bomber, a twenty-three-year-old called Kulaveerasingam Veerakumar, two years to slowly charm his way into the trust of the President's police guard, paying for their alcohol and their prostitutes.[18] The officers paid the price for their indulgences: twenty-five people were killed in the May 1993 attack, including the President.

The Black Tigers also became one of the first terror groups regularly to film their own suicide attacks, not just the pre-martyrdom videos as in Lebanon, but recording the flash and the bang of the attack itself. Stores in Kilinochchi, their administrative headquarters, sold CDs with tribute songs to the Black Tigers, along with videodiscs of their infamous attack on Colombo's airport, where fourteen suicide bombers killed seven Sri Lankan air force personnel and destroyed or damaged twenty-six aircraft. The LTTE's own radio station broadcast the details of every Black Tiger operation and put up a giant billboard on a major road that ran through the northern territories, showing women how best to exploit their deaths in battle. Other posters instructed followers how, if wounded in a firefight, their best tactic was to play dead until enemy soldiers approached, then to blow up as many as possible and themselves in the process. Suicide fighters even wore capsules containing potassium cyanide around their necks, so that in the event of a failed mission, they could bite down on the glass, ensuring a quick death and the avoidance of the interrogator's chair.[19] There are reports of twelve Tigers having swallowed such cyanide capsules after being captured by Indian troops in 1987.[20]

In all these ways, suicide bombings were developed as an offensive weapon, not a defensive one. After all, the Tamils were outnumbered by about three to one. It was, as the Tigers' political head S. Thamilchelvam was to say, virtually repeating Nirupan's statement: 'to ensure maximum damage done with minimum loss of life.'

The question that remained, though, was why? Why would these men and women give their lives up so often, so readily? There was not the cultivated fealty here, as in Japan, to a godhead emperor. There was not the fevered revolutionary rhetoric that had once inspired a generation of Russian students.

Nirupan needed to go; he had picked up his helmet and held it in his hands, rotating it impatiently, but his final words to me seemed to answer this. He spoke of the influence of his leader, of Prabhakaran's charisma: 'If he were alive now, I'd still give my life for him. I learned more from the mouth of that dear leader than I ever did from my parents.'

With that he shook my hand and limped out into the blanket of the night. He left me with the thought that, to appreciate why so many gave their lives for the Tamil cause, I needed to get to know Prabhakaran himself. The best way to do this was to go on a little pilgrimage of my own.

Devotionals are easy to find in Sri Lanka. Within ten minutes of my catching the 87 bus from Colombo to the north – a rackety affair that started off empty in the pre-dawn hours and soon was packed to bursting with swaying travellers – the conductor had jumped out and prostrated himself in front of a statue of Saint Sebastian. He then paid homage to the Lord Buddha, sprayed the fat-bellied Ganesh elephant god that sat on the dashboard with holy water, and passed money over to a roadside shrine to Lord Shiva. The hedging of bets here when it came to religion seemed commonplace; I even spotted a large statue of the Hindu monkey god, Hanuman, with huge nails piercing his blue feet, perhaps trying to woo over local Catholics to the Hindu cause.

This ubiquity of votives, idols and shrines throughout the country seemed to represent a national proclivity for worship, one that I had witnessed in many former Tigers, as well as Nirupan. One man with kohl-rimmed eyes said that dying for Prabhakaran was absolutely worth the cost. Another said the LTTE was nothing without its leader, that no one could replace him. Then there was the man who told me a tale of Prabhakaran eating ice cream: how the leader had been interrupted by his guards, saying that it was time to leave. The head of the Tamil Tigers ignored the request and carried on spooning the vanilla scoops into his mouth, so the guard came back and said, again, it was time to go. That request was ignored. The third time, though, the guard forcibly took the leader by the arm and dragged him out of the room. 'Such is my burden, they won't give me any peace,' Prabhakaran had said as he was led away.

The tale was recounted not as a description of a man's greed, but of a man's stoic commitment to the fight. An anecdote that showed the LTTE leader placed the cause above the pursuit of pleasures. To me, it seemed that he just liked ice cream, but my cynicism had no place among his followers. To appreciate a little more the roots of this pervasive devotion, I had travelled to Valvettithurai, a fishing town to the north of Jaffna. It was one of the furthest inhabited places from the capital, Colombo, but I felt the trip was worth it. After all, Prabhakaran had been born here, and birthplaces have a habit of revealing something of a person's character.

The son of an administrative officer who worked far from the government who paid his salary, Prabhakaran was a scion of privilege. In the nineteenth century, the family had owned vast tracts of land, and a Shiva temple was even constructed from those landlords' gains. The nation's lurch to independence, though, had eroded the family fortune and forced his father into the ignoble realities of work. The young Prabhakaran had watched his Tamil father struggle to learn Sinhalese when the government made it mandatory for its civil servants to do so. And he had watched the growing humiliations that his family and community had to endure as the balance of power shifted from the Tamils to the Sinhalese.

The birthplace of that future leader was Aalady Lane. Arriving, we got out of the van to have a look, parking in front of a bright-green bungalow faced by a grey wall. Beside that stood a vacant lot – a space of rubble. A ghostly poster of Prabhakaran was pasted upon a mouldy wall, next to Tamil lettering in bleached ochre paint that spelt out that this was his home. But that was all there was to see. When the conflict ended, people had been drawn to this spot, war pilgrims perhaps seeking the same thing I was – an answer as to why this quiet man had managed to inspire a generation of Tamils to die for a cause. It was a question that had concerned the triumphant army and, fearing the place could fan the flames of martyrdom, they had razed his childhood home to the ground. Visitors still carried on coming, though, pocketing the rubble as a souvenir, and so more troops returned with trucks at night to carry away the last remains of the home. But, even so, remnants remained. I walked into the area and bent down. There, nestled in the weeds was a tiny crumbling piece of white concrete. I picked it up and, rubbing it between my fingers to loosen off the soil, slipped it into my pocket.

Down the road, to the east, sat an old lady wearing a dress stamped with bright-red flowers. I walked over. Arun was already there, asking her how old she was. She answered that she was eighty, and looked up and smiled. Between her hands was a thick pole to fend off the stray dogs that would languish in the afternoon heat, barking at passing cars. Yes, she said, she knew the boy Prabhakaran.

'I called him "Praba".' She spoke in a clear voice about how he played cricket, how he would climb the local trees and steal fruit, and how a group of friends always surrounded him. She described his love for catapults: his aim was good and scurrying squirrels and languid chameleons were his victims. Perhaps she was hinting that he was violent even then, or maybe just that he was a regular kid, it was hard to tell. What I did know, though, was that as the future leader grew, his attention focused on deadlier weapons. He managed to get a copy of the book *Teach Yourself Shooting* and studied it with fierce concentration. As a fighter, he was to take apart and oil his Smith & Wesson revolver every day, and always took the lion's share of the bullets. But saying it starts with killing squirrels and ends with sending suicide bombers to their deaths would be too fanciful.

Nonetheless, others had come here before me to read in such anecdotes an understanding of Prabhakaran's early life. Journalists had chronicled how he used to steal chemicals from his school's laboratory to make home-made explosives. How his eighth-grade teacher had urged his students to take up arms against the iniquity of the Sinhalese repression.[21] Another reported how Prabhakaran was fascinated with the short-lived Tamil secessionist movement in India and, in particular, how he fixated upon the story of a Hindu priest who, in 1958, was caught and burned alive by a Sinhalese mob near Colombo.[22] I asked the woman what her memories of that child were.

'He was always on his bike' she said, 'wherever he went he had to rely on that broken pushbike.'

I had read that Prabhakaran's life was marked by super-fluidity. That he was permanently on the move; spending a few nights at one home, a few nights at another, he would, especially in his younger years, keep to the back roads and use that old Raleigh bike to avoid the authorities. In a sense, this was a secret of his longevity. He stayed away from the mechanisms of the state; even when incapacitated by jaundice he refused a visit to the hospital. He avoided the camera's lens for the same reason, destroying any photograph that might have been taken of him. Police officers were left trying to identify this scarlet pimpernel with a dated school identification card. The same caution meant he scarcely gave interviews – the journalist Marie Colvin lost her eye trying to get through the front lines to secure one with him. It was a distancing from the world's media that did him a favour, though; like Bin Laden and al-Baghdadi, it ensured his image was not sullied by overexposure and familiarity.

Such distancing worked. Prabhakaran was short and plump, with a thin, reedy voice – hardly the stuff of legend, but he ended up becoming one.[23] Followers pledged allegiance not to the cause, but to Prabhakaran himself. One brigadier, approaching the dying body of a Black Tigress, was to report that the girl called out, 'not to her mother, not to her father, not even to God, but to "Annai, Annai! (Prabhakaran)".'[24] Such was his reputation that, upon his death, one biographer described him as 'the LTTE's supreme leader, its god, its icon.'[25]

There are many examples of terrorist groups who have had enigmatic leaders, inspiring followers to converge around an ideology, motivating individuals to choose a path of self-sacrifice. Abu Bakr al-Baghdadi of ISIS, Osama Bin Laden of Al-Qaeda, Abdullah Öcalan of the Kurdistan Workers' Party (PKK) and Hassan Nasrallah of Hezbollah have all been described as charismatic figureheads of groups that have successfully utilised suicide bombing. A common characteristic of such groups is the ability of the group's leader to inspire absolute loyalty and submission from their followers.

The difference between many of these groups and the LTTE, though, is that those who blew themselves up for the Tamil Tigers did not die for a god; they died for Prabhakaran and all that he believed in (the same can be said of Kurdish fighters, too). His role was central to their deaths. He would attend ceremonies to congratulate 'martyrs' who had chosen to die, and he even claimed he was responsible for transforming his 'weak brethren into a strong weapon called the Black Tigers'.[26] Although an unlikely man whose combat fatigues clung to his belly in the northern heat, Prabhakaran had something nebulous to him that compelled others to give up their lives.

All the ex-Tigers I met had described Prabhakaran with a sense of reverence. Meeting their commander was a lifetime goal for many of his neophyte cadres. One, a broken man who talked to me at his farm, resting upon a faux snakeskin car seat surrounded by goats and chickens, seemed to rise above the oppressive conditions of the present when he spoke of how he was once summoned to meet the leader.

'We were in awe,' he said – a slowly dying man. 'When we saw him, we were not able to talk – words wouldn't come. Whatever we were thinking in our minds, he knew these things.'

It was a magnetism that tied his followers to Prabhakaran, a flowering of a particular type of love and loyalty that persists, even now, beyond his death and his lost war. Like other charismatic leaders, this was partly because 'Praba' preached upon fertile soil – his pulpit was founded upon cultural, political and social turmoil. He wanted to break down the institutions, he screamed for change, he embraced violence – the typical hallmarks of a charismatic terrorist. But he had other traits, too.

One Canadian scholar sought to quantify the role of charisma in terrorist leaders and concluded that the most charismatic of them all tended to prefer bombs over bullets. They assassinated high-level politicians, he found; they committed numerous lethal strikes and in so doing deeply wounded the government they were striking at; they rooted their violence in a purposeful strategy; and they headed organisations that had an acute sense of self-identity.[27] He might have just been describing Prabhakaran: former Tigers that I spoke to said that they feared disappointing their leader more than they did dying.

This unlikely leader appears to have known instinctively how to appeal to his followers, and how to manipulate them to achieve his own ends. Acknowledging there was a cultural reluctance in Hinduism to accept suicide, for instance, he encouraged members of the LTTE to use the euphemism *thatkodai* (to give yourself) instead of *thatkolai* (suicide) to describe the actions of the Black Tigers.[28] As Prabhakaran said, 'It is a gift of the self – self-immolation, or self-gift. The person gives him or herself in full.' It was an attempt – as Hezbollah had sought to do through language, like giving the co-driver in a suicide bombing a particular martyr's name – to reframe the suicide bomber's act. In this case, placing it not as someone who expressly kills themselves, but rather as someone who dies in the act of killing. It was a nuance that meant nothing to the victims, but was everything to those who had volunteered to die.

To help emphasise this sense of devotional sacrifice, Prabhakaran encouraged symbolism and ritualism. He designed a logo for his group: a roaring tiger, its paws curled around the stocks of two crossed rifles, its head ringed by a saintly halo of bullets. It was in direct opposition to the lion of the Sinhalese Buddhists (the Sinhalese derive their name from Simha, the Sanskrit word for 'lion'). He made celebratory holidays and rituals pivotal to the Black Tigers' lives. An 'Office of Great Heroes' responsible for the cultivation of such events was set up in Jaffna, while each morning the ritual of the camps began with a ceremony where cadres would swear allegiance to Prabhakaran himself, rather than Tamil Eelam or the Tigers. Elaborate commemorations for those killed in combat (Great Heroes' Day) and for suicide bombers (Black Tiger Day) became annual affairs. Moreover, Prabhakaran invited suicide bombers to have their last supper with him, before being sent off on their missions.[29]

In these ways, he cultivated an image of the Black Tigers as the most elite cadre in the organisation. But access to such elites came with a price. Unmarried Black Tigers were forbidden from having sex, not even permitted to hold hands, and could only marry with their commander's approval. Prabhakaran neither smoked nor drank and he expected the same from his troops, though some prohibitions were as much practical as they were about reinforcing a sense of sacrificial purpose. Once, when watching a scene in the film *Operation Daybreak*, one that showed Nazi guards eliciting a confession from a Czech dissident by threatening his family, Prabhakaran turned to a follower. 'This is why I insisted that family life is not suitable for the cause,' he said.[30]

It is well established that religions or cults that offer direct communication with their god or leader can produce acts of terror. Under the warm glow of the leader, of the godhead, the barbed realities of life seem more mundane, more painful and more intolerable. Like the effect of the gaze of the mother on a child, the devotee becomes more susceptible to doing extreme things to recapture that feeling of love. So it was with Praba. But, as I saw both in Sri Lanka and in the rise of the global jihad that we see today, devotion can produce demons.

Prabhakaran's influence is even more extraordinary when you appreciate that the Tigers did not subscribe to a fully defined political ideology. In the beginning, many Tamil militant groups, including the Tigers, had a quasi-socialist framework to their call to arms but Prabhakaran eschewed even that framing of a post-war reality. Nationalism, action and sacrifice were their only creed – a death cult built in part upon the very memories of those who died for the cause.

Prabhakaran's cultivation of this notion of sacrifice was deliberate. Tamils, for instance, traditionally cremate their dead, and this posed a problem for the LTTE. But, taking inspiration from Commonwealth World War graves, Prabhakaran ordered the remains of his fallen to be buried in neat cemeteries, providing a visible reminder of their martyrdom. An 'eternal lamp' was lit on each Black Tiger tombstone (and given they were suicide bombers, at least some of the plots would have been empty).[31] They called the cemetery Maveerar Thuyilum Illam – 'Resting Home of the Brave' – and ensured it was swept clean every day. The message for would-be suicide bombers was clear: your death is meaningful and will not be forgotten. What was important was that the hero was seen to live on in the group's collective memory; in this context it seemed to be a key, even, to immortality.

In such ways, Prabhakaran extended the cult of the personality from him to all those who died for him, each death bolstering his supremacy. As he said, 'Every Tiger is committed to end his or her life for the goal.'[32] The message was clear: if it was a goal worth dying for, then it was a noble goal indeed.

The commemoration of the fallen also hid where the real power lay. In one moment, the bomber was lionised, eulogised, held up as a hero; in another, the bomber was an expendable resource. Suicide attacks were decided by Prabhakaran in a process in which the bombers did not take part until the very last stage. There was, for instance, a four-year hiatus between the Tigers' first suicide bombing and their second. That lag is central to appreciating that, behind that strategy lay one man and his will; only when Prabhakaran felt another suicide attack was justified and supported did one occur. It illustrates a man whose charismatic leadership was so powerful that he alone would choose the timing and the manner of their death.

The Black Tigers were not just a small group either. In 2002, a reporter from *Time* magazine met a female suicide Tamil Tiger in a base in Northern Sri Lanka. Eraj Samandi described how there were more than fifty suicide bomber applicants, so many that a lottery was held to choose those who would die. As she recounted: 'The Leader pulls out two names, reads them out and the 48 who aren't chosen are all crying at first. But the two who are chosen, they are very happy and the people around them then raise them on their shoulders and are all clapping and celebrating.'[33]

Within this anecdote much can be seen. There is the intoxicating persuasiveness of the crowd; the introduction of the element of luck in the lottery system – suspending the supplicants' sense of self-will to a higher, more fateful determination; and the manner in which the entire process manoeuvred around deeper cultural beliefs of death in Tamil life.

The flipside to such resolute devotion towards him, though, was a Messianic complex. Some would later complain how Prabhakaran 'never apologised for anything he did, never critically analysed his own actions. Never.'[34] He forced his soldiers to swat flies around him because he could not stand the smell of fly spray; he adopted the gauche flamboyances of tin-pot despots and kept three leopard cubs as pets; he gorged on food, even when his men were running low on rations. He forced his followers to play a game of football he had invented called 'taraball', in which the players squatted down low and passed the ball by hand. And there was a darker side, too: he executed Tigers who displayed disloyalty or the slightest levels of insubordination, having the 'traitors" bodies displayed for all to see. He was also ruthless to those that might have challenged his power base: in the late 1980s, he set about attacking and killing hundreds of the members of rival groups, a process that has been termed a form of 'predatory rationalisation'.[35]

Despite such tyranny, his control over his followers did not diminish. Perhaps this was because he offered to many a glimpse of a world worth dying for. In the 1990s, when the Tigers ran Kilinochchi and Jaffna, there was a moment when the names of streets, newborn children and houses were all Tamil. Today, people speak of how safe the streets were then, how drug addiction and alcoholism was absent, and how there was a sense of community and moral dignity everywhere. Even now, the attraction of a separatist state as a haven of harmony still dominates the local Tamil imagination.

Prabhakaran also offered a meaningful death to those racked by poverty and oppression and, to give him his due, he practised what he preached: he was prepared to die for the cause. As the war came to its close, the Tigers' depleted forces were pushed onto a sliver of land between the Nandikadal Lagoon and the Indian Ocean. The heavy guns of the Sri Lankan army cut off hopes of escape, and Prab-hakaran handed out to his men CDs of a recent Hollywood movie. It was the 2006 film *300*, the story of Leonidas and his small band of Spartans willing to fight to the death against the overwhelming odds of the Persian army. Prabhakaran watched the film six times, perhaps imagining his death would be immortalised like this. But it was wishful thinking; as the Austrian philosopher Walter Benjamin once wrote: 'History is written by the victors', and it was true here, too. In Prabhakaran's home town, the image of a leader for whom men and women once willingly died had been effectively wiped from the face of the earth, as if he had never existed.

We got back into the van and headed further north. Passing an enormous Hindu temple, whose cornices were marked by a finial statue of a dark-skinned, pot-bellied temple guardian, we left the village and drove until the shoreline of the Indian Ocean came into view. Up ahead was Point Pedro, the northernmost point of the island. Here, in the town and hinterlands, local families could trace their lineage right back to the *Sambangarar* or 'ship people' who first inhabited this coastline, and along the side of the road, smooth-bottomed boats lay hauled up on the rocky shore. India and the trading opportunities that she represented were just over 30 kilometres away on the horizon.

It was the Palk Strait, a strip of sea that connects the Bay of Bengal in the north-east with the Palk Bay further south. Named after the Englishman Robert Palk, governor of Madras during the mid-eighteenth century, its shallow waters and reefs make it difficult for large ships to pass through, turning it into a smuggler's paradise in the war.

Getting out, we walked to the shoreline. Someone had erected a sign proclaiming 'Sri Lanka' in black ink upon weathered concrete; beneath it was a badly drawn lion. 'Distance from Dondra to Point Pedro 432km,' it stated, as if to say: this is one country, don't forget that. But, gazing across the seas towards the Indian Tamil shore, it was clear that this whole region looked northwards, not south. Moments before we had passed a statue of Marudur Gopalan Ramachandran, or M.G.R., raising his fingers in a victorious salute. It was not a Sri Lankan being celebrated, but an Indian actor who had served as chief minister of the state of Tamil Nadu, just across the water, for the ten years before his death in 1987.

The sound of Kollywood music drifted up from the roofs of villages – songs from the film industry in the Kodambakkam neighbourhood of India's Chennai province. Here the food was also different from that of the Sinhalese majority: whereas the more verdant south infused their dishes with pepper, cardamom, cinnamon and coconut, the north preferred the sweeter tastes of tamarind, and, confronted with the sweeping dry and hot winds of India, they chose spices and chillies to make their bodies produce a cooling sweat. Even the Sri Lankan tourist board says it is 'difficult to miss the profound Indian influence made obvious by the gradual switch from the singsong cadences of Sinhala to the quick-fire intonations of Tamil', noting, too, the 'hordes of kamikaze cyclists' that fill the northern streets.[36]

The Indian connection had consequences. During the war, under night skies, small ships would ply these waters, leaving India to bring weapons of war to the Tigers – a trade in bullets and bombs that sustained the conflict. It was hard to get ex-fighters to give details of this illicit commerce; the mindset of the war had seeped into their bones, and made distrust commonplace. But, over time, I managed to gather snippets of information from interviews, emails, sideways comments.

Weapons had reportedly been shipped to these shores in speedboats that only took forty-five minutes to cross from India's shores. They arrived loaded with overstock from a global weapons bazaar: Bulgarian SA-14 short-range missiles, bazookas bought from Cyprus, grenade launchers from Croatia and guns from Cambodia, Thailand and Burma. AK-47s came from Afghanistan, and mortar shells from Zimbabwe and the former Yugoslavia. Dealers in Hong Kong, Singapore and Lebanon fed the supply, while corrupt military officers selling arms from Thailand and Burma abetted it.

One Tamil arms trader called Kumaran Padmanathan, his bag packed with faked passports and dollar bills, travelled from Yangon to Bangkok to Johannesburg, lubricating relationships with funds from bank accounts in London, Singapore and Frankfurt. Almost $300 million was being raised by the Tigers a year at one point, with as much as 90 per cent funded by the overseas diaspora.

The explosives that laced the Black Tigers' suicide belts were gathered by every means conceivable, as if the Tigers were jackdaws in search of armaments. When the Sri Lankan government bought 70,000 mortar shells from Zimbabwe Defence Industries, and the Zimbabweans turned to an Israeli company, L.B.G. Military Supplies, to supply the rounds, the LTTE stepped in. The United States embassy in Colombo received a fax that claimed the Tigers had snatched the 81-millimetre mortars on the high seas.

Complex, interwoven lies underpinned this trade. A British-based Tamil set up a fake company called the 'Euro-Ukraine Consultancy Agency', then negotiated with a state-owned Ukraine company – the Rubezone Chemical Factory – the purchase of tons of hexogen, a Semtex-like plastic explosive; 50 tons of TNT; and enough electric timing caps and detonator cord to assassinate a hundred politicians. Payments were made via false accounts in London, Frankfurt, Athens and New York. Finally, the Ukrainian government delivered the explosives, believing the Bangladeshi minister of defence had dutifully signed the end-user certificate. It was a forgery but nobody seemed to notice, and so with subterfuge and lies clouding the sale, 60 tons of explosive material made its way to these northern shores aboard the *Swene*, a Tamil Tiger ship, flying the Honduran flag.[37]

At least some of these explosives were used in a suicide attack that was the deadliest terrorist act of 1996. A truck containing hundreds of pounds of high explosives ploughed through the gates of the Central Bank, a Colombo seaside high-rise. The driver detonated the massive bomb, which tore through the bank and damaged eight other buildings nearby, killing 91 people and injuring a further 1,400. Over 100 people were reported blinded by the shards of glass that sprayed the area. Still the explosives kept on coming, despite the government trying all they could to stop the trade. They even went so far as to prevent soap from being traded with the blockaded north, as they believed it was used to render their bombs waterproof.

It was an onslaught that was to force the Sri Lankan government's hand, too. Faced with Tamil resilience, stoic acceptance of death, fanatical belief in the virtues of self-rule and such charismatic leadership, the government was to turn its back upon a world that called for respect of human rights or moderation. Instead, it unleashed its version of hell upon its enemies, a counter-attack that spilt rivers of blood that were to flow into the sea up ahead of me, just along the coast.

Sri Lanka today seems to be a country freed from violence. One of the things that conveys this sense is the proliferation of peaceful Buddhist stupas that line the A9 highway: giant dun-coloured statues of the seated Siddhārtha Gautama, and white icons so bright they hurt your eyes, marking the way. But the building of these Buddhist monuments, in a part of the country so explicitly Tamil, is a deliberate assertion of cultural dominance by the victors. Within three years of the cessation of hostilities, at least thirty such statues had been constructed. One, an MP claimed, was even built upon the rubble of a demolished Hindu temple.

The visitor might get a hint of the newness of these monuments by their milky-whiteness, but other icons are less obvious. Bodhi trees line the highway too. The planting of these *ficus religiosa* was a branding of nationalism through nature: these trees claim a lineage that stretches, tree upon tree, right down to the first branches under which the Buddha is said to have gained enlightenment. The same impulse in planting was echoed in nationalist archaeologists scouring this area after the war, looking for traces of a similar Buddhist lineage.

Both were attempts to show that the Sinhalese were here long before the Indian Tamils. So it was that religion here has been tainted with a sense of military triumphalism.

Other things changed, too. Signposts that once pointed to 'Kandarodai' now read 'Kadurugoda', a Sinhalese mutation of the Tamil name. Luxury hotels are owned by Sinhalese businessmen or the military. The only flights from Jaffna to Colombo are run by the Sri Lankan air force. Meanwhile, army bases, the state's long reach up to the north, are everywhere, a mark of power encircled by barbed wire and sentry posts. On the public bus up to Kilinochchi, an officer from the logistics corps – Captain Lavik – had sat down beside me and begun a conversation. He had been silent for the first few minutes, but on seeing I was reading Samanth Subramanian's book *This Divided Island*, one that catalogued the impact of the war, he looked at it and sniffed: 'That's a Tamil name.' I said it was but that the book was balanced. He shook his head as if to say: there is no such thing as a balanced Tamil. During the conversation that followed, one that oscillated between him recounting how his uncle had been killed by a suicide bomber and me hoping he wouldn't demand to see my passport as I was only there on a tourist visa, we passed five military bases. One of the entranceways was built to look like the mouth of an enormous lion, like a Disney pastiche.

The conquering army didn't just build lions, they also made memorials. One, near Elephant Pass, was a huge mound that had a path spiralling its way to the top, upon which stood a squat square monolith. Representations of the army, air force and navy had been impressed on three sides, while the fourth displayed a curiously kitsch image of the sun and the moon. Walking up the slope Arun had remarked that the state here had invested first in memorials, long before they invested in infrastructure, and to the locals such tributes dotting the landscape were symbols not of peace, but of a continued repression. Around the base of the memorial, gardeners had planted trees from all over the island – enforcing an unfelt homogeneity through nature. These trees were now a constant reminder to the locals of the status quo: not there to remember the dead, but to tell the living they had lost.

It is not surprising the post-war landscape here lacked subtlety. The government's victory was an exercise in unbridled power. Faced with the suicidal onslaught of the Black Tigers, the Sri Lankan government had moved away from any attempt to negotiate with the LTTE to annihilating them. For the first two decades of the civil war the government's tactic was to drag the LTTE to the negotiating table. But in mid-2006, when the LTTE deliberately violated a ceasefire, the Sri Lankan government decided enough was enough.

They realised the Tigers had a fundamental Achilles' heel: that for every suicide bomber they sent to their deaths, theirs was another fighter lost. The LTTE had a limited fighting base: only 12 per cent of Sri Lanka's population were Tamils. And only some 300,000 actively supported the LTTE. Even this support base had grown weak, decimated by loss of life. By 2006, the LTTE was having to rely on conscription – not volunteers – to fill their ranks, and many of these were children. The Sri Lankan government came to the cold calculation that, no matter what human rights they would contravene, they could win the war by slaughter. Using whatever means necessary, they set about destroying the LTTE's ranks.

The armed forces' budget was boosted by 40 per cent, supported by a billion-dollar loan from China, along with lines of credit for oil and weapons from Iran, Libya, Russia and Pakistan. The government worked hard overseas to ensure the LTTE (which received about two-thirds of its funding and the lion's share of its military equipment from abroad) was alienated globally. The fact that they used suicide bombers also turned off many governments, particularly in a post-9/11 world, and the group found itself banned in some thirty-two countries. Help from crucial allies in India dried up.

The Sri Lankan government then tried a different tack. They invested in alleviating poverty across the country, including costly schemes such as the poor farmer fertiliser subsidy scheme. In short, they convinced the wider population that there was a peace worth fighting and dying for. It was an argument that worked: before 2005, the army struggled to recruit 3,000 soldiers annually; by late 2008, 3,000 soldiers a month were enlisting.[38]

There was also a marked divergence in military strategies that exploited their enemy's weaknesses and countered its strengths. Defections of senior LTTE commanders proved a significant setback for the guerrilla fighters, and emboldened the government's hand. Operations employing small, well-trained, highly mobile military units were conducted to wipe out LTTE cells operating within the capital and some large towns.

By the spring of 2009 the Tigers had been pushed, relentlessly, into a small corner of the north-east, and the government had drawn a curtain around the entire area, hoping to shield the world's eyes from what they intended to do next. Then, they wheeled in their big guns, loaded up their fighter jets and set about bombing their enemy to hell, with no offer of capitulation.

When the United Nations eventually managed to get on the ground and tried to work out how many civilians had died in the final months, they estimated about 40,000 had been killed on the coast in the north-east alone, including Prabhakaran and his leadership cadre – though others said the toll was far higher. Gordon Weiss, a UN spokesman in Colombo, was sent a text message by one of the UN's Tamil workers at the time: 'Women and kids wards shelled. God, no words. Still counting the dead bodies.'[39]

The government, backed by the heavily criticised Lessons Learnt and Reconciliation Commission, said that the loss of civilian lives was a combination of the inevitable crossfire, the LTTE murdering people and the rebels' 'refusal to let the hostages get out of harm's way'.[40]

There was no evidence presented, the Commission concluded, that the government's forces had targeted civilians. It's a claim that, when repeated to Tamils, usually makes them either laugh sarcastically or causes their eyes to flare with anger.

Such slaughter was the often-seen end game caused by the suicide bombers' acts. Extreme acts of violence enable governments to speak in binary terms: capitulate or devastate. This is the nature of suicide bombing – it eradicates all moderation and incites the most severe of responses, all too often justified in the name of counterterrorism. For the death toll that comes in the suicide bomber's wake is almost always higher than those killed in the initial blast.

At first glance, it was just a vast, gritty wasteland. There were no road signs, no indications it was anything but an expanse of dirt and sand. Except for one thing: a small shrine had been set up surreptitiously to one side. A little protest in stone, it had the flag of the Tamil Tigers draped over it.

Beyond, under an arching tree, a solitary dog gnawed at something. Since this was once a graveyard for those Tamil Tigers who had died in bomb blasts and night-time ambushes, a place where thousands of bodies had been buried, I could not help but wonder what this dog was eating. But the army had come, as they had elsewhere, without remorse, and bulldozed the lines of graves. Memory had been pulverised into dust.

To one side lay a small pile of broken headstones, and before it a parade of others had been reassembled – a jigsaw collection of defiance. This was it – about the only visible reminder that the Tamils had once dominated this land. There were other ugly reminders of the conflict; a visit to a local mental health hospital had revealed lines of equally broken men and women, their minds shattered by the weight of trauma. Then there was the student who had shared with

*A former LTTE graveyard, long since destroyed
by the Sri Lankan government*

me a picture of a birthday cake he had had made in Prabhakaran's honour – a protest in icing and sugar that could have got him months in prison. But there was little else.

When I asked former fighters if they had a photograph of the leader in their homes, they shook their heads – such a possession would have seen them back in 'education camps', or worse. The physical evidence of the conflict had been largely reduced to rubble and the heavy-handed government presence that followed.

I stood in front of this levelled necropolis and watched the sun setting behind a distant clump of Ceylon reed-bamboo. In 1993, Prabhakaran had declared: 'From the tombs of the dead martyrs who lie in rest in the womb of our soul rises the cry of freedom.' But even now that had been wiped away. This was the impermanence of suicidal protest: how an ideal once so passionately fought for could evaporate over the years. The urgency of the moment lost, as if a fever had once gripped this place and then passed.

Perhaps this was inevitable. Pierre Vergniaud, a lawyer who was pivotal to the French Revolution, once said that 'Revolution, like Saturn, devours its children.' Each attempt to overthrow an old regime has its heady success, followed by a brief honeymoon period which lasts until the revolutionaries – inevitably – begin to quarrel among themselves. This squabbling causes the once-victorious revolutionary bodies to collapse, destroying their hopes and ideals in a spectacle of political terror. The guillotine becomes the natural child of that sort of revolution.[41]

But a revolution that uses suicide bombers to achieve its goals is one that leaves nothing to devour. The violence of that revolutionary weapon drags terror into its very genesis, not its outcome. In so doing, it destroys its moral potential, while forcing its enemies into counter-actions of extremes. Accordingly, suicidal revolutionaries almost always fail in their objectives.

The traumas that such levels of violence have caused continue to haunt countless Sri Lankan citizens. In Colombo, I once took a three-wheel taxi to a meeting. The driver had been a soldier and he explained, shouting over his shoulder in the weaving traffic, how he had narrowly escaped death. Years before, a suicide bomber had detonated his belt in front of his platoon, leaving ten of them dead. Even now he bears the shrapnel of that attack in his legs.

In just over a week, I met a dozen people who had been affected directly or through the loss of a family member by suicide bombings. But there were broader consequences. Even though the Black Tigers lost, the fact that they managed to shake the Sri Lankan government to its roots was recognised by fighters the world over. Terrorists and guerrilla insurgents had seen that the Black Tigers could take on a far superior military. So, as with the kamikaze, even though the LTTE did not win their war, the promise of great potential in the suicide bomber's tactic helped fuel an ever-expanding cult of the suicide bomber.

So it was that the Black Tigers learnt from Hezbollah, who learnt from Iran, who learnt in part from the Japanese, who had learnt from the Chinese, who had learnt from the Russians. Each one refined their deadly suicidal weaponry, until the suicide bomber became the icon of revolutionary resistance the world over. And under that icon, the next phase of the suicide bomber would emerge: one where civilians would become not just the bystander to the bomber's violent act, but their very target.

Chapter 6

A House in Heaven

On 6 April 1994, a fresh-faced man pulled his vehicle up alongside a municipal bus in the centre of Afula in Israel. Though the car bore an Israeli licence plate, its driver was a nineteen-year-old Palestinian, and it carried 67kg of dynamite. The bus it pulled up alongside was filled with civilians, many of them teenagers; two Israeli junior high schools were nearby, and many pupils were heading home early for the day.

At twenty-five minutes past twelve, the bomb went off. The blast was so intense that two boys were set aflame and burned like torches for a brief, terrible moment. Eight Israeli civilians died, fifty-five more were injured. The blackened trainers of teenage boys were later photographed scattered around the burnt shell of the bus.

It was the first time in history that a suicide bomber had specifically targeted civilians, and therefore the first time that Israelis had been killed in this type of attack in Israel. If you look at a nineteenth-century English survey of the place names of Western Palestinian land, the name Afula is described as meaning "ruptured" (a woman)' in Arabic. So it was that the place that gave birth to the modern act of suicidal terror against civilians was named after a uterine rupture.[1]

It was a pivotal moment. There had been three suicide attacks in

1993 in the Occupied Palestinian Territories, but all of them had targeted Israeli soldiers, and, apart from the bombers, the only person killed was a Palestinian Arab. This time the attack was purposely aimed at killing Israeli civilians in their own country. As the *New York Times* was to report, 'underscoring the indiscriminate nature of the attack was the fact that some of the victims were Israeli Arabs, including a 30-year-old woman.'[2] The militants responsible for the massacre, the military wing of Hamas, released a statement saying: 'So that no one should make the charge that we are interested in killing Israeli civilians, we urge the settlers to quickly leave the West Bank and Gaza Strip.'

There are three memorials to the Afula dead. At the tumbledown bus station stands a gloved hand in granite, clutching a bus steering wheel. Near where the bomber detonated his explosive load stands a second, more prominent memorial – it has the appearance of a broken Star of David on a lopsided plinth, as if the bomb has knocked the monument sideways, leaving it still standing but forever altered. And right where the bomb exploded, there is a third monument: a simple testimony of the events on a rounded block of stone.

Such inscriptions, though, fail to answer the question: why were these civilian Israelis targeted? Why now? One aim seems to have been to halt the plan by Israel and the Palestine Liberation Organisation for Palestinian autonomy, a peace plan that Hamas rejected. Another was in retaliation for a mass shooting by an Israeli settler, Baruch Goldstein; he had gunned down twenty-nine Palestinians while they were at prayer at a mosque in Hebron on 25 February that year.

This new category of bombing, though, was to ignite emotions. As Palestinian mosques broadcast news of the attack, Israelis took to the streets in anger, some chanting 'Goldstein, we love you', others 'Death to Arabs'. Others still questioned the peace talks outright: 'I think that the minimum the government can do,' said a youthful

Benjamin Netanyahu, the leader of the right-wing Likud party, 'is suspend the talks and demand the PLO live up to its commitment to fight terrorism.'

Certainly, that commitment did not seem to be at the forefront of the PLO's minds. A few days later, on 13 April, twenty-one-year-old Amar Amarna entered the Hadera bus station between Haifa and Tel Aviv at 9.30 in the morning. He was carrying a bag containing over four pounds of home-made acetone peroxide explosive. Ten minutes later, as a bus was pulling out of the station, he detonated his load – shrapnel ripping through the passengers on the bus, killing six and wounding thirty. A second bomb exploded at the scene just as rescue workers arrived. This was the 'second in a series of five attacks,' a Hamas pamphlet declared ominously.[3] Something dark and terrible had begun.

It was to be the second in 114 suicide strikes that were, over the

A memorial near the site of the Afula suicide attack

years, to target the heart of Israel. About 40 per cent of these were by Hamas, a quarter by Palestinian Islamic Jihad and a quarter by the al-Aqsa Martyrs' Brigade (a secular coalition of Palestinian armed groups in the West Bank), with secular groups making up the rest. In all, since 1994, 721 people were killed and 5,098 injured in these attacks, the majority of them Israeli Jews, the vast majority by suicide belts.

These attacks were not just to usher in an age of civilians being targeted, either. It was the first time Sunnis were deploying suicide bombings in a concerted way. This was the birth of Sunni terrorism, a shift in their use by Shias and secularists, and such a change was to have significant consequences. Since they were first seen in the Middle East, to this day, at least 126 groups have deployed suicide bombers globally; of these, 96 – three-quarters – have described themselves as Sunni Muslim in outlook. These self-described Sunni Muslims have been responsible for almost 3,000 attacks. Since 1979, Sunni Islam has been the banner under which about 90 per cent of all suicide bombings around the world, and all the subsequent deaths and woundings, has been claimed.

In comparison, there has only been one explicitly Christian (in Lebanon)[4] and one Sikh (in India)[5] suicide bombing. As far as I can find, no Jewish suicide bomber has ever successfully carried out an attack.[6] This dominance of Sunni Islam in suicide attack use must give us pause for thought. It goes without saying – and this is a fact that could be repeated on every following page of this book – that this does not mean that Sunnis are by nature terrorists. Many Sunnis have been the victims of these attacks. Millions more have condemned them outright, saying that those who blow themselves up are not Muslims. To put it into perspective, suicide bombers make up about 0.0002 per cent of the global self-identifying Sunni population.[7]

But Sunni Islam and its relationship to suicidal terror cannot be ignored, especially in a book that focuses on the latter. So, we must ask, why did a Sunni suicide bomber carry out a suicide bombing here in Israel? Why were civilians targeted? And what were the consequences of such a change in tactics? Answering these questions, touching as they do on the labyrinthine complexities of the Palestinian and Israeli conflict, is no simple task.

There are the terrible conditions of Gaza – over 1.3 million Palestinians crammed into a tiny strip of land; its airspace, coast and most of its borders controlled by Israel – and the seemingly endless misery that lies within. There are the policies that Israel has been pursuing in the West Bank of building settlements since 1967, despite global condemnation, along with the construction of security barriers and severely limiting the movement of Palestinians in their own lands. There is the 1993 Declaration of Principles resulting from the Oslo peace process, leaving about 60 per cent of the West Bank under Israeli civil and security control, with another quarter under Palestinian civil control, but Israeli security control; the rest is still subject to Israeli incursions. There is the capture of all of Jerusalem by the Israelis in 1967, putting both East and West Jerusalem under its sovereignty and civil law. There is also Israel's pre-emptive attack on Egypt that drew Syria and Jordan into a regional war in the same year, leading to Israel making massive territorial gains in the West Bank, Gaza Strip, Golan Heights and the Sinai Peninsula up to the Suez Canal. There is the 1948 war that broke out after British troops withdrew and the Jewish declaration of the state of Israel, resulting in a bitter conflict with Arab troops and the establishment of the West Bank and Gaza Strip as distinct geographical units.

Within all this attack and counter-attack, some see suicide bombings as the fault of Israel and the West, pushing Palestinians to the point of mad desperation. One *Guardian* journalist painted the suicide attack as a 'Revenger's Tragedy' – a picture not of Israeli victims, but of Palestinian fightback. It was a piece concerned with the poverty of refugees, a 'collapsed' economy where people chance their lives on the streets, and it depicted the suicide bomber as 'a wounded creature'.[8] There was little stated sympathy for the lives they planned to take.

Others see suicide bombings as a peculiarly Arab problem. 'What kind of a society consciously and purposely sacrifices its own youth for political gain and tactical advantage?' asked Eli Hertz, the Jewish chairman of the Committee for Accuracy in Middle East Reporting. 'The overwhelming majority of Palestinian Arabs nurture a blind hatred of Israel. They created a cultural milieu of vengeance, violence and death – preparing their children to be sacrifices in a death cult.'[9]

In this conflict, both sides defend their position fiercely, and this fuels violence. So where to begin unpicking how suicide bombs – not just violence but specifically suicide bombings – emerged in Israel? Perhaps it is best to start with something tangible and fixed – a field. Or, more specifically, a field of flowers.

I bent down to pick a few of them: a windflower, a turban buttercup, a white rock rose, until I had gathered enough for a small posy. Opening my notebook, I slid them into the envelope at the back, capturing the memory. I was in the middle of a rocky terrace of ochre and green, surrounded by touches of red and blue and white and yellow, the snowy peaks of Mount Hermon in the distance.

In late 1992, in response to the seemingly endless first intifada that had begun in 1987 in retaliation for the Israeli occupation of the West Bank and Gaza, and the killing of a border police officer, Yitzhak Rabin's Israeli government made a decision, one they would later rue. They would deport 415 of the uprising's leaders along with other Islamic Palestinian activists, including both Hamas and Palestinian Islamic Jihad members, to here – a field of flowers in a remote part of Southern Lebanon, and leave them to their own devices. The locals call it Marj al-Zohour.[10]

Lebanon's Field of Flowers

It had been a hard winter. When the deportees first arrived in Lebanon from Palestine they had to sleep on the stony, frozen earth, but they were more resilient than Rabin would give them credit for. Within months someone had created a small garden to grow mint and spices. Near it, they erected a tent for their prayers. Then there was a tent for learning, which they called 'Marj al-Zohour University' and filled with books – from Russia, America and France. At first the local Lebanese had brought them food but the Palestinians demanded something to read instead: they needed nourishment for their souls, they said, more than their bellies. Seventeen professors were part of the exiled crowd, so a college was founded, and sixty of the exiles joined its ranks as students: their favoured subject matter was sharia law.

Other knowledge was also shared. The camp – a bit like Camp Bucca in Iraq, the American prison that gave birth to ISIS[11] – became a place where Palestinian fighters began to cultivate contacts and advance their knowledge of counter-insurgency methods. 'During the long months of deportation,' a history of Hamas recalls, 'leaders and militants were in constant discussion . . . one that elaborated the movement's new overall strategy, reorganized its structure and opened contacts with the other Islamist organizations in the region.'[12] Members of Lebanese Hezbollah and the Iranian Revolutionary Guards came to greet their – then – Palestinian brothers in arms, and from them the exiles were to learn how to carry out suicide attacks.[13] Because then, unlike today, Shias met Sunnis and Sunnis met Shias on equal ground and they spoke of violence against a common enemy – not each other.

Later, when in Israel, I met with Michael Cardash, a British-born Israeli who was once deputy head of the Israeli National Police Bomb Disposal Division, a man who had commanded in both the West Bank and Tel Aviv. He said a transfer of deadly skills undeniably happened.

'We started to see bomb devices that we knew only came from Lebanon,' he told me over supper on the seafront of Tel Aviv. In April 1994, when that suicide bomber hit the Hadera bus station, the killer had left another device, this one designed to take out the emergency units the bomber knew would come. 'There was an enormous battery in that device – one bigger than the bomb itself. The engineer had got that straight from Hezbollah. He had been one of those exiles in Lebanon.'

Hamas had considered suicide attacks before the 'Field of Flowers' – they had adopted 'in principle' the use of self-immolating terrorists in 1980. Their 'leaflet number 68' had already summoned the faithful to begin engaging in suicide missions against the Israelis.[14] But meeting with Hezbollah turned that principle into practice. Within months of those conversations in Southern Lebanon, the virus of suicide bombing had spread. As one observer of the camp wrote:

'There was no question that rather than destroying Hamas, Israel had made them stronger.'[15]

Perhaps compounding its mistake, the Rabin government allowed many of the 415 deportees back to the disputed territories over the course of the following months.[16] They returned with fire in their bellies. Many were frustrated by the failure of the Oslo Accords, a peace process designed to empower the Palestinian people with the right of self-determination. Others were driven by an internal power struggle among the Palestinians themselves – Hamas felt that Fatah, the Palestinian nationalist political party, was overshadowing the Islamic movement's influence in Judea, Samaria and Gaza.[17] So Hamas – an organisation Israel had initially encouraged as an opponent of the PLO – asserted itself in the strongest way possible.[18] Within a year, Hamas and Palestinian Islamic Jihad launched eight separate suicide attacks on Israel.

The baton was passed. The use of suicide attacks by Shia Muslims had lasted up until 1994 in Lebanon when it was mainly to end. Since that year, self-professed Sunni groups have carried out almost all suicide attacks globally done under the banner of Islam.[19]

Perhaps the significance of what happened here in this Field of Flowers has lingered. Within an hour of visiting the field, I and my fixer, Nadia, had been stopped by the Lebanese military and questioned for two hours, then told to drive to another military station an hour away where we were interrogated again, until we were told that we either had to travel to yet another centre, leave the area entirely, or risk arrest. We departed, the flowers still pressed in my notebook, suspicion barking at our heels.

It was not just here that once saw violent collaborations bloom. In October 1992, a Hamas delegation arrived in Iran to hold meetings with senior Shia leadership. In these exchanges an agreement was reportedly forged – Tehran promising to give $30 million in annual aid, along with military training for Palestinian Hamas militants in Iran and Lebanon.[20] And, seeking to trace the impact of such support, to find just how the allure of the suicide bomber had leapt from Shia to Sunni, from Iran to Lebanon to Palestine, I left those Lebanese mountains and headed, a few weeks later, to Ramallah in the central West Bank. There I had arranged to meet a failed suicide bomber.

I had not expected her to be fully veiled. Despite having lived and worked in over two dozen Muslim-majority countries, I had only once before interviewed someone who had worn a niqab – a veil that covers the face, showing only the eyes. Usually it had been the men who had spoken for their wives and daughters but, then, Itaf Elyan was no ordinary woman.

If what she said was true, had her planned suicide attack in 1987 been successful, she would have been the first Palestinian suicide bomber; the first one to attack Israel within its borders; the first female suicide bomber in the Middle East; and the first Sunni suicide bomber.

Itaf, now a woman in her fifties and dressed from head to toe in various shades of grey, said she had travelled from Palestine to Lebanon, via Syria, in 1980 to undertake militant training. She had been trained for twelve days in a PLO-run apartment in Beirut, taught how to 'use guns, how to shoot, how to prepare bombs', before heading to Jordan and from there back to the West Bank.

'Of course there was an impact on the Palestinian revolution from the Iranians,' she said. 'The Iranian revolution was in 1979, I arrived there in 1980 and though it was well known then that the Palestinian revolution was a secular revolution, when I arrived there I saw some of the guys already praying.'

'So,' I asked her, as we sat in the religious education centre that she now runs with her husband, 'did the religious nature of the Iranian revolution affect the Palestinian secular revolution?'

*Itaf Elyan – who would have been the world's first Muslim female
suicide bomber had her mission been successful*

'Absolutely, yes,' she said. 'The impact of the Iranian revolution on
the Palestinian cause was direct – through ideology. Through our discussions in the camp, we came to the conclusion the critical success
of the Iranian revolution was the adoption of a religious ideology. At
that time there was no Hamas or Islamic Jihad, but there, in Lebanon,
we tried to create the Islamic Jihad militia.'

The people in her group had Marxist and communist backgrounds,
but they had been disillusioned with the failures of their movements,
and the failure of socialism around the world to take hold. When the
Islamic revolution succeeded, it sent out a signal to everyone that
faith was required above all. It was this sense of faith that, ultimately,
was to lead to her decision to strap on a suicide vest.

'My operation was the first suicide bombing attack to be planned
in Palestine – 1987,' she said. 'We started planning it in 1985. I had

been deeply influenced by the suicide bombings in Lebanon and so asked if I could organise a suicide bombing attack here.'

Her strong Islamic beliefs were central to that decision. 'In terms of Islamic ideology,' she said, 'the thing is you don't feel that your life is going to end when you undertake a suicide attack. It's continuity – your life continues, you're moving from earth to heaven, from one place to a better place. That is why our notion of sacrifice is stronger.'

'So you're saying that sacrifice imbued with ideology makes such sacrifice more likely?' I asked.

'Exactly. It's as if you are establishing another house in heaven.'

There was a strategic point, too. She felt that the Israelis had helped suppress the news of previous non-suicide bombings – the noise of the Palestinian revolt was never heard internationally. Suicide bombings could not help but be noticed. 'Suicide attacks would really harm them and give them no way of covering it up in the media,' she said.

Her ambition to build that home in paradise, though, was thwarted. Before she was able to carry out what would have been the first planned car bomb strike in Israel – on an Israeli ministry building – the engineer who had built the bomb had been arrested. She said this bomb maker, who had learnt his skills fighting the Soviets in Afghanistan, had been tortured into giving her up and she was arrested on 2 August 1987. She claimed she was also beaten, and then sentenced to fifteen years in prison only to be released a decade later after the Israeli government reached an agreement with the PLO in Oslo in 1997. 'The 22nd of February 1997,' she said about the date of her release, her precision adding weight to her testimony.

I had one last question. I wanted to know if she had remorse about wanting to become a suicide bomber. 'Do you regret it?' I asked.

'No,' she said. 'No. Not at all.'

The Iranian and Lebanese role in the rise of the Sunni suicide bomber seems to be clear. As Ayatollah Khomeini's successor, Ali Khamenei, said in 2004: 'The Palestinians say that their popular awakening followed the teaching of the Imam Khomeini; the Lebanese say that they attribute their victory over the Zionists to the school of the Imam. The entire Islamic elite . . . conducts its victorious battles on the basis established by the political school of the Imam.'[21]

Dr Fathi al-Shaqaqi, a leading figure in the Sunni Muslim Brotherhood, has also written about how the Iranian revolution offered Sunnis a model for challenging corruption and establishing an Islamic order.[22] Shia theology, he said, encouraged rebellion against tyranny in a way not found in Sunni Islam.[23] In 1981 he created Palestinian Islamic Jihad, and in 1993 it carried out its first suicide bombing – the first of fifty-four such attacks the group undertook.[24] Al-Shaqaqi argued that these bombers were already 'doomed to death' by the powers of colonialism and imperialism, so chose instead 'the most beautiful death' by deliberately dying in defence of their homeland.[25]

This call for a beautiful death could have been straight out of Ayatollah Khomeini's playbook. Followers of Hamas and Palestinian Islamic Jihad went from rock throwing to blowing themselves up, and the Palestinian people stood with them – the national support for *shahada* (incidental death in jihad) changing to that of *istishhad* (deliberate death in jihad). At its peak, a Pew poll placed Palestinian support for suicide attacks at 70 per cent.[26]

In the Palestinians' eyes, this was born from strategic necessity: the suicide bomber was David versus the Goliath of the Israeli state. Unlike the Russian utopianists, theirs was a battle just to exist, not to create a paradise on earth. The paradise on offer was just for those who pressed the button on their suicide vests. As one author on the Palestinian conflict put it: 'The question of reward in Paradise constitutes a crucial portion . . . of [the Palestinian] worldview and plays a major role in their battle motivation.'[27]

The ever-perceptive Yasser Arafat noted this. Over time, the nominally secular Fatah was to adopt the *istishhad* approach too. What began with a Sunni innovation entered the political language of violence in Palestine. Starting with an attack in 2001, the al-Aqsa Martyrs' Brigades were to carry out at least 42 suicide attacks, killing 133 people in the process. Soon Shia concepts of martyrdom had been firmly injected into numerous Palestinian groups, both religious and secular, along with the pre-attack rituals (such as video recordings and praise for the martyr) that had first been developed in Iran and Lebanon. It was to make the second intifada, which stretched from 2000 to 2005, an intense time for suicide bombings.

The adoption of suicide bombings by Sunni groups, though, was the most notable change of all. This was, in part, because the body politic of the Sunni faith is very different from that of the Shia. For the Sunnis, there is no ayatollah, no version of the pope, no undisputed leader whose authority is an inherited part of an established structure. Unlike Shia Islam, whose clerics tend to form on hierarchical lines, Sunni Islam offered a very different host in which the culture of martyrdom could grow.[28] This observation was made to me by Sayyid Ali Fadlallah, the son of Grand Ayatollah Mohammad Hussain Fadlallah, back in Lebanon.

'Hezbollah inspired Hamas to use suicide bombings, but the Hezbollah's religious source is in Iran, Hamas is not,' he had said. 'And the difference between Shia and Sunni suicide bombers is that Shias have a centralised and precise religious authority to seek permission from. With Sunnis there is no specific hierarchy; you can never know where the fatwas are coming from. We wish the Sunnis would have one central religious authority or else the chaos will continue.'

The strict clerical organisation of Shia Islam means the leaders of their faith can both condone – and then condemn – suicide attacks. Shia dictates on suicide attacks often came from established, independently run institutions, whose leaders had the highest standards of Islamic education. In Sunni Islam, though, the hierarchy of the faith is far more horizontal. In Sunnism, there are thousands of mosques and independent schools of belief run by amateur intellectuals or self-proclaimed scholars, who have studied subjects such as engineering or medicine. Theirs has often been a narrative of opposition to the state. So when 'martyrdom-as-entry-to-paradise' was condoned in Sunni Islam, an interpretation of what that meant was opened to hordes of Sunni clerics, who were often poorly qualified to comment on such matters. This way an intellectual Wild West was born.[29]

The first head of the group responsible for most of Hamas's suicide attacks was Yahya Ayyash, who had a Bachelor of Science degree in electrical engineering. That may have helped him create suicide belts, but was not necessarily a good grounding for the theological use of them. Similarly, the founder of Palestinian Islamic Jihad was a paediatrician, and when he was assassinated an economics professor took his place. One study has found that engineers were 'over-represented among (Sunni) Islamic radicals by two to four times the size we would expect.'[30]

The issue of religious sources also fuelled the emergence of this ultimately unmanageable philosophy in the Sunni faith. Sunnis focus on the Hadiths: narratives that either quote the Prophet Muhammad on a wide range of life issues, or describe his actions and habits. The trouble is that forgery of the Hadiths has taken place on a massive scale.[31] This corruption of the literature has led to substantive disagreements over aspects relating to military jihad. In short, the theological Wild West was governed by a set of rules that no one could agree upon, a fact that lurks in the background of nearly every suicide attack today.

If, then, suicide bombing can be seen as a sort of virus, leaping from one host to another, when it jumped from the body of Shia faith to the Sunni faith, its new host was one filled with contradictions and a lack of consensus. A faith that, when confronted with the promises that suicide attacks had in terms of strategic gain, had radically to rethink its tradition of martyrdom and jihad.

We have seen how Shias look upon the martyr's sacrifice almost as a benediction – how, in the festival of Ashura, they re-enact the spilling of Hussein's blood. We have seen how secular groups began to adopt the tropes and rituals of the Shia for political and military ends. But when it comes to suicide attacks being taken up by Sunni Muslims in Israel, things were very different indeed. Sunnis, unlike Shia, had no grand heroes of self-sacrifice. The Sunni narrative was often one of conquest and victory, not death when faced with unbeatable odds. For centuries, violent martyrdom was condemned outright by most Sunni scholars. A major sticking point in adopting suicide attacks was the strong prohibition against suicide in the Sunni faith. As the Prophet Muhammad said: 'He who kills himself with something in the worldly life, will be tortured with it on judgement day.' There were no Quranic verses that sanctioned 'martyrdom' operations.

Despite this, modern martyrdom still found space within the theological world of Sunni Islam. Why was this? Partly because there existed in Sunni Islam a tradition not of sacrifice, but of jihad – the Quran has over 120 verses referring to the struggle that Muslims must undertake either collectively or individually, to defend Islam.

In many ways, the history of Sunni Islam has been precisely that: a history of jihad, dominated by the various interpretations of what was meant by this term. In the very beginning, during Muhammad's own life, jihad seemed to refer to two things – both inner conflict, emblematised by the sacrifices of Islam's believers, men and women put to the sword for their beliefs; and outer jihad – the justification for aggressive and militant expansionism under the guise of spreading the word. Muhammad spent his last decade, from 622 to 632, in a permanent state of war with those who would seek to stamp out his power base with at least ninety-five different battles recorded.

So, on the one hand you had the sacrifice of martyrs such as Sumayyah bin Khayyat, an old slave in Mecca, who was murdered for her new faith – holding aloft the idea that this was a religion for Mecca's poor and marginalised, reinforcing Islam's message of equality.[32] And on the other, you had the violent deaths of men such as Amir ibn Fuhayra in the turmoil of battle, as part of jihad-as-conquest; his final words were said to have been: 'By Allah, I have been successful.'[33]

The latter type of jihad was to have arguably more impact than the former. For Jews, their collective memory is the exile of Moses; for many Christians it is the persecution of the early saints; but for Sunni Muslims it is that of conquest – the military triumphs of the Prophet.

The tension between 'inner' jihad – the battle for one's soul – and 'militant' jihad – the battle to protect or expand the Islamic community – has lingered up to today. The history of Islam is one marked by the oscillation between the two. In the eighth century, Islamic mysticism might have led to a rise in a contemplative Islam, where Sufis even began to call themselves 'martyrs of love',[34] but when Mongol armies began to wreak havoc on large parts of the Islamic world, aggressive jihad found its voice again.

One man in particular, Ibn Taymiyyah, was to embrace the logic of militant jihad. Born in 1263, seven years after the ransacking of Baghdad, and during the reconquista – the recapture of the Iberian peninsula by Christian crusaders – he argued that the Islamic world's weakness was a result of their renunciation of true Islam. To recover its strength, he said, jihad demanded a return to a putative seventh-century version of Islam. He saw any veneration of Sufi saints as a perversion of Islam's message of God's supremacy. He insisted that strict orthodoxy was the only path to paradise.[35] Those who called themselves Muslims but ate pork, or drank alcohol, or followed the laws of man, not of sharia, were not true Muslims. In the end, Ibn Taymiyyah declared a fatwa against the Mongols, praised military jihad, and painstakingly detailed the rewards awaiting martyrs in paradise.[36]

Similarly, centuries later when the Ottoman Empire was in decline, the eighteenth-century scholar Muhammad Abd al-Wahhab also embraced the notion of militant jihad, all the time railing at the Islamic world's perceived degeneration. Seeing divisive colonialism and migration, he yearned for a return to the practices of the early Islamic age, explicitly stating that those who die in jihad are granted immediate access to paradise.[37] At first confined to the Arabian Peninsula, modern Islamic scholars were later to internationalise al-Wahhab's ideas.

One such scholar was Sayyid Qutb who, by the mid-twentieth century, saw the West as fundamental to the Islamic world's decline, blaming 'Crusaders and Jews' to this end. Qutb came from Egypt, a country to which Napoleon Bonaparte had sought to export Enlightenment through violent conquest. He concluded that, to overcome Western hegemony, the struggle for the soul of Islam had to be violent in turn.[38] As he said in his book *Milestones*: 'The honour of martyrdom is achieved only when one is fighting in the cause of Allah, and if one is killed for any other purpose this honour will not be attained.'[39]

The words of these three men – Ibn Taymiyyah, al-Wahhab and Qutb – were to find receptive ears in 1979, a pivotal year that saw the birth of Thatcherism, the Iranian revolution, China instituting the 'one child per family' rule and, crucially, the Soviet Union deciding to invade Afghanistan. This last conflict came in a global period of radical thought and angry revolution. And it was to lead the Palestinian Sunni theologian and founding member of Al-Qaeda, Abdullah Yusuf Azzam – known to some as the 'Father of Global Jihad' – to find inspiration in those three 'founding fathers' of modern jihad. From them, he extrapolated a militant jihadist rhetoric designed to help the Afghan mujahidin defeat the Soviet invaders.

In his work *Martyr – The Building Block of Nations*, Azzam took elements of their theories and upheld sacrifice in jihad as integral to the well-being of the wider Islamic community. He said the history of Islam had to be written 'with both the ink of a scholar and his blood', and only sacrifice would let Muslims be 'rescued from their decline and awoken from their sleep'.[40]

This awakening was part and parcel of a rising Arab nationalism. The thorn in the side of the Islamic world had, for a long time, been Israel. Zionist settlements in Ottoman-ruled southern Syria, later British-controlled Mandatory Palestine, and the eventual establishment of the state of Israel in 1948, rankled deeply. Nascent Arab nationalism was to find a powerful voice in the 'us and them', 'Arabs versus Jews' rhetoric that followed confrontations between Jewish immigrants and local Arabs. When Jewish communities began to build synagogues and plant crops, the Palestinians – also made up of migrants from other parts of the Arab world – began to construct national and religious identities in return. And, with every slight, every counter-attack, a concept of modern, militant jihad was slowly built.

For decades, the Arabs of Palestine referred to their ethnicity and their nationality before their faith; Islam was not central to their way of seeing themselves, their Mullahs were corrupt, their leaders weak. Instead they found inspiration in a vision of a pan-Arab community. When Yasser Arafat's Fatah guerrilla group began to oppose Israel using guerrilla warfare, it was done using the rhetoric of the Cold War, the ideologies of Arabism, and Soviet revolutionary slogans. Sacrifice was seen as virtuous, but such jihad was second to political methods, at least until the Six-Day War with Israel in 1967.

But, over time, the promises of politics faded. Amidst the poverty of West Bank homes, Palestinians found the hollow blandishments of pan-Arabism to be wanting: Israel's defeat of the Arab states in both 1967 and 1973 left an indignant scar. Lebanon, though, was different

– it offered the audacity of hope. Households across the broken streets of Gaza would watch Lebanese TV telling one central message: how, in Lebanon, the Americans, the French and the Israelis had been driven from occupied land by the might of the suicide bomber.

Liberty had been gained because the Lebanese people had sacrificed themselves, unafraid of death. If this was how Lebanon made itself free, then why not Palestine?

Such a question occupies the heart of the change that occurred, one that began with that first Sunni suicide attack against civilians in April 1994. Admittedly, in the early days military considerations often overshadowed in-depth theological discussions. Yahya Ayyash, Hamas's chief bomb maker, said suicide attacks were a way to make the Israeli occupation 'that much more expensive in human lives, that much more unbearable'.[41] But, in a sense, there was no need for the Palestinians to create dramatic theological justification; such discussions had long been had by scholars from Ibn Taymiyyah to Abdullah Azzam, and the influence of such scholarship persists up to today.

Nonetheless, suicide bombing was new in Sunnism, and it required some awkward justifications. To sidestep the tricky issue of suicide, for instance, Hamas latched on to the Quranic claim that those who die fighting God's cause will be granted a special place in paradise.[42] Didn't Muhammad, in *The Book on Government*, declare: 'The gates of Paradise are under the shadows of the swords'?[43] Didn't the Quran say: 'Never think of those who have been killed in the cause of Allah as dead. Rather, they are alive with their Lord'?[44]

It helped when others gave their backing. The influential Qatar-based preacher Al-Qaradawi, a stalwart of the Palestinian cause, was to see suicide bombings as 'evidence of God's justice . . . he has given the weak a weapon (that) the strong do not have, and that is their ability to turn their bodies into bombs.'[45] Meanwhile Muhammad Tantawi, the Grand Imam of al-Azhar, a very influential Sunni religious position, said suicide attacks were 'an act of self-defence . . . what Israel is doing would drive any Muslim to seek revenge.'[46]

These words helped plant a new seed of rhetoric in the Sunni faith – the virtue of self-sacrifice in jihad. It was a combination of the inner and outer jihad, the spiritual and the militant journey that any suicide bomber must confront when contemplating their own death as weapon. So when, in 2001, the mufti of Jerusalem and Palestine, Sheikh Ikrima Sabri, announced to the Israelis that 'as much as you love life – the Muslim loves death and martyrdom,'[47] it was a statement that reached all the way back to 633, one year after the prophet's death. For that was when the Muslim general Khalid ibn al-Walid had threatened his enemies with a similar line: 'I bring the men who desire death as ardently as you desire life.'[48]

The meme of sacrifice began to penetrate Palestinian life. Children were sent to 'paradise camps' where they were trained in the art of suicide bombing and where, the BBC reported, the boys were 'told not only that it is good to kill, but also that it is good to die.'[49] Over time, suicide bombers became celebrities, sports idols, religious heroes all rolled into one. Rallies commonly featured children wearing bombers' belts. The claims of the rewards of paradise, the extolling of suicide bombing, was done with purpose: the Palestinian leaders had to create a culture alien to the Sunni tradition. This, unlike in Iran where the ghosts of Shia martyrs framed such a cultivation, was manufactured martyrdom.

It was a manufactured idea that was greeted readily. As anyone who has visited the refugee camps of the West Bank will tell you, suffering is a constant theme, an obsession. People say they could explode under the pressure of humiliation. Martyrdom offered, then, meaning and direction; death became infused with life. Suicide bombers were believed to live for ever in paradise, their sins wiped clean, away from the hell of Gaza at least. They were not even suicide bombers, they were 'holy explosions', for whom they said – quoting

Imam Bukhari, a ninth-century Persian mystic – 'a special place was given in Paradise'.[50]

Such narratives gave hope in a time of hopelessness, purpose and power where there was none. The Palestinians, for the longest time seeing themselves as voiceless victims, began to see a chink of light in the possibility that, by dying for a cause, meaning would be given to the individual, honour to the family and liberty to the nation. As the author David Brooks wrote in the *Atlantic*, 'suicide bombing became the tactic of choice, even in circumstances where a terrorist could have planted a bomb and then escaped without injury'.[51] Suicidal jihad to some Sunnis became not just a means, but an end in itself – the same message that Khomeini promoted in Iran but without a central leader dictating what was, and what was not, acceptable. Which is why, unlike in Iran and Lebanon, civilians were to become legitimate targets.

Of the 721 people killed in Israel since suicide bombings were first seen there, 95 per cent of them have been civilians.

In Lebanon, Shiite scholars had selected military targets and mostly sought to avoid civilian harm; during Hezbollah's seventeen-year struggle with Israel in Southern Lebanon, it has never been proved that the Party of God perpetrated an attack specifically against Israeli civilians.[52] Hezbollah wanted their actions to be regarded as resistance and not criminal acts.[53] They felt bound by Islamic rules of engagement not to harm innocents.

In contrast, Sunni scholars explicitly issued fatwas permitting the killing of Israeli citizens. The Qatari cleric Qaradawi frequently said suicide attacks on civilians were not illegal under international law. Meanwhile the former Grand Sheikh of the al-Azhar, Muhammad Tantawi, designated such assaults as legitimate.[54]

This ran counter to wider Islamic teaching. The Prophet Muhammad strictly prohibited the killing of civilians in war, which he defined as servants, women, children or the elderly. The main Islamic jurisprudence schools agree 'that minors and women may not be killed, unless they actually fight against the Moslems'.[55] Some Sunni clerics, though, granted Israel a unique place in this – arguing that all Israeli civilians were fair game, as Israel was essentially a 'military barracks' by virtue of its universal conscription and the nature of its occupation of Palestinian lands.[56]

There were, roughly speaking, four types of bomber in Palestine: the religious fanatic, the exploited, the avenger and the nationalist fanatic. They reportedly displayed relatively normal personality traits. They were neither depressed nor suicidal.[57] They may not have been 'normal', they just did not exhibit psychopathology.[58] It seems they also made their decisions based on cold rationality; their deaths were not impulsive.[59] Certainly, despite claims the money the martyr's families were to receive was a motivating factor, there is no firm evidence they did it for that reason (though Saddam Hussein providing funds of up to $25,000 to the families of Palestinian suicide bombers may have sweetened a bitter pill).[60]

But what many needed was a strong idea – one that showed how they could turn their private sufferings into public empowerment.[61] Such ideas are important. The content of an armed group's ideology has been seen to be a crucial predictor as to whether its follower will strap on a suicide belt or not.[62] In short, members will be attracted to a group if it reflects their world beliefs and offers solutions, even if they are self-destructive ones. An idea so strong that one failed Palestinian suicide bomber was to later say that he 'didn't want revenge for anything . . . I just wanted to be a martyr'.[63]

Unsurprisingly, studies have concluded that 'abject poverty mixed with political frustration and military imbalance' has been a substantive reason why some Palestinians have chosen to undertake suicide attacks. By 2003, 400,000 Israeli Jews were living in the occupied territories, in explicit violation of the Fourth Geneva Convention in international humanitarian law.[64] It has been a form of colonialism that has been supported by successive Israeli governments ever since 1967. But – and this is a crucial point – there have been many other situations around the world where poverty, political oppression and military inferiority have marked a rebel movement, and its followers have not chosen to blow themselves up.[65]

There were no suicide bombers in the Peruvian Shining Path guerrilla movement. None in Nagaland or Chiapas, in the Bophuthat-swana crisis or the Namibian Caprivi conflict, in the Ugandan Allied Democratic Forces insurgency or the recent Donetsk People's Republic separation from Ukraine. With ETA in the Basque country, the Greek Revolutionary Struggle, the Cambodian Khmer Rouge and the Nep-alese civil wars, suicide bombers were absent. I have reported on many liberation wars – from Mindanao to Colombia, Somaliland to Mozambique – where similar complaints as those raised by the Pales-tinians were at the root of the conflict, and there sprouted no culture of self-martyrdom. All faced issues of poverty, isolation, persecution, prosecution and attack, but none responded with a suicide belt.

Why, for instance, have there been no Tibetan Buddhist sui-cide bombers?[66] The occupation of their land by the Chinese has been as violent as that witnessed in Palestine, but it has created a very different form of protest: the self-immolating monk. Ever since 27 February 2009, when Tapey, a novice monk from Kirti monastery, poured petrol and dropped a match upon himself in the marketplace in Ngawa City, there have been nearly 150 con-firmed self-immolations in Tibet.[67] Why did they not ignite others with them? I can only conclude that a theological interpretation of Buddhism does not permit the harming of others in their protest, whereas a Sunni-jihadist interpretation of the holy texts did so.

In those civil wars where secular suicide bombers have been deployed – Sri Lanka and the Kurdish struggle – it seems that the godlike influence of the leader, actively encouraging his supporters to die in this way, was the impetus towards their suicide bombings. But seeing suicide bombers as just part of the struggle for independence and land, as some do, fails to answer the question: what about the liberation movements that don't deploy such attackers? The thing that changes everything is the seeding – and embracing – of that notion of martyrdom.

In Palestine, then, while the 'cult' of martyrdom cannot by itself explain the increase in suicide attacks, if you take away the religious framing that first legitimised suicide bombers there, it is hard to see how it would have both caught on and persisted. But persist it did and, by attacking civilians and doing so with theological justification, Hamas opened up a Pandora's box of trouble and pain. And the one thing about Pandora's Box is that, once opened, the consequences are predictable: misery, violence and heartache. So it was that an equally predictable *danse macabre* was to take place following suicide attacks on civilians in Israel.

Soon after an explosion, as people were still screaming in agony, as ambulances were carrying victims to emergency units, Orthodox Jewish volunteers known as ZAKA (Disaster Victim Identification) would arrive at the scene in fluorescent yellow vests. It was a terrible job: to collect blood and body parts – including the remains of the bomber – and take them to a forensic centre in Jaffa. They moved swiftly: a crime scene could be cleared within three hours. They needed to; a Hebrew commandment forbids you to leave the dead unburied overnight (unless it is to honour the person who passed). In the meantime, in Jaffa, pathologists would reassemble what was left of the bodies for identification purposes. Newly developed DNA testing was, in many cases, the only means of connecting one piece of flesh with another.

With the news of a bombing, family members would also descend on the scene, calling out their relatives' names. Those unable to find their loved ones were directed to Jaffa. The pathologists there tried to be kind: no, they would say, you must not see the remains, you must remember your relative as they were. But many still wanted to touch them one last time, even if a foot was all that was left. The officials would bury the larger body parts first: torsos and heads. Smaller pieces were added later, after DNA testing confirmed who they belonged to. In this way, the graves of civilians would be re-opened and closed, each time a violation of the tomb.

A dark pattern began to emerge. People lit candles and talked of revenge, too. The Israelis scrambled fighter jets, Palestinian police stations were sometimes bombed, and tanks advanced into Jenin, Nablus and Ramallah. For some, whatever counter-response was undertaken was deemed too little, too late.

In Palestine the mood was markedly different. There would be the expected response from the Palestinian Authority – that Ariel Sharon was a warmonger and that Palestine was the casualty – but in the shacks of refugee camps, people danced the traditional *debkeh* and celebrated.

Then things appeared to return to normal, but something was lost. The debris might be removed, new martyr posters might be put up, but fear persisted long after. Municipal buses drove three-quarters empty. Perhaps the person best placed to have observed the bomber's truest impact is Gil Kleiman, a former foreign press spokesman for the Israeli police. A New York Jew, he is fast-talking, hard-nosed and vulnerable all at the same time. By his own calculations, in a role that required he attend every bombing and witness its devastation to report on it accurately, he has seen forty-eight suicide bombings up close.

He saw them come in two waves. The first was from 1994 through to 1998: twenty-four attacks in Israel and Palestine, all carried out by Hamas and Palestinian Islamic Jihad. The next, far bigger, wave began in 2000 and lasted until 2008 – during and beyond the second intifada: there were 147 attacks, carried out by at least seven groups, including secular ones such as the Popular Resistance Committees and the Popular Front for the Liberation of Palestine.

During that second wave, Gil said, there were 'more suicide bombers volunteering than they had belts – human minds connected to a bomb, the most dangerous warheads'. There were years where over half of Israel's violent deaths were from suicide bombings, not because there were no shootings – there were thousands of them – but because the suicide bombs were so lethal. These were not attacks on the structures of fortified, institutional power, but on 'soft' targets: restaurants, nightclubs, hotels and markets. So frequently were cafés attacked, it was even drily dubbed 'the war of the croissant'.

The attackers were hard to spot. 'In 1997 we were teaching security officers to look out for a religious, clean-cut, shaven, ready-to-meet-God type; you know – male, glassy-eyed. By 2001, there was no profile,' Gil recalled. They could be men or women, young or old. They could be that person sitting next to you on the bus with the rucksack.

Such random, repeated attacks, the ever-present threat, was trans-formative. Nowhere felt safe. People would get birthday party invites telling them that armed guards would be present. Parents would insist their children had mobile phones at all times. 'Terror', he said, 'does not have to do with how many are killed. It's how much effect you have on the society.'

He was once sent to a bombing scene where he had been briefed that an elderly man had been killed, and his walk to the inert body, knowing his elderly father was in the same area and not answering his phone, was the longest of his life. He took each step with his heart in his mouth until he saw the shoes poking out from the body bag and knew his father had never worn such a pair.

He developed mechanisms to cope with that sort of stress. A disassociation seeped in. You can hear it now in how Gil talks about violence: 'seeing a person's head is very indicative of a suicide bombing: the head blows off because it's the weakest link'; 'the spinal cord was found a week later on one of the hills'; 'I don't remember where we found the torso.' Someone in the Jerusalem Museum café where we were talking stared at us hard for a few minutes. Gil didn't notice.

It got to the point where he found himself deliberately taking phone calls hunched next to dead bodies at bomb scenes because that was the quietest place in the area – the dead are silent. He was once smoking a cigarette when he noticed it was wet with the blood of one of the victims. He coped by framing the events in terms of black and white: the dead were good, the killers evil. 'My message was always good people, innocent . . . against evil,' he said. 'The statue of justice has scales and a sword in her hand. Good people need to use the sword to protect good people. In a city of pacifists, one terrorist with a fork can conquer the city.' This was a justification that I had heard in many places before, and it reminded me starkly of Second Amendment cheerleaders I had met in the United States.

But there was a limit to how much he could shut things out. 'By the end of the second intifada,' he said, '20 per cent of the Israeli police bomb squad was diagnosed with PTSD. But everybody was affected by it.' For him, it was like hitting a wall. After years of chasing ambulances and morgue wagons, one Sunday morning he found himself crying uncontrollably. 'I couldn't actually breathe. I didn't leave my room for a month. Every one of the hundreds of people who I had seen murdered at suicide bombings was waiting outside my room, as if to say "You don't remember me but I was the person lying there." I had to make peace with all those people.'

Israeli society turned inwards, too. The news became too depressing for many to watch; drug use soared. 'The frequency of use of psycho-active substances is astronomic,' one addiction specialist reported.[68] Binge drinking and cannabis smoking became widespread among younger Israelis.[69] Others just left the country – the bars of Kho-San road in Bangkok or the clubs of Europe saw a steady stream of Israelis, many bringing the traumas of war with them: 'harmful, aggressive, unsociable, disrespectful' was how one Israeli living in South America described his fellow countrymen in an article called: 'Why Israelis make the worst tourists'.[70]

Gil believed things changed when, after one particularly terrible bombing in a hotel, the decision came down from on high to allow news crews to film everything. And the images of civilians being killed in that way – their bodies penetrated by the bones of their killers, by table legs, by cutlery – shown on the evening news shocked the world. It obliterated any chance of meaningful dialogue, decimated the Israeli peace activist movement, and led to many around the world seeing the Palestinians as more than just a threat, but as fundamental opposites to Jews.

Gil shared that view. 'Arab society is different from our society. That's it. I know it's not politically correct to say this, but they're brought up differently. When a mother says: "I wish I had more children to sacrifice for the cause", well, you'd never hear a Jewish mother say that. Never. An Israeli mother will say "My son died, he's a hero, I can't believe my son died." We just have a different attitude towards life.'

I asked him what he thought of this book's title, *The Price of Paradise*, and he was quick with his reply. He said the Palestinians would not call it a price, they would call it a gift. For them it was a 'gift God allowed me to kill myself'.

So the theological landscape had been set – Palestinian Sunnis had embraced self-immolation and justified the deaths of civilians in the same breath. But did such a framing fuel the use of suicide bombings? I believe so.

In a very limited sense, the suicide attacks won what the perpetrators wanted. Hamas's campaigns contributed to the Israeli withdrawal from the lands of Judea, Samaria and Gaza in the West Bank at the time of the implementation of the Oslo Accords. It also made Hamas a significant force in Palestinian politics. But in the main, the attacks just led to more death and stasis, and created a deadlock that we still see today. When I was in the West Bank, the Gaza Strip was aflame, with hundreds of burning tyres placed along the barbed wire fence to mask the view of Israeli snipers. The barely-men of the IDF still fired, though, and dozens died along that jagged border.

In Israel, suicide bombers reasserted the notion the Palestinians were seeking to stamp out an entire nation. Throughout history, I was told, the Jews had always been threatened with extermination and this threat was still there. And I felt much sympathy for this statement – it is hard not to, having visited the killing camps of Dachau and Bergen-Belsen, Auschwitz and Buchenwald. Just as it is hard not to be shocked by the comments of some when it comes to the Jews – like the Lebanese woman who spat out that they were 'not humans' and who was shocked when I reprimanded her for such monstrous inhumanity. Anti-Semitism is on the rise, and it is as much a moral imperative to separate criticism of the Israeli state from that of the Jewish people, as it is to separate criticism of armed jihadists from Muslims.

Self-defence, though, needs to be measured and proportionate. But the Israelis had the military might and the support of the US to fight back, and they did so, hard. Between 1987 and 2017, 11,357 Palestinians were reported killed by Israelis. This compares to 1,664 Israelis being killed by Palestinians.[71]

The Israeli pushback was hard indeed. Over 200 Israeli-run assassination attempts of Palestinians took place between 2000 and 2005, 80 per cent of which succeeded, sometimes killing innocents in the process.[72] And while, in 1999, the High Court of Justice in Israel outlawed torture, their attorney general was to assure torturers they would not stand trial if they could prove it was a matter of life or death.[73] What followed were Palestinians faced with sleep depriva-tion, threats against family members and punching; Amnesty said even children had been tortured.[74]

When a suicide bomber killed with a rucksack carrying explosives, the Israelis responded with jets carrying missiles. When a Palestinian attempted to kill a busful of students, the Israelis sought to wipe out every person who was behind that targeted attack. As Amnesty also reported: 'Killings of Palestinians by Israel security services or settlers have led to suicide bombings and the deaths of Israeli civilians. These have led to waves of arbitrary arrests, incommunicado detention, torture and unfair trials. The Palestinian population have been the main victims of such violations.'[75]

Violence did not just fuel violence, but added petrol to the con-flagration. A study of individual motivations of Palestinian suicide bombers during the second intifada shows that almost two-thirds were seeking to avenge the killing of a relative or in response to a specific Israeli attack. The appetite for targeting of civilians became more and more palatable to Palestinians as time went on. During the first intifada, Palestinian support for suicide bombings never exceeded 30 per cent. At the height of the second intifada, 70 per cent thought it acceptable.[76] One study found that Israeli 'targeted killings seem to be followed by an increase in the number of suicide bombings'.[77]

It seems the most vengeful Palestinians were also the most reli-gious. When forty-five insurgent leaders representing all significant factions were interviewed in 2006, every single Hamas and Palestinian Islamic Jihad fighter said they would never be willing to recognise Israel. Only 10 per cent of secular leaders said the same.[78] Perhaps when you have God on your side, you become far more immovable; religious justifications for suicide missions seem to persist long after secular ideologies fail to bring about desired results.

Many claim that Israel's tactics – assassinations, torture, enormous fences – worked. Nearly 600 suicide attacks were launched at Israel and the occupied territories between 2000 and 2005. Of these, less than 25 per cent reached their targets.[79] There was a sharp decline in suicide attacks in the years following 2004 as populations were pushed back behind unbreachable barriers. At least this is one side of the argument: that an iron fist can crush an insurgency.

The truth is more nuanced. As Hamas developed more sophisticated weaponry, it decreased its use of suicide attacks. From 2004 rockets became the weapon of choice, due to improvements in range and accuracy.[80] Qassam missiles allowed Hamas militants to strike inside Israel without having to cross heavily policed boundaries. Then, in early 2006, Hamas won a surprise victory in the Palestinian legislative elections, giving the group a mandate as a legitimate political party. Several months following their success, Yihiyeh Musa, a Hamas member of the Palestinian Legislative Council, said Hamas 'suicide bombings happened in an exceptional period and they have now stopped . . . they came to an end as a change of belief'.[81]

Despite suicide attacks in 2007 and 2008, the new policy seemed to remain in place for years. In recent times, though, there does seem to have been a change in policy by Hamas senior leadership. In December 2015, a music video posted by the official Hamas channel Al-Aqsa TV featured a would-be attacker preparing for a suicide mission, while the lyrics of a popular song in Gaza includes the line: 'The intifada is not an intifada if the bus roof doesn't fly off'.[82] In that year, Israel's security service uncovered a Hamas terrorist cell which had made advanced plans to carry out more suicide attacks;[83] there was an apparent failed suicide bombing at a checkpoint near Jerusalem in October of that year, while Hamas leaders appeared to reject a fatwa issued by a leading Muslim cleric which banned Palestinian suicide operations.[84] In short, the suicide bomber could easily emerge again as a weapon of the Palestinians.

A precedent had been established – a method of violence

institutionalised and codified – which is why the most recent suicide bomber in Gaza was not a Palestinian killing Israelis, but an
ISIS fighter killing a top Hamas commander.[85]

I had one final place to visit. I got into my car and drove out of Jerusalem, down sharp winding roads beside olive groves and cypress
trees. The way was filled with potholes and a storm was brewing
in the skies. The path took me down under a looming viaduct,
humming electricity wires hovering above. Further beyond, tucked
away overlooking a valley of green trees and bleached stone, stood
a memorial constructed from the steel of the remains of the World
Trade Center. It is the only memorial outside the US that includes the
names of all those who died in the attack of 9/11. It includes those
of five Israeli citizens.

I brought the car to a stop just as the rain began and rushed to
the empty site. A tiered auditorium circled the monument: a spiral

*A memorial to 9/11 near
Jerusalem*

of dark metal, like a black flame, imprinted with Stars and Stripes. It was a statement that, to me, said: 'You have suffered, as we in Israel have suffered.'

The rain pushed me back to the car and I sat there for a while, the windows steaming up. When I turned on the ignition to force air through, the radio came on. A song was playing, the words 'feels like heaven' on a loop. It didn't.

Chapter 7

The Devil's Face

'On a clear Tuesday morning . . .'

These are the first words of an overview of what happened on 11 September 2001, written on the website of the official memorial to that tragedy and echoed in many other reports since. Certainly, it was a day marked by blue skies. The sort of visibility pilots call 'severe clear': a cloudless one that sparkled.

Nineteen men shattered this peace. They hijacked four commercial aeroplanes, deliberately crashing two of them into the Twin Towers of New York City and a third into the Pentagon in Arlington, Virginia. Passengers on the fourth plane, Flight 93, launched a counter-attack, and the aircraft hurtled into an empty field in western Pennsylvania. That day, 2,977 people were killed, 115 foreign nationalities represented on the list of the dead. The oldest was eighty-five, the youngest just two.[1]

It was the greatest loss of life ever from a single terrorist attack; the most number of people killed in a suicide strike; the most suicide attackers to die in a combined mission; the most-witnessed mass death in the history of the world.

Suspicion was soon to fall on the group behind the trauma: the radical Sunni Islamist entity, Al-Qaeda – or 'the Base' in Arabic.

Founded in 1988, and led by the Saudi-born Osama Bin Laden, the organisation had attacked the West before, on 26 February 1993. Then, men following their creed had detonated explosives in the garage beneath the same place they were to strike on 9/11 – the World Trade Center. They managed to kill six people and injure thousands more.[2]

Over the following eight years, Al-Qaeda was to be implicated in a series of attacks on the United States around the world. These included: the shooting down of two US Black Hawk helicopters over Mogadishu, Somalia in October 1993; the killing of nineteen Americans when a military housing complex was bombed in Saudi Arabia in 1996; the suicide attacks on US embassies in Dar es Salaam and Nairobi in 1998, with 223 killed; and the suicide attack on the USS *Cole* in 2000 in the Yemen, leading to the deaths of seventeen servicemen.

These attacks were part of an orchestrated campaign that was steadily gaining momentum. In 1996, Bin Laden had called for his followers to 'launch a guerrilla war against American forces and expel the infidels from the Arabian Peninsula'. And, soon after the 1998 embassy bombings, the Federal Bureau of Investigation had placed the khaki-clad preacher on their Ten Most Wanted list. A reward of $25 million was offered for his capture.

Still, the American public did not feel Bin Laden's threat acutely. These attacks had been limited or distant. As the official report on 9/11 was to conclude: 'Neither in 2000 nor in the first eight months of 2001 did any polling organization in the United States think the subject of terrorism sufficiently on the minds of the public to warrant asking a question about it in a major national survey.'[3]

It was, indeed, a clear day for most. And then everything changed.

I had been to New York many times before this. At fifteen years old, I had backpacked across the US, ending up in the chaos of that city, and visited the World Trade Center then. The name itself seemed so imposing, so confident, that it was a daunting trip and I felt uneasy going, as if I were visiting a cathedral of some faith without knowing what the religion was. After that, I shoved the place to the back of my mind and never gave it another thought, but now I was on the Metro B train downtown, headed to a place that had influenced my journalistic life far more profoundly than that teenage visit ever had.

An automated voice told us to be alert, to stay safe, and then I was off the train, and up to West Broadway, and the memorial came slowly into view – like a skyscraper had been laid down, a sleeping giant of glass and steel.

There it was: Ground Zero.

Ground Zero – a name first used to describe Hiroshima: that point directly beneath the aerial detonation of the atomic bomb. A name given by Americans to their violent response to the kamikaze attacks. Now it was used in sorrow, but Bin Laden had partly justified his mass murder of civilians here by arguing: had the Americans not done the same in Japan, had they not created wastelands with their own atomic blasts? The devastation first born in the Manhattan Project – the research project during the Second World War that produced the first nuclear weapons – had come home.

As I passed a roadside stall, there came into view another building that was shaped like the whitened bones of an enormous whale, its ribs flaring upwards like an architectural carcass: a massive shopping centre. To its right lay the 9/11 Memorial.

Here, two huge pools were set in the footprints of the original towers. People peered in. Thirty-foot waterfalls – the largest human-made ones in North America – cascaded down, each into a void. A pair of chasms clad in granite, lined with a film of eternal, falling water. Inside lay a second void, its bottom hidden from sight, and it reminded me of that Walt Whitman line: 'the huge first Nothing'.

I was also reminded of something the historian Julia Kristeva had

The 9/11 memorial

once written: how 'monstrous and painful sights' could be so harmful as to damage our ways of mourning and representing loss; how the way we symbolise death finds itself hollowed out when faced with a perceived apocalypse. 'On the edge of silence,' she wrote, 'the word "nothing" emerges.'[4]

The cascade into these black depths was as far a cry from the classical forms of remembrance as I could imagine. I was used to the cenotaphs and plinths of war that dot Europe's landscapes, but such traditional commemoration here was deemed inappropriate and insufficient. The inspiration for this memorial had to come from a Jewish tradition: a form of remembrance gouged out by the Holocaust.

Along the parapets, around the pool, ran the names of those who had died here, incised in bronze. They stretched 212 feet on every side. I looked for an order to the listings, but the names here had been arranged by relationship, not alphabet; the idea was to preserve the bonds of family and friendship.⁵ It meant this memorial did not have the orderly regulation of a military tomb.

At one time, this space had been commemorated differently. In 2002, eighty-eight searchlights had been turned to the sky and the beams had merged into two pillars of light, four miles high, the most powerful strips of luminescence ever created. But these phantasmal towers caused some to say they commemorated more the loss of the structures than the people, and the lights were turned off.

It is rare to have public memorials directly laid upon the site of death. Here, though, almost seven hectares had become a mass grave, one where 13 million square feet of 'class A' office space, housing 400 companies and several government agencies, had once thrived. Now there stood just wavering lines of planted swamp white oaks and, among them, a Callery pear tree. They call it the 'Survivor Tree' because workers had found its damaged stump deep in the wreckage, nursed it back to health and replanted it here – 'a story,' one guide read, 'of survival and resilience'. The trees, at least, seemed to offer a natural buffer between this sacred space of loss, and the everyday profanities of the city beyond.

I walked towards the memorial exhibition building. I had arranged to meet Clifford Chanin, the executive vice-president there, and had to clear security first. Like all visitors, I had to pass through five airport security scanners– the legacy of fear of another attack –with guard dogs standing outside. Beyond this was a list of the board members of the memorial: fifty-one names (none Muslim, I noted), Billy Crystal and Robert De Niro among them. Honorary board members included four presidents – Bush Jr., Bush Snr., Carter and Clinton – then a longer list of the memorial's founders: 119 in all, including the pillars of capitalism – J.P. Morgan, Amex, Goldman Sachs, Barclays, Credit Suisse, Morgan Stanley, Walt Disney, Time Warner, Coca-Cola, Deloitte, HSBC, KPMG, Lehman's, McDonald's,

PepsiCo. America's authorities of power and wealth were guardians of this site now.

Stairs led up to a cinema and down to permanent displays and sites of remembrance. They included two core exhibitions: 'In Memoriam', which pays tribute to those killed in the attacks on 9/11 and in the 1993 World Trade Center bombing, and a three-part historical exhibition, which recounts what happened on the day, exploring what led up to the attacks, its aftermath and how it 'continues to shape our world'.

Above was a balustrade, bearing the weight of a line of flags – each for a national that died that day. It was a nod to the 180 flags that hung in the mezzanine level of the original lobbies of the World Trade Center. A coalition of nations that, according to Bruno Dellinger, a French-born survivor of the attacks, 'represented a Utopia that can only exist in New York'.

I sat down in the café and a few minutes later in walked Clifford. A bespectacled man with tight cut hair and a New Yorker executive's trimness to him, he apologised for being late. We got straight to the point. He had been working at the memorial for over a decade now, so I asked him whether he sensed there was a loss of utopia in New York after the tragedy. He was not sure. 'It was certainly a loss of a sense of safety and a growing sense of vulnerability,' he said.

Understanding and unpicking all that has happened since is hard, he said – Afghanistan, Iraq, and all the rest – but if you return to the day it all began, 9/11, a very clear sense of what happened was evident. Certainly this memorial has been a lodestar, not just for the ongoing War on Terror, but for others also trying to contemplate different tragedies. People had come to see how memorials were conceived and carried out – from those commemorating the massacre by the Norwegian Anders Behring Breivik, to authorities from the Fukushima Daiichi nuclear disaster. Others came, too – government intelligence officers, military and law enforcement – to see the point

Clifford Chanin, the Executive Vice President of the 9/11 Memorial

of origin of their daily concerns, a decade and a half later. Today the newest of their ranks are of an age that they don't remember what unfolded on that day. So, in this sense, this memorial is for them, the genesis of their service, their potential sacrifice.

I asked him what role religion had in the memorial – what role Islam played. Some people said that there was too much emphasis on the ideologies of the hijackers, others said there was not enough. Clifford had been accused of fomenting hatred, as well as of covering up the reality of who was behind the attack, but in general the theme of ideological motivation did not lace throughout the exhibits here. He admitted the shortcoming, and said there would always be a lack of nuance when trying to explain the tragedy that this place witnessed.

'We're not putting books on walls,' he said. 'It's inevitably more complicated than we can present. We could go to the beginning of

Islam, or choose any starting point between that and 9/11. It could be the Iranian revolution, the 1967 war, the anti-colonial movement, the failures of the nineteenth century, the Enlightenment, the Crusades . . . you could go right back to the creation of the new faith of Islam.'

'You can't disentangle these things,' he concluded. And I thought, yes, perhaps not in a museum, but it's essential – if we are to seek to stop history from repeating itself – at least to try.

One thousand two hundred and ninety-seven days before 9/11, on 23 February 1998, Osama Bin Laden issued a fatwa that was, effectively, to begin the War on Terror.[6] A decree filled with fiery rhetoric and bombast, it was much more emphatic than the threat he had made in 1996. He railed against US boots on the ground in the Middle East 'occupying the lands of Islam in the holiest of places, the Arabian Peninsula', and described America's involvement there as one of 'crusader armies' spreading like 'locusts, eating its riches and wiping out its plantations'.

All Muslims, Bin Laden said, had a duty to kill Americans wherever they could. They should also strive to liberate Jerusalem.[7] It was a call for death, including the sacrifice of those that would fight on the side of Allah: 'What is the matter with you . . . ye cling so heavily to the earth! Do ye prefer the life of this world to the hereafter?'

That same year he was to give an interview to ABC News.[8] The ghosts of previous suicide attacks – and responses to them – were present in that broadcast. He explicitly noted the impact of suicide bombers in Lebanon, saying how America's 'weak soldiers' had proved their worth 'in Beirut, when the Marines fled after two explosions'. He also took America's military response to the suicide bombers of the past as an example of how the US was godless.

'American history,' he said, 'does not distinguish between civilians and military, and not even women and children. They are the ones who used the bombs against Nagasaki. Can these bombs distinguish between infants and military?'

The threat of US aggression was also a central theme in his argument; what was needed, most of all, was a pre-emptive strike at the heart of American soil: 'The only way for us to fend off these assaults is to use similar means.'

By the spring of 1999, Bin Laden had held a meeting with Khalid Sheikh Mohammed, Al-Qaeda's number three, during which they started planning for such a strike inside America. It was a plan that was to take shape slowly. At first they considered targeting a nuclear power plant, but then decided against it, fearing things could 'get out of control'.⁹ They settled on a suicidal aerial assault at the centre of American power, at its icons of military might and commerce – in their eyes, at its very soul.

Why was such a plan hatched? Where had such anger and thirst for suffering come from? In many ways, it was the logical result of what Bin Laden had always sought, ever since he had formed Al-Qaeda back in 1988. Even then he said the group's central mission was to strike at the sponsors of regional tyrants in the Arab world. Their target was always the United States, for Bin Laden and his followers believed that if they could do what Hezbollah did to the US in Lebanon, they could turf America out of the Middle East. In turn, Israel, Saudi Arabia, Egypt and Turkey would fall to the new order that Al-Qaeda would usher in.

The plan of 9/11 was also the product of two other strands of thought that had emerged in Sunni Islam: the acceptability of suicidal martyrdom in jihad, and of targeting civilians in the process. These were radical shifts, as we have seen, born in Lebanon and Palestine, but something new was added to the mix with Al-Qaeda. They aligned with another strand in Sunni Islam – the rise of what is known as Salafi-jihadism.

Deriving from the Arabic word *salaf* or 'predecessors', Salafists like

Bin Laden yearned for a return to a way of life as practised by the Prophet Muhammad, his companions and the two generations of Muslims that followed them. They believed that only by returning to the fundamentals – the base – of Islam could they create an Islamic utopia. And, given the Quran and Hadiths were written at a time when strict enforcement of the rule of law was normal – with stonings and crucifixions commonplace – such a return demanded, in the eyes of Bin Laden, a conservative and rigid interpretation of the faith, overseen by an authoritarian theocrat.[10]

Salafism itself was not a new idea. The dominant Salafist interpretation is that of Wahhabism, a religious practice conceived by Muhammad ibn Abd al-Wahhab in the eighteenth century and that, today, stands as the official Saudi state ideology and basis for the country's conservative legal system.[11] So it must be stressed that neither Salafism nor Wahhabism is – in itself – inherently violent. But there are elements of both that can go, in part, to explain how, when contaminated with the rhetoric of jihad, such ideologies produced violence. Indeed, many Salafist-Wahhabists valorise the idea of military jihad. They are quick to excommunicate non-believers, and possess a stubborn black-and-white view of the world: believers on the one hand, non-believers on the other. Such dualism fuels their call for conflict because they see it as legitimate to take up arms in defence of Islam against non-believers of all kinds.[12]

Again, it must be stressed that such extreme positioning is not the view of all Salafists, and not the view of the vast majority of Sunnis, but in the hands of enough determined jihadists it rocked the world.

The view of extremists like Bin Laden was a departure from the Islamic norm. If you walk down to a local mosque in most parts of the world and ask the imam there whether the Quran calls on Muslims to fight non-Muslims purely on the basis of their beliefs, the answer would be almost without exception: no. That, many would say, could only happen if Muslims were actively persecuted.[13] The justification for most of the twentieth century's Islamic suicide attacks – in Iran, Lebanon, Palestine – was that it was self-defence, and while you may vehemently disagree with their use of martyrdom tactics to do so, it would be hard to deny that they had at least some justification in saying they were doing it to protect themselves and others.

Al-Qaeda, though, were seeking to do something very different. They ignored the 124 verses in the Quran that favoured a less aggressive approach towards non-believers.[14] Instead their inspiration was the line: 'Fight and slay the pagans wherever ye find them', an instruction that had been largely ignored before because Islam's spiritual leaders knew it would pit their religion against all others, and for its lack of humanity.[15] But not Bin Laden. As he was to say in an interview a month after 9/11: 'I tell Muslims to believe in the victory of God and in Jihad against the infidels of the world. The killing of Jews and Americans is one of the greatest duties.'[16]

Bin Laden's desire to wage jihad – a highly political and bloody jihad at that – had deep roots. While the foundations of Shia jihad were nurtured in the holy Iraqi city of Najaf, his Sunni-Salafist impulse to jihad found its intellectual soul in the hectic streets of Cairo. Egypt has long been the source of a violent – and philosophical – struggle between East and West. Ever since the eighteenth century, when Napoleon invaded the lands of the Nile seeking the prestige of empire, there had been attempts to export the teachings of the Enlightenment to North Africa. When Napoleon sent over 150 French scholars there to analyse the ancient Egyptian civilisation, it was not just to learn from Egypt, it was to force the nation to move from the 'barbarism and ignorant superstition' of the Mameluke rulers to something that resembled France.[17] But whereas what Napoleon saw when he clambered up the pyramids was the potential for conquest, many Egyptians did not. They were to see and feel the beginnings of Western oppression and exploitation – and not just them, so did countless others faced with, and still facing in some senses, murderous colonial expansion.

It took many decades for the incursion of the modern into Egypt to bear fruit, but in 1928, dismayed at the venality of the Egyptian government and filled with a desire to return to a purer, simpler time, the Egyptian schoolteacher Hassan al-Banna formed the Muslim Brotherhood. Merging the conservative strands of religious belief in Salafism with a political vision, the Brotherhood sought to create an Islamic utopia. Al-Banna and his Muslim brothers built their own society, their own hospital, factories and schools. Such building was part of a wider plan, as al-Banna wrote: 'It is the nature of Islam to dominate, not to be dominated, to impose its law on all nations, and to extend its power to the entire planet.'[18]

Slowly, over time, this notion was to grow, and the vision of that Islamic utopia was to find its most articulate form in the writings of another Egyptian, Sayyid Qutb. It was his 1964 book *Milestones* that many consider laid the foundations for modern Islamist militancy. To Qutb, the world was following an arc of history that was descending into hell, not rising to paradise. Hell, in this case, was a period of *jahiliyyah*, where ignorance and chaos would reign, where man's laws would subvert, not enlighten. For him, only by returning to the teachings of the prophets would freedom come.

Qutb advocated a kind of 'anarcho-Islam', rejecting all kinds of government, both secular and theocratic. It was a dogma partly born out of a trip to the United States, where he saw 'godless materialism and debauchery'.[19] Faced with such perceived sin, he was to develop a theory that the West was imposing its control over Muslim lands, taking advantage of the Ottoman Empire's collapse after the Great War. The leaders in these Islamic lands might claim to be Muslims, he said, but they had long ago left the path of righteousness. When Qutb saw British troops around the Suez Canal, laughing and carousing in bars, hotels and nightclubs, or the Egyptian king, Farouk, driving around Cairo in one of his red cars, seducing young women, he saw the same corruption he had seen in America.

Qutb concluded that offensive jihad against the West and its supporters was the only way for the Muslim world to redeem itself. And even though Qutb was hanged for sedition in 1966, his ideas did not die. Men like Ayman al-Zawahiri, another Egyptian who is the current Al-Qaeda leader, saw potent meaning in Qutb's view that men killed fighting for the return to purity in jihad would be honoured in paradise, to sit 'among the noblest angels'.[20]

Described as 'the philosopher of the Islamic revolution', Qutb's ideas were so influential that the official commission of inquiry into 9/11 concluded: 'Bin Laden shares Qutb's stark view, permitting him and his followers to rationalise even unprovoked mass murder as righteous defence of an embattled faith.'[21]

The notion of purity in Salafi-jihadism is important. It frames the very concept of who is and who is not the enemy with clarity, a dualism that is – in a way – reminiscent of the Zoroastrianism or Manichaeism of Iran. Secular terrorists might see their enemy as the agents of a specific government or rule, but Islamist terrorists have a wider view: they are pitted against a far greater foe. When Qutb re-energised the Quranic term *jahiliyyah*, the pre-Islamic epoch of ignorance in which paganism grew, and used it to portray any society not in his view Islamic, he was effectively to make the whole world the potential enemy.

Jihad, though, was only part of the complex strands that led to 9/11. Al-Qaeda needed, too, to find volunteers for that suicidal attack. We have seen how the culture of self-sacrificial martyrdom that first began in Iran was later to emerge in Lebanon and then to infect the Israel–Palestine conflict. But it was among the Salafi-Wahhabists that the martyr's mantra found its most fecund ground. For them, the suicide bomber became the equivalent of a medieval knight who throws himself valiantly into the enemy's lines, knowing he is very unlikely to survive (known as *al-inghimās fī 'ṣ-ṣaff*, 'plunging into the line'). Gibril Haddad, a hard-line Wahhabi sheikh, wrote that *inghimās* 'must not be viewed as reckless self-destruction, but as the highest valour and courage'.[22] It was not so different from the kamikaze, but for the fact that the Salafi jihadist's god was Allah and their enemy anyone who did not prostrate themselves to him.

Many Al-Qaeda theologians, and other Salafist jihadists, even began to consider martyrdom as an individual's religious duty (*farḍ 'ayn*) – elevating it to the same status as praying or going on pilgrimage. They not only embraced suicide bombing, but made it an integral part of their tactics. They also embraced the idea of *Al-Qadā wa-l-Qadr*, one of the six articles of faith in Islam, that states that God has already written and preordained whatever will happen. Such a theory asserts that nothing can hasten or delay one's death; this meant that anyone who truly believes cannot refuse to participate in fighting. Indeed, Salafist scholars went on to say that whoever fails to believe in *Al-Qadā' wa-l-Qadr* commits apostasy, for they doubt God's almightiness. It is a sort of theological blackmail that causes fighters to embrace death, as it is already fixed.[23]

Such theological approaches worked. Senior Al-Qaeda commanders were later to boast: 'We were never short of potential martyrs. Indeed, we have a department called the department of martyrs.'[24]

One place above all provided fertile soil for these ideas to grow: Afghanistan.[25] For militant jihadism to flourish, it needed a battlefield and a victory. Afghanistan provided both. Following the Soviet invasion of 1979, and the subsequent nine years of conflict, Afghanistan became a magnet for would-be jihadists from all over. Some 35,000 men, eyes bright with the fervour of religious rectitude, travelled to Afghanistan's mountain peaks to wage war against the Soviet menace. They brought with them funding, training camps and support networks, and there, financed by millions of US taxpayer dollars through the CIA Operation Cyclone, they learnt the art of war.

This was not a time of suicide bombing – that was to come later. But it proved the making of men like Bin Laden and Abu Musab al-Zarqawi. They found a type of macho utopia in their camps and mountain hideouts, a sort of 'pure' Islam, forged in violence, that offered a weighty sense of identity. This sense of identity was buttressed by events such as the Israel–Palestine conflict, which was framed as a battle between Jews and Muslims. That conflict, as well as wider dismay at American intervention across the world, helped cultivate international support for and awareness of a new type of martyr across a global Islamic community. In 2002, while about three-quarters of Lebanese and Palestinians saw suicide bombing as justified, so too did about half of Nigerian, Bangladeshi and Jordanian Muslims.[26] In this sense, then, the concept of suicide bombing as an acceptable form of violence seeped from Lebanon and Palestine to dozens of other countries. There it was to be taken up by Al-Qaeda – and not only suicide-terror tactics, but the entire strategy of *istishhad* (the deliberate death in jihad).[27]

So there was a shift. Traditionally, the mujahidin in Afghanistan were careful not to lose men in battle against the Soviets; martyrdom was not part of their culture. In the 1980s, they even asked the Tamil Tigers if they could supply Sri Lankan suicide attackers in exchange for money.[28] And when the CIA-sponsored Pakistan intelligence services tried to find a suicide bomber to detonate a vehicle bomb in the 1.6 mile-long Salang Tunnel, seeking to destroy the crucial north–south Soviet supply route, there were no takers. Suicide, they said, was a sin.[29]

The first recorded suicide terrorist attack by the Taliban may have been in 1992 in Afghanistan's Kunar province, when the Salafi warlord Maulvi Jamil-ur Rehman was killed by an Egyptian fighter, but this seems to have been a one-off as opposed to a change in theology or strategy.[30] It was not until the charismatic leader Ahmad Shah Massoud was killed on 9 September 2001, when Al-Qaeda operatives gained access to him by posing as journalists having disguised a bomb as a camera case, that suicide bombings began to enter the Afghan consciousness.

Still, martyrdom had its limits. For a long time, some fighters – influential Al-Qaeda commanders like Abdullah Yusuf Azzam and the morbidly obese Tameem al Adnani – had expressed concerns about taking armed jihad to nations outside the heart of Islam, and they had grave misgivings about targeting civilians. Death, though, silenced their cautioning words: Azzam was killed in Afghanistan in November 1989, while al Adnani died of a heart attack around the same time when visiting Walt Disney World in Florida.[31] These two deaths liberated their protégé – Bin Laden – and it was he who helped thousands of Muslims flock to Afghanistan, who helped fund their fight, and who would provide inspiration to some 10,000 recruits from across the Arab world, from Saudi Arabia to Algeria to Egypt. An influence that not only formed the base of Al-Qaeda, but of all the following jihadist groups it would help spawn.

What drove this Saudi zealot on? Perhaps, like Ayatollah Khomeini, early tragedy left a deep mark on him. Bin Laden's father died when he was young, in this case in a plane crash when Osama was just ten years old – his fifty-nine-year-old father was on his way to wed his twenty-third wife the night he died.[32] But it was Afghanistan where Osama, the billionaire's son, was to cut his jihadist teeth. High on the words of Qutb and others, he was said to have fought bravely in the mountainous war, leading charges against machine guns, even being wounded in a skirmish at Jalalabad airport – all events that added lustre to his image as the 'Emir of al-Qaeda'. And it was in that furnace of violence that a belief hardened that only through faith and fury could the Great Satan of American be defeated.

The withdrawal of the Soviet Union, in Bin Laden's eyes, was not because the Soviets had been beaten by the notoriously hard terrain of Afghanistan's black mountains; not because the porous border with Pakistan had bolstered the Taliban's forces with a constant flow of arms and fighters; not because the climate and food had led to so many Russians soldiers dying from dysentery and disease; and not because Moscow saw glasnost as being preferable to endless Cold War. To Bin Laden, it was because faith made his mujahidin victorious.[33]

So, when Osama returned to Saudi Arabia, Afghanistan's soil barely off his boots, and he was met with Saddam Hussein's invasion of Kuwait on 2 August 1990, he believed his faith and his fighters could take on Hussein's army. But when the Saudi royal family asked the US government, not him, to stop the Iraqi army from reaching their country, Bin Laden was mortified. He pleaded, but the Saudi government rejected his motley crew of 1,000 fighters, and instead enlisted the help of the American infidel. This confirmed to him that the demonic hordes of America must be stopped at all costs. The removal of the US from the Middle East, he became convinced, would usher in a perfect pan-Islamic state, one governed by sharia law.

It was a conviction whose extremism worried the House of Saud. In 1992, the authorities, sensing Bin Laden's plans to overthrow their government and establish an Islamic regime, forced him into exile, first to Sudan and, from there, back to Afghanistan. Returning to his old war haunts, he aligned himself with the Taliban leader Mullah Muhammad Omar, and finally his anti-American rhetoric found its voice and the support he craved.

In the meantime, many in the Muslim world looked on. They saw the devastation wrought by the US in the 'Highway of Death' in Iraq. They noted that 200,000 Iraqi soldiers had been killed, compared to the American losses of 148 soldiers in battle. They knew over 100,000 civilians were also killed.[34] They also saw the export of McDonald's and Nike, Hollywood films and the influence of the greenback, and steadily and surely, Bin Laden's support grew and grew.

'The Emir' began his wars against America slowly. First it was the bombing of the World Trade Center in 1993; then the 1996 attack on a US military housing complex in Saudi Arabia; the bombings of the American embassies in Kenya and Tanzania in 1998; and then the suicide bombing of the USS *Cole* in 2000. This attack on a US warship, while it was refuelling in Aden, killed seventeen US Navy sailors and injured thirty-nine more. As Bin Laden framed it: 'The destroyer represents the capital of the West, and the small boat represents Mohammed.' Such an analogy found support in the wider Salafist community. The Saudi cleric Hamud al-Shuaybi ruled, for example, that attacking American civilians was justified, based on the Islamic idea of *qisas*, essentially an Islamic version of 'an eye for an eye'. If the West kills innocent Muslims, Muslims can kill innocent Westerners.[35]

Another way these attacks on civilians were justified was through 'vicarious liability'. Bin Laden wrote: 'The American people have the ability and choice to refuse the policies of their government and even to change it if they want.'[36] In other words, civilians were held responsible for their governments' actions, as their governments were freely elected by the public. Democracy made everyone culpable.

The stage had been set. The jihadists' intellectual foundations had been laid in Egypt, the rhetoric of the sacrificial martyr forged in Afghanistan, and the urgency to defeat the satanic America seen in their incursion into Kuwait and their support of the Israelis in Palestine. It was only a matter of time before such strands would come together to shock the world with terror.

What Bin Laden now needed was to recruit those hijackers who would bring death to America's heartlands. There were two types of fighter required for the operation: suicide-martyrs and jihadists. This is because, even though nineteen hijackers were behind 9/11, FBI investigators were later to conclude that eleven of them did not know they were on a suicide mission. Unlike the eight 'lead' attackers, who were all trained pilots, the remaining group did not leave messages for friends or family saying their lives were soon to be over. As one US agent said: 'It looks as if they expected they might be going to prison, not paradise.'[37]

The eight who knew they were on a suicide mission were led by an Egyptian, Mohamed Atta, the pilot who was to crash the first plane into the North Tower. The oldest of the entire team at just thirty-three, he had studied architecture at Cairo University, and continued his studies in Hamburg. There he had written an urban planning thesis on the building of a truly Islamic city; the best way to begin this process was to destroy all the city's high-rise buildings, he said. He saw Islamic civilisation and Western civilisation as distinct and incompatible – only through the devastation of the latter could you build a future for the former. The place he based his thesis on was Aleppo in Syria.[38]

For Atta, the destruction of a symbol of modernity to help create a perfect Islamic world must have been captivating, for he and the lead pilots of the three planes – the Emirati Marwan al-Shehhi, the Lebanese-born Ziad Samir Jarrah and the Saudi Hani Hanjour – all travelled to Afghanistan and, eventually, were to head to the United States for flight training. For them, the theories espoused and developed by Al-Qaeda were crucial. The pilots were fired up by the belief they could kill corrupted civilians and gain access to paradise at the same time. In a way, such logic was itself a consequence of globalisation and capitalism. The idea that the actions of men and women in offices half a world away had a direct impact on the suffering of the Islamic community in Gaza or Kabul was a product of mass media, global trade and an overpowering loss of perspective. Indeed, coming as they did from a wide array of countries, the men behind 9/11 were very much the products of a post-Cold War, global community: youthful Arab males who lived abroad, wowed by but alienated from Western modernity, and who then retreated back into the confines of a male jihadist group – there to cultivate a judgemental and fundamental piety.

Globalisation was both the thing they railed against and their cover: it enabled them to mingle in the US without arousing suspicions, visiting Virginia, California, Arizona and Florida. They even booked into a motel that stood right next to the American spy organisation, the National Security Agency. It enabled them to board planes, too, without much suspicion.

The hijackers' behaviour in the days preceding 9/11 has been analysed in depth, and many have levelled the accusation of hypocrisy at them, just as they were to condemn Bin Laden for having pornography on his computers when he was killed.[39] Two of the attackers met in Las Vegas, famously going to strip clubs for lap dances, perhaps imagining the virgins who might visit them in the next life. They drank alcohol, too; when one was confronted about a bar bill, he was to say: 'There is no money issue. I am an airline pilot.'[40]

The impossible thing to know is how they reconciled such 'Western' habits with their own beliefs. Perhaps they assumed their final act of martyrdom would purge their souls of all previous sin. Indeed, we know that those hijackers who had been tasked with crashing the jets, those who knew they were soon to die, were meticulous in purifying themselves in their final hours. In Islamic custom, the dead body is cleaned, prepared for the grave. As some of the hijackers knew they would have no such burial, they were given a prep sheet that told them to shave off their body hair and to wear cologne – to prove their devotion to personal purity.[41]

In the early morning hours of 11 September, the hijackers donned button-downs and slacks and slipped collapsible knives into their pockets. Surveillance cameras at the airports recorded them proceeding through security, footage now for ever tainted by the heavy comprehension of where they were headed. When Mohamed Atta checked in at Logan airport, in Boston, his name set off an alert on the airport's security system, meaning his bags were never loaded into the plane's hold. But he and the others still walked through, something the family's victims were later to decry.

The jihadists seemed relaxed. Those that knew this was a suicide mission were looking forward to it. 'Be cheerful,' the preparation note had entreated, for once death comes 'a happy and satisfying life begins.' To those that knew the true nature of the attack, paradise had been promised to them, filled with 'the prophets, the righteous, the good and the martyrs'. And, with a final entreaty to lace their shoes tightly, it sent them to their deaths. 'Smile . . .' it said, 'for you are departing to the eternal paradise!'[42]

As you descend the 9/11 memorial you are met by the posters of the missing that covered New York's streets in the weeks after the event, projected onto a grey concrete wall. The words of Virgil, 'No day shall erase you from the memory of time', are written across another, forged from pieces of recovered steel from the wreckage of the building. Two thousand eight hundred and ninety-three blue watercolours, each for a lost life, surround that classical refrain. Watercolour and iron, modern font and ancient script; from the classical to the fleeting, the timelessness of memory to the agony of grief. Then, a small sign: 'Reposed behind this wall are the remains of many who perished at the World Trade Center on September 11, 2011' – and you were reminded that this was a repository, a mass tomb.

Beside it was a room filled with the faces of the dead. Rows upon rows of names and photographs of the victims; those that didn't have a photo were remembered by the leaf of a swamp white oak. There was Tariq Amanulla from Pakistan; Waleed Iskandar from Lebanon; Yin Ping Wong from Hong Kong; there was Ignatius, Milagors, Jorge, Mychal, Ching, Igor, Shuyin . . .

Before visiting I had researched the numerology of 9/11's grief. I knew the attacks had killed 2,606 in the World Trade Center, 246 in the aeroplanes, 125 in the Pentagon. But here, unlike any other mass memorial I had ever visited, every one of these numbers was named. You scanned the room for connections. There were three men called Michael Lynch, just three of 146 Michaels killed on that day. There were 68 Williams, 55 Richards, and 52 Patricks, too. The number of photographs of men on the walls was notable: three times as many men died as women on that day, most of them in their late thirties. These were photos that testified to the sadness that 3,051 children lost a parent that day. There were brief obituaries that showed 658 people all worked for the same company, Cantor Fitzgerald, just one of 128 companies to lose a worker. The number of men in uniform told how 343 firefighters and paramedics died – running to the scene, not away from it. And, unphotographed, how there were eleven unborn babies that also died.

Such a room had an unfathomable resonance. It was said that 20 per cent of Americans knew someone hurt or killed in the attacks, and the weight of America's grief felt heaviest right here.[43]

Beyond the memorial lay an exhibit, telling how the day unfolded, in the order that it did. It began with innocence. Framed newspapers bore news of little weight. Elizabeth Jagger on the front-page of the *New York Post*. The *New York Times* reporting on the primary elections that were gripping the city, and beside it a portentous coincidence: the story of a teacher, tracked on the Internet, being charged with hijacking a jet plane in 1971. Beside these newspapers was a little receipt – a stamp on it marked the time: 8.47. It was the last transaction that day recorded in the North Tower – a minute after the plane had struck.

'It went from that bright crisp morning to just total blackness, and then it felt like an earthquake,' an exhibit read.

Next were the first television images broadcast of the smoking building. At first it felt almost benign: glittering around the Towers were clouds of paper – reams and reams of documents and minutes and legal briefs – like a ticker tape parade. But then, to the screams from the people holding the cameras, the impact of the second plane. Only four people managed to escape from the floors above that strike.

Further along, the exhibition had a screened-off section. Behind it were photographs of some of the most memorable horrors of the day: the jumpers. Those who, unable to withstand the ferocious smoke and heat, were forced to leap to their deaths – about 200 of them. Their fall lasted as long as ten seconds, an 'end-over-end tumbling to the ground'. They were to strike the earth at just under 150mph. Some jumped alone, some in pairs and groups. The first firefighter to die that day was hit by a jumper.[44]

A note read: 'She had a business suit on, her hair was all askew. This woman stood there for what seemed like minutes, then she held down her skirt and then stepped off the ledge. I thought, how human, how modest, to hold down her skirt before she jumped.' Another: 'You felt compelled to watch, out of respect to them. They were ending their lives without a choice. And to turn away from them would have been wrong.' Five images were shown of these headlong flights. Ten deaths displayed – suicide attackers forcing people to choose how to die.

The drama continued: terror in instalments. There came the concertina collapse, killing thousands. Over 100,000 pounds of burning fuel had superheated the upper steel columns to temperatures of over 1,500 degrees Fahrenheit. When they buckled and fell, the weight of the upper floors took the rest with them. Few escaped the crush as millions of tonnes of steel and cement went straight down, filling up the New York air with pulverised particles – a lethal combination of asbestos, lead, silicon and worse. One man 'rode' the collapse down from the twenty-third floor, awakening three hours later atop a slab of concrete fifteen feet in the air, with just a broken foot.[45] But he was the exception: only twenty people made it out alive.[46] The last survivor, Genelle Guzman, was found in the ruins of the North Tower twenty-seven hours after its collapse.[47]

When the second tower collapsed, as Ian McEwan described, with 'malign majesty',[48] it was so impactful it was recorded by the only American not on Earth during 9/11, astronaut Frank L. Culberston. 'And tears don't flow the same in space', a label read beside a photograph of the devastation that he took. He later learnt that a murdered pilot in one of the planes that day was a classmate from the US Naval Academy.[49]

In Washington, the Pentagon was hit by Flight 77, slicing into a section of the building that had just undergone a $258 million re-armament, with strengthened walls and reinforced windows. Many of those walls right next to the plane's point of impact remained intact, but still 125 workers there died, along with 59 passengers and crew. Then Flight 93 crashed into an empty field. There were just four hijackers in this one, leading to a fightback that stopped even more devastation, as the hijackers crashed the plane before reaching their target. Forty passengers and crew died in that instant. 'Allah is the Greatest' was screamed nine times by that plane's pilot before the transmission ended at 10.03 a.m., a transcript read.

In all, it was the largest loss of life by a foreign attack on American soil. In many cases, the victims vanished. Only 60 per cent of bodies were identified when the Twin Towers collapsed.[50] Two hundred and ninety-one were recovered 'intact', the others made up of almost 20,000 body parts. Among the wreckage, making the task all the harder, were the remains of rats, pigeons and even T-bone steaks from the Windows on the World restaurant that had been on the top floor. During the search, rescue dogs found so few living people that it caused them to stress out because they believed they had failed. Their handlers had to regularly hide in the rubble so as to give the rescue dogs a successful find, keeping their spirits up.[51]

The rest of the unfound dead were issued death certificates by judicial decree, the only real evidence being their absence. And there are still question marks. 'We have DNA profiles from remains that don't match anything on the reference side,' the assistant director of the Office of the Chief Medical Examiner has said.[52]

Such absence pervades the entire tragedy. The memorial is a void, a cascade into the dark. The perpetrators are elusive shadows. Even one of the World Trade Center's most vocal survivors, and president of its support group, Tania Head, was later found out to have lied – she was not even in the city on 9/11.

The dying did not end on that day, either. At least three people were later to succumb from smoke inhalation, and over 1,100 were diagnosed with cancer as a result of 'exposure to toxins at Ground Zero',[53] with nearly 70 per cent of rescuers later to develop lung problems.[54] An estimated 410,000 people were exposed to the dangerous toxin asbestos in the dust-filled air that clouded New York's streets. Other tragedies followed. Ninety-one days after the attack, Pat Flounders, a widow from that terrible day, shot herself in grief – 9/11's first direct suicide victim.[55]

The displays tried to infuse the mountain of loss with a sense of humanity. Here were small items, intimate belongings: a mariner's cross; hotel room keys; a Blackberry phone; slippers. But it proved hard for me to find meaning in such everyday objects. Then again, people seek meaning in something – anything – following such surreal trauma. The top search on Google the week following 9/11 was for the babbling prophecies of Nostradamus. In that end-of-days catastrophe, others saw, in the billowing smoke of the burning towers, the Devil's face appear.[56] Church and synagogue attendance in Manhattan rose by 20 per cent. And, soon enough, conspiracy theories emerged: it was the Jews, the US government, the buildings were rigged with explosives.

Such a search for hidden meaning was understandable. The enemy was, at first, elusive. There were no strident political demands, no statements issued. At first Bin Laden even denied involvement. Perhaps he wanted to make it seem as if the planes were an act of God

– a terrible visitation as a direct consequence of American foreign policy.

If it was not only meaning that people sought, it was life. Nine months after 9/11, there were 20 per cent more births in New York City compared to the same month in the years before. Within ten days of the attack the US magazine website *Salon* was to refer to 'terror sex' – the urgent need to engage, to feel. As *Shortbus*, a film about the search for sexual liberation in New York after 9/11, framed it: 'It's just like the sixties, only with less hope.'[57] Alcohol intake in Manhattan in the week after 9/11 spiked by 25 per cent compared to the year before; tobacco and dope consumption also rose. Many Americans say that something was lost on that day – a sense of self-confidence, perhaps. A turn away from America, as Nabokov would have it, as a 'lovely, trustful, dreamy, enormous country', to something else – one where a country emptied of good becomes a potential habitat for evil.[58]

The broader reverberations were immediate. That day, all planes in the air – some 4,000 – were immediately ordered to land, the man doing the ordering on his first day on the job.[59] The only private plane allowed to fly after the attacks was one from San Diego to Miami transporting anti-venom to a man bitten by a deadly snake. It was accompanied by two jet fighters.[60] Many planes were diverted northwards; Canada found itself housing and feeding over 33,000 waylaid passengers.[61] Millions took to the roads instead; it has been estimated that 9/11 caused an extra 1,600 people to die in automobile accidents because they switched their travel plans from flying to driving.[62]

So great was the change that scientists later analysed the weather following the three-day flight ban over the US; they found the days were a little warmer and the nights cooler, suggesting that the exhaust trails that planes leave in the sky shield the earth from the sun during the day and trap heat at night. Scientists also found that whales' stress levels plummeted immediately following 9/11: all the halted ship traffic reduced the levels of low-frequency noise in the oceans, the tone that whales use to communicate with.[63]

There were other reverberations over the long term. With respect to financial cost, the United States' wars in Iraq, Afghanistan, Pakistan and Syria and the additional expenditure on Homeland Security and the Departments of Defense and Veterans Affairs, have been estimated to be more than $5.6 trillion since 9/11. The direct losses associated with 9/11 were to top $80 billion – so great that they caused insurance companies to end automatic coverage of terrorist-induced damages.[64] A total of $4.2 billion was spent on compensation to cover the health of those who worked at Ground Zero after the attacks. The US government also paid an average of $1.8 million to the families of the victims.[65] Wall Street's big institutions, though, were too big for the terrorists. According to the City of New York's Comptroller's office, in the first quarter of 2002, the city's economy contracted by 4 per cent. It went on to shrink for another two years. But New York's famed resilience came to the fore and, by 2004, its economy was growing again by nearly 5 per cent every three months.[66]

The media's response was predictable and engulfing. Almost 28,000 9/11-based articles were published by the British press alone in the year following the attacks. In the decade following the strikes, 1,742 books were written about the day.[67] The CBS 9/11 programme, broadcast in March 2002, holds the record for the world's highest audience for a TV documentary. And into the coverage seeped assumptions and stereotypes, nationalism and bellicosity. Over 150 songs were banned from the airwaves by one radio network in the months afterwards, including 'Bridge over Troubled Water' and 'Imagine', for being too downbeat or pacifist.[68] Anger was the order of the day – 338,000 copies of Toby Keith's album Unleashed flew off the shelves in the first week of its release in early 2002; one song – 'Courtesy of the Red, White and Blue (The Angry American)' – contained the

line 'We'll put a boot in your ass / It's the American Way'.[69] Another
song spoke of raising 'our glasses against evil forces'.

The following morning, the New York Times ran a headline:
'America's Emergency Line: 9/11'. It was the first use in print of the
nine-eleven name by which the attacks became known. Other words
– the Taliban, Al-Qaeda, radicalism, Islamism, extremism, the Axis
of Evil – also seeped into the lexicon of the everyday, but the word
that stuck was 'freedom'. It was used not just as rhetoric but as analysis. America's liberties were seen to be part of the reason why the
US East Coast had been attacked, and the notion of freedom became
quickly intertwined with the language of vengeful violence – the
Statue of Liberty was soon depicted hoisting an assault weapon in her
copper fist. From French fries becoming 'freedom fries' to Operation
Enduring Freedom, for President Bush, freedom was part of that
divine battle he was waging: 'the Almighty's gift'.[70]

There was a surge of patriotism and memorial. Flagpoles, dedica-
tions and crosses were made, many using steel from Ground Zero,
and even more American flags appeared in front of millions of homes
across the States than usual. The National Aeronautics and Space
Administration (NASA) even took metal from the rubble and used
it on Martian rovers as a tribute to those who had died.

Such patriotism reflected a wider split that occurred. On the one
side was the Salafi-jihadist movement: men who had prostrated
themselves to the idea there was no free will, that Allah would dictate their future, one where violence would bring about a return to
a premodern world. A side where the suicide bomb could usher in
an Islamic utopia bolstered by draconian laws and purified by its
rejection of capitalism.

On the other side was a world framed by 'freedoms'. The free
market, freedom of speech, the freedom of capitalism and democracy.
'Al-Qaeda is to terror what the mafia is to crime,' Bush was to opine.
'But its goal is not making money; its goal is remaking the world –

and imposing its radical beliefs on people everywhere.' This was, as we shall see, a rhetoric that was to mutate over time, to include the freedom to torture, to rip up human rights, to make money out of war and, even, to bomb cities far away under the banner of liberty.

These two visions underpinned the competing ideologies of violence from the very beginning, and came to define much of what was to flow afterwards – what was, to some, a cosmic clash of civilisations. As Israeli Prime Minister Ariel Sharon said after the attack: 'The fight against terrorism is an international struggle of the free world against the forces of darkness.' An 'Infinity War', even; as President Bush was to say, portentously: the 'war on terror begins with al Qaeda, but it does not end there'.[71]

When Bin Laden was eventually to speak to the world in the weeks following the attacks, he was to echo this shift. To him the world had entered a new era, where 'life or death does not matter'. As he told an interviewer: 'The awakening has started'.[72]

Chapter 8

Global Jihad

Nine-eleven was to mark the turning point of suicide bombing, transforming it into a global phenomenon. Since that September day, at least 115 militant groups[1] have conducted suicide attacks in 51 countries.[2] The overwhelming majority of these have been Salafi-jihadist groups. The leading six perpetrators of those attacks – ISIS, the Taliban, Al-Qaeda, Boko Haram, Al-Shabaab and Jabhat al-Nusra – are, today, common names on front pages the world over.

That day was also to cause a fundamental change in the users and tactics of suicide attacks. Between 1991 and 2001, just a quarter of all global suicide bombings were by Sunni militants – most of these in Palestine and Israel. In the decade after 9/11, 98 per cent of attacks were by Sunni Salafists; no new nationalist or secular group has adopted suicide bombings in over a decade.

The number and frequency of suicide bombings also increased massively. In the decade before 9/11, there were 151 suicide attacks worldwide. In the decade that followed, there were 3,155 suicide attacks. A rise so extreme that, today, the suicide bomb is a metonym for Sunni Islamist terror, a dark icon for the twenty-first century. In the minds of many, an entire religion has been tainted by a small sector of a small group of one strand of Islam.

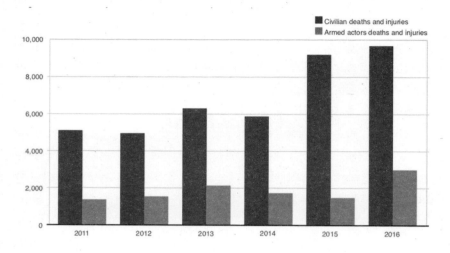

Global deaths and injuries from suicide attacks
(2011–2016) from AOAV's dataset

What was behind this marked rise in Salafi-jihadist suicide bomb-ings? In large part it is because there has been, in the last two decades, a significant proliferation of ultraconservative religious ideas among Sunnis around the world, ideas that have been framed much through the prism of jihad. In addition, there has also been a sense of a global persecution among many Muslims, especially with the United States-led military intervention in Iraq, Afghanistan and beyond, a belief that has led a vocal and deadly minority of Muslims to want to defeat 'crusaders' in the Prophet's lands.

Other factors have also played a role. A rise in social media and Internet access has meant new networks have been created and exploited by militant recruiters. On top of this there have been power grabs for political supremacy by numerous religious jihadists, with suicide attacks used as a strategic weapon. And there has been an increasing 'normalisation' of violence throughout the Islamic world, spurred on by the swelling of unemployed and young Muslim men in ever-growing cities – men ripe for radicalisation.³ Into the mix throw poverty, discontentment with globalisation, despair at political corruption, depression, sectarianism and coercion and you can see that the driving forces of this surge of suicide attacks find their roots deep in the chaotic social fabric of modernity.

Even experts in terrorism struggle to keep track of this evolution of terror. Over time the number of militant groups has, like mushrooms in a forest, multiplied. One estimate says there are thirty-six active terror groups in Pakistan alone.⁴ On the eve of 9/11 there were about 400 men who pledged allegiance to Al-Qaeda. Today, despite a claimed dip in support when ISIS was gaining ascendancy, the group has a hundred times that number, with as many as 20,000 followers in Syria, close to 10,000 in Somalia, up to 5,000 in Libya and Yemen and yet more spread across the Sahel, Maghreb, Indonesia and South Asia.⁵

Within a few minutes of joining the messaging chat service Telegram, I find a group that praises such a global vision of Islamist struggle. 'We are fighting,' one post reads, 'the national jihad from Kashgar to the shores of the Atlantic, from the peaks of the Caucuses to Somalia and Central Africa. We gather together as one nation, fighting one battle on multiple fronts, not as narrow national organisations afraid of being called terrorists.'

I scroll down and there are links to videos. A few, I am sure, might be illegal to share in the UK. I scroll down some more. It was on this platform, using the private chat service, that ISIS plotted their strikes on Paris. One channel has an advert asking for funds to sponsor the family of a mujahid; I have no way of knowing who posted it or where.

Whereas before I could travel to distinct places to trace the development and impact of the suicide bomber – Russia, Japan, Lebanon, Sri Lanka, Israel, the US – now the whole world seems a possible destination, a dilution that frustrates a plan to go to this particular city or that bomb site to comprehend its driving forces. I am further hindered by the fact that, for many would-be and current suicide bombers, the journalist has become a legitimate target. In 2016, about three-quarters of the seventy-four journalists who were killed were targeted by Islamist groups.[6] I have personally known journalists murdered by jihadists; when I travelled to report for the BBC from Mogadishu in late 2004, the tension was so ramped up that it was no surprise to me when, within eighteen months, the British journalist Kate Peyton and the Swedish reporter Martin Adler were killed there. In terms of the terrorists' propaganda of the deed, the murder of a journalist is logical and desirable.

These realities, along with the obvious fact that successful suicide bombers are no longer around to interview, cannot be ignored. In Palestine, I could sit with a failed suicide bomber, outside a prison cell wall, and not be terrified. In Lebanon, I could be held and interrogated by Hezbollah and not feel, as the captive Brian Keenan did, that it was the beginning of an evil cradling. But with the global jihad things changed – journalists have been paraded in jumpsuits and had their throats cut. While I was writing this book, a secondary suicide bomb was deliberately set off in Kabul, killing nine journalists; the bomber knew that the press pack would gather twenty minutes after a previous suicide bombing. He mingled with those reporters before he detonated his belt, carrying a camera as if one of them.[7]

I have interviewed present-day jihadists; from meeting Al-Qaeda murderers shackled in prison in Hargeisa in Somaliland, to being blindfolded and led to meet members of the Moro Islamic Liberation Front in the Philippines, since 9/11 a large part of my reporting on violence has been focused on analysing and cataloguing the rising Salafi-jihadist threat. But the hallmark of that threat is its very secretiveness – few reporters have ever managed to interview a modern-day jihadist preparing for a suicide mission.

Even the most compelling film made in the last few decades about such fighters – called *Dugma: The Button* – by the Norwegian Pål Refsdal, which followed a group of would-be suicide bombers fighting for Jabhat al-Nusra in Syria – was notable for the fact that none of the people filmed carried out an attack. As Pål said to me, 'Two of them are dead, but they were killed in combat, not suicide bombings.'

When I called him in Norway to ask whether he had feared for his life in making that film, he said that al-Nusra was far less worrying in that regard than, for instance, ISIS. Al-Nusra, he said, were more concerned with targeting military groups than killing civilians. But, then again, he had already experienced the dark side of trying to record the violence of militants. The Taliban had kidnapped him in 2009, during which time he converted to Islam.

I asked Pål what drove the men he filmed to volunteer for suicide bomb missions. 'The foreigners' motives were purely religious,' he said, 'but with the Syrians there was a lot of personal history involved. Suicide bombing would be less attractive without religion – but people always try to find a higher purpose with their fight, a reason why they were willing to sacrifice their life. But one Saudi that I filmed seemed to be doing it to secure a place for his parents in paradise; the impression that I got was that he was being pressured by his father to do it, and that he didn't really want to do the operation.'

Complex group drivers and hard-to-fathom personal impulses add to the already difficult task of speaking to the would-be suicide bombers in the first place. So, when trying to unravel this amorphous and elusive global threat, I decided to start by creating a list of the countries where Salafist jihad has spread, and, like an oncologist faced with the historic scans of an ailing body, traced the spreading cancer of suicide bombings around the world.

Within twelve months of September 2001, five countries were to see Salafist suicide attacks in lands where they had never been seen before. It first began in Bin Laden's hideout, Afghanistan, with the murder of a leading political player just days before 9/11. Then, after the Twin Tower attacks in the US, the allure of that weapon seeped from the rugged mountains of the Tora Bora, down to neighbouring Pakistan and China, before emerging in Bangladesh. It appeared, too, in Uzbekistan and then, a few years later, attacks were seen in Tajikistan and Kazakhstan.

When the US responded to 9/11 by invading Iraq in 2003, looking for weapons of mass destruction that never existed, the suicide bomber appeared there, too, this time with a vengeance. Iraq, along with the Palestinian upsurge in bombings during the second intifada, thrust the suicide bomber into almost everyday news, and the bombers' violent allure soon spread east and west, north and south. Within two years, Saudi Arabia, Egypt, Jordan and Qatar were all hit by suicide strikes. By 2006, Syria had witnessed this spreading form of violence in a terrible foreshadowing of what was later to unfurl there.

The entry of suicide bombers into Africa, starting with Tunisia in 2002 and then Somalia in 2006, also saw its spread through that continent. Algeria, Mauritania, Uganda, Nigeria, Libya, Mali, Niger, Djibouti and Cameroon all succumbed to its deadly logic in quick succession. And once embedded in these countries, it gained a devastating momentum. Despite 2015 being the first time suicide bombers were used in Cameroon and Chad, that year alone saw thirty-four separate suicide attacks in those two countries, fuelled by the glut of cheap explosives that followed the overthrow of Gaddafi in Libya.

Europe, too, began to feel the suicide bomber's threat. Starting with the 7/7 Tube attacks in 2005 in the UK, bombers were to appear in Sweden in 2010, Bulgaria in 2012, and then in Ukraine, France, Belgium and Germany.

And so it spread. By 2015, twenty-one states globally were witness to suicide bomb attacks – the most countries ever impacted in one year.[8] Compare that to 1992, when just one country – Sri Lanka – was hit.

It was almost as if the suicide bomb had become a sort of franchise operation. Just as Misha Glenny focused on 'McMafia' with modern crime gangs, this was a form of 'McJihad', with suicide bombers as a signature 'dish'.[9] ISIS, for instance, established relationships with a wide range of partners. These included Boko Haram in West Africa and other affiliated groups in Sinai, Libya, Yemen and Afghanistan. Besides carrying out suicide attacks in most of these countries, ISIS also claimed responsibility for, or inspired, other attacks in Germany, Sweden, France, Belgium, the UK, the US and Turkey.

To name-check the proliferation of suicide attacks in so many countries, by so many militants, would swiftly become an exercise in bookkeeping. Groups merge and split, leaders are killed and new leaders rise to power. Each group is the product, to some degree, of powerful local forces and regional political realities, responsive to such things as levels of employment, poverty, corruption and disaffection. But irrespective of local dynamics at work, the attraction of the suicide bomb remains a constant theme.

In May 2014, President Barack Obama said that Al-Qaeda central was no longer the major threat, but rather 'decentralized affiliates' were the real enemy. 'Technology and globalization', he said 'has put power once reserved for states in the hands of the individual, raising the capacity of terrorists to do harm.'[10] The suicide bomb – one that caused a superpower to withdraw from a conflict and injected extreme religious ideas into the conduct of war – was at the centre of that power struggle, embraced by Sunni militants like no other.

This wholesale adoption of the suicide bomb has led to incredible levels of violence. Over the decades, secular suicide bombers have killed, up to the end of 2017, about 2,300 people. Shia bombers have killed over 1,300. Sunni militant bombers, though, have been responsible for almost 33,000 deaths.

The main reason for this is that there have been so many Sunni groups adopting this terror tactic. International Salafi-jihadism has radically altered the relationship between some Muslims and their traditional spiritual and political leaders – offering instead an alter- native, bottom-up political movement in which any 'devout' Muslim can participate. And for some devotees, the martyrdom operation stands at the pinnacle of that call to arms.

This partly explains why, in countries where there has been a breakdown of power, suicide bombs have been so quick to appear. The one thing that links the main centres of suicide bombings since 9/11 – Iraq, Afghanistan, Pakistan, Syria, Nigeria, Yemen and Somalia – has been their political instability, pervasive poverty, and the fact they have all seen actual or attempted regime change. Perhaps in the maul of anarchy and scarcity, death seems less terrifying, and paradise more alluring.

Since 9/11 there has also been a significant change in targeting tactics. In the ten years before 9/11, about 75 per cent of all targets of suicide bombs were security forces or political parties. In the decade that followed, 65 per cent of targets were civilians.

Why did this happen? Partly it was because 9/11 pushed suicide bombings into a 'no-go' zone for many non-Salafist liberation move- ments or militant groups. So synonymous did suicide attacks become with a certain form of terror, that some groups realised they would never be seen as 'freedom fighters' if they attacked with a suicide vest – they'd just be labelled as fanatics. As the world cried out at the devastation in Manhattan, many instinctively knew a sea change had occurred.

Mohammad Hussein Fadlallah, *spiritus rector* of the most radical of the Lebanese Shiites, identified the new mood: 'Nothing can justify the murder of thousands of innocent civilians,' he said. 'No religion justifies such a thing.'[11]

But to many Salafi-jihadists, it was just the beginning. Their field of battle had transformed into one of total, global war, where civilians were intrinsically seen as the enemy – part of a worldwide, 'military-industrial' complex. As one of the foiled 2008 transatlantic suicide bombers was to say: 'We're not targeting innocent civilians. We're targeting economic and military targets.'[12] In truth, he was targeting tourists and business people, but he was too drunk on self-righteousness to see that.

So while the suicide attack of 9/11 was, in part, the consequence of a martyrdom cult that Shia clerics like Fadlallah helped to create, that view of martyrdom mutated. And the place where that mutation was most painfully felt was in the tempestuous crucible of Iraq.

'It's getting worse, I'm telling you, it's getting worse every day.' And you could see from the eighteen-year-old's eyes that he meant it. We had just missed, by about two minutes, a 'contact' – the military term for a firefight. Then a message over the radio relayed that the commanding officer's vehicle had been targeted by a rocket attack, crippling the front of his jeep.

It certainly felt like it was getting worse. The night before, over the space of one hour the regiment's soldiers had been fired upon with four rocket-propelled grenades (RPGs), along with two other improvised explosive devices (IEDs). The base had gone into lockdown and the soft-top vehicles we had been driving around the streets of Basra were no longer deemed safe. The troops were put on the highest alert possible – a Scottish soldier had already lost an eye in the previous night's violence.

It was 4 April 2004, and I was in Iraq reporting on the role of the now disbanded Argyll and Sutherland Highlanders, following a small platoon of sixteen men as they went about their duties. These Scots were there to train up the Iraqi Civil Defence Corps and patrol the dry lands that stretched around the southern Iraqi city of Basra. This was not meant to be a 'hot' war zone, but within days of arriving, we had been shot at, had bricks thrown at us, and now this.

That dawn, dozens of militants belonging to Moqtada Sadr's Mehdi Army had stormed the Basra governor's office. These Shia forces had come chanting: 'No to America, we'll sacrifice ourselves to Sadr', and fired their AK-47s into the air, waving pictures of their leader as they did so. A few days before, on 31 March, four armed contractors from the American security company Blackwater had been killed in Fallujah, 600 kilometres to the north-west. Their bodies had been beaten and burned, and the world watched on as footage showed their charred corpses being dragged through the city streets, then hung over a bridge crossing the Euphrates River.

It was a year into the coalition invasion of Iraq and things were not going to plan. That 2003 invasion, beginning on 20 March, was the start of what the US dubbed Operation Iraqi Freedom, and in the maelstrom of violence that was beginning to engulf Iraq, the soldiers and I witnessed a transformation from freedom to quagmire.

'I thought I was dead, everybody did,' one soldier told me as he washed blood from his arm, pierced by shrapnel wounds. A crowd of two hundred had turned on his platoon and he and his comrades had only just escaped, their armoured cars left as blackened pieces of metal scrap. They had been hit by ten RPGs, their faces streaked with black carbon and their hands shaking as they slipped the rounds from their magazines. In all there were twenty-four separate attacks on the British troops in less than a day. But what they were going through here was just one part of what was unfurling, like a spreading fire, right across the country.

In 2002, there were 54 suicide bombings around the world, 39 in Israel or Palestine. In 2004, there were 116 bombings, 51 of them here in Iraq. During the two weeks I spent with the British military, a suicide bomber injured six people in Baqouba, 30 miles north-east of Baghdad. Another drove his car bomb into the house of a

US-appointed local Iraqi police chief south of Baghdad, wounding seven. Two more were killed when a Sunni militant self-detonated in the municipal council building in the northern Iraqi city of Kirkuk, while two US soldiers and five Iraqi civilians were injured when a suicide bomber blew up his car close to US army vehicles in northern Iraq. It was the start of years of trauma. Over the next decade, Iraq was to see over 1,400 attacks that killed and injured almost 56,000 people.

Such strikes were in large part retaliation for the coalition occupation, and trying to unpick why British and US troops were here was part of the reason I had sought a military-embed as a BBC journalist. It was an invasion that many say was never justified, but the shadow of 9/11 was so great it blinded reason – a common feature of the suicide attacker's impact. And in seeking justice for 9/11, Iraq's name had been there from the beginning. Sitting in a secure bunker in those September days, the American Defense Secretary, Donald Rumsfeld, said out loud: 'You know, we've got to do Iraq.' When the others with him – including Dick Cheney and Colin Powell – expressed their astonishment, saying Iraq had nothing to do with the attacks, Rumsfeld rebuffed them, saying: 'There just aren't enough targets in Afghanistan. We need to bomb something else to prove that we're, you know, big and strong and not going to be pushed around.'[13]

Shortly afterwards, at President Bush's behest, Condoleezza Rice was to get a request for a 'Survey of Intelligence Information on Any Iraq Involvement in the September 11 Attacks'. The responding memo found no 'compelling case' that Iraq had either planned or carried out the strikes, nor any evidence that Saddam Hussein had cooperated with Bin Laden on unconventional weapons.[14]

But the Bush administration was hell-bent on proving Iraq had a connection, even if falsehoods had to be sown. So there was the false claim that Mohammed Atta had met an Iraqi intelligence agent in Prague; that Iraqi intelligence was behind the 1993 World Trade Center bombing; and that Saddam was running a terrorist training camp near Baghdad. The biggest lie of all came from the Libyan Al-Qaeda operative Ibn al-Shaykh al-Lib. Under torture in Egypt, he claimed his fellow militants had received biological and chemical weapons training from the Iraqi government. By February 2004, al-Lib was to recant his confession, but it was too late. Truth in the face of terror had been cast aside – American troops were already on the ground.

Nothing good grew from the lie. Within days of the invasion, a suicide attack was used against the coalition troops. On 25 March 2003, an unnamed insurgent destroyed a tank with his bomb – the news item not revealing more – but the day before the coalition had condemned the Iraqi troops for their 'perfidy' on the battlefield.[15] It was the first of at least 867 suicide attacks against coalition forces in Iraq over the years.

At first, groups such as Jama'at Al-Tawhid Wa'al-Jihad or Al-Qaeda in Iraq were behind the attacks.[16] These were men seeking to rid Iraq of the foreigners' presence – their ranks almost entirely from Iraqi Sunnis.[17] Disenfranchised following the overthrow of their patron, Saddam Hussein, they took their fight to US forces; it was, in a sense, a long time coming.

Like Bin Laden, the first Gulf War in 1990 had outraged many of these fighters – they despaired at seeing US boots on the ground and believed such presence was part of a wilful attempt to weaken the Islamic world. In that despair, they were to find solace in the messages of political Islam, something that Saddam himself actively nurtured. When he launched his 'Enhancement of Islamic Belief' campaign in the early 1990s, restricting drinking and gambling, imposing the strict sharia punishment of amputation for theft, and building one of the world's largest mosques – the Saddam Hussein Mosque – in Baghdad, he helped reinforce that Islamist message: the West was corrupt, the Jews were pulling the strings, and Israel should be stopped.[18]

Saddam was also actively to attract jihadists to his fold. As early as 1982, he had made alliances with a variety of Islamist groups, and thousands travelled to Iraq for training in the 1990s. He actively supported Palestinian suicide bombers with funds.[19] Saddam permitted, too, the opening of ultra-conservative mosques and Islamic universities; Abu Bakr al-Baghdadi, for instance, the leader of ISIS, graduated from Saddam University for Islamic Studies with a PhD in 2007;[20] while Saddam's religious police – in a dark foreshadowing of ISIS – were reportedly using swords to behead alleged prostitutes, leaving their heads 'on the doorsteps of their homes'.

It was not just what Saddam had laid down, though; external voices also fuelled the call for suicidal terror. On 11 February 2003, Bin Laden released an audiotape, aired on Al Jazeera, calling on Iraqis to carry out such attacks. On 21 March, Hamas and Palestinian Islamic Jihad also joined that call. Just over a week later, on 29 March, four US soldiers were killed by a suicide car bomb in Najaf.[21] The attacker, a junior Iraqi army non-commissioned officer, was posthumously awarded two medals by Saddam Hussein. 'This is the blessed beginning on the road of sacrifice and martyrdom,' a pro-Saddam news broadcast said.[22] Within a year of the invasion, one military review concluded: 'Suicide bombings had become firmly embedded in the Iraqi insurgent armamentarium.'[23]

By 2007, there was a suicide attack almost every day in Iraq – 291 attacks during a year that was to be dubbed the Bloody Circus.[24] And while the main perpetrator might have been Al-Qaeda in Iraq, responsible for 45 per cent of Iraq's attacks over the years, the group was not alone: at least eleven other groups sent so-called martyrs to their deaths.[25]

One reason why Iraq had become so violent was that there was a fundamental alteration in how suicide bombs were deployed there. In 2003, around 95 per cent of suicide attack targets in Iraq were military or political. In 2007, 60 per cent of victims were civilians.

As in Israel, the suicide bomber's focus had shifted from men in uniform to seemingly anyone and everyone. This was partly because the militaries and police had learnt from the sort of violence that I had witnessed in Basra. They excelled at bunkering down, reducing the threat to themselves; but it was also because the targeting had changed. Sunni-jihadists sought to kill not just coalition forces but Shias too, and this new sectarianism was to lead to a bloodletting that Iraq had never before seen.

On 31 August 2005, about a million Shia pilgrims gathered at the shrine of Al-Kāẓimīya in Baghdad. They were there to mark the anniversary of the death of their seventh imam, praying at the grave of that spiritual leader. The mass of people stretched from the mosque, right across the River Tigris, down to Sadr City, clogging the bridge that spans the smooth waters below. A mortar attack on the crowd early in the day had killed sixteen and injured many more, and the gathering was on edge. So, when word began to spread that there was a suicide bomber in their midst, the mass of people panicked. In the ensuing stampede, over a thousand died – some were trampled to death, others drowned after jumping in the river. Most of the victims were women and children. Their fear was, by then, hard-wired. Before that crush of bodies, since the start of the war, fifty-two suicide attacks had been carried out specifically targeting civilians, killing almost a thousand more.

Why did such a targeting occur? Simply put, some radical Salafi-jihadists just expanded the target of martyrdom operations to include not only the 'crusader infidel', but other Muslims as well. What started as attacks on Western civilians – murdered journalists at Kurdish checkpoints or foreign workers blown up at New Year's Eve parties in Baghdad – was to switch to the targeting of Iraqi Shiites – in a land where they make up about 60 per cent of the population.

In March 2004, this new ferocity struck home. In a series of attacks on the holiest day of the Shiite Islam calendar – the festival of Ashura – up to a dozen suicide bombers targeted crowds of worshippers in Baghdad and Karbala, killing at least 178 people. It was Iraq's worst day of violence since the fall of Saddam Hussein. In Karbala, the bombers chose the most crowded places, where thousands had gathered after a morning ceremony of ritually beating themselves. They were easy targets.[26]

Initially, blame was directed at the Americans and Israelis, but the atrocity fitted precisely with the aims spelt out by Abu Musab al-Zarqawi, the militant deemed most responsible for turning an insurgency against US troops into 'a Shia–Sunni civil war'.[27] Sometimes known as 'Sheikh of the slaughterers', it was he who had called for a campaign of 'martyrdom operations and car bombs' aimed at Shiites, and who had dismissed them as 'the lurking snake, the crafty and malicious scorpion, the spying enemy, and the penetrating venom'. To him, the Shia worshipped the grave, venerated idols and violated the name of Islam. In Iraq, he claimed, they were cutting a deal to give them 'two-thirds of the booty for having stood in the ranks of the Crusaders against the mujahedeen.' As one analysis has it, to al-Zarqawi, 'the only solution for the Shia was . . . a final one.'[28]

Al-Zarqawi was the sort of thug who would call for such genocide. A Jordanian high school dropout who had spent time in prison for drug and sex offences, he had embraced a violent form of Islam before heading to Afghanistan to cut his jihadist teeth, meeting Bin Laden and Ayman al-Zawahiri there in 1999. By all accounts the two Al-Qaeda leaders did not take to him, finding him brash and headstrong. But he was charismatic and dynamic, and eventually they put him in charge of a training camp in Herat, western Afghanistan. It was here that he met an ideologue whose radical writings were to prove crucial in his subsequent calls for blood-letting. Abu Abdullah al-Muhajir's writings – contemplating the merits of torture, assassinations, beheading, biological weaponry – provided religious cover for the most brutal of excesses, including the murder of Shia as infidels and their Sunni collaborators as apostates.

It was a form of violent excess that quickly went global. About two hours after the bombings in Iraq, a Shiite procession in the Pakistani city of Quetta was also attacked, with at least two men blowing themselves up in the process. It was a justification for violence against civilians that was to be adopted by many others; about two-thirds of Al-Qaeda's and Boko Haram's suicide bomb victims have been civilians, and just under half of ISIS's.

Admittedly, not all Salafist groups embraced the targeting of civilians. The Taliban was notably reticent, at least until 2017. Just 10 per cent of their victims have been civilians, and the same with Jabhat al-Nusra. Still, when you rank the terror groups most responsible for civilian deaths from suicide bombs, the top fifteen are Sunni militants, with the LTTE coming in sixteenth.

What drove al-Zarqawi to demand such attacks on Muslims, and for his field commanders and followers to heed that cry? Sectarianism was not new; enmity between Sunnis and Shias had been around for a long time. The Afghan mujahidin destroyed dozens of Shia villages long before the Taliban came along. Radical Sunnis in Pakistan had murdered thousands of Shias since 1990, often shooting them down in mosques as they worshipped. And the Iran–Iraq war was, for many, framed as a battle between Sunnis and Shias.[29]

But Sunnis and Shias have coexisted peacefully for a much longer time than they have been in conflict. The divisions at play today are ones where ancient grievances have been brought to the fore by current tensions. Such tensions in Iraq were, in part, magnified following the arbitrary divisions laid down by the Franco-British pact called the Sykes–Picot Agreement that carved up the Middle East over a hundred years ago. The divisions helped lead to a political situation in Iraq where a Sunni minority ruled over a Shiite majority for decades. So, when the Sunni Saddam Hussein was overthrown and the US permitted a Shiite government to take over, and that government proceeded to marginalise Iraqi Sunnis, tensions were set at an all-time high.

Certainly the issue of whether you are a Shia or a Sunni is acutely felt in Iraq. There, in the land where biblical tradition has it that Cain killed Abel, the ancient fault lines of faith are pronounced. The split between the different interpretations of the Islamic faith stands at roughly 50 per cent Shia to 40 per cent Sunni, with other religions making up the rest. Such a sharp distinction is not universally felt throughout the Muslim world; one survey in 2014 found that 74 per cent of Muslims in Kazakhstan and 56 per cent of Muslims in Indonesia identified themselves as neither Sunni nor Shia, but just Muslim. In Iraq, however, only 5 per cent said they were 'just a Muslim'.[30]

When new post-Hussein anti-terrorism laws began jailing ranks of Sunni Iraqis without charge, and other laws focused on punishing former Baath party Sunni loyalists, the lines of division were laid painfully bare. Seen to be Iraq's equivalent to Germany's denazification after the Second World War, the American-led policies of removing public sector employees and the dissolution of the Iraqi military, which led to the unemployment and loss of pensions of as many as 500,000 men, opened the wounds wider.[31] As one of President Bush's nominees to head the general staff, US Navy Admiral Michael Mullen, pointed out, American policy 'proved more divisive than helpful, created a lingering vacuum in governmental capability that still lingers, and exacerbated sectarian tensions'.[32]

It was a division that outside interests sought to manipulate to their own ends, part of a wider 'regional cold war' between Sunni Saudi Arabia and Shiite Iran. When Iran used Hussein's downfall to support Shia militias in Iraq, Saudi Arabia began funding militant groups in Iraq, and beyond, in response to the feared increase of Iranian influence. A 'Great Game' emerged in Iraq, and then in Syria, between the two great powers in the region – the Iranians and the Saudis – one that continues to this day.

Just having a Sunni–Shia split, however, does not explain why the Sunnis would volunteer to die attacking their Shia neighbours in suicide bombings. Catholic and Protestant divisions in Northern Ireland, for instance, may have been terrible but never led to that specific tactic being used. The recent history of the Democratic Republic of Congo might have been one of civil war and corruption, with up to six million lives lost – either as a direct result of fighting or because of disease and malnutrition – but suicide bombers have never appeared in Kinshasa.

Why Iraq gave birth to such suicidal violence against Shias can – in part – be explained by certain religious texts that influenced men like al-Zarqawi. Such documents cannot be ignored; as one study of jihadists has found, 'religious ideals can influence individual and collective choices', especially when they have a 'moral or practical appeal for the believer, seen to help address the everyday realities of life'.[33] Naturally, cause and effect are hard to unpick – but the repeated use of suicide bombings by groups influenced by these texts, and the absence of suicide bombings by groups who do not think such doctrine holds sway, highlights their importance.

One religious justification that stands out was a fatwa issued by the medieval theologian Ibn Taymiyyah. His ruling was called the Mardin fatwa, after the fortress in south-eastern Turkey where he compiled the edict in the thirteenth century. It was in response to the debate as to whether the town – which had a mixed population of Muslims and non-Muslims – was part of *dar al-Islam* (a realm of peace, safe for Muslims) or *dar al harb* (a realm of war, where Islam is under threat).[34] Ibn Taymiyyah said Mardin was neither. Instead, it was a third domain, where Muslims should be treated as they deserved; if they deviated from the path of righteous Islam, they should be treated as unbelievers.[35] In doing this, Ibn Taymiyyah made it 'permissible' for the likes of Al-Qaeda to attack fellow Muslims if they were deemed apostates.[36] Al-Zarqawi, writing in 2005, was to claim Ibn Taymiyyah 'said: "Allah made it lawful to kill people as much as necessary for the good of humanity." As He said: "*Fitna* [temptation into heresy] is worse than killing".'[37]

It was an argument that fundamentally changed the nature of suicide bombings. In his influential book *Dying to Win*, Robert Pape argues that the 'bottom line is that suicide terrorism is mainly a response to foreign occupation', where 'a foreign power has the ability to control the local government independent of the wishes of the local community.' But such a view, while it may explain why Hezbollah attacked foreign soldiers, or the Black Tigers blew themselves up in Sinhalese barracks, does not fully explain why a global jihad was to emerge with Shias at the front line of harm. Yes, the presence of American troops in Iraq, Afghanistan and beyond has provided tangible targets that have undeniably fuelled the rise in bombings, but this does not explain why there have been places witnessing suicide attacks that have no discernible foreign power present: Bangladesh, Jordan, Morocco, Pakistan and Uzbekistan to name a few. These were attacks not against an occupying power, but on mosques and markets filled with fellow nationals.

A battle for power, resources and territory cloaked in theological garb, the global jihad can almost be described as a modern Reformation, but in this case using the purgatorial fire of the suicide bomb instead of the stake and pyre. Over the following years, Iraq saw over 500 suicide attacks on civilians alone, and it did not stop there; now anyone was a possible target, be they Shia or Christian or apostate.

What individual motivations drove these men (and sometimes women) to become suicide bombers is something we will come to later, but the suicide bomb's allure to many groups was not just down to fatwas and ideologies. To fully appreciate how global jihad took such hold, two other fundamental elements need to be looked at: the growth of access to the Internet, and high levels of international financing. These two drivers of globalisation helped disseminate such toxic beliefs and convictions in an age where media and money fuelled suicide bombing the world over.

The sound is terrible and the camera's colour balance so off that the wall behind her is bright green and her red beret glows intensely, and all the while the cameraman jerkily manipulates the focus as she speaks. Sometimes she does not even look into the lens, but talks to someone to her side, as if in a café over a coffee and a cigarette. With the sound off you would not know she was talking about her impending death.

This is said to be the first 'martyrdom video'.[38] It was made to record the 1985 'martyrdom' of Sana'a Mehaidli, the seventeen-year-old who blew herself up in Lebanon.[39] Her backers appreciated that for her act to have the most significant effect, it needed to be heard throughout the country. So her final message was captured and distributed widely on VHS and Betamax cassettes.

From such beginnings, a new genre emerged – the suicide bomb video. There had already been some attempts at capturing the final moments of bombers on film, but they had been amateur ones; the Black Tigers in Sri Lanka, then Hezbollah, then Hamas all began to use it. But in the Second Chechen War (1999–2009), the propaganda machine kicked in, when Saudi Arabian-born Chechen military leader Ibn al Khattab embraced comprehensive filming of all operations. The Chechens had a clear purpose: to build a political and funding base; to recruit people to the cause; and to network with sympathetic groups. They infused the coverage of their suicide attacks with Islamic justifications and sang verses from the Quran: 'Let those fight in the way of Allah, who sell the life of this world for the other', ran one popular line.

It was in Iraq, though, that the martyrdom video came into its own. DVDs of coalition troops being blown up and shot at became standard fare throughout Iraq and many Arabic-speaking lands; I even saw British troops watching them in their base in Basra.

Realising the importance of such messaging, jihadi groups went on to establish media arms of their own: Al-Qaeda set up 'The Cloud' in 2001, and ISIS later established the 'Jihad Media Battalion'. Their output was prolific. As one soldier serving in Iraq wrote: 'DVDs [of suicide attacks] were so common that our soldiers were trained to expect an imminent attack if a civilian was spotted filming them with a video camera.'[40] By 2007, 'The Cloud' was pushing out ninety-seven videos in just one year – a sixfold increase from a few years before – ranging from long-form documentaries to shorter clips in formats suitable for iPods and mobile phones.

As time went on, and editing software became cheaper and easier to use, a certain baroque bravado started to seep into the films. Jihadists filled them with combusting banners, echo-chamber Quranic recitations and 3D animations, and a distinctive style emerged. They began with a lengthy introduction, where logos fizzed and exploded in a simulation of fire; this was followed by a justification for the 'martyrdom' about to be witnessed. 'Zionist-Crusaders' and the 'treacherous' rulers of the Arab world (especially the House of Saud) were pitted against the Muslim '*umma*' (community) and its mujahidin fighters. Footage of falling bombs, destroyed buildings and civilian casualties hammered home this struggle – an uneven fight where the crusaders were the ones killing innocent civilians under the guise of the War on Terror. To balance this iniquity, suicide attacks were shown to be a necessary weapon – the suicide bomber integral to the restoration of dignity, the expulsion of the infidel from Islamic lands, and the overthrow of corrupt heads of state.

Then there was the biography of the martyr. Here the suicide bomber spoke of their search for paradise and their love of Allah: 'If

I die, do not cry for me. I will be in Heaven waiting for you,' is one line by an immature Pakistani bomber that sums up many of their final words.[41]

The videos then end with either a film or an animation of the attack. Getting this right was important. Take the case of Humam al-Balawi, a Jordanian doctor and suicide bomber, who carried out his attack on Camp Chapman, a CIA base in Afghanistan in December 2009. It was said his martyrdom operation was postponed for several days to allow his handlers to get the necessary footage.[42]

The trend, over time, has been one of increasing sophistication. As one jihadi wrote: 'Everything about the special effects scenes breathed Hollywood, yet it was not, what we had instead was a powerful masterpiece that was Islamic to the core.'[43] In some ways, the suicide video had become as important as the bombing itself.

The filming and editing over, the next step was dissemination. Because if suicide bombing is, in a way, a form of grotesque political theatre, then it demands an audience. Films were first distributed by VHS and Betamax, and, from time to time, TV channels aired them. Then they were loaded onto websites, such as azzam.com, and when these sites were shut down, the clips began to crop up on message boards and on social media platforms such as Facebook and Twitter. Then, as Internet penetration in the Middle East and North Africa almost doubled over the last five years,[44] and uptake of social media swept across the region, the ability of the call to jihad to reach hundreds of millions of people saw terror messaging spread through other online networks. 'Social media,' one analysis reported, 'is no longer virtual: it has become an essential facet' of jihad – disseminating real-time information of conflicts and revealing the existence of new 'spiritual authorities' to possible recruits.[45]

If the first Gulf War was the first globally televised war, this new, suicidal global jihad is the first one that has been tweeted. Jihadists appeared grinning before suicide car bombs; pictures were posted of

Syrian suns glinting through the trigger guard of a handgun; bullets were used to spell out a jihadist's Twitter handle.[46] This was not just global jihad, but jihad through a smartphone filter. From Jordan to Mauritania, Pakistan to Palestine I have met dozens of young men, their phones filled with videos of violence, their message apps linked to more like them. In one Mogadishu Internet café, I witnessed one bearded youth listlessly watching two pop-up screens on his computer. The first showed a porno film – a blonde woman in the fake throes of ecstasy – the other was a page filled with flowing words of Arabic, and above it was the black standard of Al-Qaeda: both offering him a false promise of paradise.

In such a way, the outrages of distant conflicts were brought into the homes and minds of disenfranchised men and women the world over. On the one hand, smartphones brought messages that offered a sense of identity – the loving embrace of an empowered Islamic community, a narrative of victory, a sense of purpose in days of disbelief. On the other they channelled all the rage and frustration that modernity brings in its wake, with America and her Western lapdogs as the cause of all their woes. For we live in a simultaneous era of hyper-connectivity and fury, where social media bolsters our own sense of injustice while simultaneously offering up a stream of random, discrete messages that, in turn, depress or infuriate. And from such media, the call for more, not less, violence was born.

Where, though, did these groups get their weapons from and who has supported them? Certainly money needs to lubricate the wheels of war and it is no small business, either. Estimates of the Taliban's annual revenue are as much as $2 billion, while Al-Shabaab has created their own Ministry of Finance.[47] ISIS was even said to have smuggled $400m out of Iraq and Syria during its recent retreat.[48]

Admittedly, the financial cost of a suicide bomb is not – in itself – that high. The 2005 attacks on the London transport system were costed by the UN at about $14,000. The Pentagon has said a suicide vest costs as little as $1,200 and a suicide car bomb has been put at $13,000 (the car was the main expense).[49] Other attacks have been said to cost more: the Bali bombings were estimated to be $50,000, the Madrid bombings €100,000[50] and the attacks on 9/11 as much as $500,000.[51]

Regardless of these specific costs, suicide bombers generally die for a cause that is headed by a group, and the running of such groups costs far more. There is substantial expenditure in maintaining an organisation and disseminating its ideology: food, transport, communications, training, media output, salaries, safe houses and bribes all cost money. Despite all the promise of a cashless paradise awaiting the martyr, without money that promise would wither on the vine.

First and foremost, these groups rely on influential funders to help meet their outgoings. Since 9/11 one country more than all others has been accused of holding the purse strings for many a Salafi-jihadist: Saudi Arabia. As a US Senate Intelligence Committee chair once said, the appearance of their violent ideology was 'a product of Saudi ideals, Saudi money and Saudi organisational support'.[52] Indeed, Saudi support for Salafi-jihadism is said to go – at least until recently – right to the top, including the present monarch, King Salman bin Abdulaziz. Salman was the royal family's main fundraiser for fighters in Afghanistan during the 1980s and in the Balkans in the 1990s. Saudi Arabia once even held a telethon to fund the families of Palestinian 'martyrs'.[53]

The Saudi government has repeatedly rejected the accusation that it has been involved in terror funding.[54] And, yes, there has yet to be a smoking gun that shows the House of Saud has been directly funding suicidal terrorism, but the opinions of governments, armed as they are with intelligence services, supports the notion that Saudi Arabia is, indeed, the powerful hand that steers. Leaked emails from the office of Hillary Clinton, then US Secretary of State, contain one that reads: 'The governments of Qatar and Saudi Arabia are providing clandestine financial and logistic support to [ISIS] and other radical Sunni groups in the region.'[55] Joe Biden, then-US Vice-President, also once said Saudi Arabia and other Gulf States were pouring 'hundreds of millions of dollars and tens of tons of weapons into anyone who would fight against Assad'. This included al-Nusra, Al-Qaeda, and ISIS.[56]

The thing that has protected Saudi Arabia from too hard a scrutiny has, of course, been oil. As the world's largest exporter of petroleum, the black stuff has bought them a deadly form of discretion. Richard Clarke, who served under three presidents on the National Security Council staff, wrote: 'For several years prior to September 11, the United States government provided the Saudis with information about al Qaeda members in the Kingdom. That information seemed to disappear into a black hole.'[57] Blind eyes have been repeatedly turned. For instance, then British Prime Minister David Cameron ordered a report into foreign funding of terrorist groups in 2015, with a focus on Saudi, but his Home Office said it might never be published.

This reticence to ask too many awkward questions is best understood in acknowledging that both the UK and the US sell billions of dollars of weapons to Saudi Arabia. British arms companies were granted 636 military export licences for Saudi Arabia between 2012 and 2017, worth around £5.2 billion in total. In 2017, the United States signed a $110 billion arms deal with the Kingdom.[58] Such deals mean Saudi Arabia is seen as an ally by the West and not a threat. The British government has said it is in the UK's 'security and prosperity interests' to maintain a good relationship with Saudi. And in 2016, John Brennan, then director of the CIA, called the Saudis 'among our very best counter-terrorism partners globally'. He did so while speaking at the 9/11 Memorial and Museum.

It is not just Saudis, either. The government and ruling family of Qatar have also been repeatedly accused of funding Al-Qaeda, the

Taliban, Hamas and several regional affiliates of the Muslim Brotherhood and, for a long time, Doha permitted local fundraising for radical Islamist groups.[59] Qatar-based individuals have been named as Specially Designated Global Terrorists and placed under sanctions by the likes of the US, the UK and the UN, for providing financial assistance to terror organisations. Some of these individuals appear to enjoy close relations with senior members of the government and the Al Thani ruling family.[60]

In 2015, the US State Department reported that 'entities and individuals within Qatar continue to serve as a source of financial support for terrorist and violent extremist groups, particularly regional Al-Qaeda affiliates.'[61] One Qatari charity, for instance, tweeted it 'supports the mujahedeen with weapons and ammunition'.[62] More than twenty high-ranking Taliban families are also believed to reside in Qatar, and there is a Taliban office in Doha.[63] Qatar has even reportedly paid $1 billion – crammed into suitcases – for the release of twenty-six members of a royal family falconry party in southern Iraq and about fifty militants captured by jihadis in Syria. As much as $300 million was given to Islamist groups in Syria, most of that to Tahrir al-Sham, a group with links to Al-Qaeda. It was a deal that was, in part, to trigger a decision in June 2017 by the United Arab Emirates, Bahrain, Saudi Arabia and Egypt, to cut diplomatic ties and transport links to Qatar, alleging it fuels extremism and terrorism.[64] Qatar has repeatedly denied all these allegations.

Other states, like Kuwait, have also been accused of being centres of fundraising for 'terrorist groups in Syria'.[65] The Bahraini government, which has an MP who boasts he sponsored 1,640 Sunni mujahidin,[66] has been said to have been 'nurturing and nourishing extremist groups . . . to counter the so-called "Shiite threat"'.[67] The United Arab Emirates (UAE) has also fallen under suspicion, in the belief that Dubai's glittering skyscrapers might be used as a hub for terror financing.[68]

The skyline of Dubai – an impenetrable source of jihadi funding

Outside the Gulf, other nations have also aided the Salafi-jihadist. It is, perhaps, one of international diplomacy's worst kept secrets that the Pakistani Intelligence Service (ISI), has funded and provided weapons to the Taliban. After all, the Taliban's central command, the Quetta Shura, is based in Quetta, while the former head of Afghanistan's intelligence service released documents in July 2016 that he said proved Pakistani government funding of the Taliban had occurred.[69]

Another country involved in that Great Game is Iran. There are supposedly four Taliban training camps in Iran – in Tehran, Masshad, Zahedan and in Kerman province – and leaked diplomatic cables claimed Iran trained the Taliban on how to attack coalition forces.[70] The group also has an office in Iran, which opened in 2012.[71] Today reports proliferate that Iran's support for the Taliban is to stem the ascendance of ISIS in Afghanistan.[72]

State sponsorship of terror groups though, while hard to quantify and harder still to prove, is just one side of the coin. As state support to certain jihadist groups has waxed and waned post-9/11, Salafi-jihadist groups have, like modern multinationals, sought to diversify their funding models: capitalism and its systems have seeped into the very organisations that seek to dismantle it.

The methods that jihadist groups employ to self-finance their suicide attacks – from purchasing explosive component parts to compensating bombers' families and loved ones – are complex and continually evolving. One highly lucrative area of profit has been in the exploitation of natural resources;[73] at one time, ISIS controlled over 300 oil wells and production facilities, running 60 per cent of Syria's oil sector, earning up to $2.5 million a day.[74] They even signed a 'devil's agreement' with Damascus natural gas supply, effectively creating a joint venture with the Assad regime.[75]

There are other ways that the natural world has been exploited to further the violent urges of men. The Taliban brings in considerable funds from illicit lapis lazuli,[76] emerald and talc mining,[77] while Al-Shabaab has earnt a fortune from charcoal production – netting as much as $50 million per year – leading the UN to impose a ban on its export.[78] The illicit sugar trade between Somalia and Kenya has also been exploited, with trucks taxed as much as $1,000 each time they pass through an Al-Shabaab checkpoint.[79]

Human exploitation is another source of funds, with the kidnapping of Westerners much favoured. It is estimated that Al-Qaeda and its direct affiliates have raised at least $125 million in ransom money between 2008 and 2014.[80] In 2012, the late leader of Al-Qaeda in the Arabian Peninsula (AQAP), Nasser al-Wuhayshi, said that over half his budget in Yemen came from such ransoms.[81] A decade ago, Al-Qaeda would behead its hostages, but today they find them more valuable alive, even procuring medical attention for them if required. So valuable has kidnapping become that suicide terror groups now intentionally target nationals whose governments have a record of paying up. In abductions in Yemen, for instance, AQAP received over $20 million in 2013 for the release of two Finns, an Austrian and a Swiss national, while Canada paid out $700,000 for two of their diplomats.[82] Since 2013, millions have been paid to them for the release of Turkish, Fijian, Lebanese, Syrian and Italian citizens, with as much as $150 million received for just one American.[83]

The Taliban is one of the most prolific kidnapping groups in the world, making tens of millions of dollars from it. A Westerner can earn as much as $200,000, and in some cases the Taliban has received $20 million for hostages.[84] It doesn't have to be only Westerners, either. It is also Boko Haram's largest source of revenue.[85] The most infamous case of Boko Haram kidnapping is the so-called Chibok girls' case where, on the night of 14 April 2014, they abducted 276 female students from a state school in Borno State; the group's leader Abubakar Shekau later claimed he would sell them as slaves.[86]

Other forms of exploitation persist. Some terror groups squeeze money out of aid and reconstruction projects. Al-Shabaab employs a 'Humanitarian Coordination Officer' in charge of dealings with aid agencies; fees to operate and distribute aid reach as high as $10,000.[87] One unnamed UN agency official said they gave 10 per cent of its project budget to Al-Shabaab in 2009.[88]

Other terror groups use Islamic charities to source funds. Accusations have been levelled at the Kuwait-based African Muslims Agency, the Red Crescent Society of the UAE, the Saudi-based al-Islah Charity, the International Islamic Relief Organisation, Dawa al-Islamiyya and the al-Wafa Charitable Society for helping raise money for terror groups.[89]

Crowdfunding websites and virtual currencies like bitcoin have also been exploited – both systems that help hide donors and beneficiaries.[90] In addition, money is often transferred using the *hawala* method, a decades-old honour-based system in which an individual gives money to an agent, who in turn pays the same amount of money to someone on the receiving end, who finally bequeaths the money to the intended payee. It is a system that is almost untraceable, and a natural benefit for terrorist groups.[91] In 2016, for instance, Norwegian police seized $1.4 million in undeclared cash at Oslo airport, which was allegedly going to be shipped to Somalia through the UK by a *hawala* agent.[92] Following the Paris suicide attacks, Western Union received 75 subpoenas identifying over 850 people who may have been involved in such illicit transfers. It was such a crackdown that ISIS was forced to ask its supporters to send funds via Bosnia.[93]

Many terror groups that control territory also use taxation and extortion as a source of income. In 2015, it was estimated that around five million people lived under Boko Haram control, with up to 75 per cent of households in this area being taxed.[94] Similarly, a Somali intelligence official has said that Al-Shabaab made $9.5 million from taxes on farms in the Jubba valley in 2014 alone.[95] Boko Haram has also used children, the elderly and the mentally ill to raise money through begging.[96]

Outside the exploitation of resources, kidnapping and extortion there have been other, often unexpected, routes of funding. ISIS was reported to have raised funds from anything from fish farming to car dealerships.[97] Illicit archaeological digs were also established, with ISIS netting 20 per cent of the profits from antiquity finds.[98] I once posed as a buyer in a high-end antique market in London, and was quoted the price of about £20,000 for an ancient Mesopotamian lintel. A British Museum expert on Iraqi history not only later identified where it was from, but even found a reference to it in one of his books on famous Iraqi digs. It had been looted in the days following the American invasion, and the beneficiaries of that sale were as murky as the trade it was sold into: when confronted about selling pillaged artefacts, the Lebanese owner of the shop said he was selling it for a friend, and did not know anything about its provenance.

Foreign fighters coming from Europe to join the likes of ISIS were also said to have raised 'significant' funds from the use of 'petty theft, fraudulent loan applications, social insurance fraud, and sophisticated VAT fraud'.[99] Would-be jihadists were encouraged to fund their jihad by mugging people on the streets,[100] pilfering from churches,[101] selling stolen vehicles,[102] and abusing welfare payments.

It appears that terror groups are willing to raise funds from activities forbidden in Islam. Al-Shabaab has been known to resell imported heroin to criminal groups in Nigeria.[103] Al-Qaeda in the Maghreb, along with others, is reportedly raising revenue by 'taxing' the estimated 40 metric tonnes of cocaine smuggled through West Africa each year en route from Colombia, Peru and Bolivia to Europe, generating an estimated $800 million.[104] And, given that Afghanistan's poppy plant export stands at $2.8 billion and represents 13 per cent of the country's GDP,[105] and that the country supplies up to 90 per cent of the world's heroin,[106] it would be a principle too far, it appears, for the Taliban to ignore this cash cow. If anything, they have cultivated its production: in 2016, figures were released showing that opium production in Afghanistan had increased by 43 per cent from the year before,[107] with some estimates suggesting heroin makes up as much as one-third of the Taliban's annual income.[108] Hashish and smuggled cigarettes bring in significant additional funds.[109]

All this goes to show that the ways and means in which the major Salafi-jihadist groups raise funds to carry out suicide bombings are complex and often nefarious. Some might see a dark irony in the means they employ for their ends – people smuggling, drug running, prostitution rackets, gambling, extortion, robberies. Do they see these abusive, irreligious activities as being acceptable? Do they believe that their god will forgive them in the Great Reckoning? These questions remain unanswered in the murky world of trans-border payments and illicit transfers.

While money is one thing, jihadists getting their hands on explosive materials is another. Much of the material they need for their suicide bombs comes from stolen military ammunition. There are numerous stories of groups raiding arms depots and factories to supply their deadly arsenals; from Al-Qaeda's attack on an ammunition factory,[110] to Al-Shabaab seizing 'tonnes of weapons' after clashes with the Kenyan military,[111] but there are dozens of other ways in which suicide bombers obtain bombs.

The mass proliferation of weapons throughout the Afghanistan-Pakistan region, the Middle East and North Africa have undoubtedly fuelled the global rise of suicide bombings. During the 1980s, Saddam Hussein was the largest importer of military equipment in the world: up to 12 per cent of the entire global weapons export market was sent to Iraq.[112] When war broke out, such munitions stockpiles were left exposed; about 90 sites in Iraq saw the theft of military materials, with over 342 tonnes of high explosives stolen from Baghdad in October 2004 alone.[113]

When Muammar Gaddafi fell in 2011, his billion-dollar stockpiles of munitions were also distributed like sweets to various factions.[114] NATO air strikes, furthermore, didn't destroy the armament storage sites, but just spread unexploded ordnance across open fields.[115] Widespread and systematic looting by various armed groups ensued. Following such a spree, as UN experts noted, there was a sharp increase in improvised bombs. Even in 2016, weapon transfers out of Libya were continuing, 'in particular to terrorist groups' in Nigeria, Egypt, Gaza, Syria, Tunisia, Algeria, Mali and Niger.[116]

The Taliban has used both explosive materials left behind by the

Soviet–Afghan War and more modern American and Australian explosives that have fallen into their hands.[117] Poorly managed supply lines and a lack of proper inventory checks may be behind these thefts;[118] a report by the US government itself acknowledged a real potential for its own bought weapons 'to fall into the hands of insurgents'.[119] As the US withdrawal from Afghanistan took place, the Taliban raided their empty barracks, looting some 150 American Humvees, some of which were used in suicide car bomb attacks in February 2016 in southern Helmand province.[120]

Then there is Syria. In the years immediately preceding the outbreak of the civil war, Syria bought over $5.3 billion of arms.[121] Stories abound of ISIS capturing Iraqi, Chinese and Russian missiles. In June 2014, the UN Security Council estimated that ISIS had gained control of sufficient weapons 'to arm and equip more than three Iraqi conventional army divisions (about 40,000 soldiers)'.[122] ISIS also reportedly used science facilities such as the University of Mosul to perfect their suicide bomb-making skills.[123]

This is not all. In places where manufactured explosives are hard to obtain, suicide bombers have improvised. In Nigeria, Boko Haram has armed their suicide bombers with dynamite and detonators stolen from construction sites to do this.[124]

Overall, a combination of entrepreneurialism, military strategy and guile have helped arm and fund suicide bombers the world over – a complex interplay of funding and hard-to-control precursor chemicals that make suicide bombing an impossibly hard weapon to beat, something that cannot be discounted when trying to track its pernicious rise.

One final thing that had an undeniable influence on the spread of the suicide bomber has been this: Salafi-jihadists have not, on the whole, operated in isolation, railing at the world. Instead, they have been interconnected, networked groups, sharing information and skills with other terror groups, particularly when it comes to military skills and bomb-making expertise.

Shared histories are common. ISIS emerged from an Al-Qaeda affiliate organisation in Iraq, and Boko Haram had close connections with Al-Qaeda in the Islamic Maghreb. The Taliban famously provided sanctuary and assistance to Al-Qaeda operatives in Afghanistan, while Talib fighters were, in turn, trained by Iraqi jihadists in suicide bombings, leading to a dramatic rise in attacks.[125] In Central Asia, ISIS benefited from the experience of former Islamic Movement of Uzbekistan (IMU) members, who joined the group in Afghanistan.[126]

When you begin to trace the connections between the many groups that use suicide bombers, you quickly create a spider's web of subterfuge and violence. Boko Haram has sent fighters into Libya to assist ISIS troops.[127] ISIS fighters may have fled northern Libya down to the south, using smuggling routes controlled by Boko Haram.[128] Sometimes the influence is direct: in August 2016, ISIS installed Abu Musab al-Barnawi as the new Boko Haram leader. Boko Haram also received explosives training by the Al-Qaeda operative Khaled Bernaoui as far back as 2006.[129]

Al-Qaeda in the Arabian Peninsula (AQAP) have also reportedly exchanged explosive materials, money and personnel across the Gulf of Aden with Al-Shabaab.[130] The Persian Gulf is so porous the Somali government has labelled it a 'terrorist borderland like the area between Afghanistan and Pakistan'.[131] The fact that Al-Shabaab was able to produce sophisticated suicide bombs and hide them in laptops, designed to be taken onto planes, says to many that the AQAP's leading bomb maker, Saudi-born Ibrahim al-Asiri, had a hand in their making.[132]

Such relationships can be transformative. Aligning themselves with a group that uses suicide bombing can even lead to other long-established terror groups adopting its use. When the Filipino jihadist group Abu Sayyaf declared their allegiance to ISIS in 2016, it was reported shortly afterwards that a Moroccan suicide bomb maker was killed fighting alongside them in Mindanao.[133] The following year, a regional Philippines military commander spoke of a likely threat of suicide bombs being seen in the fierce battle for Marawi City, with militants running at his troops with grenades in their hands.[134] By late July 2018, a suicide attack had been targeted at a military checkpoint in the south, killing eleven. ISIS claimed responsibility.[135]

In this way, the physical networks of knowledge that have fuelled the spread of suicide bombings cannot be overestimated. All too often, in this digitally interconnected world, we tend to forget the importance of physical realities to the mechanisms of violence: the impact of geography, face-to-face meetings, and the warped bravery that comes when men gather and pray together. Such things are even more critical when it comes to convincing someone to die for a cause – after all there is a limit to the seductiveness of a YouTube video.

So prolific and widespread has the spread of suicide attacks been in the last two decades that explaining the root causes and the separate inclinations of each and every Salafist group would take up page upon page. But what is clear is that suicide bombings have risen on a tide of theological justification, terror propaganda, funded support and groups merging and communicating. Each terror group may use suicide bombers differently, but each benefited from this four-pronged reality.

The result, in a sense, has been the birth of one terror group to rule over all others: the Islamic State. Whether it is known as ISIS, IS, ISIL or Daesh, it is a group that has, in a way, become the epitome of the modern suicide bombing threat. A group that embodies so many of the strands of suicide bombing that we have seen so far. One where a search for utopia has met a military-strength strategic purpose; where religious doctrine has blended with a search for statehood;

where the justification for killing civilians has aligned with an apocalyptic vision; whose media outputs and funding platforms have been sophisticated and developed; and where, underpinning it all, resides a strident and ugly interpretation of Islam and the paradise that awaits those who die in its name.

In a sense, ISIS is the terrible and logical product of decades of suicidal violence: a perfect storm that is the State of Terror.

Chapter 9

The State of Terror

In 2015, a memory stick was smuggled out of Syria – stolen from ISIS's internal security police. It contained data on who had travelled to join ISIS's ranks, scans of questionnaires filled out by volunteers from fifty-one countries. Such form-filling was a formalisation of terror: blood group, date of birth, civil status, education level, knowledge of sharia, previous involvement in jihad, even hearing levels.[1] And among them, 149 volunteers had indicated their desire to become a martyr.[2] There was a waiting list of people wanting to die and they divided them into nationality and age. There were even two types of martyrs listed: 'suicide bomber' or 'suicide infiltrator' – the latter a relatively new development, a fifth-columnist role. One who would join the forces of the Syrian army, only to turn on their fellow troops in a murderous attack.[3]

This data also revealed that the majority of the volunteers were young men, their peach fuzz beards testimony to that; 69 per cent of suicide bombing recruits were under thirty. Most had headed into Syria via Turkey, were single and had no children. A third were either students or unemployed. The majority had completed secondary-level education and a quarter had attended universities. And yet, despite this relatively high level of education, only 3 per cent of suicide martyrs said they had a deep comprehension of sharia law, with many describing their understanding as 'basic'. Only 13 per cent declared any previous experience of jihad.[4]

In addition to these files other sources offer clues as to the emotional impulse that drove such men to become suicide bombers. A deep search online – most sources are now hard to find owing to crackdowns on ISIS propaganda – led to me finding twenty-one ISIS suicide videos: dead men talking.[5] Predictably, their final words were steeped in religion, a fervour bookended by the 'promised' paradise. The reward for their deaths, they were convinced, was the 'green birds of Jannah' – the souls of fighters in the afterlife. A suicide bombing, one said, is the 'hardest, most impactful force on the enemies of our religion, and it is the quickest path to Allah'. Their visions of paradise were told in a matter-of-fact way, without doubt or uncertainty. One was adamant his martyred death was 'the path to the *hourias*' (the virgins of paradise). Another said: 'This deed is only for Allah. It does not have any goal for reputation or for nationalism.' Overall, the words 'Allah', 'attack', 'brothers', 'path' and 'jihad' dominate. 'I only fight to bring victory to Allah,' said one; 'We will not rest until Allah's sharia is established on earth,' said another. One ended his diatribe with the words: 'I fight only to bring victory for this religion.' One fighter mentioned Allah thirty-nine times in his short video, another eleven times in just five sentences.

They were half-grown men with hearts bursting so much with ideology that it seeps into their final speeches with a quasi-erotic sensuality. Words like 'bliss', 'longing', 'body', 'hearts', and 'beautiful' fill their breathless passages. They speak in short, urgent sentences, but in a language of extremes and polarities. The words of martyrdom – 'sacrifice', 'angels', 'exalted', 'glorified' – are stacked up against the words of angry victimhood – 'tyrants', 'sacrifice', 'infidels'.

They lionise their own deaths, too; one says he hopes his body will burn like a volcano. Others express their joy at being surrounded by so many tonnes of explosives, a death embraced. 'Don't you see how [jihadists] are advancing to death fearlessly, laughing,' one said, 'yet death is escaping them, so they chase it until they reach it, they chase death to write history again.'

Another says that, with their lives, they are telling the world 'here is the heaven, here is the jihad market, here is the house of Islam'.

Many focus on their deeds as being acts to punish their enemies, either as payback for crimes against fellow Sunni Muslims, or, simply, to punish the enemy for being 'filthy' apostates or infidels. They often use the word '*rawafidh*', a derogatory word meaning 'rejectionist', to describe the Shia, or they denigrate those they fight as 'pigs'. As one shouts into the camera lens: 'We have prepared explosive cars for you to destroy your thrones. By Allah, we will rub your noses in the soil and rip you to pieces.'

For all the bravado, though, fear of pain still seems to lurk in their testimonies. As the Syrian fighter, Abu, cried out: 'One pinch, I will only feel a pinch, this is what the Prophet, peace be upon him, told us, the martyr feels only a pinch.' As another says: 'The prophet told us the martyr only feels an ant bite.'

What these entry forms and death videos do not do, though, is offer wider context. They might reveal personal details of what sort of fighters entered ISIS and what their inner preoccupations were, but they do not give answers as to why ISIS came into being, and what drove its popularity.

Broadly speaking, ISIS grew out of the chaos that followed the US invasion of Iraq, the bitter child of those violent parents Al-Qaeda in Iraq (AQI) and the Islamic State in Iraq (ISI). But what caused that child to mature was a more complex array of forces: the disenfranchisement of Sunnis by the Iraqi Shia prime minister; the power vacuum created by the US's withdrawal from Iraq in 2011; the violent breakdown created by the Syrian civil war; the fear of a dominant Iran that fuelled Sunni power politics; the failure of the 2011 Arab

Spring to offer tangible reform; and the lingering effects of years of vicious sectarianism.

More directly, ISIS was also born from – appropriately – a suicide bomb. In 2013, its leader Abu Bakr al-Baghdadi launched his 'Breaking the Walls' campaign, seeking to free several militant prisoners. Conducting suicide attacks on prisons across Iraq, including a strike on Abu Ghraib, he released a swarm of jihadi fighters who would go on to form the core structure of the group.[6] Many of the top cadres of ISIS's leadership underwent torture or abuse in those jails, feeding into later calls for vengeance.[7]

But such things do not fully explain the sheer numbers of suicide bombers that ISIS has deployed. They do not explain, either, the complete joy with which these bombers embraced their deaths. To me, the reason that ISIS fighters embraced the suicide bomb so fervently is that, in many ways, ISIS embodied the precise traits and factors that had driven previous organisations towards suicidal violence. They were, in a sense, the perfect host in which the suicide bomb virus could take hold.

The search for utopia that we see in ISIS's desire for a caliphate, for example, mirrors the utopian impulse that led the first suicide bomber, a Russian, to kill his Tsar. The use of suicide bombs as a strategic weapon of war, summed up in ISIS's wave of bombers, reflects a militarism honed by the Japanese kamikaze in the first half of the twentieth century. The virtues of Islamic martyrdom that ISIS so embraced can, in a way, be traced back to the Iranian revolution. The role of the charismatic leader, with Baghdadi central to ISIS's use of suicide bombers, reminds us of the cultish charisma that inspired a generation of Tamil Tiger suicide attacks. The theological justification to kill civilians, one adopted by Hamas in the 1990s, is furthered in ISIS's barbarism. Finally, the global jihad that Al-Qaeda embraced became, in a sense, ISIS's fundamental trademark: a call to Muslims everywhere.

*The border to Syria taken in Jordan – when I was there in 2016,
ISIS fighters could be heard fighting on the other side*

Al-Qaeda, it has been said, is to Trotsky as ISIS is to Stalin. While
Al-Qaeda and Trotsky bided their time, hoping for the world to ignite
in revolution, both ISIS and Stalin sought to build their vision through
violent empire-building.[8] For ISIS, such an empire is their dream of
a caliphate – a state under the leadership of an Islamic steward
called the caliph, a religious successor to the prophet Muhammad
and leader of the entire Islamic *umma*. To its followers, such a state
constitutes a very real utopia, one where the hypocrisies of human
power are revealed as false, and where the word of God alone can
create harmony and love. It has a powerful allure; armies of jihadists
from around the world flocked to join ISIS's ranks, seeking a home
where they could live as heroes, not just a battleground where they
could die as martyrs.

ISIS was not the first to create a caliphate. One had existed for centuries, ultimately disbanded in 1924 by Kemal Atatürk, the Western-looking ruler of Turkey. But the idea of a caliphate persisted in the Islamist imagination; within a few years of its dissolution, the hope for its recreation was articulated by the founder of the Egyptian Brotherhood. What Baghdadi did, though, on 29 June 2014, when he raised ISIS's black flag over Mosul and declared himself 'Caliph Ibrahim', was to grab destiny by the throat and create a very real place, not one of dreams.

It was a utopia that came with a price from the very beginning. ISIS fighters would cut off the arm that smokers used to raise the cigarette to their lips; they would execute those who dared drink alcohol; if a woman ventured from her home without her husband or chaperone, or not veiled, there would be consequences just as terrible; and if a man failed to pray five times a day he would be lashed.

But despite these onerous restrictions, the vision of the caliphate's utopia to its followers was, like the Russian utopia envisaged by the People's Will, one of boundless horizons. After the group took Mosul, it sent out a bulldozer into the desert, towards the Syrian–Iraq border, and demolished the berm that separated the two lands. To hammer the point home, they released a video called 'The End of Sykes–Picot' – a reference to the secretive agreement between Sir Mark Sykes and François-Georges Picot of Britain and France in 1916 to create what became the borders of Iraq and Syria. The bearded jihadi fronting the film, probably now long dead, called Baghdadi 'the breaker of barriers', and said there were no countries, just Muslims.[9]

For a time, the vision held. By January 2015, ISIS was in control of almost 90,800 square kilometres (35,000 square miles), albeit mostly desert scrub. And, at its height, over half of ISIS's media output was to show how virtuous and lovely life in that desert scrub could be.[10] One British fighter, Abu Rumaysah, wrote a forty-six-page travel document for visitors. He described a place that proves 'the superiority of Islam over all other ways of life' and a land that promised – of all things – Kinder Surprises, Cadbury's chocolate, fruit cocktails and, in a curious turn of phrase, 'an exquisite Mediterranean climate that has all the markings of a plush holiday resort'.[11]

When he boasted that the caliphate had as good coffee as any found in 'your local Costa', he revealed not only the banality of evil, but also that the Islamic State was not seeking to dismantle the mechanisms of Western capitalism. Their conception of a perfect state may have been unrelentingly violent, but underneath it all there was no economic vision of alternatives, and in that sense it was quite humdrum.

I had once met the author of this booklet, almost a decade before the caliphate was declared. Then he was still called by his birth name, Siddhartha Dhar, and was a spokesperson for the British Islamist group, Al-Muhajiroun. I had travelled to north London to interview the organisation's co-founder, Anjem Choudary. At the time, in August 2005, Al-Muhajiroun was deeply reviled in the UK, in part for hosting a conference a year after 9/11 called 'The Magnificent 19', in reference to the numbers of hijackers, and the government swiftly banned the group. Siddhartha spoke to me as I was leaving, and he claimed that Islam had demography on its side, that Muslim women were producing far more children than Western women, and it was only a matter of time before the whole world was Islam. I had asked him if he had ever been to Latin America, aware that there were only about four million Muslims there in an area of almost 700 million inhabitants, and he didn't answer me. When I emailed him later to ask if we could meet, interested to find out more about his ideological beliefs, he never replied.

Ten years later, his vision of utopia was an ISIS one, offering redemption and empowerment in equal measure. It was 'a brighter picture of jihad' that rooted economic, political and legal systems in Islam, where religious and social lives were perfected and where the

state could expand until the entire Muslim world was under its juris-
diction. ISIS even articulated an ecological vision, publishing articles
that praised the diversity of the natural world under the caliphate.[12]

Such hyperbole is predictable. Whereas nationalistic utopias look
at the past to find meaning, imperial utopias stare forwards, their
ambition being to create a better civilisation than the nations they
seek to usurp. And such empires usually argue that self-sacrifice is
needed to enable their leaders to achieve their goals.

ISIS also offered something else, particularly to those frustrated
by the lack of change the Arab Spring had truly achieved. Whereas
liberals promised local democratic reform, ISIS guaranteed riches
and rewards in both this life and heaven.

To ISIS suicide bombers, their own violent death was, in this way,
a win-win. It would create both an earthly utopia (the establishment
of the caliphate) and grant them the keys to heaven. This logic comes
out in the caliphate fighters' testimonies. On 25 March 2016, three
ISIS suicide bombers targeted checkpoints around Aden, Yemen. One
of them, Soheib al-Wiqari, recorded a video saying they were 'willing
to put our blood and our lives on the line in order to see God's rule
on Earth'. While Abu Aisa al-Ansari, who detonated his bomb at the
entrance of a military training camp in Yemen in February 2016,
said: 'The "suicide operation" is the easiest way to heaven.' 'Here,'
another jihadi bomber said, 'is the home of the Caliphate; here is the
devotion, here is dignity.'

The allure of such a society was, for many, great. In May 2015, a
family of twelve from Luton in the UK travelled to Raqqa in Syria
seeking 'a land that has established the Shariah, in which a Muslim
doesn't feel oppression . . . in which a parent doesn't feel the worry of
losing a child to the immorality of society . . . in which the sick and
elderly do not wait in agony'.[13] The family members ranged from one
to seventy-five years old. ISIS, in this way, was not just a terror group
that sought inexperienced men; they offered a home for entire fami-

lies, and entreated non-fighters, such as doctors and nurses, dentists and accountants to come to fill the ranks of the faithful.

It was, in part, the reason why so many Tunisians sought to join ISIS's ranks: their own revolution had failed them.[14] To those Tunisians, ISIS must have been seen to be incorruptible, at least compared to their own country's dishonest leaders. ISIS's feeder countries were often poverty-stricken, with their largest numbers coming from the lower half of the world's underdeveloped nations.[15] After all, the caliphate would give away a house, home furnishings, and $1,200 in cash to ISIS fighters who wished to marry.[16]

What more could you ask for?

On 1 March 2017 *The Times* ran a headline that read: 'ISIS waging "kamikaze" war with a thousand suicide bombers'.[17] The ghosts of the kamikaze have often been raised by journalists seeking a glib description of a suicide bomber, but here the journalist might well have had a point. Because, like the Divine Wind forces of the Japanese emperor's army, ISIS embraced the suicide bomber as an intrinsic weapon of war.

In their early years, like other jihadist groups, ISIS focused on the age-old rivalry of the Sunnis and the Shias that had emerged in Iraq. These included two of the most massive suicide bombings against Shias in Iraqi history: a strike on a market in Khan Bani Saad in July 2015, killing 121 people, and on a bazaar in Karrada in Baghdad, murdering 325 more. Such carnage was intended to cause deep political rifts, and added to the impression that the Iraqi government could not protect its citizens.[18] In the theatre of sectarian warfare in Iraq, where the Iran-sponsored Popular Mobilisation Units (PMU) were accused of massacring Sunnis,[19] such violence was seen by ISIS as a way of forcing fence-sitters into joining their camp. This has been, in large part, why ISIS suicide bombings have often occurred during the Muslim holy month of Ramadan – they wanted to outrage.[20] And why, when you look at those who joined ISIS's ranks, you find that many are from places where Sunnis feel 'under threat'.

Many of their volunteers, for instance, came from the North Governorate of Lebanon, a place that produced about 70 per cent of Lebanon's foreign fighters – the north long being a centre of sectarian tensions between the local Sunni and Alawite communities.[21] Other Sunni fighters came from Muharraq Island, located outside Bahrain's capital Manama, part of the archipelago in the Persian Gulf that has produced about 79 per cent of Bahrain's total foreign fighters. It's a place that maintains close ties with Bahrain's royal family, a Sunni family ruling over a majority Shia country, and is itself majority Sunni.[22]

But, over time, ISIS's targeting of civilians changed. Their suicide bombers shifted from militant foreigners targeting civilians, to attacks being carried out by local insurgents on military targets.[23] Mosques and marketplaces gave way to roadblocks and military bases, showing that it was not just blind fury that motivated ISIS's use of suicidal terror but something approaching dark logic. Between December 2015 and November 2016, 84 per cent of ISIS's suicide operations were against military targets.[24] This compares to its predecessor – the Islamic State of Iraq (ISI) – which only used suicide bombers attacking security targets 20 per cent of the time.

One video released during that surge illustrates this shift in shocking detail. The footage is from a drone, hovering high above the dusty streets of Mosul in northern Iraq, and shows a sequence of huge, radiant explosions – flashes of ochre and debris hurled high. Each clip of death follows the same pattern: a heavily built ISIS suicide truck is circled in green, the soon-to-be victims highlighted in their tanks in red. The vehicle drives slowly alongside, almost casually, and then there is a powerful flash of light. Then the filming drone jerks a little as the pressure waves ride upwards, hitting it like a kestrel in a storm. Each blast is the assured death of at least one ISIS fighter and the likely killing of many of their enemies, burnt alive in the fireballs that ensued.

Wave after wave of ISIS suicide bombers are seen dying, and killing and maiming, with over forty suicide attacks captured on film in less than a year's fighting. What the drone does not convey is the terror felt by the petrified teenagers in uniform, on guard, scanning the horizon for the dusty plume of their personal approaching apocalypse. The fear of the tank crews as they see these rhinoceros-like lorries come barrelling towards them. They don't impart the agonising screams of men burned alive in broiling metal or the smell of burning flesh.

These waves of suicide attacks, death piled upon death, constitute the largest deployment of suicide strikes in recent history, as high – if not on occasion higher – as kamikaze attacks of over seven decades ago. In 2011, there were an average of seventeen suicide attacks each month around the world. In 2015, there were seventy-six. The following year, at least according to ISIS's claims, they were carrying out suicide attacks at a higher monthly rate than all other militant groups combined for the previous five years.

ISIS employed everyone and anyone in these 2016 attacks. There were old men with hardly any teeth left in their mouths, sporting full white beards;[25] there were the disabled in wheelchairs;[26] there were children with learning disabilities;[27] and there were, after a time, women, despite ISIS's early reservation about using females in violent jihad.[28] All hoisted into the trucks they were soon to drive to their deaths.

Combined, these men, women and children evolved the suicide bomber's art into a form of warfare that sent terror into the hearts of their enemy and challenged the technical and military might of nations. As one security adviser put it, it was akin to 'close air or artillery support for an army that lacks planes to support their conventional operations'.[29]

With such military tactics, ISIS sent in waves of suicide attackers

strapped into heavily fortified trucks, to pound their enemy's positions. This was a method used by Iraq's Baathist military under
Saddam Hussein, some of whom were later to join ISIS's ranks.
Each of the leaders of ISIS's military council, for instance – with
one exception – was a former Baathist officer, and they even had
an ex-Baathist 'Minister of Explosives' in charge of the group's IED
campaigns.[30] Several high-ranking foreign fighters also influenced
ISIS's strategy; defensive tactics used in Mosul were similar to those
deployed by Chechen jihadis in the 1990s, though in the past it was
heavy bombardments that the Chechens employed – in this case the
guided missiles were trucks driven by men.[31] Their tactics evolved
to take into consideration other weapons too; one ISIS film showed
a drone armed with two bombs taking off and dropping them over
a crowd of soldiers. Two fell to the ground and the others scattered
and, as people chased to the scene, a white suicide bomb car arrived
and exploded next to an armoured vehicle. Improvised air strikes
and ground strikes combined – a deadly mix.

Such tactics proved effective. During ISIS's offensive of Ramadi,
they aimed a bulldozer packed with explosives at the city's security
perimeter and, in obliterating it, allowed around thirty more armoured
suicide bombs to flood the city.[32] ISIS also used so-called *inghimasi*
operations in an unprecedented manner.[33] Such missions are derived
from the Arabic word *ghamassa*, meaning to plunge oneself into
something. ISIS often used this as a tactic during raids; *inghimasi*
fighters charging their enemies with guns, trying to penetrate enemy
lines, before 'plunging' into their midst to detonate their suicide
vests.[34] The tactic was surprisingly effective; one American soldier
was killed three miles behind the front lines of Mosul in May 2016 by
an ISIS bomber, highlighting just how far behind enemy lines these
operations could reach.[35]

To fuel this surge ISIS's suicide bomb production, like the kamikazes', took place on a 'quasi-industrial scale.'[36] The fact that ISIS

captured such vast swathes of territory allowed them to manufacture and modify these huge car bombs at remote sites with seeming
impunity. Welded together with iron and steel, they looked like something from a Mad Max film.[37] One report found component parts of
these suicide bombers from fifty-one companies in twenty different
countries, while dud bombs dropped by coalition planes, leftover
munitions from the US-led invasion of Iraq and weaponry seized in
battle, were all repurposed for deadly use.[38] ISIS even established a
secret factory in Turkey where it produced hundreds of suicide vests,
as well as building suicide car bombs disguised as ambulances.[39] Such
subterfuge was used in November 2016, when security checkpoints
in Tikrit and Samarra in Iraq were targeted by false ambulances,
leaving twenty-one dead.[40]

In their bid to secure a paradise in heaven and on earth, it seems,
ISIS would be prepared to flout every covenant and every decency.
And so, perhaps, the analogy with the kamikaze goes too far. Because
even though the Japanese flouted the Geneva Convention and placed
their fervent nationalism above compassion and moderation, they
still had boundaries. With ISIS it was as if they violated the fundamental rules of war not just because it was an effective tactic, but
because it was part and parcel of burning the world to the ground
– so that they could raise their utopia from its ashes. And it was this
yearning for the apocalypse that was to make ISIS such a terrifying
enemy.

When confronted with the possibility that the world is going to
end, death takes on a new meaning. That, at least, seems to be a
central theme among ISIS suicide bombers. The motivation for
their deaths is radically different from many bombers before them.
Unlike Hezbollah and Hamas, for instance, while ISIS funded its
fighters in general, it did not provide particular financial incentives
for its suicide bombers. Nor did it dedicate much time or resources

to martyrdom videos; fame does not appear to have been a driving factor for those who attacked and died for ISIS. In an analysis of over a month of monitoring ISIS's reports of eighty-two suicide bombings, only one biography came up. The most an ISIS bomber could have hoped for was, in general, a brief news bulletin or perhaps a picture. Even then, notoriety was not assured: real names were almost never given.

The sacrifices of these nameless men were, instead, placed at the altar of often hard-to-fathom sacred values – philosophies so deep and so unmovable that these men forsook their families, communities and lives for them. One study of captured ISIS insurgents concluded that these 'abstract' ideas, not earthly motivations, had compelled many to fight – ideas about the end of the world, the final battle and the return of a great Islamic age. Such abstract ideas, the researchers found, could trump even 'group loyalty in willingness to fight'.[41]

These millenarian ideas in ISIS, I would argue, were different from those of many previous suicide bombers because, for ISIS fighters, their fight had become a truly apocalyptic one. Hamas and Boko Haram, Al-Qaeda and the Taliban may have had moments where they talked about the imminent end of the world, but they did not put such a vision at the front and centre of their messaging.

Certainly the apocalypse dominates ISIS's messages. 'When will the last day come?' asks a character in the British director Peter Kosminsky's carefully observed 2017 television series *The State*. The answer is taken from a book called *The Islamic Understanding of Death and Resurrection*,[42] and it is stark. 'When piety has given way to pride, and truth to lies. When children are born out of wedlock. When usury, adultery, homosexuality and the obedience of men to their wives prevail. When sex is performed in public places, and there is no Imam to lead the faithful in prayer. When people compete with one another to construct high buildings. When earthquakes increase. Does any of this sound familiar? It's happening now. The hour is approaching.'[43]

Like the Old Testament, the early chapters of the Quran are packed with this menace – a final reckoning between good and evil. Such framing reinforced in the minds of ISIS's troops that there was a terrible battle being fought between good and evil – 'us' and 'them'. As Zarqawi stated: 'There are only two camps: the camp of truth and its followers, and the camp of falsehood and its factions. So choose to be from one of the two camps.'[44] And the presentation of the world as embroiled in a great battle between good and evil reinforced the idea that for paradise to be reached a great sacrifice needs to be offered; the heavenly balance wills it.

ISIS fighters were to embrace this vision like no other, seeing such destruction as a prerequisite for their utopia to be ushered in. In 2014, they published the second issue of their recruitment magazine *Dabiq*. The front cover was dramatic: a still from Darren Aronofsky's epic film *Noah*. The wooden ark, like the fisherman's boat in the Japanese woodcut *The Great Wave off Kanagawa*, was shown tossed upon a broiling sea. The title above the granite waves spelt out 'The Flood'. Inside you could read articles about ISIS's humanitarian work caring for orphans, but the cover story dominated: would-be jihadists were warned of the forthcoming 'Day of Judgment'. And for those who did not submit to ISIS's will? 'The punishment . . . drowning in the flood.'

Their unrelentingly violent propaganda film *The Clanging of the Swords IV* was also to channel this apocalypticism. It begins with the line: 'My lord, (grant us) the victory that you promised.' This is a direct reference to the 'end of times' prophecy that heralds the glorious reappearance of the final Mahdi (the Twelfth Imam). In such a time, an evil creature called 'al-Dajjal' is predicted to appear (often translated as the Antichrist), and everyone will be judged for their deeds. The sky, they say, will rip apart; the sun will rise in the West and Jesus will descend, wrapped in a robe, onto a minaret in

Jerusalem.[45] This last sign has always struck me as curiously under-reported about the millenarianism of ISIS: the world's most feared Islamist terror group believes in the Second Coming of Christ with as much fervour as any Midwestern American Christian.

There will, too, be moral decline, earthquakes and public for-nication. A mountain of gold will be discovered at the mouth of the Euphrates that hundreds will fight and die over, and a black banner will fly over 'Khorasan' – referring to a historical region that once encompassed north-eastern Iran, southern Turkmenistan and northern Afghanistan. Jihadists neatly interpreted these last two premonitions as being the black gold of the Iraqi oil fields and the even blacker flag of ISIS.[46] But it is not just oil and the hoisting of the ubiquitous black flag that will herald Armageddon. ISIS says that war against Christians is the clearest sign of the great reckoning, a belief underpinned by a Hadith that speaks of a final battle between Romans and Muslims waged close to the town of Dabiq,[47] with occu-pation by foreign armies and the diminishment of Islam integral to that.[48] Furthermore, the caliphate has to sack Istanbul before being defeated by an army headed up by the anti-Messiah. That mass sac-rifice – leaving just a few thousand jihadists standing – will bring in the new dawn.

Such millenarianism pervaded the intellectual framing that led to ISIS's creation. Al-Zarqawi called Shiites the 'followers of "al-Dajjal"', and deliberately set about ordering their torture and the defilement of their corpses. He announced that a 'war against Islam' was being waged, a framing that contributed significantly to the mass mobi-lisation of foreign fighters.[49] It's easy to dismiss such claims as the mutterings of madmen: there is no place for the apocalypse outside Hollywood and psychiatric institutions. But to do so would fail to appreciate some fundamental elements that underpin the beliefs and motivations of their suicide bombers (and it is not just ISIS – one study found that over half of Muslim adults in nine out of twenty-three countries surveyed believed the return of the Mahdi was imminent and would happen in their lifetime).[50]

Many of ISIS's actions can be explained away in terms of economics and politics. Their pragmatic oil trade with the Assad regime; their official apology after attacking a unit of the Israeli Defence Forces;[51] even their heavily staged executions of prisoners can be considered as strategic acts.[52] But ISIS is far from consistently rational, at least in a secular sense: their decision to attack the US, French, Russian, Syrian, British and Turkish militaries at the same time;[53] their battle to protect that supposedly strategic but meaningless town of Dabiq,[54] or the vast amount of propaganda they spewed out, only makes sense when you look at such strange decisions through the prism of their 'end of days' mentality. Those fighters who die are not looked upon with pity, but envied as martyrs who have found their salvation. Loss is victory.

It is an end-of-days framing that pervades much of what they do. How they embrace the idea that to succeed, hundreds of thousands of their fighters have to die. It explains why, when American aid worker Peter Kassig was beheaded in 2014, along with sixteen Syrian soldiers, the masked British militant known as 'Jihadi John' said to the camera that they were there, in Dabiq, 'waiting for the remainder of your armies to arrive'.[55] And why, when ISIS lost that town, they stopped publishing a magazine under that name but instead launched an English-language report called *Rumiya* – the Arabic for Rome. The conquest of Rome, another apocalyptic sign, may in their eyes take longer, but it still is a teleology that many fighters sign up to.

Within all this, the suicide bomber's sacrifice has become a necessary precursor to victory. So while some historians have concluded that suicide attacks are 'unlikely among members of a coalition with no imaginable prospect of staving off defeat', this does not hold with regard to ISIS.[56] They undertake suicide attacks even with defeat staring them in the face – an apocalyptic movement that seeks not its sustainability, but its own spectacular destruction.

In January 2015, ISIS released a 22-minute video that showed the lone figure of a captured Royal Jordanian Air Force pilot dressed in an orange jumpsuit, standing in a cage. The twenty-six-year-old, Moaz al-Kasasbeh, had been imprisoned on Christmas Eve the year before, when his F-16 fighter jet suffered mechanical problems and crash-landed close to the de facto ISIS capital Raqqa. In the hours before the release of the video, the group's Twitter supporters had deployed the Arabic hashtag #SuggestAWayToKillTheJordanianPilotPig, offering up ways the pilot could be executed. One person suggested death by chainsaw, another by melting him with acid. Feed him to a caged crocodile, tweeted another.

They chose to pour petrol over him and set him alight, and filmed his agonised death in what could be described as a pornography of violence. ISIS said it was punishment in 'equal retaliation' to the suffering the pilot had caused with his plane's bombs. After his cries ended, they dumped rubble on his corpse – in remembrance of the homes he had bombed.[57] It was an execution rooted in the retributive Islamic notion of *qisas*; usually used by families seeking redress from a slight, ISIS adopted it as a form of rough justice. They also published a fatwa citing an obscure text describing how a companion of the Prophet, Khaled Ibn al-Walid, also burned apostates.[58] But Iraq's most senior Sunni mufti, Sheik Mahdi al-Sumaidaie, claimed that Kasasbeh's execution was a violation – that the prophet Muhammad ordained 'that only God can punish with fire'.[59]

That being said, visible punishment in Islam is not a new thing. Throughout the Muslim world, punishment has often been kept in the public eye, with football stadiums being used for executions in Libya,[60] Afghanistan[61] and Iran.[62] It follows the Quranic stipulation that a party of people should bear witness to the penalty to ensure it

is an impactful, public deterrent. In 2016, 75 per cent of all death pen-
alties globally (675 out of 900) were in Islamic-majority countries,[63]
and all thirteen countries in the world where apostasy is punishable
by death are also Muslim majorities.[64]

But this combination of harsh punishment and public display
reached its height under ISIS. At least 2,000 people appear to have
been executed by the terror group.[65] People were killed for having
derogatory remarks about ISIS on their phones; a bride was beheaded
for wearing make-up on her wedding day; thirteen-year-old girls,
trafficked as sex slaves, were murdered because they 'stirred up'
trouble. The depravity did not stop there. Children were employed
as executioners: one was filmed beheading a man on a playground
roundabout, another – about four years old – shooting a man in the
face.

Into this mix of punishment seeped the motif of the suicide bomb.
Captured soldiers were filmed strapped into suicide vests, which
were then detonated from a distance. One video showed the footage
spooling backwards, so their exploding bodies were seen to recon-
stitute themselves, the blast rushing inwards. And just as the suicide
belt became a weapon of punishment, so too did the suicide bomber.

ISIS has used the suicide bomb to punish the Shia for their apostasy, to harm Christians for their government's 'crusades' in Muslim
lands, and to punish people like the Yazidis for, in their eyes, wor-
shipping the Devil. What started years before with the targeting of
that school bus in Afula in Israel, gained momentum with the strike
on lower Manhattan by Al-Qaeda, transformed into attacking Shias
under Zarqawi, before finding its natural home in ISIS. In total,
about a quarter of ISIS's suicide bomb targets have been civilians,
and the impact of this religious war has been devastating – about
15,000 killed or injured. So vicious were the attacks on Shias that al-
Zawahiri, Al-Qaeda's current chief, had even said they should cease.

'Can the mujahedeen kill all of the Shia in Iraq?' he asked, 'Has any

Islamic state in history ever tried that?'[66] But the plea went unheeded and the attacks continued, leading Al-Qaeda to break with the group in early 2014, with al-Zawahiri saying his group was 'not responsible' for the actions of its former affiliate. ISIS continued regardless. When Abu Dujanah Al Shami died in Aleppo in July 2016, his last words in his death video were: 'My message to the *rawafidh* [Shia apostates], we have prepared suicide car bombs for you so as to destroy your shrines, we will humiliate you and blow you into pieces.' Such attacks on Shias were so concentrated, so wilful, that the US secretary of state even described them as genocide.[67]

In targeting Shias, what ISIS did, alongside all the stonings and beheadings, was to make the suicide bomber a punitive arm of its state – public and visceral. It was a concept that had been laid out by the writer Abu Bakr Naji in his book *The Management of Savagery*. In it, he praised 'punishment that establishes the justice which is missing from the earth'. Then, using a justification once employed by medieval inquisitors who claimed burning at the stake cleansed the heretic's soul, he wrote that punishing Shias proves 'a greater mercy to humanity than the awful torment of God being sent down directly upon them'.

To Abu Bakr Naji, jihad had to be 'violence, crudeness, terrorism, frightening [others], and massacring' – all a necessary stage through which the *umma* must pass.[68]

ISIS called for the spectacle of violence, designed to challenge Western ideas of punishment and power to the very core. Centuries ago, state-sanctioned punishment was not that unlike ISIS's: exposed, physical and theatrical. But today, especially in Western nations, it is contained, secretive and dispassionate, where the state's sentencing has reformed from physical torture to something that now targets the mind and soul of the sentenced. The pillory was abolished in France in 1789 and in England in 1837. The public exhibition of prisoners in France ended in 1848. Branding stopped in 1834 in England, two years earlier in France. By 1848, public executions had been effectively phased out in most of Western Europe, with some notable exceptions. In its place, a form of 'judicial reticence' influenced physical punishment; the punishment's effectiveness became based not on its violent intensity, but rather on its calculated and timed inevitability.

Instead of the executioner's axe or the noose, punishment in the West altered over the nineteenth century to become ordered, bureaucratic and deeply clinical. The sort of public executions that were to follow the Tsar's murder in 1882 were prohibited and in their place came other horrors: mechanised slaughter in concentration camps, death by lethal injection using sterile needles and, up to today, the use of solitary confinement. The Eastern State Penitentiary in Philadelphia had, by 1829, over 250 men and women in solitary. Charles Dickens described it as burying men alive, an act 'which no man has a right to inflict upon his fellow creature'. By 2005, the US Bureau of Justice Statistics listed almost 82,000 prisoners confined to 'restricted housing'.

To ISIS, the suicide bomber was seen as 'God's holy weapon', but the West had different ways to impose a secular hell. The ultimate form of deprivation is not the unending silence of the grave, but the confinement of the soul in a tiny room. And there you must remain: unable to produce, unable to realise your potential. People in solitary have bitten off their fingers, ripped off their testicles, and even blinded themselves. About half of those in US prisons who kill themselves do so when in solitary, including biting into the arterial veins in their wrists or diving head first off their beds.

Time, too, has seeped into the management of the modern criminal in the West. The often brutal repetition of a schedule in a modern-day prison is the hallmark of its punishing nature: imagine knowing that breakfast is the same time, every day, for the rest of your life. The suicide bomber, though, is not regimented by time. Their attacks are the opposite: unpredictable and fluid. Their punishment is exacted without warning.

ISIS suicide bombers, then, by being public, savage and unexpected were intended to be a direct challenge to Western legal doctrines, part of an arsenal of punishments that sought to wrest justice from the hands of men and give it back to God.

A utopian vision, a strategy, an apocalyptic ideology – all these may have contributed to a surge of suicide attacks under ISIS, but other factors were at play too. One notable feature was how much ISIS presented itself as a vast pseudo-family – a commune for whom ISIS fighters vowed to give their life. Such a sense of bonding created a group logic that could bend individual personalities towards horrific behaviour.[69] It has long been noted that outside a group, bombers may doubt themselves. As one analysis of suicide attackers in Palestine concluded: when you got a would-be martyr alone, 'there was a lot more nuance, flexibility and doubt . . . whereas in the group they're convinced of what they're saying.'[70]

But with ISIS that sense of conviction that their sacrifice was worth it was, as with the Tamil Tigers in Sri Lanka, reinforced by a deliberate process. Communication with friends and family was cut off, music and television banned, and would-be bombers found themselves endlessly educated about the importance of jihad. Elders would lecture acolyte jihadists about the lives and deaths of previous martyrs, they would be reminded about the inevitabilities of sickness and old age. And these bonding rituals transformed jihad and self-sacrifice into something more than just a core belief in a faith; they became tradition – even a form of performance.[71] Through such means a culture of martyrdom was created.

For many, ISIS's jihad offered a fresh start. Like the Foreign Legion where you are allowed to take a new name, in ISIS the past was another country. Passports were burned, a strict dress code enforced, and then, once the initiates made their *bay'ah* – an Islamic practice of declaring allegiance to a particular leader – their sins were forgiven.

Whatever they did in a previous life (*jahiliyyah*) was wiped clean, embraced as they were by their new band of brothers.

These brothers died together. Of the fifty-one suicide bombings listed in the magazine *Dabiq*, twenty-five were undertaken by groups of bombers, implying a sense of camaraderie and unity in death. An October 2015 strike on a meeting of Saudi, Emirati and Yemeni officers in Aden was a coordinated operation by four bombers who had planned and prepared for the attack together. Backing out of such a strike would, one imagines, have been seen as a betrayal of the group, shameful for both the individual and his family. Like the kamikaze, once you had agreed to become a martyr, a loss of face in backing out might have been a powerful factor in ensuring attacks were completed.

Everywhere the search for meaning and heroism is present. With modern-day fighters, the allure of travelling to a distant land – a similar appeal that caused George Orwell to head off to the International Brigades in the late 1930s, there to fight with the Republicans against the fascists in the Spanish Civil War – is marked.[72] An *esprit de corps* is pervasive. Unlike the West, where social isolation is relatively common and the number of people living on their own has doubled in recent years,[73] communities are still very strong in many Muslim-dominant countries. Family and friends, neighbourhood chatter, influential teachers and imams, radicalised work colleagues, soccer-team jihadism, and, increasingly, the virtual dynamics of online chat rooms and social media have all created conditions where a violent ideology has the opportunity to find roots.[74] Many studies, for instance, have shown that young adults more involved in civil society were also more likely to engage in political violence, which comes as a surprise to read when balanced against the media's focus on mass shooters who all too often turn out to be angry and isolated loners.[75]

Defence of the Islamic community – the *umma* – is central to this search for meaning. One analysis found the indignation of Muslims being humiliated was present in 40 per cent of ISIS propaganda, more than in Al-Qaeda's or Jabhat al-Nusra's.[76] This sense of a permanent threat was deeply alluring, creating the idea of the underdog, rooting a sense of identity in what ISIS was not, as much as what it was (not a place of humiliation and not part of the dominant, corrupt Western order).

A community requires leadership – and ISIS found that in a man called Baghdadi. Such was the devotion he inspired that, at the beginning of 2017, ISIS used seventeen suicide car bombs to help him flee Mosul. And many more suicide bombers have pledged allegiance to him; before a Syrian national launched an attack in Ansbach, Germany in July 2016, killing himself and injuring fifteen others, he recorded a will where he vowed loyalty to the 'Emir ul-Mu'minin' ('Emir of the Faithful').

Who was this man for whom others would die? Born in 1971 in Samarra in Iraq, the son of illiterate farmers, Abu Bakr al-Baghdadi grew up in a simple, one-windowed home. His early life was like that of so many other Iraqi boys – he loved football and played in a team called 'the Mullahs'. One thing, however, differentiated him from the others: his voice. So beautiful was it that he would be asked to lead prayers, and he quickly gained a reputation for his extensive knowledge of the Quran. But, over time, things changed. He began to see sin everywhere, he gave up football, and retreated more and more into a life framed by a deep yearning for a glorified past. When the Americans invaded in 2003, he was a cleric in a mosque, his belly full of anger and his head brimming with a belief in the virtues of a political Islam.

By 2004, such tensions were to find form in violent attacks against the Americans, and Baghdadi was arrested for founding a militant group, Jeish Ahl al-Sunnah al-Jamaah, in the Sunni communities around his home city. At thirty-three years old, he was sentenced to four years in Camp Bucca, both a prison and a school of Islamist terror for the 24,000 prisoners there. It held two groups – extremists on the one side and former members of Saddam's army on the other – two factions that would, ultimately, conjoin to form ISIS. Both were realising, at the time, that the US invasion, sold as a war of liberation, was rapidly becoming a grinding occupation.

Within that prison, Baghdadi began to frame an articulation of wholesale terror. Outside the penitentiary walls he saw just filth and corruption that urgently needed to be cleansed. 'Degradation,' he once said, cannot be erased, 'except by sacrificing souls and lives, spilling blood, scattering carnage, skulls, martyrs and injured all along the way.'[77] Others in the jail began to defer to this fierce orator, a man who believed the teachings of the Quran could not be interpreted, but had to be read literally. He was cold and aloof, a man who could claim direct lineage to the Prophet Muhammad and who possessed a sort of detached self-assuredness. That, and the PhD he held in Islamic studies from the Islamic University of Baghdad, meant he was a force to be reckoned with.

When al-Zarqawi was killed in June 2006, Baghdadi was eventually to step into his shoes. He had smuggled out of prison, written in his underpants, the contact details of potential allies for the forthcoming jihad. Phone numbers were called and, pretty soon, Baghdadi was heading up a crew of killers. He then approached the Baathist fragments of the old rule – ideological enemies who had a common hatred of the US and the Shia-led Iraqi government – and the idea of an Islamic State began to take shape.

Soon he was to develop a reputation as a hard-nosed battlefield strategist, making him an attractive option to jihadists searching for a fight. He clearly had enough charisma to persuade people to die for his cause. ISIS's first claimed suicide attack was on 6 August 2006, just two months after Baghdadi's release from prison. More followed, and in their first five years, the Islamic State of Iraq was to launch over a hundred suicide attacks, all in Iraq, with almost 2,200 people killed and a further 6,000 wounded, about half of them civilians.

By 2011, the US recognised the importance of the man behind this threat and offered $10 million for his capture or death. The clamp-down that followed was severe and, increasingly, the group found it hard to operate in Iraq; in 2007 they carried out thirty-three suicide attacks there, in 2012 it was just eight. Undeterred, they were to find fertile ground in neighbouring Syria, and the suicide bomb virus was spread yet again. The rising dissent in Syria against Assad offered an opportunity for Baghdadi to capitalise on, and he sent jihadists to Syria to help foment civil war. His aim: to establish a caliphate and, in so doing, to control both sides of the Iraqi–Syrian border.

In 2013, there were four suicide strikes in Syria; in 2014, there were forty-nine. And just as the newly formed Islamic State in Iraq and Syria (ISIS) gained ground in Syria, it found its teeth again in Iraq, too: 2014 saw the group launch at least 130 suicide attacks there. A foothold had been established, so much so that, in July 2014, when Baghdadi climbed the *minbar*, or pulpit, of the Grand Mosque of al-Nuri in Mosul to anoint himself as leader of a new caliphate, thousands followed his call. After all, he fulfilled the necessary pre-conditions of being the caliph: he was – as it was decreed the caliph must be – not disfigured, his lineage was sound, and he had the bearing of a leader. He offered not just brutality, but an alternative exercise of power to an existing system that so many young jihadists felt failed by. He promised to 'trample the idol of nationalism and destroy the idol of democracy'.

This is not to paint a picture of a moral man. Baghdadi has a cold and cruel heart; he has reportedly raped women, including the Ameri-can hostage Kayla Mueller and a fourteen-year-old Yazidi girl.[78] But such things were, to many ISIS fighters, part of the spoils of war – sex-slaves were common and violence was virtue. It is incontestable that his allure worked on many. In 2017, I managed, via an interpreter, to speak to an ISIS bomber who was preparing for his final mission in Syria. What emerged in that encrypted conversation was that the bomber was doing it because of his fierce loyalty to Baghdadi; he would, he said, die gladly for the caliph. And he did. 'He is our father,' the man said, 'I do what I do for him, and for Allah.'

There is one final and crucial attribute for being a successful cult leader: the art of survival. Despite being the world's most wanted man, Baghdadi has managed to escape death many times. Of the forty-three founding members of ISIS, as of May 2018, Baghdadi is the last man standing.[79] In part this is because he, like the Tamil Tiger Prabhakaran, lives in the shadows. He, unlike those he said he would lead, clings to life.

Alongside visions of utopia, strategic logic, apocalyptic signalling, notions of punishment and cultish brainwashing, the final element of ISIS – in my eyes – that led it to create 'the perfect storm' of suicide attacks was because it was a shadowy product of globalisation.

On a basic level, this is down to the fact that ISIS's ranks were made up of Tunisians, Iraqis, Syrians, Emiratis, Russians, Dagestanis, Egyptians, Chechens and Moroccans, among others.[80] Even German, Australian, Irish, British and French jihadists had blown themselves up in a dusty street in Syria and Iraq, with nationals from the West making up 7 per cent of the volunteers. Saudis reportedly made up an astonishing 60 per cent of ISIS suicide bombers in Iraq,[81] while a very high number of Tajik fighters also joined the suicide brigades. In all, it is believed that ISIS recruited men from over eighty countries.[82]

Even the mujahidin in Afghanistan did not boast such a diverse set of volunteers, and certainly not so many willing to blow themselves up. So, while ISIS can trace its ideological heritage and leadership to Al-Qaeda, along with ideas of political Islam that emerged in Egypt in the 1960s, its rise in recent years has been fuelled by other, broader influences.

Cheap flights and increased global migration patterns, the embracing of social media, the politics of identity, alienated post-modern youth – all the hallmarks of globalisation can be seen in ISIS. The most notable of these, in a sense, has been the role of social media and the smartphone in ISIS's ascent. As a recruitment tool and a disseminator of its terror, the ability of terror groups to circumvent state-ordained broadcasting companies has meant the digital lens has become intrinsic to the suicide bomber's act.

Weeks after its capture of Mosul in 2014, ISIS began to push out those videos of suicide attacks, their calls to arms and their tweets in a flood. They were striving to popularise their brand in an avalanche of media, inject themselves into a global conversation and, in turn, force any rival jihadist groups into the shadows. At their height, they were releasing thirty-eight new items per day, including full-length documentaries, photo essays, audio clips and pamphlets, all in a range of languages.[83]

Admittedly, despite its notoriety, the ultra-violence for which the group is notorious formed but a fraction of its overall media output. Portrayals of public works projects, civil society events and economic development were as likely to appear in their offerings as suicide bombings; *Dabiq*'s issue 9, for instance, included a glossy four-page spread on healthcare in the caliphate. Nonetheless the darkness dominated for, in terms of view count, military operations and martyrdom videos were always ISIS's most popular content. The group's media wing, al-Furqan, understood this and embraced the status of a violent pariah.[84] They spent extensive time filming operations, using multiple cameras to record suicide attacks from different angles and even attached GoPro cameras to AK-47s and sniper rifles to give viewers a video game-like first-person view of the action.

They also maximised the reach of these films by using multiple platforms – Facebook, YouTube, Tumblr, Telegram to name just some – in a saturation bid. During the offensive on Mosul in 2014, their Twitter followers generated 40,000 tweets in a single day, with at least 45,000 pro-ISIS accounts online in those autumn months.[85] And, at its height, a third of those handles were extolling the value of martyrdom.[86]

The territorial collapse of the Islamic State, though, put paid to this outpouring. By December 2017, its media output was 90 per cent down from the pinnacle of the so-called caliphate in the summer of 2015. Lost territory, jihadist lives and even sense of direction in the organisation has rendered it a shadow of its previous media self. Once obsessed with a utopia born from a millenarian struggle, its output has become more infused with what has been described as 'military denialism' – militant and rebellious, holding the caliphate up as an embattled but still defiant pseudo-state.[87] But it is clear that, for the moment at least, the writing is on the wall.

Their surge of suicide bombers did not, in the end, break down the walls that ISIS sought to destroy. But, then again, it might be too soon to say what real damage they truly caused.

Chapter 10

On Europe's Shores

On 17 October 2017, the BBC led the news with the story that ISIS's 'capital' had fallen to US-backed forces.[1] Raqqa had been 'liberated'; the Syrian Democratic Forces – a military coalition made up of Kurdish People's Protection Units and smaller Arab factions, helped by US-led coalition air strikes and special forces – had driven ISIS from its heartland.

Undoubtedly, the victory was hard won. Aerial footage showed Raqqa as a skeleton city, a mottled landscape of debris and dust.[2] High-rises had had their facades ripped off, homes crushed by air strikes were now just piles of rubble. Rumour had it the town's feral cats, surviving on corpses, had begun to go bald, and its urban birds had lost their feathers. The war had stripped everything of life, and the images broadcast around the world of the devastation rekindled that quote from the Vietnam War: 'It became necessary to destroy the town to save it.'[3]

In the final days, reports emerged of 500 ISIS female fighters lying in wait, armed with suicide vests – ready to wage a last-ditch battle. But such suicide bombers could not turn back the tide. While ISIS still held some footholds along the Euphrates River Valley, the terror group had been broken.

From that wreckage, though, rose the question: what was to become of the surviving 30,000 foreign fighters who had once joined ISIS's ranks? The fear was that, with the caliphate destroyed, these jihadist fighters would return to their birth countries and bring the dogs of war with them. Many might be forced to remain in Syria and Iraq; when some jihadists burned their passports, they burned their bridges. But others were intent on returning, as the BBC article that proclaimed ISIS's defeat was to conclude: 'For all the reasons that brought it about, [ISIS] and everything it represented will still be around in one form or another for a very long time to come.'[4]

It was of little surprise to read, the same day ISIS was said to be defeated, a different, less reassuring BBC headline: 'MI5 boss Andrew Parker warns of "intense" terror threat'.[5] The UK's intelligence service chief said there was 'more terrorist activity coming at us, more quickly'. The British secret service had 500 live operations looking at 3,000 individuals involved in extremist activity in the UK alone; the intensity of counterterrorism operations was the highest Parker had seen in his thirty-four-year career. The next month he said he was expecting some of the 800 Britons who had joined ISIS to return. Later, he claimed that between April 2017 and May 2018, a dozen ISIS attacks had been thwarted in Britain.[6]

It was not just the British authorities that feared returning suicide bombers. A leaked internal French anti-terror police report relayed there were as many as ninety 'kamikaze terrorists-in-waiting' already in the EU, preparing to attack.[7] In July 2017, Interpol circulated a list of 173 suspected members of ISIS, all supposedly trained to mount suicide attacks in Europe,[8] and NATO's Secretary-General, Jens Stoltenberg, said the West was facing its 'biggest security challenges in a generation.'[9]

Although it is important to take such official warnings with a pinch of salt – nothing wins the hustling for tight government budgets like a terror threat – these concerns were not unwarranted. Some of the suicide bombers who had struck both Paris and Brussels had entered Europe having been trained in northern Syria by ISIS. According to one of ISIS's fighters, the terror group had invested 'a lot in sending their people to Europe, and it won't be over soon'.[10] It was a threat articulated by another ISIS fighter: 'When we descend on the streets of London, Paris and Washington . . . not only will we spill your blood, but we will also demolish your statues, erase your history and most painfully, convert your children'.[11]

Concern about returning jihadists was just part of the problem. Yes, a few times men had been able to travel back to the heartlands of Europe to wreak havoc, but of the dozens of attempted or realised jihadi attacks that had already occurred within the EU, most had been by 'lone wolves' who had pledged allegiance to the group from afar. Since 9/11, there have been twenty-two suicide bombers in Europe – all either born or resident there, and all but one were Islamist extremists.[12] There have been other attacks: bombs detonated among unwitting commuters; unprovoked stabbings; people mown down by trucks and vans; journalists and concertgoers murdered with semi-automatic machine guns. But the other problem was that the suicide bombings of Europe have been some of the most shocking and disturbing attacks the West has seen since the Second World War. By targeting busy cities, their explosions, as well as their preceding gunfire, have killed or injured over 2,676 people.

It has been a spate of attacks that has coincided with ISIS's rise and fall. Over half of all Europe's suicide bombings have been since November 2015, and they have been responsible for two-thirds of the damage. These suicide attacks caused a tsunami of concerns: the challenges of multiculturalism; the security risks implicit in accepting refugees; the role of Islam in the West; and, again and again, questions about what would drive men to commit such harm. Why would they do this? What compelled them to die for a cause that was often so nebulous, so distant?

Remembering the Manchester dead

Since the 7/7 attacks on London, hundreds have tried to articulate what these men's attraction to jihad was, each seeking to understand this new threat on Europe's shores. And all too often their answers say as much about the people doing the asking (and their funders) as it does about the men who took lives so resolutely on Europe's streets. Economists see factors of unemployment and poverty; humanitarians see disadvantage, discrimination and racial hostility at play; ardent nationalists see incompatibilities with the West's way of life; atheists, and holy men, see dark religious influences; liberal sociologists see the alienated and dispossessed; psychologists see depressives.

Reading through the analyses, I remembered that Whitmanian phrase: 'I am large, I contain multitudes' – a multitude of explanations that might all be partly true and still not wholly sufficient. In the end, even the families of six of Europe's bombers said they had no idea what caused their sons to do what they did; the lawyers for the Moroccan family of Najim Laachraoui, the man who was part of that attack on Brussels in March 2016, said that 'for them, Najim has been dead for three years'.[13]

I felt that the best way to navigate through this confusion was to seek something physical: to interrogate the very places that gave birth to such terror, so far from the heartlands of Islam. Not what drove men to travel to Syria and Iraq to give up their lives there, but what led men to pick up arms in the Western countries they called home. So I decided to travel to a city that has been a notable source of Europe's jihadist threat: the minster town of Dewsbury in West Yorkshire.

A number of places have become centres of Islamist extremism across Europe. In the UK, Luton, Birmingham, Portsmouth, High Wycombe, Barking in east London, Shepherd's Bush in west London and Manchester have all produced foreign fighters. In Belgium, Molenbeek produced both one of the Paris suicide bombers and the presumed mastermind of those attacks, Abdelhamid Abaaoud, along with a raft of other jihadists. In France, the *banlieue* of Sevran has been called a 'caliphate 40 minutes from Paris',[14] while Nice and the southern town of Lunel have often been cited as centres of concern. In Germany, 43,185 people are said to be members of Islamist groups – many coming from Bremen, Wuppertal, Remscheif and Solingen – all major centres of textile manufacture – as well as others from Dinslaken, Hildesheim, Wolfsburg, Braunschweig, Würzburg, Ansbach and Nuremberg – the last three lying within a 65-kilometre radius of each other.

Given there are so many cities of concern across Europe, choosing just one place to find answers to why Europe has produced twenty-one Islamist suicide bombers who died with '*Allahu Akbar*' on their lips was always going to be a difficult thing to do. Britain has produced many jihadists of Pakistani descent; France and Belgium have had many with Tunisian and Moroccan roots; Germany has seen many individuals with Syrian and Iraqi backgrounds;[15] while in America the Uzbek immigrant community has been the focus of attention, after five fatal terror incidents have involved people with links to that Central Asian country.[16] Even going to all these countries would still not provide all the answers.

But Dewsbury seemed as good a place as any to start, not least because a day before I set off, two men there had had midnight raids on their homes, arrested on suspicion of 'the commission, preparation or instigation of acts of terrorism'. It led the *Sun* newspaper to report: 'Cops "foil terror plot on British leisure centre"'.[17] The *Daily Mail*, meanwhile, focused on the part of Dewsbury where the arrests took place: Savile Town. That area, it reported, 'has gained notoriety as a hotbed of Islamist extremists in recent years, being home to Britain's youngest convicted terrorist and the 7/7 mastermind'.[18] The arrested men, it turned out, were innocent – released a few days later, without charge – but few papers mentioned that.[19] To the nation, it appeared that Dewsbury had just produced yet more devotees of terror.

'Suicide bombing seems to have become a new Yorkshire tradition' was a typical headline about the town.[20] The *Daily Mail* had also previously run a story called: 'Where even the ice cream lady wears a burka: how Dewsbury, the once great textile town of the North, has undergone a terrifying transformation'. The text said that 'Dewsbury has become a breeding ground for ISIS jihadis'.[21]

It seemed there was something of deep concern about this former mill town. Three of the four suicide bombers who had murdered fifty-two people in London in July 2005 had come from nearby. It had produced Britain's youngest suicide bomber, Talha Asmal, who was just seventeen when he and three others blew themselves up in 2015, attacking Iraqi forces near an oil refinery south of Baiji, killing eleven. Talha had travelled to Iraq with Hassan Munshi, the brother of Britain's youngest convicted terrorist Hammad Munshi, another Savile Town resident.

Savile Town seemed, in the popular imagination, to be the epitome of the sort of place where extremism could flourish. It had seven mosques, some of which occupied the space of pubs long closed down. The town also boasted a sharia court, criticised in a House of Lords report for discriminating against women in divorce proceedings. As the polemicist Rod Liddle would have it, the place was 'a little quadrant of hell created by arrogant, deluded, well-meaning white liberals infused with the multicultural ethos'.[22]

At first glance, it was hard to see what the fuss was about. The town, built beside the slow-flowing River Calder, had once housed the cheap labour that did the backbreaking jobs of the wool mills in the late 1950s. The rows of terraced houses were the same as any town in Yorkshire: tan stone and neat lines that spoke of history and tradition. The road signs reflected this heritage; Mill Street was the main artery, while around it ran streets with solid, naturalistic names: Headfield, Thornhill, Warren, Pentland. When I visited, the main road was lined with hairdressers and chippies, vets and supermarkets. Washing hung from garden lines, and the air was filled with the tinkling sound of an ice cream van playing 'Greensleeves'. This was very much England.

But, after a while, you began to see signs of a culture that was not native to Yorkshire. Indian and Pakistani immigrants had come here to toil in those dark, satanic mills, and others had followed them, bringing their customs, their faiths. The boys walking to lessons at the mosque's *madrasah* school wore distinctive Islamic clothes, variants of the shalwar kameez from the Indian subcontinent. There were young girls wearing hijabs, laughing on the swings. And there were women, too, surrounded by their skipping children, walking to the shops, dressed in black niqabs.

I parked beside a tatty banner that had been hung on some railings. It spoke of a fundraising project for 'Peace', 'Tolerance' and 'Respect'; they wanted half a million pounds to renovate the Madni Masjid mosque with a 'dedicated floor exclusive for sisters'.

I got out of my car and walked towards a park bench. The sun was out, it felt like the first day of spring, and people were leaving their homes to blink in its glare, while others headed for midday prayers. Children, like in those sepia photographs of old mill towns, played in the street, kicking balls around and sitting on worn front steps, but they were not white, poor kids like in those old pictures. They were all of Asian descent.

'Watcha doin' mister?' asked a little girl, who had appeared by my car, her head wrapped in a dark blue hijab. I turned and smiled. 'Just here to visit,' I said.

'Why would you want to do that?' she asked, without malice – just the singsong words of a child, her accent of Yorkshire.

'I'm writing a book, and thought I'd write a little about this place,' I said. She nodded, thinking that was a good enough answer, and skipped away. But I felt she was asking me that question because I was out of place – there were no white people on this street. I was on that road for over four hours and did not see another Caucasian face the whole time. This seemed to be normal, too: government inspectors had recently visited a non-faith state secondary school near here and found that the Pakistani and Indian pupils there estimated the population of Britain to be between 50 per cent and 90 per cent Asian, they saw so few white British. Of the 4,033 residents there, only 48 are white Britons, and the rest are of Pakistani or Indian descent.[23]

Coming as I did from London, home to 270 nationalities and 300 different languages, different races and creeds were for me an everyday sight. But here, in Savile Town, I was struck by just how monocultural it was. And not just here: in Blackburn, Birmingham, Burnley and Bradford, voter records show wards with between 70 per cent and 85 per cent British Asian populations.

For me, these are awkward observations and are ones that have to be discussed carefully. I believe Britain has gained a great deal from immigration; my paternal grandparents were Peruvian and my father came to Britain, not speaking a word of English, in the 1950s. My grandfather, Pablo Antonio Bernal, had been a political prisoner in Lima many years ago. He was wrongfully arrested for storing bombs under his bed (they were, in fact, his sister's boyfriend's – a radical Marxist) and he had been tortured, his feet beaten until he could no longer walk. Britain offered, to him, a security and respect for human rights that he always praised. Without immigration, my family would not exist.

But, then again, not to debate immigration – and integration – in the context of European suicide bombers would lead to journalistic inquiry falling short because we know that those jihadists who have blown themselves up in the cities of Europe have all been troubled by a profound crisis of identity. Every one of those bombers had either been born overseas, or his parents had been, and theirs was a ferocious struggle of belonging and displacement.

A term often used is that of 'cultural marginalisation' – men caught between two worlds: the society in which they were raised or lived, and the ideologies and cultures of their or their parents' origin. Such tensions are unquestionably seen in the statements and videos the bombers left.[24] They railed against the racism they experienced, felt disdain for the way Western women dress, saw corruption and decadence everywhere, even among their own. As one bomber put it, his fellow European Muslims are 'too busy watching *Home and Away* and *EastEnders*, complaining about the World Cup, drinking alcohol, to care about anything'.[25]

Their sense of alienation was compounded by the fact that the majority of Europe's bombers did not integrate into the wider, indigenous community.[26] It is hard to know their private lives fully, but few appear to have had white friends. Then again, how could they, I thought, when their neighbours were – like here in Dewsbury – non-white, and the local white community didn't make an effort to mingle (and why should they, you might ask). Salafi-jihadism offered them the warm embrace of an identity they had never felt in Europe.[27]

Here, in Savile Town, you could see such 'cultural marginalisation' at work. The Muslim community had done what many an immigrant diaspora has always done: stuck together. Liverpool is home to the first Chinatown in Europe; New Malden in south-west London houses some 20,000 Koreans; London has more than 800,000 British Jamaicans, many in Brixton. But Muslim communities like this one in Savile Town were different from Chinatowns or Little Koreas, because an association with terror had tainted these streets. This is the legacy of the suicide bomber: the coverage they garner, and the fear they engender, contaminates and spreads, labelling and pointing accusatory fingers along the way.

The major problem with such a tainting is that the Muslim community in Britain is one of substance, numbering over four million people – about one in twenty citizens. Between 2001 and 2011, the number of people identifying themselves as Muslim grew by some 1.2 million people, more than any other group in the UK. This was an expansion primarily fuelled by immigration and higher birth rates. Other parts of Europe have seen similar growth levels, with over a million Muslim refugees from Syria recently entering Germany. Between 2010 and 2016, the Muslim population of Europe rose by six million; a 'medium' migration prediction claims that Muslims could reach 11.2 per cent of Europe's population in 2050.[28] That growth, and the implication that it might bring greater terror threats, fuels populist fears.

This fear is exacerbated by the fact that conservative Islamic views are often visibly present in Asian communities. In 2016, one survey found 23 per cent of Muslims supported the introduction of sharia law instead of British laws in some areas of the country; a third refused to condemn people who would hurt those who mocked the Prophet; while four times more Muslims sympathised with suicide

bombings than the rest of the British population.[29] Though such polls
have to be taken with a measure of caution – they arguably highlight
the limitations of bias and poor questioning in surveys – they make
for potent headlines.[30]

Overall, there does seem to have been a hardening of beliefs along
'traditional markers of faith', particularly among younger British
Muslims.[31] One survey in the West Midlands found South Asian
Muslims born there are more likely to wear Islamic dress than their
parents. Some have attributed this to second- and third-generation
British-born Muslims being intensely aware of suffering experienced
by the *umma* and their responsibilities towards it.[32] Discrimination
against Muslims, both real and perceived, is a source of real frustration that heavily contributes to the identity crisis of many teenage
Muslims;[33] as one major review found, many British Muslims from
South Asian backgrounds do not feel they belong to Britain, in large
part because of xenophobia and bias.[34]

Such xenophobia has doubtless been exacerbated by the media
reporting of Muslims. The British bomber, Kabir Ahmed, who died
in Iraq, had pointed the finger at the media precisely for this, saying
the reporting on the War on Terror had contributed to a global
anti-Muslim environment. It's not an unreasonable claim: one 2015
study showed that, over twenty-five years, the portrayal of Islam and
Muslims in *New York Times* headlines was more negative than that of
cancer, alcohol or cocaine. In total, the study found no positive words
in the top twenty-five associations with Islam and Muslims.[35] You
could argue these features were reflecting the violence perpetrated
by Muslims so what else could the paper do, but such a deluge of
leaders and reports (including, perhaps, even this book), undeniably
play a part in making some Muslims feel they are a set-upon minority.

These tensions are further heightened by European political controversies such as banning or criticising the wearing of burkas and
the burkini. More recently, the US 'Muslim travel ban', led former

President Barack Obama to warn President Donald Trump about the consequences of falling 'into the trap of painting all Muslims with a broad brush and [implying] that we are at war with the entire religion'.[36] The most impactful of these political controversies was the decision to go to war in the Middle East, the reverberations of which are still being felt today. Framed as a clash of civilisations by some, 'Crusaders' and 'Jihadists' pitted against each other, it is not hard to see how some might feel their Muslim identity and faith are under attack.

Retaliation for such military actions has, without a doubt, been a leading motivation in European suicide bombings.[37] As the ringleader of the 7/7 bombers in London, Mohammad Sidique Khan, said: 'Our democratically elected governments continuously perpetuate atrocities against my people all over the world . . . Until you stop the bombing, gassing, imprisonment and torture of my people we will not stop this fight. We are at war and I am a soldier'.[38]

He was not the only one to say so. In Germany, the Ansbach suicide attacker, a Syrian asylum seeker, left a video that blamed Germany's participation in the bombing of ISIS. Bilal Hadfi, one of the suicide bombers in the November 2015 Paris attacks, cried out that Western governments were killing Muslim mothers, fathers and children, and destroying their homes in their bombing campaigns.[39]

What is curious, though, is that for the most part, these were militants who had never been touched directly by war. One European bomber had seen the horrors of Iraq, one had been to a jihadist training camp in North Africa, and a few had fought in Syria, but most had never lived under the flight path of war jets, nor had they been woken by the sounds of bomb blasts. Still, they were men who felt the plight so intensely and so personally of those who did, that they would die in revenge.

Having said this, cultural isolation, anger at a perceived war on Muslims, identity crises, are complaints and slights felt by many

Muslims in Britain, and yet the vast majority of them do not retaliate with violence. So, the fact that Islam in Europe has homogeneous communities, or is riven with identity politics, is alone insufficient to explain the rise of the suicide bomber there.

Why was it, then, that here in Savile Town some boys and men were so radicalised? And why were some of those prepared to die for their beliefs? And, more importantly, why were 99.99 per cent of the Muslim community in the UK not driven to such violence? I needed to focus beyond the wider Muslim community, to look for more specific explanations.

Poverty is often cited as a driver of extremism, and it was not hard to see poverty here in Dewsbury's streets. Walking down Foundry Street in the city centre an hour or so before, I noted a Ladbrokes, Subway, Age UK, Greggs, and Money Shop. Thirty per cent of local businesses here had shut down in recent years, and the Polish woman running a store in Dewsbury's city centre complained that business was so slow she was thinking of returning to Kraków. The city Arcade, once a handsome line of shops, had been closed down long ago, and loose gravel and chip wrappers swirled in front of its dirty, empty windows. I stopped outside one of the nearby estate agents – devoid of customers – and saw you could get a three-bedroom house here for £50,000.

If Dewsbury was poor, Savile Town seemed poorer. Poverty, where it exists in the UK, tends to hit South Asian communities harder than most. One in ten adults from a Pakistani or Bangladeshi background is unemployed, compared with one in twenty-five white British people. Sixty per cent of women from Pakistani and Bangladeshi backgrounds are out of work, making them the least likely of any ethnic minority in Britain to be employed as adults. Such communities also disproportionately live in the most deprived areas in England: the most depressed tenth of England, economically speaking, is home to a third of all Pakistanis and Bangladeshis.[40] So it may have been easy for me to note the house prices in Dewsbury, but even these were out of reach for many; Pakistanis are more likely to rent than any other ethnic group in the UK.

Work here, what there is of it, is often low-paid or low-skilled. In Britain, one in four Pakistani men are taxi drivers, while two in five Bangladeshi men work in restaurants. And, as with all cultures, where there is poverty, other ills will flow. Drugs, alienation, marginalisation, depression may not be the four horses of the apocalypse, but they can certainly create a fertile environment for jihadist recruitment. The low-level poverty seen here in Dewsbury bore the same patina of everyday despair I had seen in run-down Muslim neighbourhoods in Brussels, France and Germany.

In general, Muslim minorities in Europe are ranked among the lowest of all economic groups, while the rate of unemployment remains high – sometimes twice the average – among Muslim youth. Most of Europe's Muslims are employed in low-skilled and low-paid jobs, and it was not that much different with Europe's suicide bombers. Three of them were electricians, but most of the rest were struggling with financial difficulties long before they decided to die for their faith. Seventeen of the twenty-two bombers were unemployed when they died.

While it would be easy to conclude from this that unemployment was a driving force in terrorism, many of these bombers rejected Western beliefs of capitalism and employment, so their lack of jobs might be reflective of their ideological stance, as opposed to a causal factor for violence. Nonetheless, those jihadists who were unemployed before joining ISIS's ranks were more likely to tick the tag 'suicide bomber' when they filled out their application forms than employed volunteers.[41] This is in line with studies that have shown that young men with skills and training who cannot find work are more likely to justify violence as a means to an end.[42]

Alongside poverty, a lack of access to tertiary education may also have had an impact.[43] Fifteen of Europe's suicide bombers did not finish their higher education or go to college. This observation, however, cannot paint a full picture; a third had been enrolled at university, some of whom were interested in studying sharia and Islam. Radicalism and violence have had a long tradition in universities, and some studies have found that more educated Salafists are also more prone to violence, so it would be wrong to say that suicide bombers are just those suffering from low levels of education. Of those jihadists who did have higher levels of education, many studied natural sciences, mathematics or technology. It has been suggested that a more binary, 'black-and-white' approach taken in these subjects means that a 'good-and-evil' jihadist narrative is somehow more attractive.[44]

There has been considerable focus on Islamic education and the specific role that it has played in the rise in terror in Europe. It is clear why some journalists are worried about that link: in the UK, there are an estimated 2,000 *madrasahs* – religious centres of Islamic teaching – attended by more than 250,000 British Muslim children.[45] A significant proportion of the financing of these *madrasahs* and private schools has come from overseas funders – particularly Saudi Arabia – from those seeking to promote the messages of Salafism and Deobandism, a revivalist movement within Sunni Islam. In February 2018, such funding and influence led the chief inspector of Britain's schools to warn of the danger of supported faith schools actively perverting education. She called for 'muscular liberalism' to combat those who, 'under the pretext of religious belief . . . use education institutions, legal and illegal, to narrow young people's horizons, to isolate and segregate, and in the worst cases to indoctrinate impressionable minds with extremist ideology'.[46]

On the way here, I had driven past a school called the Paradise Primary. While there is no suggestion it has been implicated in extremism, their curriculum was certainly steeped in the Islamic faith: 'As part of our Ramadan challenge,' one school announcement said, 'children were encouraged to learn the 99 names of Allah.'[47] Other schools in the area took this legitimate religious focus to the next, more worrying, stage. In 2015, it was reported that the 'Institute for Islamic Education' in Dewsbury had told parents their children faced expulsion if they associated with non-Muslims. Documents handed to parents said that pupils were forbidden from 'socialising with outsiders'.[48]

But are these worries and concerns too knee-jerk? I believe so. I have not seen any evidence that Europe's suicide bombers were graduates of such faith schools – none at all. The problem seems more that such schools offer a visible presence that, in the media fury that follows a terror attack, provides a ready target. Given such establishments rarely let journalists in, and that what they preach is often hidden from view, their existence in areas that have been linked to extremism gives rise to such concern.[49] Again, the death of the suicide bomber leads to the living being accused, perhaps too forcefully, in their ghostly stead.

The concerns surrounding education have been sufficient, though, for the UK government, and others around Europe, to launch campaigns seeking to address the radicalisation of Muslim youth. One major initiative has been the 'Prevent' campaign, designed to stop people at risk from joining extremist groups. About twenty people a day were referred to the scheme in 2016, with about half of them fifteen years old or under. In cases where ideology was noted, just over half were related to Islamist extremism (then again, the majority of referrals led nowhere and were dismissed). The UK government says its strategy is working; that 150 people, including 50 children, were stopped from heading to Iraq and Syria because of it. But the Muslim Council of Britain and the National Union of Teachers say it makes Muslim students feel persecuted and more open to radicalisation as a result.[50]

If education, though, was not a consistent factor in the radicalisation of Europe's suicide bombers, did mosques play a part? After all, for all the bombers a professed faith was front and centre. Salman Abedi, the Manchester bomber, murdered those children 'out of a love of Islam', his sister claimed.[51] The London bomber Mohammad Sidique Khan said: 'Our religion is Islam . . . This is how our ethical stances are dictated.'[52]

Seeking answers, I walked over to one of the many mosques in Savile Town, conscious of the fact that mosques have been seen to be so pivotal in radicalisation in Europe. The former French Prime Minister Manuel Valls called for a temporary ban on foreign funding of French mosques[53] and shut down twenty of them on suspicion of their preaching radical Islam.[54] The Belgian prime minister announced a similar threat of closure in 2015.[55] And in Vienna in 2017, seven mosques were closed, an authoritarian position that did not stop the Austrian city from being declared the world's most desirable city to live in the following year.

Bans and closure, though, are very much the exception; the defence of free speech and the right to practise religion in Europe prevents such practices. In Britain, some of the more fire-and-brimstone imams and ideologues came here because the ideas they once expounded in their birth countries were considered too dangerous.[56] And these are men who, according to a UK government report, 'are keen to take religion backwards and away from 21st Century British values'.[57]

Undercover footage has captured imams in Britain saying: 'We love the people of Islam and we hate the people of kuffar (meaning infidels)!',[58] and calling for adulterers, gay men and apostates to be murdered. As one imam was heard to cry out: 'Kill him! You have to kill him, you understand. This is Islam.' And those imams who talk of love, not murder, have been threatened in turn.[59]

In 2017, one imam called Kamran Hussain was imprisoned for preaching to children in a mosque about eighty miles south of

Dewsbury, that 'martyrdom was the supreme success, greater than any other success'.[60] In 2018, twenty-five-year old Umar Haque was also found guilty of training up children to attack as many as thirty landmarks across London. When his sentence was handed down, Haque cried out from the dock: 'You will clearly see Islamic State establish itself in the Arabian peninsula and that droughts will affect Europe and America.'[61]

Given it only takes one person to become a suicide bomber, even a handful of such preachers can have a concerning influence.[62]

The mosque I went to visit was called the Masjid-e-Umar – a two-storey, dun-coloured building in the heart of Savile Town. I had asked for an interview before I arrived, but the phone had only been answered once, and I was told to call back. It had been like this in many mosques in the area – there was an evident reluctance to speak to journalists. Walking in, the immediate sensation was of silence. The carpets here were thick and this, combined with heavy curtains and solid walls, stifled all sound. Men were still praying inside, and, taking off my shoes to place them in the neat rack that lined a wall, I asked if I could speak to the imam. A young man dressed in black came out, his chin covered with a wispy beard. Yes, he was the imam, but he wasn't able to speak, he said, he had to go to work. Perhaps I could talk to Ekbal, and he pointed out an older man still focused on his prayers beyond the partition glass, and with that, he was gone.

After a while, Ekbal Ibrahim Patel came out and, following a few words explaining my purpose, he led me into a small back room filled with prayer mats, bottles of water, chairs and children's lap desks. Born in Malawi, he had been living here in Dewsbury for almost fifty years, but even now, at sixty-one, his accent was unmistakably Indian. He was considered a sort of spokesman for the mosque's community, he said. Wearing a shalwar kameez, he tucked his bare feet under the chair and nodded for us to begin.

The Masjid-e-Umar mosque in Dewsbury

I asked him about himself. He ran a company selling mass-spectrometry scientific instruments up the road, with assets approaching half a million pounds, and prayed five times a day in this mosque. Cutting to the chase, I asked him about the issue of extremism in the mosques in Dewsbury, and why so many men from here had been implicated in terrorism.

'It's totally misrepresented,' Ekbal said, '99.99 per cent of mosques in West Yorkshire is mainly to preach the ways of Islam and to teach people how to read Quran,' he said. 'Politics never comes into mosque. The mosque would not allow it.'

If the mosque was not at fault, then, I asked him, why have there been more than a few jihadists coming from the region? 'It is a misrepresented meaning of jihad,' he said. 'The younger generation are using the wrong word, which has nothing to do with what it is meant to.'

This was a valid point. Jihad to most Muslims means an inner struggle, not an outer, violent one, but, I said, it can't be denied that suicide bombers do die with the word jihad on their lips, surely? No, he replied, the problem was that everyone assumes nowadays that Muslims are doing it, but they could be Hindus, Christians or atheists.

'Islam is the most growing religion in the world,' he said. 'Politically, do they want it to continue? Or do they want to stop it?'

I was confused. He seemed to be saying that governments were somehow complicit in the suicide bombers' rise, seeking to trim the rising wings of the Islamic faith. To me, it sounded like a conspiracy theory and, certainly, conspiracy theories play a powerful part in the context of suicide bombers. A few years ago, I had been invited on to a news show in Islamabad to talk about terrorism in Pakistan; it was an influential weekly show, one even respected.

'So, Mr Overton, thank you for coming here to discuss the pressing issues of the day,' the interviewer had said, using the florid and formal language the media often deploys in Pakistan. 'Isn't it true that the majority of suicide bombers in Pakistan are, in fact, Americans?'

It had left me open-mouthed, trying to tread the line between laughing out loud and answering in a way that didn't show contempt. Perhaps such questions were, in a way, predictable. Pakistan as a nation seems to have embraced the conspiracy theory. 'Bored of mundane explanations for the country's problems,' one op-ed in the largest English-speaking daily went, 'we eagerly come up with alternative theories to keep things exciting – and, more often than not, the media also joins the conspiracy chorus.'[63] And what a chorus it is: Malala Yousafzai is a CIA agent; the floods of 2010, which killed 2,000, were caused by secret US military technology; killer rats have been genetically modified to terrorise Muslims. In a world where the Pakistani government is obsessively secretive, rationalism has been flung into the shadows.

It is not helped by the fact that some things that might look like conspiracy turn out to be true. The CIA did, in fact, use a polio vaccination campaign in Waziristan to spy on people there.[64] Pakistani civilians have been killed en masse by US drones despite the CIA denying this to be the case.[65] As the Pakistani Prime Minister Imran Khan has explained: Pakistanis are 'lied to all the time by their leaders. If a society is used to listening to lies all the time ... everything becomes a conspiracy.'[66]

In many ways, the conspiracy theory has become a potent recruitment tool for groups that perpetrate suicide attacks. They offer suspicions and outrages that fuel men's and women's decision to die so violently. In a way, if the suicide belt is the terrorist's ultimate weapon, the conspiracy theory is their ultimate narrative. And perhaps the most dominant of all such beliefs is of a Jewish secret society that controls the world from the shadows. One where rabbis tell their congregation to poison the waters;[67] where Jews train animals to kill and to spy, including eagles,[68] sharks,[69] dolphins[70] and vultures;[71] and where the organs of the dead are also harvested.[72]

Conspiracy theories, though, do more than create a permanent, nebulous enemy. They reinforce a sense of identity for those who feel they are under attack. They cause like-minded people to become more likely to associate with like-minded people. They force people to take extreme positions. After all, if the Jews were seeking to take over the world, and have been doing so for millennia, then surely they need to be stopped? They also help justify the use of violence, because if there *is* an eternal battle being waged, then only extreme measures can end it. As Richard Hofstadter wrote in 1964, addressing the paranoia of American politics: 'The paranoiac spokesman sees the fate of conspiracy in apocalyptic terms – he traffics in the birth and the death of whole worlds, whole political orders, whole systems in human values. He is always manning the barricades of civilization.'[73]

I felt the conspiracy theory that this elder in Dewsbury seemed to be espousing was part of that suspicion. Suicide bombers were not Muslim. The Jews were behind 9/11. ISIS was an invention by Western intelligence agencies to discredit Islam.[74] Baghdadi's real name is Elliot Shimon, and he was trained by Mossad.[75]

This distancing is, to some degree, to be expected. Few want to have their religion and cultural identity linked to something as abhorrent as the wilful murder of children using a bomb. As Raza Habib Raja, a Pakistani Muslim writing in the *Huffington Post*, puts it: 'Conspiracy theories appeal to our fundamental and deeply held conviction that a Muslim cannot do anything which would bring a bad name to Islam and lead to adverse consequences to the Muslim community.'[76] But, to me, such a distancing was dangerous; the idea that others are at fault serves to stop any attempt to address the issue directly. And they add to this permanent sense of grievance, an imagined conspiracy that can never be truly defeated.

Ekbal was still speaking. It seemed he was no longer suggesting that suicide bombers were not Muslims, but now was saying that they were pushed to it through terrible acts of violence. 'What happens when a human being gets to a state of total defencelessness,' he said, 'when his own wife or daughter is raped in front of him, abused badly, even putting a knife through their private parts? What does that human being become? He has no longer the meaning of life, and he begins hating the people who have done it to him.'

Had there been any evidence that Europe's suicide bombers' families had been raped and their families sexually assaulted with knives? No. But he was trying to find reasons for the unreasonable and his words were beginning to unravel. I noted how quickly he had taken a question about suicide bombers straight to conspiracy theories and the discussion of the mutilation of a daughter's genitals.

'The persecution of Muslims has been a factor,' he said, changing tack, 'when you see in the Middle East how Muslims have been treated. These various groups that keep forming – Al-Qaeda, ISIS

– do so in retaliation to violence. But one of the biggest culprits is the Internet, and what's available online. That is where the major problem lies.'

The issue was always somewhere else, culpability displaced. Ekbal was not an expert on suicide bombings, nor was he an elected official. But, in a way, it was revealing to hear his thoughts and opinions, ones not often recorded in the media. And he ended with another conspiracy theory.

'These so-called terrorists,' he said, 'who created them? Let's find out these answers – they are not coming from an Islamic country. We need to get to the bottom of that.'

I found such words sadly inevitable: the expected denial that suicide bombers have anything to do with the community they come from. In some parts, I sympathised: diaspora communities are often encouraged to integrate; 'not making a fuss' is an implicit agreement between the immigrant and the host country. But I also found his refusal to recognise any link between these suicide bombers and either Islam or the people of Savile Town telling; there would be no public admission from the mosques of Dewsbury that there was a concern here. And perhaps that was part of the problem.

Idris was more forthcoming. A devout Deobandi Muslim who runs a mobile phone shop on the edges of Savile Town, he offered nuance where I thought I would not find any. 'These terrorists are not engaging with the community,' he said, busy fixing a phone with deft hands, 'they are not attending the mosques and there is not a mosque that I know of that would condone this stuff.'

He said that the media apportions too much to the influence of local imams and men like Ekbal. Perhaps they give these men the same weight as the Christian Church does to its priests and pastors, he said. 'Most of these imams preach in Arabic and their words are general – they don't have the competence to condemn terrorism, even. They are not community leaders; all they do is lead prayers five times a day. There is no system in place to discuss such things as suicide bombings.'

Perhaps he was right. Local mosques are rarely the end-site of radicalisation; some European jihadists travelling to Syria and Iraq rarely visited a mosque. Two of the Brussels suicide bombers, Khalid and Ibrahim El-Bakraoui, were said to have never worshipped locally at all. And despite calls for the Muslim 'community' to do something, the mosque did not foster that same sense of community as, say, the Christian church. The mosque was where you went to pray, and that was it.

'There's no single leader of Savile Town. No one who is up there who everyone else looks up to,' said Idris. He said that that the community should do more to integrate – 'it's very, very insular here' – but he was adamant that mosques were not the place to look. So, where else, then, could such radicalisation have taken place?

It felt like I was trying to take a photograph and was being forced to focus more and more. From that wide view of ethnic minorities and communities wrapped in poverty, right down to local centres of education and mosques. Until I was focusing on the very intimate and personal relationships these young British men cultivated on their road to martyrdom.

On occasion, such close connection seems to have been crucial in this regard. Some British jihadists who left to join ISIS did so with family or friends, and four of Europe's suicide bombers were siblings. The UK-born suicide bomber Fatlum Shalaku, who blew himself up in May 2015, was encouraged to go to Syria by his brother Flamur, who later died on the front line in Iraq. The Brussels attacks were by the brothers Khalid and Ibrahim El-Bakraoui. And Brahim Abdeslam, who was a bomber in the Paris attacks, planned the murders with his brother Salah, who was also supposed to blow himself up that day but ended up not detonating his device.

But explaining the road to jihad solely in terms of the influence of family would be too much. As we have seen already, there are many instances where the family express shock at their relative's actions. Some of this might be a matter of saving face. The mother of Bilal Hadfi, one of the Paris suicide bombers, said she knew nothing of her son's radicalisation, but then forgot to mention he had left for Syria in 2014. Both she and the mother of Brahim Abdeslam also said their sons had no intention of killing people, which seems curious given they had voluntarily strapped a suicide bomb to their chests.

Sometimes that mask slips. When, in 2014, Englishman Abdul Waheed Majid drove a truck bomb into the walls of Aleppo prison in central Syria, aiming to release those incarcerated there, his brother, Hafeez Majid, said he was proud of him. Had it not been for his ethnicity and religion, his brother said, he'd have been treated as a hero in Britain.

Other intimate communities can also play a role. Radicalisation in prison has often been cited as a concern: at least four European suicide bombers had previously spent time serving custodial sentences, two being apparently radicalised there. Kabir Ahmed from Derby, an hour's drive from Dewsbury, who died in Iraq in 2014, was another suicide bomber who had spent time locked up. In an interview he did for the 'ISIS show' while he was in Syria, he said that being a prisoner made him embrace jihad, how months in his cell contemplating the struggle of other Sunni Muslims in war-torn countries led him to join the jihadi cause. While Khalid el-Bakraoui, one of the Brussels suicide bombers, said he was inspired to take up jihad during his time in incarceration after having had a vivid dream during which he saw the Prophet Muhammad.[77]

Redeeming the self from old sins through the purifying explosion of a suicide attack is a theme commonly found in the narratives of suicide bombers. When a German ex-soldier convert to Islam joined ISIS and blew himself up in Iraq, the magazine *Dabiq* claimed he had once fought against Muslims in Afghanistan, and that his death redeemed him in Allah's eyes. This pattern of 'sin' and 'redemption' is consistent enough for MI5 to say that some jihadists hold a 'misguided belief that participation in jihad might help atone for previous wrongdoing'.[78]

Patterns of redemption and atonement are often seen in jihadists. Men who had previous lives of drug taking and petty crime suddenly see the light. It is a narrative that, in itself, might make the explosive light of a suicide bomb seem symbolically meaningful to the bomber – a purification by fire. In addition, while conversion to Islam is not in any sense a predictor of violence, and the majority of Western converts will never have anything to do with jihadi terrorism, it can't be ignored that Western converts are overrepresented among jihadists. Of fifty-eight individuals linked to ISIS-related plots in the West between July 2014 and August 2015, 29 per cent were converts to Islam. Converts also accounted for 67 per cent (twelve out of eighteen) of Americans involved in committing or planning an ISIS-related attack, despite comprising only 20 per cent of Muslims in the US.[79] The same pattern has been found among convicted British jihadists: converts constitute an estimated 3 per cent of Britain's 2.8 million Muslims, yet were involved in 31 per cent of jihadi terrorism convictions in the UK between 2001 and 2010.[80]

Perhaps the most infamous of these converts was nineteen-year-old Germaine Lindsay who, on 7 July 2005, boarded a Piccadilly line train in London and detonated his bomb near Russell Square, killing himself and twenty-six others, injuring hundreds more.[81] Lindsay had converted to Islam shortly after his mother, Maryam McCleod Ismaiyl, had taken up the faith in 2001. He had also married one of Britain's most infamous converts to Islam, Samantha Lewthwaite, better known as the White Widow. Another convert was Jamal al-Harith, born Ronald Fiddler, a British Islamic State fighter who carried out a suicide bombing in Iraq in 2017. Al-Harith was a former

Guantánamo Bay detainee who was released from that US detention camp in 2004 and successfully claimed compensation after saying British agents knew about or were complicit in his mistreatment.[82]

But what would lead these neophytes to a suicide bombing death – converts whose eyes had been opened wide to a violent form of jihad?

As that religious leader in Dewsbury, Ekbal, said to me, the Internet and social networks have played a role in this. ISIS successfully used this tool to convince European youth to join its ranks. For example, Talha Asmal, the young Dewsbury suicide bomber, was reportedly recruited online.

'He was certainly groomed,' one person I spoke to in Savile Town who knew the local boy, said. 'I knew him well. It was like I'd see him every day and then one day, poof, it was like someone had flipped a switch.' It is well established that social media – who you follow and who you block – creates echo chambers that can, in turn, lead the susceptible towards extreme views. The anonymity it offers leads to people saying what they feel, without fear of prosecution. This has been called 'toxic disinhibition', where people 'explore the dark underworld of the Internet, places of pornography and violence, places they would never visit in the real world'.[83]

It is, undoubtedly, a place where conspiracy theories flourish, and the logic of sacrifice might even be sown. The question, though, is this: if the Internet or computer games are behind young men becoming violently radicalised, what made them susceptible to that message? And the one thing that does seem to stand out, above all else, is their age. We know that Europe's twenty-two suicide bombers were, on average, young – the average age was a little under twenty-seven years – about nine years older than the average US white male mass shooter.[84] It is an issue of age that speaks to a sort of generational revolt, where a lack of a 'grand project' leads sec-ond-generation Muslims and native converts to see radical Islam as a deadly vehicle that fits in with their idealism.[85] It is a nihilism that speaks more to an Islamification of radicalism than a radicalisation of Islam.[86] As the French political scientist Olivier Roy has written: 'If we are truly living – in Dame [sic] Thatcher's immortal words – in a world to which there is no alternative, nihilism is exactly the form of anti-politics one would expect to find in this age of civic exhaustion.'[87]

When they say they love death more than we love life, theirs is a yearning for a radical transition, for a new *ancien régime*, a restitution of a golden age that never was.[88] Infused with a form of cultural iconoclasm, these men have such delusions of grandeur that they believe their deaths will change the world. In this way, Islam offers an appealing anti-world-order philosophy, one that the disintegrating international left-wing movements now fail to provide.[89] For men whose young lives have pasts blighted by poverty, racism, criminality, absent father figures, drug addiction and other failures, jihadism provides a sense of inclusion and group solidarity so powerful that its followers would even sacrifice their lives for it.[90]

When suicide bombers targeted Paris, then, they attacked not just a football stadium or a rock concert, but rather the ghosts of Voltaire and Napoleon, the Enlightenment and the Crusades. They were striking at the icons of Western corruption – Paris, a city described by ISIS as the 'capital of prostitution and vice'.[91]

Perhaps some of them were railing at their own vices when they died. As Daniel Koehler, a senior fellow at George Washington University's Program on Extremism, has said, ultra-violent ideologies 'explain what is wrong in your life, and tie your personal frustration into a global struggle – the global conspiracy against Islam'. This, in turn, gives people 'a chance for significance, for living out a positive, heroic life' through violence.[92]

Dewsbury, then, was only to offer up partial clues to working out why suicide bombers appeared in Europe, because the community for which they died was not in Dewsbury. It was elsewhere: a community of the imagination – a global, utopian Islamic community.

Along the way a host of factors play their parts: hermetic communities; a failure of multiculturalism; the grinding humiliations of poverty; the rhetoric of mosque and school; the role of family and friends; conspiracy theories and the Internet. But the ultimate reason someone turns to suicide bombing is a combination of the external factors of the group and the world, and the inner, psychological drives that lead them to their terrible, violent deaths. And, if we are to comprehend the age of the suicide bomber truly, it is to this world we must now turn: a journey inwards, if such a journey can ever be undertaken, a search for psychological explanations deep in the suicide bomber's mind.

Chapter 11

Inner Demons

In August 2017, President Donald John Trump took to the podium to discuss his counterterrorism strategy. In front of a wall of cameras, he was to label jihadi terrorists as 'losers'.[1] His message was clear: he would expose the 'false allure of their evil ideology', and make it self-evident they would 'find no glory in this life or the next'.

'They are nothing but thugs and criminals and predators,' he said, getting into his stride, 'and, that's right, losers.'

Losers: a fraternity epithet for a global jihad that has taken too many lives, dragged a superpower into grisly quagmires around the world and drained hundreds of billions of dollars from Western public health and education services. Yet it is a phrase that, to many, is alluring. When a suicide bomber acts, particularly if that bomber is from the West, the news pack heads to the family home, there to glean anything that might suggest the bomber was a misfit, a sociopath, a failure. The immediate instinct is to create a psychological profile of why this person chose to murder, and to die in so doing; it is far easier to package someone as a psychopathic degenerate than to explain the complex interplay of faith and fury that leads someone to kill in the way they do.

One of the first times that the phrase 'loser' was used by the US president in this context was to describe the Manchester bomber, Salman Abedi.[2] After Abedi's murderous attack in 2017, hundreds of column inches were devoted to him. We learnt of a misfit called 'Dumbo' because of his big ears, of a 'wild youth of booze and taking drugs',[3] of a man who 'wasn't a strict Muslim at all'[4] but one 'known to police for a string of crimes such as theft and assault'.[5] He was, the reporting concluded, 'not very bright',[6] a benefit scrounger who was a 'nobody'.[7]

Perhaps with Abedi such profiling was accurate, but from 9/11 onwards, the 'seedy secrets' of jihadist bombers have been a mainstay of journalism after the horrors of the event.[8] Be it the revelation a would-be suicide-bomber on the Washington Capitol had once sold ecstasy pills or been to sex clubs, or the disclosure that three of the four 7/7 London bombers had criminal records, *post hoc* reporting has always sought to highlight the hypocrisy of the martyr's myth.

Not heroes, but zeroes.

In some respects, this is what newspapers do: after a scandal, they track down people's failings and paint them in lurid colours. Theirs is the gaze of the modern panopticon – social control through exposure and ridicule. With suicide bombers the humiliation of the media 'stocks' is frustrated – only their memories can be sullied – but by painting a picture of the bomber as a failure or misfit, a sense of social control is re-established, even if such control is illusory. The narrative is that if the terrorists are the losers, then the other side must be winning.

But if you were able, for a moment, to suspend the horror of their deeds and try to examine the bomber without a surge of hatred and bile, what does such scrutiny reveal? While we have looked at the personalities of those who have encouraged suicide bombers to their deaths – men like Khomeini, Prabhakaran, Bin Laden – what of the adherents who do their bidding? Is there, indeed, a personality type of a suicide bomber?

*

The path to any suicide bombing is both a collective and an individual one. On a group level, it involves a variety of potent forces: a search for utopia; the strategic logic of violence; nationalistic fervour; charismatic leaders; seductive ideologies. Such themes can be traced with relative clarity, evident to a greater or lesser extent in the shadow of each suicide bomber.

Digging down to individual motivations, though, means we are confronted by far greater complexities – a black honeycomb of distinct needs, experiences, desires and vexations. The chemistry of the group ignites these personal urges. Very few blow themselves up without doing so under one banner or another. If a hunger striker starved to death without saying why, they would be seen as victims of pathology, like anorexia. The same applies to a suicide bomber; someone who blows themselves up without reason is reduced to psychopathy. Someone who blows themselves up for an ideology is, generally, not – despite the efforts of some to frame such terrorists purely in psychopathic terms.

The mental state of bombers is poorly understood. This might be because, as one of the few in his profession to interrogate the inner drivers towards terrorism has noted, too few psychologists 'take terrorism as their primary interest'. They 'wade in, publish a paper or two and then depart'.[9] And even then the focus has been on the surviving victim, not the perpetrator. This is inherent to the inquiry: successful suicide bombers cannot be interviewed, while survivors of their deeds often have terrible PTSD. But the result is that, as a 2017 report concludes, 'psychology cannot currently offer clear answers as to why some people become involved in terrorism when most do not'.[10]

'What is often referred to as "the radicalization process" is shrouded in uncertainty', that paper concluded, 'presented largely via metaphor, and rarely subject to the kind of rigorous, data-driven hypothesis testing one expects of psychological science.'

Into that uncertainty, some have ventured. Professor Adam Lankford, for instance, a criminology professor at the University of Alabama, goes so far as to assert that 'far from being psychologically normal, suicide terrorists are suicidal'. He believes that suicide bombers suffer from serious mental trauma and can be seen to demonstrate traits such as suicide ideation, or have formulated suicide plans or have previously attempted suicide. 'They kill themselves,' he says, 'to escape crises or unbearable pain.'[11]

Other reports had been far less assertive; when the Pakistani journalist Nasra Hassan interviewed almost 250 people who were either recruiting and training bombers or preparing to go on a suicide mission themselves in the late nineties, he said pretty much the opposite. 'None of the suicide bombers,' he wrote, 'conformed to the typical profile of the suicidal personality. None of them were . . . depressed.'[12] Another major analysis of five studies on the psychologies of bombers, also reported that 'terrorists are not truly suicidal and should not be viewed as a subgroup of the general suicide population'.[13]

So I arranged an interview with Lankford over Skype, to delve a little more into his theory. 'Many who volunteer for suicide terrorism have never engaged in terrorism before,' he said over a line that kept breaking up, 'and they have shown no interest in being "regular" terrorists . . . The people committing these attacks are mostly coming from desperate communities where mental illness is off the charts.'

To him, the jihadist image of paradise was a powerful incentive, allowing them to commit suicide without all the moral baggage that often comes from such an act. 'A large number of these bombers are religious more in name than anything else; if you have decided you wanted to die, anyone who tells you something that would make that more comforting – you would latch onto that.'

But if they were all depressed, how would they be able to motivate themselves to undertake such, often complex, attacks, I asked. After all, 9/11 took years of planning. 'There are peaks and valleys – at their lowest people don't commit suicide,' he said. 'But those who are on the uptick, they can get excited about the idea of killing themselves as it will be a relief to their pain . . . Suicide can be a rational response to wanting to escape pain and future suffering.'

Lankford was, after a fashion, lucid in his argument. He believed the strong stigma against suicide in Islam meant that many who wanted, desperately, to die chose to don the mantle of the suicide bomber to achieve that end. 'It is,' he said, 'a loophole . . . the only way to kill yourself without violating religious or cultural beliefs.'

In many ways, it is clear how Lankford comes to his conclusions: those who blow themselves up often articulate sentiments that, from a white, Western, male psychologist's perspective can only be seen as suicidal intent. They talk of the desire for a better life in the next world, they speak of apocalypses and suffering, they see their deaths as being a positive thing in a world dragged down by immorality. Liberals – including me – who are uncomfortable with labelling things as 'ideological' seek other explanations because if you begin to frame everything as such, it can lead you to intolerances of faiths that are deeply destructive.

Lankford cites one study as 'best evidence' in his claim that suicide bombers are suicidal.[14] It is a small, unblinded review of fifteen failed Palestinian bombers in Israel compared to non-suicide bomber terrorists. The Israeli study states that 'some of the would-be martyrs but none of the control and organizers groups' participants displayed sub-clinical suicidal tendencies. Significantly more martyrs than control group members displayed symptoms of depression.'[15]

So, yes, some suicide bombers certainly do have histories of clinical depression, and that is a plausible explanation. But I had a nagging feeling that Lankford believed he had found one central argument that summed up all suicide bombers and bent anything that didn't fit that narrative to his will. What about the self-immolating monks of Tibet or the IRA hunger strikers? Suicide seemed a terrible resort to some in those grinding struggles – but neither group had resorted to suicidal violence.

When I met suicide bombers who were not able to complete their missions in Sri Lanka, Lebanon and Palestine, none of them – when asked – said that they were ever unduly depressed, and all of them denied it emphatically when I asked if they might have been trying to commit suicide. Mine is a small cohort, but other studies have shown that the proportion of bombers demonstrating suicidal tendencies is just 30 per cent.[16] Some studies certainly offer nuance: Tajik suicide bombers are said to suffer disproportionately from personality disorders, while Palestinians – on the other hand – do not.[17]

Perhaps many bombers see their actions more as a lifting of a veil – a tiny prick of pain that will then immediately send them to a better world, filled with green birds of paradise. Perhaps even, weaned on video games that cause you repeatedly to die trying to complete the game, they see their deaths as a 'reboot'. It comes as no surprise that there are numerous parallels between the video game *Call of Duty* and many ISIS propaganda videos.[18]

It seems too much to say that there is a single psychological profile that can explain the motives of all suicide bombers. People become extremists for a wide variety of reasons: feelings of honour, redemption, heroism, alienation and revenge all factor into an individual's choice to carry out a suicide bombing. And when confronted by such broad reasons, some will seek singular explanations – because an enemy that you can recognise, you can defeat.

Which is possibly why, after the argument 'they are mentally ill', the next go-to suggestion by many is that suicide bombers are just off their faces on drugs.

On 6 February 2015, a suicide car bomb was driven towards a military checkpoint in Benghazi, East Libya, the birthplace of the 2011 protests that toppled Libya's former leader Muammar Gaddafi. From a distance, a jihadist filmed, with shaking hands, the last moments of one of his 'brothers'. A sharp flash of red and yellow filled the screen and, at that moment, a father and son were murdered, and twenty more civilians were injured by the echoing blast.

The driver was a young man who went by the name of Aba Talheh. When ISIS released footage of his final moments, they included an interview. It shows Aba grinning, swaying in the front seat of his vehicle, packed in on all sides by tank rounds, which he pats lovingly. He speaks about the nymphs that are soon to greet him in Paradise, and how the '*murtadeen*', or apostates, are soon to be 'shown the light' by the weapons that surround him. But the most notable thing about this video was that Aba Talheh is clearly high on drugs. His pupils are dilated, his voice slurred, his head lolling.

Undeniably, there is some evidence that drug taking has a role in some suicide attacks. It's a neat explanation for how people muster the courage to end their lives, and one that leads to reports that tramadol is the suicide bomber's drug of choice, at least according to a breathless *Newsweek* headline in 2017.[19] That article argued that a rise in trafficking of the synthetic opioid throughout West Africa and the Middle East, one often found in the pockets of suicide bombers, was destabilising the entire Sahel region. Another, more scholarly work, suggested that we were witnessing 'a new chapter in the misuse of psychoactive drugs' in suicide attacks.[20]

These claims were repeated in the *Guardian*: suicide bombers were 'plied with dates stuffed with tramadol' before being sent on missions.[21] Other reports said a 'chemical courage' drug produced in Lebanon, called Captagon, was fuelling ISIS suicide attacks in Syria.[22] One teenager claimed in a CBS interview that ISIS gave him the anti-anxiety drug Zolam before he went into battle: 'That drug makes you lose your mind,' he said. 'If they give you a suicide belt and tell you to blow yourself up, you'll do it.'[23] While another told interviewers that his jihadist 'teacher' gave him 'an injection that made him feel aggressive'.[24] The abuse of scopolamine and Pentothal, with names like Congo, Bazooka and Abu Malaf, drugs that can turn young men into mindless jihadists, has also been reported.[25]

Such reports ring a little hollow. Drugs are commonplace in conflict and their use is not exclusive to jihadist bombers. During the Second World War, methamphetamine, synthesised in Germany in 1937, was distributed by some German and Allied commanding officers to treat fatigue among exhausted troops.[26] The Third Reich was rife with drugs, especially cocaine, heroin and crystal meth.[27] The Vietnam War was also infamously filled with drug taking, the US military plying their soldiers with cocktails of amphetamines, steroids and opiates to help them endure extended combat operations.[28] So endemic was it there that the British philosopher Nick Land described that conflict as 'a decisive point of intersection between pharmacology and the technology of violence'.[29]

The use of drugs in conflict is as old as the existence of both, and certainly cannot, alone, explain the widespread use of suicide bombers. But what is as revealing, perhaps, is the reason why many journalists were drawn to the specific framing of drugs as being integral to the suicide bomber's act, as opposed to the broader reality that drugs were part and parcel of war. Perhaps, like depression, it offers a more straightforward, logical reason as to why people commit such deadly acts.

As one review of the mental state of ISIS members concluded, there was too much of a tendency to 'overuse mental health problems as a "silver-bullet" explanation for terrorist involvement'.[30] As well as fitting into the view the terrorist was not pious, clean or upright – but depraved and demonic – it also suggests that ideology is not at play. There exists a disinclination among both Western intelligence agencies and some liberal professors to concede that people might be willing to sacrifice their own lives for a cause, and a god, without being intoxicated or depressed when they do so.

The truth is that, yes, they are intoxicated, but often more on the promise of paradise than on something else. But if it is not depression or the drugs taken to ease the pain that have fuelled the suicidal martyr's rise, has it been another profoundly motivating factor: sex?

'My dear family, please forgive me,' read the handwritten letter that was found, unsent, in the dusty halls of an ISIS training compound in eastern Mosul. 'Don't be sad and don't wear the black clothes [of mourning]. I asked to get married and you did not marry me off, so, by God, I will marry the 72 virgins in paradise.'[31]

Similar words were also said by Omar al-Jazrawi, a Jund al-Aqsa-affiliated bomber who launched an attack in Hama, Syria in August 2015. His suicide bomb, he was to tell a camera lens, was 'the path to the *hourias*'. 'Ten metres from here,' he claimed, 'seventy-two *hourias* pray for us so that we can reach them.'

Then there was the seventeen-year-old Pakistani boy caught in Afghanistan wearing a bomb vest, intent on killing the governor of Jalalabad. He, too, believed his promised virgins would be at the site of his martyrdom, watching and waiting to take the bomber to paradise. They would make his dismembered body whole again so he could sleep with them.[32]

These three tales are some among many that align the male martyr's death with the paradisiacal promise of supplicant nymphs. It is a tale of seventy-two virgins that has not only preoccupied the fevered imaginations of many a modern jihadist but those of head-line writers, too. It was a promise first embraced by the modern age during the fierce fighting of the Iran–Iraq War. There, in rousing speeches on the Iranian front lines, religious officials told Shia soldiers that seventy-two virgins awaited them in the next life.[33] Those propagandists took their cue from previous teachings; the ninth-century Hadith of the Persian al-Tirmidhi said that, along with a place in paradise, instant relief from pain and terror, and being anointed with dignity, the martyr would be offered 'seventy-two wives among the *houris*, and he may intercede for seventy of his close relatives.'[34]

The *houris*, other Hadiths were to say, are 'beautiful, lovely-eyed and full-breasted' mystical beings, 'virgins' who inhabit paradise. They are mentioned four times in the Quran,[35] and it was said that the prophet declared: 'The smallest reward for the people of Paradise is an abode where there are 80,000 servants and 72 wives.'[36]

Such a prophecy, particularly in the minds of ardent Salafi-jihadists, opened the doors to unbridled fantasy. One book, *The Maidens of Jannat*, first published in Pakistan in 2002 and distributed in the UK from a shop in Leicester, promised men they would get 500 wives, 4,000 virgins and 8,000 previously married women in the next life.[37] 'The women of Jannat will be far more superior than the women of this world,' the book claims, going on to assert that 'the pleasures of Jannat will last forever.' It describes a place where you can shape-change, grow crops instantaneously, and where women's beauty derives from their being 'fair-skinned'. The maidens, it appears, are created from the spice saffron – a marked improvement on earthly humans who are made from sand. Furthermore, they will be free from impurities such as 'menstruation, urine, excreta, and saliva', being, instead, as pure as 'preserved eggs'. They will be clothed in seventy layers of cloth, and all women will be the same age – thirty-three years old – but all will permanently increase in beauty; 300 servants will bring the martyr 300 plates of food in the morning and evening; they will have sex with 100 virgins in one morning.

Above all, there will be unfettered adoration. As the book says, 'Whenever he will go to a wife, she will say to him, "I swear by Allah, there is nothing in Jannat more beloved to me than you."'

Such adoration will happen the moment the suicide bomber dies, with his wives rushing to him 'as if they are a breastfeeding camel who has found her lost child in an empty and barren land'. But all this has a price. The book even has it as a subtitle: 'The Price of Jannat'.

To receive such splendours, you have to 'fight in the path of Allah', it entreats, 'kill the enemy or [be] killed'.

Such claims, despite sounding ludicrous, appear to have wider traction in the Muslim world than many might think. After all, 96 per cent of Muslims in Turkey say they believe in angels, 99 per cent of Tunisians say they believe in Heaven, as do 88 per cent of Palestinians.[38] It has even caused ISIS wives to write poetry that talks of their worries that their soon-to-be martyred husbands might find the *houris* more attractive than them.[39]

There are, though, theological complications in such decadent visions of paradise. Nowhere in the Quran does it mention the numbers of virgins awaiting the dead. And it seems that the beautiful-eyed young women are available to all male Muslims, not just martyrs. That is, indeed, if any women are waiting at the gates at all: the Quran says there will be '*hur*' for the martyr in paradise, a word that early commentators took to mean 'virgins'. In Aramaic, though, '*hur*' means 'white', and was more commonly used to refer to 'white grapes' or 'raisins'.

Clearly, the promise of sexual delights in paradise has rooted itself deep in many a young jihadist's imaginings, one that no amount of debate on semantics or semiotics will change. One suicide bomber in Israel was found to have wrapped Kleenex tissue around his penis, reportedly because he hoped to preserve himself for those anticipated orgies in paradise.[40]

Such sexual fantasies about what awaits them in heaven might, in part, stem from the complex relationship that many Salafi-jihadists seem to have with sex. One word that regularly appears in their online posts is the Arabic word *fitna*, meaning both social chaos and seduction. The disorder they see in the world, and the temptations of sin, seem intertwined in their minds – a world where women are the physical incarnation of *shahwa* (desire), a seductress sent by the Devil.

In this way, ISIS's murder of gay men, their holding of sex-slave markets and their widespread sex with children all point to jihadists deeply uncomfortable with sex. A discomfort summed up in an edict issued by the terror group that reads: 'It is permissible to have intercourse with the female slave who hasn't reached puberty if she is fit for intercourse.'[41] And some have argued that such a discomfort with sex, an obsession with virgins in paradise, and a sexual violence that permeates much of the journalism surrounding jihadist groups, is spurred on by the fact Islam is the only dominant world religion that says its adherents can have many wives.

We do know that the impact of polygamy, particularly in traditional Islamic cultures, is to produce a large number of young men of low status who cannot find a wife. Older, wealthier men might have a second, third or fourth bride, but each time they take on a wife, it means one fewer for the younger, unemployed men in a community. Across all societies, this mismatch appears to increase violent crimes, such as murder and rape, even after taking things such as poverty and population levels into consideration. In South Asia, for instance, polygamy appears to have 'played a role in aggravating societal instability, violent crime and gang formation'.[42] In short, the more polygynous the society, the more young men face the distinct possibility of ending their lives childless, making them a prime candidate for social unrest.[43] As Christopher Hitchens said in his anti-theist polemic *God Is Not Great*, the jihadist's 'problem is not so much that they desire virgins as that they are virgins'.[44]

We know, for instance, that Umar Farouk Abdulmutallab, the twenty-three-year-old Nigerian charged with trying to detonate a bomb on a Northwest Airlines flight over Detroit on Christmas Day, 2009, was lonely and sexually repressed. 'I think I feel lonely,' he complained on an Internet forum, 'the natural sexual drive awakens and I struggle to control it.' It led the *New York Post* to report that 'the bomb wasn't the only thing burning in his pants'.[45]

However, polygyny by itself, while it might increase violence, is insufficient to explain all suicide bombings. Eighteen of the twenty most polygynous nations in the world are in sub-Saharan Africa and the Caribbean, and they are not the heartlands of suicidal terror. While those countries have very high levels of violence, such violence tends to be civil war or gang-related, often with guns, not suicide bombings. So polygyny in itself is not sufficient cause.

But that mixture of sexual frustration, youth, a lack of a partner, the belief that death is not the end, the glorification of the martyr, and the complex interplay of sexual politics can undeniably impact, even in the most unexpected of ways.

When visiting the West Bank, I had met with a man called Murad Tawalbeh. In 2002, aged just nineteen, Murad had decided to become a suicide bomber. It was a decision made after a friend of his, a young man of the same age, had been killed by an Israeli military sniper. Murad had been protesting with the teenager at the Jalameh checkpoint when his brother-in-arms had fallen, shot in the chest. There was blood everywhere.

Murad's decision was the culmination of a long road of frustration. A daily sense of injustice had cast a permanent shroud over their lives, he said, and he had seen the success of the Lebanese in expelling the Israelis with suicide attacks, so why not use that weapon here? But there were other reasons, too.

'Imagine me coming to your house, occupying your house and insisting you have sex with your mother or sister, what would you do?' he asked.

I hesitated in my note-taking because there was absolutely no evidence that Israeli troops forced people to do that. He sensed my scepticism, and so elaborated, though his example was not one of forced incest. 'During the first intifada,' he said, 'there was a checkpoint controlled by soldiers near Jenin. These soldiers stopped a taxi

Murad Tawalbeh - a Palestinian would-be suicide bomber

and picked on a guy and a girl sitting in the car, and made him kiss her. The Israeli soldiers hit the man until the girl begged him to kiss her. It's one of the things that the Israelis do to control us.'

I had heard such tales of sexual humiliation in conflict before, so I pursued the point, posing the questions raised by those who view jihad as partly a consequence of sexual frustration.

'Humanity's urge to have children is great,' I said. 'You were nineteen, you had no children, you would have died with no genetic legacy – did you ever think about that? Was there a sense you were going to leave nothing behind?'

'I didn't have the chance to live a normal life, so what I was doing was dying to give others a chance to a better life,' he replied. 'How could I get married and have children destined to live the same horrible life I was living? It would be so cruel to them.'

'So, in your eyes, that reproductive instinct was stopped,' I said, 'because you feared bringing a child into hell?'

He leant towards me – an intense man with hollowed, gaunt features – and pulled out his smartphone. Flicking through the images, he stopped at one. It was an image of a dead Palestinian baby.

'She was killed in Gaza,' he said. 'I didn't want to see my daughter or son in the same situation. If I can't protect my child, why bring it into the world?'

He pushed the image closer. 'Look at the picture, imagine this is yours, what could you do?' he said. 'When I went to carry out the attack, I left a letter for my family, and the only picture I left was this picture – Iman Haju from Gaza.' I later learnt that she was three and a half months old when an Israeli tank shell hit her grandparents' home in the city of Khan Yunis in May 2001, killing her instantly.[46]

This sounded to me like a form of punitive altruism – a sincere attempt to help others that in so doing harms others or oneself. Such misguided belief is seen by many to be a critical factor in the modern suicide bomber – indeed, the only thing on which there is 'full consensus between scholars' who have analysed the socio-psychology of suicide attacks is that defining temperament of altruism.[47]

The surge of feel-good neurotransmitters like serotonin that comes from selfless acts has been marked as a possible reason why some might die so willingly for others, driven by 'a variety of neuro-hormonal pathways and mechanisms that have only just begun to be understood.' Moreover, it spoke of the reality that nearly all suicide bombers believe that what they are doing is for the absolute good.

That image of the dead child haunted Murad so much that, even though he prays, his decision to blow himself up was motivated by that death, not his own. The tropes of Sunni martyrdom were not central to his mission: he did not shave his body; did not believe in seventy-two virgins awaiting him; did not pray excessively. He put on his best T-shirt, kissed his family as they slept, and slipped out into the pre-dawn to meet his brother, a well-known Palestinian fighter. The brother helped him put on the suicide vest – a bulky brown contraption with tubes made of iron – crying and kissing him as he did so. Murad, on the other hand, remained calm.

Did he think that his death would be a hard one, I asked.

'Death is difficult, but it is not more difficult than our life,' he said. He talked about the mission matter-of-factly. He paid seventy shekels for a taxi to take him to Haifa, arriving there at seven that morning. The town was waking up, and he waited, ordering a shawarma for breakfast, the belt strapped to him.

The crowds slowly gathered.

He got up and walked to the town's main market, intent on detonating. There, though, among the Israeli commuters and early morning shoppers, he saw a young woman with a child, barely eighteen months old, and at that moment everything changed.

'I started thinking that I am here to stop the killing of babies, so I couldn't imagine myself killing another baby,' he said. 'Immediately I left.'

He went to a barren patch of land near the market and discarded the explosive belt, but then, on returning to the town, he was arrested by Israeli police officers after they found him wandering around without a valid permit. The belt was soon discovered, and he was sentenced to seven years in prison, released on 7 April 2008: 'I spent seven years in prison in order to prevent this girl from dying,' he said.

In interviewing him, I was conscious his words could have been intentionally tuned to give a sense of humanity to Palestinian terror violence. Even though he claimed that ISIS gave Islam a bad name, I could not help but think of the many civilians Hamas had killed in their vengeance attacks, just as he reminded me of the many civilians the Israelis had killed. But what was most striking was how much the life and death of a baby motivated him; to kill and not to kill – altruism was rooted in both impulses.

Framing the humiliations of the Palestinians as he had done in overtly sexual terms, and describing how two babies influenced his failed suicide mission, made me think some potent psychological forces drove his impulses to kill and to save: cultural optics of honour and heroism, martyrdom and selflessness, fuelled by the ever-present indignities of Israeli occupation. And these were tensions that existed in him still.

I finished the interview with a final question: 'Can you imagine a time for suicide bombers to come back to Palestine?' I asked.

He said one word in reply.

'Soon.'

When it comes to sex and the suicide bomber, as ever, complex dynamics exist. How do you interpret, for instance, the curious case of the suicide bomber Abdullah Hassan al-Asiri, who on 27 August 2009, tried to kill Muhammad bin Nayef Al Saud, a prominent member of the House of Saud, at his home in Jeddah?

The bomber, who had concealed an explosive device in his rectum, detonated the device, killing himself and wounding bin Nayef. The standout part of the story is that his teacher had told the bomber that the only way he would be able to conceal sufficient explosives in his anus was to loosen the sphincter walls. To do this, al-Asiri had let his teacher regularly sodomise him.[48]

With this attack, what was the motivation? Was it the promise, as stated by the bomber, of seventy-two virgins? Or was al-Asiri gay and this was a way of dying as a hero without facing the opprobrium of family? Or, like Murad, was it because he didn't want to build a life for himself in this corrupted world? Or was he sexually abused and subsequently suicidal?

Such sexual complexities seem to dominate in the current surge of Salafist suicide bombings. Yes, there are some stories of kamikaze pilots visiting sex slaves before their deaths in the Second World

War; one so-called 'comfort woman' remembered how one of the
pilots, despite raping her each time they met, said he was in love
with her, and that she had given him a venereal disease. 'He said he
would take the disease to his grave as my present to him,' she recalled
years later.[49] But for many, if not most, kamikaze, the honour codes
they adhered to meant they flew to their deaths as virgins. Indeed,
perhaps recognising just how many virgins there were, the Japanese
government arranged for groups of very young girls and women to
gather at kamikaze airbases, there to ease the pilots' fears before their
missions, repair their uniforms and serve them their last meals. These
women were to become known as the Nadeshiko, after the pale-pink
blossoms they threw at the departing planes, and were perhaps fan-
girls and mother substitutes in the eyes of those about to die – but
they were not nymphs.

That promise of virgins firmly resides in the fevered imaginings
of today's jihadists. Then again, the idea of virgins and suicide
bombers inflames wide curiosity and prurience. The 1980s band
The Kamikaze Sex Pilots had a song called 'Sharon's Been Deflow-
ered and Defoliated' that included the line: 'She's been given the
taste of Paradise'. Today, in Okinawa, 'Kamikaze Girls' is a website
for the only escort service there, offering sex 'to non-Japanese
speaking customers'.[50]

It is a fascination that has turned into humour. Many cartoons
depict the suicide bomber being met in paradise by troops of virgin
men;[51] by angry women who don't want to have sex;[52] by seventy-two
Catholic nuns;[53] or just by other suicide bombers, trapped in hell,
demanding answers.[54] Even reporters are known to infuse their
reporting with sexual metaphor: *Newsweek*'s coverage of ISIS asked
what was causing the 'orgy' of suicide strikes during Ramadan in
2017.[55]

But one area of sex and gender that seems to hold the greatest
interest of all is the media's fascination with something that has

been held up as the epitome of modern-day evil: the female suicide bomber.

On 8 June 2014, a middle-aged woman approached the army barracks of the 301 Battalion in Gombe, in north-eastern Nigeria, seated upon a motorbike. The base was on high alert, the troops having received a tip-off that the terror group Boko Haram was planning an attack. Seeing her, one of the soldiers flagged the rider to stop, and walked over to carry out a search. When he got close, people were later to say, she hugged him. The two were enveloped in the blast of her suicide bomb.

It was said to be the first use of a female suicide bomber by Boko Haram.[56] Nineteen further attacks by women occurred globally that year; of them, 85 per cent were by those Nigerian Salafists. The next year was worse: globally, 124 women undertook *istishhadi* operations, 120 of them in the West of Africa.

In Boko Haram, sex and gender dynamics were unmistakably at play. That first Nigerian female bomber would likely have been offered a beauty makeover before her death. Henna – brown swirls in beautiful lace-like patterns – would have been applied to her feet. Her hair would have been brushed and straightened with care. And, when the suicide bomb had been strapped around her waist, it could well have been covered by a beautiful dress, bought for the occasion. They might even have gifted her a matching headscarf.

She may have also been given a choice: marry a jihadist or volunteer for the 'mission'. She could have been given money for the task, and she certainly would have received hours of religious teaching, instructing her to submit to Allah's will. In such lessons, she was probably taught that to kill would grant her entry to paradise.

In recent years, so many women in Nigeria have become or have been forced to become suicide bombers that they are referred to as *annoba*, which means something like 'epidemic'. The problem

is so bad that a huge billboard stands in Maiduguri, the home of
Boko Haram, stating: 'Stop Terrorism'. Its image is of an angry girl,
explosives strapped to her chest, a detonator in her young fists. A
government video has also been produced: 'Do not allow them to
tie explosives on you,' says a young woman in it, 'it is dangerous.'[57]

Every suicide attack by women from 1985 to 2000 appears to
have been motivated by secular goals. Since 2000, however, religiously motivated terrorists have carried out the majority of suicide
attacks by women.[58] While groups such as Hezbollah, the Kurdish
PKK, the Tamil Tigers in Sri Lanka, Hamas and Chechen fighters
all used women and girls to carry out suicide attacks, Boko Haram
has outstripped any one group in terms of scale. Since that June
day, hundreds of women and girls have carried out attacks: in
Nigeria, Cameroon, Chad and Niger. Such violence is not entirely
unexpected; Boko Haram is thought to be one of the deadliest
militant groups in modern times. Since 2009 they have killed over
27,000 civilians in Nigeria alone.[59] But while at first mainly young
men carried out the attacks, inspired by Boko Haram's Salafist ideology, when the Nigerian military responded with extreme force,
the number volunteering dropped significantly, so Boko Haram
started sending women, often kidnapping and coercing young girls
in the process.

But it cannot be said that all Boko Haram suicide bombers were
'victims'. Research by a doctoral candidate at Yale University has
found that many women married into Boko Haram, even against
their parents' wishes. 'There was a 100 per cent better treatment
under Boko Haram,' a commander's wife who had been 'rescued' by
the army told the researcher, Hilary Matfess. 'There were more gifts,
better food, and a lot of sex that I always enjoyed.'[60]

There seem to be many tactical reasons for Boko Haram to use
female suicide bombers. Strategically, women draw less suspicion
than men and so have an advantage in reaching their targets. Sol-

diers may not want to conduct body searches, while the women's use of pregnancy outfits and baggy clothing make it easier to disguise explosive vests. As women are not routinely soldiers, using them as bombers also does not reduce the fighting strength of a terror army.

Crucially, it seems, female suicide bombers provide a greater 'propaganda of the deed' than male bombers. Their act feeds off deep fears of the femme fatale, giving rise to countless newspaper reports and a small library of academic research. A new generation of scholarly work has emerged on gender and violence.

To some degree, the interest in suicide bombings and gender is disproportionate. Yes, secular suicide-bombing campaigns in Lebanon, Palestine and Sri Lanka saw women play an often substantial role, and Chechen rebels and Boko Haram have used (or abused) women repeatedly in suicide bombings. But in other parts of the world, in areas where suicide bombings are continuously felt, such as Iraq, Syria, Afghanistan, Pakistan, Turkey and the European Union, the repeated demographic for suicide bombers is that of young, single men.

All Europe's suicide bombers, for instance, have been male. Even when one woman, Hasna Ait Boulahcen, was reported to have blown herself up as French police raided the place where she was staying, it was later found out that she had not done so.[61] Of the 122 ISIS fighters who said they were happy to be suicide bombers on their application forms, all were male. In *Dabiq*, of the ninety-eight suicide attackers identified, none were women. The Chicago database on suicide bombings says only 8 per cent of known suicide bombers since 1974 have been women.

Young men being the main perpetrators of violence is nothing new; cultural influences, adolescent rebellion and heightened testosterone levels have all been cited as reasons for this. But, on their own, they are not convincing explanations as to why some men choose to be suicide bombers and some do not. I have met both jihadists and ultra-violent gangs in Central America, and when it comes to meeting 'angry young men', there is not much that separates the two, but you don't get the Mara Salvatrucha gang members blowing themselves up. So while the philosopher Frantz Fanon might once have argued that 'violence is man re-creating himself', that impulse cannot explain the male dominance in suicidal violence.

Why, then, are men so over-represented in suicide attacks?

One of the main reasons seems to be because women are not seen as acceptable fighters in many schools of Salafi-jihadist thought.[62] Rather than don a suicide vest, they should stay at home, procreate and bring up the next generation of fighters.[63] Islam, one jihadist manifesto reads, 'gives man dominance', whereas women have 'the divine duty of motherhood'. Men are defined by 'movement and flux', whereas women consist of 'stillness and stability'; if people start mixing up gender roles, 'the base of society is shaken, its foundations crumble and its walls collapse'.[64]

What this means is that the female suicide bomber possibly looms larger in the public imagination than it does on the field of conflict. Of those attacks listed by the Chicago Suicide Attack Database where the gender of the bomber was known, about 8 per cent have been women. And while this database has not recorded the surge of female suicide bombers by Boko Haram, it also does not include the male kamikaze units of World War Two. What it shows is that female suicide attacks, globally, have been the exception and not the norm.

The attention that they get is sometimes disproportionate to the damage they have – overall – caused. They do not differ much in terms of the amount of harm they inflict: men and women on average kill about ten victims per attack and wound half a dozen. But people latch on to the idea of the murderous female and begin to see wider patterns at work in their deaths.

Scholars have written about issues such as emancipation and freedom from traditional gender roles, particularly in women bombers in the PKK and the LTTE.[65] Issues of gender are plainly evident in the analyses; some say that female bombers are often unmarried or widows; they are on the verge of being divorced by their husbands; they cannot have children or have lost custody of their children; or they have been accused of adultery.[66] In some instances, the re-establishment of 'honour' by a female suicide bomber seems to have been a strong impetus. According to UNICEF, in 1999 more than two-thirds of all murders in the West Bank and the Gaza Strip were 'honour' killings.[67] By putting on a cloak of religion, the female suicide bomber was reportedly able to expunge that 'shame'. There have also been claims that Al-Qaeda in Iraq insurgents raped women and then told them the only way for them to redeem their honour was to become suicide bombers.[68]

The one aspect where the female suicide bomber in the Muslim context differs from the male suicide bomber seems to be the fact that the allure of virgins in paradise does not hold sway. Rather, she is (as are male bombers) offered the prospect of interceding on behalf of seventy-two relatives on Judgment Day.[69]

Using female suicide bombers is also said to shame men into action. When Al-Qaeda in Iraq lost ground and a large number of militants to the US-led coalition, they posted online a message from al-Zarqawi, asking: 'Isn't it a shame for the sons of my own nation that our sisters ask to conduct martyrdom operations while men are preoccupied with life?'[70]

To law enforcement, the use of female suicide bombers poses a considerable challenge. When I spoke to the Israeli police spokes-person Gil Kleiman in Israel, he said that when the Palestinian groups started using female suicide bombers, they 'crossed the Rubicon . . . to a very dark area'. It posed problems for young men at checkpoints, as suspicion fell on anyone and everyone, and women needed to be patted down and checked. Following Hamas's first use of a female suicide bomber attack, their spiritual leader Sheikh Ahmed Yassin accepted this change, saying it was 'a new development in resistance against the enemy',[71] and it provided the group with a wider pool of potential recruits. Such a shift was backed by a fatwa that said women could carry out suicide bombings without having to gain permission from their husbands.[72]

Such fatwas were necessary. Many Middle-Eastern jihadist ideologues have explicitly excluded women from becoming bombers; Salafi-jihadists see women as having a role in their struggle, but their place is in the home, not on the battlefield. Jihadists of all stripes are 'fearful of fighting alongside women on the battlefield because this will inevitably lead to a sexual revolution that would supplant jihad altogether'.[73] And so these jihadist groups, like ISIS, tend to have only used female suicide bombers as a last resort – as a form of defence, not attack. As the Zawra' Foundation – a female-orientated propaganda outlet aligned with ISIS – reported: a woman can self-detonate only if she is 'in a hospital or a public place attacked by the kuffar . . . and she has a [suicide] belt with her'.

Over time, ISIS's battle altered from offensive to defensive and eventually women were issued with suicide vests, threatening to detonate if anyone tried to surrender.[74] In that maelstrom, some ISIS female bombers may have been deployed. On 8 July 2017, an image emerged from Mosul of a young woman cradling a baby.[75] Moments after the image was captured, the woman was said to have detonated a bomb, killing herself and her child, and injuring others. By mid-July, more than thirty women were reported to have undertaken suicide missions.[76] According to Elizabeth Pearson, an associate fellow at the Royal United Services Institute in London, such use of female suicide bombers represents a final act of desperation and 'signals the erosion of the gender binary that upheld the principles of the Islamic State project'.[77]

To me, though, writing about female suicide bombers is, to a degree, unnerving. We live in an age where the optics of opinion are being challenged like no other time in history. 'Checking your privilege' is not a catchphrase, it is an urgent call to seek balance and empathy, to strive 'to avoid sanctimony'.[78] Intersectionality – an attempt to see how interlocking systems of power impact the most marginalised in society – is more than a buzzword, it is a political call to arms. It has led to people being told to 'stay in their lanes' when discussing issues of race, education, sexuality, class, age, gender, ethnicity, culture, language, creed and disability.

As a white, straight, middle-class, middle-aged, male Caucasian, a Londoner, an English-speaking, Christian-raised writer, a man whose work is based mainly on researching and advocating non-violence, I have to consider deeply the person I am writing about here: likely a black, semi-literate, adolescent, Muslim female who is about to commit a truly violent act. The gulf that exists between us is more than significant – I sometimes fear it to be blinding and stifling.

Yet, for precisely the things I am, for exactly what my privilege means, I am also a potential target of that suicide bomber. If by chance or design, I were in her sight when she detonated her vest, I would be her unwitting victim. To me, this breaks down some of the debate about 'staying in lanes'. The need to recognise the 'other' in the suicide bomber – the need to penetrate their inner motivations, in whatever measured way we can – is a moral imperative. First, because all of us are potential victims unless we are followers of their ideology, and second, because if we do not seek to analyse them, then the only alternative to stop them seems to be through hard, brute force.

Empathising without condoning, understanding with awareness of the limitations of that understanding, are – in this case – the truest drivers of non-violence.

So in a bid to know more, I reached out to the world's foremost expert on female suicide bombers: Mia Bloom, a Professor of Communication at Georgia State University. Our initial communication, in a way, summed up why I wanted to speak to her: 'Happy to help any serious researchers,' she said to me on Twitter. 'That said, I am a critical reviewer so no snowflakes need apply. Experience has shown that overly insecure entitled males do not succeed around me.' She sounded perfect.

When we eventually got to talk, I asked her whether there was a difference between male suicide bombers and female suicide bombers. In a way, she said, not that much. 'There are common features that contribute to what we would call motivation,' she said. 'It could be about injustice, it could be about anger, it could be about humiliation. A diversity of answers – anything from personal experiences as a child, a desire to do something for your people, feeling like you had no other choice. These aren't going to change based on gender.'

For her, gender came most into play when it related to the issue of altruism. For women, Bloom said, the promise of virgins was 'far less persuasive than the ability to intercede for some of your relatives . . . so you're helping not just your people, you're also specifically helping your family'.

'Is there a difference between a female religious and secular suicide bomber?' she asked rhetorically. 'They both think that they're doing an altruistic act, but the nature of the altruism changes. One thinks she's doing it for the people and the land, and the other one might think she's doing it for Allah. But there's still this notion of the willingness to make a sacrifice. Now this contrasts significantly with some Israeli research that makes the argument that all female suicide bombers are suffering from sexual abuse.'

She said she had found no evidence of that, or that they killed themselves because they were particularly depressed. However, she said, what she had discovered was that 'when terrorist organizations shift tactics, from hard targets like military bases or things run by the state, to soft targets that are mostly civilians, then that's where you often see a shift from male to female'. And she was clear on another 'advantage' – that female suicide bombers can get as much as 'eight times more media attention' than men.

Were there, I wondered, any special benefits for female suicide bombers in paradise, then, if the virgins were not a particular allure? 'The female suicide bomber is also granted the right to sit by Allah's side,' she said. 'Any physical imperfection that they had on earth disappears; that might be more persuasive for women. If there's some sort of physical imperfection, or they've been injured in some way, they're made whole again in the afterlife.'

I asked if this equal status was important, if it gave them a better position in the social order in paradise? 'Everyone who goes to paradise would theoretically be equal,' she said. 'Apparently, the women in Jinnah don't menstruate.'

It was a detail that struck me – after all, if such particulars can be articulated to the would-be suicide bomber, do they not reassure that a paradise is, indeed, awaiting them? I was reminded of Shakespeare's famous lines in Hamlet, when the Prince contemplates his own death, and how the staying hand prevents us from prematurely shuffling off this 'mortal coil':

> The undiscover'd country from whose bourn
> No traveller returns, puzzles the will
> And makes us rather bear those ills we have
> Than fly to others that we know not of.

Perhaps, I thought, those little details about menstruation or the exact numbers of relatives you can take with you transform the afterlife from being an 'undiscover'd country' to one very much like home. An articulated vision of paradise that acts as a lure – not death, but a new, golden life.

In trying to get to grips with the psyches of male and female suicide bombers, I felt like I had hit the outer wall of understanding. I had managed to track the group dynamics and historical driving forces behind the suicide bombers' rise, and seen those deadly strands coalesce in the barbarity of ISIS and others. I had also sought out the more specific drivers of such violence, and that had led me from community, to family, to the internal demons that might compel someone to blow themselves up.

While it was always obvious that there would be no single answer, no neat explanation, one thing stood out for me: a wide variety of personal circumstances need to apply before someone might consider a suicidal terror attack. And that person needs a banner to act under, too. But perhaps the very reason why the suicide bomber is so hard to identify and beat is that so much lies hidden away, in personal visions of paradise that we may never truly grasp. When faced with a library of explanations, the compass needle always seemed to point, at least in modern jihad, to two things: the group dynamic that promised paradise through violence, and the personal dynamic where a form of pathological altruism found allure in that promise.

Who is the best person to enlighten as to why this bomber or that bomber decided to strap on a vest? A fellow fighter? An imam? A journalist? A victim? Each perspective is rooted in privilege or disadvantage, anger or despair. My own privilege in being able to write this book puts me at an automatic distance: I do not have to resort to violence to make myself heard. But those who could most fully describe the modern suicide bomber's motivation – the Salafi jihadists – are perhaps too close, too invested in the justification of violence to offer a measured critique.

Perhaps, too, there has to be a limit to empathy. Understanding is important, but it cannot obscure the fact these bombers died in the act of murder. If we give them too much of a voice, then do we do those they harmed a disservice?

Faced with that thought, it feels necessary not to concentrate only on the lives and deaths of suicide bombers the world over, but to examine what their acts did to their unwitting victims.

Chapter 12

The Mountain of Victims

At least a quarter of a million people have been killed or injured by suicide attacks since the Tsar of Russia was assassinated in 1881.

It's a mountain of victims that is higher than the peaks created by those harmed by the two atomic bombs in Japan.[1] Greater than the casualty lists of the Battle of Gettysburg, the first day of the Somme, Pearl Harbor and the Battle of Khe Sanh, all combined. But unlike those massacres, the suicide bombers' toll spreads across decades and continents, conflicts and insurgencies, making it a body count that is hard to contemplate. But, when the death toll is counted, it is found that suicide attacks, on average, produce six times more fatalities and twelve times more casualties than conventional bombings.[2]

It's a death toll estimate that probably falls short. When the fog of war descends, killings and injuries all too often go unrecorded. But a quarter of a million is a large enough figure for anyone, and an important one to consider. After all, there cannot be development without security, and you cannot establish if a place has security without knowing first just how many people are being killed and injured. Casualty records help reveal systemic patterns: whether terrorists are targeting a certain community, whether the government response is proportional and justified, whether things are getting better or worse.

Such figures are deeply political. Some governments even actively discourage casualty numbers being published, fearing they show they are losing a conflict, or killing too many civilians in the process. For this reason, the former US Commander General Tommy Franks said in Iraq: 'We don't do body counts.'[3] The International Committee of the Red Cross finds the recording of the dead so political, it refuses not only to publish its figures, but also to explain why it does not do so.[4] Official death tolls following a suicide attack are also sometimes lower than the numbers of the dead stated by witnesses. Gravediggers in Nigeria, for instance, were reported saying they had buried three times the number of people officially claimed after two blasts ripped through a mosque and market in May 2018 in the town of Mubi, Adamawa State.[5]

I have felt this political sensitivity for casualty figures up close. I was once asked to stand before an entire assembly of the world's diplomats at the United Nations, a 'high-level' meeting in Geneva. There I said that Pakistan was among the top five countries most impacted by suicide attacks in the previous year. Within seconds of descending the podium, I was surrounded by four of its diplomats, all animated and concerned.

Things are getting better, they said, with a flurry of hand gestures – it was much worse a year ago. Yes, I agreed, it was. In 2013, Pakistan was the third-worst impacted country in the world by suicide attacks. In 2014, the year I was referencing, it was the fourth, overtaken by Syria. They proceeded to send me emails challenging my data, and when I showed them my figures were robust, diplomatic silence ensued.

Perhaps this is because a sensitive political question today is whether governments are killing civilians in their counter-terrorism efforts. This concern is a relatively recent phenomenon: in the nineteenth century about 10 per cent of war casualties were civilians; by the Second World War it was about 50 per cent. Today, it stands anywhere between 75 and 90 per cent, something we know all too well with the quagmire of Syria and Iraq.[6] We do know that when explosive weapons are used in towns and cities, about nine out of ten people killed or injured will be civilians. And the deliberate targeting of civilians has meant that, as we have seen, about twenty-nine civilians have been harmed on average in each suicide attack over the last eight years.

The international response to this reality of civilian deaths has been slow, but the changing nature of conflict has finally seeped into the global debate. The first Geneva Convention only focused on the military, and it has only been relatively recently that organisations such as Human Rights Watch and Amnesty International have sought to secure global disarmament measures aimed at reducing civilian harm. Significant changes from such efforts have ensued: the international treaties banning landmines in 1997, and cluster munitions in 2008, have had impact. But no such ban on suicide vests exists: ISIS tends not to listen to UN directives. So that mountain of the dead continues to expand and expand.

Men constitute the majority. The Chicago Suicide Attack Database shows that, between 1982 and 2016, where gender was known, 90 per cent of those killed were men, as were 92 per cent of those wounded.[7] It is a pattern of harm that is seen in closer analyses, too. About 80 per cent of those who died in the Twin Towers of 9/11 were men;[8] three-quarters of those killed in Iraq by suicide bombers between 2003 and 2010 were also men.[9] This is unsurprising – when suicide bombers attack military or police bases, they are generally targeting men. And given that so many suicide bombs detonate today in majority-Muslim countries – lands where men dominate street life – when suicide bombers attack civilian crowds, it is predictable men will be killed or maimed.

The Ariana Grande concert attack in Manchester that killed twenty-two people was unusual in this regard. On that day many more females were killed – fifteen – causing it to be regarded by some as a misogynistic attack.[10]

How people die from this type of bomb makes for uncomfortable reading. Some victims are instantly killed by the detonation – a blast so powerful it can stop a heart and rupture internal organs in a microsecond. At a speed of about five kilometres per second, it can kill anything in close proximity.[11] But it is not just the first blast that causes harm; when that force hits something like a wall or a door, the rebound can be even worse – amplified by as much as nine times.[12]

It was for this reason the London bombings on 7/7 were so deadly. The narrow confines of the carriages focused the blast's energy and caused the explosion to act like a terrible scythe among the morning commuters. The train at King's Cross was in the worst place of all when the bomber detonated: a single, tight tunnel. This fact, combined with thick crowds, meant that four times as many people died there as did at Aldgate and Edgware Road.

One analysis of almost a thousand casualties from a dozen suicide attacks in Israel concluded that those who were in a closed space at the time the bomb went off suffered the most severe injuries, and had to undergo the most emergency room and surgical interventions. Bombings in the open caused fewer severe injuries and deaths, but a higher number of overall casualties.[13]

Then there are the 'tertiary' blast injuries – a blast that can be so powerful it throws people against walls, doors, ceilings and floors, where hard concrete fractures and dislocates. But the harm does not stop there. There are the thermal effects of a blast, a surge of heat so blistering that those standing too close are incinerated alive. At King's Cross, the bomber's furnace reached 2,000° Celsius – eighteen people who died in that carriage had burns to over 80 per cent of their bodies. Clothes become torches, people combusting in their own nylon dresses and cotton shirts. The exposed parts of the body – face, neck and hands – are scorched instantly.

Parts of the bomber's vest or case, the shrapnel they have packed around it, and bits of the bomber's flesh and bones blast out at thousands of feet a second. These can rip a body apart. In the London attack, thirty-six people died from having their legs blown off, while fourteen had their arms amputated. And, if the blast is strong enough, other things become shrapnel too. Pieces of concrete, shards of glass, anything displaced or fractured by the detonation can penetrate and kill. So extensive is the impact that US Homeland Security says you are only safe from a suicide bomber's vest 110 feet away – about twice the length of a bowling lane.[14]

The measurement of such distances and codification of such harm has become a dark science. Sub-sections of governments the world over are dedicated to examining the terrorists' weapon. I once was invited to join a 'group of experts' seeking to analyse the impact of explosive weapons, hosted by the Geneva International Centre for Humanitarian Demining, and by far the most informed people in the room were lecturers from Cranfield University. These were men and women who had made it their life's work to predict what happens in those seconds after a bomb goes off. They calculate the energy levels and distribution of explosions. They run tests on the formation and velocity of fragments. They would, unlike me, be able to work out how, mathematically, the fragmentation of a suicide bomber's blast can be represented as:

Where the bomber stands, what type of explosive is used, how old the primer is, where the victims are positioned, how much space there is surrounding them, even the weather conditions – all can dictate a blast's lethality. And all that chaos – that line between whether you live or die on that day – can be reduced to the terrible neatness of an equation.

Equations, though, are clearly not an appropriate public response to terror-related deaths. How should they be remembered? The German philosopher Walter Benjamin stands out: 'It is more difficult to honour the memory of the anonymous, than that of the renowned.'[15] Unlike the suicide bomber who, all too often, leaves a final video, is named in the news, is analysed and investigated, the victims they leave behind are silent, especially outside the West where their memory is often unrecorded and publicly unlamented.

Theirs was not a death foreseen. They often did not have the chance to leave a final farewell, and in the suddenness of their deaths people struggle to fill the void.

For some, memorials are created. The Church of the Saviour on the Spilled Blood may have remembered the first victim of the first suicide bomber, the Tsar of Russia, as if he were the fallen Christ, but today's mass killings of civilians have proved far harder to memorialise. Where formal sites of memory and mourning of a terror attack have been established, like for those who died in 9/11, the language of such memorials often seems to have been borrowed from Holocaust monuments. They are often gloomy, sombre places that urge us to contemplate, and where laughter and joy are excluded.

For many, remembrance is done in intimate ways: people leave bouquets and teddy bears at the site of harm, there for the dirt of a city to cover them; they light candles; they buy benches and have them inscribed with the names of the dead.

But the majority of those killed by suicide attacks are not remembered in such ways at all. The West might construct memorials, but the places where suicide attacks are most prevalent do not grieve in this way. The most you find in Pakistan or Iraq, Turkey or Lebanon is a scorched piece of tarmac, or shrapnel marks on a building. In areas already wrapped in the cloak of war, the suicide bomb might take lives, but leaves little in return.

This makes describing the dead the hardest part of writing this book. I could visit sites of destruction on the global trail of suicide attacks, and write about how such harm came about, or I could write

about what states do to prevent this harm. But here – in the centre
of this book – lie the dead.

How not to make the deaths of suicide bomber victims the most
significant part of their lives? In the West, many victims of the suicide
attacks of 9/11, 7/7, Paris or Manchester will be remembered in the
public eye – with the digital immortality offered on Google, social
media and news sites – for the death they died rather than the life
they lived. I find this troubling because it seems as if the terrorists
'won' in this sense; their ugly ideology marked a civilian's life that had,
all too likely, absolutely nothing to do with their religious delusions,
so why in death too?

With that thought in mind, I reached out to one family and asked
if I could meet them to talk about the son they had lost in a terror
attack, to learn as much about the life that was cut short, as well as
the cutting short of that life. And, in a way, by getting to know the
history of that man, I hoped to show that behind each statistic was
a life once full of promise.

Dr Stuart Murray was waiting for me outside his home. He was
looking out at the public park that lay beyond his front drive to a
pond. He turned and looked at me, a little apprehensively. He smiled
a thin smile and shook my hand, his wariness to be expected: I was
just another journalist who had descended, unwanted, into his life
to speak to him about his dead stepson, and I would have felt the
same. But he was all kindness and ushered me into the kitchen to
meet his Turkish wife, Figen.

She had prepared food, and we sat down in the adjoining dining
room where she laid out the dishes: roasted chicken and fresh salad
and warm bread. We smiled at each other again. It was strained,
though I took comfort from the fact that her son, Martyn Hakan
Hett, would have approved of someone writing about his life.

After all, Martyn was the consummate showman, forever in the limelight, the focus of attention. Stuart and Figen had a large family. Both had children from previous partners, and they had two more children together: five in all: Daniel, Martyn, Emma, Louise and Nikita. But, from what I was to glean, Martyn was perhaps the most rambunctious of the lot.

We began slowly; a little about their lives was revealed. Stuart was a GP in a local practice. Figen, a dark-haired woman in her late fifties, used to be a mental health counsellor. But she had not been able to go back to work since 22 May 2017, the day she found out that Martyn had been killed at the Ariana Grande concert in the Manchester Arena.

Martyn was her second eldest, after Daniel. Two sons to an Englishmen she had met when living in Aschaffenburg, an ancient Bavarian town that sits on the River Main. Her parents had settled there after fire and flood had wiped out the family business in Turkey, and though she was agnostic, the fact that she came from an Islamic culture was something that played out a little in the reporting on her son's murder by a Muslim extremist.

Hers was not a religious family, but it was conservative. She was not allowed to mix with young German boys growing up, make-up was not permitted, and when her mother caught her sister wearing tight-fitting jeans, there was hell to pay. She took the first chance she could to get out, and falling in love with that Englishman was a ticket to ride. She soon found herself with two small boys living under the heavy skies of the north of England. Martyn, the younger, was born on 15 December 1987.

By then, she had found work as a secretary and was doing translations in the evenings from English to German for the extra money. It was not an easy time. Her marriage was falling apart and Martyn was a boisterous boy, always getting into trouble; she was exhausted most of the time.

'Drama followed him,' she said, remembering the time when he got

his head stuck in a ladder, or when he somehow pulled down a line
of street lights in Turkey on a family holiday, plunging the seafront
into darkness. Things may have changed in her life – she left her
first husband and moved in with Stuart within a few weeks of their
meeting – but the constant was Martyn and his energy.

'His personality was infectious,' Stuart said, 'he was a people-magnet
from the very beginning.'

He was always acting, performing, playing up. He'd charge you
ten pence to watch him do a show, and was forever in front of the
camera, asking to be adored. His creativity sometimes overflowed as
he grew up. Trouble stalked him, like the time he filmed his mother
chatting to a cat, and then overlaid the footage with moans and
groans, turning the banal into the obscene. Or when he plastered car
windscreens at his school with photocopied images of a schoolgirl
posing in her underwear, leading to social services to be called.

When he took his mother to one side, aged sixteen, saying he had
something important to say, it was Figen who cut in: 'You're going
to tell me that you're gay. Either that or you want a sex change.' His
mother had known long before he did.

As he got older, dark clouds of depression began to form, and
Figen was to become his rock in those storms of sadness. When his
boyfriend broke up with him, when his depression was so severe he'd
ring her up and say he was feeling suicidal, Figen was there, phone
to hand. She stopped talking for a moment and looked at her plate.

'It's funny,' she said, 'ever since he died I keep on losing my phone,
misplacing it. I never once lost it when he was alive.'

I sensed that she missed his neediness. This flamboyant man – captured in endless selfies – needed his mother more than the adoration
of strangers. Still, people flocked to him. After he died, there were so
many who said to his parents they were Martyn's best friend, people
his parents or sisters had never heard of; an old boyfriend once
remarked that being with Martyn was like being with a celebrity.

Beyond us a door was open, leading out to a garden lawn warming in the spring sunshine. A bee, the first I had seen this year, buzzed briefly into the house and I remarked upon it. Stuart said: 'That's probably Martyn sending a message.'

Figen laughed – on her arm was a tattoo of a bee, an emblem for Manchester. That northern city had been such a hive of activity during the Industrial Revolution that seven bees were included in the crest of its coat of arms to reflect the industriousness of the place. Following the murder of twenty-two people at the concert, many Mancunians had had one tattooed in solidarity.

A tattoo in remembrance of Martyn was apt – he was famous in his own right for having an image of the character Deirdre Barlow from Coronation Street on his calf. He even went on a television series called *Tattoo Fixers* to have it 'upgraded' from just her name to her full face, staring out from behind bars. His tattoo, though, was to be a source of immense upset in the hours following the attack. Surely, his loved ones asked, someone could identify his body with such a distinctive image tattooed upon it? But they couldn't or wouldn't.

In many ways, Martyn was the opposite of the man who killed him. He was popular, gay, media-savvy, seemingly full of life. He liked how his friends called him a 'one-man hen night' and once claimed his 'life peaked when he met Mariah Carey'. The last time he was seen alive, he was carrying two glasses full of wine. 'One for Martyn and one for Martyn,' Stuart said, laughing. He had been locked out of the Ariana Grande concert after leaving to go to the toilet before the final song, and had stood in the foyer, singing right up to the moment of his death.

Stuart was answering some office emails when the news came on about an incident at the concert hall. He didn't think anything of it until Louise, Martyn's sister, came through the door saying that her phone kept going, people looking for Martyn. Figen, who had gone to sleep early, was up in an instant.

'You don't normally get out of bed that way,' Stuart said, thinking back. But she knew something was amiss.

'I told her not to worry. That he'll be pissed somewhere,' he said. Martyn had been kicked out of concerts before for singing too loudly. But Figen had stayed up, watching the news unfold, and she knew.

'You know what,' she had said to her daughter, sitting there in the early hours, fixated on the news, 'he's dead. There's an emptiness. I can't feel him any more.'

Martyn had been the second nearest to the bomber when the explosion hit. It killed him instantly.

For Martyn, death was to cut short great changes in his own life. He had already hosted four leaving parties for a trip he was about to make to the United States – a haphazard crisscrossing of the country in a manner that reflected his impulsiveness, but a trip that was to mark a new chapter in his life. He was going there, he said, to think about his future. He had been offered a significant promotion at work and changes were in the wind. And, in the moment he was killed, he was wonderfully drunk.

The conversation began to waver. Memories were raw now, unfiltered, and the recollections of Martyn intermingled with the chaos of events that followed. Figen and Stuart had travelled into the city to the site people worried about their loved ones were advised to go, the Etihad Stadium. They expected to find hundreds there, but few families were present. Mobile phones meant that most were able to make contact quickly after the event. Only the ones whose calls were not being answered had come. Then, after certainty had crept in with each passing hour, they were ushered into a room and told that Martyn had died.

It took five more days until they were able to see him.

'Nothing,' said Figen, 'prepared you for the coldness of his body when you hugged him.' Perhaps I can take a picture of you with your hands next to his tattoo, the nurse had said, and they had done so but didn't know why anyone would want to look at such a thing.

And, in a sense, that was it. There was the funeral: two white horses and a chariot, a coffin covered with images of Martyn's beloved soap stars and singers. But when the crowds had left, and the journalists had stopped calling, there was a void. Figen had always been, even with him as a grown man, his caregiver. Always there, always picking up the pieces, and now there was nothing. No calls in distress saying he had lost his wallet and he couldn't get home. No dramas in the night. No laughter.

'It was not a natural death,' Figen said. 'It was an extraordinary death. Had Martyn died of a terminal illness, it would have been different. But this . . . this makes me feel like I am in a different universe. My son. My son was murdered.'

She keeps on finding nuts and bolts in the strangest places, places where you'd not expect to, and while she's not a religious person, these small finds shock her; she puts them in her pocket. After all, it was nuts and bolts that took her son from her. I asked in what ways his death had changed her, and she was considered in her reply. 'When I see a woman with a headscarf,' she said, 'I think: "I bet you feel really uncomfortable in this country."'

'And when I see a young Muslim man on a plane, a guy with a beard, I think – in a calm way: "You could blow this plane up."'

Since the killings, her life has changed. Her daughter says sometimes she feels not just that she has lost a brother, but a mother as well. Figen campaigns for the rights of families of victims of terror attacks. She has travelled to the European Parliament, spoken to countless reporters, and educated herself on why a young jihadist would do such a terrible thing. It has led to a sort of understanding – accepting there was a deep dissatisfaction among many Muslims with the West's War on Terror.

'The 9/11 attack in New York,' she said, 'yes – that is directly linked to what happened in Manchester. Some of the decisions that our government has made, going to war in Iraq, have upset these people deeply. Our foreign policy is to blame.'

I saw this attempt towards empathy as painfully admirable, but others did not. One said her stoicism was inappropriate, that she should be more upset. 'With your attitude,' the troll had written, 'your son deserved to die.'

After many hours of talking, it was clear the weight of memory was draining the two of them, and I said I had to go. It would be futile to try to capture the nuances of a life in a few hours, but what we had done, remembering Martyn with all his highs and lows, felt meaningful. For his mother and stepfather, it was a form of catharsis and, for me, it offered context. The suicide bomber's act is so disruptive, it goes against our concept of fairness and love, respect and tolerance, and threatens to blot out everything with its horror. But here, in the quiet hours of a Mancunian afternoon, a semblance of balance was found again.

While the news that follows a suicide bombing usually focuses on how many people were killed, there are many more who will survive the attack. In the last eight years, for every civilian killed in a bombing, three have survived, albeit injured.[16] This figure is also likely to be on the low side. Journalists often report on the critically harmed, not the walking wounded, particularly in areas where accurate reporting is often fraught with difficulties, like Iraq and Syria.

In places where inquests on terror attacks take place, and where better records are kept, the numbers recorded as injured are often far higher. In the 7 July 2005 attack in London, 52 people were killed, but 775 people at the four scenes were to survive with various injuries. In 2016, in the Brussels attacks, 32 people died, yet over 300 people were recorded injured. In the Manchester bombing in 2017, 22 people were murdered, but over 800 were eventually deemed to have suffered injuries.

Part of this is down to the nature of the device. Improvised explosive weapons have been found to be more injurious than manufactured explosives such as rockets or mortars; they have a greater chance of resulting in multiple amputations (70 per cent compared to 10 per cent), as well as genital injury.[17] Some harm is hard to survive: if an arm is ripped off in the blast, it is unlikely the victim will live to see the day out. Extreme burns are usually fatal. But there seem endless ways in which a person can be scarred for the rest of their lives if they survive an attack.

In the 7/7 bombing, forty-nine different types of injuries were noted by doctors among the 775 survivors. Laceration was the most common, while injuries to hands, lung contusions, inhalation injuries, fractured ribs, objects piercing the eye, deep thermal burns and piercings by metal shrapnel were each recorded numerous times. The nature of the blast radiating upwards and outwards, particularly with seats and other passengers in the way, meant many commuters were scalped.[18] Many more were deafened; even people standing eight metres away had their eardrums ruptured, with over sixty-five survivors suffering 'tympanic membrane rupture' that day – the most common of all injuries sustained.

Some were 'degloved' – where a swathe of skin was ripped off, severing the blood supply – a trauma powerfully summed up in its naming. Spleens were ruptured, eyes gouged out, mandibles fractured; and then there lay a single line that recorded 'penetrating human foreign body'. The bombers' bodies had become weapons, with a dozen victims found to have 'human tissue implanted' in them.[19]

Other damage is also hidden. When, in 2001, a suicide bomber attacked a group of Israeli civilians, a thirty-one-year-old woman had bone fragments extracted from her wounds – not her own, but those of the terrorist. It was found he had hepatitis B, leading the hospital to immunise his victim against that virus.[20] That threat of HIV or other blood-borne diseases is ever-present; at least one victim from the 7/7 bombings was put on post-exposure HIV prophylaxis.[21]

Such a litany of ways to be harmed inevitably creates potent challenges to medics. After an attack, they are confronted with an unexpected surge of the wounded. The injuries are the type of trauma seen in conflicts, yet doctors and nurses are not braced with anticipation like a military medical unit on a war footing. For this reason, research has shown suicide bomb victims are often 'over-triaged' as much as 59 per cent of the time – an unintentional overestimation of the urgency of a patient's condition, prioritising their management unnecessarily.[22]

This is to be expected. Some of the wounded will be on the edge of death; one survey of Israeli suicide bomb victims found, compared to other trauma incidents, they were more likely to need blood transfusions and intubations, suffered more chest injuries and were more likely to have an emergency thoracotomy (an incision into the chest, to gain access to organs within). Overall, a quarter of those casualties suffered severe-to-critical injuries, compared to about 10 per cent of victims of non-terrorist explosive trauma.[23] As one surgeon described after the Manchester bombings: 'Short of any military experience, which I don't have, nothing can prepare you for that scale of injury on each individual patient and collectively as a group of patients.'[24]

The medical literature that documents such injuries proves visceral reading. In one case in Israel, a girl presented unconscious, with no apparent wound. It was only after a methodical search that an almost invisible cut was found inside her mouth: a nail from the terrorist's bomb had penetrated the fourteen-year-old girl's brain.[25] Such tiny metal pieces, nuts and bolts that frequently pack suicide vests and cars, cause terrible damage. Of over 1,155 Israeli suicide bomb patients, more than half had to have X-rays to find such shrapnel.[26]

It is not unknown for suicide bomb shrapnel to be tainted with excrement, the bombers actively seeking to cause post-blast infections. Rotting animal testicles and faeces were discovered in the backpack of suspected extremist Abderamane Ameroud, a man shot in the leg at a tram stop in Brussels in April 2016.[27] In February of that year, ten terrorist suspects were also arrested in Morocco: jars were seized that contained dead rats, vomit and shredded nails.

Other factors play a role in injury profiles. In Israel, it was found that women caught up in a bombing suffered from more burns to their lower extremities than men because they were wearing skirts, not trousers, at the time of the blast.[28] Children are less likely to survive a suicide bomb than adults, and require more specialist paediatric services if they survive. Even the time of day you are injured might influence the healing outcome. Researchers in the UK discovered that wounds that occur in the daytime heal up to eleven days quicker than those that happen at night, while NHS records showed those who were burnt at night took 60 per cent longer to heal than those injured during the day.[29] And these were the immediate impacts of the bomb. But for those that survived an attack, it was the beginning of a journey that would last, in many respects, for a lifetime.

Shehan Baranage is a busy man. A Sri Lankan Buddhist, he runs media affairs for the Ministry of Education, and long after his colleagues have departed the faded corridors of their government offices, he can be found, sitting at his desk, filled with restless energy. Painfully thin, and wearing a shirt that threatened to engulf him, he was answering two mobile phones and filling out a form when he greeted me. Outside, the Sri Lankan day was fast turning to dusk, and in the gloaming he showed no signs of slowing down.

'Hello,' he said, warmly. He was once a TV journalist and still had that air of self-assurance that often comes with the territory. Indeed, it was about this time that I wanted to talk to him because when he

Shehan Baranage – the survivor of a suicide bomb attack in Sri Lanka

was a twenty-nine-year-old political reporter, a few days before the
start of the new millennium, he had been a victim of a Black Tiger
bombing.

It was the final day of public speeches on 18 December 1999, in
the run-up to the Sri Lankan elections, and Shehan was covering the
presidential race. A trusted member of the press pack, he had been at
all the main rallies and had a knack for the job. His university thesis
had been about the electoral process in Sri Lanka since 1948, and
he could read the political landscape better than most. Something
about this final day of speeches at Colombo's town hall, though, didn't
seem quite right; he had called his editor with that hunch, asking for
a second crew to cover it. He'd never done that before – there was
something amiss, he was sure of it.

Dusk was fast approaching when the long, impassioned speeches were coming to an end. Rain was falling gently and the president seeking re-election, Chandrika Kumaratunga, had just descended from the podium. Shehan had rushed to a clear spot by the edge of the stage, hoping to put a question to the incumbent president as she walked towards her bulletproof Mercedes-Benz.

It was then that the bomb went off. A Black Tiger, attempting to climb a security fence, had been blocked by three security guards and had taken that moment to trigger his vest. 'The President's guards fell on her in that moment, screaming for assistance,' he said. 'Some even died by electric shock as the TV broadcast wires fell.'

The explosion knocked Shehan off his feet, and in those slowed-down moments after the blast, he could feel other people's flesh – hands and legs – hit him as he fell.

As a child, he had been told how to react to an emergency: lie in a prone position. So there he lay, eyes shut tight, thinking he was about to die, terrified his hands and legs had been blown off, obeying the orders of a lesson taught long ago. Slowly, he opened his eyes and saw his jacket and trousers had been blown clean off him. Then he began to check himself. 'Legs, hands . . . intact. Ears . . . OK. And then I tried to stand.' What he could not see was that the blast had caused both his lungs to collapse, so when he tried to get up, he fell back down, gasping for breath. But at least he was breathing.

Soon rescuers came for him and carried him to a police bus. They put him on last, knowing that when they arrived, he'd be the first one taken off and treated. Kumaratunga's driver, two bodyguards and the deputy inspector general of police all lay nearby, dead. Twenty people died that day, though up to thirty-six were reported killed in the media; among the dead was Shehan's camera assistant.

Within four hours, Shehan was in an operating theatre, surgeons trying to stop his life ebbing away. Minutes before they put him under, he saw a news bulletin: the networks were reporting on his death. He spent almost nine hours in surgery and had forty-eight

stitches that ran from his throat right down to his stomach, and more
suturing to patch up the 3-inch hole in his lower back. His liver was
shattered, his diaphragm damaged. When he came to, he found that
he had lost 6 feet of intestines, had shrapnel taken out of his liver,
knee, ankle and shin. Even then, he still had six pieces of metal shards
embedded deep in his body.

His father, who was in Australia at the time, had called the sur-
geon. 'Don't rush,' the medic had said, 'your son has a week to die.
If you have time, come. But if he survives, it will be by luck – purely
God's gift.'

But Shehan fought. Another operation took out more shrapnel and
he somehow survived that; others did not and he would awake to
find beds in the ward emptied overnight. He persevered, and three
weeks later managed to swing his atrophying legs off his mattress,
and stood up. Doctors, nurses and paramedics, he said, cried with joy.

The virtues from his past life gave strength to his new, traumatised
one: the fact that he neither smoked nor drank speeded his recovery.
But there were things that no amount of healthy living would heal –
today, seventeen years after the attack, the shock of the bombing still
lingers. A chest pain haunts him, but they cannot find the source of
his discomfort and, as an MRI scan would disrupt the metal shards
that lie embedded within, they never will. His spine was severely
damaged and it means he cannot climb steps without triggering the
pain. The only way he can live without agony is through constant
distraction; when he is focused or under pressure he can manage
the hurt, but when silence descends the only thing he can feel are
jagged edges.

I asked if he ever got help for post-traumatic stress, but he said no;
nothing was offered, he just carried on. Such is the reality in most
developing nations. I once oversaw a survey of dozens of survivors
of a bombing in Pakistan and only one of them had had counselling.
To me, Shehan seemed to need it. It took him seven years to go near

the town hall, and even now, he hides behind the curtains at night if a lightning storm rages over Colombo. His wife says she is married to a man who can never stay still.

Pain and fear: these are the hidden and private burdens that linger long after the bomber has struck. Deep, personal, intimate hells that no one else can truly know – reverberations that echo through a lifetime.

'Did it reduce your belief in humanity?' I asked.

'Not even an inch,' he replied. And, to be frank, I didn't believe him.

The long-term injuries from a suicide bomb are difficult to quantify; some will be left with extreme physical disability, others with searing memories of the atrocity. To give a clear-eyed overview of such trauma is hard. Patients are often compartmentalised, sent to one clinic or another. A panoply of care, at least in countries that can afford it, is made available to the victim: plastic surgeons, nephrologists, cardiologists, orthodontists, psychiatrists, vascular surgeons, urologists, ophthalmologists . . . a lengthy list of medics who might be tasked with repairing the terrorist's damage.

In this sense, Emily Mayhew is pretty unique. As full of energy as she is of facts, hers is a rare calling – she is the only historian in residence working in a science department in the UK. The department she is in – Bioengineering at Imperial College – is a global centre of excellence in analysing the trauma that comes from explosive weapons. Emily's role in that team is to ensure that, within all the scientific analysis of blast impact and effect, a human voice is heard. She was the perfect person to meet to discuss the nuanced, long-term impact of the suicide bomb on those that survive.

She had once worked in retail, using the words that so easily trip off her tongue to convince shoppers in Harrods to buy baubles. Today her motivation was for compassion, not profit. Hers was a storyteller's eye, one that peered over the surgeon and saw the patient beneath;

there to record what they were suffering at the time, what they had suffered and what they were going to suffer.

Within minutes of meeting at her offices in Imperial College's campus in Albertopolis, just off Exhibition Road in London, we were talking about antibiotic resistance, long-term physiotherapy, horticultural therapy and the fact that the human body is terribly efficient at absorbing the shock of a bomb, and not in a good way. Then she told me something striking. Those that live after an explosion, she said, sign a 'deal with death': a price paid for surviving a blast. 'When you nearly die,' she said to me over coffee, 'all your inflammatory responses are activated, to such an extent that they never really go back to normal. In a sense, it is like a tsunami, a devastation that the bomb leaves behind.'

This was a relatively new observation. For years people were treated for the injuries sustained in the bomb blast, but the possibility that such an explosion had damaged their entire biological system was not addressed. She talks now of a 'casualty continuum', seeking a healthcare approach that appreciates how the inflammatory damage incurred at the point of wounding can linger far into the future, never going away.

Traumatic brain injuries, growth hormone deficiencies and persistent post-concussive symptoms such as headaches can remain for years after an attack, even in those who may not have realised they were so seriously affected by the blast.[30] In some, the shockwaves can trigger a form of brain atrophy that can lead to behavioural changes, memory loss and intellectual impairment. In short, the bomb can cause a cascade akin to Alzheimer's.[31] Medical papers talk of things such as 'oxidative stress', 'microglial activation', 'blood-brain barrier dysfunction' and the 'activation of neuroendocrine-immune systems' – changes in the body that are also seen in devastating auto-immune disorders such as multiple sclerosis. One study found that those who experienced the impacts of explosive violence in the Second World

War were more likely to have diabetes as an adult.[32] Clearly being in the path of an explosion can bring both expected and unexpected health consequences.

Awareness raising by people like Emily has meant that the focus on post-trauma care has come on in leaps and bounds, particularly driven by soldiers' charities pushing for it. There is one story that Emily likes to tell people about recuperation, and that is the story of chickens. These, she says, are a sort of litmus test used on patients recovering from suicide bombs or roadside explosions. The thinking goes like this: give them a chicken and then wait and see what happens. If the chicken thrives under the patient's care, then the doctors are upbeat about the future. If the chicken starts to waste away, or die, the patient needs more help.

Sometimes complications hinder recovery. She described something called 'heterotopic ossification': the presence of bone in soft tissue where bone normally does not exist and is often found in people who have lost an arm or a leg following an explosive attack. It is estimated that between 60 per cent and 80 per cent of amputees injured in such events have developed this condition.[33] It is an ossification that appears to be triggered by the blast itself; the explosion transforms cells, turning ones that are not bone-forming into ones that are.[34] This was extraordinary to hear: the suicide bomber's blast can change our very cell structure.

Other reverberations were felt. Emily had noted that many of those she had interviewed who had survived an explosive attack had lasting problems with their teeth. Their bodies change shape and sag. It is almost like they are ageing prematurely, the blast killing them slowly. 'When people say "He was never the same after the war", they mean it literally,' she said. It is as if they signed a pact with death the day they survived the blast, but it was a contract that would hound them to an early grave.

It is not just physical changes, of course. The psychological impact of terror strikes is well documented. A widely researched topic on terror attacks, second only to papers on the 9/11 attacks, is that of post-traumatic stress disorder or PTSD.[35] This is to be expected, given the numbers: for every person physically harmed in a terrorist attack, between four and fifty times the number of people will display signs of psychological trauma.[36] Thirty-five per cent of people who saw 9/11 unfold at close quarters had developed PTSD within four years.[37]

There is the possibility that a Western focus on PTSD, where patients are encouraged to relive a suicide attack to 'externalise' their memories, has meant that emotional trauma is not only being more diagnosed but might even be overstated. It has led some to talk about 'the invention of post-traumatic stress disorder',[38] whereas those who 'repressed' their emotions following a major traumatic event have been found to report 'fewer PTSD symptoms, fewer additional anxiety disorders, less depression, and less physical disability' than those that openly displayed anxiety.[39] But in developing nations it is clear that there is extensive psychological trauma that remains woefully unaddressed.

Muteness, rage attacks, bed-wetting, insomnia, endless nightmares – these were the findings of social workers in 2017 at the Iraqi refugee camp of Hasansham, one that housed those fleeing the waves of suicide attacks in western Mosul. Over half of the 1,500 children there were said to be severely traumatised and in need of urgent psychological support – a generation of children damaged. As the veteran correspondent, Anthony Loyd, wrote about a four-year-old: 'He had seen death before . . . He still, when he is angry, wants to kill . . . Social workers dealing with traumatised children fleeing Mosul after two years of ISIS rule say that his case is unexceptional.'[40]

Even those distanced from an attack can still be affected by it. In Israel, a correlation between the media's coverage of political violence, including suicide bombings, and the anxiety felt by the general population has been made.[41] In the wake of the Manchester bombings, one survey found that a quarter of people in the UK population were found to have had elevated stress symptoms.[42] And after 9/11, many Arab Americans were said to be 'doubly traumatised'; the attacks that caused deep upset to many were an upset further compounded by later harassment and profiling. Among such communities, rates of depression and anxiety were found to be higher than among the general public and other minorities. Half of 601 adult Arab Americans surveyed detailed an emotional state that would have been diagnosed as clinical depression.[43]

Not all is bad news, though. There are occasionally some positive consequences of suicidal terror. One study assessed the impact of 9/11 on the rate of suicides in England and Wales, and concluded that the number of those killing themselves reported in that month was significantly lower than other months in the same year, and in any September during the previous twenty-two years. The terror attacks – and the media reporting of them – appeared to have had a brief but significant inverse effect on suicide rates.[44] It was something that was said to support the sociologist Émile Durkheim's theory that external threats create group integration within a society and that social cohesion lowers the suicide rate.

Wanting to know if this held true for other major suicide attacks, I checked the UK's Office of National Statistics. Did the same apply for the London Tube bombings of 7/7? With 394 people killing themselves in July 2005, that month saw fewer suicides than any July in the previous twenty-five years.[45] It seemed to support the 9/11 thesis: major suicide attacks might, for a brief period, stop others from killing themselves.[46]

Having said this, there is little other light that can be found from such terror attacks, no matter how hard you look. They are, for instance, too disparate and haphazard to have led to specific medical advances; it is a violence that takes and does not give back.

There are other, unexpected and unwitting victims of the suicide bomber that exist beyond the reach of blast and shrapnel. With a death not only comes the wrenching grief of loss that I saw with Martyn's family but often other hardships: there can be long-lasting consequences, especially in conservative cultures, if a man dies in a terror attack. All too often these men are the family's primary bread-winners and, in communities where women often stay at home, their widows might be forced even to prostitute themselves to keep their families fed. Others might have to remarry, causing the children from the previous marriage to risk abuse from the incoming father. And knowing how many men are killed by suicide attacks, this is a very real issue for many.

For those that survive, the injuries they suffer can also bring challenges to their loved ones. Depending on the height of the bomber when they detonate their vest, suicide bombs often cause head injuries to those around them, and the resulting brain injuries can have an overwhelming impact on a victim's family. Bathing and feeding someone who needs around-the-clock care can destroy partnerships (a burden that seems to affect spouses more than parents).[47] Sleep problems, dissociation, and severe sexual dysfunction are also often seen in people surviving explosive trauma, putting enormous strains on a marriage.[48]

And, even though they garner the least sympathy of all, the families of suicide bombers are also often deeply impacted by their children's actions. One British mother, speaking at a fundraising event for a counter-extremism foundation, put it powerfully when, on finding her jihadist son had died, she said she was devastated because he 'was killed after being brainwashed into pursuing a murderous cause', but at the same time she was also relieved because it 'meant that he could no longer harm innocent people'.[49]

There is one last, terrible piece of the jigsaw worth reporting when it comes to the suicide bomber's victims, and that is when the suicide bombers themselves are also the victims in the attack.

On the morning of 17 April 1986, security guards working for El Al airlines at London's Heathrow airport found 1.5 kilograms of Semtex explosives in the bag of Anne-Marie Murphy, a five-months pregnant Irishwoman who was attempting to fly with 375 fellow passengers to Tel Aviv. A timed triggering device was also discovered in her bag – a calculator in disguise. She said she was unaware of the contents – her Jordanian fiancé, Nezar Hindawi, had given her the bag. He, she said, had sent her to meet his parents before marriage. The court believed Murphy, and Hindawi was found guilty by a British court at the Old Bailey, who sentenced him to forty-five years' imprisonment. It is said to be the longest determinate, or fixed, criminal sentence in British legal history.

El Al airlines had been targeted in a similar way before. In 1971, a Dutch and a Peruvian girl had been duped into carrying a bomb onto another flight to Tel Aviv. The following year, two British women were also conned into doing the same. Such discoveries led to some in the airline security industry to stress that racial profiling would fail to identify these hidden threats.[50]

It was a devious new form of terror, where even the bomber was unaware of their actions. And it was not just those betrayed by love who were coerced; those with cognitive difficulties have also been abused in this way. When I was working at the Bureau of Investigative Journalism, interrogating the Iraq War Logs as leaked to us by WikiLeaks, we uncovered the story of an Iraqi doctor who had allegedly sold lists of eleven patients with special needs to Al-Qaeda in Iraq. Remote control suicide belts were to be strapped onto them, set to detonate in busy markets. At least two women were 'used in the 1st February 2008 dual suicide attack on local markets', the logs reported. Those explosions in a pet market killed at least 73 people and wounded 150 more.[51] This was not an isolated case. On 4 April 2008, a 'mentally retarded' teenage boy was also blown up at a funeral north-east of Baghdad, killing six and injuring thirty-four others at the same time. The US army log recorded that he had the 'facial features of a person with Down's syndrome', part of an 'ongoing strategy' to recruit people with learning difficulties.

Such atrocities continue to this day. The UN Committee on the Rights of the Child reported in 2015 that ISIS had used 'mentally challenged' children.[52] Videos released by ISIS show a man with Down's syndrome firing an AK-47. This is of little surprise – a group that would throw gay men off roofs, crucify, behead and set fire to their prisoners, lost its humanity the moment it was born.

Then there is that other terror: the bomber who is forced to undertake an attack because if they do not their families will be butchered. These are usually referred to as 'proxy' or 'human bombs', and it was a tactic infamously used by the Provisional Irish Republican Army (IRA) in Northern Ireland during the Troubles and later adopted by FARC in Colombia, Palestinian terrorists, and by rebels in the Syrian civil war.[53]

In the early 1970s, the IRA would usually give the man they had forced to drive a car bomb towards a checkpoint enough time to flee before they detonated the device, but by the 1990s they took the tactic to the next stage. Three men, each said to be 'collaborators', were strapped into vehicles and forced to drive at British military targets, but this time they were not given the chance to escape. The first strike, on a checkpoint in Coshquin in Londonderry in the early hours of an October day in 1990, proved to be the deadliest, killing both the driver and five soldiers. The next, in Cloghoge, killed one soldier, but the proxy survived. While the last, in Omagh, killed no one – the detonator was faulty.

In the Coshquin attack, the 'collaborator' who was murdered was a forty-two-year-old Catholic chef called Patrick Gillespie. His 'crime' had been cooking for the soldiers at a local British base: enough to warrant his murder. Bishop Edward Daly, the cleric famously photographed during Bloody Sunday in 1972 waving a red-stained handkerchief after British troops opened fire on demonstrators, spoke at Gillespie's funeral. The IRA and its supporters, he railed from the pulpit that day, were 'the complete contradiction of Christianity . . . their lives and their works proclaim clearly that they follow Satan'.[54] It was a condemnation that had an effect. A combination of technical glitches on two further efforts and this attack from the Catholic Church were to stop the IRA from embracing the tactic, and it was non-violent sacrifices, such as the hunger strikes, that garnered far more support for the movement.

Other forms of coercion have also been used. Salafist groups have raped young men, leaving them in such a state that they become suicidal and accept the wearing of a bomber's vest accordingly. Following an autopsy of an Algerian militant bomber in 2009, it was shown he had 'a large tear in the anus . . . which confirms sexual abuse'.[55] There is also evidence that at least some Iraqi male teenagers have been forced to train as suicide bombers and do so under fear of reprisals against their families. This use of teenagers is a double form of abuse: the threat to a family member and the coercion of a child.

Child suicide bombers are a horror hard to grasp. In Japan, about 3,000 kamikazes were 'boy pilots', drawn from a special programme set up to train young Japanese men to die for their country.[56] It is likely that some were under eighteen when they flew to their deaths.[57]

It was, though, in the Middle East that the child suicide bomber was openly lauded and praised. The first recorded child suicide bomber in that region was also the first Muslim suicide bomber: Mohammed Hossein Fahmideh, the thirteen-year-old boy who fought and died in the Iran–Iraq War. The first Muslim female suicide bomber was also a child, the Lebanese teenager Sana'a Mehaidli, just sixteen when she died.

From such raw 'firsts', others followed; the Palestinian Islamic Jihad reportedly recruited children as young as thirteen,[58] while the Coalition to Stop the Use of Child Soldiers says that 'at least nine Palestinian children carried out suicide bombings against Israeli soldiers and civilians between October 2000 and March 2004'.[59] In the last seven years, 14 per cent of all suicide bombings – one in seven – have been by kids, a reality that is part of a wider issue of child soldiers being recruited by Salafist groups. In 2017, the number of children in conflicts across the Middle East and North Africa was found to have more than doubled in a year.

Half of all child suicide bombers have been in Iraq, a third in Syria and almost all the rest in countries where Boko Haram operates, such as Nigeria or Cameroon. Al-Shabaab in Somalia has also been known to use children as young as eight years old,[60] while ISIS allegedly once used a four-year-old.[61] In August 2016, a thirteen-year-old boy bombed a wedding in Turkey, killing fifty-one people – a sign that child bombers were even encroaching into mainland Europe. That attack, along with so many others in Syria and Iraq, was carried out under ISIS's orders.

Some of ISIS's bombers were so young they could barely see over the steering wheel of the cars they were driving;[62] by as early as 2014, reports were coming out of thirteen-year-old boys turning up at checkpoints, suicide bomb vests padlocked to them by ISIS fighters.[63] The terror group were to cultivate this atrocity; as one failed child suicide bomber said: 'There were four older men who would teach us about heaven . . . Twenty-four hours a day.'[64] Another said ISIS 'planted the idea in me that Shiites are infidels and we had to kill them'.[65] If he did not carry out his mission, he was told, Shiites would rape his mother.

Others had no parents to fear for. 'Thanks be to God, we want to kill ourselves, to kill the enemies of God, even if they were our father,' one was filmed saying, but his father was already dead, along with five of his uncles. The parents were Yazidis mown down by ISIS fighters in 2014, and their children had been captured and brainwashed. As the boys said: 'When we were in Sinjar, we used to worship the Devil.'[66] They were to blow themselves up in the eastern alleyways of Mosul.

ISIS realised children were a useful and expendable tool. They released films of young boys sleeping with AK-47s, waking early for their military training, screaming out jihadist slogans in orderly lines, ISIS black banners wrapped around their heads. Young teen-agers were forced to wear suicide vests while conducting non-suicide missions, such as guarding or patrolling, and told to detonate their vests if necessary.[67]

Sometimes ISIS parents even sent their children to their deaths: videos have emerged of fathers kissing their sons goodbye as they climbed inside cars filled with explosives.[68] According to Reuters, a young girl, aged about nine, blew herself up in the last month of 2016 at a police station in the Syrian capital, Damascus. Her parents had sent both her and her sister on their deadly missions.[69]

How could anyone do such a thing? One film on the operation to retake Mosul captured a radio interview where a father of a soon-to-be child suicide bomber was interviewed. 'I encouraged him because it's the key to Heaven,' the father said. 'Yes, we brainwashed him, but we brainwashed him with the Holy Quran and its verses . . . I hope my other sons will take the same path.' And, in that Humvee filled with smoke, the light glaring through sand-stained windows, a Kurdish fighter listened in. He looked at the radio, dragged on his cigarette and said, in a flat voice: 'Fuck off.'[70]

But given how malleable and trusting children can be, the fact that terror groups use them as suicide bombers is, perhaps, not that unex-pected. Boko Haram, renowned for its brutal treatment of civilians, sent at least forty-four children to their deaths in this way in 2015.[71]

They abducted children on their errands, strapped suicide vests to them and then sent them back home, only to detonate the bomb when they were back with their families.[72] Overall, about one-fifth of all their suicide attacks have been carried out by children, mainly by young girls, often drugged.[73]

The Taliban recruits its child bombers from *madrasahs* on the Pakistani side of the Afghan border because along the wild length of the north-west frontier lie thousands of such unregulated schools.[74] There, free education and board are provided, enough to create a prime recruiting ground for Taliban groomers. The pupils are told that foreign forces are raping women and children; that Americans are burning the Quran; and that their deaths will ensure their parents find a place in heaven.[75] Some are given amulets containing Quranic verses. These, they are told, will allow them to survive the blast of their loose-fitting suicide vests. And, in an echo of what the Iranians were to do with their child soldiers, the Taliban gives others a necklace of keys that will open up the gates of paradise to them after their attack.[76]

In all these terror groups, such use of children has a strategic rationale. It does not 'waste' adult soldiers who are better trained for conventional fighting; children are less likely to be suspected as suicide bombers and are often easier to coerce.[77] Such Salafist coercion likely constitutes the most extensive brainwashing of children as suicidal weapons in history.

This poses a massive headache for Western intelligence services which are acutely fearful of what might happen to such children in years to come, given their early-age radicalisation. Children have been included on a list of 173 ISIS European jihadists who might, in the future, strike their countries of birth.[78]

These challenges have contributed to the myriad threats to militaries and police forces the world over, and it is the response to those threats that has changed modern warfare and law enforcement in profoundly impactful ways.

Chapter 13

Endless War

As the dust settled over New York after September 2001, horror quickly turned to anger and anger to revenge. President Bush's top officials 'cast aside diplomatic niceties' and vowed violence. Stand with us, they said to the world, 'or face the certain prospect of death and destruction'.[1] A few days later the US threatened to bomb Pakistan 'back to the stone age' unless it joined the fight against Al-Qaeda.[2] It was part of a wider plan: President Bush had just authorised the CIA to wage war globally, signing off on something called the 'Worldwide Attack Matrix'. It proposed operations against terrorists in eighty countries.[3]

Sixteen years later that matrix was firmly in place, seemingly to the letter. In July 2017, a Pentagon press release announced, 'some 8,000 special operators are in 80 countries around the world'.[4] Eighty countries: the matrix fully operational. Almost half the planet had been dragged, one way or another, into the War on Terror, and the twenty-first century was to feel the mark of that September day like stigmata.

The elusive fight has led to American boots being seen on the ground far beyond the original target of the mountains of Afghanistan. While there are still 15,000 US soldiers fighting in and around Kabul,[5] there are as many as 4,000 troops in Syria,[6] and more still in Somalia,[7] Yemen,[8] Niger, Cameroon, the Central African Republic, Uganda and South Sudan. The list goes on, with unexpected places seeing mission creep. In recent years the US has deployed at least 1,500 troops to the Sahel and sub-Saharan regions, with little open debate and even less clear a strategy.[9] In 2008, the US Africa Command, the umbrella group for American military operations on the continent, inherited 172 missions in Africa. By 2017, there were 3,500 missions – a 1,900 per cent increase.[10] Suicide bombers followed; that year, US soldiers were targeted by suicide attacks not just in Afghanistan[11] and Iraq,[12] but in Niger, Yemen and Mali, too.[13]

Such a link between an ever-expanding field of operations and suicide bombings seems undeniable. The Twin Towers were attacked in part because of US intervention in the Middle East, so when the US responded by putting more troops on the ground, first in Central Asia, then in the Middle East, then Africa, it was perhaps inevitable this would foment nationalistic and sectarian backlashes; coalition forces provided a visible enemy to attack. As one study of over 138 countries between 1981 and 2005 found, foreign intervention was 'likely to increase the use of suicide attacks by regime challengers'.[14] Even the head of Britain's MI5 said that the invasion of Iraq 'increased the terrorist threat by convincing more people that Osama Bin Laden's claim that Islam was under attack was correct'.[15]

Since 2001, over twenty-nine countries have witnessed suicide attacks on military or security units around the world – over 3,385 strikes harming about 75,000 soldiers and bystanders. And, in the main, such attacks have spread along with counterterrorism efforts. When you look at a graph of attacks on military personnel over the years, it has the appearance of a wave hitting the side of a harbour wall – a relatively calm sea until about 2004 and then sudden peaks, with 2007 and 2014 being high points. If you take a second graph

– that of US mobilisation of troops around the world – and place it over the first, you will see that the ebbs and flows match.

You cannot say that it is entirely a case of 'cause and effect': troops might be mobilised to combat a suicidal threat as much as creating one, but the consequences of this threat, from a military perspective, have been great. Suicide bombers, it would not be too much to say, have effectively changed the manner in which modern militaries wage war.

In a sense, the entire War on Terror is a conflict defined by the improvised explosive device (IED). These are the weapon of choice for Salafi-jihadist groups and have proved so impactful they have been called the 'artillery of the twenty-first century', responsible for about 70 per cent of foreign military casualties in Iraq and Afghanistan.[16] Of these IEDs, suicide bombers hold a special, terrible place in the hearts of soldiers – they can harm troop morale, cause them to shelter behind sandbags and limit their ability to move freely around. Soldiers stop their foot patrols and instead sit in enormous armoured vehicles, speeding through villages or across farmers' fields in their heavy wheels, wrecking crops and crushing goodwill in the process. As the Joint IED Defeat Organisation, a dedicated Pentagon agency established in 2006, said of suicide bombs: 'No other widely available terror weapon has more potential for mass media attention and strategic influence.'[17] And, right from the start of that internecine war, such weapons have caused havoc and mayhem – from the moment they were first used in the maelstrom of Iraq.

US Private First Class Michael Russell Creighton-Weldon felt that he was on top of his game. That Saturday, 29 March 2003, he was twenty years old, in great shape and was doing what he thought was God's work. He had recently got engaged but, for him, the call of duty meant he had gone to Iraq instead of to church and, in a way, his fiancée understood – Michael's mother, after all, had been a sergeant major.

Next to him stood another Michael, M.E. Curtin, a twenty-three-year-old, newly minted corporal from New Jersey. He had never expected to go to war, but that had all changed on 11 September 2001. Two days later he had graduated from the US Army's basic training school at Fort Benning, Georgia, and 563 days later there he was, manning a checkpoint, with three comrades from the army's 3rd Infantry Division outside the Iraqi city of Najaf, about 100 miles south of Baghdad.

On the other side of the dusty road stood Private First Class Diego Rincon, a Colombian in American fatigues. Even though his family had emigrated to *el Norte* when he was five years old, he was not yet a US citizen, just one of nearly 40,000 members of the US military who did not have citizenship. Rincon had a bad feeling that day. A week before he had written a letter to his mother saying he believed he was soon to die; he asked her forgiveness for any wrong done to her. His mother said reading it was like someone pouring a bucket of iced water over her.

The fourth man in the group was Sergeant Eugene Williams. He had been assigned to the 2nd Battalion, 7th Infantry Regiment, 3rd Infantry Division and was twenty-four years old; he was missing home cooking like you wouldn't believe. A laid-back man, who loved R & B, he was planning on finishing a demo tape to showcase his singing when his tour ended. Originally from Chicago, he lived in Wahiawa in Hawaii with his wife, Brandy Delacruz. They had a three-year-old daughter, and there was a second one on the way.

Four men from across the United States – Florida, Hawaii, New Jersey and Georgia – all in Iraq hunting for weapons of mass destruction and seeking to change a regime of violence, but without a clear vision of how to stop its replacement being violent, too.

They saw a taxi approach. Its driver stopped his car and beckoned to the four soldiers, so they walked over, weapons at the ready. Then, without saying a word, the driver flipped a switch and he and those four Americans were killed in an instant. It was to be the first suicide attack against US troops in Iraq.[18] It happened just ten days into Operation Iraqi Freedom (before 19 March, the mission in Iraq was called Operation Enduring Freedom), and while almost eighty coalition soldiers had already been killed since the war began, this was the first use of this particular weapon against the military.

It was to prove a significant game changer because it was the moment the US high command realised they were fighting something more than the incompetent vestiges of Saddam Hussein's Baathist army. They had not encountered a suicide bomber before in this campaign (and given there were no Iraqis involved in 9/11 perhaps they assumed that suicide attacks had not infiltrated Iraqi culture). But that was no longer the case, and if someone was willing to blow himself up in this fight, they thought, perhaps a deeper ideology was at work – the start of an unyielding insurgency.

Taha Yassin Ramadan, Iraq's Vice-President, said it was an Iraqi military officer who had driven that taxi. 'This is only the beginning,' he said.[19] Iraq could send enough 'martyrs' to kill thousands of Americans. Over time, jihadist volunteers from Saudi Arabia, Europe, Syria, Kuwait, Jordan and North Africa tried to blow up American troops on Iraqi soil. They could reach anywhere, it seemed. When, in April 2007, a bomber managed to get through checkpoints and armed guards right into the heart of the most fortified place in the country, Iraq's parliament inside the Green Zone, seeking to destroy those who would ally themselves with the Americans, the message was clear: nowhere was safe. Suicide attacks seemed to be a weapon that was almost impossible to defeat. As a 2006 US military review concluded: 'As combat operations against insurgencies become more successful, and the enemy loses more and more of his trained supporters, he will turn to less trained, but potentially more dangerous options . . . the suicide bomber.' They, the report ended, with a touch of despair, 'can be anyone.'[20]

It was a report that was framed by an unstated question, one that has been asked ever since 9/11: how can you stop an attack that cannot be deterred by the threat of death? Suicide bombers trounced the safeguards that 'mutually assured destruction' offered. They were motivated by something that defied the normal ways the US measured and monitored an enemy, so, even though the US Central Command Director of Operations, Major General Victor Renuart Jr., said at the time of that first bombing that it would not change the coalition's operational strategy, the surge of attacks on his troops absolutely did. It led to US strategists saying that their primary guiding principle was to 'prevent attacks by terrorist networks before they occur'.[21] In this way, the suicide terror threat created a warfare of denial: the US sought to stop suicide bombers from enjoying the sanctuary of rogue states that they could use as a launching pad for their terror.[22]

For many soldiers, the traditional logic of war was challenged. 'When you fight someone who wants to survive, I always felt like my teammates and I could make better decisions or predictions,' a former marine who fought in Fallujah in 2004, told *Time* magazine. But with suicide bombers, he said, the idea of a conventional war went out of the window. 'You would much rather obliterate every building, torch every plant and leave no one alive rather than patrol in at close quarters for an unpredictable encounter with a madman with no intent to surrender.'[23] In this febrile environment, anybody became a potential enemy.

On 6 September 2008, a pickup truck travelling down a highway in Ninewah province, north-west Iraq, came across a US convoy driving in the opposite direction. The driver of the vehicle was an elderly man, with cataracts, and, perhaps not realising what to do when faced with an oncoming military truck, failed to slow down. The soldiers, fearing a suicide car bomb, tried to get the driver's attention. They shouted and waved and raised weapons, but the driver kept coming.

Then, as per their manual, the soldiers fired a warning shot; the old man tried to stop, but his brakes were threadbare and he lost control. Seeing such erratic driving, the soldiers opened fire again and riddled the car and the man with bullets.

This was just one of the hundreds of stories of civilians being killed in Iraq, ones where civilians approaching checkpoints or convoys were shot by terrified, trigger-happy US soldiers. Six hundred and eighty-one civilians were killed in similar checkpoint stand-offs between 2004 and 2009, at least thirty of them children. And with each year, as the occupation continued, that death toll mounted, alongside a rising number of suicide attacks. In 2004, there were 22 civilian deaths at checkpoints. In 2005, there were 300.

Overall, more than five times the number of civilians were killed during such 'escalation of force' incidents than actual insurgents. It was an accumulation of tragedy that led a 2007 US operations handbook to note that, in Iraq, there was 'a perception that coalition forces engage in indiscriminate killing'.[24] It was only when Lieutenant General David Petraeus intervened, insisting that his soldiers be better trained to react and orders to fire minimised, that the death rates dropped. Even then, from May 2006 to the end of 2009, there were still 320 further civilian deaths.[25] And it is impossible to record the countless moments where civilians were forced to take off their shirts and trousers to show that they were not concealing bombs – humiliations that could rankle and radicalise.[26]

The ever-present threat of suicide bombers at roadblocks raised other issues, too. Major Roger Davies, a UN counterterrorism adviser who specialises in IED technology, once told me how nervous Iraqi soldiers might well have waved through suspicious-looking trucks on many an occasion, terrified that the driver was about to detonate their payload. 'And one reason why there were so many bombings in Baghdad,' he said to me, 'was because security was circumvented – it was nobody's interest to stop a vehicle.'

There was, over time, a wider transformation of US military tactics. When American troops first arrived in Afghanistan and Iraq, they fought a conventional war – mechanised units, cluster bombs, cruise missiles – the sort of tactics that you can't face down an insurgency with, especially one that uses suicide bombers. Suicide attacks forced security forces into a 'functional stop' of their operations eight times out of ten.[27] Missions were bogged down, and troops began to arm their fortified trucks with heavy machine guns. Immensely expensive mine-resistant ambush-protected (MRAP) vehicles were ordered, and soldiers were wrapped in thick armour.

Troops also put up massive concrete structures and bunkered down behind them. They called these ready-made blocks things like 'Jersey' and 'Colorado', all the way up to the twelve-foot tall and seven-tonne wall named 'Alaska'. Thousands of these were put up, each costing over $600; the Americans used them to force traffic into roadblocks, attempting to thwart roaming suicide car bombs and sniper fire. But there was overuse: one brigade erected over 30 miles of wall, separating themselves from the rest of Iraq in what they called 'safe communities' – the implication being that the rest of Iraq was unsafe.[28] One 3-mile, 12-foot high wall was even put up in Baghdad, separating Sunnis and Shias.[29]

In a sense this bunkering down worked, leading one US major to describe such concrete barriers as 'the most effective weapon on the modern battlefield'.[30] But something was lost. An environment akin to siege warfare emerged, with soldiers putting up as many as ten dozen concrete barriers in one night. And what this image of hard-faced men tucked inside huge trucks living behind massive walled compounds did for the local opinion of these foreign armies is self-evident.

As David F. Eisler, a captain in the US Army who wrote a paper called 'Counter-IED Strategy in Modern War',[31] said to me: 'If you subscribe to the notion that the conflict we were fighting was primarily a counter-insurgency one, one that necessitated being onside with the people, then arming ourselves with heavy weaponry and bunkering down did not seem to be, intuitively, the right response. The suicide bomber hampered the hearts and mind capacities of the coalition.'

'Our strategic response to the threat of suicide attacks,' he said, 'was the opposite of what the theory of counter insurgency would have you do.' If you can't get within 10 metres of an Iraqi or Afghani farmer to ask him about issues in his community, fearing he might self-detonate, then you are never going to find out what is going wrong in local communities. And, as one US Army lieutenant colonel has recently admitted, almost two decades into the War on Terror, his military 'lacks a comprehensive strategy for countering and eliminating the drivers of violent extremism'.[32]

There were other impacts, too. In an attempt to stop the devastation of the suicide bomber, eye-watering amounts of money were spent. As of late September 2017, the wars in Iraq, Afghanistan, Pakistan and Syria, the spending on Homeland Security, along with the running costs of the Departments of Defense and Veterans Affairs had, since the 9/11 attacks, cost the US taxpayer more than $4.3 trillion.[33] This spending was the direct consequence of a war that began with suicide attacks, but the threat of ongoing suicide bombings presented its own costs. On 5 August 2007, the US House of Representatives made $500 million available to the Joint IED Defeat Fund,[34] and this was just the start of it. Between 2006 and 2015, in Afghanistan the counter-IED force spent $17 billion.[35] As one counter-IED report noted: 'The military is always searching for better vehicles and equipment to defeat what is, at its core, a homemade device made for a fraction of the cost of our technological countermeasures.'[36]

This military spending was part of the suicide bombers' plan. Al-Qaeda had always wanted to erode US military power by making their government haemorrhage money. As Bin Laden said: 'Each of Al-Qaeda's dollars defeated one million American dollars, thanks to Allah's grace.'[37]

One of the most significant costs incurred by the US government was in their attempt to defeat the suicide bomber with technology. In 2008, nearly 60 per cent of the Joint IED Defeat Organization's $4.4 billion budget was devoted to developing counter-IED technologies.[38] Radar scanners, devices that cause a bomb to explode prematurely and X-ray equipment armour for vehicles and personnel were all developed to stop the suicide bombers in their tracks.

Untold millions were also spent on technologies such as the 'stoichiometric diagnostic device', something that can decipher the chemical signature of explosive materials through metal or concrete.[39] Further millions were pumped into developing a high-strength aluminium and graphite fibre 'Sabot round' that, when fired, can pierce through metal like a knife through butter and obliterate an oncoming suicide car in seconds.[40] The US army also issued a contract of up to $48.2 million for the development of the 'Counter-Bomber', a device with two video cameras that emit low-level radiation beams, supposed to be able to detect bombs hidden under someone's clothing.[41]

But the most effective response when faced with an approaching bomber, they discovered, was the deadliest one: the headshot. And the weapon entrusted with doing that was the US military's M2 machine gun. Nearly six feet long and weighing 128 pounds with its tripod, it fired up to 550 rounds per minute. With a maximum range of four miles, it was one of the mounted infantryman's best defences against a lumbering suicide car bomb. In the fourteen years following the terror attacks of 9/11, the US Department of Defense issued contracts for small arms, parts and ammunition that, if fulfilled, would have reached over $40 billion. Not all of these bids were to stop suicide bombers, but such contracts show a tendency towards buying weapons most effective against incoming suicide strikes. Over $1.6

billion was spent on machine guns, almost 112,000 of them bought for US troops.[42] It was, as the American journalist C.J. Chivers was to note, a 'shift in many American units from being foot-mobile to vehicular, as grunts buttoned up within armored trucks and needed turret-mounted firepower to defend themselves'.[43]

Such expenditure has and will have consequences for the American people. One Harvard review noted that the massive spend on military defence, alongside compensation for wounded soldiers and pensions for veterans, will lead the United States to face 'constraints in funding investments in personnel and diplomacy, research and development and new military initiatives'. This does not even acknowledge the amounts that could have been spent on US hospitals and schools, welfare and support instead. As the review concluded: 'The legacy of decisions taken during the Iraq and Afghanistan wars will dominate future federal budgets for decades to come.'[44] In 2000, before the economic impact of 9/11 struck, there was no US deficit for that year; the federal government spent $236 billion less than it received in revenue. It was the most the government had 'underspent' since at least 1929.[45] In 2019, the US deficit is estimated to top $984 billion.

Yet, even when confronted by such an immense deficit, security spending still goes on. For 2019, Donald Trump proposed a 12 and 13 per cent increase in Homeland Security and Defense Department spending respectively.[46] Simultaneously, deep cuts in other US departments were also announced: the Environmental Protection Agency is scheduled to suffer cuts of 25 per cent, Housing and Urban Development, 14 per cent.

The suicide bomb added one final aspect to soldiers' roles. It forced them to become more adept at gathering forensics and biometrics: seeking fingerprints and DNA after the device has gone off, trying to find out what forces were behind the attack. And that led to the global development of counter-IED initiatives, particularly in the most affected regions of the Middle East, North Africa and the Sahel.

Today, at least 327 different organisations are engaged in attacking suicide-bombing networks around the world.[47]

It is an uphill struggle for many of these organisations, though. Unlike in the US, many counter-IED units are often under-resourced. Simple things such as bomb defusing equipment are absent, while others struggle to contain cross-border trade of materials that go into making suicide bombs. The fact that suicide bombs can be made up of a wide range of materials poses a particular challenge: how can you stop a trade in fertiliser that could be both used in agricultural work, as well as being transformed into weapons of destruction? Many militaries also remain heavily reliant on help from other nations or charities, while others have an unequal approach to addressing the issue, despite sharing common borders. This means that a suicide bomber can plot their strike in a poorly governed nation (like Somalia) and cross over to strike terror in the heart of another (like Kenya).[48]

Overall, the complexities of stemming the tide in suicide bomb materials, protecting soldiers on the ground and defeating an enemy that by its very use of weapons sees deception as a virtue, has led states to distance themselves from the battlefield. At the peak of the war in Iraq and Afghanistan, in 2007, over 1,000 US soldiers were killed overseas.[49] In 2017, there were twenty-one families in the US awarded a 'Gold Star' for losing their son or daughter in combat in some distant, foreign field.[50]

As American troops withdrew from the field of battle, two things happened. First, they began to be spread thinly, fighting a wide number of insurgencies in a seemingly ever-increasing number of countries. Second, the US sought instead to project power from afar. In this way, the development of modern-day air power has to be seen partly as a response to the potential harm wrought by suicide bombings, and partly the result of a hyper-connected world, where each Western soldier's death is seen as a death too many. Steadily and surely, drones and air-dropped bombs began to replace Humvees and large military camps, and the consequences of that are still being felt today.

Chris Woods is the sort of journalist that governments and businesses should fear. An intense man, he is an intensely focused investigative reporter and, without him, I am sure the world would not know half of what they know about the US's covert drone war.

He came to me in the spring of 2011 when I was running the Bureau of Investigative Journalism. He seemed discontented with the failure of the media to do the sort of investigations he felt were urgently needed. So when he walked into my office and said that he was on to a big story, an important one, I listened. The CIA, he explained, had claimed they had not killed a single civilian in their drone strikes against terrorists in Pakistan. I had not heard much about such operations. The media had not focused on them, and the areas the drones were striking were largely out of bounds for many Western reporters. Since the US journalist Daniel Pearl had been captured and beheaded by Al-Qaeda in Pakistan in 2002, the coverage of places like Waziristan and the Swat valley seemed minimal.

But we agreed he should see if it stood up as a story and, by July 2011, we published a story headlined 'US claims of "no civilian deaths" are untrue'.[51] Statements by President Obama's chief counterterrorism adviser John Brennan that there hadn't 'been a single collateral (civilian) death' in Pakistan since August 2010 were shown to be a lie. Instead, we exposed that, up to that point, at least 116 CIA 'secret' drone strikes there had killed at least forty-five bystanders – six of them children.

It was the start of a much bigger story. Chris's team went on to find that less than 4 per cent of those people killed in drone strikes on Pakistan were named members of Al-Qaeda, calling into question then US Secretary of State John Kerry's claim that only 'confirmed terrorist targets at the highest level' were fired at.[52] The team raised significant concerns about the legality of such strikes over foreign soil;[53] about whether 'double tap' drone strikes were targeting the rescuers at the sites of the initial attacks;[54] and whether drones were being used to extra-judicially kill European nationals.[55]

It was this use of drones that led some to conclude there is 'a dark shadow on claims that CIA drones are proportional'.[56] And by the summer of 2016, the White House officially acknowledged it had, in fact, killed dozens of civilians. Chris and his team were even contacted by Obama's advisers and briefed on this admission.

Drone warfare is important to focus on because it was the sort of weapon the suicide bomber inadvertently pushed to the fore of modern conflict. Suicide bombers created conditions where the enemy, by being nebulous and a permanent, anonymous threat, evacuated militaries from the battlefield and thrust them into the air. When drones began to offer 'precision' strikes from a distance – especially from about 2007 onwards – they seemed to present a new way to beat the suicide bomber.

It was their supposed targeted efficiency that caused Donald Trump to believe he could 'bomb the shit out' of ISIS, and why drone strikes in Yemen and Somalia tripled under his first year in power.[57] In a way, he was following the same logic as President Obama, under whose presidency there were ten times more drone strikes than under President George Bush.[58] The US Air Force was said to be flying as many as seventy drone sorties a day in 2018, an increase from about fifteen a day ten years before.[59]

But the word 'precision' in 'precision warfare', especially when it comes to air strikes, is a contentious adjective. As Lieutenant Colonel Jill Long of the United States Air Force writes, 'the term "precision" does not imply, as one might assume, accuracy', but rather a 'discriminate targeting process'. 'By using a word that has such specific meaning in the mind of most civilians,' she says, 'it is easy to see how a gap in understanding and expectations has been fostered.'[60]

Precision, for instance, ignores the fact that a drone or air strike on a would-be suicide bomber can go terribly wrong because of electronic countermeasures, sandstorms, poor weather, or a human operator screwing up. And it fails adequately to convey how imprecise air strikes are in the first place. The accuracy of a weapon is gauged by what is termed the 'circular error probability' (CEP). What this means is that, in tests, missiles are fired and an imaginary circle is then drawn around the 50 per cent of strikes that land closest to the target. This circle becomes the CEP and its radius defines the weapon's accuracy. The bombs that hit outside that circle are ignored, even if they land miles away. Furthermore, such testing is carried out by the manufacturers, not impartial observers, and then backed up by militaries that arguably have a vested interest in saying they are using precise weapons of war.

The awkward truth is that a suicide bomber is still – despite all the modern advances of technology – more accurate than a manufactured guided missile system.

And even if a government's bombs hit their targets, those bombs cause shrapnel capable of eviscerating anything over a significant distance. As one drone pilot described, his payload could 'slice and dice anyone within a twenty-foot radius . . . Even those out to fifty feet might not escape its wrath'.[61] The US military field manual says that 'safe distances for unprotected troops are approximately 1,000 meters for 2,000-pound bombs and half a kilometre for 500-pound ones. Even protected troops are not entirely safe within 240 meters of a 2,000-pound bomb'.[62]

I have been to the borders of Syria and the conflict zone of Ukraine – with a tape measure in hand – to measure the kill zone of mortar strikes and Grad missile attacks and to see how far those weapons harm. But in the areas where drones are most felt, like Northern

Waziristan, Somalia and Yemen, reporters and researchers fear to tread, so exact evidence of the drone's harm is not recorded in detail. In addition, journalism is stretched thin; the lack of people buying newspapers has stripped down foreign desks, and the numbers of foreign correspondents have fallen. The result is a relative lack of scrutiny, on the ground, of the actual effect of those air weapons designed to take out terror cells.

If it were not for journalists like Woods, the US government could have carried out its missions in relative silence. For instance, a 2017 investigation established that, since 9/11, the Pentagon has failed to publicly list a substantial number of its air strikes in Iraq, Syria and Afghanistan.[63] The British Ministry of Defence, meanwhile, claimed for many months – at least until it was shown not to be the case – that 'in the hundreds of airstrikes that the RAF has carried out in Iraq, we have had absolutely no civilian casualties reported'.[64] Besides all this, any man killed by a US drone who is of combatant age is automatically said to be a terrorist, not a civilian, so we will never know the real figures of the innocent dead.[65] Nonetheless, as one US drone operator said about these strikes, they show to the American people that the US government is 'doing something without . . . putting Americans at risk'.[66] There are consequences to such displays of power, though.

One of these impacts is the drone's effect on notions of a 'just war'. Chivalry – the ancient code of conduct that once determined the medieval rules of conflict – was founded on the idea that the knight would be present on the battlefield upon his horse (hence the derivation of the word from the French *cheval*). These mounted soldiers helped mould the rules of war as a form of insurance; if captured, then a fee could be paid for their release. The subsequent development of the laws of conflict was born from this idea of insurance: soldiers adhered to conventions because they wanted to be treated in such a way if they themselves had to surrender. Drones, however, take the modern soldier away from the risk of harm. Should a drone operative be given a campaign medal, for instance? What does distanced warfare do to perceptions of bravery, fair play and honour? Compare the actions of a drone pilot – safe in a secure compound in Nevada – to that of a suicide bomber approaching a military outpost in Kandahar or Kano. From the perspective of a jihadist, the former is a coward hiding behind technology; the latter is a lion among men.

The other major impact lies in that fact that any civilian deaths from such attacks have become a jihadist's propaganda dream. In 2011, I had asked Pratap Chatterjee, a British Sri-Lankan investigative journalist, to travel to Islamabad to report on the US use of drones throughout Pakistan. There he had met elders and young men from Waziristan, a province in northern Pakistan, who had travelled to the capital city to discuss the impact of US drone strikes in their communities. Among the group was a sixteen-year-old called Tariq Aziz, who wanted to learn basic photography to help document these strikes. The teenager had a reason to do so – about eighteen months before, a drone missile had killed his cousin. The philanthropist Jemima Khan had donated the cameras, and the group gathered to listen to ways in which these devastating strikes across their country could be stopped.

Seventy-two hours later, Tariq was killed by one of those CIA drones, along with his twelve-year-old cousin Waheed Khan. On Monday 31 October 2011, the two boys had travelled to pick up his newly-wed aunt, to take her back to the town of Norak. Two hundred yards from her house, two missiles had struck their car, killing them both. Neither of the boys had been involved in terror activities; they were two more dead children in a creeping war that has claimed the lives of so many.

For many Muslims, Tariq's death – and countless others like it – are seen as proof of a heartless and evil enemy, and they fuel the call for more suicide attacks and more violence. When, in 2009, a Jordanian suicide bomber killed several people at a US outpost in Khost, Afghanistan, the bomber posthumously appeared in a video urging jihadists to avenge the death of Baitullah Mehsud, the Taliban chief who was killed by a CIA-controlled drone.[67] And when, a year later, the same group attacked a police station in Lakki Marwat, Pakistan, their spokesman said that Pakistani forces would continue to be targeted because its 'government has allowed America to launch drone attacks on us'.[68]

Data proving a relationship between drone strikes and retaliatory suicide bombings is limited, but there were 396 suicide attacks across Pakistan from 2009 to 2016, and during the same period, the Bureau recorded 375 drone strikes. Broken down year by year, the figures show a moderately positive correlation between the two, and comparing drone and suicide strikes in Yemen seems to reveal an even stronger relationship. As Chris Woods said to me, 'Armed drone use and suicide bombings have always been intimately connected. Many early targets of the US drone-targeted killing programme were implicated in the 9/11 atrocities. In turn, terrorist groups have often used the pretext of drone strikes as justification for further atrocities – though whether those attacks might anyway have happened is far less clear.'

Certainly, dead women and children in the rubble of homes destroyed by drone or air strikes are included as standard fare in jihadist suicide bombing videos. As is footage of an interview with a US Air Force colonel, where he says civilian deaths are sometimes permissible if they stand in the line of fire of a critical target. Other jihadist videos show Marc Garlasco, former chief of high-value targeting at the Pentagon, saying that as many as thirty civilians could be killed in a high-value target strike before the Secretary of Defense or President had to be consulted.[69] Even a US Department of Homeland Security-funded project found that 'high-profile killings' by their government, 'either had no influence or were associated with a backlash effect'.[70]

As criminologist Andrew Silke at the University of East London, who has conducted many interviews with imprisoned jihadists in the UK, says: 'The government does not like to hear that someone became a jihadist because . . . airstrikes blew up a bunch of civilians in Mosul.'[71]

An important caveat needs to be made here: the US's use of drone attacks in Pakistan and beyond has sometimes had terrible consequences, but it has never been equal to the horror of ISIS suicide attacks on civilians. Drone strikes seek specific targets. Jihadist suicide attacks were often indiscriminate. Drone missiles are not nuclear bombs, and they are, ostensibly at least, regulated by national and international laws.

But it is what the drone represents that, to many, is the thing that has a far wider impact. In 2011, another investigation by the Bureau revealed that Iranian Press TV had faked dozens of accounts of US drone strikes, claiming that 1,370 people had been killed in fifty-six drone strikes in Somalia. There was no evidence of the reported incidents.[72] The subtext of this subterfuge was that the Iranian-backed channel knew that they could stir up anger against the West by claiming its drones had killed innocent people.

In much of the Islamic world, the very things that the West decries in the suicide bomber's actions, Western militaries stand accused of doing. The ISIS suicide bomber that killed at least seventy people in a Pakistan hospital?[73] But wasn't there that American gunship in Afghanistan that decimated a hospital operated by Médecins Sans Frontières, killing more than thirty staff members and patients?[74]

That suicide bomber who dressed as a woman to kill fourteen in a refugee camp?[75] Yes, but in Syria, didn't eight SAS troops also use subterfuge to dress in burkas so they could penetrate enemy lines?[76]

What about the injustice of what suicide bombers do? Then name one coalition general or politician who has been prosecuted for breaching the Geneva Conventions; for the invasion of Iraq; prisoner treatment at Abu Ghraib and Guantánamo; extraordinary rendition; extrajudicial killings . . . all arguably illegal actions that have been justified in the name of defence.

ISIS coming to fight in the streets of Europe? Well, much of the hostility toward drones is born from the belief that the US is violating concepts of sovereignty.[77]

Yes – you may say – these are not equivalences, but many Muslims that I have spoken to do not see that nuance. Such perceived double standards even led to US General Stanley McChrystal saying that drones are hated on a 'visceral level' by Muslims under attack and, if used carelessly, the American public 'should not be upset when someone responds with . . . a suicide bomb in Central Park'.[78]

But this is what the suicide bomb has helped do: it has stretched the boundaries of warfare, creating a form of 'total' war that does not just mean armies bringing conflict to the doorsteps of civilians, but meaning civilians themselves have become militarised, and everyone has become a potential target. And that stretching has eroded the lines between war and peace, allowing war and all its horrors to come home, in ways both unexpected and profound.

When the Russian government was confronted with the suicide attack that killed their Tsar, they responded with an iron fist. Gallows were erected, nooses were made, graves were dug. Hundreds were to die.

When the Japanese government confronted the American military with kamikaze pilots, the US responded with an atomic fist. The Manhattan Project unleashed death over Nagasaki and Hiroshima. Tens of thousands died.

When Al-Qaeda launched its attack on the eastern seaboard of the United States in September 2001, the US government responded with a global first, a counter-strike that seems without end. Operations Iraqi Freedom, New Dawn, Enduring Freedom, Inherent Resolve,

Freedom's Sentinel – each blending and bleeding into the other. Hundreds of thousands died.

Unquestionably, American lives have been lost in these conflicts: as of August 2018, 6,957 American servicemen and officials have been reportedly killed in Iraq and Afghanistan, part of US losses in some twenty-eight countries and four seas since 9/11. In addition, there have reportedly been 1,464 non-US, Allied troop deaths in those two countries.[79]

But civilian deaths in Iraq are even higher. They have been estimated to stand between 181,916 and 204,133, as of August 2018,[80] while in Afghanistan, 37,000 were killed.[81] When you include the deaths of combatants, Iraq has seen 288,000 killed,[82] while a 2016 study put Afghanistan's death toll at 111,000, though that figure is likely to be several thousand higher today. The same review found the spread of violence into Pakistan to have caused almost 62,000 deaths there.[83] So what started with a suicide attack that killed nearly 3,000 people mutated, expanded and devoured.

In total, something approaching half a million people have been killed in areas targeted by the United States, and this does not even include Syria or Yemen or Nigeria or Somalia or beyond. The gyre of violence widened and widened, spiralling far beyond the original atrocity. This is what suicide bombings do – they kill, and then their impact kills again and again as people try to seek revenge for the horror. And within all that tragedy something else happens: the violence that was once exported begins to turn, and – eventually – comes home to haunt us all.

Chapter 14

Police States

As the War on Terror has marched on, and unsuspecting nations have woken up to news that a suicide bomber has targeted their citizens, their police and intelligence forces have found themselves unexpectedly staring at a blood-spattered crime scene where the motives are wrapped in ideology and the main perpetrator, being dead, lies far beyond the application of justice.

Like the military, many law enforcement units have been transformed by this threat and – inevitably, perhaps – have steadily become more militarised in the process. In an attempt to reduce the risk of attack, military-grade weapons have been bought and, increasingly, police tactics have begun to look like special forces operations: men in black with blacker guns in city streets.

This seems inevitable given recent attacks. The sudden alteration of a city into a place of mass shootings and mass deaths from explosions changes everything. The rush of phone calls to emergency services; the chaos of a terrorist attack that moved through the night like a terrifying monster, where stadiums, cafés, restaurants and concert halls were all targeted in heartless succession; and the testimonies of those who saw their friends, their children, their loved ones die at the hands of a cruel militant. All these combine to show how quickly cities can become war zones, and how everything is transformed in such moments. The emergency services, often displaying extraordinary levels of heroism, rush towards, not away from scenes of violence; first responders find themselves faced with injuries a lifetime of car crashes will never present; and everywhere horror, in all its surreal and painful forms, leaves its mark.

So, when a nation wakes up to learn that 130 of its citizens have been killed on the streets of Paris, or 22 have been murdered in Manchester, or almost 400 in Baghdad, its politicians, faced with intense media reporting and the public demand for order and safety, have seemingly only one choice: to implement a 'hardening' of law and order.

Over time, while the military might be at the very 'tip of the anti-terrorism spear',[1] many other branches of government have been forced to adapt to suicidal terrorism. As the White House's National Strategy for Combating Terrorism made clear in 2006, the US had knocked down those 'old orthodoxies that once confined our counterterrorism efforts' and ensured they now involved 'the application of all elements of . . . national power and influence'.[2]

Nations at war inevitably see the language and the legacy of violence seep back into their own systems. In the War on Terror it is perhaps most evident with weaponry: in US police forces, M4 carbine assault rifles replaced the standard pump-action shotgun, grenade launchers were acquired, MRAPs purchased. Since 9/11, the US Defense Department has donated some five billion dollars' worth of military kit to local government, with a further thirty-four billion dollars given in grants to help them buy their own security equipment. It was a torrent of spending to defeat a nebulous threat – one that led, for instance, a relatively quiet backwater like Brevard County in Florida to acquire two armoured personnel carriers, thirteen helicopters and 246 assault rifles.[3]

It has not just been a US phenomenon. In the UK, a country that historically prides itself on its unarmed police force, there has been a similar creeping militarisation. A typical police armoured car now could contain Glock 17 pistols, Benelli Super 90 shotguns, Heckler & Koch MP5s, G36 carbines, SIG Sauer rifles and G3 sniper rifles. Tasers are commonplace, used over 11,000 times in 2016, an increase of about 50 per cent from 2010.[4] In May 2018, it was announced that British police could be 'routinely armed' to respond to terror threat in rural areas.[5]

These are, clearly, not unjustified reforms – terror attacks have often blighted Britain in the past. But such armament was not commonplace during the Irish Troubles, even when IRA bombs killed people in British pubs, parks, shopping centres and hotels and there were shootings across the country.[6] What is different, it seems, is that the modern wave of terror has often been marked by suicidal attacks, and that extremism has dictated the response.

There has also been a substantial expansion of counterterrorism police. Before 9/11, fewer than two dozen full-time officers were working on counterterrorism in the New York Police Department. Now there are more than a thousand, and today the NYPD has offices in London, Abu Dhabi, Singapore and Tel Aviv.[7] The GSG9, the 'elite' German police squad, increased in size by over a third in 2018.[8] The French President, Emmanuel Macron, has recently set up a 'National Counterterrorism Centre'.[9] In Britain, it was announced that 'anti-terror police' were to be given a new £50 million HQ and training centre in London,[10] alongside the London Metropolitan Police creating 600 more armed-officer posts.[11]

Such growth seems sadly inevitable; the resources to carry out a surveillance operation on a prospective Salafi-jihadist are considerable. It reportedly takes as many as sixty people to follow a single suspect around the clock.[12] The cost in 2019 of British police counterterrorism was set at £757m.[13] Between 2002 and 2017, the

US spent 16 per cent of its entire discretionary budget on the coun-terterrorism fight.[14]

In all this spend and expansion, people point the finger at pro-portionality. Between 2007 and 2016, it was noted that, on average, Islamic jihadist immigrants killed two Americans each year. Compare this to the numbers killed by lawnmowers (69), being hit by a bus (264), falling out of bed (737), or being shot by another American (11,737).[15]

But the devastation that just one suicide bomber could cause means measured proportionality is an inevitable casualty. The fear that a suicide bomber could detonate a 'dirty bomb' using a truck in downtown London or Paris or LA, keeps intelligence and police officers awake at night.[16] The myriad ways that harm could be wreaked upon a population seem endless, like the counterterrorism report that talks of the 'possibility of suicide bombers infecting themselves with contagious disease before mingling with a population'.[17]

Weapons and personnel and fear are a lethal mix, and it comes as no surprise that the militarisation of police forces has led to the deaths of people with nothing to do with terrorism. A review of police shootings in the UK over the last decade shows that the majority of those killed were not terrorists, nor were they armed or carrying a loaded gun. It would be an exaggeration to claim these killings are directly linked to counterterrorism, but even serving and ex-police officers say that firearms change the 'power dynamic' of policing and 'there will be more deaths as a result'.[18] I asked the Home Office what evidence they had scrutinised to ensure that the arming of more police might not cause more people across the board to be shot by those officers. None, they said – there was no evidential justification for arming everyday police (and I stress 'everyday' – large city centres need to have armed response units).

We do know that, in the US, the militarisation of the police has had a major impact. Since 9/11 there has been a significant rise in the number of SWAT teams, 'no-knock operations' and unarmed civilians killed by deadly police overreaction. There are estimated to be between 50,000 and 80,000 SWAT raids per year in America, spiking from about 3,000 in 1980.[19] In 2017 alone, 987 people were shot and killed by US police officers.[20] This is just the dead: my charity, Action on Armed Violence, asked police units in the ten most violent cities in the US how many people were shot and injured by their forces in recent years. For every person killed, it was revealed, on average another two were wounded – a toll that is often lost in the reporting.

Again, these shootings cannot all be laid at the door of counter-terrorism methods, but weapons purchased by counterterrorism funds and distributed in the name of heightened national security have exacerbated an already tense situation. This is something that should serve as a warning to any police force that decides that terrorism necessitates the mass arming of its officers.

In the UK, one of the notable tragedies born in the suicide bomber's wake was the death of Jean Charles de Menezes. On 22 July 2005, officers from the London Metropolitan Police's SCO19 firearms unit rushed down the escalator of Stockwell Tube station, and on the platform's edge shot a young man, eight bullets ending an innocent life. Menezes – a twenty-seven-year old Brazilian electrician – was wrongly identified as a suspected suicide bomber. His death came two weeks after the 7/7 bombings and emotions were running high. Officers involved in the shooting were to testify that Menezes was wearing suspicious clothing and fitted the ethnic profile of the suspect – this despite the fact he was wearing jeans and a denim jacket and the suspect they were looking for was Somalian.[21]

The only sure way to stop a suicide bomber in their tracks is by obliterating the 'brain stem' – the medulla oblongata, the part of the brain responsible for controlling heartbeat and breathing – located at the top of their spine. This is why Menezes died with seven shots to the head and one to his shoulder.[22] But these shoot-to-kill tactics seem more suited to a special forces unit, not a police operation. No surprise, then, to learn that the firearms unit that shot Menezes had trained with the British Special Air Service (SAS).[23]

As Menezes's death made clear, the danger posed by the suicide bomber can be so extreme, and can cause such heightened emotions, that the limitations of minimum force or the presumption of innocence are disregarded. Operation Kratos, the guidelines developed by the Metropolitan Police Service for dealing with suicide bombers, was still deemed 'fit for purpose' by the Association of Chief Police Officers a year after the Menezes shooting.[24] It laid out that police should shoot for the head, and that warning a suspect before opening fire could result in the suspect detonating. That particular operation was dropped, but today, if an officer believes someone poses a threat to their life, or to the lives of others, it is still said that lethal force may be used.[25]

Admittedly, given the consequences of a successful bombing, the British police's response has, over the years, been admirably balanced. In May 2013, Fusilier Lee Rigby was brutally murdered in a south London street by Michael Adebolajo and Michael Adebowale, two jihadists who claimed they had been commanded by God to kill a soldier. A Met Police armed response vehicle reached the scene and the two attackers rushed at the officers, brandishing knives and a cleaver, along with an unloaded gun. They later claimed they wanted the officers to shoot them dead and make them martyrs, but the police showed an incredible level of restraint and only wounded the men, giving the pair first aid afterwards. Such heroism should not be forgotten, just as the courage of those who rush to the scene of countless other attacks to save lives, not take them, should not be.

Nonetheless, in the climate of tension that exists after a terrorist attack, militarised policing has created what has been described as a 'significant and real change in the level of violence Western democracies now consider legitimate in dealing with "terrorist" suspects'.[26] Certainly, the War on Terror has seen some police and intelligence forces crossing legal and ethical lines, breaking the logic of 'policing by consent'.[27] Former US Attorney General John Ashcroft called such a model a 'new paradigm in prevention'[28] – shoot first, ask questions later. And it is a preventive strategy that has found its most concerning forms in the application of the law.

In the aftermath of the 9/11 attacks, countries across the world rushed to put in place stringent counterterrorism measures. And, as suicide terrorism spread in the years that followed, so too did the testing of the law, at times running up against, and at other times breaching, fundamental principles of human rights.

Such overstep has taken many forms, but perhaps the most notorious response to the atrocity of 9/11 of all has been the opening of a US detention facility to hold terrorism suspects at Guantánamo Bay in Cuba. Arriving off planes hooded and shackled, men in bright-orange jumpsuits were locked in outdoor cages, held incommunicado, and detained without charge. It was intended as the end of the line for the 'worst of the worst' and Guantánamo became a 'legal black hole' where neither US nor international law applied, with the detainees being called 'enemy combatants'. In short, the US government responded to suicidal terror with a living terror of its own.

Guantánamo Diary, the first account to be written by a prisoner while interned at the infamous American prison camp in Cuba, is a serrated read indeed. It lists experiences of torture, threats and humiliation over the course of a thirteen-year incarceration, including an 'odyssey of detention' from Mauritania to Senegal, Afghanistan to Jordan and finally to Guantánamo. In it, Mohamedou Ould Slahi, the book's author, a Mauritanian national who was incarcerated between August 2002 and October 2016, lists the violations he endured. This includes being sexually assaulted, force-fed saltwater, subjected to a mock execution, left in a freezing room with threadbare clothes, and all the time repeatedly beaten and kicked. It is filled with throwaway sentences that leave you speechless. To obey the order that his toilet had to be kept dry, he had to use his 'only uniform to dry the toilet up and stayed soaked in shit'.[29]

Since Guantánamo opened on 11 January 2002, 780 detainees have passed through its gates. Of these, 731 have been released without charge, many after being held for years. Nine detainees have died in detention,[30] six from suspected suicide.[31] At least fifteen of those detainees were children at the moment of their incarceration. Mohammed el Gharani was only fourteen years old when he was imprisoned. He was released in 2009 after spending seven years, a third of his life, under that unrelenting Cuban sun. A judge found that the evidence against him lacked credibility.[32] Despite being a child, he was still allegedly tortured.[33]

Torture, indeed. Men and boys in 'Gitmo' have been reportedly strapped down and force-fed through their nostrils, a horrendously painful technique that the UN Human Rights Commission has labelled as torture.[34] Beatings and humiliations have been alleged: men claiming they had their heads forced down toilet bowls and the cistern flushed so they almost drowned; that garden hoses have been thrust down their mouths and the water turned on; that their testicles have been crushed and chemicals thrown into their faces.[35]

This is one side of the story. The detainees themselves seem like hard men indeed, men who stand accused of funding terrorism; of assassination plots; of training up suicide bombers; of having had close relationships with Bin Laden and Al-Zawahiri. Their biographies list them as forgers, weapon smugglers, bomb-making experts and would-be suicide bombers. Ramzi-Bin al-Shibh is held there, a man who was supposedly 'slated to be one of the 11 September hijacker pilots'. Walid Bin Attash is said to have been behind the attack on the USS *Cole* in 2000 and to have supervised the training of two of the 9/11 attackers. Khalid Skaykh Muhammad is said to have been 'the driving force' behind 9/11, too.[36]

But, and this is the fundamental problem, these allegations are just that – allegations. Not tried and tested in open court, not subject to the very rules of civilisation and liberty that this War on Terror is supposed to be defending. And yet, despite promises from Barack Obama that he would shut down this illegal holding,[37] as of August 2018, forty detainees remain.[38] Only seven of them face any kind of charges.

Guantánamo is, to some degree, the most visible open wound that the butcher-surgeon's cure for suicide bombing has created. The means by which some of those detainees arrived at that detention facility highlighted other concerns. Many were subjected to the CIA's covert 'extraordinary rendition' programme – the extrajudicial transfer of a terror suspect to other countries. This rendition programme made use of 'black sites' – secret prisons run by the CIA – to hold suspects without bringing them to the US or charging them with a crime. Afghanistan, Lithuania, Morocco, Poland, Romania and Thailand all had such centres and, in total, at least 136 people were extraordinarily rendered or held by the CIA in secret, with fifty-four governments participating along the way.[39] Much of this has been carried out with a cast-iron sense of impunity.

In 2018, for instance, the Trump administration's nominee for CIA director, Gina Haspel, was heavily criticised for overseeing a CIA black site in Thailand in 2002. During this time, detainees were waterboarded – subjected to simulated drowning – and Haspel later was to order the destruction of more than a hundred videotapes recording such techniques. Despite these revelations, and Haspel's offer to withdraw her nomination, Trump's team reaffirmed its desire for her to take on the role.[40]

Some victims of extraordinary rendition have sought redress through other courts. Khaled El-Masri, a German national of

Lebanese descent, was abducted while on holiday in Macedonia, having been mistaken for an Al-Qaeda suspect with a similar name. He was held there in secret before being handed over to a CIA rendition team at Skopje airport, where he was severely beaten, sodomised with an object, shackled and hooded. El-Masri was then flown to a secret prison outside Kabul known as the Salt Pit, where he suffered further abuse. On 13 December 2012, the European Court of Human Rights (ECtHR) held that Macedonia had violated El-Masri's rights, and found that his treatment had amounted to torture.[41] Other cases have been brought to the ECtHR against Italy, Poland, Romania and Lithuania.

In the UK, the government has reached settlements with victims of rendition operations in which it has been complicit. In May 2018, it finally apologised to Libyan dissident Abdel Hakim Belhaj and his Moroccan wife, Fatima Boudchar, after they were kidnapped in Thailand on the basis of British intelligence. They were held and abused at a secret prison, then rendered to Libya on a CIA plane where they were tortured at the hands of Gaddafi forces. Belhaj was sentenced to death. Boudchar was five months pregnant at the time.[42]

The harm suffered by many can never be undone. At the secret CIA-run Salt Pit prison in Afghanistan, one detainee – Gul Rahman – froze to death after a CIA case officer 'ordered guards to strip him naked, chain him to the concrete floor, and leave him there overnight without blankets'.[43] At that CIA black site in Thailand, a Saudi-born Palestinian, accused of playing a key role in Al-Qaeda, was waterboarded eighty-three times.[44] Other 'enhanced interrogation techniques' included forced rectal feedings, threats of sexual and physical abuse against suspects and their families, and mock executions.[45] A CIA operative was later to say the black sites where such things went on were the nearest thing they had ever seen to a dungeon.[46]

In such ways, after 9/11, did 'the gloves come off'.[47] And although former President Obama signed an executive order on his second day in office banning so-called enhanced interrogation techniques, President Trump has repeatedly asserted his belief that 'torture works', claiming 'we have to fight fire with fire'.[48] As a columnist in the New Yorker was to write, if the processes to stop Trump using torture with impunity fail, then the US is 'truly lost in a vortex of self-perpetuating evil. We will have abolished something deep and essential in the soul of America. We will be a dungeon on a hill.' [49]

One fear is that of precedent; Mark Fallon, a man who has served for thirty years as a US counter-intelligence officer, summed this up when he noted that 'once torture is accepted in limited doses, it begins to spread like a virus.'[50] What might start as the torture of a known terrorist can quickly mutate into other abuses. The fact that migrant children have been separated from their mothers; and the repeated shooting of unarmed black men by white US police officers; the reality that 50,000 American youths, age seventeen and younger, are held in juvenile prisons or other confinement facilities on any given day – perhaps all these abuses have roots in a system where empathy has, since 9/11, long been lost. Indeed, it is hard sometimes to see who the real terrorists are.[51]

The US is not the only country where serious moral and ethical dilemmas in relation to counterterrorism have been raised. There is evidence that UK special forces helped teach US interrogators the dark arts of combating 'R2I' – resistance to interrogation.[52] These were techniques originally honed in Northern Ireland and used against IRA suspects.[53]

In addition, two months after the 9/11 attacks, the UK pushed through the Anti-Terrorism Crime and Security Act 2001. This allowed for foreign nationals, suspected of involvement in terrorism, to be indefinitely imprisoned without charge or trial. For three years, a number of men were detained under this Act, without knowing why they had been incarcerated.[54] In 2004, the House of Lords intervened, saying it was unlawful.[55]

The time limit for how long you could be held before being charged with an offence was also tested. After the 7/7 bombings, the UK Terrorism Act of 2006 increased that time from fourteen to twenty-eight days. In Australia, it is twelve days; in France, it is six; and in the US, Germany and New Zealand, just two.[56] In 2005, Prime Minister Tony Blair's government tried to extend this further – from twenty-eight days to ninety days – but it was rejected in the Commons.[57] A compromise was reached and, from January 2011, the maximum pre-charge detention limit in the UK stands at fourteen days, the longest of any comparable democracy.[58]

The challenges posed by suicide bombers have not just shaped the manner in which intelligence agencies and police forces approach suspects. In some instances, they have transformed the very mechanism of the law itself. Special courts or procedures to try terrorism suspects have been created, many of which erode internationally recognised rights to a fair trial, and deny terror suspects the necessary protections of due process.

Most notably, the US created a military commission system at Guantánamo. Under this process, prisoners are not allowed to see the evidence against them and can be prosecuted on hearsay, with limited ability for the defendant to challenge the source. They can find themselves accused on evidence obtained under torture, and the prisoner's right to choose their counsel or be guaranteed a speedy trial are absent.[59] In short, the principles the West takes for granted as a bulwark against the despotism of the state are in danger of being thrown out of the window, especially when the argument 'we are doing this to stop another 9/11' is used.

Again, where the US led, others followed. In the UK, the Justice and Security Act 2013 expanded so-called 'secret courts'. Under such courts, wrote the human rights charity Reprieve, 'the side opposing the Government is excluded from the courtroom, along with the press and the public, and is unable to hear or challenge evidence used against them'.[60] Any secret intelligence introduced by the government can only be seen by the judge and by security-vetted 'special advocates'; those who represent the accused cannot then disclose what they have seen, even to the prisoner.

Other freedoms have been challenged. In the UK, when the House of Lords prevented foreign nationals being held in indefinite detention, the Home Office established the 'Control Orders' scheme in 2005. Those suspected of condoning or supporting suicide bombing, and other forms of terrorism, were effectively placed under house arrest, faced with a curfew of up to eighteen hours per day.[61] This caused such an uproar that it forced the government to amend it. In January 2012, control orders were replaced with terrorism prevention and investigation measures (TPIMs), but this, according to the human rights group Liberty, was an illusory panacea – effectively a 'control order-lite'.[62]

Once in place, such laws have been used in matters that seem to have little to do with terrorism. There was the man detained and questioned for taking a picture of a British town hall;[63] the police force in the north-east of England accused of using anti-terror laws to find out details of a whistle-blower seeking to expose racism in its ranks;[64] the detention for nine hours in Heathrow of the partner of Glenn Greenwald, the American journalist responsible for reporting the revelations of the American whistle-blower, Edward Snowden;[65] and the Labour party member and pensioner who was forcibly removed from a political conference because he voiced his dissent about the Iraq War. These are just some of the ways in which laws put in place to stop terror attacks in Britain have been subverted to muzzle free speech, intimidate journalists and stifle political debate.

Similar tensions between security and freedoms have been seen elsewhere. The November 2015 suicide attacks in Paris saw then-

French President François Hollande declare a nationwide state of emergency, granting state authorities sweeping powers. Included in these powers was the ability to place under house arrest anyone whose 'behaviour constitutes a threat to public order and security'.[66] Under this provision, suspects could be confined to their house for up to twelve hours a day, forced to stay within the boundaries of a particular district, and required to check in at a police station three times a day. As of November 2017, when France's state of emergency was officially ended, and a new anti-terrorism law came into force, forty-one Muslims had been subject to this house arrest.[67]

The suicide bomb threat justified further erosions, including the right to privacy. Deploying the argument that, at any moment, the suicide bomber is able to act, French police have been allowed to carry out random searches of persons and properties without a warrant, at any time of the day, and without prior warning.[68] Accusations quickly began to emerge that such searches had been conducted in a violent and discriminatory manner.[69] Human rights groups have accused French police of injuring and traumatising people in the process.[70]

All these actions have been justified in the name of security. Concerns about suicidal terror have seeped so deeply into the judicial processes of nations that, if we were to look at what rules are in place today and time-travelled back to 10 September 2001, we might blench at what has been done since in our names.

Some are acutely aware of the danger that minute modifications to the rule of law can, cumulatively, cause a landslide. Eliza Manningham-Buller, the former head of Britain's MI5, has said we should 'be deeply cautious of anything that leads to security being seen as the opposite of liberty'.[71] When she discovered the role MI6 had had in abductions that led to suspected extremists being tortured, it was reported that she banned some of their agents from working at MI5's headquarters in London.[72]

I know a few people who work or have worked for the intelligence services in Britain, and they are among the most level-headed people I have met. They recognise the burdens of responsibility that come with the task. One of them described to me how they broached the idea of supplying jihadists with dud explosive materials in sting operations, so that when the terrorist walked into a crowded place and sought to set off their vest, only the detonator would explode. The trouble with that, they were told, is that a police officer might then shoot the terrorist, and it would – in effect – be the killing of an unarmed man. The idea was dropped.

But for every measured civil servant, intelligence agent or law enforcement officer, there are others who subscribe to that notion that we can only sleep in our beds because rough men stand ready to do violence on our behalf, even if that means extending the parameters of the law. When many of these issues were being debated hotly in the UK press, a poll found that 34 per cent of the population said governments should be allowed to use some degree of torture in some instances.[73]

It is a creeping normalisation of state violence that led the investigative journalist Andrew Fowler to conclude that 'there is a real possibility that the overreach of national security laws in the west will damage the very commodity that [they are] supposedly designed to protect: security and liberty.[74]

I reached out to David Luban, a Professor in Law and Philosophy at Georgetown University, a man who has written extensively on human rights since 9/11, to ask him about his view on this impact on civil liberties. 'Opportunistic governments love the idea that they can wave the red flag of fighting terrorism to expand their power and whack the pesky human rights community,' he replied. 'It's also a way executives can push against the courts – and the courts go along. A case in point: in 1999 Israel's Supreme Court banned torture. Last December (2017) they gutted that decision, in a "ticking bomb" case. So, yes: the War on Terror has devastated world commitment to human rights.'

Other nations have followed the lead taken by Europe and America. In Tunisia, in December 2003, the parliament passed a law to 'support the international effort to combat terrorism and money laundering'.[75] Human rights organisations immediately criticised the law as heavily restricting people's freedom and beliefs; within five years of the new law being passed, almost 1,000 Tunisians had been detained, charged or convicted of terrorism.[76] According to a 2015 Tunisian counter-terrorism law, a protestor that damages a police car or a government building could be charged with terrorism and punished with a minimum of six years of prison.

In Morocco, following a Casablanca terrorist attack in 2003 that killed forty-two people, a new law was passed that expanded the definition of terrorism, strengthened the power of authorities and introduced severe sentences for inciting terrorism; 2,112 suspects were charged with terrorist offences after the bombings, of whom 903 were convicted and 17 were sentenced to death.[77] Human Rights Watch described the legal process as routinely subject 'to serious human rights violations'.[78]

In Bangladesh, the 2006 Information Communication Technology Act (ICTA) was introduced as a means of combating terrorism on the Internet and allowing the government to engage in surveillance without judicial oversight.[79] It made it an offence to publish 'fake, obscene or defaming information in electronic form',[80] a wording described as 'so vague that law enforcers can interpret it as they will to arrest anyone, anytime'.[81] In a 2012 amendment of the Anti-Terrorism Act 2009, an Act that has a broad and vague definition of what terrorism is, the punishment for financing terrorism was upgraded to death.[82]

Similar loose wording of what 'terrorism' means, and the heavy-handed application of judicial force to combat it, has been seen in

Russia, where a 2016 amendment to a Federal Counter-Terrorism Act was said to severely undermine freedom of expression in particular on the Internet, as well as other rights including privacy and freedom of religion.[83]

Globally the pattern is clear: terrorism legislation, often justified in the immediate aftermath of a suicide bombing, has been used around the world to weaken, not strengthen, human rights.

The issue is further complicated by the fact that would-be suicide bombers see such liberties as an Achilles heel. In a 2015 publication by ISIS intended as a terror guide for lone jihadists, entitled 'How to Survive in the West', there is a line that makes you stop and think. It says that Cage, a London-based advocacy organisation which aims 'to empower communities impacted by the War on Terror', has information on their website about what 'questions you have to answer, what you can say "No Comment" to, and what you can answer with a lawyer.'

Given this, it is no surprise the jihadist poses a fundamental challenge to the rule of law. If the state oversteps the mark and is seen as being violent, unjust or morally corrupt, then terrorism may itself seem legitimate and justified to the disenfranchised and dissolute.[84] But if the state does not stop suicidal killers, then it is seen as weak. It is a quandary further complicated by the fact that there are significant economic opportunities to be found in all this, in the place where counterterrorism meets capitalism.

To say that the War on Terror has lined the pockets of some would be an understatement. There have been billions made in its waging, the details of which are hidden behind a cloak of 'security' and 'national interest'. While it might be a battle that governments have thrown themselves into, the real victors of this fight have been the private sector and their profit margins. So, when the Counter-Terrorism Expo in London launched its website for their 2018 show, it was no surprise they posted two UK government reports at the bottom: 'Strategy for Countering Terrorism' alongside 'Increasing Security Exports'.[85]

The latter was unabashed. 'Significant opportunities' were identified for Saudi Arabia, a country knee-deep in Salafist rhetoric and funding; 'billions of pounds' of sales opportunities were envisaged in Qatar. Throughout the Gulf, the UK government concluded, 'significant resources' were available for 'building security capabilities', the whole region being 'critically important to UK security and prosperity'.

The snake eats itself. The very region responsible for the rise in Salafi-jihadism and suicidal terror funding is also seen as the jewel in the crown for the UK's security exports against ideological terror. 'Opportunities exist globally,' said the UK government, 'particularly in developing nations and those facing a specific terrorist threat'; the global security industry was worth some £571 billion in 2016, it said, boasting an annual growth rate of 10.3 per cent. To find out a little more about this often opaque industry, I decided to visit the 2017 Security Expo in west London, hosted in the cavernous hall of Olympia.

At first, it seemed like any other exhibition: rows upon rows of cubicles, each manned by smartly dressed men and women armed with glossy brochures. But the thing that distinguished this expo was the overriding marketing of the ever-present threat. On entry, immediately to the right, stood a large display listing the day's talks: 'Are we doing enough,' one asked, 'to prevent and stop the next attack?' It seemed not. As an interview said in a magazine being handed out: 'We need people to realise that [the victim] could be them, and it could happen tomorrow.'

'Security forces have to be lucky all the time,' read another article, 'while the terrorists only need to be lucky once.' The rationale was that nothing, in the fight against terrorism, was enough.

The shadow of the suicide bomber was everywhere. Talks touched on 'Rehabilitating Jihadis'; 'Lone Wolves'; 'The Art of the Possible – Tackling Suicide Terrorism'; and 'Why We Need a Trained Population to Combat Terrorism'. Here, the head of security for Westminster Cathedral was presenting on 'Adversarial Risks to Places of Worship'; the former security head of the Los Angeles Museum of Art was discussing terror threats to the cultural heritage sector; someone was offering up a case study of 'Good Practice in Hotels' in relation to counterterrorism; while the head of security from King's College in London was talking on security in the education sector.

There were security lectures about the terrorists' threat to the National Health Service, royal palaces, theme parks, stadiums, railways, shipping routes, oil supplies, nuclear transport, the Houses of Parliament, and fire services. There were 'Safer Cities' roundtables, featuring senior city officials from Barcelona, Brussels, Melbourne, London and The Hague, all witness to recent suicide attack threats. In all, over 250 sessions were crammed into two days, each of them dealing with the threat of terror to various sectors. It seemed summed up by the seminar called 'Desperate Times . . . Extreme Measures.'

These were just the talks. Packed throughout the hall were dozens of different security products for sale because here, underpinning the terror threat, lay commercial opportunities. Companies were selling blast-resistant buildings; mobile checkpoints; advanced emergency warning systems; surveillance drones with names like 'Sparrow-Hawk'; 'bomb blast protection' glass; and 'blast resistant' automatic sliding doors. Others had created robotic targets for live-fire weapons training, and one firm had developed a programme that allowed soldiers and police to practise counterterror operations using 'virtual reality' suits in a simulated computer setting – suicide bombers had gone virtual.

Men walked the corridors in blue suits and polished shoes, eyeing up the goods. Ex-military and ex-police officers found their natural territory here; the whole day passed and I did not see one black face and only a handful of women. That said a great deal about the real bases of power in Western culture.

Training was on offer everywhere with 'next generation techniques' for counter-IED work. One group ran a forensic course, teaching 'how terrorists are taught to manufacture' suicide bombs, 'according to genuine jihadi' bomb-making instructions.[86] There was a conference on offer that explored 'non-racial profiling'; how not to let a suicide bomber's 'good looks' fool you; and insights into the recruitment and training of 'the suicidal terrorist'. Universities, too, had realised the profitable potential of such courses: University College London was offering an MSc in countering organised terrorism, costing £25,800 to overseas students.

Counterterrorism here had been professionalised, regulated and monetised. A business advertised job opportunities for '1000s of suitable security professionals', while the British Institute of Facilities Management handed out guidance notes. 'Terrorism,' their pamphlet warned, 'is an issue that is not going to go away anytime soon.' It will be, they suggested, a major problem for the next three decades at least.

'There really is no excuse for not taking action on this,' they said, and offered up a security audit, asking whether your office had a 'challenge culture' to anybody not wearing a pass, whether your windows were blast protected, and whether a 'clear desk' policy out of working hours was in place. And I couldn't help but think that such a list, in the hands of a paranoiac or a martinet, could become a cudgel.

What was clear was just how much suicidal terror had infected the mindsets and offerings of this room. I stopped at one stall. The man there helped run an airline consultancy service. He, like many others that day, was reluctant to be quoted directly but did say that suicide bombers had radically transformed his industry. Nine-eleven, the shoe bomber and the underpants bomber had all had a monumental impact, but then again, the defining thing about the airline industry was that any calamitous event was immediately thrust into the public eye. 'If we were able to hush everything up,' he said, 'we wouldn't be such a target.'

Years of working in an industry facing such a threat had made this man cautious. He had just come back from Freetown in Sierra Leone and said it was like being in a British airport in the 1970s. He had seen lapses in security that would make the public think twice about boarding a plane.

That language of fear had been transformed into a sales pitch. One brochure had an image of a chameleon in a forest. 'You might not have spotted the threat', ran the text below, and there, hidden in the jungle canopy, was a lurking terrorist in black. Another said that 'any perimeter can no longer be considered as impenetrable'.

One of the main ways of averting such a threat was through the monitoring of the public, evident in the dozens of organisations here selling surveillance equipment. One company, Asqella, had developed 'sub-millimetre wave camera technology' that could scan crowds for 'concealed threats', such as a suicide vest. 'Seeing the Unseen' was its promise, and it marketed their product with the line: 'it can also be hidden from sight as a completely covert operation', meaning that people could be screened without their knowing. While it claimed no sensitive 'anatomical details' were revealed, there was no concern raised about secretly screening people. When I asked the company's chief about this, he said it was 'inaccurate' to say that they encouraged such use, despite having it in their marketing materials.[87]

There were devices, too, that could identify explosive materials, offering 'forensic quality trace detection' in seconds. These were able to detect 'less than a billionth of a gram' of explosives, with 'near to zero' rates of false positive or false negative findings. Such a device, the manufacturer – Mass Spec – promised, could review cargo, freight and over 900 people an hour, with analysis taking less than four seconds. Another system, by Radio Physics, was said to be able to detect a suicide bomb vest over 30 metres away.

It was not just bodies that could be tracked for explosives – emotions were being monitored too. One business had created a surveillance system that could 'detect any signs of aggression'. Another had developed CCTV software that sought to replicate the mechanisms by which humans recognise each other, creating an autonomous identification process that could potentially analyse the gait of a would-be bomber and issue an alert before they have even triggered their bomb.

Such forms of surveillance have consequences; some see in the West a 'paranoid surveillant racism', through which Muslim populations are viewed as threatening death and destruction.[88] Such nuance was not uttered here. Technological advances, instead, seemed to supersede ethical considerations. A nervous speaker was hosting one side event. His team, SilentTalker, had developed a product with Manchester University that, effectively, detected deception. Theirs was a system of psychological profiling that combined image processing with artificial intelligence and was able – they claimed – to identify when a person was lying. In telling a lie, we unconsciously perform micro-gestures, and their system picked up on these twitches and flinches. 'The applications,' the presenter said, 'are virtually endless.'

'Especially in the hand of a despot,' I thought.

Overall, such surveillance systems could gather a mass of information – information that, to some, provided opportunities. Companies offered services to analyse such data, promising a 'rich history of responses and actions' that 'eliminated doubt'. Surveillance developed to counter the external threat of terror seemed, here, to be inverted – the cameras of the corporation not only pointing outwards at the ever-present threat of attack but also to scrutinise the threat within. Corporations said this data could be shared with 'internal and external stakeholders'.

It raised a fear: how what was first justified as a security measure could, rapidly, become a different form of control. With such analytical tools, you could not only ascertain security threats but also 'gain a better understanding of your people'. The panopticon justified by terror could be inverted and used to monitor more than just terrorists.

'If you have nothing to hide, you have nothing to worry about,' was how one seller put it, but to me, lines of privacy were being blurred. The interest here was global sales, and there seemed little stopping surveillance equipment being sold to states with draconian laws and a culture of extrajudicial killings. Foreign officials walked around, some in the military uniforms of their homelands; this was a global industry, seeking – above all – to win lucrative contracts. One pamphlet, aimed at 'Homeland Security Solutions', was in Arabic. Other companies were to boast of work in Sierra Leone, Egypt, Pakistan, Sudan and Afghanistan. Their products had taglines such as 'from the battlefield to the street' – the creep of militarisation into a peace setting. Here, the phrase 'originally designed for the military' was seen as a product benefit.

Above all the UK crowed about its expertise in fighting terrorism. The legacy of combating the IRA, and the War on Terror, had meant – as the chairman of the UK Security Expo, the Rt. Hon. Lord West of Spithead, was to say in a brochure – 'the UK is ideally suited to being the global centre of excellence for security given our long history in counter-terrorism'. The fightback against the suicide bomb was, it seems, a marvellous business opportunity to Lord West and everyone else here.

In this way, government policy intersected with industry, and security aligned with capitalism. Not just here, either. In the US and the EU, former political aides and generals have become homeland-security lobbyists.[89] One notable peddler of influence was Michael Chertoff, former US Secretary of Homeland Security, who co-founded a lobby group soon after he left the job in 2009. One of his clients was Rapiscan, the producers of airport body scanners. Under Chertoff, the US government had purchased the machine and, when out of government, Chertoff sought to crank up the orders. When the underwear bomb plot failed, Chertoff was across the media, arguing for more full-body scanners in airports.[90] The Transportation Security Administration (TSA) was soon to order $173 million worth of the new machines, despite warnings that UK Home Office officials were not 'persuaded that they would work comprehensively against terrorist threats to aviation'.[91] But fear – and the protection it leads us to desire – sells.

The logic of the selling of security is neatly summed up in a book called Top Secret America, where the authors write that hundreds

Arms and security conferences like this one in Las Vegas have been the source of huge profits during the War on Terror

of billions of dollars have been spent on defeating suicide bombers without a real questioning of 'what they were getting for their money'. 'And even if they did want an answer to that question, they would not be given one,' it reads, 'both because those same officials have decided it would gravely harm national security to share such classified information—and because the officials themselves don't know.'[92]

Capitalism meets fear and fear meets secrecy – the ultimate hard sell. And you could not help but feel in that hall that it was, in part, because of those seductions of profits and patronage that alternative ways to combat the Salafi-jihadist threat – one that almost two decades years of war had not defeated – were not adequately considered.

In October 2017, the European Union announced it was to spend €118.5 million on projects to 'better enhance the protection of public spaces'.[93] The list of projects was extensive: security barriers, protective urban landscape design, the protection of sports and cultural events, raising public awareness, tackling terrorist financing, supporting law enforcement, regulating explosive precursors, improving dialogue with the private sector ... it went on. The press release seemed to describe a Sisyphean task at best.[94]

When a threat can come from anywhere, everywhere is affected. In 2017, the photographer Edmund Clark held an exhibition at the Imperial War Museum in London, focusing on the impact such a reality had had around the world. Through photographs of hotels used in rendition seizures, Guantánamo Bay communal areas and the interiors of control order homes, Clark showed the architecture of counterterrorism at work. And underpinning it was his concern that 'terror affects all of us'. As he said, 'Our daily lives, our own personal spaces are in some way implicated in or contaminated by terror and the fear of terror and the measures that our governments claim are needed to protect us from the threat of terrorism.'[95] The language and architecture of terror has seeped into the very fabric of society.

In places most beset by suicide bombings, this is extreme and overt. Anyone driving around the streets of Lahore or Basra or Abuja will testify to how hotels, compounds and office blocks are often like fortresses, with body scanners and jagged-glass rimmed walls. Here, the luxury of the aesthetic is lost to the necessity of security; barbed wire and sandbagged entrances transform cities into militarised zones. I once had to hire a dozen armed security guards in Mogadishu for protection, each of them demanding to be given a bonus to buy the low-level amphetamine khat for the job, too. The hotel we stayed in was a stronghold. In this way lives are truncated by terror, hemmed in and reduced.

But even in less impacted environments, the urban landscape has been slowly transformed. It has led the Royal Institute of British Architects (RIBA) to publish a manual on 'good design that creates a sense of security without a siege mentality';[96] to New York City installing 1,500 security barriers;[97] and to 'rings of steel' being thrown up around London.[98] The most striking instance I could find of such new architecture was the installation of a reflecting pool for the headquarters of Devon Energy in Oklahoma City – they had built a protective moat.[99] These were the fears of an epoch fixed in space.

Such transformations should concern us because, as Winston Churchill once said, 'We shape our buildings and afterwards our buildings shape us.'[100] If cities slowly evolve into becoming defensive centres, does that defensiveness affect the way we see the world and alter our very nature? We might often be blind to such things, but do security barriers and cordons and their hard geometries harden us in turn?

Unquestionably, for terrorists, destroying a public space can be as symbolic as harming the people that inhabit it. The Eiffel Tower, the Golden Gate Bridge, the Vatican, Disneyland and the UK Houses of Parliament have all been cited as targets eyed up by Salafi-jihadists.

The Statue of Liberty and Mount Rushmore have even had their surfaces scanned so they can be reconstructed if they are destroyed by an attack.[101]

The threat also haunts public events. In the run-up to New Year's Eve 2017, headlines reported how, at celebrations marking the end of a year defined by repeated terror attacks across the world, the menace of terror loomed large. 'You will see an increase in heavy weapons, bomb squad personnel, radiological detection teams, and our technology to include over 1,000 cameras in and around the area of Times Square for the event,' the NYPD's chief of counterterrorism said.[102] Some Hogmanay celebrations were cancelled, the cost of counterterrorism security cited as the reason.[103] One front-page headline even warned of 'SAS snipers on streets for New Year's Eve'.

Tourism seems to be the canary in the mine in all of this. Nine-eleven saw US air passenger numbers drop by half; the year following saw a decline in ticket sales for the first time in two decades. This had real consequences: American Airlines and United Airlines cut 20,000 jobs, and the Caribbean saw a 13.5 per cent decline in US visitors, resulting in about 365,000 people being laid off work.[104] Manchester, London and Paris, following attacks there, all experienced significant visitor drops, too. And places with more of a prevalence of suicide attacks – vast swathes of the Middle East, for instance – remain empty of visitors. Suicide bombers, in this way, reduce our horizons – either with sandbags or torn-up travel plans.

In 2016, I travelled to Jordan and visited the southern city of Petra to see the rock-cut architecture of the Nabataean Kingdom. The place was virtually deserted, save for local Jordanians and a small group of American men. These Americans all had the uniform beards, beige fatigues, wraparound sunglasses and desert boots of US military contractors. There were virtually no other tourists. Such a drop-off in numbers is reactive to terror – in December that year, one of Jordan's biggest Crusader castles was attacked by jihadists, killing ten, including a Canadian tourist. The terrorists' suicide belts were later found by the police.[105]

In Turkey, tourist sites were deliberately targeted by Salafists, with more than 40 people killed and 239 wounded when three suicide bombers detonated their vests in 2016 at Istanbul's Ataturk International airport, adding yet more woe to an already dire tourism situation that had seen a 28 per cent drop in visitor numbers.[106] Early that year, a suicide bomber killed at least ten in Istanbul's Sultanahmet square, most of them German tourists.[107] Perhaps it is no surprise that in CNN's 'Places to Visit in 2018' article not one Muslim-majority country was recommended.[108]

It is reasonable to say that suicide bombers have tainted the entire global foreign travel experience. Before 9/11 there was a relative laxity when it came to airport security. Security was hitherto in place – the days of international air travel with no checks or screenings was disrupted in the 1960s after a flight from the US to Cuba was hijacked. But after the attacks on the Twin Towers, things became very serious. Knives of less than four inches were banned altogether, and families were refused access 'airside' where they once were able to wave their loved ones away on a plane.

In the US alone, 60,000 security screeners were hired, many from an 'aggrieved underclass'. The writer Paul Theroux said of them: 'Like many instant officials involved in private security in America . . . they are, on the whole, intolerably rude.'[109] Perhaps this is because humour is anathema to the security search; dozens of people have been arrested for making jokes about having a bomb in their bag when passing through airport security. It has led to extreme responses, such as the pilot who quipped, as a security guard inspected his tweezers, 'Why are you worried about tweezers when I could crash the plane?' He was arrested.[110]

It is not just a sense of humour that has been lost. Baggage and passenger screening was estimated, in the fifteen years after 2001, to have cost as much as $100 billion.[111] A radicalised petty thief called Richard Reid – the 'shoe bomber' mentioned earlier – changed things even further. His failed attempt to detonate explosives packed into his shoes during an American Airlines flight to Miami on 22 December 2001 was to cause passengers the world over to go through the ritual of removing their shoes when passing through airport checking – a remarkable impact of one man on the entire globe.

Liquids over a certain level were also banned. Passenger IDs had to replicate the name on their ticket. Jackets had to be taken off and security pat-downs became routine. Pilots could apply to carry guns. Cockpit doors were fortified and locked. Children were no longer allowed that thrilling visit to the pilot's side. The actions of an ugly few tainted the journeys of billions and security queues were created that stretched seemingly for ever (a three-hour wait was cited to the US Senate)[112] causing untold flights to be missed.

The ripples and reverberations of these security measures emerged in unexpected ways. For some, dignity in labour was created: jobs were created for the new roles of armed air marshals or screener guards. For others, dignity was lost: a body-scanning machine had to be scrapped after it was found that the image of the passenger showed them to be practically naked, alongside fears of there being radioactive exposure, too.[113] Even people who fit outside the 'profile' have been subjected to humiliations, like the eighty-eight-year-old traveller in a wheelchair who suffered a prolonged search following the identification of a bulge in her colostomy bag.[114]

Debates erupted about passenger profiling. In the US, Arabs, Muslims and Latinos appear to have been specifically targeted for screening, despite repeated assurances from the Department of Homeland Security that they do not profile passengers on their ethnicity, race or religion.[115] 'Flying while Muslim' has even become a phrase – with untold numbers of passengers in hijabs or thawbs stopped. Many think it only sensible to interrogate people who adhere to a religion, a subset of a subset of which is responsible for most suicide attacks today.[116] But this is, again, the uncomfortable situation that a minority wielding terror can bring to bear – one where any 'male with a fresh shave and lighter skin on his lower face', could be considered a possible Muslim zealot, according to an internal US government document.[117]

Despite all this, though, the fear of the suicide bomber sneaking through persists. In 2011, a year and a half after Umar Farouk Abdul-mutallab – the so-called underwear bomber – passed through airport screening in Amsterdam and boarded a Christmas Day flight with plastic explosives sewn into his undergarments, the US screening system was found to be falling short 'in significant ways'.[118] More recently, the US's Minneapolis–Saint Paul International airport failed 95 per cent of security tests conducted.[119]

Different nations also have different standards of scrutiny. In Baghdad, on certain flights, you have to be dropped off four miles away from the airport and then shuttled in by taxi. After that, you undergo six separate security clearances before you can board the aircraft.[120] In Egypt, however, where a bomb was smuggled on board a Russian airliner at Sharm el-Sheikh airport, killing 224 people in 2015, it was said by the British foreign secretary that they had a 'cultural problem' with security implementation.[121] Security guards there were reportedly seen taking cash to let passengers skip the security queues.[122] Kenya, Rwanda and Tanzania are also said to be currently using the failed Rapiscan scanners, despite their showing a repeated inability to identify guns, bombs or knives hidden by Teflon or in the folds of a passenger's clothing.[123]

Heightened security has even led to deadly violence. In December 2005, Rigoberto Alpizar, a Costa Rican-born American citizen, was shot and killed on the tarmac of Miami International airport when two federal air marshals opened fire, hitting him eleven times. They believed he was about to detonate explosives hidden in his bag.

Onlookers said the mentally ill Alpizar never mentioned a bomb, and none was found.[124]

The fact that air marshals are armed is a concern in itself, offering possible violent passengers a way to seize a gun. It's a quandary made starker when you read of a passenger finding a loaded gun in the aeroplane toilet, an absent-minded air marshal having left it in there.[125] Others contend that for all the precautions, there are still security gaps: box-cutter knives are still allowed on certain flights, while body cavity searches are not performed on passengers.[126]

The central challenge is that whatever steps are taken to address the threat of suicide bombers getting on board a plane, there will be those who seek to find a way around them. AQAP's online magazine, 'Echo of Battle', released in February 2010, outlined ways to confuse security equipment designed to pick up explosive residue.[127] Such scheming means that, while security is today seen as a standard feature of any trip, the lurking shadow of the bomber persists, and this presents a hostage to fortune. In October 2017, Moscow had 130 fake bomb calls on one day alone, forcing the removal of 100,000 people from all four Moscow airports, five railway stations, and several shopping malls, hotels, schools and offices. No explosives were found.[128] In November of that year, in Oxford Circus in London, Christmas shoppers were hit by rushing pedestrians as a rumour of a terror attack spread, partly spurred on by a terrified celebrity tweeting he was under attack. A number were injured, with nine needing hospital treatment; there were no terrorists.[129]

In turn, such fear can itself be manipulated. It is not in the interests of security services to underestimate the security threat posed by jihadists, and the 'sexing up' of a threat of imminent attack is all too common. US intelligence agencies in 2002 said that the number of trained Al-Qaeda operatives in the US was between 2,000 and 5,000, yet in 2003, FBI Director Robert Mueller told the Senate Intelligence Committee his agency had yet to identify even one Al-Qaeda cell in the US.[130] He saw shadows in this absence: 'I remain very concerned about what we are not seeing,' read one sentence highlighted in bold in the submitted text.[131] No Al-Qaeda cell was ever found.

The reason for this sexing up is innate. Those whose focus is to prevent suicide bombings will, to a degree, see danger everywhere. Given that a successful suicide attack can cause devastating damage, any threat deemed credible by a security agency has to be one taken very seriously indeed. And, just as the clichéd turkey does not vote for Christmas, neither would an intelligence agency seek to downplay a threat – after all, budgets and livelihoods are involved here.

The most infamous instance of this came when the CIA 'grossly exaggerated' the threat of weapons of mass destruction held by Saddam Hussein in Iraq.[132] But there have been plenty of other moments when we have been told that a suicide attack was imminent when it was not. In 2003, the British Prime Minister Tony Blair deployed tanks in Heathrow after being told by security services 'to do nothing, deploy the military, or close Heathrow airport'. When there was no attack (and would tanks deter a suicide bomber anyway?), some claimed the deployment of the military was more to encourage the growing number who opposed the war in Iraq to support the government's line.[133]

Having met many counterterrorism experts in researching this book, I understand why such red alerts are issued, and yet no bombing happens. Much is done in the shadows, and we never hear about the many attacks that have been prevented. This is, again, the terrorists' weapon: anything that is seen to overstep the mark in stopping a suicide bombing can be decried as an erosion of human rights, and an evisceration of civil justice. Precisely what the terrorist wants. But still, the threat lurks – creating a fear that spreads from infecting the likes of militaries, the police and the judicial process, to one that affects the core of our societies.

Chapter 15

Generation Terror

In the end, what are jihadist suicide bombings? They are disproportionate, lack perspective and are marked by an extreme absence of
empathy. They violate civil rights, seek to destroy democratic ideals,
and set out to harm the canons of multiculturalism and freedom of
speech. In essence, they aim to destroy the things social liberalism
seeks to be.

But while it is often said that Salafi-jihadists pose the greatest threat
to that political ideology, other dangers lurk. Because when the state
fails to moderate its response to terror – to keep their response well
defined, limited and controlled – counterterrorism policies have
been shown, repeatedly, to pose an equal threat, if not a greater one,
to social liberalism. This is not a new observation, but with suicide
attacks escalating in the heart of the West, it is an observation worth
repeating.

We are now in our eighteenth year of the War on Terror, and
during that time we have seen, again and again, one more military
incursion, one more legislative bill, one more police raid. Alone, these
changes look sometimes measured, sometimes contained, and always
fiercely justified. But combined, they have helped alter the body politic in ways that have yet to be truly tested, and have transformed our

own relationship with the state. Things once held as inviolable – the right to speak and write freely, protection from arbitrary arrest and punishment, even being told why you have been detained – have been tried and often cast aside in the name of security. Boundaries have been crossed that set dangerous precedents.

'In the name of security' is a term that should possibly concern us as much as the phrase 'another suicide bombing'. In recent months it has been used to justify the destruction of private property,[1] the pushing back of migrants adrift at sea,[2] the collation of customer data by social media companies,[3] the imposition of tariffs on free-trade partner goods,[4] the criminalisation of online speech,[5] the murder and mistreatment of terror suspects,[6] and the storage of our personal data by governments.[7]

It is a phrase that has rooted itself in the heart of political life – challenging empathy, charity and, ultimately, our sense of humanity. And it is what has been said and done in the name of security that lies at the very heart of how the suicide bomber has shaped the modern world.

On 15 December 2017, the *Daily Mail* – a newspaper said to be the most influential in Britain – ran a front-page story.[8] 'Another Human Rights Fiasco!' read the headline. 'Iraqi "caught red-handed with bomb" wins £33,000 because our soldiers kept him in custody for too long.'

It was yet another attack by that publication on such legislation. 'Too often the courts decide the human rights of terrorist suspects are more important than the human rights of victims,' a retired colonel was quoted as saying. Human rights were, yet again, seen to be frustrating the interests of national security.

In previous editions, the *Daily Mail* had denounced European human rights legislation as an 'insult' that 'imperilled' Britain, 'shielded' terrorists, helped jihadists 'avoid justice', and freed prisoners, allowing them 'to kill'.[9] The paper had lobbied hard for the release of a British soldier imprisoned after executing an injured militant on the dusty plains of Afghanistan.[10] And, on a daily basis, it obsessively reported on migration, terrorism and the growth of Islam in the UK.

The problem with the Iraqi bomb story, though, was that there was no evidence the arrested man – Mr Abd Al-Waheed – was a jihadist.[11] As his London lawyer said to me: 'The judge held that the evidence about being caught "red-handed" was a fabrication. The forensic evidence demonstrated that Mr Al Waheed could not have been handling explosive materials. It soon became apparent to his interrogators that he was innocent.' A doctor also testified that Mr Al Waheed 'appears to have been deliberately beaten' while in custody. Eventually, after about six weeks and forensic tests that confirmed Al Waheed was indeed innocent, he was released. He was later to be diagnosed with PTSD.

A man had been arrested, beaten, imprisoned for weeks and deeply traumatised, and then forced to wait ten years to get a measure of compensation. Yet his case was not highlighted as an abuse of military justice, but rather a 'human rights fiasco'. I was struck by how corrosive this sort of journalism was, so filed a complaint with the Press Standards Organisation in London. This eventually led to the paper publishing two separate corrections – not the first time the *Daily Mail* had been caught out when railing against human rights legislation.

A few years before, the paper had run the story: 'Human right to make a killing'. It claimed that judges at the European Court of Human Rights had handed 'taxpayer-funded pay-outs of £4.4 million' to terrorists and criminals.[12] But the amount was exaggerated, as was the allegation about the people it went to. Again, it led the *Mail* to publish a correction with the line: 'Many applicants are of good character with no criminal connections.'[13]

This is a paper that has published a cartoon of migrants entering

Europe accompanied by rats, invoking an ugly stereotype of sub-humans once used by Nazi apologists.[14] A paper that has employed the columnist Katie Hopkins, who has called Islam a 'Religion of Murder', and who had asked, after one London terror attack, 'How many more attacks must pass before we acknowledge these are no longer the acts of "extremists"?'[15] Hopkins was even to rail against nuance in reporting on suicide attacks; to her, journalism that sought to contextualise terror was guilty of 'shape-shifting, neutering, dulling down, dampening'. Nuance itself was denounced as 'politically correct language'.[16]

These doubts about both the virtues of human right legislation, as well as the liberal desire to analyse a problem in the hopes of solving it, are suspicions held by the right-wing press in general, particularly when it comes to terror. This is concerning. The state, with its military and judicial power, is always going to be a blunt instrument, but the press, I believe, needs to be more than that. It should offer explanation, pose counter-arguments and challenge the seats of power.

In the aftermath of the Manchester attack, though, these necessary bulwarks against the abuse of power were thrown out of the window. It was reported with praise that soldiers were 'flooding Brit streets' to protect its citizens 'packed with firepower to take out terrorists'.[17] Few asked whether the fact 'up to 3,800 troops' were being deployed across the nation was proportional or strategically justified.[18] Instead, the *Daily Telegraph* reported that visitors thought 'the sight of soldiers in camouflage, carrying rifles was reassuring'.[19]

When the *Daily Express* reported that SAS troops were '"posing as homeless beggars across UK streets" to foil attacks', they did so with praise, not disquiet.[20] But the idea there might be armed men in disguise on British streets, attempting to stop something as random and covert as a suicide bomber, worried me. So I submitted a freedom of information request to the government to find out if this was true or not. I was not asking where such soldiers might be, nor how many, nor what they were posing as. I just wanted to know whether this was happening or not. My request was rejected because of 'national security' – the British public are not allowed to know if the government uses undercover soldiers on our streets.

Such concern was never voiced in the original article; outrage at the terrorists' act had silenced criticism, while calls for urgent action had supplanted analysis and contemplation. Nuance and context were actively shunned. When Jeremy Corbyn, the British Labour party leader, said that the UK needed a response to the Manchester bombing that 'fights rather than fuels terrorism', the *Sun*, Britain's most popular newspaper, screamed in outrage. They attacked him for 'linking Manchester bombing to government's war on terror just four days after atrocity left 22 dead', and ran with a front-page headline that read 'Corbinexcusable'.[21]

It was a heavy-handed smear, especially given that the sister of Salman Abedi said her brother had carried out the attack to avenge air strikes on Syria. 'He saw children – Muslim children – dying everywhere, and wanted revenge', she told the *Wall Street Journal*.[22] Just as it ignored the fact the British government accepted their own military intervention would cause a backlash. On 10 February 2003, one month before the Iraq war began, the UK's Joint Intelligence Committee – the main government advisory body on intelligence matters – released a white paper called 'International Terrorism: War With Iraq'. It concluded that the threat from terrorism to the UK 'will be heightened by military action against Iraq. The broader threat from Islamist terrorists will also increase in the event of war, reflecting intensified anti-US/anti-Western sentiment in the Muslim world, including among Muslim communities in the West.'[23]

It was not the first time an attempt towards a more subtle interpretation of the drivers of suicide bombings was denounced. When, in 2015, the former Deputy Prime Minister John Prescott said 'we've played a huge part in making [British jihadists] want to leave Britain and take up arms in a foreign land', he was condemned as an 'apologist for terror'.[24] And, two days before the 2017 general election, 'Apologists for Terror' was, again, the *Mail*'s headline as they devoted fourteen pages to accusing the Labour party's three most influential MPs – Jeremy Corbyn, John McDonnell and Diane Abbott – of devoting 'their lives to befriending the enemies of Britain while undermining the very institutions that keep us safe in our beds'.[25]

But, you might ask, why should we listen to a terrorist's motivation? Their victims were never given such respect. My answer is this: if we do not, then how can we truly defeat the rise of such terror? It is, perhaps, predictable to want to respond to the suicide bomber's terror with hard and blunt force, but have such responses – military intervention in Afghanistan and then Iraq and beyond – led to a reduction of the terror threat? I would say not. As I write this in August 2018, the MI5 terror threat level for the UK is severe – the second highest it can be. Pointing this out, though, does not win friends.

Attempts to try to comprehend the motivations of a suicide bomber are often rewarded with *ad hominem* attacks. When Nicolas Henin, a French journalist and former hostage of ISIS, spoke to the BBC about the need to ensure justice, not revenge, was meted out to its adherents, the comments on social media were immediate and predictable: 'Bonkers!'; 'Bring back hanging!'; 'Fool!'; and 'Stockholm Syndrome?' were just the first few of a long line of insults.

Similarly, the comments section under news articles following the Manchester attack also showed an urgent desire for revenge: 'we need internment and we need capital punishment for these people and their supporters'; 'we are at war and no room for political correctness'; 'we need to toughen up and really hurt these idiots!' came the replies in their thousands.[26]

Twitter, Facebook and twenty-four-hour rolling news on our smartphones mean that, even though the vast majority of us are not present at a suicide bombing, the terrible nature of such events can touch us all, and we vent our fury in turn. Just as 9/11 saw the greatest loss of life ever broadcast live in history, so too were the killings of London, Manchester, Brussels and Paris brought instantly into our living rooms and our everyday consciousness. One study found suicide bombings get twelve times more coverage than other terrorist attacks.[27] They also get more attention than other kinds of explosive violence – such as air strikes.[28]

The collective fascination with the suicide bomber is, perhaps, not that surprising. It is a form of violence that provokes a host of responses: from our morbid fascination with the act of suicide, our amazement at the mindset of someone who would kill and die in such a way, to the illicit allure of seeing a mutilated body, suicide bombings are inherently laden with meaning and changing perspectives. We are confronted, for instance, by the fact that a photograph of a body at the scene of a bombing might be either victim or perpetrator – meaning our response to such an image could change in an instant.

A suicide bomb seems, in some ways, one of the most extreme instances of our witnessing the pain of others. So much so that it renders photographs of the suicide bomber's acts – from the burning towers of Manhattan to the masked face of a victim of 7/7 – darkly iconic in turn. It is something fixed. Something rejected. The actions of 'the other' distilled.

Hollywood's scriptwriters have noted these themes, even before 9/11. Many blockbusters have a pivotal moment where a central protagonist blows themselves up for the good of others. This form of 'benevolent' self-sacrifice is often integral to the 'hero's journey', that lodestar for many a scriptwriter. As Joseph Campbell, whose research into myths inspired Star Wars, once said, 'A hero properly is someone who has given his life for something bigger than himself.'[29] And there are many films where the hero, faced with a non-human threat, blows themselves up to save their team or the world. This is the case with extra-terrestrials in *Independence Day*,[30] *Edge of Tomorrow*,[31] and *Aliens*;[32] with asteroids in *Armageddon*[33] and *Deep Impact*;[34] with zombies in *I Am Legend*[35] and *Village of the Damned*;[36] and with skull-crawlers in *Kong: Skull Island*.[37]

Blockbuster sci-fi and fantasy films have also begun to include suicide bombings against other humans. In *Guardians of the Galaxy* and *Star Wars: The Last Jedi*, female characters blow themselves up to defeat their nemesis and to save others. In *Star Trek: Into Darkness*, Starfleet operative John Harrison detonates a bomb that kills him and all of London's 'Section 31 installation' in return for a medical intervention that could save his daughter's life.[38] In the X-Men franchise *Logan*, the 'glorified truffle hunter' mutant Caliban (who can sniff out other mutants) detonates two grenades inside his cell, killing himself and his guards, with the final words: 'Beware of the light.'[39] While in the film adaptation of Tolkien's *The Lord of the Rings*, an Orc suicide bomber breaches Helm's Deep in a suicide attack.[40]

In these ways, the suicide bomber has entered mass culture, distanced from the horror of the terrorist act, and often framed altruistically. There can be, Hollywood tells us, good suicide bombers – albeit pitted against aliens, meteorites, zombies, dinosaurs or psychopaths – both reflecting and buttressing a deep public fascination with themes such as suicide, murder, martyrdom and evil.

On a wider level, such fascination raises questions as to whether the focused reporting on suicidal terror is purely in the public interest, or whether a mawkish fascination fuels column inches that follow any such atrocity. It would, of course, be impossible to separate the two – both can coexist. But such themes – death, sacrifice, brutality – are so emotive, so potent, that they wield considerable power, which is why any analysis of the impact of the suicide bomber needs to look at what the atrocity – and the reporting of it – does to our own political cultures.

*

Terrorism is, almost inevitably, a political act, aiming to change the path of the many to the will of the few. But just as terrorism seeks to manipulate us all, so too can governmental responses to terror be spun for other ends. Politicians are animals of expediency, so it is perhaps inevitable that their reactions to such atrocities – emboldened by a press seeking answers, assurances and payback – can sometimes be disproportionate or unconnected to the actual threat.

The Australian politician Michael Howard, for instance, was said to have used 'fear-arousing rhetoric' about the Islamist threat in order 'to support his political purposes'.[41] President Barak Obama was accused of being 'politically motivated' when he approved a terror threat warning about Pakistan, seen by some as an attempt to justify an escalation in US drone strikes there.[42] And Theresa May, responding to the Manchester 2017 attacks by putting armed soldiers on British streets in the middle of national elections, was charged with 'politicising' the attack.[43]

Fear is a profoundly political creature, and we know that terror can bend an entire society towards a political position. In Israel, terror attacks have been shown to cause people to favour parties of the right over the left.[44] In Madrid, when Al-Qaeda set off train bombs that killed 192 people in 2004, the subsequent victory of the Socialist party was put down to the fact that their politicians had not supported the war in Iraq.[45] This is no surprise. Clearly, terrorists want their acts to have a direct political impact, and in many cases, the timing of a suicide attack reflects this.[46] But political responses to suicide bombings have also become a political tool, used to further doctrines and embolden party lines.

When Donald Trump said in his 2016 presidential election campaign he was going to destroy ISIS, he was showing himself as harder and tougher than Hillary Clinton. He didn't even hide the raw logic of capitalism that framed his speech, saying he'd bomb Iraqi and

Syrian oil pipelines, too: 'You'll get Exxon to come in there and in two months . . . they'll rebuild that sucker, brand new – it'll be beautiful.'

To Trump, counterterrorism was no longer a necessity, but a virtue – and a profitable one at that.[47] It was no surprise when he, as president, was to apply the argument of 'national security' to justify his levy on some metal imports to the US, threatening the escalation of a trade war. American aluminium and steel, he told a cabinet meeting in March 2018, 'are vital to our national security . . . They are the bedrock of our defence industrial base.'

This political expediency has created a climate where some mainstream politicians show their true, ugly colours, as when former Australian Prime Minister Tony Abbott, said 'Islamophobia hasn't killed anyone';[48] when the Hungarian Prime Minister, Viktor Orbán, said 'Hungary doesn't want "Muslim invaders"'; when Geert Wilders, the far-right Dutch politician, said in 2017: 'Islam and freedom are not compatible'.

Of all politicians, perhaps predictably, Donald Trump appears to have been the most divisive. When he said that 'Islam hates us',[49] called for a ban on Muslims entering the United States, considered racial profiling[50] or said 'radical Islam is coming to our shores', he was stoking populist fears.[51] Furthermore, his planned responses were inconsistent with the evidence: of the 180 people charged with jihadist terrorism in America since 9/11 (or who had died before being charged), only 11 came from the seven countries banned in Trump's order.[52] If anything, Trump's words and actions emboldened Salafi-jihadism because they proved to its followers that this was, indeed, a clash of civilisations – something President Obama had always been keen to avoid.[53] But Trump played the mainstream card and the people approved – 60 per cent of Americans supported the move to impose a travel ban.[54]

Suicide attacks also lead to politicians overstating the risk. In May 2017, the then US Secretary of Homeland Security John Kelly told

CNN the American public would 'never leave the house' if they knew what he knew about terrorist threats.[55] If such a claim had been made in Pakistan, or Iraq, or Syria, I would get it. But in the United States, it was a curious claim to throw out there. After all, in the sixteen years after 9/11, jihadists killed 103 people inside the United States.[56] In just one decade, between 2005 and 2015, 301,797 Americans died from gun deaths.[57]

This combination of political expediency and fearmongering leads some politicians to respond with tokenism – the need to be seen to be doing something in the face of crime and terror. It is a tokenism often supported by legislators who legislate to justify their salaries – leading, as we have seen, to mission creep. One that represents, as Human Rights Watch said, 'a broad and dangerous expansion of government powers to investigate, arrest, detain, and prosecute individuals at the expense of due process, judicial oversight, and public transparency'.[58]

So we have seen politicians call for, or implement, round-the-clock surveillance by CCTV; centralised identity card registers; large-scale collection of communications; and stripping jihadists of their citizenship. Politicians will often seek to expand the horizons of their control, too, and the War on Terror has seen – in the name of security – demands for access to encrypted messaging apps to be granted; for people to be prosecuted for posting messages supporting terror online; even for just owning ISIS propaganda (something my harddrive is full of). These measures might all seem reasonable to many given the urgency of the threat, but the issue is this: once such liberties have been lost, or sentences passed down, what other erosions will occur? Where does it end?

The cumulative effect of the media's representation of, and political engagement with, Islamist terror has been, as we have seen, a rise in Islamophobia. In 2016, a US poll found that cancer had a better public image than Muslims there.[59] A possibly more balanced

survey still found that 61 per cent of Americans hold an unfavourable view of Islam.[60] It is not just in the US; in 2015, 55 per cent
of the British public said there was a clash between Islam and the
values of British society.[61] In the same year, a *Guardian* poll found
that 65 per cent agreed that Islamophobia was widely prevalent in
Britain.[62]

Such findings are the tip of an extensive body of research that
points to increasing disapprobation of Muslims and Islam after
2001.[63] Though the reasons behind this increase are not just tied to
terrorism (issues such as sex grooming and female genital mutilation
add to the discomfort), the suicide bomber looms large. And, as
the British philosopher Bertrand Russell once wrote, 'collective fear
stimulates herd instinct, and tends to produce ferocity toward those
who are not regarded as members of the herd'.[64]

Such ferocity is real. After 9/11, violence against Muslims jumped
in America. According to the FBI, 28 hate crimes in 2000 were found
to be anti-Islamic; in 2001, there were 481 such attacks. In the UK,
hate crime has also risen, with a 600 per cent spike in offences pro-
voked by religious hatred against British Muslims recorded in the
aftermath of the 7/7 London bombings.[65] Meanwhile three-quarters
of American Muslims polled in 2017 said that they faced a lot of
discrimination, with half saying it was getting worse.[66]

At its most extreme, such anger has erupted into violence. This
was evident when Anders Behring Breivik, the Norwegian who
killed eight people with a bomb in Oslo and a further sixty-nine at a
summer camp, published a manifesto that said resistance against an
Islamic invasion of Europe was his motivation for the atrocities he
was about to commit. Before the 2017 Finsbury Park attack, when a
man drove a van into a crowd of people outside a London mosque,
killing one, the right-wing 'ultra-nationalist' Tommy Robinson said
that militias would be set up to clean 'out this Islamic problem'.[67]
And Ukrainian neo-Nazi Pavlo Lapshyn was found to have placed

three bombs in mosques in Walsall, Tipton and Wolverhampton, two months after murdering Mohammed Saleem, a grandfather walking back home from his mosque in Birmingham.[68]

One analysis of terror attacks between January 2012 and September 2016 in the US, Australia, UK, France and Germany has shown that far-right and Islamist terror attacks tended to spike at the same time.[69] Admittedly, followers of the far right have not conducted suicide attacks, nor killed as many people, but they have found themselves stuck in a sort of dark symbiosis with Salafi-jihadism – both groups feeding off the other's venal rhetoric, both justifying violent intolerance in response.

More generally, a perception of Islam as a religion of terror has fuelled concerns about immigration causing a loss of national identity. When the *Daily Mail* reports a 'staggering' number of asylum-seeking juveniles – 4,210 living in council care – prone to radicalisation,[70] describes the French capital as 'Powder Keg Paris' owing to 300,000 'illegal immigrants', or runs front-page headlines that warn of 'UK Muslim Ghettos', it sets a tone that infects public debate. The European Commission against Racism and Intolerance (ECRI) picked out reports similar to these for 'offensive, discriminatory and provocative terminology' in their reporting on immigration, terrorism and the refugee crisis, ones that contributed 'to creating an atmosphere of hostility and rejection'.[71]

That atmosphere is certainly heightened. One survey found that 59 per cent of Europeans believe refugees increase the likelihood of terrorism.[72] In 2017, 64 per cent of American Republicans polled said that Muslim tourists posed a national security threat.[73] Surveys from the Czech Republic[74] to Canada[75] have shown, again and again, that people link immigration with an increased risk of suicide bombings.

Perhaps the irony here is that many of these migrants are, themselves, fleeing the madness of explosive violence. Between 2015 and

2016, 1.3 million people claimed refugee status on Europe's shores, a mass of people not seen since the Second World War, most fleeing the violence of Syria. In 2016, my charity conducted interviews with over 250 of these refugees and more than a third said they had witnessed suicide attacks.[76] Yet the very presence of refugees – intensified by concerns, for instance, that 73 per cent of asylum claimants were male – has ignited an equally explosive debate in Europe.[77]

It has led to calls for repatriation. European nations sent almost 10,000 Afghan asylum seekers back in 2016 – nearly triple the number in the previous year – despite a resurgent Taliban presence and a growing ISIS threat there.[78] It has caused some countries to refuse refugees. The EU has even sued Hungary, Poland and the Czech Republic for denying residency to asylum seekers,[79] while in 2015, Britain granted asylum to more Albanians than people from war-torn Iraq.[80]

The vocal links made between suicide bombers and Muslim migrants have also challenged the pillars of multiculturalism. This is something polemicists have been saying since the early years of the War on Terror, but it has become so mainstream that a recent UK government report even said: 'Too many public institutions . . . have gone so far to accommodate diversity and freedom of expression that they have ignored or even condoned regressive, divisive and harmful cultural and religious practices, for fear of being branded racist or Islamophobic.'[81] A 2018 Pew study found that between a third and half of Europeans felt that Islam was incompatible with their national values.[82]

Overall, such concerns have helped fuel the rise of right-wing politicians, across the board. The relative popularity of Marine Le Pen, President of France's National Rally political party (previously named National Front), is due in no small part to her saying things such as: 'We do not want to live under the yoke of the threat of Islamic fundamentalism.'[83] Similarly, after winning its first parliamentary seats, AfD – 'Alternative for Germany' – vowed to fight 'an invasion of foreigners' into the country.[84]

From Geert Wilders of the Dutch Party for Freedom, to the Italian, populist Five Star Movement, to the Swedish SD party, Islamophobia has been a continual theme in the rise of right-wing power. Naturally, the ascendency of extreme right politics is not just a result of Islamist terrorists. A sense of disenfranchisement from politics, the influence of social media, a sentiment that labour is not being adequately rewarded, and the export of manufacturing jobs have all played their part. But the spectre of a dangerous, spreading Islam is a constant in many a far-right group's arsenal of concerns.

Such concerns seem to have even contributed to Britain's decision to leave the European Union in the Brexit referendum. Even though very few migrants from the EU to the UK are Muslim, a fear of Islamist extremism was present in that vote. A poster was produced by the Leave campaigners that read 'Breaking Point', depicting a column of Muslim Syrian refugees in the Balkans; the insinuation was that the barbarians were at the gates and that terrorism would follow them. Brexiteers such as Dominic Cummings were adamant such campaigns were pivotal to their success: 'Would we have won without immigration?' he wrote in an op-ed. 'No.'[85] Since their victory they have shown their true colours even more: the official Leave EU team tweeted that 'British multiculturalists feed Islamic fundamentalism. Londonistan, built on the sad ruins of English Christianity.'[86]

Such fears have become part and parcel of contemporary political rhetoric. In September 2018, the former foreign secretary and arch-Brexiteer, Boris Johnson, attacked the UK government's plan for a 'soft Brexit', saying it had 'wrapped a suicide vest' around the British constitution and 'handed the detonator' to Brussels.[87]

When in Dewsbury, I had travelled to the outer edges of Savile Town, to visit the Leggers Inn, the only surviving pub in the area. There I asked the lunchtime drinkers whether they had voted Brexit and all of them had said yes. 'Why?' I said, and their responses were the same: they wanted to stop the Muslims coming over. They knew that Europe wasn't the source of those Muslims, but it was a vote to say that they had had enough; I had put the same question to a dozen other white people in Dewsbury, and their answers were identical. Europe is being Islamised, they told me, either by Muslims having kids or by migration, and it has got worse. Brexit was their chance to stop it. It offered the people of Dewsbury a legitimate, even respectable, way to voice their concerns. The vote helped channel their concerns about Muslims – as potential terrorists, as 'un-British', as incompatible with the West – into a legitimate expression of dissent.

It would be wrong to say suicide bombers caused Brexit, but the suicide bomber is at the heart of national fears of Muslim extremism, and anti-immigrant rhetoric in British print and social media has been explicitly framed around concerns for our national security. The trauma of suicidal violence has spread beyond its casement and evoked sentiments that have, in turn, had seismic political effects.

Perhaps it is no surprise, then, to find such cultural anxiety has been manipulated. Russian-government funded social media accounts have posed as Muslims online, there to push out lies that Hillary Clinton admitted the US 'created, funded and armed' Al-Qaeda and ISIS, or that Osama Bin Laden was a 'CIA agent'.[88] Other Russians have pretended to be American, calling for things such as 'No More Mosques in America'.[89] One Russian-run account claimed that a Muslim woman ignored victims of the Westminster Bridge terror attack in March 2017, a lie that was to be picked up and reported as truth by sections of the British national press.[90]

All these fallacies were designed to stimulate British and American nationalism and, in so doing, loosen transnational ties. Such meddling led Guy Verhofstadt, the Brexit coordinator of the European Union, to say on Twitter that: 'Europe has a fifth column in its ranks: Putin's cheerleaders who want to destroy Europe & liberal democracy from within.'[91] It is not hyperbole: one review found that in those German cities where Facebook use was higher than average, there were more attacks on Muslim refugees than in places where Facebook was less popular.[92]

What future impact this representation of Muslims, and the responses to it, will have on politics is unknown. The perception of devout Muslims as being incompatible with the traditions of the West, the fear that such devotion can slide into violence, and the concern that armed jihad will become a permanent threat in Europe and beyond is one that will not go away any time soon.

The hope is that such concerns will not be solely framed in the language of pogroms or pig-headed intolerance, but to stop that from happening will require the threat of the suicide bomber to end. This will not just necessitate nation states to take action, but the global community to come together – something that that community has so far struggled to do.

It was a thin crowd. The room had been booked last minute, and the meeting had been announced even later, but given the subject matter, attendance felt low. I looked down at my speaking notes; I had written that 2016 had seen almost 46,000 deaths and injuries from explosive weapons and a great swathe of these were from suicide bombs.[93] I wanted to stress to the room the omnipresence of such attacks: how, of the ten worst incidents that year, five were by jihadists blowing themselves up.

Such news, though, seemed no news at the United Nations. It was yet another chance for me to give evidence here, but this debate felt increasingly sidelined. There were a few diplomats from East Africa, a handful from Western Europe, one from the former Eastern Bloc. Next to me sat the Afghan ambassador – there because the only resolution passed in the UN that directly addressed IEDs had been tabled by his beleaguered nation. It was a poor turnout. Elsewhere in the UN headquarters in New York larger gatherings had formed; in particular, countries without nuclear weapon capabilities were talking about banning nukes. But here, in this room, the weapon that has killed the most people in the twenty-first century – except for guns – did not warrant a decent discussion.

It was disheartening. Not least because I knew the institutional liberalism that had led to the creation of the United Nations had worked before: the global community has had a long history of coming together in an attempt to stop certain weapons being used. They did so against poison gas in 1925 and biological weapons in 1972. Over time, other terrible forms of violence were condemned by many nation states – spike pits (1980), blinding lasers (1980), napalm (1980), chemical weapons (1993), anti-personnel landmines (1997), cluster bombs (2008) and nuclear weapons (2017) have all had bans seeking to reduce their use. Suicide bombs, though, have taken more lives than the most egregious of these, and yet no one has designed a logo or started a pressure group (apart from my charity's) to stop them.

In part, the problem lies with the very nature of suicide bombs. Other heinous explosive weapons like landmines and cluster munitions have, thanks to the work of charities, been eradicated from many conflict zones. Why? Because people lobbied their governments to ban the production of weapons, ending their manufacture on state-sanctioned assembly lines. Clearly, there are no formal production lines for suicide vests that can be shut down in the same way. And those people that use suicide bombs – 'non-state actors' as the UN likes to call them – do not take much notice of international weapon bans.

There are also no simple ways to prevent precursor explosive chemicals getting into the 'wrong' hands. As we have seen, the materials to make suicide vests are everywhere – chemical industries, on a daily basis, make tonnes of ingredients that could be turned into a

The UN in New York – when it comes to suicide bombings
is it a case of doing too little, too late?

bomb, from paint thinner to fertiliser, bleach to hair dye. Stopping the supply of such compounds presents a challenge that befuddles both nations and organisations like the UN alike.

But just because something is difficult does not mean it should not be attempted. Such an attempt, though, requires strong political will, and there are no major backers here. The US has been relatively silent, as has the rest of the UN Security Council, except for France. Most have focused instead on their own national counterterrorism initiatives, or relied on transnational groups like NATO who mainly approach the suicide bomb threat from a military perspective. There are also virtually no charities debating suicide bombings, and history has shown that it is the voices of charities like Human Rights Watch that cause weapons to be banned.

In my eyes, seeking a global ban on suicide bombings would reinforce what other laws say (the targeting of civilians, for instance, is forbidden under international humanitarian law), and would send out a clear message of condemnation and stigmatisation. This might sound naive, but if a weapon becomes sufficiently loathed, even the most hardened jihadist might falter before its use, particularly those who seek, one day, to sit at the table of power. Once poison gas was considered a weapon of virtue – capable of breaking the quagmire of trench warfare – but today even despots would not publicly praise its use. As Human Rights Watch has argued about other weapons bans, banning a weapon can influence 'even those that do not join the treaty'.[94]

Perhaps more importantly, a ban could lead to proper financing and a concerted political will to stop the proliferation of the suicide bomb. This is needed because those UN measures that have been put in place to stop bombers are largely underpowered, underfunded, and at times unheeded. [95]

So why are charities and pressure groups so quiet when it comes to calling for global action against suicide bombings, compared to – say – calling for an end to drone strikes? In part, it is because of priorities: the funding and political will lies more around creating a 'landmine-free world' than talking about suicide vests. The 1997 Anti-Personnel Mine Ban Convention established political commitments that meant that, in 2016, thirty-two donors contributed $479.5 million for mine action worldwide, a 22 per cent increase from the year before.[96] That year, there was no global money made available for any attempt to address specifically the spread of suicide bombings.

To put that into context: English-language media reported on 256 suicide bombings in 2016, causing 9,680 civilian deaths and injuries. That year, thirty-six civilians were reported killed or injured by landmines. The actual figures for both are higher – this is just relying on newspaper reports to monitor harm – but the fact remains that the funding and attention placed on certain weapons at the UN does not always reflect the damage such weapons have caused.[97]

What this means is that demining agencies have, in the words of one senior British officer to me, ended up 'clearing houses in Mosul and other liberated areas [in Iraq], which goes beyond the scope of demining' even though such operatives don't 'have the training or threat assessment knowledge' to do so. Meanwhile major demining agencies, such as the Mine Action Group, have ended up claiming that many devices 'that are currently being described as IEDs are in fact landmines'; a statement that ignores the harm suicide vests and car bombs have wreaked.[98]

The broader reluctance to address the issue of suicide bombings is also because UN and humanitarian agencies seek to remain 'neutral' – they cannot be seen to be taking sides in a conflict.[99] Trying to address the driving causes of suicide attacks would challenge this impartiality, civil society members argue. But the clearance of any IED is 'inherently political';[100] Salafist jihadists see demining agencies like the Mines Advisory Group or the HALO Trust as being mere extensions of Western power.

In the end, my talk to the United Nations felt insignificant, depressingly so. To address the suicide bomb threat requires far more engagement, a more imaginative and diverse approach than the UN seemed able, or willing, to envisage. It means getting demining agencies, militaries and police, intelligence services, religious and cultural leaders, and civil society to come together: some to address the supply chains for improvised bomb materials, some to counter radicalisation, some to oversee the urgent need of assistance to the thousands of victims from suicide attacks. But nobody seems to want to implement such a complex and radical plan, and the fact that suicide bombs are infused with a noxious form of ideology makes many diplomats swerve away. I have repeatedly been told not to mention Islam in talks I have given at the UN about suicide attacks.

One attempt to create a wide-reaching, joined-up approach has been tried. In 2015, there was a global meeting held of intelligence officers, police forces and military chiefs in Canberra, Australia, to talk about countering the IED threat – put together by Interpol.[101] It was the first time such a meeting had taken place. Unfortunately, it was not repeated. The desire to hold a follow-up summit was hampered when the British Metropolitan Police allegedly refused to guarantee the safety of attendees at a proposed London meeting: unless they could cordon off streets, they said, their hands were tied.

There is one more reason why the international community fails to address the rising threat of the suicide bomber, and that is because, on a fundamental level, the suicide bomber has created a mentality that puts nationalism before collaboration, and infuses everything with a sense of defensiveness. Diplomatically, this has occurred on a very physical level: ever since embassies were attacked in Lebanon, security walls and blast-resistant blockades have been erected around national outposts the world over. Al-Qaeda's bombings of American embassies in East Africa furthered this need, and 9/11 made it permanent.

More significantly, counterterrorism intelligence is not shared, and complex levels of security clearance mean even those best suited to stopping the spread of suicide bombings are not briefed. One chemical industry expert told me that the British government had approached him, asking for help. When he asked what chemicals most concerned them in terms of bomb production, they said he did not have security clearance for such information. Another Interpol officer in charge of counterterrorism work told me he had once written a report on IEDs and had it circulated to police forces around the world. On returning home from his posting, he discovered he did not have the security clearance to read the report he had written.

Secrecy, a lack of funding, an absence of strong political leadership, a disquiet born from the fact suicide bombs are improvised, a belief it is 'another agency's responsibility', a lack of pressure from charities and lobbyists, and the reality that, when you pick at the issue of suicide bombings, you often reach tricky issues of ideology, mean that the UN, and many other international bodies, have failed to come together to address its threat. And in a sense, the limits of an organisation like the UN in addressing the actions of individuals, not states, are fully exposed by this failure; a limitation that questions the capacity of the UN to live up to its guiding principles – where everyone has a right to 'security of person'.[102]

Conversely, it seems that UN resolutions are getting longer and less intelligible, its structures have become increasingly Byzantine, and its mandates more and more confused. This institution, designed to avoid and resolve nation-upon-nation conflict, finds itself perplexed and puzzled when confronted with the proliferation of jihadists, for whom nations and borders are held in contempt and whose goals seem as rooted as much in theology as in politics. Over the decades, the UN has honed its approach to dealing with 'conventional' wars, but when faced with the shadowy and mutating world of 'non-state actors' it finds itself at a loss. Admittedly, some states have tried. The French government has been arguably the most proactive – engaging with the private sector to try to stop the illicit spread of explosive materials, for example – but others have not matched their lead.

In many ways, this collective failure has harmed the UN itself. When a suicide bomber targeted their Assistance Mission in Iraq on the afternoon of 19 August 2003 at the Canal Hotel in Baghdad, at least twenty-two people were killed, including the UN Special Representative, Sérgio Vieira de Mello. It was a bombing that resulted in the withdrawal, within weeks, of most of the 600 UN staff members from that country.

Such a targeting of humanitarian workers has been a repeated feature since 9/11. The Aid Worker Security Database shows that, between 2004 and 2013, there was a 300 per cent rise in severe attacks in which a staff member was killed, injured or kidnapped.

Roadside bombs have prevented aid agencies from driving down specific routes. Suicide bombings – such as the January 2016 attack that saw a car packed with explosives rammed into Beach View Hotel in Somalia's capital – have targeted areas where international staff gather, leading to unknowable numbers of UN and humanitarian workers refusing posts or leaving jobs.[103]

In response, UN and aid agencies have adopted security measures. But these responses, like 'bunkering down' or driving in armoured vehicles, have led to locals associating them with military or police operations, while other security measures – like putting certain areas off-limits – have inhibited access to the very populations that agencies seek to deliver aid to. When, in June 2016, a humanitarian convoy finally reached Bama, Borno State's second largest city, they found a Nigerian community destroyed. The graves of 1,233 people, including 480 children, were discovered.[104] These deaths may have been avoidable, but the route to the camps was filled with Boko Haram suicide bombers, preventing access.

The UN, then, not only finds itself struggling to address the driving forces behind suicide attacks, but also discovers its ability to operate is often hampered by Salafi-jihadist violence. In this way, the suicide bomber affects political responses, both national and international, in complex and influential ways – and invariably either frustrates the counter-response or pushes it to the political right. And what such failures to solve the problem of Salafi jihadism do to us – to our own view of the world – is deeply worrying.

Murder, to quote the poet W.H. Auden, is unique in that it abolishes the party it injures, so that society must take the place of the victim, and on their behalf demand atonement or grant forgiveness. But suicide bombing is unique also in that it abolishes the perpetrator as well, so that society is denied its chance to enforce justice or find resolution. This double injury – I believe – goes to the very heart of why the suicide bomb has led us down paths to extremes. It disrupts the natural balance of things; it contaminates everything.

Yes, in the immediate aftermath of a suicide event, good sometimes comes out. During the aftermath of 9/11, those injured were not crushed by panicked crowds, they were calmly assisted even in the maelstrom of confusion.[105] That same orderly quality has been noted in responses to suicide attacks in London, Moscow and Madrid.[106] But for the most part, such attacks just leave pain.

We have seen how the victims of attacks have to live with the physical and mental scars, but people far away from the incident are still affected. In 2004, Dmitri Trenin of the Moscow Carnegie Center commented on the Moscow subway suicide bombing that killed forty-one people and talked about its impact on the nine million Muscovites who use the subway daily. 'Every time I go down into the underground I wonder if I will finish my journey,' he said. 'Now nine million people are feeling they are playing Russian roulette.'[107] A poll after the event found that 59 per cent were afraid to ride the metro.[108]

Such small and often hidden fears are hard to capture, but they can seep into the constitution of a city. When writing this book on the London underground, I was stopped by a policeman and asked what I was doing. The young woman next to me had seen me writing about suicide attacks and had informed a Transport for London officer. So attuned was she to the notion of an attack, she was nervously responding to the Underground's tannoy mantra: 'See It, Say It, Sorted' – the urban soundtrack to Generation Terror.

Even when the immediate threat of terror dissipates, even when we feel that things have returned to normal, they haven't. Over time, this anxiety – often understated, but still lurking – can impact the way we see the world.

The roads that lead to a suicide attack are complex, and yet a desire to understand such complexities is another casualty. We strive for simple and straight answers instead: as Primo Levi once wrote, 'Without a profound simplification the world around us would be an infinite, undefined tangle that would defy our ability to orient ourselves and decide upon our actions.'[109] But while simplicity might make it easier to condemn the suicide bomber – calling them 'evil' or a 'loser' – such a resolute view of the world inhibits us, as a society, from finding ways to stop that violence from recurring, and so the War on Terror drags on.

The outcome of this is a 'normalisation' of violence – and the responses to it – something that is seen in distinct and concerning ways. The story of seven-year-olds being invited by police to an open day to brandish replica guns, encouraged to 'shoot terrorist' targets.[110] Of holiday planes being evacuated because people were overheard

In many parts of the world, security checks have become part of the fabric of the city, like the scanners here in St Petersburg's underground – near the site of the world's first suicide bomb

having a suspicious – but entirely innocent – conversation.[111] Of Ihsan Abualrob, a Palestinian student at Durham University who was called a 'suicide bomber' and then beaten up by three men after saying 'Merry Christmas' to them.[112] Of the 'black budget' report leaked by US intelligence agent Edward Snowden that detailed sixteen spy agencies and more than 107,000 employees that make up the US intelligence community.[113] Of thousands of small and unexpected ways that terror transforms our lives, and the lives of the people we love, and sullies them with the language of fear and intolerance.

It is not surprising, too, that we read of the mental anguish caused by the War on Terror everywhere. From Ariana Grande saying she had PTSD following the attack on her concert in Manchester,[114] to US drone pilots suffering from waves of sickness, outbursts of skin welts and lingering digestive problems as the memories of their remote war come back to them,[115] psychological trauma stalks the sites where suicide bombers have struck.

Writing this book, I spoke to and heard the testimonies of dozens of people who had survived terror incidents. They share their stories in different ways. Some wish to remain anonymous, fearful that speaking out will somehow invite the trauma to return. Some cry without realising it, their tears coming as they remember the smell of the explosion, the pools of blood. Some feel guilty, knowing that they survived while others fell. Some rock nervously in the telling; others talk in calm, steady voices as if they weren't even there. They speak of their children waiting for them at home; of parents nervously texting where they are; of the noise of the ringing mobile phones of the dead, never to be answered.

Strangely, few seem to focus on the men that did this to them. They talk almost as if the people who perpetrated the violence were ghosts – a sideshow to their ordeal. And in a sense, they were – strangers up to the point of violation.

Above all, memories mark. As one survivor of the Paris attacks of November 2015 said: 'What's most horrible about this is that the violence we're subjected to is such that it completely dehumanizes us. It pushes us to be indifferent to the suffering around us.'[116]

I was once asked to speak at a gathering of the Felix Club – former members of the British Army bomb disposal squad – and some were visibly suffering from their memories. A few drank until they could barely talk, while others talked so fast they struggled to catch their breath. The room was a painful battlefield of failed marriages, health problems and insomnia. The year I gave that talk, 2012, both the British and US militaries reported that suicides of serving soldiers or ex-servicemen had outstripped battlefield deaths.[117] The US Department of Veterans Affairs said veteran suicide was even worse, running at twenty-two a day.[118] And each of those men and women has children or partners, parents or friends who, in turn, are impacted by that anguish.

Every family who has had someone harmed in an attack is left largely on their own, rebuilding their lives as well as they can.

For the rest of us, the danger is that we become desensitised, accustomed to violence. Whether by watching images of refugees drowning off Europe's coastline, or seeing videos of skeleton cities bombed in the Middle East, we so quickly can become hardened not only to the fear of the suicide attack but also to the very real consequences of what terrorist violence has led to. The suicide attack, and the responses to it, can take on a patina of predictability and, in that predictability, a distancing occurs. It silently reduces us. Individual death may be felt intensely, but when so many strangers are involved, our response becomes muted. After a fashion, we look away.

For the best of us, outrage slides into apathy, condemnation mutates into a lack of conviction. For the worst, impassioned words become infused with calls for retaliatory violence and intense hatred. And if the worst prevails, the age of the suicide bomber is going to last for a very, very long time to come.

Chapter 16

Paradise Lost

I had conjured up in my mind an image of a long cord, made from all the flags of the countries ever affected by the suicide bomber's blast. It was a rope that started off as a single thread: Russian political assassins, denoted by the brilliant yellow of the Russian imperial banner – the first suicide bombers. Then, after decades, I had envisaged a thickening of the line. The military colours of Asia seen as the armies of the East began using coordinated suicide attacks: first the Chinese, then the whites and reds of the Rising Sun wrapped around the foreheads of Japanese kamikaze. The cord would thin again, until green could be seen – the Iranian revolution of the Middle East. From there, the colours would begin to spread. First Lebanon's flag, then other nations in the region such as Kuwait and Iran. Alongside them, you could trace the orange of the Sri Lankan Tamil Tigers, as well as the colours of an occasional Indian assassination.

By now you could see the threads twisting and strengthening, other colours added to the mix. There are Palestinian bombs and then a burst of attacks in Israel. A bombing in Algeria and a Kurdish backlash in Turkey, mostly minority nationalist movements against perceived despots. Then a new wave of Islamic nationalist movements would appear: the violence of the Chechens and the Kashmiris, and the black flag of Al-Qaeda heralding a new stage of the cord. Beginning in Afghanistan, then Kenya and Yemen, the most noticeable knot in the rope denotes the horrors of 9/11. After that, the War on Terror changes the colours entirely.

Suicide bombings in Iraq herald a new age of Sunnis attacking Shias and from there, the rope widens, fatter and thicker. The colours of other Muslims countries show through: Morocco, Pakistan, Indonesia, Saudi Arabia, Uzbekistan, Egypt, Qatar, Bangladesh, Somalia, Nigeria, Mali, Tunisia, Cameroon, Kyrgyzstan and, of course, Syria. Once a country is touched, violence seems to be seen again and again: suicide bombings stick. And, if you look hard enough into the rainbow-coloured mix, you can see other – largely Christian – countries beginning to show. The flags of Spain, Britain, Bulgaria, Belgium, France, Germany, Sweden, Georgia, Finland and Ukraine all appear. There are other, isolated strikes even harder to see – solitary attacks in Argentina, Bolivia, New Zealand – the rope stretches onwards and onwards.

There is always the hope that the rope will end one day. Perhaps suicide bombings will burn themselves out. Ready-to-buy drones, after all, are attractive to non-state groups that want a targeted weapon in their arsenal. In 2017, ISIS carried out dozens of drone strikes with disturbing accuracy: they appear to have been able to drop bomblets into the top hatches of vehicles and the psychological effect this had on troops was noticeable – on hearing drones, soldiers would flee.[1] But drones do not carry the same propagandist potency as suicide attacks.

Instead, the fear is that, in a bid to secure greater publicity and impact, the suicide bomb will just get deadlier: a dirty bomb in a major city. Even the spectre of the nuclear suicide bomber has been raised: in 2016, it was reported that North Korea had established an infantry unit whose members were trained to carry atomic devices in backpacks. In the event of war, the soldiers were instructed to infiltrate the South before detonating their weapons.[2]

As I write this in the autumn of 2018, in the last week alone, attacks have happened in Afghanistan, Somalia, Libya, Nigeria and Syria, with Turkish police narrowly foiling one attack. This weapon has evolved into a standard weapon of armed conflict today, and the risk of it being seen again in Western nations remains ever-present. In the year it took me to write this book, suicide bombings were witnessed in twenty-one countries.

To cut the rope – to stop the infernal spread of the appeal of this terrible weapon – requires a far more imaginative response than the ones tried to date. Bullets and bombs have not only failed to stop the bomber's rise but have fuelled it. And along the way, such violence has caused immeasurable pain and heartache. But what can be done to stop that cycle of violence? How can the allure of paradise be stopped?

I have produced a suicide bomb video. Having watched so many jihadist videos extolling the virtues of murder and the merits of sacrifice, I felt something had to be done. So, a team and I set about hiring a director, finding a cast of actors and producing a short film.

The thinking behind it was relatively simple: in the hundreds of suicide bomb videos that exist, almost all end with the deadly blast. Theirs are the pageantry of propaganda, the sound and the fury, but all end in the same way, with the agony of those gathered around. The long-term suffering that followed a bomb blast was never conveyed by the jihadists and rarely by the mainstream media. Seeking to redress this, we captured testimonies from victims of a suicide attack in Pakistan, we got actors to voice their words, applied make-up to replicate their injuries, and wrapped it all in the quasi-mystical, bombastic format used in so many jihadist videos.

The film offered an alternative view: the victims talked about how their lives had been altered for ever, they spoke of the pain of seemingly endless hospital visits, the financial and emotional cost that had drained them of joy. It was, in one way, a reclaiming of the story. For when culture challenges violence as seriously as violence challenges culture, there is still hope.

The logic behind it was this: the more Salafi extremists are seen to be using faulty religious justifications to harm civilians, the more there could be a backlash among the Muslim community. The film challenged the promise of paradise – the argument that a 'good' Muslim killed in a suicide attack will also go to heaven. But what happens to a 'good' Muslim, we asked, who has had their legs blown off, or is blinded? Where is the theology that justifies that living hell? There is none.

Such narratives can be – must be – presented. How Muslims are the overwhelming victims of suicide attacks; how suicide is forbidden in Islam; how terror groups are exploiting young men and women to their own ends; how the current supporters of suicide attacks lack the religious authority to justify such attacks.

A video is not going to do that alone, clearly, but it is a start. Religions have the capacity both to create and to disavow their most dangerous zealots. Christianity, undeniably, has a brutal history; it is marked by the tragic pogroms that once swept Europe but, by and large, Christianity has evolved. It has rejected the violence of coercion, and recognised that saving souls by burning people at the stake is immoral. Pope John XXIII's reforms showed that the Catholic Church could face modernity. Likewise, the Japanese have rejected their kamikaze past. The Sinhalese in Sri Lanka have not sought to resort to suicide bombing. The Shias have largely disavowed this weapon.

As I write, in my room stands a collection of items picked up around the world. A coin from the church in St Petersburg that commemorates a fallen Tsar; a black and white photograph of six Japanese women raising garlands as a kamikaze plane prepares for take-off; the posy of dried flowers from a Lebanese field where Shias once taught Sunnis how to carry out their martyrdom missions; a rolled-up poster from a bygone age encouraging people to 'Visit Palestine'; a piece of crumbled concrete, retrieved from the remains of Prabhakaran's childhood home. These are dark mementoes, yes, but they all speak towards something, too. How suicide bombers have flared up and then been rejected by the communities where they once took root.

A similar rejection within the Sunni faith – a form of Islamic *aggiornamento* – is needed. For this to happen, it must be widely accepted that a warped framing of Islam plays a role in suicide bombings, that the promise of paradise reached through violence is a potent driver. Merely saying that suicide attacks are 'un-Islamic' is insufficient. Stressing there is a 'better' way both allows for the issue of faith to be discussed without immediately reaching the accusation that all faith inevitably results in violence; and it provides a point from which dialogues of non-violence can flow. So while, in the interest of free speech, ultra-conservative religious messages should be able to be expressed so long as they do not incite violence or recruit jihadists, the active encouragement of moderate forms of Islam is needed. As one Lebanese woman said to me: 'The media should stop inviting old, bearded men to talk on TV, and focus instead on interviewing young, educated modern Muslims. It is not Islamist extremism; it is extremism that uses Islam as a facade.'

There have been attempts. In Morocco, a new school for imams from across the world focuses on 'inner jihad' – the personal struggle – and not the 'glory of terrorism'.[3] Elsewhere, prominent Islamic scholars, jurists and preachers have denounced the violence carried out by ISIS and their kin. The former Imam of the Grand Mosque in Mecca, Sheikh Adel al-Kalbani, condemned ISIS as a product of Salafism, and said that the movement needed to take a hard look at itself. Al-Kalbani, himself a Salafist, criticised Salafism's desire for 'blind re-enactment' of the Prophet's times. Elsewhere, the remains of suicide bombers have been refused an Islamic burial, sending out a potent message that the Muslim community is turning its back on the jihadist and their violent death. States should inter their remains in unmarked and lonely graves.[4]

Other ways forward have begun. In March 2010, a group of scholars gathered in Mardin to discuss the medieval fatwa issued by Ibn Taymiyyah that has been used to justify attacks on civilians. The delegates agreed the original Mardin fatwa was inappropriate for modern times, and should not be used by extremist armed groups.[5] While in January 2018, over 1,800 Pakistani clerics from different schools of Islam issued another fatwa that said suicide bombings were 'haram', or forbidden under Islamic law.[6] Some fighters have listened to these words; the Libyan Islamic Fighting Group once agreed 'it is forbidden to kill women, children, elderly people', while also saying – perhaps about the subterfuge of a suicide attack – that 'betrayal is prohibited'.[7]

It would, however, be wrong to lay the entire blame on theology when it comes to contemporary suicide bombings. The allure of paradise is a potent trigger, and such allure requires ideological underpinning, but the other conditions that justify such sacrifice also need to be addressed.

To prevent calls for revenge, states need to uphold human rights; they need to ensure that breeding grounds for extremism are not created in prisons, schools or mosques; they need to combat Islamophobia; to insist that the trials and punishments of Muslims accused of terror are subjected to a transparent and fair process; to address high levels of unemployment and widespread socio-economic deprivation among many Muslim communities; to create victim-assistance programmes; and to recognise the fact that many societies around the world have concerns about immigration and the failures of liberal policies on race and religion.

This list could go on. Countering extremism is notoriously hard. When the then Secretary-General Ban Ki-moon revealed the UN's plan of action to do so in January 2016, there were over seventy recommendations made, ranging from development policy initiatives, to youth empowerment, to gender equality to human rights.

But there are four fundamental points that I believe should be addressed head-on.

The first is that the United Nations needs to up its game. A ban on suicide bombing would send out a clear message of priorities, and create political commitments and funding to address the complex issues that underpin the weapon's rise. This needs to spread beyond demining operations – any approach has to accept suicide bombings are built upon both social and ideological grounds. And funding could help charities, businesses, trade officials, police units, UN agencies, militaries and others come together to respond imaginatively and creatively to this terrible weapon. Without there being a coherent and systemic approach to combating the cult of the suicide bomber, there is little hope the spread of this weapon will be curtailed.

The second point is that we should seriously assess the impact Western foreign policy has had on the Middle East and North Africa to avoid past mistakes. This does not mean accepting the conspiracy-laden narratives presented by jihadists. Nor is it realistic to assume that Western policies towards the region going back for decades can be completely altered. But the inadvertent arming of future jihadi groups through the US's and other states' oftentimes uncontrolled supply of arms and explosives to the Middle East should be stopped. Air strikes have been shown, repeatedly, to fuel support for Salafi-jihadism, while carrying out secret drone strikes bolsters the claims the West is waging an eternal, subversive battle against Islam. These must be ended.

The third challenge lies in stopping the conflicts in which the vast majority of today's suicide bombings and their casualties are found. NATO and other states have focused on state-building activities to do this, often initiating violent regime change to induce democratisation and economic growth. They do so believing peace can be built by creating democracies, but after two decades this approach has failed to work. Partly this is because you cannot export democracy down the barrel of a gun. Partly because such interventions fail to take into account the political reality of the Middle East, specifically the Arab states. Traditional Arab-Islamic concepts of war and peace seem more based on immediate conflict resolution, seeking a return to the status quo, than wholesale transformation and reform. Peace-building initiatives need to reflect the cultural conditions of the region, and not merely act as a 'sticking plaster' of Western sensibilities.

Fourth, states should be profoundly aware of the failures of history when it comes to countering suicide bombers. Much of the media might seek hard and retributive justice, but history has shown that man's ability to overstep the mark, generate mission creep and abuse human rights in the name of national security is all too predictable. The conditions to produce a suicide attack are complex: the means to counter such attacks need to be as well.

In the end, it is in our own responses to suicide attacks where we have the most significant capacity to act. When we look back to find out how we arrived at the place we find ourselves in now, we should not be blinded by the carnage brought by terrorism, but also see the ensuing violence justified to crush that threat. We must remind ourselves how the Tsar's blind repression of anarchists fanned the flames of tyrannical Communist revolt. How the US high command's justification for the devastating use of nuclear weapons to defeat the feared kamikaze ushered in the Cold War. And how the calamitous invasions of Iraq and Afghanistan were decided before the dust had settled on downtown Manhattan.

This is a view that reveals starkly how nearly every attempt to stamp out the suicide bomber since they first appeared in the nineteenth century has claimed more lives than the original bombing ever did.

Knowing this, the words of Martin Luther King Jr. should sound in our ears: 'The ultimate weakness of violence is that it is a descending spiral, begetting the very thing it seeks to destroy. Instead of diminishing evil, it multiplies it ... Violence merely increases hate ... Returning violence for violence multiplies violence, adding deeper darkness to a night already devoid of stars.'

Ultimately, the notion of paradise obtained through violence needs to be broken. And we need to realise we cannot break that notion through violence.

Today, confronted by global jihad, there are tangible steps all of us can take to help do this. I asked Nima Elbagir – an old friend and Emmy-award winning Sudanese-born CNN reporter – what her motivations to challenge extremism have been and she responded quickly: 'Never give up on engaging.'

'When friends I grew up with were beginning to espouse increasingly conservative ideology,' she told me, 'what really helped was their mother was well versed in the Koran and engaged them on issues of theology, quoting appropriate verses and Islamic scholars to refute what they were reading online. Too often we allow ourselves to be intimidated by the one-upmanship of "I'm a better Muslim than you", and we should be more willing to have these debates – however contentious – rather than allow young men and women to become increasingly isolated.'

Engagement seems to be the key. If you are not a Muslim, then perhaps read the Quran or visit a mosque on an open day. And – most fundamentally – accept that non-Muslim Russians, Chinese, Koreans, Japanese, Germans, Italians, British, Indians, Sri Lankans and Americans have all, in one way or the other, used their bodies as an explosive weapon since the death of the Tsar of Russia almost 140 years ago. The ideological conditions that can create a suicide bomber are not just Islamic ones, offering proof that this death impulse can be counteracted. Blaming a single religion is not how to do it.

Overall, the cycle of violence and hate can be eroded if we seek to recognise and speak to each other. This is not to say we should all sit around in a vast circle, singing 'Kumbaya'. But more listening on both sides about the concerns and fears of those who might be seen as 'the other' is a significant step.

If a newspaper reports on a story that is wrong, if a columnist writes something that is bigoted, then challenge them, report them to a press regulator, voice your disavowal. But also be open-minded: follow people on social media whose opinion you do not like, read articles that offend your sensibilities. As Dostoevsky said, 'While nothing is easier than to denounce the evildoer, nothing is more difficult than to understand him.'

If there is a protest about drone strikes or air campaigns, go along. Tweet at politicians that such attacks have been shown to fuel, not end, terrorism. Get angry when civil liberties are eroded; join a group that disavows torture. Be aware of what is being done in your name to combat terror: read about the erosions of freedom of speech and judicial process. And then act as your conscience dictates.

But listen, too. When you hear people furious at immigration or concerned about Islam, try to comprehend their fears – merely shouting at each other isn't working. Get involved in the debates that surround all these concerns. And all the time, I hope, do so by saying that non-violence is the only way to address this situation. Threatening to kill people who have already embraced the notion of paradise-through-death will never work.

Funded, wide-ranging and humanitarian counterterror work; considered peace-building; attempts at religious reformation; the rhetoric and the practice of inclusivity, diversity and tolerance: these are what states and institutions should aim to achieve. Empathy, humanity and the permanent search for nuance: these are actions we must perform ourselves.

These small steps are essential, because the routes that lead to any suicide bombing are always an accumulation of unseen slights and offences, and so the road away from it can be, too. We can carve an alternative passage – all of us – when we talk about non-violence because that is not just a way to peace, but also a path to love.

Notes

Prologue

1   There is an argument that the first suicide bomb attack happened in 1706, as the French were besieging Turin. There, the besiegers penetrated the tunnels that formed part of the citadel. One of the Turinese, Micca, found himself with too short a fuse to escape and yet left enough gunpowder to block the French attack. He ordered his companions back before destroying the tunnels, killing himself in the process. This story, though, fits more into a 'sacrifice in the moment of battle' death than a premeditated suicide attack – defensive rather than offensive. Instead, I place the Tsar's murder in 1881 (see Chapter 1) as the start of the suicide bomb era.

2   In 2017, on average, thirty civilians were killed or injured by each suicide bombing. This compares to eleven from air-strikes and two from landmines.

3   This is a calculation based on four attacks in Russia, at least seven in China in pre-Second World War conflicts, 7,465 in Japan during the Second World War, 5,430 between 1974 and 2016, and 244 in 2017. Sources: Gerald W. Thomas, 'Suicide Tactics: The Kamikaze During WWII', Air Group 4 – 'Casablanca to Tokyo', http://www.airgroup4. com/kamikaze.htm; Chicago Project on Security and Terrorism (CPOST). 2016. Suicide Attack Database (12 October 2016 Release), http://cpostdata.uchicago.edu/; Jennifer Dathan and James Kearney, 'The Burden of Harm: Monitoring Explosive Violence in 2017', Action on Armed Violence, April 2018, https://aoav.org.uk/wp-content/ uploads/2018/04/Explosive-Violence-Monitor-2017-v6.pdf

4   This is from the Chicago Suicide Database which lists, where gender

is known, 110,878 victims with 101,733 being male, and where of 3,221 attackers (where gender is known) 2,886 were male. As this database does not include the Second World War or before, taking into account the number of men killed by – and constituting – the kamikaze, then it is likely that much more than 90 per cent of victims and perpetrators are male throughout history.

5   Sam Prince, 'ISIS Uses 4 Year-Old Boy as Suicide Bomber After Executing His Father', *Heavy.com*, 5 January 2016, https://web.archive.org/web/20160107223155/http://heavy.com/news/2016/01/new-isis-islamic-state-news-pictures-videos-child-boy-suicide-bomber-four-years-old-al-shirqat/

6   Richard Wheatstone, 'Japanese park explosions caused by "suicidal" 72-year-old ex-soldier blowing himself up', *Mirror*, 23 October 2016, https://www.mirror.co.uk/news/world-news/japanese-suicide-pensioner-blows-himself-9108705

1. Utopia's Weapon

1   The National Library of Russia, 'The Western Manuscripts Collection: Modern Historical Manuscripts from the 16th–20th Centuries', accessed 14 May 2018, http://nlr.ru/eng/coll/manuscripts/westscripts2.html

2   Sankar Muthu, *Enlightenment against Empire* (Princeton: Princeton University Press, 2009), 260–1.

3   Crane Brinton, *The Anatomy of Revolution* (New York: Vintage,1965), 202.

4   Ibid. 202.

5   Ibid. 199–200.

6   Albeit the things I sought were inherently the things I knew. As Walter Benjamin once wrote: 'Every image of the past that is not recognized by the present as one of its own concerns threatens to disappear irretrievably.' (*Theses on the Philosophy of History*)

7   Christine D. Worobec, *Peasant Russia: Family and Community in the Post-Emancipation Period* (Dekalb, IL: Northern Illinois University Press, 1995), 34.

8   E.J. Hobsbawm, *Revolutionaries; Contemporary Essays* (New York: Pantheon Books, 1973), 143.

9   Albert Resis, 'Das Kapital Comes to Russia', *Slavic Review* 29, no. 2 (1970): 219–37.

10   www.marxists.org/archive/lenin/works/1920

11   Curiously, the People's Will may have also contributed to

Dostoyevsky's death. In January 1881, while searching for members of the terrorist organisation, the Tsar's secret police carried out a search in the apartment of one of Dostoyevsky's neighbours. On the following day, Dostoyevsky suffered a pulmonary haemorrhage, the first of three that would lead to his death. Some claim that the stress of the search helped precipitate the stroke.

12   Boris Mironov, 'The Development of Literacy in Russia and the USSR from the Tenth to the Twentieth Centuries', *History of Education Quarterly* 31, no. 2 (1991): 229–52.

13   According to Woodcock, a well-known historian of anarchism, the concept of 'propaganda by deed' can be traced back to an Italian, Carlo Pisacane, who had written that ideas emanate from deeds and that intellectual propaganda was an empty gesture.

14   By July 1881, just a few months after the death of the Tsar, an international congress of anarchists met in London and officially adopted the policy of 'propaganda by deed'. Andrew Carlson, *Anarchism in Germany.* 1: *The Early Movement* (Metuchen, N.J.: Scarecrow Press, 1972), 62–3.

15   Walter Laqueur, *A History of Terrorism* (New York: Routledge, 2017).

16   Other intellectuals influenced too – the Frenchman Pierre-Joseph also advocated a non-authoritarian form of socialism and was the first person to declare himself an anarchist. His 1840 book *What is Property?* concluded that 'property is theft' and he called instead for 'federalism and mutualism'. Federalism was to replace centralised governments with local communities; mutualism was to run society based on small, mutually supporting economic groups.

17   Mikhail Bakunin, *Statism and Anarchy*, ed. Marshall Shatz (Cambridge: Cambridge University Press, 1990), 214.

18   This was possibly inspired by the words of the first German Communist, Wilhelm Weitling, who announced to a crowd of shocked onlookers, 'founding the kingdom of heaven' would only be achieved 'by unleashing the furies of hell.' Paul Thomas, *Karl Marx and the Anarchists,* Library Editions: Political Science, Volume 60 (London: Routledge, 2013), 291.

19   Thomas, *Karl Marx and the Anarchists,* 291.

20   Still, they had limits. When James Garfield, the President of the United States, was assassinated in 1881, the People's Will condemned the use of terrorism in such a democracy as the United States. Terrorism, they argued, could only be justified in extreme circumstances.

21   Edvard Radzinsky, *Alexander II: The Last Great Tsar,* trans. Antonina Bouis (New York: Free Press, Simon and Schuster, 2006), 107.

22   However, he was more lenient in Finland, where he encouraged

independence – partly to thank them for service in Crimea, and partly to create a wedge between Russia and Sweden. To this day he is still known there as 'the good Tsar'. See Harald Haarmann. *Modern Finland: Portrait of a Flourishing Society* (Jefferson, NC: McFarland & Company, Inc., 2016), 211.

23 Other groups in the Russian Empire emerged, focusing on assassinations and robbing banks to finance their activities. The Armenians (Hunchaks) and the Poles were first. Then the Balkans exploded, where many groups (e.g., Internal Macedonian Revolutionary Organization, Young Bosnia, and the Serbian Black Hand) found the boundaries of states recently torn out of the Ottoman Empire unsatisfactory.

24 The funds, for example, to subsidise the peasants to buy land proved to be insufficient.

25 This is no surprise: his was a lineage of overachievers. His great-grandfather discovered the liver's lymphatic vessels; his father invented plywood; his brothers revolutionised the oil industry of the Caspian Sea, running what was – at the time – the largest company in Russia and one that once employed a young Joseph Stalin. See: M. Nobel, 'The Dynamite King and the Russian Rockefellers', *Економічний нобелівський вісник*, No. 1 (7) (2014): 3–9, http://duan.edu.ua/uploads/vidavnitstvo14/ekonomichnij-nobelivskij-visnik-114/7587.pdf

26 William S. Dutton, *One Thousand Years of Explosives: From Wildfire to the H-Bomb* (Philadelphia: John C. Winston, 1960), 147–52. Norman Gardiner Johnson refers to the story of Nobel's cut finger and collodion as a 'legend'. *Encyclopaedia Britannica*, 1970 ed., s.v. 'Explosives'.

27 He went on to publish *The Science of Revolutionary Warfare* in Chicago in 1885. One year later, a local anarchist newspaper praised dynamite's power: 'A pound of this stuff beats a bushel of ballots,' said its editor 'and don't you forget it.' His readers agreed. A bomb thrown soon afterwards was to kill seven policemen, breaking up a strikers' gathering in the city's Haymarket Square.

28 Mikhail Frolenko, quoted in Gavin Cameron, *Nuclear Terrorism: A Threat Assessment for the 21st Century* (New York: Palgrave Macmillan, 1999), 67.

29 Avrahm Yarmolinsky, *Road to Revolution: A Century of Russian Radicalism* (Princeton: Princeton University Press, 1986), 276.

30 A thought that Dostoyevsky summed up when he wrote: 'What is to be done with the millions of facts that bear witness that men, fully understanding their real interests, have left them in the background and rushed headlong to meet peril and danger . . . ? Fyodor Dostoyevsky, *Notes from Underground* (1862), planetebook.com, 27.

NOTES

441

31 *Economist*, 'For jihadist, read anarchist', 18 August 2005, http://www.economist.com/node/4292760

32 Yves Ternon, 'Russian Terrorism, 1878–1908', in *The History of Terrorism: From Antiquity to ISIS*, ed. Gérard Chaliand and Arnaud Blin (Oakland, CA: University of California Press, 2016), 133.

33 Avrahm Yarmolinsky, *Road to Revolution*, Chapter 14.

34 John Gray, *Black Mass: Apocalyptic Religion and the Death of Utopia* (London: Penguin Books, 2007), 28.

35 Thomas More, *Utopia*, trans. Ralph Robinson, in *Three Early Modern Utopias*, ed. Susan Bruce (Oxford: Oxford University Press, 1999), 38.

36 Martin Anthony Fletcher, 'My sons, the jihadists', *The Times* magazine, 11 October 2014, http://www.martinanthonyfletcher.com/my-sons-the-jihadists-the-times-magazine/

37 Friedrich Nietzsche, Essay 3 of *The Genealogy of Morals* (1887), 10.

38 Marc Ferro, *Nicholas II: Last of the Tsars*, trans. Brian Pearce (New York: Oxford University Press, 1995), 14.

39 See the very impressive Geoffrey Hosking, *A History of the Soviet Union* (London: Fontana Press, 1985).

40 Richard Bach Jensen, 'The Pre-1914 Anarchist "Lone Wolf" Terrorist and Governmental Responses', *Terrorism and Political Violence*, 26:1, 2014, 86–94.

41 Simon Dubnow, *History of the Jews in Russia and Poland*, 3 volumes, trans. I. Friedlaender (Philadelphia: Jewish Publication Society of America, 1916–1920), 15, 1905, 247–58.

42 Ferro, *Nicholas II: Last of the Tsars*, 13.

43 Nicholas Riasanovsky, *A History of Russia* (New York: Oxford University Press, 1977), 362.

44 Aleksei Vassilyev, *The Ochrana: The Russian Secret Police* (London: G.C. Harrap, 1930), 93–5.

45 New Mexico Museum of Space History, 'International Space Hall of Fame: Nikolai I. Kibalchich', accessed 14 May 2018, http://www.nmspacemuseum.org/halloffame/detail.php?id=14

2. Divine Winds

1 Alex Kerr, *Dogs and Demons: The Fall of Modern Japan* (London: Penguin Books, 2001), 15.

2 BBC News, 'Japan police arrest Korean suspect in Yasukuni shrine bomb', 9 December 2015, http://www.bbc.co.uk/news/world-35048140

3 Bryan Walsh, 'The Last Refuge of Kamikaze Ideology', *Time*,

12 April 2007, http://content.time.com/time/world/
article/0,8599,1609931,00.html

4   David McNeill, 'Kamikaze shrine that turns history on its head',
     Independent, 7 April 2004, https://www.independent.co.uk/news/world/
     asia/kamikaze-shrine-that-turns-history-on-its-head-55160.html

5   https://www.youtube.com/watch?v=DTCxd-24gtM

6   https://www.youtube.com/watch?v=WNDI6BK7lWA

7   There was an attack on HMAS *Australia*, a heavy cruiser, on
     21 October 1944, shortly before the Battle of Leyte Gulf in the
     Philippines, and a strike a few days later when a Mitsubishi G4M
     bomber crashed into the USS *Sonoma* and sank it in the same seas.

8   Richard Frank, *Downfall: The End of the Imperial Japanese Empire*
     (New York: Random House, 1999), 311.

9   John Toland, *The Rising Sun: The Decline and Fall of the Japanese
     Empire, 1936–1945*, Vol. 2 (New York: Random House, 1970), 568.

10   Made of cheap metal and wood, they were never actually used, as
     Japan surrendered before mass production could begin.

11   Steven J. Zaloga, *Defense of Japan 1945* (Oxford: Osprey Publishing,
     2010), 42–52.

12   Kim Hyung Jin, 'Opponents try to block memorial for Korean
     kamikaze', Associated Press, 10 May 2008, https://www.japantimes.
     co.jp/news/2008/05/10/national/opponents-try-to-block-memorial-
     for-korean-kamikaze/#.Wlnoaq2caT8

13   Ko-Shu Ling, 'Taiwanese kamikaze looks back', *Kyodo*, 15 May 2014,
     https://www.japantimes.co.jp/news/2014/05/15/national/taiwanese-
     kamikaze-looks-back/#.Wlnozq2caT8

14   One of the first recorded instances of a soldier using explosives
     expressly to die rather than surrender was during the Belgian War
     of Independence in 1830. Jan Carolus Josephus van Speijk, a Dutch
     naval lieutenant in command of a gunboat, found himself fighting
     against the Belgian independence movement. He said he would rather
     die 'than become an infamous Brabander'. So when, on 5 February
     1831, a gale blew his gunboat into the Antwerp quay, and Belgians
     began to quickly storm his ship, demanding that the Dutch flag be
     hauled down, Van Speijk chose death over surrender. He turned
     and fired a pistol into a barrel of gunpowder in the ship's magazine,
     killing himself, dozens of Belgians and twenty-eight of his thirty-one
     crewmen. Again, this is not a suicide bomb but rather an act of
     desperation carried out in the thick of battle.

15   Hao Jin, '与日本坦克同归于尽的奥运英雄', 文史博览, no. 9 (2012), 39. There
     are some claims that in 1804, when the United States was at war
     with Barbary pirates on the North African coast, a ship called the

USS *Intrepid* was turned into a massive suicide boat bomb to destroy the Barbary fleet. However, I find this claim unlikely. Even though the *Intrepid* did blow up, killing its crew, the fuses on the explosives had been set for fifteen minutes, granting time to escape. It was the discovery of the plot and an attack on the *Intrepid* that was more likely to have detonated the explosives early, and it was only later presented as an act of sacrificial heroism.

16 Xu Feng, '雨花台上血花飞——抗日名将高致嵩殉国前后,' 文史春秋, no. 10 (2015), 50.

17 Peter Harmsen, *Shanghai 1937: Stalingrad on the Yangtze* (illustrated ed.) (Havertown, Pennsylvania: Casemate, 2013),112. And http://blog. creaders.net/u/11445/201703/284205.html

18 http://www.hoplite.cn/templates/hpjhzto050.html

19 http://news.ifeng.com/history/zhongguojindaishi/ detail_2012_03/30/13568589_0.shtml

20 Jonathan Fenby, *Modern China: The Fall and Rise of a Great Power, 1850 to the Present* (New York: HarperCollins, 2008), 284. During China's turbulent history there are instances of many military units, ranging from platoon-size formations to entire brigades, comprising thousands of troops adopting the name 'Dare to Die Battalions'. We do not know if all soldiers calling themselves such were intent on their own deaths: their name could be little more than a war cry, designed to terrify their enemies, but the earliest example of such Dare to Die units, called Si Shi (死士 – those who do not fear death), existed during the Shang Dynasty (1600 BCE–c. 1046 BCE). Early documents also recount how three columns of the king of Yue's armies charged into the enemy, only to commit suicide there en masse. The soldiers of the opposing army – the Wu clan – were so shocked by this behaviour that it caused them to falter, opening up a chance for Yue's army to defeat them. During the Han Dynasty, too, a Chinese military tactic emerged that was called 'Xian Chen' (陷); these were units responsible for incredibly dangerous tasks such as scaling the walls of forts to break the enemy's siege – death for them was almost a foregone conclusion.

21 Joseph Esherick, ed., *Remaking the Chinese City: Modernity and National Identity, 1900 to 1950* (Honolulu: University of Hawaii Press, 2002), 132.

22 Ryan Schultz, '"Because We Were Japanese Soldiers": The Failure of Japanese Tactics at Changkufeng and Nomonhan and Lessons Left Unlearned' (BA Thesis, Oberlin College, 2011), 8 and 27. See also: https://www.youtube.com/watch?v=_TQxodxIeeI

23 Schultz, "Because We Were Japanese Soldiers", 39.

24   http://news.ifeng.com/history/zhongguojindaishi/special/
     kangzhanwangshangjinianguan/detail_2011_03/08/5027613_3.shtml
25   Hanna Reitsch, *The Sky My Kingdom: Memoirs of the Famous German
     World War II Test Pilot* (Philadelphia: Casemate Publishers, 2009).
26   Antony Beevor, *Berlin: The Downfall, 1945* (London: Viking, 2002),
     238.
27   *International Herald Tribune*, '1965: Viet Cong Suicide Unit
     Strikes', 1 June 2015, https://iht-retrospective.blogs.nytimes.
     com/2015/06/01/1965-viet-cong-suicide-unit-strikes/
28   Francis Pike, 'The development of a death cult in 1930s Japan and
     the decision to drop the Atom Bomb', *Asian Affairs* 47.1 (2016): 1–31.
     This article has proved invaluable to my research and while I cite the
     original sources herein, the guidance to search for these sources has
     come mainly from Pike's own work.
29   Wires guided the torpedo to a range of 1,800 metres, allowing the
     missile to speed 4 metres under the water, its trajectory followed by
     a small mast that just broke the water's surface. Innovatively, this
     torpedo was powered by the very wires that steered it. Brennan
     had discovered how to make a device move forwards by pulling it
     backwards. To demonstrate this, he had taken a cotton reel and put
     a pencil through the hole in the centre; then, by resting either end of
     this pencil on two books, and pulling the cotton thread from beneath,
     he had seen the bobbin roll forwards. The harder he tugged, the
     quicker the cotton unwound, and the faster the reel was propelled the
     other way. The British government liked the design and agreed to pay
     £110,000 for it – a scandalous amount at the time.
30   A filing for a 'land torpedo' was also submitted in the final days of the
     First World War by an American – acknowledging that it had become
     'quite a problem to conduct military operations from trench to trench'
     – possibly the greatest understatement in the history of patents.
     https://www.google.co.uk/patents/US1407969
31   BBC News, 'Iran buys kamikaze dolphins', 8 March 2000, http://news.
     bbc.co.uk/1/hi/world/middle_east/670551.stm
32   Michael Evans, 'Donkey "suicide" bombing is latest tactic against
     patrols', *The Times*, 30 April 2009.
33   Michael G. Lemish, *War Dogs: A History of Loyalty and Heroism*
     (Washington, DC: Brassey's, 1999), 89–91.
34   John Hall, 'Is ISIS developing suicide CHICKENS? Pictures appear
     to show bombs strapped to hens by bird-brained jihadis', *Daily Mail*,
     20 July 2015, http://www.dailymail.co.uk/news/article-3167978/
     Bird-brained-ISIS-jihadis-developing-suicide-chickens-strapping-
     homemade-bombs-hens-encouraging-wander-enemy-camps.html

35 Burrhus F. Skinner, 'Pigeons in a pelican', *American Psychologist* 15.1 (1960).

36 https://www.youtube.com/watch?v=vGazyH6fQQ4

37 Noah Shachtman, 'Unleash the Cats of War!', *Wired*, 20 June 2007, https://www.wired.com/2007/06/unleash_the_cat/

38 Alexis C Madrigal, 'Old, Weird Tech: The Bat Bombs of World War II', *Atlantic*, 14 April 2011, https://www.theatlantic.com/technology/archive/2011/04/old-weird-tech-the-bat-bombs-of-world-war-ii/237267/

39 Mohammed Hafez, 'Dying to be Martyrs: The Symbolic Dimensions of Suicide Terrorism', in *Root Causes of Suicide Terrorism: The Globalization of Martyrdom,* ed. Pedahzur (London, New York: Routledge, 2006).

40 Imperial Rescript to Soldiers and Sailors (*Gunjin Chokyuyu*).

41 Stephen S. Large, *Emperor Hirohito and Showa Japan* (Abingdon: Routledge, 1998), xxxiv.

42 Allan R. Millett and Williamson Murray (eds.), *Military Effectiveness, Volume 3, The Second World War* (New York: Cambridge University Press, 2010), 37.

43 In Japan there is a phrase that is not found easily in other cultures: *Mono No Aware*. It translates into an acute sensitivity to the transience of lovely things. Within its three words lies an awareness that everything of beauty will fade, and yet there also exists a simultaneous rich joy at the short-lived beauty. The cherry blossom, above all else, provokes this strong emotion.

44 Yamamoto Tsunetomo, *Hagakure: The Secret Wisdom of the Samurai*, iBooks, 49.

45 Richard B. Frank, *Downfall: The End of the Imperial Japanese Empire* (New York: Random House, 1999), 29.

46 Some of these suicides in Okinawa may have been less than voluntary, though. In 2008 an Osaka Prefecture court ruled that 'the military was deeply involved in the mass suicides'. David Pilling, *Financial Times*, 12 April 2008.

47 Bill Gordon, 'Censored Suicide', Kamikaze Images, May 2006, http://www.kamikazeimages.net/stories/fujii/index.htm

48 Bill Gordon (trans.), 'Crash Attack With New Wife On Board', Kamikaze Images, March 2012, http://www.kamikazeimages.net/stories/crashattack/index.htm

49 Associated Press, 'Japan's real kamikaze pilots: survivors debunk stereotype in stories of sacrifice', 17 June 2015, https://www.thenational.ae/world/japan-s-real-kamikaze-pilots-survivors-debunk-stereotype-in-stories-of-sacrifice-1.100796

50   Chiyomi Sumida, 'Priest tells of kamikaze pilot training during WWII', *Stars and Stripes*, 25 January 2015, https://www.stripes.com/news/pacific/priest-tells-of-kamikaze-pilot-training-during-wwii-1.325764

51   A total of 708 non-commissioned army officers died as kamikaze pilots, while the total death toll of army air force officer-class kamikaze pilots was 621. In the navy, 1,732 petty officers died as kamikaze pilots compared with 782 officers: See Yuki Tanaka, 'Japan's Kamikaze Pilots and Contemporary Suicide Bombers: War and Terror', *The Asia Pacific Journal: Japan Focus* 25 (2005).

52   Flight Petty Officer Matsuo, aged twenty; in Naitō, *Thunder Gods,* 114.

53   Rumi Sakamoto, 'Mobilizing affect for collective war memory: Kamikaze images in Yūshūkan.' *Cultural Studies* 29.2 (2015): 158–84.

54   Hasegawa Shin, aged twenty-three, *Making Sense of Suicide Missions*, 38.

55   Flight Petty Officer Kameda, aged nineteen; in H Naitō, *Thunder Gods: The Kamikaze Pilots Tell Their Story* (Tokyo: Kodansha International, 1989), 114.

56   Tsunetomo, *Hagakure: The Secret Wisdom of the Samurai*, 20. The most obvious example of this is the tale of the 47 Rōnin (master-less samurais). In 1701, Asano Naganori, daimyo of the Akō domain, drew his sword and assaulted Kira Yoshinaka in the Edo Castle because of a slight on his honour. Asano was immediately ordered to commit *seppuku* (ritual suicide by disembowelment) for this breach of etiquette, and he obliged. His retainers plotted for two years and enacted a vendetta culminating in the successful assassination of Kira at his mansion. This, in turn, led to their ritual suicide.

57   Sumida, 'Priest tells of kamikaze pilot training during WWII'.

58   Richard P. Hallion, 'Precision Weapons, Power Projection, and the Revolution in Military Affairs', Air Force Historical Studies Office, 26 May 1999, https://web.archive.org/web/20090505052709/http://www.airforcehistory.hq.af.mil/EARS/Hallionpapers/precisionweaponspower.htm

59   This is the number given at the Yakasuni shrine. Other historians put the number at 3,912 or 3,862. See: Steve Zaloga, *Kamikaze: Japanese Special Attack Weapons 1944–45*, 12.

60   https://www.c-span.org/video/?307521-1/world-war-ii-veterans-mark-victory-japan-day

61   Paul J. Chara Jr. and Kathleen A. Chara, 'Posttraumatic stress disorder among survivors of a kamikaze attack', *Psychological Reports*, 89.3, 2001, 577.

62   Daniel A Kitchen, 'Kamikaze, the Ultimate Sacrifice', Kamikaze Images, August 2007, http://www.kamikazeimages.net/stories/lct746/index.htm

63   https://diogenesii.files.wordpress.com/2012/09/wilfred-burchett-in-hiroshima1.pdf The terrible effects of radiation sickness were also not included in calculations: Oppenheimer had so misjudged the fallout from his first New Mexico atom bomb test that the US were considering using it to invade the third biggest island of Japan and most south-westerly of its four main islands, Kyushu.

64   *New York Times*, 'First Atomic Bomb Dropped on Japan; Missile Is Equal to 20,000 Tons of TNT; Truman Warns Foe of a "Rain of Ruin"', 6 August 1945, 'http://www.nytimes.com/learning/general/onthisday/big/0806.html#headlines

65   Harry S. Truman Presidential Library and Museum, 'Harry S. Truman to Roman Bohnen, 12 December 1946. Truman Papers, President's Secretary's File. Atomic Bomb'.

66   There are some awkward truths to this idea that the rejection of the Potsdam Accord was a driving cause of the use of the atom bomb. After all, the official written military order to use the atom bomb was sent out on 25 July – the day before, not after, the Allies issued their Potsdam Proclamation. But after the war, President Truman asserted that he decided to drop the atomic bomb after Japan failed to respond to the terms laid out in the proclamation.

67   PBS, 'The Atomic Option', http://www.pbs.org/perilousfight/psychology/the_atomic_option/

68   Eric. M. Bergerud, *Fire in the Sky: The Air War in the South Pacific* (Basic Books Reprint edition, 2001), 675.

69   https://www.youtube.com/watch?v=sDfuau2SfVE

70   Ralph Raico, 'Harry Truman and the Atomic Bomb', excerpted from John Denson (ed.), 'Harry S. Truman: Advancing the Revolution' in *Reassessing the Presidency: The Rise of the Executive State and the Decline of Freedom*, Mises Institute, 24 November 2010. If American casualties at Okinawa had been replicated pro rata in Operation Downfall the total number of US casualties would have been 2.7 million with some 485,000 troops killed. British casualties would have numbered some 540,000 with 97,000 deaths – more than a third of British troops who died in the Second World War. These numbers do not include the estimated British forces casualties from the invasion of Thailand planned for 18 August, nor the likely murder of Allied POWs and civilian internees by Japanese troops. In total, between 25 and 35 million people died in the Pacific War (including the Second Sino-Japanese War), of whom about 5 million were combatants.

71   Ryan Browne, 'Why did the U.S. bomb Hiroshima?', CNN, 27 May 2016, http://edition.cnn.com/2016/05/27/politics/hiroshima-obama-explainer/index.html

72   J. Samuel Walker, 'The Decision to Use the Bomb: A Historiographical Update', *Diplomatic History* Volume 14, Issue 1 (January 1990): 97–114, https://doi.org/10.1111/j.1467-7709.1990.tb00078.x

73   Barton J. Bernstein, 'Why We Didn't Use Poison Gas in World War II', *American Heritage,* Vol. 36, Issue 5, August/September 1985, https://www.americanheritage.com/content/why-we-didn't-use-poison-gas-world-war-ii

74   Today, in Japan, only 14 per cent say the bombing was justified, versus 79 per cent who say it was not. Bruce Stokes, '70 years after Hiroshima, opinions have shifted on use of atomic bomb', Pew Research Center, 4 August 2015, http://www.pewresearch.org/fact-tank/2015/08/04/70-years-after-hiroshima-opinions-have-shifted-on-use-of-atomic-bomb/

75   Hal Gold, *Unit 731: Testimony* (North Clarendon: Tuttle Publishing, 2007), 53.

76   Doug Long, 'President Harry S Truman', accessed 16 May 2018, http://www.doug-long.com/truman.htm; Gar Alperovitz, *The Decision to Use the Atomic Bomb*, material quoted from 563.

77   Article 22 of The Hague Convention of 1907 Respecting the Laws and Customs of War on Land states: 'The right of belligerents to adopt means of injuring the enemy is not unlimited.' And: *New York Times,* 'Atom Bomb Loosed on Nagasaki', 9 August 1945, http://www.nytimes.com/learning/general/onthisday/big/0809.html

78   Barbara Moran, *The Day We Lost the H-Bomb: Cold War, Hot Nukes, and the Worst Nuclear Weapons Disaster in History*, iBooks, 33.

79   BBC News, 'How Japan's youth see the kamikaze pilots of WW2', 3 November 2017, http://www.bbc.co.uk/news/world-asia-39351262

80   Mamoru Iga, *The Thorn in the Chrysanthemum: Suicide and Economic Success in Modern Japan* (Berkeley: University of California Press, 1986), 156.

81   Jewish Telegraphic Agency, 'Memorial Service in Puerto Rico for Victims of 1972 Lod Massacre', 9 June 1982, https://www.jta.org/1982/06/09/archive/memorial-service-in-puerto-rico-for-victims-of-1972-lod-massacre

3. The Rise of the Martyr

1   Some have put the date of his death at 10 November 1980.

2   *Iran Analysis Quarterly* Vol. 2 No. 4 (July–September 2005), http://web.mit.edu/isg/IAQ242005.pdf

3   Free Stamp Catalogue, '2012, Martyr Mohammed Hussein Fahmideh',

https://www.freestampcatalogue.com/sirp31212-martyr-mohammed-hussein-fahmideh-s-s

4   George S. Cuhaj, ed., *Standard Catalog of World Paper Money, Modern Issues, 1961–Present* (F+ W Media, Inc., 2015), 528.

5   Navideshahed, 'Martyr Fahmideh, everlasting role model', 2 November 2016, http://navideshahed.com/en/news/385053/martyr-fahmideh-everlasting-role-model

6   An excellent article to read on this matter, and to which I am indebted, is: Matthias Küntzel, 'Ahmadinejad's World', 30 July 2006, www.matthiaskuentzel.de/contents/ahmadinejads-world

7   Richard Kreitner, 'September 22, 1980: Iraq Invades Iran, Beginning the twentieth-century's Longest Conventional War', *Nation*, 22 September 2015, https://www.thenation.com/article/september-22-1980-iraq-invades-iran-beginning-the-twentieth-centurys-longest-conventional-war/

8   Kevin Sullivan, 'The (Plastic) Key to Understanding Iranian Martyrdom', RealClearWorld, 3 May 2013, https://www.realclearworld.com/articles/2013/05/03/iran_martyr_state_plastic_paradise_keys.html. See also Reza Aslan, *No God But God: The Origins, Evolution, and Future of Islam* (New York: Random House, 2006), 190.

9   Read Ramita Navai's book *City of Lies* to get an idea of how hard it is to find the truth in Iran.

10   Baham Nirumand, 'Krieg, Krieg, bis zum Sieg', in *Iran-Irak: 'Bis die Gottlosen vernichtet sind'*, eds. Anja Malanowski and Marianne Stern (Reinbek: Rowohlt, 1987), 95–6.

11   Reuter, *My Life is a Weapon*, 47.

12   Christiane Hoffmann, 'Vom elften Jahrhundert zum 11. September. Märtyrertum und Opferkultur sollen Iran als Staat festigen', *Frankfurter Allgemeine Zeitung*, 4 May 2002.

13   However, this ranking did not bring as much social mobility as was gained by the families of those who had been killed. See: Amir Taheri, *Holy Terror: The Inside Story of Islamic Terrorism* (London: Hutchinson, 1987), 81.

14   Elaine Sciolino, 'Martyrs Never Die', excerpt from *Persian Mirrors: The Elusive Face of Iran* (2000), PBS, https://www.pbs.org/wgbh/pages/frontline/shows/tehran/inside/martyrs.html; and Reuter, *My Life is a Weapon*, 50.

15   Sciolino, 'Martyrs Never Die'.

16   A combination of figures from the Chicago Suicide Attack Database (up to end of 2016), and AOAV's dataset for 2016, 2017 and 2018.

17   Peace be upon him.

18   https://www.timeanddate.com/holidays/iran/. Good Friday is a holiday

in Egypt and commemorates religious martyrdom; however, it is not considered here as this study aims to shed light on Islamic belief systems.

19   Khosrokhavar and Macey, *Suicide Bombers: Allah's New Martyrs*, 21.

20   Vali Nasr, *The Shia Revival: How Conflicts in Islam Will Shape the Future* (New York: W.W. Norton & Company, 2006), 49.

21   The University of Chicago Library: https://www.lib.uchicago.edu/collex/exhibits/graphics-revolution-and-war-iranian-poster-arts/new-battle-karbala/

22   Garret Nada, 'Politics and Art of Iran's Revolutionary Tulips', US Institute of Peace, 23 April 2013, https://iranprimer.usip.org/blog/2013/apr/23/politics-and-art-iran%E2%80%99s-revolutionary-tulips

23   Amir Taheri, *The Persian Night: Iran under the Khomeinist Revolution* (New York: Encounter Books, 2009), 87.

24   Thomas L. Friedman, *From Beirut to Jerusalem* (New York: Macmillan, 1995), 202.

25   Jacqueline Anne Braveboy-Wagner, ed. *Diplomatic Strategies of Nations in the Global South: The Search for Leadership* (New York: Springer, 2016), 200.

26   Dawud Gholamasad and Arian Sepideh, *Iran: Von der Kriegsbegeisterung zur Kriegsmüdigkeit* (Hannover: Internationalismus Verlag, 1988), 15.

27   Richard L. Rubenstein, *Jihad and Genocide* (Lanham, MD.: Rowman & Littlefield, 2010), 153.

28   Daniel Brumberg, 'Khomeini's Legacy. Islamic Rule and Islamic Social Justice', in *Spokesmen for the Despised: Fundamental Leaders of the Middle East*, ed. R. Scott Appleby (Chicago & London: University of Chicago Press, 1997), 56.

29   Ruhollah Khomeini, *Islamic Government: Governance of the Jurist* (1971), 1.

30   Mehdi Abedi and Gary Legenhausen, eds., *Jihad and Shahadat: Struggle and Martyrdom in Islam* (The Institute for Research and Islamic Studies, 1986), 20.

31   Bernard K. Freamon, 'Martyrdom, Suicide, and the Islamic Law of War: A Short Legal History', *Fordham International Law Journal* 27 (2003): 299.

32   Ali Shariati, 'Red Shi'ism (the religion of martyrdom) vs. Black Shi'ism (the religion of mourning)', Iran Chamber Society, accessed 17 May 2018, http://www.iranchamber.com/personalities/ashariati/works/red_black_shiism.php

33   Freamon, 'Martyrdom, Suicide, and the Islamic Law of War'.

34 Arshin Adib-Moghaddam, ed., *A Critical Introduction to Khomeini* (Cambridge: Cambridge University Press, 2014), xxiii.

35 After all, Iran was a land that produced what some see as the first 'society of the dead': the Assassins were a secret order led by the mysterious 'Old Man of the Mountain' that carried out targeted killings.

36 Norman Cohn, *Cosmos, Chaos and the World to Come: The Ancient Roots of Apocalyptic Faith* (New Haven: Yale University Press, 1999), 88.

37 Jacques Duchesne-Guillemin, *The Hymns of Zarathuštra*, trans. M Henning (London, 1952), 18.

38 Cohn, *Cosmos, Chaos and the World to Come*, 96.

39 Ramita Navai, *City of Lies; Love, Sex, Death and the Search for Truth in Tehran* (London: Weidenfeld & Nicolson, 2014), 23.

4. Back to Barbarism

1 ShiaWatch, 'Alerts', 22 November 2013, http://www.shiawatch.com/article/541

2 *New York Times*, 'Around the World; Deaths Now Put at 30 in Beirut Bomb Blast', 17 December 1981, https://www.nytimes.com/1981/12/17/world/around-the-world-deaths-now-put-at-30-in-beirut-bomb-blast.html

3 Karla Vallance, 'Iraqi Embassy in Beirut racked in "kamikaze" hit', *Christian Science Monitor*, 16 December 1981, https://www.csmonitor.com/1981/1216/121619.html

4 Nizar Qabbani, 'A Poem to Balqis (1981)', on Lebanonfirst (blog), 19 April 2005, http://tripolilebanon.blogspot.co.uk/2005/04/it-is-sad-when-people-talk-about-nizar.html

5 This is based on the Chicago Suicide Database, but it is likely to be more: certainly some bombings I was told about and later verified were not listed by Chicago.

6 Others at first claimed the attack, saying it was by the Kurds, others accusing former Iraqi Prime Minister Nouri al-Maliki, of having being involved. See: Abdelhak Mamoun, 'Al-Maliki to be arrested in Lebanon after claims of his involvement in bombing in 1981', *Iraqi News*, 30 November 2014, https://www.iraqinews.com/iraq-war/al-maliki-arrest-lebanon-claims-involvement-bombing-1981/

7 'Baath Party', *Encyclopaedia Britannica*, 2007.

8 Jerrold Post, *The Mind of the Terrorist: The Psychology of Terrorism from the IRA to Al-Qaeda* (New York: Palgrave Macmillan, 2007).

9   Augustus Norton, *Amal and the Shi'a: Struggle for the Soul of Lebanon* (Austin: University of Texas Press, 1987), 68–9.

10   Robert Fisk, *Pity the Nation: Lebanon at War* (Oxford: Oxford University Press, 2001), 556.

11   Jeffrey Lewis, *The Business of Martyrdom: A History of Suicide Bombing* (Annapolis, MD: Naval Institute Press, 2012), 71.

12   Fisk, *Pity the Nation: Lebanon at War*, 468.

13   They formally announced their existence in an open letter in 1985.

14   Israel Ministry of Foreign Affairs, 'Highlights of Main Events 1982–1984', 28 November 2000, http://www.mfa.gov.il/mfa/foreignpolicy/mfadocuments/yearbook6/pages/highlights%20of%20main%20events-%201982-1984.aspx

15   Ronen Bergman, *The Secret War with Iran: The 30-Year Clandestine Struggle against the World's Most Dangerous Terrorist Power* (New York: Simon and Schuster, 2008), 64.

16   Joseph Croitoru, *Der Märtyrer als Waffe. Die historischen Wurzeln des Selbstmordattentats* (München: Hanser, 2003), 132.

17   David Hirst, *Beware of Small States: Lebanon, Battleground of the Middle East* (London: Faber and Faber, 2010), 196.

18   J Flint, '39 killed in US embassy bombing', *Guardian*, 19 April 1983.

19   Bernard Gwertzman, 'Reagan Calls Bombing Cowardly', *New York Times*, 19 April 1983, http://www.nytimes.com/1983/04/19/world/reagan-calls-bombing-cowardly.html

20   Rassemblement Canadien pour le Liban, 'IX: War in Lebanon', accessed 17 May 2018, https://library.cqpress.com/cqalmanac/document.php?id=cqal83-1198422

21   Hirst, *Beware of Small States*, 193; James McManus, 'Suicide bombers kill 170 troops; Iran and Syria suspected in Beirut raids', *Guardian*, 24 October 1983.

22   Robin Wright, *Sacred Rage: The Wrath of Militant Islam* (New York: Simon and Schuster, 2001), 72.

23   Leaked US intelligence reports named two men: Imad Mughniyeh, an explosives expert trained by Yasser Arafat's elite troop Force 17; and Mustafa Badredin, a member of al-Dawa. Mughniyeh later became one of the most wanted terror suspects in the world, believed to be behind numerous abductions – including that of Terry Waite. See: Timothy J. Geraghty, *Peacekeepers at War: Beirut 1983 – the Marine Commander Tells His Story* (Dulles, VA: Potomac Books, Inc., 2009), 185.

24   Hala Jaber, *Hezbollah: Born with a Vengeance* (New York: Columbia University Press, 1997), 82.

25   Muhammad Munir, 'Suicide Attacks and Islamic Law', *International Review of the Red Cross*, vol. 90, no. 869, 2008.

26 Geraghty, *Peacekeepers at War: Beirut 1983*, 185.

27 Steven V. Roberts, 'House Democrats Draft Resolution on Beirut Pullout', *New York Times*, 1 February 1984, http://www.nytimes.com/1984/02/01/world/house-democrats-draft-resolution-on-beirut-pullout.html

28 Jack Moore, 'Trump Administration Says War on Terror Began Before 9/11 with Hezbollah Attack on US Troops', *Newsweek*, 24 October 2017, http://www.newsweek.com/trump-administration-says-war-terror-began-911-hezbollah-attack-us-troops-691653

29 Ahmad Nizar Hamzeh, *In the Path of Hizbullah* (London: Syracuse University Press, 2005), 89.

30 Jaber, *Hezbollah*, 29.

31 This data is from the Chicago Suicide Attack Database – it might err on the low side, as many attacks listed on its database are unattributed.

32 These groups combined have carried out at least twenty-five attacks over the years, killing 1,299 people and injuring 1,670.

33 Agence France Presse, 'Hezbollah suicide bomber kills Israeli soldier in Lebanon', 20 March 1996.

34 Simon Engelkes, 'A Blood Wedding: Hezbollah's Shuhada and its Culture of Martyrdom', American University of Beirut, Department of Political Studies, 2015.

35 Tatyana Dronzina and Rachid El Houdaïgui, eds., 'Contemporary suicide terrorism: Origins, trends and ways of tackling it', Vol. 101, IOS Press, 2012, 32.

36 Thanassis Cambanis, *A Privilege to Die: Inside Hezbollah's Legions and Their Endless War Against Israel* (New York: Free Press, 2011), 111.

37 Joyce M. Davis, *Martyrs: Innocence, Vengeance and Despair in the Middle East* (New York: Palgrave Macmillan, 2003), 214.

38 Joseph Alagha, 'The Pedagogy of Martyrdom among Female Suicide Bombers', *Sociology International Journal* 1(2) (2017), http://medcraveonline.com/SIJ/SIJ-01-00008.php

39 CNN iReport, 20 February 2009, http://ireport.cnn.com/docs/DOC-217031

40 https://www.youtube.com/watch?v=2BidlsybYVU

41 Khrais, Bilal. 'Lebanon's women warriors' http://www.aljazeera.com/programmes/general/2010/04/2010413115916795784.html

42 Christopher Dickey, 'Young Lebanese Seek New Martyrdom: Suicide Bombers Emerge as Martyrs', *Washington Post*, 12 May 1985, https://www.washingtonpost.com/archive/politics/1985/05/12/young-lebanese-seek-new-martyrdom-suicide-bombers-emerge-as-martyrs/cb779208-7a56-4e48-a5ec-eea5cb863fd5/?utm_term=.4cfc7e8987b9

43   Muhammad Hussayn Fadlallah, 'Al-Islam wa al-mantaq al-quwwa' (Beirut, 1987).

44   Munir, 'Suicide Attacks and Islamic Law'.

45   https://www.youtube.com/watch?v=VKWXiQAudAk

46   John Elster, 'Motivations and Beliefs in Suicide Missions', in *Making Sense of Suicide Missions*, ed. Diego Gambetta (New York: Oxford University Press, 2006), 237–8.

47   Christoph Reuter, *My Life Is a Weapon: A Modern History of Suicide Bombing* (Princeton: Princeton University Press, 2004), 65.

48   Ami Pedahzur, *Suicide Terrorism* (Cambridge: Polity, 2005).

49   Nicholas Blanford, *Warriors of God: Inside Hezbollah's Thirty-Year Struggle Against Israel* (New York: Random House, 2011), 216.

50   Rafael Israeli, 'A Manual of Islamic Fundamentalist Terrorism', *Terrorism and Political Violence*, 14(4) (January 2002), 30.

51   Christopher E. Whitting, 'When David became Goliath' (Master's thesis, US Army Command and General Staff College, 2001), 82.

52   Munir, 'Suicide Attacks and Islamic Law'.

53   Andrew Kohut, 'Global Opinion Trends 2002–2007: A Rising Tide Lifts Mood in the Developing World, Sharp Decline in Support for Suicide Bombing in Muslim Countries', Pew Global Attitudes Project, 24 July 2007, http://www.pewglobal.org/files/pdf/257.pdf

54   Ali Mamouri, 'Suicide bombings on the rise among Shiites', *Al-Monitor*, 17 December 2013, https://web.archive.org/web/20171007013053/https://www.al-monitor.com/pulse/originals/2013/12/suicide-bombing-increase-shiite.html

55   Reuters, 'Yemen's Houthis attack Saudi ship, launch ballistic missile', 30 January 2017, https://www.reuters.com/article/us-yemen-security-saudi/yemens-houthis-attack-saudi-ship-launch-ballistic-missile-idUSKBN15E2KE

5. Death in Paradise

1   https://www.youtube.com/watch?v=LTZn32ENM1s

2   Chicago Project on Security and Terrorism (CPOST) Suicide Attack Database (2016) http://cpost.uchicago.edu/

3   The deadliest attacks included the Central Bank bombing in Colombo with 91 killed, and 1,400 injured (31 January 1996); the Dehiwala train bombing with 64 dead and 400 wounded (24 July 1996); the Bandaranaike International Airport attack with 7 Sri Lankan Air Force personnel killed (24 July 2001); and the Digampathana truck bombing

that attacked 15 military convoys leaving as many as 112 dead and over 150 injured (16 October 2006).

4   Alex Perry, 'How Sri Lanka's Rebels Build a Suicide Bomber', *Time*, 12 May 2006, http://content.time.com/time/world/article/0,8599,1193862,00.html

5   K. Ratnayake, 'Suicide bomb blast in Sri Lanka threatens ceasefire', World Socialist Website, 9 July 2004, https://www.wsws.org/en/articles/2004/07/sril-j09.html

6   Gandhi's assassination was also LTTE's only suicide operation conducted outside the territory of Sri Lanka.

7   Reuters, 'Chronology – Assassinations of political figures in Sri Lanka', 19 January 2007, http://uk.reuters.com/article/uk-srilanka-assassinations-idUKCOL15928620061110?mod=related&channelName=worldNews

8   Amy Waldman, 'Masters of Suicide Bombing: Tamil Guerrillas of Sri Lanka', *New York Times*, 14 January 2003, http://www.nytimes.com/2003/01/14/world/masters-of-suicide-bombing-tamil-guerrillas-of-sri-lanka.html

9   Djan Sauerborn, 'Political Violence Revisited: The Liberation Tigers of Tamil Eelam', in *Terrorism Revisited: Islamism, Political Violence and State-Sponsorship*, eds. Paulo Casaca and Siegfried O. Wolf (Cham: Springer International Publishing AG, 2017), 183.

10 Ami Pedahzur, *Suicide Terrorism* (Cambridge: Polity Press, 2005), 70–97.

11 Asoka Bandarage, *The Separatist Conflict in Sri Lanka: Terrorism, Ethnicity, Political Economy* (London: Routledge, 2009), 105.

12 Bandarage, *The Separatist Conflict in Sri Lanka*.

13 V.S. Sambandan, 'Living through the bombs', *Frontline*, Vol. 17 Issue 09, 29 April–12 May,2000, 13, and Ely Karmon, 'The role of intelligence in counter-terrorism', *Korean Journal of Defense Analysis* 14.1 (2002): 119–39.

14 Robert Pape, 'Tamil Tigers: Suicide Bombing Innovators', *Talk of the Nation*, 21 May 2009, transcript at: http://www.npr.org/templates/transcript/transcript.php?storyId=104391493.

15 Pape, 'Tamil Tigers'.

16 Benjamin Dix, 'A critical analysis of suicide terrorism focusing on the Liberation Tigers of Tamil Elam', MA dissertation, University of Sussex 2011.

17 Rohan Gunaratna, 'Suicide terrorism: a global threat' in *Jane's Intelligence Review* 12 (4) (2000): 52–5.

18 Rajan Hoole, 'The Premadasa Assassination', *Colombo Telegraph*, 21 June 2014, https://www.colombotelegraph.com/index.php/the-premadasa-assassination/

19   Charu Lata Joshi, 'Ultimate Sacrifice: Faced with harassment and economic deprivation, young Tamils are ready to give up their lives', *Far Eastern Economic Review* 163, no. 22 (2000): 64-76. See: http://www.essex.ac.uk/armedcon/Countries/Asia/Texts/SriLanka011.htm.

20   Amy Waldman, 'Masters of suicide bombing: Tamil guerrillas of Sri Lanka', *New York Times* 1, 2003, 14.

21   Jyoti Thottam, 'Prabhakaran: The Life and Death of a Tiger', *Time*, 19 May 2009, http://content.time.com/time/world/article/0,8599,1899590,00.html

22   *Hindu*, 'The making of a militant leader', 19 May 2009, http://www.thehindu.com/todays-paper/tp-opinion/The-making-of-a-militant-leader/article16599489.ece

23   *Independent*, 'Peter Popham: Prabhakaran talked of peace. But the man I met was doomed to die in action', 18 May 2009, http://www.independent.co.uk/voices/commentators/peter-popham-prabhakaran-talked-of-peace-but-the-man-i-met-was-doomed-to-die-in-action-1687198.html

24   Anita Pratap, *Island of Blood: Frontline Reports from Sri Lanka, Afghanistan and Other South Asian Flashpoints* (London: Penguin Books, 2002).

25   Anuj Chopra, 'Sri Lanka: Can Tamil Tigers go on without their leader?', *Christian Science Monitor*, 18 May 2009, https://www.csmonitor.com/World/Asia-South-Central/2009/0518/p06s04-wosc.html

26   Diego Gambetta, ed., *Making Sense of Suicide Missions* (Oxford: Oxford University Press, 2006), 64.

27   David C. Hofmann, 'The Influence of Charismatic Authority on Operational Strategies and Attack Outcomes of Terrorist Groups', *Journal of Strategic Security* 9.2 (2016): 14–44.

28   Bruce Hoffman and Gordon H. McCormick, 'Terrorism, Signaling, and Suicide Attack', *Studies in Conflict and Terrorism* 27.4 (2004), 243–81.

29   Tony Birtley, 'Sri Lanka's Black Tigers', Al Jazeera, 23 July 2007, http://www.aljazeera.com/news/asia/2007/07/2008525183414716851.html

30   Samanth Subramanian, *This Divided Island: Stories from the Sri Lankan War* (London: Atlantic Books, 2014), 51.

31   Sauerborn, 'Political Violence Revisited', 193.

32   Waldman, 'Masters of Suicide Bombing: Tamil Guerrillas of Sri Lanka', *New York Times*

33   Perry, 'How Sri Lanka's Rebels Build a Suicide Bomber', *Time*.

34   Subramanian, *This Divided Island*, 85.

35   Jagath P. Senarartne, *Political Violence in Sri Lanka, 1977–1990: Riots,*

Insurrections, Counter-insurgencies, Foreign Intervention (Amsterdam: VU University Press, 1997), 85.

36 Sri Lanka Travel, 'Northern Sri Lanka', accessed 18 May 2018, http://www.srilanka.travel/northern-sri-lanka

37 This impressive investigation was Raymond Bonner, 'Tamil Guerrillas in Sri Lanka: Deadly and Armed to the Teeth', *New York Times*, 7 March 1998 *https://www.nytimes.com/1998/03/07/world/tamil-guerrillas-in-sri-lanka-deadly-and-armed-to-the-teeth.html*

38 With thanks to Peter Layton for providing this argument: Peter Layton, 'How Sri Lanka Won the War', *Diplomat*, 9 April 2015, https://thediplomat.com/2015/04/how-sri-lanka-won-the-war/

39 Gordon Weiss, *The Cage: The Fight for Sri Lanka and the Last Days of the Tamil Tigers* (London: The Bodley Head, 2011), 128.

40 *Sunday Times (Sri Lanka)*, 'LLRC calls for Rule of Law, not rule of men', 18 December 2011, http://www.sundaytimes.lk/111218/Columns/political.html

41 Crane Brinton, *The Anatomy of Revolution* (New York: W.W. Norton & Company Inc., 1938), 112.

6. A House in Heaven

1 E.H. Palmer, *The Survey of Western Palestine: Arabic and English Name Lists Collected During the Survey* by Lieutenants Conder and Kitchener, R. E. Transliterated and Explained by E.H. Palmer (*Committee of the Palestine exploration fund* 1881), 142. See https://archive.org/details/surveyofwesternp00conduoft/page/n3

2 Clyde Haberman, 'Arab Car Bomber Kills 8 in Israel; 44 are Wounded', *New York Times*, 7 April 1994, http://www.nytimes.com/1994/04/07/world/arab-car-bomber-kills-8-in-israel-44-are-wounded.html

3 While Hadera was the first official bombing, it was actually the third attempt at one, part of a trial-and-error phase during which Hamas bomb maker Yahya Ayyash perfected his craft. In addition to two failed attempts and the bombings on 6 and 13 April 1994, Ayyash would eventually be responsible for the deaths of at least thirty-nine people in five more attacks. He would also teach others, like his friend Hassan Salameh, how to make bombs.

4 The target of the attack was Lebanese Christian leaders, in an attempt to stop Lebanese Christians from aligning too closely with Israel: Ihsan A Hijazi, '5 Die in Lebanon Suicide Bomb Attack', *New York Times*, 13 November 1985, http://www.nytimes.com/1985/11/13/world/5-die-in-lebanon-suicide-bomb-attack.html

5   *Hindustan Times*, 'How mastermind of Punjab CM's assassination was caught', 29 November 2015, https://www.hindustantimes.com/punjab/how-mastermind-of-punjab-cm-s-assassination-was-caught/story-xl85pJjBAm92d6ieuqRHhP.html

6   However, Samson did reputedly use his brute strength to pull down a temple's pillars upon himself, killing thousands of Philistines along with him.

7   Pew Research Center, 'Mapping the Global Muslim Population', 7 October 2009, http://www.pewforum.org/2009/10/07/mapping-the-global-muslim-population/

8   Kevin Toolis, 'The revenger's tragedy: why women turn to suicide bombing', *Guardian*, 12 October 2003, https://www.theguardian.com/world/2003/oct/12/israel

9   Eli E. Hertz, 'Sacrificing Children', Arutz Sheva, 9 August 2011, http://www.israelnationalnews.com/Articles/Article.aspx/10486

10   *Ma'an News*, '1992 mass deportation of Hamas members', 23 July 2009, http://www.maannews.com/Content.aspx?id=214068 and Clyde Haberman, 'Israel Expels 400 From Occupied Lands; Lebanese Deploy to Bar Entry of Palestinians', *New York Times*, 18 December 1993, http://www.nytimes.com/1992/12/18/world/israel-expels-400-occupied-lands-lebanese-deploy-bar-entry-palestinians.html

11   Terrence McCoy, 'Camp Bucca: The US prison that became the birthplace of Isis', *Independent*, 4 November 2014, http://www.independent.co.uk/news/world/middle-east/camp-bucca-the-us-prison-that-became-the-birthplace-of-isis-9838905.html

12   Paola Caridi, *Hamas: From Resistance to Government,* trans. Andrea Teti (New York: Seven Stories Press, 2012).

13   Bruce Hoffman, *Inside Terrorism* (New York: Columbia University Press, 2006), 148.

14   Anat Kurz, Maskit Burgin and David Tal, *Islamic Terrorism and Israel: Hezbollah, Palestinian Islamic Jihad and Hamas* (Tel Aviv: Papyrus, Tel Aviv University, 1993), 174.

15   Brother Andrew, *Light Force* (London: Hachette, 2011).

16   Jessica Stern, *Terror in the Name of God: Why Religious Militants Kill* (New York: Harper Collins, 2003), 47.

17   Shaul Mishal and Avraham Sela, *The Hamas Wind: Violence and Coexistence* (Tel Aviv: Miskal Yedioth Ahronoth Books and Hemed Books, 1999), 78–80.

18   Robert Fisk, *The Great War for Civilisation: The Conquest of the Middle East* (New York: Vintage Books, 2007), 498.

19   Kelly F. Kafeyan, 'Sunni and Shiite Martyrdom: A Comparative Analysis of Historical and Contemporary Expressions' (Master's

Thesis, Naval Postgraduate School Monterey, California, 2010), http://
calhoun.nps.edu/bitstream/handle/10945/5061/10Dec_Kafeyan.
pdf?sequence=1

20 David Hirst, *Beware of Small States: Lebanon, Battleground of the
    Middle East* (London: Faber and Faber, 2010), 222.
21 MEMRI, Special Dispatch, 9 June 2004.
22 The book, *al-Khomeini: al-Hall al-Islami wa al-Badeel* [Khomein: An
    Islamic Solution and Alternative], was first published in 1979. See also:
    Abu-Amr, Ziad, *Islamic Fundamentalism in the West Bank and Gaza*
    (Bloomington: Indiana University Press, 1994).
23 Bernard K. Freamon, 'Martyrdom, Suicide, and the Islamic Law of
    War: A Short Legal History', *Fordham International Law Journal*,
    Volume 27, Issue 1 (2003): 358.
24 Fathi al-Shaqaqi was assassinated on 21 October, 1995 in Malta. It is
    widely believed that the Israeli Mossad carried out the killing.
25 Robert Fisk, 'Ugly End For Man Who Laughed at Death', *Independent*,
    30 October 1995, http://www.independent.co.uk/news/world/ugly-
    end-for-man-who-laughed-at-death-1580134.html
26 Pew Research Center, 'Concerns About Islamic Extremism on
    the Rise in the Middle East', 30 June 2014, http://www.pewglobal.
    org/2014/07/01/concerns-about-islamic-extremism-on-the-rise-in-
    middle-east/pg-2014-07-01-islamic-extremism-11/
27 Raphael Israeli, *Islamikaze: Manifestations of Islamic Martyrology*
    (London: Routledge, 2004), 218.
28 Rainer Brunner, 'Shi'ite Doctrine ii – Hierarchy in the Imamiyya',
    Iranicaonline, 1 October 2010, http://www.iranicaonline.org/articles/
    shiite-doctrine-ii-hierarchy-emamiya
29 Kafeyan, 'Sunni and Shiite Martyrdom'.
30 Diego Gambetta and Steffen Hertog, 'Engineers of Jihad', *Sociology
    Working Papers* 2007–10, Department of Sociology, Oxford University,
    10. Another analysis discovered that having an education in the
    humanities and social science had an apparent 'opposite impact' on
    creating Sunni jihadists. See Martin Rose, 'Immunising the mind: How
    can education reform contribute to neutralising violent extremism',
    (London: British Council Working Paper, 2015), https://www.
    britishcouncil.org/sites/default/files/immunising_the_mind_working_
    paper.pdf
31 Daniel W. Brown, *Rethinking Tradition in Modern Islamic
    Thought* (Cambridge: Cambridge University Press, 1999), 93.
    You can download the book here: https://www.scribd.com/
    document/116836545/Rethinking-Traditions-in-Modern-Islamic-
    Thought-Daniel-w-Brown

32   Christian Szyska, 'Martyrdom – A Drama of Foundation and Transition', *Future Islam* (blog), accessed 22 May 2018, http://www.futureislam.com/inner.php?id=NDI5

33   'The Story of the Tragedy of Bi'r Ma'oona', *Stories of the Sahabah* (blog), accessed 22 May 2018, http://storiesofthesahabah.tumblr.com/post/44194259506/tragedyofbirma-oona

34   David Cook, 'Martyrdom (Shahada)', in Oxford Bibliographies Online – Islamic Studies (25 October 2012), http://www.oxfordbibliographies.com/view/document/obo-9780195390155/obo-9780195390155-0124.xml

35   'Ibn Taymiyyah', *Encyclopaedia Britannica*, accessed 22 May 2018, https://www.britannica.com/biography/Ibn-Taymiyyah

36   Shiraz Maher (ed.), *Salafi-Jihadism – The History of an Idea* (London: C. Hurst & Co., 2016).

37   Alastair Crooke, 'You Can't Understand ISIS If You Don't Know the History of Wahhabism in Saudi Arabia', *Huffington Post*, 30 March 2017, http://www.huffingtonpost.com/alastair-crooke/isis-wahhabism-saudi-arabia_b_5717157.html

38   Sayyid Quṭb, *Milestones*, Issue No. 512, trans. S Badrul Hasan (International Islamic Publishers, 1981).

39   Ibid.

40   Sheikh Abdullah Azzam, 'Martyrs: The Building Blocks of Nations – Will of the Shaheed' (2001), https://english.religion.info/2002/02/01/document-martyrs-the-building-blocks-of-nations/

41   BBC News, 'Analysis: Palestinian suicide attacks', 29 January 2007, http://news.bbc.co.uk/1/hi/world/middle_east/3256858.stm

42   Quran, Chapter 3, Verse 169, Surah Al 'Imran, https://quran.com/3/169

43   Tom Holland, *Millennium: The End of the World and the Forging of Christendom* (London: Abacus, 2008), 83.

44   Quran, 3:169.

45   Magdi Abdelhadi, 'Controversial preacher with star status', BBC News, 7 July 2004, http://news.bbc.co.uk/1/hi/uk/3874893.stm

46   Mardawi Al-Rashed and Marat Shterin, *Dying for Faith: Religiously Motivated Violence in the Contemporary World* (London: L.B. Tauris & Co. Ltd, 2009). He reversed his position in 2003 and condemned suicide attacks entirely, refusing to sanction an attack against civilians, only against combatants. However, for him all Israelis counted as combatants due to the country's policy of universal conscription and its harsh politics in the Palestinian territories.

47   Hoffman, *Inside Terrorism*, 148.

48   Scott Atran, 'Genesis of Suicide Terrorism', *Science*, Vol. 299, Issue 5612 (7 March 2003): 1534–9. https://doi.org/10.1126/science.1078854

49   Jeremy Cooke, 'School trains suicide bombers', BBC News, 18 July
     2001, http://news.bbc.co.uk/1/hi/world/middle_east/1446003.stm
50   Shaykh Muhammad Saalih al-Munajjid, '47048: Is the Throne above
     the seventh heaven?', Islam Question & Answer, 23 April 2004, https://
     islamqa.info/en/47048
51   David Brooks, 'The Culture of Martyrdom: How Suicide Bombing
     Became Not Just a Means but an End', *Atlantic*, June 2002, https://
     www.theatlantic.com/magazine/archive/2002/06/the-culture-of-
     martyrdom/302506/
52   Judith Palmer Harik, *Hezbollah: The Changing Face of Terrorism*
     (London: I.B. Tauris, 2005), 168. There are always possible exceptions
     to the rule. On 18 July 1994, a suicide car bomber targeted a Jewish
     community centre in Argentina, killing 85 and wounding more than
     200. The Argentinian authorities said the attacker was a Hezbollah
     fighter – Ibrahim Hussein Berro – funded by Iran. Hezbollah
     rejected this, saying that Berro had died in Southern Lebanon while
     fighting Israel. Independent investigators found the Argentinian
     investigation riven with incompetencies and lies, and that no proper
     autopsies or DNA tests had been done. In a May 2007 interview,
     James Cheek, President Clinton's ambassador to Argentina at the time
     of the bombing, told the paper *La Nación* that 'there was never any
     real evidence [of Iranian responsibility]. They never came up with
     anything.' So even that lone accusation of Hezbollah targeting civilians
     remains clouded by doubt.
53   Kafeyan, 'Sunni and Shiite martyrdom'.
54   Freamon, 'Martyrdom, Suicide, and the Islamic Law of War', 367.
55   Mohammed M. Hafez, *Manufacturing Human Bombs: The Making of
     Palestinian Suicide Bombers* (Washington, D.C.: United States Institute
     of Peace, 2006), 65.
56   Freamon, 'Martyrdom, Suicide, and the Islamic Law of War', 365.
57   Atran, 'Genesis of suicide terrorism', 1537.
58   Donatella Marazziti, Antonello Veltri and Armando Piccinni, 'The
     Mind of Suicide Terrorists', CNS Spectrums, Volume 23, Special Issue
     2, September 2017, 1–6, 3.
59   Ibid., 5.
60   See BBC News, 'Palestinians get Saddam funds', 13 March
     2003, http://news.bbc.co.uk/1/hi/world/middle_east/2846365.
     stm; or *Sydney Morning Herald*, 'Saddam stokes war with
     suicide bomber cash', 26 March 2002, https://www.smh.com.au/
     articles/2002/03/25/1017004766310.html
61   David Hofmann and Lorne Dawson, 'The Neglected Role of
     Charismatic Authority in the Study of Terrorist Groups and

Radicalization', *Studies in Conflict & Terrorism* (2014), 360, http://
dx.doi.org/10.1080/1057610X.2014.879436. Angela Gendron, 'The
Call to Jihad: Charismatic Preachers and the Internet', *Studies in
Conflict & Terrorism* (2016), 48, 57, http://dx.doi.org/10.1080/1057
610X.2016.1157406

62   Djan Sauerborn, 'Political Violence Revisited: The Liberation Tigers of
Tamil Eelam', in *Terrorism Revisited: Islamism, Political Violence and
State-Sponsorship*, eds. Paulo Casaca and Siegfried O. Wolf (Cham:
Springer International Publishing AG, 2017), 191.

63   James Bennet, 'In Israeli Hospital, Bomber Tells of Trying to Kill
Israelis', *New York Times*, 8 June 2002.

64   Fisk, *The Great War for Civilisation*, 522.

65   Basil Saleh, 'Palestinian suicide attacks revisited: a critique of current
wisdom', *Peace and Conflict Monitor* (2004), 237.

66   Sam Harris, *The End of Faith: Religion, Terror, and the Future of
Reason*, iBooks, 450.

67   *Free Tibet*, 'Tibetan Monk Dies After Self-Immolating in Eastern
Tibet', 20 May 2017, https://freetibet.org/news-media/na/tibetan-
monk-dies-after-self-immolating-eastern-tibet

68   Ayelett Shani, 'What Drives Israelis to Drug Addiction?' *Haaretz*, 15
January 2016, https://www.haaretz.com/science-and-health/.premium-
what-drives-israelis-to-drug-addiction-1.5390670

69   Miriam Schiff et al., 'Exposure to terrorism and Israeli youths'
cigarette, alcohol, and cannabis use', *American Journal of Public Health*
97.10 (2007): 1852–8.

70   Michelle Hites, 'Why Israelis Make the Worst Tourists', *Haaretz*, 31
March 2014, https://www.haaretz.com/opinion/.premium-why-israelis-
make-the-worst-tourists-1.5341538

71   B'Tselem, 'Statistics', accessed 22 May 2018, https://www.btselem.org/
statistics

72   Robert J. Brym, 'Six lessons of suicide bombers', *Contexts* 6.4 (2007):
42.

73   Chaim Levinson, 'Torture, Israeli-style – as Described by the
Interrogators Themselves', *Haaretz*, 24 January 2017, https://www.
haaretz.com/israel-news/.premium-israeli-style-torture-as-described-
by-the-interrogators-themselves-1.5489853

74   Amnesty International, 'Israel and Occupied Palestinian
Territories 2017/2018', accessed 22 May 2018, https://www.
amnesty.org/en/countries/middle-east-and-north-africa/
israel-and-occupied-palestinian-territories/report-israel-and-occupied-
palestinian-territories/

75   Robert Fisk, 'Amnesty condemns Israelis and Palestinians for rights

abuses', *Independent*, 8 September 1998, http://www.independent.
co.uk/news/amnesty-condemns-israelis-and-palestinians-for-rights-
abuses-1196948.html

76 Bader Araj, 'Harsh state repression as a cause of suicide bombing: the
case of the Palestinian–Israeli conflict', *Studies in Conflict & Terrorism*
31.4 (2008): 291.

77 Edward H. Kaplan, Alex Mintz and Shaul Mishal, 'Tactical prevention
of suicide bombings in Israel', *Interfaces* 36.6 (2006): 553–61.

78 Jeff Goodwin and James M. Jasper, eds., *The Social Movements Reader:
Cases and Concepts* (Chichester, UK: John Wiley & Sons, 2014), 243.

79 Brym, 'Six lessons of suicide bombers', 42.

80 Amos Harel, 'Hamas Weapons Capability Increased Four-fold
Over Last Five Years', *Haaretz,* 5 April 2011, https://www.haaretz.
com/1.5147022

81 Conal Urquhart, 'Hamas in call to end suicide bombings', *Guardian*, 9
April 2006, https://www.theguardian.com/world/2006/apr/09/israel

82 *Times of Israel*, 'Hamas calls for suicide bombings in Israeli buses', 7
February 2006, https://www.timesofisrael.com/hamas-calls-for-suicide-
bombings-in-israelis-buses/

83 Gili Cohen, 'Hamas Terror Cell Planning Suicide Attacks in Jerusalem
Uncovered, Shin Bet Says', *Haaretz,* 22 December 2016, https://www.
haaretz.com/israel-news/.premium-hamas-terror-cell-planning-
suicide-attacks-uncovered-shin-bet-says-1.5477291

84 Adnan Abu Amer, 'Hamas leaders reject fatwa forbidding suicide
attacks', *Al-Monitor*, 20 December 2016, https://www.al-monitor.com/
pulse/originals/2016/12/palestinian-fatwa-suicide-operations-israel.
html

85 *Israel Today*, 'Hamas Gets Taste of Its Own Medicine in Gaza Suicide
Bombing', 20 August 2017, http://www.israeltoday.co.il/NewsItem/
tabid/178/nid/32215/Default.aspx

7. The Devil's Face

1 *New York Magazine*, 'Death, destruction, charity, salvation, war,
money, real estate, spouses, babies, and other September 11 statistics',
September 2014, http://nymag.com/news/articles/wtc/1year/numbers.
htm

2 Scott Stewart, 'A Look Back at the 1993 World Trade Center Bombing',
Stratfor, 26 February 2015, https://worldview.stratfor.com/article/look-
back-1993-world-trade-center-bombing

3 National Commission on Terrorist Attacks upon the United States, *The*

9/11 Commission Report: Final Report of the National Commission on Terrorist Attacks Upon the United States (Government Printing Office, 2011).

4 Julia Kristeva, *Black Sun: Depression and Melancholia,* trans. Leon S Roudiez (New York: Columbia University Press, 1989), 223.

5 Linda Tischler, 'At 9/11 Memorial, Name Placements Reflect Bonds Between Victims, Thanks To Algorithm', 5 May 2011, *Fast Co Design*, https://www.fastcodesign.com/1663780/at-911-memorial-name-placements-reflect-bonds-between-victims-thanks-to-algorithm

6 Federation of American Scientists, 'Jihad Against Jews and Crusaders: World Islamic Front Statement', 23 February 1998, https://fas.org/irp/world/para/docs/980223-fatwa.htm

7 Mark Juergensmeyer, *Global Rebellion: Religious Challenges to the Secular State, from Christian Militias to Al-Qaeda* (Berkeley: University of California Press, 2008), 202.

8 *New York Times*, 'The World; Osama bin Laden, In His Own Words', 23 August 1998, http://www.nytimes.com/1998/08/23/weekinreview/the-world-osama-bin-laden-in-his-own-words.html

9 Yosri Fouda, 'We left out nuclear targets, for now', *Guardian*, 4 March 2003, https://www.theguardian.com/world/2003/mar/04/alqaida.terrorism

10 The challenge of their literal readings of the Quran and the Hadiths is that – like with the Bible – therein lurks pre-scientific prejudice and assumptions that jar to the modern ear. If you took the words of the writings of al-Bukhari's Hadith at its word, for instance, you would be led to believe that a child will resemble the parent who climaxed first (55:546); that Satan causes yawning (73:245); that the Devil sleeps in your nose (54:516); that if Beelzebub urinates in your ear, you will oversleep (54:492); that keeping a dog as a pet will lead to a reduction of the number of good deeds a man does in this life (67:389); and that you should wipe yourself with an odd number of stones after defecating (4:163).

11 'Wahhabism' is seen as a pejorative term by many of its followers and is a contested term in Saudi Arabia.

12 For more on this, see Shiraz Maher, *Salafi-Jihadism: The History of an Idea* (London: Hurst & Co, 2016).

13 Chapter 60, Verse 8, Surah al-Momtahana of the Quran; Chapter 60, Verse 9, Surah al-Momtahana of the Quran; Chapter 2, Verse 190, Surah al-Baqara of the Quran.

14 Bernard K. Freamon, 'Martyrdom, Suicide, and the Islamic Law of War: A Short Legal History', *Fordham International Law Journal*, Volume 27, Issue 1; (2003): 315, note 48.

15   Chapter 9, Verse 5, Surah al-Tawba of the Quran.

16   CNN, 'Transcript of Bin Laden's October interview', 5 February 2002, http://edition.cnn.com/2002/WORLD/asiapcf/south/02/05/binladen. transcript/

17   Melanie Byrd, 'The Napoleonic Institute of Egypt', *Napoleonic Scholarship: The Journal of the International Napoleonic Society*, Volume 1, Number 2, December 1998, https://www.napoleon-series. org/ins/scholarship98/c_institute.html

18   Mitt Romney, *No Apology: The Case for American Greatness* (New York: St. Martin's Press, 2010), 67.

19   Jim Muir, '"Islamic State": Raqqa's loss seals rapid rise and fall', BBC News, 17 October 2017, http://www.bbc.co.uk/news/world-middle-east-35695648

20   Sayyid Quṭb, *Milestones,* Issue No. 512, trans. S. Badrul Hasan (International Islamic Publishers, 1981), 151.

21   National Commission on Terrorist Attacks Upon the United States, *The 9/11 Commission Report*, 52.

22   Ami Pedahzur and Arie Perliger, 'The Changing Nature of Suicide Attacks: A Social Network Perspective', *Social Forces*, Volume 84, Issue 4 (June 2006): 1987–2008.

23   Shiraz Maher and Alexandra Bissoondath, 'Al-Qadā'wa-l-Qadr: motivational representations of divine decree and predestination in salafi-jihadi literature', *British Journal of Middle Eastern Studies* (2017): 1–15.

24   Fouda, 'We left out nuclear targets, for now'.

25   Maher, *Salafi-Jihadism: The History of an Idea*.

26   Pew Research Center, 'A Rising Tide Lifts Mood in the Developing World', 24 July 2007, http://www.pewglobal.org/2007/07/24/a-rising-tide-lifts-mood-in-the-developing-world/

27   Benjamin T. Acosta, 'Palestinian precedents: The origins of al-Qaeda's use of suicide terrorism and Istishhad', in *Political Islam from Muhammad to Ahmadinejad: Defenders, Detractors, and Definitions*, ed. Joseph Morrison Skelly (Santa Barbara: Praeger Security International, 2010), 198–9.

28   Navid Kermani, 'Roots of terror: suicide, martyrdom, self-redemption and Islam', *openDemocracy*, 21 February 2002, https://www. opendemocracy.net/faith-europe_islam/article_88.jsp

29   Steve Coll, *Ghost Wars: The Secret History of the CIA, Afghanistan, and bin Laden, from the Soviet Invasion to September 10, 2001* (New York: Penguin, 2004).

30   Thomas Rid and Marc Hecker, *War 2.0: Irregular Warfare in the Information Age* (Westport; London: ABC-CLIO, 2009), 166, and

Ahmed Rashid, *Descent into Chaos: The US and the Disaster in Pakistan, Afghanistan, and Central Asia* (New York: Penguin Books. 2008), 366.

31   It led Azzam's son to say that had he lived, 'there would have been no September 11'. https://www.youtube.com/watch?v=zoEMuYOa3dU

32   Steve Coll, *The Bin Ladens: An Arabian Family in the American Century* (New York: Penguin Press, 2008), 118.

33   Jonathan Steele, '10 myths about Afghanistan', *Guardian*, 27 September 2011, https://www.theguardian.com/world/2011/sep/27/10-myths-about-afghanistan

34   BBC News, 'Flashback: 1991 Gulf War', 20 March 2003, http://news.bbc.co.uk/1/hi/world/middle_east/2754103.stm

35   Maher, *Salafi-Jihadism – The History of an Idea*.

36   Ibid.

37   David Rose, 'Attackers did not know they were to die', *Guardian*, 14 October 2001, https://www.theguardian.com/world/2001/oct/14/terrorism.september111

38   Daniel Brook, 'The Architect of 9/11', *Slate*, 8 September 2009, http://www.slate.com/articles/news_and_politics/dispatches/features/2009/the_architect_of_911/what_can_we_learn_about_mohamed_atta_from_his_work_as_a_student_of_urban_planning.html

39   Ashley Collman and Louise Boyle, 'Osama bin Laden had an "extensive" porn collection – but officials are refusing to release details because of its "nature"', *Daily Mail*, 21 May 2015, http://www.dailymail.co.uk/news/article-3090394/Officials-refuse-release-Osama-bin-Laden-s-extensive-porn-collection-nature.html

40   Dan P. Lee, 'The Hijackers: Who Were They?', *New York Magazine*, 27 August 2011, http://nymag.com/news/9-11/10th-anniversary/hijackers/

41   Certainly it was a constructed ritual, possibly learnt from the Pashtun tribesmen of Afghanistan, who shave their bodies before going into battle. Juliet Lapidos, 'Hair Today, Gone Tomorrow', *Slate*, 25 March 2008, http://www.slate.com/articles/news_and_politics/explainer/2008/03/hair_today_gone_tomorrow.html

42   Government Exhibit BS01101T, accessed 23 May 2018, http://www.vaed.uscourts.gov/notablecases/moussaoui/exhibits/prosecution/BS01101T.pdf

43   *New York Magazine*, 'Death, destruction, charity, salvation, war, money, real estate, spouses, babies, and other September 11 statistics.'

44   Dennis Cauchon and Martha Moore, 'Desperation forced a horrific decision', *USA Today*, 2 September 2002, https://usatoday30.usatoday.com/news/sept11/2002-09-02-jumper_x.htm and Jim Dwyer, 'Vast

Archive Yields New View of 9/11', *New York Times*, 13 August 2005, http://www.nytimes.com/2005/08/13/nyregion/nyregionspecial3/vast-archive-yields-new-view-of-911.html

45   Nick Sywak, 'Surfing the Collapse', *New York Magazine*, 27 August 2011, http://nymag.com/news/9-11/10th-anniversary/surf-to-safety/

46   Matthew Shaer, 'Survivor, Last Pulled Out', *New York Magazine*, 27 August 2011, http://nymag.com/news/9-11/10th-anniversary/last-survivor/

47   Joanna Walters, '9/11: "I was the last person pulled alive from the rubble of the Twin Towers"', *Daily Express*, 10 September 2011, https://www.express.co.uk/expressyourself/270365/9-11-I-was-the-last-person-pulled-alive-from-the-rubble-of-the-Twin-Towers

48   Ian McEwan, 'Only love and then oblivion. Love was all they had to set against their murderers', *Guardian*, 15 September 2001, https://www.theguardian.com/world/2001/sep/15/september11.politicsphilosophyandsociety2

49   Nick Greene, 'September 11, 2001 Terrorist Attacks – 9/11 Attacks', *ThoughtCo*, 19 March 2017, https://www.thoughtco.com/twin-towers-from-space-3071240

50   John M. Butler, *Advanced Topics in Forensic DNA Typing: Methodology* (San Diego, CA; Waltham, MA: Academic Press, 2011), 284.

51   *AllCreaturesLargeandSmall* (blog), 'Tribute and Memorial to the Search and Rescue Dogs of 9-11: Words and Images', 9 September 2011, https://allcreatureslargeandsmall.wordpress.com/2011/09/09/tribute-and-memorial-to-the-search-and-rescue-dogs-of-9-11-words-and-images/

52   Michael Idov, 'Unidentified Remains', *New York Magazine*, 27 August 2011, http://nymag.com/news/9-11/10th-anniversary/unidentified-remains/

53   CNN, 'More than 1,100 have cancer after 9/11', 11 September 2013, https://edition.cnn.com/2013/09/11/health/911-cancer-treatment/

54   Matt Mauney, 'Asbestos, 9/11 and the World Trade Center', Asbestos.com, 6 February 2018, https://www.asbestos.com/world-trade-center/

55   Charles Laurence, 'Death of World Trade Center victim's loyal dog tips widow into suicide', *Daily Telegraph*, 16 December 2001, https://www.telegraph.co.uk/news/worldnews/northamerica/usa/1365469/Death-of-World-Trade-Center-victims-loyal-dog-tips-widow-into-suicide.html

56   Mark Jacobson, 'Satan's Face', *New York Magazine*, 27 August 2011, http://nymag.com/news/9-11/10th-anniversary/satans-face/

57   Rachel Baker, 'Terror Sex', *New York Magazine*, 27 August 2011, http://nymag.com/news/9-11/10th-anniversary/terror-sex/

58   Ellen Pifer, ed., *Vladimir Nabokov's Lolita: A Casebook* (Oxford: Oxford University Press on Demand, 2003), 103.

59   Judy Faber, 'FAA Manager Relives Events Of Sept. 11', CBS News, 25 April 2006, https://www.cbsnews.com/news/faa-manager-relives-events-of-sept-11/

60   Discovery Channel Videos, 9/11 Snakebite, https://web.archive.org/web/20140308105753/https://www.discovery.com/tv-shows/other-shows/videos/i-was-bitten-9-11-snakebite.htm

61   Transport Canada, 'Four Days in September', accessed 23 May 2018, https://www.tc.gc.ca/eng/mediaroom/infosheets-fourdays-fourdays-6433.htm

62   James Ball, 'September 11's indirect toll: road deaths linked to fearful flyers', *Guardian*, 5 September 2011, https://www.theguardian.com/world/2011/sep/05/september-11-road-deaths

63   *Wall Street Journal*, 'Unplanned 9/11 analysis links noise, whale stress', 9 February 2012, https://www.wsj.com/articles/APacaea2ac7b53461a81e686f1874dd1b5

64   Walter Enders and Todd Sandler, *The Political Economy of Terrorism* (New York: Cambridge University Press, 2011).

65   Kenneth Feinberg, *Who Gets What: Fair Compensation after Tragedy and Financial Upheaval* (New York City: PublicAffairs, 2012).

66   John Mervin, 'Wall Street and the aftermath of 9/11', BBC News, 6 September 2011, http://www.bbc.co.uk/news/business-14798711

67   Alizeh Kohari, 'Is there a novel that defines the 9/11 decade?', BBC News, 28 August 2011, http://www.bbc.co.uk/news/entertainment-arts-14682741

68   Robert Hilburn, 'Judging Songs by Their Titles', *Los Angeles Times*, 19 September 2001, http://articles.latimes.com/2001/sep/19/entertainment/ca-47192

69   https://www.youtube.com/watch?v=ruNrdmjcNTc

70   *Salon*, 'Freedom is the Almighty's gift', 17 November 2003, https://www.salon.com/2003/11/17/bush_frost_int/

71   *Washington Post*, 'Text: President Bush Addresses the Nation', 20 September 2001, http://www.washingtonpost.com/wp-srv/nation/specials/attacked/transcripts/bushaddress_092001.html

72   Jason Burke, 'Al-Qaida leadership battle: who can replace Osama bin Laden?', *Guardian*, 2 May 2011, https://www.theguardian.com/world/2011/may/02/al-qaida-leadership-osama-bin-laden

8. Global Jihad

1   These were: Aden-Abyan Army, Aisha Umm-al Mouemeneen,
Ajnad al-Sham, Al Madina Regiment, Al-Haramayn Brigades, Jaysh
al-Islam, Majlis al Shura, Al-Mourabitoun, al-Qanoon, Amjad Farooqi
Group, Arab Resistance Movement, Al-Rashid Brigades, Army of
Palestine, Believing Youth Group, Benghazi Revolutionaries, Shura
Council, East Turkistan Islamic Movement, Free Sunni Brigade,
Gakayev Group, Gatia Pro-Government Militia, Gazotan Murdash
group, Haqqani Network, Hizbal Islam in Somalia, Islambouli
Brigades of Al-Qaeda, Islamic Army in Iraq, Islamic Jihadist Union,
Islamic Pride Brigades in the Land of the Nile, Islamic State – Hijaz
Province, Jamaat Ansarullah, Jund al-Islam, Jund al-Sham, Kamtapur
Liberation Organization, Karwan-e Naimatullah, Khalid ibn al-Walid
Army, Lebanese Islamic Jihad (Hezbollah), Liwa Ahrar al-Sunna,
Mujahidin Indonesia Timur, Muslim Brotherhood, Partisans of the
Sunni, Popular Resistance Committees, Sergokala Bandit Group
(Abdu-Salam), Shumukh al-Islam, Shura Council of Benghazi
Revolutionaries, Soldiers of the Prophet's Companions Group, Syrian
Tawhid and Jihad, Tajamo Ansar al Islam, Teyrêbazên Azadiya
Kurdistan, Yekineyen Parastina Gel, 1920 Revolution Brigade, Ahrar
ul-Hind, Hezbollah, Iraqi government, Islamic Front (Syria), Islamic
Unity Brigades, Jamaa Al-Islamiya Al-Alamiya, Kurdistan Freedom
Falcons, Lashkar-e Islam, Lashkar-e Taiba, Mujahedi Masr, Turkistan
Islamic Party, Ahrar ash-Sham, Ansar al-Mujahedin, Fatah al-Islam,
Free Syrian Army, Harakat ul-Mujahidin, Hizbul Mujahedin, Jamaatul
Mujahideen Bangladesh, Lashkar-e-Jhangvi, Mujahideen Youth
Movement, Revolutionary People's Liberation Party/Front, Suqour
al-Sham, Great Eastern Raiders Front, Nusra and Jihad Group in
Greater Syria, Ansar al-Islam, Assirat al-Moustaqim, Jaish Ansar
al-Sunnah, Jaish-e-Muhammad, Abdullah Azzam Brigades, Islamic
Movement of Uzbekistan, Jundullah (Iran), Chechen Separatists, Hizb-
i-Islami, Jemaah Islamiya, Jundullah (Pakistan), Ansar al-Sharia, Jaish
al-Fatah, Mujahideen Shura Council, Popular Front for the Liberation
of Palestine, Taliban (Pakistan), Ansar Beit al-Maqdis, Kurdistan
Workers Party, Movement for the Oneness and Jihad in West Africa,
Caucasus Emirate, Riyadus Salikhiin, Jamaat-ul-Ahrar, Lashkar-e
Jhangvi Al-almi, Al-Qaeda in the Land of the Islamic Maghreb,
Ansar al-Sunna, Jama'at Al-Tawhid Wa'al-Jihad, Al-Qaeda Central,
Liberation Tigers of Tamil Eelam, Palestinian Islamic Jihad, Hamas,
Al-Aqsa Martyrs' Brigade, Al-Qaeda in the Arabian Peninsula, Jabhat
al-Nusra l'Ahl as-Sham, Al-Shabaab, Islamic State of Iraq, Al-Qaeda

in Iraq, Boko Haram, Islamic State of Iraq and Syria, Tehrik-i-Taliban Pakistan, Islamic State, and Taliban (IEA).

2   These were Afghanistan, Algeria, Bangladesh, Belgium, Bolivia, Bulgaria, Cameroon, Chad, China, Djibouti, Egypt, Finland, France, Georgia, Germany, India, Indonesia, Iran, Iraq, Israel, Jordan, Kazakhstan, Kenya, Kuwait, Kyrgyzstan, Lebanon, Libya, Mali, Mauritania, Morocco, Niger, Nigeria, Pakistan, Palestine, Qatar, Russia, Saudi Arabia, Somalia, Spain, Sri Lanka, Sweden, Syria, Tajikistan, Tunisia, Turkey, Uganda, Ukraine, United Kingdom, United States, Uzbekistan and Yemen.

3   William McCants, 'Trump's Misdiagnosis of the Jihadist Threat', Brookings Institution Markaz Blog, 11 November 2016, https://www.brookings.edu/blog/markaz/2016/11/11/trumps-misdiagnosis-of-the-jihadist-threat/

4   South Asia Terrorism Portal, http://www.satp.org/

5   Bruce Hoffman, 'The resurgence of Al-Qaeda', Lowy Institute: *Interpreter*, 13 March 2018, https://www.lowyinstitute.org/the-interpreter/resurgence-al-qaeda

6   James Rothwell, 'Majority of the 74 journalists killed in 2016 were "targeted deliberately," says Reporters Without Borders', *Daily Telegraph*, 18 December 2016, https://www.telegraph.co.uk/news/2016/12/18/majority-74-journalists-killed-2016-targeted-deliberately-says/

7   Saeed Kamali Dehghan, Akhtar Mohammad Makoii and Haroon Janjua, 'Ten journalists among 36 killed in Afghanistan attacks', *Guardian*, 30 April 2018, https://www.theguardian.com/world/2018/apr/30/kabul-explosions-hit-city-centre-attack

8   The countries affected were Nigeria, Iraq, Afghanistan, Turkey, Syria, Yemen, Chad, Cameroon, Pakistan, Lebanon, Kuwait, France, Saudi Arabia, Somalia, Libya, Egypt, China, India, Bangladesh, Mali and Tunisia.

9   Misha Glenny, *McMafia: A Journey through the Global Underworld* (Toronto: House of Anansi, 2008).

10   Catherine A. Traywick, 'President Obama at West Point: Watch the Speech, Read the Transcript', *Foreign Policy*, 28 May 2014, http://foreignpolicy.com/2014/05/28/president-obama-at-west-point-watch-the-speech-read-the-transcript/

11   Richard Bonney, *Jihad: From Qur'an to Bin Laden* (London and New York: Palgrave Macmillan, 2004), 304.

12   BBC News, '"Suicide videos": What they said', 4 April 2008, http://news.bbc.co.uk/1/hi/uk/7330367.stm

13   Cullen Murphy and Todd S. Purdum, 'Farewell to All That: An Oral

History of the Bush White House', *Vanity Fair*, February 2009, https://www.vanityfair.com/news/2009/02/bush-oral-history200902

14   H. Res. 1345 Referred to Committee House (RTH), 'Impeaching George W. Bush, President of the United States, of high crimes and misdemeanors', 15 July 2008, https://www.gpo.gov/fdsys/pkg/BILLS-110hres1345rth/html/BILLS-110hres1345rth.htm

15   CNN, 'Pentagon: Iraqi forces engaged in "deadly deception"', 25 March 2003, http://edition.cnn.com/2003/US/03/24/sprj.irq.pentagon/index.html

16   The former responsible for twenty-eight suicide attacks in 2003 and 2004; the latter for twenty-one.

17   Steve Negus, 'The Insurgency Intensifies', *Middle East Report*, Vol. 232 (Autumn, 2004), 23.

18   Indeed, the country was not completely devoid of suicide strikes before foreign boots arrived upon Iraqi soil. The regime-founded paramilitary praetorian unit Fedayeen Saddam carried out a suicide bombing against Kurdish opposition parties in July 2000. Kyle Orton, 'Islamic State as the Saddam regime's afterlife: the Fedayeen Saddam', *openDemocracy*, 18 November 2015, https://www.opendemocracy.net/arab-awakening/kyle-orton/islamic-state-as-saddam-regime-s-afterlife-fedayeen-saddam

19   Ewen MacAskill, 'Murders and mutilation in Iraq revealed', 3 November 2000, http://www.friends-partners.org/lists/stop-traffic/1999/att-Iraqi_execution.txt

20   Orton, 'Islamic State as the Saddam regime's afterlife: the Fedayeen Saddam'.

21   Patrick E. Tyler, 'Suicide Attack in Central Iraq Kills 4 US Troops', *New York Times*, 29 March 2003, https://www.nytimes.com/2003/03/29/international/worldspecial/suicide-attack-in-central-iraq-kills-4-us-troops.html

22   Sean Rayment, 'Suicide bomber kills troops as Saddam unleashes "martyrs"', *Daily Telegraph*, 30 March 2003, https://www.telegraph.co.uk/news/worldnews/northamerica/usa/1426101/Suicide-bomber-kills-troops-as-Saddam-unleashes-martyrs.html

23   Robert J. Bunker and John P. Sullivan, *Suicide Bombings in Operation Iraqi Freedom*, Land Warfare Paper 46W (Arlington, VA: Institute of Land Warfare, Association of the US Army, September 2004)

24   'Iraq: The Bloody Circus', 16 November 2006, http://creativity-online.com/work/iraq-the-bloody-circus/5594

25   Islamic State of Iraq, Jama'at Al-Tawhid Wa'al-Jihad, Ansar al-Sunna, Mujahideen Shura Council, Jaish Ansar al-Sunnah, Ansar al-Islam, 1920 Revolution Brigade, Soldiers of the Prophet's Companions

Group, Partisans of the Sunni, Islamic Army in Iraq and the Arab Resistance Movement.

26 In Iraq, when suicide bombers have attacked civilian crowds, on average, twenty people have been killed. When the military have been targeted, about eight people have, on average, been killed; sandbags and body armour save lives.

27 *New York Review of Books*, 'The Mystery of ISIS', 13 August 2015, http://www.nybooks.com/articles/2015/08/13/mystery-isis/

28 Michael Weiss and Hassan Hassan, *ISIS: Inside the Army of Terror* (updated edition) (New York: Simon and Schuster, 2016), 31.

29 Saddam Hussein knew this exquisitely – to secure the loyalty of the Iraqi Shia population during the war, he not only allowed more Shias into the Ba'ath Party and the government, but also paid for the restoration of Imam Ali's tomb. Efraim Karsh, *The Iran–Iraq War 1980–1988* (London: Osprey Publishing, 2002).

30 Michael Lipka, 'The Sunni-Shia divide: Where they live, what they believe and how they view each other', *Pew Research Center*, 18 June 2014, http://www.pewresearch.org/fact-tank/2014/06/18/the-sunni-shia-divide-where-they-live-what-they-believe-and-how-they-view-each-other/

31 https://www.youtube.com/watch?v=Ga5CcwMHKBI

32 Tom Regan, 'Mullen's Plain Talk About US Mistakes in Iraq', *NPR News Blog*, 1 August 2007, http://archive.li/OtFiy#selection-513.0-513.47

33 Masooda Bano, *The Rational Believer: Choices and Decisions in the Madrasas of Pakistan* (Ithaca, NY: Cornell University Press, 2012), 8–9.

34 Yahya Michot, 'Ibn Taymiyya's "New Mardin Fatwa". Is genetically modified Islam (GMI) carcinogenic?', *The Muslim World* (April 2011), http://www.muslimphilosophy.com/michot/ITA-Mardin-Conference.pdf

35 Michot, 'Ibn Taymiyya's "New Mardin Fatwa"', 16.

36 An argument used by Salafist leaders such as Abu Bakr al-Baghdadi, Abubakar Shekau, Hibatullah Akhundzada, Abu Mohammed al-Jawlani and Ahmed Umar Abu Ubaidah.

37 'Abu Mus'ab Al-Zarqawi: Collateral Killing of Muslims is Legitimate', 7 June 2005, https://scholarship.tricolib.brynmawr.edu/bitstream/handle/10066/4809/ZAR20050518P.pdf?sequence=3. Sometimes, the theological justification of attacks on Shias was tortuous. When al-Zawahiri explained why Muslims needed to take up arms, he said: 'Imam Ahmad said: "We heard from Harun bin Ma'ruf, citing Abu Wahab, who quoted Amru bin al-Harith, citing Abu Ali Tamamah bin Shafi, that he heard Uqbah bin Amir saying, 'I heard the Prophet

say from the pulpit: "Against them make ready your strength."''''' Yet, through such crude interpretations, a generation of Salafi-jihadists have concluded the murder of the Shia should be celebrated.

38 https://www.youtube.com/watch?v=bQtgLCSIoF0

39 However, this ignores the reported instance of the bride who climbed into the cockpit with her Kamikaze husband in 1945.

40 Jay Sekulow, *Rise of ISIS: A Threat We Can't Ignore* (iBooks: Howard Books, 2014), 13.

41 Nick Meo, 'Video Diaries of Taliban's Boy Suicide Bombers', *Sunday Telegraph*, 31 May 2009.

42 Joby Warrick, *The Triple Agent: The al-Qaeda Mole who Infiltrated the CIA* (New York: Doubleday, 2011), 160. So important are these as tools that cameramen have been killed while documenting the attacks. The most famous Tamil Tiger attack, the assassination of Rajiv Gandhi, is a case in point.

43 Abu Rumaysah al Britani, 'A brief guide to Islamic State 2015', 18 May 2015, https://archive.org/details/Khilafah2015

44 Statista, 'Internet penetration rate in the Middle East compared to the global internet penetration rate from 2009 to 2017', accessed 25 May 2018, https://www.statista.com/statistics/265171/comparison-of-global-and-middle-eastern-internet-penetration-rate/

45 Joseph A. Carter, Shiraz Maher and Peter R. Neumann, '#Greenbirds: Measuring Importance and Influence in Syrian Foreign Fighter Networks', The International Centre for the Study of Radicalisation and Political Violence, http://icsr.info/wp-content/uploads/2014/04/ICSR-Report-Greenbirds-Measuring-Importance-and-Infleunce-in-Syrian-Foreign-Fighter-Networks.pdf

46 Sam Jones, 'Jihad by social media', *Financial Times*, 28 March 2014, https://www.ft.com/content/907fd41c-b53c-11e3-af92-00144feabdc0

47 Tom Keatinge, 'The role of finance in defeating al-Shabaab', RUSI Whitehall report 2–14, December 2014.

48 *Economist*, 'The jihadists' rainy-day fund: Islamic State has been stashing millions of dollars in Iraq and abroad', 22 February 2018, https://www.economist.com/middle-east-and-africa/2018/02/22/islamic-state-has-been-stashing-millions-of-dollars-in-iraq-and-abroad

49 Dina Temple-Raston, 'How Much Does A Terrorist Attack Cost? A Lot Less Than You'd Think', *NPR*, 25 June 2014, https://www.npr.org/sections/parallels/2014/06/25/325240653/how-much-does-a-terrorist-attack-cost-a-lot-less-than-you-think

50 Nikos Passas and Andrea Gimenez-Salinas Framis, 'The Financing of Al Qaida's Terrorism: Myths and Realities', *Review of Penal and Criminal Law*, 2nd Semester, no.19 (2007), 511. https://www.

researchgate.net/publication/39655965_La_financiacion_del_
terrorismo_de_Al_Qaeda_mitos_y_realidades

51   National Commission on Terrorist Attacks Upon the United States,
     Monograph on Terrorist Financing, Staff Report to the Commission
     (Washington, DC: 2004), 13. http://govinfo.library.unt.edu/911/staff_
     statements/911_TerrFin_Monograph.pdf

52   Jeff Stein, 'The Saudi Role in Sept. 11 and the Hidden 9/11 Report
     Pages', *Newsweek*, 7 January 2015, http://europe.newsweek.com/
     saudi-arabia-911-george-w-bush-barack-obama-prince-bandar-bin-
     sultan-bob-297170?rm=eu

53   Sekulow, *Rise of ISIS*, 52.

54   Ian Black, 'Saudi Arabia rejects Iraqi accusations of Isis support',
     Guardian, 19 June 2014, https://www.theguardian.com/world/2014/
     jun/19/saudi-arabia-rejects-iraqi-accusations-isis-support

55   Patrick Cockburn, 'We finally know what Hillary Clinton knew
     all along – US allies Saudi Arabia and Qatar are funding Isis',
     Independent, 14 October 2016, https://www.independent.co.uk/voices/
     hillary-clinton-wikileaks-email-isis-saudi-arabia-qatar-us-allies-
     funding-barack-obama-knew-all-a7362071.html

56   Adam Taylor, 'Behind Biden's gaffe lie real concerns about allies'
     role in rise of the Islamic State', *Washington Post*, 6 October 2014,
     https://www.washingtonpost.com/news/worldviews/wp/2014/10/06/
     behind-bidens-gaffe-some-legitimate-concerns-about-americas-
     middle-east-allies/?utm_term=.4fd3d0599e7c

57   Richard A. Clarke, *Against All Enemies* (iBooks: Free Press, 2004), 751.

58   Martin Williams, 'FactCheck Q&A: Is Saudi Arabia funding ISIS?',
     Channel 4 News, 7 June 2017, https://www.channel4.com/news/
     factcheck/factcheck-qa-is-saudi-arabia-funding-isis

59   Lori Plotkin Boghardt, 'The Terrorist Funding Disconnect with
     Qatar and Kuwait', *Washington Institute*, 2 May 2014, http://www.
     washingtoninstitute.org/policy-analysis/view/the-terrorist-funding-
     disconnect-with-qatar-and-kuwait

60   David Andrew Weinberg, 'Analysis: Qatar still negligent on
     terror finance', *Long War Journal*, 19 August 2015, http://www.
     longwarjournal.org/archives/2015/08/analysis-qatar-still-negligent-on-
     terror-finance.php

61   US Department of State, Middle East and North Africa Overview,
     Country Reports on Terrorism 2015, Chapter 2 http://www.state.gov/j/
     ct/rls/crt/2015/257517.htm

62   https://www.defenddemocracy.org/content/uploads/projects/LWJ_1.png

63   BBC News, 'How Qatar came to host the Taliban', 22 June 2013, http://
     www.bbc.co.uk/news/world-asia-23007401

64   Erika Solomon, 'The $1bn hostage deal that enraged Qatar's Gulf
      rivals', *Financial Times*, 6 June 2017, 4.

65   US Department of the Treasury, Remarks of Under Secretary for
      Terrorism and Financial Intelligence David Cohen before the Center
      for a New American Security on 'Confronting New Threats in
      Terrorist Financing', 4 March 2014, https://www.treasury.gov/press-
      center/press-releases/Pages/jl2308.aspx

66   http://www.twitlonger.com/show/m276g2

67   Alaa Shehabi, 'Why Is Bahrain Outsourcing Extremism?' *Foreign
      Policy*, 29 October 2014, http://foreignpolicy.com/2014/10/29/why-is-
      bahrain-outsourcing-extremism/

68   Diplomatic cable 10ABUDHABI33_a, UAE FM DISCUSSES
      TALIBAN FINANCIAL FLOWS AND REINTEGRATION WITH
      AMB. HOLBROOKE AND TREASURY A/S COHEN, 25 January
      2010, https://wikileaks.org/plusd/cables/10ABUDHABI33_a.html

69   Reuters, 'Former Afghan spy chief says letters show Pakistan supports
      militants', 15 July 2016, http://www.reuters.com/article/us-afghanistan-
      taliban-pakistan-idUSKCN0ZU2L8

70   OS Afghanistan/Iran/Security, 'Taliban being taught at secret camps in
      Iran', 21 March 2010, https://wikileaks.org/gifiles/docs/32/323433_-os-
      afghanistan-iran-security-taliban-fighters-being-taught.html

71   Middle East Online, 'Did the Taliban leader visit Iran before his
      death?', 22 May 2016, http://www.middle-east-online.com/?id=225362

72   France24 Arabic, 'Has Iran joined forces with the Taliban against
      Islamic State?', 27 May 2016, http://www.france24.com/ar/20160527-
      قارعة-في-الصحف-معركم-الرقة-زيارة-هشوري-هميا-احتجاجات-قانون-نونع-لم

73   Financial Action Task Force, 'Financing of the Terrorist Organisation
      Islamic State in Iraq and the Levant (ISIL)', February 2015, http://
      www.fatf-gafi.org/media/fatf/documents/reports/Financing-of-the-
      terrorist-organisation-ISIL.pdf

74   Janine Di Giovanni, Leah McGrath Goodman and Damien Sharkov,
      'How Does ISIS Fund Its Reign of Terror?', *Newsweek*, 6 November
      2014, http://europe.newsweek.com/how-does-isis-fund-its-reign-
      terror-282607?rm=eu

75   Erika Solomon and Ahmed Mhidi, 'Isis Inc: Syria's "mafia-style" gas
      deals with jihadis', *Financial Times*, 15 October 2015, https://www.
      ft.com/content/92f4e036-6b69-11e5-aca9-d87542bf8673

76   Al-Araby, 'Report: the Taliban finance their wars through lapis
      lazuli in Afghanistan', 7 June 2016, https://www.alaraby.co.uk/
      society/2016/6/7/قرري-الطالبان-تمول-حروبها-من-مناجم-اللازورد-بأفغانستان. Global
      Witness, 'Afghanistan's famous lapis mines funding the Taliban and
      armed groups, new investigation shows', 6 June 2016, https://www.

globalwitness.org/en/press-releases/afghanistans-famous-lapis-mines-funding-taliban-and-armed-groups-new-investigation-shows/

77   *Middle East Press*, 'Talc – a source of funding for the Taliban and IS derived from European products', 6 October 2016, http://middleeastpress.com/arabic/التكفاغناستان-تمصدر-تمويل-طالبان/ and US Department of State in Peshawar, 'Indigenous funding for militants in Swat', Cable 09PESHAWAR105_a, 22 May 2009, https://wikileaks.org/plusd/cables/09PESHAWAR105_a.html

78   Journalists for Justice, 'Black and White: Kenya's Criminal Racket in Somalia', November 2015, https://www.jfjustice.net/downloads/1457660562.pdf

79   UN Security Council, Somalia Monitoring Group Annual Report 2015.

80   Rukmini Callimachi, 'Paying Ransoms, Europe Bankrolls Qaeda Terror', *New York Times*, 29 July 2014, http://www.nytimes.com/2014/07/30/world/africa/ransoming-citizens-europe-becomes-al-qaedas-patron.html

81   *New York Times*, 'Al-Qaeda Letter on the Importance of Kidnapping Revenue', 29 July 2014, https://www.nytimes.com/interactive/2014/07/30/world/africa/31kidnap-docviewer2.html

82   New York Times, 'Letter from Leaders of Al-Qaeda in the Islamic Maghreb to a Sahara-Based Militant Commander', 29 July 2014, https://www.nytimes.com/interactive/2014/07/29/world/africa/31kidnap-docviewer1.html

83   Consortium Against Terror Finance, 'Funding Al Nusra Through Ransom: Qatar and the Myth of 'Humanitarian Principle', 10 December 2015, stopterrorfinance.org/stories/510652383-funding-al-nusra-through-ransom-qatar-and-the-myth-of-humanitarian-principle

84   Sami Yousafzai and Ron Moreau, 'How the Taliban's French hostages were freed', *Daily Beast*, 1 July 2011, http://www.thedailybeast.com/articles/2011/07/01/taliban-s-french-hostages-how-they-were-freed.html

85   US State Department, 'Remarks of Undersecretary Cohen at CSIS', 2 June 2014, https://www.treasury.gov/press-center/press-releases/Pages/jl2415.aspx

86   James Cockayne and Summer Walker, 'Fighting Human Trafficking in Conflict', United Nations University, Workshop Report September 2016, https://collections.unu.edu/eserv/UNU:5780/UNUReport_Pages.pdf

87   Tom Keatinge and Royal United Services Institute for Defence and Security Studies, *The Role of Finance in Defeating Al-Shabaab*. RUSI, 2014.

88   Valter Vilkko, 'Al-Shabaab: From External Support to Internal Extraction – A Minor Field Study on the Financial Support from the Somali Diaspora to al-Shabaab', Uppsala Universitet, 2011.

89   LTC Geoffrey Kambere, 'Financing al-Shabaab: the vital port of Kismayo', Global Ecco, August 2012, https://globalecco.org/en_GB/financing-al-shabaab-the-vital-port-of-kismayo

90   Financial Action Task Force, 'Emerging Terrorist Financing Risks', October 2015, http://www.fatf-gafi.org/media/fatf/documents/reports/Emerging-Terrorist-Financing-Risks.pdf

91   US State Department, Countries/Jurisdictions of Primary Concern – Somalia, Bureau of International Narcotics and Law Enforcement Affairs, 2016 International Narcotics Control Strategy Report (INCSR), http://www.state.gov/j/inl/rls/nrcrpt/2016/vol2/253429.htm

92   Ellen Omland, 'Misstenker skatteunndragelse stoppet postpakke med 11 millioner kroner', NRK, 30 August 2016, https://www.nrk.no/norge/mistenker-skatteunndragelse_-stoppet-postpakke-med-11-millioner-kroner-1.13102585

93   Magnus Ranstorp, 'Microfinancing the Caliphate: How the Islamic State is Unlocking the Assets of European Recruits', Combating Terrorism Center at West Point, CTC Sentinel, Vol. 9 Issue 5, May 2016, https://www.ctc.usma.edu/posts/microfinancing-the-caliphate-how-the-islamic-state-is-unlocking-the-assets-of-european-recruits

94   Morten Bøås, 'Fears, rumours and violence: Boko Haram's asymmetrical warfare', openDemocracy, 22 January 2015, https://www.opendemocracy.net/open-security/morten-b%C3%B8%C3%A5s/fear-rumours-and-violence-boko-haram%E2%80%99s-asymmetrical-warfare

95   UN Security Council, Somalia Monitoring Group Annual Report 2015.

96   Financial Action Task Force, 'Terrorist Financing in West Africa', October 2013, http://www.fatf-gafi.org/media/fatf/documents/reports/tf-in-west-africa.pdf

97   Stephen Kalin, 'Islamic State turns to selling fish, cars to offset oil losses: report', Reuters, 28 April 2016, http://uk.reuters.com/article/us-mideast-crisis-islamicstate-finances-idUKKCN0XP2CV

98   Samuel Andrew Hardy, 'Khums: an un-Islamic tax for an Islamic antiquities market?' Conflict Antiquities (blog), 17 August 2014, https://conflictantiquities.wordpress.com/2014/08/17/syria-iraq-islamic-antiquities-trafficking-tax/

99   Magnus Ranstorp, 'Microfinancing the Caliphate'.

100   Ibid.

101   Local Germany, 'Cologne gang "stole from churches to fund Isis"', 20

October 2015, https://www.thelocal.de/20151020/cologne-gang-stole-from-churches-to-fund-isis

102   Magnus Ranstorp, 'Microfinancing the Caliphate'.

103   Judith Van Der Merwe, 'The Crime-Terror Continuum: the Case of Africa, Part Two', *Aberfoyle International Security*, 2 January 2014, http://www.aberfoylesecurity.com/?p=778

104   Kathleen Caulderwood, 'Drugs And Money in the Sahara: How the Global Cocaine Trade Is Funding North African Jihad', *International Business Times*, 6 May 2015, http://www.ibtimes.com/drugs-money-sahara-how-global-cocaine-trade-funding-north-african-jihad-1953419

105   Kriti Shah, 'Poppy Production: The Taliban's Cash Cow', *Diplomat*, 24 March 2016, http://thediplomat.com/2016/03/poppy-production-the-talibans-cash-cow/.

106   Joseph V. Micallef, 'How the Taliban gets its cash', *Huffington Post*, 14 November 2015, http://www.huffingtonpost.com/joseph-v-micallef/how-the-taliban-gets-its_b_8551536.html

107   BBC News, 'Afghanistan opium production up 43 per cent – UN drugs watchdog', 23 October 2016, http://www.bbc.co.uk/news/world-asia-37743433

108   Shah, 'Poppy Production: The Taliban's Cash Cow'.

109   Micallef, 'How the Taliban gets its cash'.

110   Al Jazeera, 'Scores Killed in Yemen Arms Factory Blasts', 28 March 2011, http://www.aljazeera.com/news/middleeast/2011/03/201132810029276777.html

111   http://www.youm7.com/story/2016/4/12/اب-لصور-حركم-لكلا-شبابلا-تس-نوحت-علىـ
طانان-م-نأس-لحمـ-وذخاء-رئ-يجلاـ-يش/2671732

112   Amnesty International, 'Iraq: Taking Stock: The Arming of Islamic State', Index number: MDE 14/2812/2015, 7 December 2015, https://www.amnesty.org/en/documents/mde14/2812/2015/en/

113   Jeremy Binnie and Joanna Wright, 'Infernal Machines', *Small Arms Survey* (2013): 233, http://www.smallarmssurvey.org/fileadmin/docs/A-Yearbook/2013/en/Small-Arms-Survey-2013-Chapter-10-EN.pdf and James Glanz and William J. Broad, 'Looting at Weapons Plants was Systematic, Iraqi Says', *New York Times,* 13 March 2005, http://www.nytimes.com/2005/03/13/world/middleeast/looting-at-weapons-plants-was-systematic-iraqi-says.html?register=google (25 July 2016).

114   Bonnie Docherty, 'Explosive Situation: Qaddafi's Abandoned Weapons and the Threat to Libya's Civilians', *International Human Rights Clinic* (2012): 10, http://hrp.law.harvard.edu/wp-content/uploads/2012/08/libyareport.pdf

115 UNMAS, 'Libya', Updated March 2018, http://mineaction.org/ programmes/libya

116 United Nations Security Council, 'Letter from the panel of experts on Libya established pursuant to resolution 1973 (2011) addressed to the President of the Security Council', S/2016/209, 9 March 2016, http:// www.securitycouncilreport.org/atf/cf/%7B65BFCF9B-6D27-4E9C-8CD3-CF6E4FF96FF9%7D/s_2016_209.pdf

117 Rafael Epstein, 'Taliban Receives Stolen Supplies', *Sydney Morning Herald*, 2 August 2010, http://www.smh.com.au/national/taliban-receive-stolen-supplies-20100801-111gw.html

118 C.J. Chivers, 'Arms Sent By U.S. May Be Falling Into Taliban Hands', *New York Times*, 19 May 2009, http://www.nytimes.com/2009/05/20/ world/asia/20ammo.html?_r=1&scp=1&sq=ammunition%20 chivers%202009&st=cse

119 Special Inspector General for Afghanistan Reconstruction (SIGAR), 'Afghan National Security Forces: Actions Needed to Improve Weapons Accountability', SIGAR 14–84 Audit Report (2014):12, https://www.sigar.mil/pdf/audits/SIGAR-14-84-AR.pdf

120 Mujib Mashal, 'Taliban, Using Humvees Stolen From Army, Attack Check Post', *New York Times*, 13 February 2016, http://www.nytimes. com/2016/02/14/world/asia/taliban-humvee-attack-afghanistan. html?ref=world&_r=0

121 Richard F. Grimmett, 'Conventional Arms Transfers to Developing Nations, 2003–2010', US Congressional Research Service, 22 September 2011, https://fas.org/sgp/crs/weapons/R42017.pdf

122 Grimmett, 'Conventional Arms Transfers to Developing Nations, 2003–2010', 19.

123 http://www.qoraish.com/qoraish/2014/12/قنبلة-عادها-الشفرقة-من-انتاج/ مخبترات-جماه/

124 Reuters, 'Boko Haram Steals Dynamite in Raid on Lafarge Nigeria Plant: Sources', 6 November 2014, http://www.reuters.com/article/ us-nigeria-violence-idUSKBN0IQ10F20141106

125 Thomas H. Johnson, 'Taliban adaptations and innovations', *Small Wars and Insurgencies*, Vol. 24 Issue 1 (February 2013).

126 Dawood Azami, interview, 25 July 2016.

127 http://www.alarab.co.uk/?id=80304

128 http://www.middle-east-online.com/?id=228651

129 Jacob Zenn, AOAV interview, 6 October 2016.

130 http://alkhaleejonline.net/articles/1466074198892826800/حركة-الشباب-الصومالية-وخطرها-علي-الامن-الخليجي/

131 http://www.aljazeera.net/news/reportsandinterviews/2015/4/26/والع-الشباب-الصومالية-بين-القاعدة-وتنظيم-الدولة

132   Analysts at International Crisis Group in Nairobi, interview, 21 July 2016.

133   Roel Pareño, 'Slain Moroccan terrorist training Abu Sayyaf in suicide bombing – military', *Philippine Star*, 15 April 2016, www.philstar.com/headlines/2016/04/15/1573214/slain-moroccan-terrorist-training-abu-sayyaf-suicide-bombing-military

134   Greg Cahiles, 'AFP: Plans of suicide bombings inside and outside of Marawi City', CNN Philippines, 24 July 2017, http://cnnphilippines.com/news/2017/07/23/afp-plan-suicide-bombing-marawi-city.html

135   Manuel Mogato, 'Suicide bomb attack kills 11 in south Philippines', *Independent,* 31 July 2018, https://www.independent.co.uk/news/world/asia/philippines-suicide-bomb-attack-dead-isis-rodrigo-duterte-a8471586.html

9. The State of Terror

1   The spreadsheet can be accessed here: https://aoav.org.uk/wp-content/uploads/2016/11/2016_10_03-AOAV-IS-docs-suicide-bombers-database.xlsx

2   146 were identified from registration forms and the remaining three were identified from exit forms.

3   http://www.alhadathnews.net/archives/113554 [Arabic]

4   Of those, the majority (70 per cent) experienced jihad in Syria or Libya, with most of them (67 per cent) gaining their expertise with Syrian Al-Qaeda affiliate Jabhat al-Nusra.

5   Since this report, almost all have been taken down. For transcriptions of the testimonies below please go to: https://aoav.org.uk/2017/understanding-rising-cult-suicide-bomber-introduction

6   Kareem Raheem and Ziad al-Sinjary, 'Al-Qaeda militants flee Iraq jail in violent mass break-out', Reuters, 23 July 2013, http://www.reuters.com/article/us-iraq-violence-idUSBRE96L0RM20130723; and Tim Arango and Eric Schmitt, 'Escaped Inmates From Iraq Fuel Syrian Insurgency', *New York Times*, 12 February 2014, http://www.nytimes.com/2014/02/13/world/middleeast/escaped-inmates-from-iraq-fuel-syria-insurgency.html?_r=2

7   *Bureau of Investigative Journalism*, 'Allegations of Prisoner Abuse by US Troops after Abu Ghraib', 23 May 2011, https://www.thebureauinvestigates.com/stories/2011-05-23/allegations-of-prisoner-abuse-by-us-troops-after-abu-ghraib

8   *Economist*, 'The new strife', 14 May 2016, https://www.economist.com/news/special-report/21698440-there-one-god-yet-different-forms-islam-are-fighting-their-own-version

9   *Belfast Telegraph*, 'Video: Islamic state media branch releases "The end of Sykes–Picot"', 1 July 2014, https://www.belfasttelegraph.co.uk/video-news/video-islamic-state-media-branch-releases-the-end-of-sykespicot-30397575.html

10   Charlie Winter, 'Documenting the Virtual "Caliphate"', *Quilliam Foundation* 33 (2015).

11   Abu Rumaysah al-Britani, 'A brief guide to the Islamic State 2015', 18 May 2015, https://archive.org/details/Khilafah2015

12   Charlie Winter, 'Apocalypse, later: a longitudinal study of the Islamic State brand', *Critical Studies in Media Communication* 35.1 (2018): 103–21.

13   Graeme Wood, *The Way of the Strangers: Encounters with the Islamic State* (New York: Random House, 2017), xxiii.

14   Iheb Guermazi, 'But what was so appealing about ISIS?', *openDemocracy*, 30 October 2017, https://www.opendemocracy.net/north-africa-west-asia/iheb-guermazi/but-what-was-so-appealing-about-isis-tunisian-story

15   Sabina Alkire, Christoph Jindra, Gisela Robles and Ana Vaz, 'Multidimensional Poverty Index 2016: Brief methodological note and results', OPHI Briefing 42, University of Oxford (2016).

16   Amir Abdallah, 'ISIS leader Abu Bakr al-Baghdadi grants $1,200, house and furnishings to members who wish to marry', *Iraqi News*, 31 August 2014, https://www.iraqinews.com/features/isis-abu-bakr-al-baghdadi-grants-1200-house-furnishings-members-wish-marry/

17   Richard Spencer, 'Isis waging 'kamikaze' war with a thousand suicide bombers', *The Times*, 1 March 2017, https://www.thetimes.co.uk/article/isis-waging-kamikaze-war-with-a-thousand-suicide-bombers-gtb9nzn9z

18   Renad Mansour, 'ISIS Is Switching Tactics in Iraq. Baghdad Needs to Get Its Act Together', *DefenseOne*, 10 August 2016, http://www.defenseone.com/ideas/2016/08/isis-switching-tactics-iraq-baghdad-needs-get-its-act-together/130637/

19   Abdulla Hawez, 'Iraq's Shia Militias Accused of War Crimes in Fight Against ISIS', *Daily Beast*, 6 August 2016, http://www.thedailybeast.com/articles/2016/06/08/iraq-s-shia-militias-accused-of-war-crimes-in-fight-against-isis.html

20   2014 was the only year where the monthly average of IED incidents was higher than the number of attacks carried out during Ramadan in Iraq.

21   Alawites are a sect deriving from Twelver Shia Islam that incorporates syncretistic elements. Although often considered a variation of Shia Islam, it could also be seen as its own religion. Syria's president Bashar al-Assad is an Alawite.

22 Al-Wasat, ‹البحريني تركيا يكلع البنيان نصرة لك «عاد»: «مدوأ الأيادي لبيعة‹ الغبادي›, 27 July 2014, http://www.alwasatnews.com/news/907176.html

23 Charlie Winter, 'War by Suicide: A Statistical Analysis of the Islamic State's Martyrdom Industry', International Centre for Counter-Terrorism – The Hague Research Paper February 2017, https://icct.nl/wp-content/uploads/2017/02/ICCT-Winter-War-by-Suicide-Feb2017.pdf

24 Jamie Grierson, 'Isis has industrialised martyrdom, says report into suicide attacks', *Guardian*, 28 February 2017, https://www.theguardian.com/world/2017/feb/28/isis-has-industrialised-martyrdom-says-report-suicide-attacks.

25 Sara Malm, 'Geriatric jihadi: Elderly suicide bomber drives armoured truck full of explosives towards Iraqi base before blowing himself up as gloating ISIS fighters watch', *Daily Mail*, 8 March 2016, http://www.dailymail.co.uk/news/article-3482349/Geriatric-jihadi-Elderly-suicide-bomber-drives-armoured-truck-explosives-Iraqi-base-blowing-gloating-ISIS-fighters-watch.html

26 Clarion Project, 'ISIS Video: From Wheelchair to Suicide Bomber', 3 September 2017, https://clarionproject.org/video-disabled-rehab-isis-style/

27 Andrew Buncombe, 'Isis militants are "using mentally challenged children as suicide bombers and crucifying others", says UN body', *Independent*, 5 February 2015, http://www.independent.co.uk/news/world/middle-east/isis-militants-are-using-mentally-challenged-children-as-suicide-bombers-and-crucifying-others-says-10024847.html

28 Conor Gaffey, 'ISIS just started using female suicide bombers, but Boko Haram has been doing it for years – and shows no sign of stopping', *Newsweek*. 12 August 2017, http://www.newsweek.com/isis-boko-haram-nigeria-suicide-bomber-649790

29 Mitch Prothero and Mike Giglio, 'ISIS Suicide Bombers in Mosul are Terrifyingly Effective', *BuzzFeed*, 17 December 2016, https://www.buzzfeed.com/mitchprothero/suicidal-isis-car-bombers-are-unleashing-hell-in-mosul?utm_term=.mvmnNPWzZ#.fcplqa5j7

30 This minister was identified in 2016 as Khairy Abed Mahmoud al-Taey, better known by his *nom de guerre* Abu Kifah, of whom almost nothing is known. See Amman al-Youm, الأردني زيادي ئسي آسي‹لمجلس‹ شورى عاد‹, 24 September 2016 – http://bit.ly/2h83XzZ

31 Ibid.

32 Robert J Bunker, 'Daesh/IS Armored Vehicle Borne Improvised Explosive Devices (AVBIEDs): Insurgent Use and Terrorism Potential', *Trends Institution*, 2 February 2016, http://trendsinstitution.org/?p=1692

33 Interview with Charlie Winter, 22 July 2016.

34   Ibid.

35   http://www.dailysabah.com/arabic/world/2016/05/03/
      american-killed-in-combat-in-iraq-while-working-as-adviser-to-
      kurdish-peshmerga-1462284702

36   Conflict and Armament Research, 'Tracing the Supply of Components
      Used in Islamic State IEDs: Evidence from a 20-month investigation
      in Iraq and Syria', February 2016, http://www.conflictarm.com/
      wp-content/uploads/2016/02/Tracing_The_Supply_of_Components_
      Used_in_Islamic_State_IEDs.pdf

37   The Soufan Group, 'The Devastating Islamic State Suicide Strategy',
      29 May 2015, http://soufangroup.com/tsg-intelbrief-the-devastating-
      islamic-state-suicide-strategy/

38   Conflict and Armament Research, 'Tracing the Supply of Components
      Used in Islamic State IEDs'.

39   Metin Boyutu, 'ISID atölye kurmus, canlı bomba yelegi üretmis', CNN
      Turk, 5 May 2015.

40   BBC News, 'Iraq suicide attacks: Ambulances used in Tikrit and
      Samarra', 6 November 2016, http://www.bbc.co.uk/news/world-
      middle-east-37888028

41   Ángel Gómez et al., 'The devoted actor's will to fight and the spiritual
      dimension of human conflict', *Nature Human Behaviour* 1 (2017):
      673–79, https://www.nature.com/articles/doi:10.1038/s41562-017-
      0193-3

42   Jane Idelman Smith and Yvonne Yazbeck Haddad, *The Islamic
      Understanding of Death and Resurrection* (New York: Oxford
      University Press, 2002), 66.

43   Springfield Springfield, 'The State (2017) s01e01 Episode Script:
      Episode 1', Accessed 4 June 2018, https://www.springfieldspringfield.
      co.uk/view_episode_scripts.php?tv-show=the-state-
      2017&episode=s01e01

44   *Dabiq Magazine*, 'A call to Hijrah', September 2014.

45   Quran 4:157; 17:49–52; 18:94; 33:63; 44:10; 84:1.

46   Matthew Henry Musselwhite, 'ISIS & Eschatology: Apocalyptic
      Motivations behind the Formation and Development of the Islamic
      State', (MA Thesis, Western Kentucky University, 2016), 7, 28–30, 53,
      82, 124.

47   Hadith No. 6924, Kitab al-Fitan, Sahih Muslim, http://
      www.sahihmuslim.com/sps/smm/sahihmuslim.
      cfm?scn=dspchaptersfull&BookID=41&ChapterID=1204

48   Musselwhite, 'ISIS & Eschatology'.

49   Marc Sageman, *Leaderless Jihad: Terror Networks in the Twenty-First
      Century* (Philadelphia: University of Pennsylvania Press, 2008), 75–88.

50   Pew Research Center, 'The World's Muslims: Unity and Diversity:
      Chapter 3: Articles of Faith', 9 August 2012, http://www.pewforum.
      org/2012/08/09/the-worlds-muslims-unity-and-diversity-3-articles-of-
      faith/

51   Chloe Farand, 'Isis fighters "attacked Israel Defence Forces unit,
      then apologised" claims former commander', *Independent*, 25 April
      2017, http://www.independent.co.uk/news/world/middle-east/
      isis-israel-defence-force-apology-attack-unit-golan-heights-defense-
      minister-moshe-ya-alon-a7700616.html

52   Michael Weiss and Hassan Hassan, *ISIS: Inside the Army of Terror*
      (New York: Regan Arts, 2015), 97–109.

53   Craig Whitlock and Ellen Nakashima, 'Islamic State's seemingly irrational
      strategy may have roots in an apocalyptic vision', *Washington Post*, 16
      November 2015, https://www.pressherald.com/2015/11/16/seemingly-
      irrational-isis-strategy-may-have-roots-in-an-apocalyptic-vision/

54   Samuel Osborne, 'Syrian rebels attack Dabiq – the town Isis believes
      will be site of an apocalyptic "final battle"', *Independent*, 15 October
      2016, http://www.independent.co.uk/news/world/middle-east/
      isis-syria-dabiq-islamic-state-daesh-apocalypse-propaganda-army-
      forces-attack-battle-a7362921.html

55   BBC Monitoring, 'Dabiq: Why is Syrian town so important for
      IS?' 4 October 2016, http://www.bbc.co.uk/news/world-middle-
      east-30083303

56   John Orbell and Tomonori Morikawa, 'An evolutionary account of
      suicide attacks: The kamikaze case', *Political Psychology* 32.2 (2011):
      297–322.

57   Jethro Mullen, Ashley Fantz and Dana Ford, 'Jordanian pilot's
      father: "Annihilate" ISIS', CNN, 5 February 2015, https://edition.cnn.
      com/2015/02/04/world/isis-jordan-reaction/index.html

58   Jim Hoft, 'ISIS Distributes Fatwa to Justify "Burning Sentence"
      of Jordanian Pilot Moaz al-Kasasbeh', *Gateway Pundit*, 4
      February 2015, http://www.thegatewaypundit.com/2015/02/
      isis-distributes-koranic-verse-of-prophet-mohammad-burning-
      apostates-to-justify-todays-pilot-torching/

59   Associated Press Baghdad, 'Muslim clerics denounce "savage" Isis
      murder of Jordanian pilot', 6 February 2015, https://www.theguardian.
      com/world/2015/feb/06/muslim-clerics-denounce-jordanian-pilot-
      execution-kasasbeh

60   Amnesty International, '"Public execution" in football stadium shows
      Libya's descent into lawlessness', 22 August 2014, https://www.amnesty.
      org/en/latest/news/2014/08/public-execution-football-stadium-shows-
      libya-s-descent-lawlessness/

61   Tom Williams, 'From mass spectatorship to mass murder: a
      history of stadiums', *Spectator*, 25 June 2016, https://www.spectator.
      co.uk/2016/06/from-mass-spectatorship-to-mass-murder-a-history-of-
      stadiums/

62   National Council of Resistance of Iran, 'Iran: Public execution at
      sports stadium', 22 September 2016, http://www.ncr-iran.org/en/news/
      human-rights/21162-iran-public-execution-at-sports-stadium

63   Capital Punishment UK, 'World', accessed 4 June 2018, http://www.
      capitalpunishmentuk.org/world.html

64   Louis Doré, 'The countries where apostasy is punishable by death',
      Indy100, accessed 4 June 2018, https://www.indy100.com/article/the-
      countries-where-apostasy-is-punishable-by-death--Z110j2Uwxb

65   Judith Tinnes, 'Counting Lives Lost – Monitoring Camera-Recorded
      Extrajudicial Executions by the "Islamic State"', accessed 20 August 2018,
      http://www.terrorismanalysts.com/pt/index.php/pot/article/view/483

66   Ben Kiernan, *Blood and Soil: A World History of Genocide and
      Extermination from Sparta to Darfur* (New Haven: Yale University
      Press, 2007), 604.

67   United States Department of State, Bureau of Democracy, Human
      Rights, and Labor, 'Syria 2016 International Religious Freedom
      Report', accessed 4 June 2018, https://www.state.gov/documents/
      organization/269158.pdf

68   Abu Bakr Naji, *The Management of Savagery: The Most Critical Stage
      Through Which the Umma Will Pass*, trans. William McCants (John M.
      Olin Institute for Strategic Studies, Harvard University, 2006).

69   Sharon Begley, 'Alternative Peer Groups May Offer Way to Deter Some
      Suicide Bombers', *Wall Street Journal*, 8 October 2004, https://www.
      wsj.com/articles/SB109717844208239500

70   Ibid.

71   Mohammed M. Hafez, 'Rationality, Culture, and Structure in the
      Making of Suicide Bombers: A Preliminary Theoretical Synthesis and
      Illustrative Case Study', *Studies in Conflict and Terrorism* 29, no 2.
      (2006), 177.

72   Stratfor, 'The Islamic State Continues Long Tradition of Using Foreign
      Fighters', 17 September 2014, https://worldview.stratfor.com/article/
      islamic-state-continues-long-tradition-using-foreign-fighters

73   Vanessa Barford, 'Is modern life making us lonely?' *BBC
      News Magazine*, 8 April 2013, http://www.bbc.co.uk/news/
      magazine-22012957

74   Scott Atran, 'The romance of terror', *Guardian*, 19 July 2010, https://
      www.theguardian.com/commentisfree/belief/2010/jul/19/terrorism-
      radical-religion

75   Mercy Corps, 'Examining the Links between Youth Economic
      Opportunity, Civic Engagement, and Conflict: Evidence from Mercy
      Corps', Somali Youth Leaders Initiative', January 2013, 3–4, https://
      www.mercycorps.org.uk/sites/default/files/somaliabrief_2_13_13.pdf
76   Emman Ed-Badawy, Milo Comerford and Peter Welby, 'Inside the
      Jihadi Mind: Understanding Ideology and Propaganda', Centre
      on Religion & Geopolitics, Tony Blair Institute for Global Change
      (October 2015), 31.
77   PBS, 'The Secret History of ISIS', 17 May 2016, http://www.pbs.org/
      wgbh/frontline/film/the-secret-history-of-isis/
78   Judit Neurink, 'Isis leader Abu Bakr al-Baghdadi repeatedly raped US
      hostage Kayla Mueller and turned Yazidi girls into personal sex slaves',
      Independent, 14 August 2015, http://www.independent.co.uk/news/
      world/middle-east/isis-leader-abu-bakr-al-baghdadi-exposed-as-serial-
      rapist-of-hostages-who-made-women-his-personal-10456237.html
79   Martin Chulov, '"We will get him"': the long hunt for Isis leader
      Abu Bakr al-Baghdadi', Guardian, 15 January 2018, https://www.
      theguardian.com/world/2018/jan/15/long-hunt-for-isis-leader-abu-
      bakr-al-baghdadi
80   Interview with Charlie Winter.
81   http://www.alhayat.com/Articles/5095504/السعودي-نويفن-ندروا-60-%D9-%AA-
      من-لعملي-تايح-نارتنال-رايح-عمي-ل-دعاش-في-لعراق
82   The Soufan Group, 'Foreign Fighters: An Updated Assessment
      of the Flow of Foreign Fighters into Syria and Iraq', December
      2015, http://soufangroup.com/wp-content/uploads/2015/12/TSG_
      ForeignFightersUpdate3.pdf
83   Winter, 'Documenting the Virtual Caliphate'.
84   Winter, 'Apocalypse, later: a longitudinal study of the Islamic State
      brand'.
85   Jessica Stern and J.M. Berger, ISIS: The State of Terror (London:
      William Collins, 2015), 171.
86   Ed-Badawy, Comerford and Welby, 'Inside the Jihadi Mind'.
87   Winter, 'Apocalypse, later: a longitudinal study of the Islamic State
      brand'.

10. On Europe's Shores

1   BBC News, 'Raqqa: IS "capital" falls to US-backed Syrian forces',
     17 October 2017, http://www.bbc.co.uk/news/world-middle-
     east-41646802
2   https://www.youtube.com/watch?v=qJDu7cKFA6M

3   Stephen L. Carter, 'Destroying a Quote's History in Order to Save
    It', *Bloomberg*, 9 February 2018, https://www.bloomberg.com/view/
    articles/2018-02-09/destroying-a-quote-s-history-in-order-to-save-it

4   Jim Muir, '"Islamic State": Raqqa's loss seals rapid rise and fall', BBC
    News, 17 October 2017, http://www.bbc.co.uk/news/world-middle-
    east-35695648

5   Gordon Corera, 'MI5 boss Andrew Parker warns of "intense"
    terror threat', BBC News, 17 October 2017, www.bbc.co.uk/news/
    uk-41655488

6   BBC News, 'MI5 chief: Russia trying to undermine European
    democracies', 14 May 2018, http://www.bbc.co.uk/news/uk-44104260

7   https://www.youtube.com/watch?v=gK2AP3LZwH4q

8   Lorenzo Tondo, Patrick Wintour and Piero Messina, 'Interpol
    circulates list of 173 suspected members of Isis suicide brigade',
    Guardian, 21 July 2017, https://www.theguardian.com/world/2017/
    jul/21/isis-islamic-state-suicide-brigade-interpol-list?CMP=Share_
    iOSApp_Other

9   NATO, 'Remarks by NATO Secretary General Jens Stoltenberg at the
    38th Meeting for Friendship amongst Peoples in Rimini, Italy', 24
    August 2017, https://www.nato.int/cps/ic/natohq/opinions_146470.
    htm?selectedLocale=en

10 Martin Chulov, 'Losing ground, fighters and morale – is it all over
    for Isis?' *Guardian*, 7 September 2016, https://www.theguardian.com/
    world/2016/sep/07/losing-ground-fighter-morale-is-it-all-over-for-isis-
    syria-turkey

11 Abu Rumaysah al-Britani, 'A brief guide to the Islamic State 2015', 18
    May 2015, https://archive.org/details/Khilafah2015

12 Instances of suicide attacks in Turkey, Russia and other states that
    fall within Europe are addressed elsewhere in this book. The only
    European bomber who was not a Muslim was a nineteen-year-old
    Finnish man who blew himself up in 2002, killing seven and
    wounding 166. This man – Petri Gerdt – detonated his rucksack in
    the Myyrmanni shopping mall in Helsinki near a group of children
    watching a clown show; his motivation remains unknown, his father
    arguing he was intending to carry the bomb into the forest to blow it
    up for fun, though this would not explain why he had packed his bag
    with shrapnel.

13 Action on Armed Violence, 'Understanding the rising cult of the
    suicide bomber: Appendix 2 – Suicide bombers from Europe
    (Brussels attacks)', 1 January 2017, https://aoav.org.uk/2017/
    understanding-rising-cult-suicide-bomber-appendix-2-suicide-
    bombers-europe-brussels/

14　Ahmed Meguini, 'Menaces sur Nadia Remadna, Sevran est devenu un Khalifa à 40 minutes de Paris', *Laicart* (blog), 15 March 2016, http://laicart.org/sevran-devenu-khalifa-a-40-minutes-de-paris/

15　Counter-Extremism Project, 'Germany: Extremism & Counter-Extremism', accessed 5 June 2018, https://www.counterextremism.com/countries/germany

16　Natasha Christian, '"Patterns of radicalisation": Uzbekistan's history with terrorism and the US', *SBS News*, 3 November 2017, https://www.sbs.com.au/news/patterns-of-radicalisation-uzbekistan-s-history-with-terrorism-and-the-us

17　John Shammas, 'Terror Plot Foiled: Cops "foil terror plot on British leisure centre" as dad and son arrested in raids', *Sun*, 4 April 2018, https://www.thesun.co.uk/news/5967999/dewsbury-terrorist-arrest-leisure-centre/

18　Mark Duell, 'Father and son, aged 52 and 21, are arrested in West Yorkshire over a plot to carry out a terror attack on a "leisure complex"', *Daily Mail*, 3 April 2018, http://www.dailymail.co.uk/news/article-5573081/Two-men-arrested-suspicion-terror-plot.html

19　Martin Shaw, 'Two Dewsbury men arrested by anti-terror police are released without charge', *Huddersfield Daily Examiner*, 7 April 2018, https://www.examiner.co.uk/news/two-dewsbury-men-arrested-anti-14504491

20　Rod Liddle, 'Suicide bombing seems to have become a new Yorkshire tradition', *Spectator*, 20 June 2015, https://www.spectator.co.uk/2015/06/how-on-earth-was-it-that-a-suicide-bomber-issued-from-savile-town-in-dewsbury/

21　Sue Reid, 'The breeding ground for jihadis where even the ice cream lady wears a burka: How Dewsbury, the once great textile town of the North, has undergone a terrifying transformation', *Daily Mail*, 15 June 2015, http://www.dailymail.co.uk/news/article-3125530/The-breeding-ground-jihadis-ice-cream-lady-wears-burka-great-textile-town-Dewsbury-undergone-terrible-transformation.html

22　Liddle, 'Suicide bombing seems to have become a new Yorkshire tradition'.

23　According to the latest (2011) census.

24　Huma Haider, 'Radicalisation of diaspora communities', Governance and Social Development Resource Centre Helpdesk Research Report, 16 January 2015, http://www.gsdrc.org/docs/open/hdq1187.pdf

25　BBC News, '"Suicide videos": What they said', 4 April 2008, http://news.bbc.co.uk/1/hi/uk/7330367.stm

26　Doron Zimmermann and William Rosenau (eds.), 'The Radicalization of Diasporas and Terrorism', *Zürcher Beiträge zur Sicherheitspolitik* Nr.

80, Center for Security Studies ETH Zurich (2009), http://www.css.
ethz.ch/publications/pdfs/ZB-80.pdf

27   Ibid.

28   Pew Research Center, 'Europe's Growing Muslim Population', 29
      November 2017, http://www.pewforum.org/2017/11/29/europes-
      growing-muslim-population/

29   ICM (for Channel 4), ICM Muslims survey for Channel 4. Available
      at: https://www.icmunlimited.com/wp-content/uploads/2016/04/
      Mulims-full-suite-data-plus-topline.pdf

30   Miqdaad Versi, 'What do Muslims really think? This skewed poll
      certainly won't tell us', *Guardian*, 12 April 2016, https://www.
      theguardian.com/commentisfree/2016/apr/12/what-do-muslims-
      think-skewed-poll-wont-tell-us

31   Sundas Ali, 'Second and Third Generation Muslims in Britain: A
      Socially Excluded Group? Identities, Integration and Community
      Cohesion', University of Oxford Working Paper (2008).

32   Tahir Abbas and Assma Siddique, 'Perceptions of the processes
      of radicalisation and de-radicalisation among British South Asian
      Muslims in a post-industrial city', *Social Identities* 18:1 (2011): 119–34,
      DOI: 10.1080/13504630.2011.629519.

33   Dina Al Raffie, 'Social Identity Theory for Investigating Islamic
      Extremism in the Diaspora', *Journal of Strategic Security* 6:4 (2013):
      67–91. DOI: http://dx.doi.org/10.5038/1944-0472.6.4.4. Available at:
      http://scholarcommons.usf.edu/jss/vol6/iss4/4

34   Abbas and Siddique, 'Perceptions of the processes of radicalisation
      and de-radicalisation among British South Asian Muslims in a post-
      industrial city'

35   Owais Arshad, Varun Setlur and Usaid Siddiqui, 'Are Muslims
      Collectively Responsible? A Sentiment Analysis of the New York
      Times', 416LABS, 2015, http://416labs.com/nytandislam

36   Kim Ghattas, 'The United States of Islamophobia', *Foreign Policy*, 5
      July 2016, http://foreignpolicy.com/2016/07/05/the-united-states-of-
      islamophobia/

37   Abbas and Siddique, 'Perceptions of the processes of radicalisation
      and de-radicalisation among British South Asian Muslims in a post-
      industrial city'.

38   House of Commons, 'Report of the Official Account of the Bombings
      in London on 7th July 2005', HC1087, 11 May 2006, https://www.
      gov.uk/government/uploads/system/uploads/attachment_data/
      file/228837/1087.pdf

39   James Rothwell and Josie Ensor, 'Isil releases beheading video
      featuring Paris attackers', *Daily Telegraph*, 24 January 2016, http://

    www.telegraph.co.uk/news/worldnews/islamic-state/12119003/Isil-releases-new-beheading-video-featuring-Paris-attackers.html

40 Louise Casey, 'The Casey Review: A review into opportunity and integration', 5 December 2016, https://assets.publishing.service.gov.uk/government/uploads/system/uploads/attachment_data/file/575973/The_Casey_Review_Report.pdf

41 Shanta Devarajan et al., 'Economic and Social Inclusion to Prevent Violent Extremism', *Middle East and North Africa Economic Monitor* (Washington, DC: World Bank, October 2016), DOI: 10.1596/978–1- 4648-0990-3. License: Creative Commons Attribution CC BY 3.0 IGO.

42 Mercy Corps, 'Examining the Links between Youth Economic Opportunity, Civic Engagement, and Conflict: Evidence from Mercy Corps' Somali Youth Leaders Initiative', January 2013, 3–4, https://www.mercycorps.org.uk/sites/default/files/somaliabrief_2_13_13.pdf

43 Migrant Integration Policy Index 2015, 'Key Findings: France 2014', http://www.mipex.eu/france

44 Mubaraz Ahmed, Milo Comerford and Emman El-Badawy, 'Milestones to Militancy: What the lives of 100 jihadis tell us about a global movement', Centre on Religion & Geopolitics, Tony Blair Institute for Social Change, April 2016, https://institute.global/sites/default/files/inline-files/IGC_Milestones-to-Militancy.pdf

45 Rahila Bano, 'Is it safe for children to study the Koran online?' BBC News, 26 June 2013, https://www.bbc.co.uk/news/uk-23060976

46 Richard Adams, 'Teaching union criticises Ofsted chief over hijab ban for young girls', *Guardian*, 30 March 2018, https://www.theguardian.com/education/2018/mar/30/teaching-union-criticises-ofsted-chief-amanda-spielman-over-hijab-ban-for-young-girls

47 Paradise Primary Newsletter No. 23, July 2016, https://www.paradiseschool.org.uk/images/NewsletterJuly2016Final.pdf

48 Caroline Mortimer, 'Muslim boarding school rated "good" by Ofsted threatens to expel pupils for mixing with "outsiders"', *Independent*, 25 July 2015, http://www.independent.co.uk/news/uk/home-news/muslim-boarding-school-rated-good-by-ofsted-threatens-to-expel-pupils-for-mixing-with-outsiders-10415952.html

49 When I asked Ofsted for details of how many of its inspectors spoke Urdu, the reply came back: 'We do not routinely collate information about languages spoken by inspectors.' https://www.whatdotheyknow.com/request/460482/response/1114960/attach/html/4/Overton%20FOI.pdf.html

50 BBC News, 'Reality Check: What is the Prevent strategy?' 4 June 2017, http://www.bbc.co.uk/news/election-2017-40151991

51 Robert Mendick, Victoria Ward and Ben Farmer, 'How Manchester bomber Salman Abedi took his twisted revenge out of "love for Islam" after being radicalised by Isil preacher', *Daily Telegraph*, 26 May 2017, https://www.telegraph.co.uk/news/2017/05/25/manchester-bomber-salman-abedi-took-twisted-revenge-love-islam/

52 BBC News, 'London bomber: Text in full', 1 September 2005, http://news.bbc.co.uk/1/hi/uk/4206800.stm

53 Associated Press, 'France plans mosque funding foundation to stop radicalisation from abroad', 1 August 2016, https://www.theguardian.com/world/2016/aug/01/france-plans-mosque-funding-foundation-to-stop-radicalisation-from-abroad

54 Yasmeen Serhan, 'France's Disappearing Mosques', *Atlantic*, 1 August 2016, http://www.theatlantic.com/news/archive/2016/08/french-mosques-islam/493919/

55 Christian Oliver, 'Belgian PM threatens to close "certain radical mosques"', *Financial Times*, 20 November 2015, https://www.ft.com/content/765af108-8c7b-11e5-a549-b89a1dfede9b

56 Rachel Bryson, 'For Caliph and Country: Exploring How British Jihadis Join a Global Movement', Tony Blair Institute for Global Change, 28 September 2017, https://institute.global/insight/co-existence/caliph-and-country-exploring-how-british-jihadis-join-global-movement

57 Casey, 'The Casey Review', 129.

58 Andrew Anthony, 'When did the police start collaring television?' *Guardian*, 12 August 2007, https://www.theguardian.com/commentisfree/2007/aug/12/comment.television

59 Lizzy Davies, 'Death threats for French Imam who preaches peace with Jewish neighbours', *Guardian*, 16 January 2009, https://www.theguardian.com/world/2009/jan/16/death-threats-Imam-france

60 Emily Pennink and James Cartledge, 'Hate preacher Imam Kamran Hussain jailed for telling kids martyrdom better than school', *Birmingham Mail*, 28 September 2017, https://www.birminghammail.co.uk/news/midlands-news/hate-preacher-Imam-kamran-hussain-13687505

61 Sky News, '"Teacher" guilty of recruiting "army of children" for London attacks', 2 March 2018, https://news.sky.com/story/teacher-guilty-of-recruiting-army-of-children-for-london-attacks-11273094

62 In the UK, six individuals seem to have had a remarkable impact on Salafist rhetoric: Abu Hamza al-Masri, Abdulla al-Faisal, Abu Qatada al-Filistini, Omar Bakri Mohammad, Anjem Choudary and Hani al-Sibai.

63 Pervez Hoodbhoy, 'What is the wildest conspiracy theory pertaining

to Pakistan?', *Herald* (Pakistan), 19 June 2015, https://herald.dawn.
com/news/1153068

64   BBC News, 'White House: CIA has ended use of vaccine programmes',
      20 May 2014, http://www.bbc.co.uk/news/world-us-canada-27489045

65   Chris Woods, 'US Claims of "No Civilian Deaths" Are Untrue',
      Bureau of Investigative Journalism, 18 July 2011, https://www.
      thebureauinvestigates.com/stories/2011-07-18/us-claims-of-no-
      civilian-deaths-are-untrue

66   Mehdi Hasan, 'Inside jobs and Israeli stooges: why is the Muslim
      world in thrall to conspiracy theories?', *New Statesman*, 5 September
      2014, https://www.newstatesman.com/politics/2014/09/inside-jobs-
      and-israeli-stooges-why-muslim-world-thrall-conspiracy-theories

67   Diaa Hadid, 'Mahmoud Abbas Claims Rabbis Urged Israel to Poison
      Palestinians' Water', *New York Times*, 23 June 2016, https://www.
      nytimes.com/2016/06/24/world/middleeast/mahmoud-abbas-claims-
      rabbis-urged-israel-to-poison-palestinians-water.html?mcubz=3

68   Yasser Okbi, 'Hezbollah: We Have Captured an Israeli Spy Eagle in
      Lebanon', *Jerusalem Post*, 16 October 2013, http://www.jpost.com/
      Middle-East/Hezbollah-We-have-captured-an-Israeli-spy-eagle-in-
      Lebanon-328880

69   Yasmine Fathi, 'Expert shoots down conspiracy theory blaming Israel
      for shark attacks', *Ahram Online*, 6 December 2010, http://english.
      ahram.org.eg/NewsContent/1/64/1343/Egypt/Politics-/Expert-shoots-
      down-conspiracy-theory-blaming-Israe.aspx

70   Nina Strochlic, 'Hamas Arrests "Israeli Spy" Dolphin', *Daily Beast*, 20
      August 2015, http://www.thedailybeast.com/hamas-arrests-israeli-spy-
      dolphin

71   Haaretz, 'Saudi Arabia "Nabbed Israeli-tagged Vulture for
      Being Mossad Spy"', 4 January 2011, http://www.haaretz.com/
      world-news/saudi-arabia-nabbed-israeli-tagged-vulture-for-being-
      mossad-spy-1.335171

72   Jonny Paul, 'Haiti Organ Harvesting Claims False', *Jerusalem Post*,
      14 February 2010, http://www.jpost.com/International/Haiti-organ-
      harvesting-claims-false, and Reuters, 'Israel blasts Palestinians after
      accusations of organ-harvesting', 4 November 2015, http://www.
      reuters.com/article/us-israel-palestinians-un/israel-blasts-palestinians-
      after-accusations-of-organ-harvesting-idUSKCN0ST32420151104

73   Richard Hofstadter, 'The Paranoid Style in American Politics', *Harper's
      Magazine*, November 1964, https://harpers.org/archive/1964/11/the-
      paranoid-style-in-american-politics/5/

74   Middle East Media Research Institute, 'Istanbul Friday Sermon
      by Syrian Cleric Mohammad Basem Dahman: The U.S. Created

ISIS to Distort the Image of Islam', 19 June 2017, https://memri.org/tv/istanbul-friday-sermon-syrian-cleric-u.s.-created%20isis-to-distort-islam, and Katie Forster, 'Egyptian state media claims Isis is "made up" and 9/11 was carried out by West to justify war on terror', *Independent*, 15 September 2016, http://www.independent.co.uk/news/world/middle-east/egyptian-911-inside-job-state-media-war-on-terror-isis-made-up-al-ahram-noha-al-sharnoubi-columnist-a7308926.html

75 Makia Freeman, 'ISIS Is a US-Israeli Creation. Top Ten "Indications"', GlobalResearch, 5 April 2016, http://www.globalresearch.ca/isis-is-a-us-israeli-creation-top-ten-indications/5518627, and Anas Chihab, 'Former CIA Agent: "The ISIS Leader Abu Bakr Al Baghdadi Was Trained by the Israeli Mossad"', *Moroccan Times*, 17 July 2014, http://themoroccantimes.com/2014/07/6414/nsa-documents-reveal-isis-leaderabu-bakr-al-baghdadi-trained-israeli-mossad

76 Raza Habib Raja, 'Why Are Conspiracy Theories So Rampant In The Muslim World?' *Huffington Post*, 7 July 2017, http://www.huffingtonpost.com/entry/why-are-conspiracy-theories-so-rampant-in-muslim-world_us_595fa09de4b08f5c97d068f0

77 *Dabiq Magazine*: online magazine used by the Islamic State in Iraq and Sham for propaganda and recruitment.

78 Alan Travis, 'The making of an extremist', *Guardian*, 20 August 2008, https://www.theguardian.com/uk/2008/aug/20/uksecurity.terrorism

79 Robin Simcox, 'We Will Conquer Your Rome: A Study of Islamic State Terror Plots in the West', Henry Jackson Society, 2015, http://henryjacksonsociety.org/wp-content/uploads/2015/09/ISIS-brochure-Web.pdf

80 Scott Kleinman and Scott Flower, 'From convert to extremist: new Muslims and terrorism', *Conversation*, 24 May 2013, http://theconversation.com/from-convert-to-extremist-new-muslims-and-terrorism-14643

81 Counter-Extremism Project, 'Germaine Lindsay', accessed 5 June 2018, https://www.counterextremism.com/people/germaine-lindsay

82 Gordon Rayner, 'British man who launched Isil suicide attack was Guantanamo Bay detainee awarded £1m compensation', *Daily Telegraph*, 22 February 2018, http://www.telegraph.co.uk/news/2017/02/21/british-man-launched-isil-suicide-attack-guantanamo-bay-detainee/

83 John Suler, 'The online disinhibition effect', *CyberPsychology & Behavior* 7.3 (2004): 321–6.

84 John Haltiwanger, 'White Men Have Committed More Mass Shootings than Any Other Group', *Newsweek*, 2 October 2017, http://www.

newsweek.com/white-men-have-committed-more-mass-shootings-any-other-group-675602

85   Olivier Roy, 'France's Oedipal Islamist Complex', *Foreign Policy*, 7 January 2016, http://foreignpolicy.com/2016/01/07/frances-oedipal-islamist-complex-charlie-hebdo-islamic-state-isis/

86   Emma-Kate Symons, 'ISIL is really a revolt by young Muslims against their parents' generation', *Quartz*, 3 December 2015, http://qz.com/562128/isil-is-a-revolt-by-young-disaffected-muslims-against-their-parents-generation/

87   Suzanne Schneider, 'The Death Drive Revisited: On Olivier Roy's "Jihad and Death"', *Los Angeles Review of Books*, 2 April 2018, https://lareviewofbooks.org/article/the-death-drive-revisited-on-olivier-roys-jihad-and-death/

88   Shiraz Maher, 'Parsons Green, and why more attacks on the West by Islamic State are inevitable', *New Statesman*, 22 September 2017, https://www.newstatesman.com/2017/09/parsons-green-and-why-more-attacks-west-islamic-state-are-inevitable

89   Isaac Chotiner, 'The Islamization of Radicalism', *Slate*, 22 June 2016, http://www.slate.com/articles/news_and_politics/interrogation/2016/06/olivier_roy_on_isis_brexit_orlando_and_the_islamization_of_radicalism.html

90   Marion van San, 'Lost Souls Searching for Answers? Belgian and Dutch Converts Joining the Islamic State', *Perspectives on Terrorism* 9.5 (2015): 47–56.

91   Max Fisher, 'Here is ISIS's statement claiming responsibility for the Paris attacks', *Vox*, 14 November 2015, https://www.vox.com/2015/11/14/9734794/isis-claim-paris-statement

92   Julia Ioffe, 'The Road to Radicalism in Charlottesville', *Atlantic*, 16 August 2017, https://www.theatlantic.com/international/archive/2017/08/charlottesville-radical-terrorism/536973/

11. Inner Demons

1   CNN, 'Trump calls terrorists "losers"', 22 August 2017, http://edition.cnn.com/videos/politics/2017/08/22/president-trump-afghanistan-war-plan-terrorists-predators-losers-sot-ac.cnn

2   Jon Sharman and Kim Sengupta, 'Salman Abedi: Police probe Libyan links of Manchester bomber who killed 22', *Independent*, 23 May 2017, http://www.independent.co.uk/news/uk/home-news/salman-abedi-lpolice-probe-ibya-links-isis-manchester-bombing-ariana-grande-concert-a7752361.html

3   Amanda Devlin and David Hughes, 'Killer Unmasked: Who was
    Salman Abedi? Manchester bombing attacker who left 22 dead at
    Ariana Grande concert', *Sun*, 22 May 2018, https://www.thesun.co.uk/
    news/3626664/salman-abedi-manchester-bombing-terror-attacker/

4   Dean Wilkins, Gordon Tait and Chloe Mayer, 'Party Animal:
    Manchester bomber Salman Abedi's friends reveal wild youth of
    booze and drug-taking – and how he was nicknamed DUMBO
    because of his big ears', *Sun*, 25 May 2017, https://www.thesun.co.uk/
    news/3644061/manchester-bomber-salman-abedi-friends-youth-
    terror-attack/

5   Steph Cockroft, 'Manchester bomber WAS known to police: GMP
    chief admits terrorist, 22, had a string of convictions for theft,
    receiving stolen goods, and assault from the age of just 16', *Daily
    Mail*, 30 May 2017, http://www.dailymail.co.uk/news/article-4555088/
    Manchester-bomber-known-police.html#ixzz54ciKNbLO

6   Esther Addley, Nazia Parveen, Jamie Grierson and Steven Morris,
    'Salman Abedi: from hot-headed party lover to suicide bomber',
    Guardian, 26 May 2017, https://www.theguardian.com/uk-news/2017/
    may/26/salman-abedi-manchester-arena-attack-partying-suicide-
    bomber

7   Lizzie Dearden, 'Manchester attack victim's mother urges public to
    forget "nobody" terrorist on first anniversary', *The Independent*, 20
    May 2018, https://www.independent.co.uk/news/uk/home-news/
    manchester-arena-attack-bomb-anniversary-martyn-hett-figen-
    murray-a8359481.html, and Robert Mendick, Martin Evans and
    Victoria Ward, 'Exclusive: Manchester suicide bomber used student
    loan and benefits to fund terror plot', *Telegraph*, 27 May 2017, http://
    www.telegraph.co.uk/news/2017/05/26/exclusive-manchester-suicide-
    bomber-used-student-loan-benefits/

8   Toby Harnden, 'Seedy secrets of hijackers who broke Muslim laws',
    Daily Telegraph, 6 October 2001, http://www.telegraph.co.uk/
    news/1358665/Seedy-secrets-of-hijackers-who-broke-Muslim-laws.
    html

9   Andrew Silke (ed.), 'Preface', in *Terrorists, Victims and Society:
    Psychological Perspectives on Terrorism and its Consequences*
    (Chichester, West Sussex: Wiley, 2003), xix.

10 John G. Horgan, 'Psychology of terrorism: Introduction to the special
    issue', *American Psychologist* 72.3 (2017): 199.

11 Adam Lankford, 'Martyr myth: Inside the minds of suicide bombers',
    New Scientist, 3 July 2013, https://www.newscientist.com/article/
    mg21929240-200-martyr-myth-inside-the-minds-of-suicide-bombers/

12 Nasra Hassan, 'Are you ready? Tomorrow you will be in Paradise . . .'

The Times, 14 July 2005, https://www.thetimes.co.uk/article/are-you-ready-tomorrow-you-will-be-in-paradise-282b9r6t83c

13   Ellen Townsend, 'Suicide terrorists: Are they suicidal?' *Suicide and Life-Threatening Behavior* 37.1 (2007): 35–49.

14   Adam Lankford, 'Ten Years After 9/11: The Suicide Angle', *Huffington Post*, 12 September 2011, https://www.huffingtonpost.com/dr-adam-lankford/ten-years-after-911-the-s_b_956462.html

15   Ariel Merari et al., 'Personality characteristics of "self martyrs"/"suicide bombers" and organizers of suicide attacks', *Terrorism and Political Violence* 22.1 (2009): 87–101.

16   Murad Ismayilov, 'Conceptualizing Terrorist Violence and Suicide Bombing', *Journal of Strategic Security*, vol. 3, no. 3 (Fall 2010): 109.

17   Domenico Tosini, 'A Sociological Understanding of Suicide Attacks', *Theory, Culture and Society*, vol. 26, no. 4 (2009): 196–7.

18   Matthew Hall, '"This Is Our Call of Duty"': How ISIS Is Using Video Games', *Salon,* 1 November 2014, https://www.salon.com/2014/11/01/this_is_our_call_of_duty_how_isis_is_using_video_games/

19   Ludovica Iaccino, 'Why Tramadol is the Suicide Bomber's Drug of Choice', *Newsweek*, 13 December 2017, https://www.newsweek.co.uk/why-tramadol-suicide-bombers-drug-choice-534884

20   Guillaume Fond and Oliver Howes, 'Pharmacoterrorism: the potential role of psychoactive drugs in the Paris and Tunisian attacks', *Psychopharmacology* 233.6 (2016): 933–5.

21   Monica Mark, 'Boko Haram leader calls for more schools attacks after dorm killings', *Guardian*, 14 July 2013, https://www.theguardian.com/world/2013/jul/14/boko-haram-school-attacks-nigeria

22   Hannah Lucinda Smith, '"Chemical courage" drug produced in Lebanon, Captagon, fuels Isis suicide bombers in Syria', *The Times*, 5 August 2017, https://www.thetimes.co.uk/article/chemical-courage-drug-produced-in-lebanon-captagon-fuels-isis-suicide-bombers-in-syria-b7tsqgn7o

23   Holly Williams, '15-year-old ISIS fighter describes atrocities', CBS News, 21 October 2014, https://www.cbsnews.com/news/15-year-old-isis-fighter-describes-atrocities/

24   Waslat Hasrat-Nazimi, 'After injection, ready for a suicide bombing', *Deutsche Welle*, 24 August 2014, http://www.dw.com/en/after-injection-ready-for-a-suicide-bombing/a-17874018

25   Jasper Hamill, 'Junkie Death Cult: ISIS turns recruits into "mass murder machines" by getting them hooked on DRUGS', *Sun*, 13 July 2016, https://www.thesun.co.uk/news/1437516/isis-turns-recruits-into-mass-murder-machines-by-getting-them-hooked-on-drugs/

26   Ray J. Defalque and Amos J. Wright, 'Methamphetamine for Hitler's

Germany: 1937 to 1945', *Bulletin of Anesthesia History* 29.2 (2011): 21–4.

27   Norman Ohler, *Blitzed: Drugs in Nazi Germany* (London: Penguin UK, 2016).

28   Lukasz Kamienski, 'The Drugs That Built a Super Soldier', *Atlantic*, 8 April 2016, https://www.theatlantic.com/health/archive/2016/04/the-drugs-that-built-a-super-soldier/477183/

29   Nick Land, *The Thirst for Annihilation: Georges Bataille and Virulent Nihilism* (London: Routledge, 2002), 33.

30   Emily Corner and Paul Gill, 'Is There a Nexus Between Terrorist Involvement and Mental Health in the Age of the Islamic State?' *CTC Sentinel* 10, no. 1 (2017): 1.

31   Stephen Kalin, '"Don't Be Sad," Islamic State Suicide Bomber Wrote To Family', *Huffington Post*, 28 February 2017, http://www.huffingtonpost.co.za/2017/02/28/dont-be-sad-islamic-state-suicide-bomber-wrote-to-family_a_21845890/

32   Robert Baer, 'A Talk With a Suicide Bomber', *Time*, 20 July 2007, http://content.time.com/time/world/article/0,8599,1645461,00.html

33   Adam Lankford, *Human Killing Machines: Systematic Indoctrination in Iran, Nazi Germany, Al-Qaeda, and Abu Ghraib* (Lanham, MD: Lexington Books, 2009), 105.

34   Hadith collection, Sahih at-Tarmidhi' from at-Tarmidhi, https://muflihun.com/tirmidhi/20/1663

35   44:54, 52:20, 55:72 and 56:22.

36   From Sheikh Palazzi, who quoted Ibn Kathir in his Tafsir of Surah Al-Rahman (55, verse 72), who quoted Daraj Ibn Abi Hatim, who quoted Abu-al-Haytham Abdullah Ibn Wahb, who quoted Abu Sa'id Al-Khudri, who was quoting the Prophet Muhammad.

37   Moulana Abdullah Nana, *The Maidens of Jannat (Paradise)* (Karachi: ZamZam Publishers, 2004). Available at: http://www.islamicbulletin.org/free_downloads/women/maidens.pdf

38   Pew Research Center, 'The World's Muslims: Unity and Diversity: Chapter 3: Articles of Faith', 9 August 2012, http://www.pewforum.org/2012/08/09/the-worlds-muslims-unity-and-diversity-3-articles-of-faith/

39   Joanna Paraszczuk, 'Will My IS Militant Husband Prefer His Houris Over Me When He's Dead?' *Radio Free Europe Radio Liberty*, 27 July 2015, https://www.rferl.org/a/islamic-state-wives-jealous-of-militant-husbands-virgins-in-heaven/27154374.html

40   As'ad Abukhalil, 'Sex and the suicide bomber', *Salon*, 7 November 2001, https://www.salon.com/2001/11/07/islam_2/?v=html

41   Anthony Loyd, 'The Mosul street in which the caliphate died', *The*

Times, 15 July 2017, https://www.thetimes.co.uk/article/the-street-in-which-the-caliphate-died-zggs5nk3c

42 Valerie M. Hudson and Andrea M. Den Boer, '"Bare Branches" and Danger in Asia', *Washington Post*, 4 July 2004, http://www.washingtonpost.com/wp-dyn/articles/A24761-2004Jul2.html

43 Satoshi Kanazawa, 'The evolutionary psychological imagination: Why you can't get a date on a Saturday night and why most suicide bombers are Muslim', *Journal of Social, Evolutionary, and Cultural Psychology* 1.1 (2007): 7.

44 Christopher Hitchens, *God Is Not Great: How Religion Poisons Everything* (Toronto: McClelland & Stewart, 2008).

45 Leonard Greene, 'Sex torment drove him nuts', *New York Post*, 30 December 2009, https://nypost.com/2009/12/30/sex-torment-drove-him-nuts/

46 Ḥaim Gordon, Rivca Gordon and Taher Shriteh, *Beyond Intifada: Narratives of Freedom Fighters in the Gaza Strip* (Westport, CT and London: Greenwood Publishing Group, 2003), 129.

47 Adolf Tobeña, 'Suicide attack martyrdoms: Temperament and mindset of altruistic warriors', in *Pathological Altruism,* ed. B. Oakley, A. Knafo, G. Madhavan & D.S. Wilson (New York: Oxford University Press, 2011), 212.

48 https://www.youtube.com/watch?v=m-Ojb1-Dy8U

49 Joshua D. Pilzer, 'Music and dance in the Japanese military "comfort women" system: a case study in the performing arts, war, and sexual violence', *Women and Music: A Journal of Gender and Culture* 18.1 (2014): 1–23.

50 http://www.kamikaze-girls.com

51 Steve Straub, 'What ISIS fighters might find their 72 heavenly virgins really are perfectly illustrated with one cartoon', *Federalist Papers*, 13 February 2015, https://thefederalistpapers.org/political-cartoon/what-isis-fighters-might-find-their-72-heavenly-virgins-really-are-perfectly-illustrated-with-one-cartoon

52 https://www.flickr.com/photos/58551403@N06/6479937145

53 Obamacartoon.blogspot.com, 'Osama's 72 Virgins', August 2010, http://obamacartoon.blogspot.co.uk/2010/08/osamas-72-virgins.html

54 Raymond Ibrahim, 'The Houris: Islam's "Sexual Superwomen"' published under '72 Virgins Plus 4 More For ISIS Mosul Defenders', Hla Oo's Blog, 26 November 2016, http://hlaoo1980.blogspot.co.uk/2016/11/72-virgins-plus-4-more-for-isis-mosul.html

55 Callum Paton, 'ISIS Suicide Bombing Orgy During Ramadan: Why are Islamic State Group Militants Attacking Shiite Muslims During the Holiest Month in the Islamic Calendar?' *Newsweek*, 10 June 2017,

http://www.newsweek.com/why-are-isis-suicide-bombers-attacking-shia-muslims-ramadan-623588

56   Tanya Narozhna and W. Andy Knight, *Female Suicide Bombings: A Critical Gender Approach* (Toronto: University of Toronto Press, 2016), 102.

57   *New York Times*, 'Boko Haram strapped suicide bombs to them. Somehow these teenage girls survived', 25 October 2017, https://www.nytimes.com/interactive/2017/10/25/world/africa/nigeria-boko-haram-suicide-bomb.html

58   Paige Whaley Eager, *From Freedom Fighters to Terrorists: Women and Political Violence* (Aldershot, UK and Burlington, VT: Ashgate, 2008), 172.

59   Gbenga Akingbule, 'Death Toll Climbs From Boko Haram Massacre in Nigeria', *Wall Street Journal*, 1 February 2016, https://www.wsj.com/articles/death-toll-climbs-from-boko-haram-massacre-in-nigeria-1454365261

60   Hilary Matfess, *Women and the War on Boko Haram: Wives, Weapons, Witnesses* (Zed Books, London, 2017).

61   Lizzie Dearden, 'Hasna Ait Boulahcen: Family of woman wrongly accused of suicide bombing say she was "murdered" during police raid', *Independent*, 21 January 2016, https://www.independent.co.uk/news/world/europe/hasna-ait-boulahcen-family-of-woman-wrongly-accused-of-suicide-bombing-say-she-was-murdered-during-a6824516.html

62   Nelly Lahoud, 'The neglected sex: The jihadis' exclusion of women from jihad', *Terrorism and Political Violence* 26, no. 5 (2014): 780–802.

63   Simon Cottee and Mia Bloom, 'The Myth of the ISIS Female Suicide Bomber', *Atlantic*, 8 September 2017, https://www.theatlantic.com/international/archive/2017/09/isis-female-suicide-bomber/539172/

64   Charlie Winter (trans.), 'Women of the Islamic State: a manifesto on women by the Al-Khanssaa Brigade', Quilliam Foundation (2015).

65   Meytal Grimland, Alan Apter and Ad Kerkhof, 'The Phenomenon of Suicide Bombing: A Review of Psychological and Nonpsychological Factors', *Crisis*, vol. 27, no. 3 (2006), 109.

66   Thayer and Hudson, 'Sex and the Shaheed'.

67   UNICEF Information Newsline, 'UNICEF Executive Director targets violence against women', 7 March 2000, https://www.unicef.org/newsline/00pr17.htm

68   Jay Sekulow, *Rise of ISIS: A Threat We Can't Ignore* (iBooks), 36.

69   https://twitter.com/memrireports/status/793361509996978176

70   Christopher Dickey, 'Women of Al-Qaeda', *Newsweek,* 11 December 2005, http://www.newsweek.com/women-al-qaeda-113757

71   Al Jazeera, 'Soldiers killed in Gaza resistance attack', 15 January 2004, http://www.aljazeera.com/archive/2004/01/2008410102321532586. html

72   http://www.sahab.net/forums/index.php?showtopic=42460

73   Lahoud, 'The neglected sex'.

74   Loyd, 'The Mosul street in which the caliphate died'.

75   Josie Ensor, 'Chilling Picture Shows Female Isil Fighter Holding Child Moments before Detonating Suicide Vest', *Daily Telegraph*, 10 July 2017, https://www.telegraph.co.uk/news/2017/07/08/chilling-picture-shows-female-isil-fighter-holding-child-moments/

76   Jack Moore, 'ISIS Unleashes Dozens of Female Suicide Bombers in Battle for Mosul', *Newsweek*, 5 July 2017, http://www.newsweek.com/isis-female-suicide-bombers-battle-mosul-631846

77   Elizabeth Pearson, 'Why ISIS Female Suicide Bombers Mean the End of the Caliphate Dream', *Newsweek*, 18 July 2017, http://www.newsweek.com/why-isis-female-suicide-bombers-mean-end-caliphate-dream-637892

78   Gaby Hinsliff, '"Check your privilege" used to annoy me. Now I get it', *Guardian*, 27 December 2017, https://www.theguardian.com/commentisfree/2017/dec/27/check-your-privilege-racism-sexism-education-income

12. The Mountain of Victims

1   Atomicarchive.com, 'The Atomic Bombings of Hiroshima and Nagasaki', accessed 8 June 2018, http://www.atomicarchive.com/Docs/MED/med_chp10.shtml

2   Mia Bloom, *Dying to Kill: The Allure of Suicide Terror* (New York: Columbia University Press, 2005).

3   Joshua Keating, 'Half a Million Deaths is a Statistic', *Slate*, 18 October 2013, http://www.slate.com/blogs/the_world_/2013/10/18/new_study_estimates_half_a_million_casualties_from_iraq_war_but_how_reliable.html

4   Isabelle Vonèche Cardia, 'The International Committee of the Red Cross: Identifying the Dead and Tracing Missing Persons – A Historical Perspective', in *Violence, Statistics, and the Politics of Accounting for the Dead* (Cham: Springer, 2016), 84.

5   *Straits Times*, 'Gravediggers say 86 killed in Nigeria suicide bombing, three times official toll', 3 May 2018, https://www.straitstimes.com/world/africa/gravediggers-say-86-killed-in-nigeria-suicide-bombing-three-times-official-toll

6   Randolph Martin, 'An Introduction to NGO Field Security', in Kevin
      M. Cahill (ed.), *Emergency Relief Operations* (New York: Fordham
      University Press, 2003), 227.

7   In total, where gender was known, 23,993 people were killed and
      65,514 injured by suicide bombers.

8   CNN, 'September 11th Terror Attacks Fast Facts', 24 August 2017,
      https://edition.cnn.com/2013/07/27/us/september-11-anniversary-fast-
      facts/index.html

9   Madelyn Hsiao-Rei Hicks et al., 'Casualties in civilians and coalition
      soldiers from suicide bombings in Iraq, 2003–10: a descriptive study',
      Lancet 378.9794 (2011): 906–14.

10   Emily Crockett, 'Why Manchester Bomber Targeted Girls', *Rolling
      Stone*, 23 May 2017, https://www.rollingstone.com/culture/culture-
      features/why-manchester-bomber-targeted-girls-127591/

11   Yoram Kluger, 'Bomb explosions in acts of terrorism – detonation,
      wound ballistics, triage and medical concerns', *Israel Medical
      Association Journal (IMAJ)* 5.4 (2003): 235.

12   One article describes it as such: 'In a closed environment a single
      Friedlander waveform is abolished. Multiple peaks and a sustained
      waveform results in a quasistatic pressure (QSP) development. This
      results in a propagated increase in the primary blast field area and
      subsequent increased number of primary blast injuries.' See Dafydd
      S. Edwards and Jon Clasper, 'Blast Injury Mechanism', in *Blast Injury
      Science and Engineering,* ed. Anthony M.J. Bull, Jon Clasper and Peter
      F. Mahoney (Cham: Springer International Publishing, 2016), 87–104.

13   Yona Kosashvili et al., 'Medical consequences of suicide bombing mass
      casualty incidents: the impact of explosion setting on injury patterns',
      Injury 40.7 (2009): 698–702.

14   US Department of Homeland Security Office for Bombing
      Prevention, 'IED and Explosive Effects Fundamentals', DHS-
      MITG-253 Version 4, accessed 8 June 2018, https://www.
      eiseverywhere.com/file_uploads 170e63337bebca0287c1aaf3509af6d2_
      IEDExplosiveEffectsFundamentals.pdf

15   Walter Benjamin, 'On the Concept of History' (2009), https://folk.uib.
      no/hlils/TBLR-B/Benjamin-History.pdf

16   A sample of 135 suicide attacks in Israel between 2000 and 2005 found
      fewer in this heavily militarised zone, with 3.7 fatalities per incident
      and 24.2 people injured. See: Michal Mekel et al., 'Terrorist suicide
      bombings: lessons learned in Metropolitan Haifa from September
      2000 to January 2006', *American Journal of Disaster Medicine* 4.4
      (2009): 233–48. In Iraq, meanwhile, for every two civilians killed,
      about five people were injured but survived. See: Madelyn Hsiao-Rei

Hicks et al., 'Casualties in civilians and coalition soldiers from suicide bombings in Iraq, 2003–10: a descriptive study', *Lancet* 378.9794 (2011): 906–14.

17　Shane Smith, Melissa Devine, Joseph Taddeo, et al., 'Injury profile suffered by targets of antipersonnel improvised explosive devices: prospective cohort study', *BMJ Open* 2017; https://bmjopen.bmj.com/content/7/7/e014697

18　Hasu D.L. Patel, and Steven Dryden, 'Clinical Forensic Investigation of the 2005 London Suicide Bombings', in *Blast Injury Science and Engineering,* ed. Anthony M. J. Bull, Jon Clasper and Peter F. Mahoney (Cham: Springer International Publishing, 2016), 122.

19　Dafydd S. Edwards et al., 'Prophylaxis for blood-borne diseases during the London 7/7 mass casualty terrorist bombing: a review and the role of bioethics', *Journal of the Royal Army Medical Corps* 162.5 (2016): 330–4.

20　Itzhak Braverman, David Wexler and Meir Oren, 'A novel mode of infection with hepatitis B: penetrating bone fragments due to the explosion of a suicide bomber', *Israel Medical Association Journal* (IMAJ) 4.7 (2002): 528–9.

21　Arul Ramasamy, Anne-Marie Hill and Jon C. Clasper, 'Improvised explosive devices: pathophysiology, injury profiles and current medical management', *Journal of the Royal Army Medical Corps* 155.4 (2009): 265–72.

22　Eric R. Frykberg and J.J. Tepas 3rd, 'Terrorist bombings. Lessons learned from Belfast to Beirut', *Annals of Surgery* 208.5 (1988): 569.

23　Limor Aharonson-Daniel, Yoram Klein and Kobi Peleg, 'Suicide bombers form a new injury profile', *Annals of Surgery* 244.6 (2006): 1018.

24　Steph Oliver, '"A night of horror": Medics relive night of the Manchester Arena bombing', *Sky News*, 26 December 2017, https://news.sky.com/story/a-night-of-horror-medics-relive-night-of-the-manchester-arena-bombing-11184467

25　M. Stein and A. Hirshberg, 'Limited mass casualties due to conventional weapons: a daily reality of a level 1 trauma center', in *Terror and Medicine*, eds. J Shemer and Y Shoenfeld (Berlin: Pabst Science, 2003), 385.

26　Limor Aharonson-Daniel, Yoram Klein, and Kobi Peleg. 'Suicide bombers form a new injury profile', *Annals of Surgery,* 244, no. 6 (2006): 1018. https://www.ncbi.nlm.nih.gov/pubmed/17122628

27　Laurence Norman, 'Belgian Suspect Ameroud Said to Have Carried Potentially Toxic Material', *Wall Street Journal*, 9 April 2016, https://www.wsj.com/articles/belgian-suspect-ameuroud-said-to-have-carried-potentially-toxic-material-1460210505

28 Yona Kosashvili, Mark I. Loebenberg, Guy Lin, Kobi Peleg, Feigenberg
    Zvi, Yoram Kluger, and Amir Blumenfeld. 'Medical consequences
    of suicide bombing mass casualty incidents: the impact of explosion
    setting on injury patterns.' *Injury* 40, no. 7 (2009): 698–702.

29 Nathaniel P. Hoyle et al., 'Circadian actin dynamics drive
    rhythmic fibroblast mobilization during wound healing', *Science
    Translational Medicine* 9.415 (2017). https://www.ncbi.nlm.nih.gov/
    pubmed/29118260

30 Institute of Medicine, *Gulf War and Health, Volume 9: Long-Term
    Effects of Blast Exposures* (Washington, DC: The National Academies
    Press, 2014).

31 Ann C. McKee and Meghan E. Robinson, 'Military-related traumatic
    brain injury and neurodegeneration', *Alzheimer's & Dementia: the
    Journal of the Alzheimer's Association* 10.3 (2014): S242–S253.

32 Sarah Knapton, 'World War 2 left toxic legacy of ill health and
    depression', *Daily Telegraph*, 21 January 2014, https://www.telegraph.
    co.uk/history/world-war-two/10584595/World-War-2-left-toxic-
    legacy-of-ill-health-and-depression.html

33 Kate V. Brown et al., 'Comparison of development of heterotopic
    ossification in injured US and UK Armed Services personnel with
    combat-related amputations: preliminary findings and hypotheses
    regarding causality', *Journal of Trauma and Acute Care Surgery* 69.1
    (2010): S116–S122, and D.S Edwards, J.C. Clasper and H.D.L. Patel,
    'Heterotopic ossification in victims of the London 7/7 bombings',
    Journal of the Royal Army Medical Corps 161.4 (2015): 345–7.

34 F.S. Kaplan, D.L. Glaser, N. Hebela et al., 'Heterotopic ossification',
    JAAOS 12.2 (2004): 116–25.

35 A.P. Silke and J. Schmidt-Petersen, 'The golden age? What the 100
    most cited articles in terrorism studies tell us', *Terrorism and Political
    Violence* 29.4 (2015): 692–712. http://dx.doi.org/10.1080/09546553.201
    5.1064397

36 Richard H. Beinecke, 'Addressing the mental health needs of victims
    and responders to the Boston Marathon Bombings', *International
    Journal of Mental Health* 43.2 (2014): 17–34.

37 C. North, D. Pollio, R. Smith et al., 'Trauma exposure and
    posttraumatic stress disorder among employees of New York City
    companies affected by the September 11, 2001 attacks on the World
    Trade Center', *Disaster Medicine & Public Health Preparedness* 5.2
    (2001): S205–S213.

38 Derek Summerfield, 'The invention of post-traumatic stress disorder
    and the social usefulness of a psychiatric category', *BMJ* 322, no. 7278
    (2001): 95–8.

39   Sarah A. Palyo and J. Gayle Beck, 'Is the concept of "repression" useful
      for the understanding chronic PTSD?' *Behaviour Research and Therapy*
      43, no. 1 (2005): 55–68.

40   Anthony Loyd, 'My four-year-old son just wants to behead people',
      The Times, 10 December 2016, https://www.thetimes.co.uk/article/
      my-four-year-old-son-just-wants-to-behead-people-395x8l8gn

41   Michelle Slone, 'Responses to Media Coverage of Terrorism', *Journal of
      Conflict Resolution*, Vol. 44, no. 4 (2000): 508–22.

42   Menachem Ben-Ezra, Yaira Hamama-Raz and Michal Mahat-Shamir,
      'Psychological reactions to the 2017 Manchester Arena bombing: A
      population-based study', *Journal of Psychiatric Research* 95 (2017):
      235–7.

43   M. Amer and J. Hovey, 'Anxiety and depression in a post-September
      11 sample of Arabs in the USA', *Social Psychiatry and Psychiatric
      Epidemiology* 47.3 (2012): 409–18.

44   E. Salib, 'Effect of 11 September 2001 on suicide and homicide in
      England and Wales', *British Journal of Psychiatry* 183.3 (2003): 207–12.

45   Office for National Statistics, 'Suicides by month of occurrence,
      1981 to 2015', 7 April 2017, https://www.ons.gov.uk/
      peoplepopulationandcommunity/birthsdeathsandmarriages/deaths/
      adhocs/006905suicidesbymonthofoccurrence1981to2015

46   However, with both counts two things need to be qualified. First, that
      there has been a steady and slow decrease in the number of completed
      suicides in England and Wales in the past few decades: 5,752 killed
      themselves in 1981 compared to 4,892 in 2015. Second, that there is
      a lag period between suicides occurring and being reported, which
      might lead to a muddying of the waters. Nonetheless, it seems highly
      likely that both major attacks, which each garnered thousands of
      media reports, deterred some from suicide.

47   Sofie Verhaeghe, Tom Defloor and Mieke Grypdonck, 'Stress and
      coping among families of patients with traumatic brain injury: a
      review of the literature', *Journal of Clinical Nursing* 14.8 (2005):
      1004–12.

48   Briana S. Nelson Goff et al., 'The impact of individual trauma
      symptoms of deployed soldiers on relationship satisfaction', *Journal of
      Family Psychology* 21.3 (2007): 344.

49   'My Son the Jihadi', https://www.youtube.com/
      watch?v=pN5IV6wUFbM

50   Aviation Security International, 'Ann-Marie Murphy and the Hindawi
      Affair: a 30th-anniversary review', 13 April 2016, https://www.asi-mag.
      com/ann-marie-murphy-hindawi-affair-30th-anniversary-review/

51   Michael Howard, 'Bombs strapped to Down's syndrome women kill

scores in Baghdad markets', *Guardian*, 2 February 2008, https://www.theguardian.com/world/2008/feb/02/iraq.international1

52 Stephanie Nebehay, 'Islamic State selling, crucifying, burying children alive in Iraq – UN', Reuters, 4 February 2015, https://in.reuters.com/article/mideast-crisis-children/islamic-state-selling-crucifying-burying-children-alive-in-iraq-un-idINKBN0L828E20150204

53 Hannah Allam and Austin Tice, 'Accounts of Syria rebels executing prisoners raise new human rights concerns', *McClatchy DC Bureau*, 3 August 2012, http://www.mcclatchydc.com/news/nation-world/world/article24733633.html

54 *New York Times*, 'Evolution in Europe: Bishop Rebukes I.R.A. for Car Bomb Attacks', 28 October 1990, https://www.nytimes.com/1990/10/28/world/evolution-in-europe-bishop-rebukes-ira-for-car-bomb-attacks.html

55 *Pink News*, 'Al-Qaeda accused of using male rape to "create" suicide bombers', 4 February 2009, http://www.pinknews.co.uk/2009/02/04/al-qaeda-accused-of-using-male-rape-to-create-suicide-bombers, and Carol Forsloff, 'Al-Qaeda Accused of Using Male Rape to Recruit Suicide Bombers', *Digital Journal*, 1 July 2009, http://www.digitaljournal.com/article/275122#ixzz546CO6kiV

56 Emiko Ohnuki-Tierney, *Kamikaze Diaries; Reflections of Japanese Student Soldiers* (Chicago: University of Chicago Press, 2006).

57 As an aside, the 'Kamikaze Kids' were an American male basketball team in the 1970s in Oregon – possibly not a moniker that would be used today. OregonLive, 'McArthur Court memories: Best eras – Tall Firs, Kamikaze Kids or something else?' 5 March 2010, http://blog.oregonlive.com/behindducksbeat/2010/03/mcarthur_court_memories_best_e.html

58 P.W. Singer, 'Transcript: Books: "Children at War"', *Washington Post*, Live Q&As, 12 June 2006, http://www.washingtonpost.com/wp-dyn/content/discussion/2006/05/22/DI2006052200785.html

59 Child Soldiers Global Report, 2004, p. 292. https://web.archive.org/web/20060421014945/http://www.child-soldiers.org/document_get.php?id=966

60 Andrew Wasike, 'Somalia: Rights Group – Al Shabab Forcibly Recruits Children', *Deutsche Welle*, 15 January 2018, http://allafrica.com/stories/201801160071.html

61 Gemma Mullin, 'Sick ISIS militants strap explosives to four-year-old boy and blow him up after executing his dad', *Daily Mirror*, 5 January 2016, https://www.mirror.co.uk/news/world-news/sick-isis-militants-strap-explosives-7121510

62 Yasmin Jeffery, 'ISIS child suicide bomber who can barely see over

steering wheel shown detonating car blast in sickening video', *Daily Mirror*, 26 January 2017, http://www.mirror.co.uk/news/world-news/isis-child-suicide-bomber-who-9695386

63   CBS News, 'Iraqi officers try to defuse suicide belt on boy in video', 18 December 2014, https://www.cbsnews.com/news/iraqi-officers-try-to-defuse-suicide-belt-on-boy-in-video/

64   Alex Rossi, 'Islamic State training child suicide bombers in special camp', *Sky News*, 18 December 2016, https://news.sky.com/story/islamic-state-training-child-suicide-bombers-in-special-camp-10700852

65   Tim Arango, 'A Boy in ISIS. A Suicide Vest. A Hope to Live', *New York Times*, 26 December 2014, https://www.nytimes.com/2014/12/27/world/middleeast/syria-isis-recruits-teenagers-as-suicide-bombers.html

66   Diana Magnay, 'Yazidi children turned into suicide bombers by Isis', *Channel 4 News*, 27 February 2017, https://www.channel4.com/news/yazidi-children-turned-into-suicide-bombers-by-isis

67   Action on Armed Violence, 'Understanding the rising cult of the suicide bomber: Current threat zones – Iraq', 1 January 2017, https://aoav.org.uk/2017/understanding-rising-cult-suicide-bomber-current-threat-zones/

68   'ISIS Child Kisses Father, Says Goodbye Before Suicide Mission for al-Baghdadi' https://www.youtube.com/watch?v=jN7-HTZulV8

69   *Snopes*, 'Jihadi Parents' Kiss Child Suicide Bombers Goodbye', 22 December 2016, https://www.snopes.com/jihadi-parents-kiss-child-suicide-bombers-goodbye/

70   'Mosul offensive: Fighting ISIS on the frontline in Iraq', *Channel 4 News*, https://www.youtube.com/watch?v=Zx6U3x2M3XA

71   Alexander Smith, 'Boko Haram's Use of Child "Suicide" Bombers Skyrocketed Last Year: U.N.' *NBC News*, 12 April 2016, http://www.nbcnews.com/storyline/missing-nigeria-schoolgirls/boko-haram-s-use-child-suicide-bombers-skyrocketed-last-year-n554591

72   Joseph Erunke, 'Suicide bombing: Boko Haram adopting new tactics – Army', *Vanguard*, 18 July 2017, https://www.vanguardngr.com/2017/07/suicide-bombing-boko-haram-adopting-new-tactics-army/

73   BBC News, 'Boko Haram crisis: "Huge rise" in child suicide bombers', 12 April 2016, https://www.bbc.co.uk/news/world-africa-36023444

74   Dawood Azami, 'How the Taliban groom child suicide bombers', BBC World Service, 15 December 2014, http://www.bbc.co.uk/news/world-asia-27250144

75   Ibid.

76   Ibid.
77   Vivian Salama and Zeina Karam, 'Islamic State group recruits,
      exploits children', *Military Times*, 23 November 2014, https://www.
      militarytimes.com/news/your-military/2014/11/23/islamic-state-
      group-recruits-exploits-children/
78   Jack Moore, 'Children Included on List of 173 ISIS Suicide Bombers
      Who Could Strike Europe', *Newsweek*, 4 August 2017, http://www.
      newsweek.com/children-included-list-173-isis-suicide-bombers-who-
      could-strike-europe-646388

13. Endless War

1   R.W. Apple Jr., 'After the Attacks: News Analysis, No Middle
     Ground', *New York Times*, 14 September 2001, http://www.nytimes.
     com/2001/09/14/us/after-the-attacks-news-analysis-no-middle-
     ground.html
2   BBC News, 'US "threatened to bomb" Pakistan', 22 September 2006,
     http://news.bbc.co.uk/1/hi/world/south_asia/5369198.stm
3   Bob Woodward and Dan Balz, 'At Camp David, Advise and Dissent',
     Washington Post, 31 January 2002, http://www.washingtonpost.com/
     wp-dyn/content/article/2006/07/18/AR2006071800702.html
4   Jim Garamone, 'Special Ops Capabilities Relevant Around the World,
     Commander Says', *US Department of Defense News*, 22 July 2017,
     https://www.defense.gov/News/Article/Article/1255158/special-ops-
     capabilities-relevant-around-the-world-commander-says/
5   John Haltiwanger, 'The Forever War: U.S. Military Now Has 15,000
     Troops in Afghanistan and That Number Could Soon Increase',
     Newsweek, 9 November 2017, http://www.newsweek.com/forever-war-
     us-military-now-has-15000-troops-afghanistan-706573
6   Andrew deGrandpre, 'A top U.S. general just said 4,000 American
     troops are in Syria. The Pentagon says there are only 500.' *Washington
     Post*, 31 October 2017, https://www.washingtonpost.com/news/
     checkpoint/wp/2017/10/31/a-top-u-s-general-just-said-4000-
     american-troops-are-in-syria-the-pentagon-says-there-are-only-
     500/?utm_term=.c4ec668c1032
7   Kyle Rempfer, 'US troops support Somali forces on the ground,
     hit al-Shabaab terrorists from the sky', *Military Times*, 20 January
     2018, https://www.militarytimes.com/flashpoints/2018/01/19/
     us-troops-support-somali-forces-on-the-ground-hit-al-shabaab-
     terrorists-from-the-sky/
8   Paul Szoldra, 'US troops are on the ground inside Yemen for an

offensive against al Qaeda', *Business Insider UK*, 4 August 2017, http://uk.businessinsider.com/us-troops-yemen-2017-8

9　Wesley Morgan and Bryan Bender, 'America's shadow war in Africa', *Politico*, 12 October 2017, https://www.politico.com/story/2017/10/12/niger-shadow-war-africa-243695

10　Nick Turse, 'The U.S. military is conducting secret missions all over Africa', *Vice*, 25 October 2017, https://news.vice.com/story/us-military-secret-missions-africa

11　Kathy Gannon, 'Pentagon says 2 U.S. service members killed in Afghanistan suicide bombing attack', *Chicago Tribune*, 2 August 2017, http://www.chicagotribune.com/news/nationworld/ct-us-service-members-killed-afghanistan-20170802-story.html

12　Song Lifang, '3 suicide bombers killed in attack on U.S. forces in northern Iraq', *Xinhua*, 17 September 2017, http://www.xinhuanet.com/english/2017-09/17/c_136616273.htm

13　WBUR, 'A Closer Look At U.S. Combat Deaths In 2017', 29 December 2017, http://www.wbur.org/hereandnow/2017/12/29/2017-us-combat-deaths

14　Seung-Whan Choi and James A. Piazza, 'Foreign military interventions and suicide attacks', *Journal of Conflict Resolution* 61.2 (2017): 271–97.

15　Eliza Manningham-Buller, *Securing Freedom* (London: Profile Books, 2012), 29.

16　International Institute for Strategic Studies, 'IEDs: the home-made bombs that changed modern war', 10 September 2012, https://www.taudfonline.com/doi/abs/10.1080.13567888.2012.727282

17　Ibid.

18　Rajiv Chrasekaran and William Branigin, 'Suicide Bombing Kills 4 Soldiers', *Washington Post*, 30 March 2003, https://www.washingtonpost.com/archive/politics/2003/03/30/suicide-bombing-kills-4-soldiers/4f45d74c-8688-481b-bf23-ea68edf1bbdc/?utm_term=.af66d9224a69

19　CNN, 'Iraq promises more suicide bombings', 29 March 2003, http://edition.cnn.com/2003/WORLD/meast/03/29/sprj.irq.car.bomb/index.html

20　DCSINT Handbook No. 1, *A Military Guide to Terrorism in the Twenty-First Century*, 'Suicide Bombing in the COE', US Army TRADOC 2006 Version 4.0

21　White House, *The National Security Strategy of the United States of America* (Washington D.C.: March 2006), https://www.state.gov/documents/organization/64884.pdf

22　Ibid.

23 Mark Thompson, 'The Fight for Mosul: Kamikaze 2.0', *Time*, 19 October 2016, http://time.com/4535914/mosul-iraq-suicide-video/

24 Center for Army Lessons Learned (CALL), *Escalation of Force Handbook*, July 2007, https://www.globalsecurity.org/military/library/report/call/call_07-21.pdf

25 Emma Slater, 'Hundreds of Civilians Gunned Down at Checkpoints', *Bureau of Investigative Journalism*, 23 May 2011, https://www.thebureauinvestigates.com/stories/2011-05-23/hundreds-of-civilians-gunned-down-at-checkpoints

26 As an example, please see: Reuters, 'An Iraqi special forces soldier checks men for explosive belts as they cross from Islamic State controlled part of Mosul to Iraqi forces controlled part of Mosul', 5 March 2017, http://news.trust.org/item/20170305071813-jvp60/

27 Andrea Beccaro and Claudio Bertolotti, 'Suicide attacks: strategic perspective and Afghan war', *Security, Terrorism and Society* 1.2 (2015): 21–59. See shorter version here: https://www.ispionline.it/sites/default/files/pubblicazioni/analysis_283_beccaro.bertolotti__2015.pdf

28 John Spencer, 'The Most Effective Weapon on the Battlefield is Concrete', *Modern War Institute*, 14 November 2016, https://mwi.usma.edu/effective-weapon-modern-battlefield-concrete/

29 Mark Tran, 'US builds Baghdad wall to keep Sunnis and Shias apart', *Guardian*, 20 April 2007, https://www.theguardian.com/world/2007/apr/20/iraq.usa

30 Spencer, 'The Most Effective Weapon on the Battlefield is Concrete'.

31 David F. Eisler, 'Counter-IED Strategy in Modern War', *Military Review* 92.1 (2012), https://pdfs.semanticscholar.org/f750/295434e9e8553a70afa8e4a16c8ab88b50f7.pdf

32 Edward Powers, 'The Military's Role in Countering Violent Extremism', (The United States Institute for Peace, 7 June 2017), https://www.usip.org/publications/2017/06/militarys-role-countering-violent-extremism

33 See: Neta C. Crawford, *Costs of War: US Budgetary Costs of Post-9/11 Wars Through FY2018: $5.6 Trillion* (Providence, RI: Watson Institute for International and Public Affairs, Brown University, 2017), http://watson.brown.edu/costsofwar/papers/2017/USBudgetaryCostsFY2018

34 Clay Wilson, 'Improvised explosive devices (IEDs) in Iraq and Afghanistan: Effects and Countermeasures', (Washington D.C.: Congressional Research Service, Library of Congress, 2007).

35 Beccaro and Bertolotti.

36 David F. Eisler, 'Counter-IED strategy in modern war', *Military Review* 92.1 (2012), 9.

37 Assaf Moghadam, *The Globalization of Martyrdom: Al-Qaeda, Salafi*

Jihad, and the Diffusion of Suicide Attacks (Baltimore: Johns Hopkins University Press, 2008), 38.

38   Glenn Zorpette, 'Countering IEDs', IEEE Spectrum, 29 August 2008, https://spectrum.ieee.org/aerospace/military/countering-ieds

39   Steve Grossman, 'Car Bomb Detector Employs a Revolutionary New Approach', RFDesign, 9 November 2005, https://web.archive.org/web/20080225154402/http://rfdesign.com/military_defense_electronics/news/car_bomb_detector/

40   https://www.youtube.com/watch?v=-x9ykqGHI_0

41   https://vimeo.com/138903827

42   Iain Overton, Adam Jarvis-Norse, Jennifer Dathan and Mia Lombardi, 'US Department of Defense spend on guns in "War on Terror" revealed', Action on Armed Violence, 24 August 2016, https://aoav.org.uk/2016/us-department-of-defence-spend-on-guns-and-ammunition-in-the-war-on-terror-revealed/

43   C.J. Chivers, 'How many guns did the U.S. lose track of in Iraq and Afghanistan? Hundreds of thousands', *New York Times*, 24 August 2016, https://www.nytimes.com/2016/08/23/magazine/how-many-guns-did-the-us-lose-track-of-in-iraq-and-afghanistan-hundreds-of-thousands.html

44   Linda J. Bilmes, 'The financial legacy of Iraq and Afghanistan: How wartime spending decisions will constrain future national security budgets', HKS Faculty Research Working Paper Series RWP13-006, March 2013, https://research.hks.harvard.edu/publications/workingpapers/citation.aspx?PubId=8956

45   Kimberly Amadeo, 'U.S. Deficit by Year: Compared to GDP, Increase in Debt and Events', *Balance*, 16 February 2018, https://www.thebalance.com/us-deficit-by-year-3306306

46   *Washington Post*, 'What Trump proposed cutting in his 2019 budget', 16 February 2018, https://www.washingtonpost.com/graphics/2018/politics/trump-budget-2019/?utm_term=.cdd20adf63c5

47   Action on Armed Violence, 'Counter-IED actors: AOAV's global list', 30 December 2016, https://aoav.org.uk/2016/counter-improvised-explosive-devices-c-ied-mapping/

48   Harun Maruf, 'Al-Shabab Claims Somalia, Kenya Attacks', Voice of America, 24 May 2017, https://www.voanews.com/a/is-claims-responsibility-for-somalia-bombing/3868856.html

49   John Haltiwanger, 'Under Trump, U.S. Military Deaths in War Zones Are Up for the First Time in Six Years', *Newsweek*, 20 November 2017, http://www.newsweek.com/trump-us-military-deaths-war-zones-are-first-time-six-years-716981

50   Meghna Chakrabarti, 'A Closer Look At U.S. Combat Deaths In

2017', WBUR radio, 29 December 2017, http://www.wbur.org/
hereandnow/2017/12/29/2017-us-combat-deaths

51   Chris Woods, 'US Claims of No Civilian Deaths Are Untrue',
        Bureau of Investigative Journalism, 18 July 2011, https://www.
        thebureauinvestigates.com/stories/2011-07-18/us-claims-of-no-
        civilian-deaths-are-untrue

52   Jack Serle, 'Only 4 per cent of Drone Victims in Pakistan Named as
        Al-Qaeda members', *Bureau of Investigative Journalism*, 16 October
        2014, https://www.thebureauinvestigates.com/stories/2014-10-16/only-
        4-of-drone-victims-in-pakistan-named-as-al-qaeda-members

53   *Bureau of Investigative Journalism*, 'Drone Strikes Are Illegal According
        to Prominent Pakistani Lawyer', 16 January 2014, https://www.
        thebureauinvestigates.com/stories/2014-01-16/drone-strikes-are-
        illegal-according-to-a-prominent-pakistani-lawyer

54   Chris Woods, 'Bureau Investigation Finds Fresh Evidence of CIA
        Drone Strikes on Rescuers', *Bureau of Investigative Journalism*,
        1 August 2013, https://www.thebureauinvestigates.com/
        stories/2013-08-01/bureau-investigation-finds-fresh-evidence-of-cia-
        drone-strikes-on-rescuers

55   Jack Serle, 'RAF Drone Strike: Syria Deaths Means At Least 10 Britons
        Now Killed By Drones in West's War on Terror', *Bureau of Investigative
        Journalism*, 7 September 2015, https://www.thebureauinvestigates.com/
        stories/2015-09-07/raf-drone-strike-syria-deaths-means-at-least-10-
        britons-now-killed-by-drones-in-wests-war-on-terror

56   Megan Braun and Daniel R. Brunstetter. 'Rethinking the criterion for
        assessing CIA-targeted killings: Drones, proportionality and jus ad
        vim', *Journal of Military Ethics* 12.4 (2013): 304–24.

57   See: Luke Mogelson, 'The Recent History of Bombing the Shit Out
        of 'Em', *New Yorker*, 20 April 2017, https://www.newyorker.com/
        news/news-desk/the-recent-history-of-bombing-the-shit-out-of-em
        and Jessica Purkiss, 'Trump's First Year in Numbers: Strikes Triple in
        Yemen and Somalia', *Bureau of Investigative Journalism*, 19 January
        2018, https://www.thebureauinvestigates.com/stories/2018-01-19/
        strikes-in-somalia-and-yemen-triple-in-trumps-first-year-in-office

58   Jessica Purkiss and Jack Serle, 'Obama's Covert Drone War in
        Numbers: Ten Times More Strikes Than Bush', *Bureau of Investigative
        Journalism*, 17 January 2017, https://www.thebureauinvestigates.com/
        stories/2017-01-17/obamas-covert-drone-war-in-numbers-ten-times-
        more-strikes-than-bush

59   Greg Jaffe, 'The watchers: Airmen who surveil the Islamic State
        never get to look away.' *Washington Post*, 6 July 2017, https://www.
        washingtonpost.com/world/national-security/the-watchers-airmen-

who-surveil-the-islamic-state-never-get-to-look-away/2017/07/06/
d80c37de-585f-11e7-ba90-f5875b7d1876_story.html

60   Jill A. Long, 'The Problem with Precision: Managing Expectations for
      Air Power' (Master of Strategic Studies thesis, US Army War College,
      Carlisle Barracks, PA, 2013).

61   Matt J. Martin and Charles W. Sasser. *Predator: The Remote-Control
      Air War Over Iraq and Afghanistan – A Pilot's Story* (Minneapolis,
      MN: Zenith Press, 2010).

62   *Field Manual 3–19.40: Tactics, Techniques, and Procedures for Fire
      Support for the Combined Arms Commander* (Washington DC:
      Department of the Army, 1 August 2001).

63   Andrew deGrandpre and Shawn Snow, 'The U.S. military's stats
      on deadly airstrikes are wrong. Thousands have gone unreported',
      Military Times, 5 February 2017, https://www.militarytimes.com/
      news/your-military/2017/02/05/the-u-s-military-s-stats-on-deadly-
      airstrikes-are-wrong-thousands-have-gone-unreported/

64   UK Ministry of Defence and the Rt. Hon. Sir Michael Fallon MP, 'RAF
      conduct first airstrikes in Syria', 3 December 2015, https://www.gov.uk/
      government/news/raf-conduct-first-air-strikes-in-syria

65   Conor Friedersdorf, 'Under Obama, Men Killed by Drones Are
      Presumed to Be Terrorists', *Atlantic*, 29 May 2012, https://www.
      theatlantic.com/politics/archive/2012/05/under-obama-men-killed-by-
      drones-are-presumed-to-be-terrorists/257749/

66   Khalil Dewan, 'Q&A: Drone Wars through the eyes of a US Sergeant',
      Huffington Post, 8 March 2017, https://www.huffingtonpost.
      com/entry/qa-drone-wars-through-the-eyes-of-a-us-sergeant_
      us_597f47efe4b06b305561d28a

67   David Batty and agencies, 'Killer of CIA agents in Afghanistan calls
      for revenge', *Guardian*, 9 January 2010, https://www.theguardian.com/
      world/2010/jan/09/cia-bomber-vows-revenge-us-video-taliban

68   Dawn, 'At least six killed in US drone strike', 12 September 2010, https://
      www.dawn.com/news/958116/at-least-six-killed-in-us-drone-strike

69   Mark Benjamin, 'When is an accidental civilian death not an
      accident?' *Salon*, 30 July 2007, https://www.salon.com/2007/07/30/
      collateral_damage/

70   Jennifer Varriale Carson, 'Assessing the Effectiveness of High Profile
      Targeted Killings in the "War on Terror"', *Criminology & Public Policy*
      16, no. 1 (2017): 191–220.

71   Peter Byrne, 'Anatomy of terror: What makes normal people become
      extremists?', *New Scientist*, 16 August 2017, https://www.newscientist.
      com/article/mg23531390-700-anatomy-of-terror-what-makes-normal-
      people-become-extremists/

72　Emma Slater and Chris Woods, 'Iranian TV station accused of faking reports of Somalia drone strikes', *Guardian*, 2 December 2011, https://www.theguardian.com/world/2011/dec/02/iranian-tv-fake-drone-somalia

73　Gul Yousafzai, 'Suicide bomber kills at least 70 at Pakistan hospital, IS claims responsibility', Reuters, 8 August 2016, https://www.reuters.com/article/us-pakistan-blast/suicide-bomber-kills-at-least-70-at-pakistan-hospital-is-claims-responsibility-idUSKCN10J0I7

74　Emma Graham-Harrison and Dr Kathleen Thomas, 'Inside the Kunduz hospital attack: "It was a scene of nightmarish horror"', *Guardian*, 10 April 2016, https://www.theguardian.com/world/2016/apr/10/kunduz-afghanistan-attack-medecins-sans-frontieres

75　Andrew Griffin, 'Suicide bomber dressed as woman kills 14 in Iraq refugee camp', *Independent*, 3 July 2017, http://www.independent.co.uk/news/world/middle-east/iraq-refugee-suicide-baghdad-bomber-dressed-robe-camp-all-covering-disguise-displaced-a7820371.html

76　Nick Gutteridge, 'Dressed to kill! SAS heroes don BURKAS for raid on ISIS bunker to take down jihadi chief', *Daily Express*, 18 January 2016, https://www.express.co.uk/news/world/635517/Islamic-State-ISIS-SAS-burkas-raid-headquarters-Syria-Raqqa-jihadi-leader?utm_source=traffic.outbrain&utm_medium=traffic.outbrain&utm_term=traffic.outbrain&utm_content=traffic.outbrain&utm_campaign=traffic.outbrain

77　Al Jazeera, 'Pakistan: State of the nation', 13 August 2009, https://www.aljazeera.com/focus/2009/08/2009888238994769.html

78　Chris Woods, *Sudden Justice: America's Secret Drone Wars* (New York: Oxford University Press, 2015), 285.

79　http://www.icasualties.org/

80　https://www.iraqbodycount.org/

81　The figures for Afghanistan are based on 31,000 deaths as of August 2016 (http://watson.brown.edu/costsofwar/costs/human/civilians/afghan), around 1,900 for the second half of 2016 (https://unama.unmissions.org/afghanistan-record-level-civilian-casualties-sustained-first-half-2016-un-report and https://www.aljazeera.com/news/2017/02/afghan-civilian-casualties-2016-170206062807210.html), approximately 3,400 in 2017 (https://unama.unmissions.org/afghanistan-10000-civilian-casualties-2017-un-report-suicide-attacks-and-ieds-caused-high-number); and 763 deaths in the first quarter of 2018 (https://unama.unmissions.org/latest-un-update-records-continuing-record-high-levels-civilian-casualties-2018).

82　https://www.iraqbodycount.org/

83   Watson Institute for International and Public Affairs, Brown
      University, 'Human Costs of War: Direct War Death in Afghanistan
      and Pakistan (Oct 2001–July 2016) and Iraq (Oct 2001–April 2015),
      August 2016, http://watson.brown.edu/costsofwar/figures/2016/direct-
      war-death-toll-iraq-afghanistan-and-pakistan-2001-370000

14. Police States

1   Arthur Rizer and Joseph Hartman, 'How the War on Terror Has
     Militarized the Police', *Atlantic*, 7 November 2011, https://www.
     theatlantic.com/national/archive/2011/11/how-the-war-on-terror-has-
     militarized-the-police/248047/

2   US National Security Council, 'Overview of America's National
     Strategy for Combating Terrorism', accessed 13 June 2018, https://
     georgewbush-whitehouse.archives.gov/nsc/nsct/2006/sectionI.html

3   Dexter Filkins, '"Do Not Resist" and the Crisis of Police Militarization',
     New Yorker, 13 May 2016, https://www.newyorker.com/news/news-
     desk/do-not-resist-and-the-crisis-of-police-militarization

4   Alan Travis, 'Police Taser use in England and Wales rises to rate of 30
     times a day', *Guardian*, 13 April 2017, https://www.theguardian.com/
     uk-news/2017/apr/13/police-use-of-tasers-rises-england-and-wales

5   Lizzie Dearden, 'British police could be "routinely armed" to respond
     to terror threat in rural areas', *Independent*, 17 May 2018, https://www.
     independent.co.uk/news/uk/home-news/police-armed-routine-uk-
     terror-attacks-target-missed-recruitment-a8354926.html

6   Reuters, 'Timeline – Worst IRA bomb attacks on mainland
     Britain', 16 May 2011, https://uk.reuters.com/article/
     uk-britain-security-bombings/timeline-worst-ira-bomb-attacks-on-
     mainland-britain-idUKTRE74F31Q20110516

7   *New York Magazine*, 'NYPD: Looking for terrorists, the police look at
     everyone else.' 27 August 2011, http://nymag.com/news/9-11/10th-
     anniversary/nypd/

8   *Local Germany*, 'Elite German anti-terror unit to grow by third and
     move to Berlin', 15 January 2018, https://www.thelocal.de/20180115/
     elite-german-anti-terror-unit-to-grow-by-third-and-move-to-berlin

9   Anne-Sylvaine Chassany, 'Emmanuel Macron to establish French
     counter-terror task force', *Financial Times*, 7 June 2017, https://www.
     ft.com/content/39d8656c-4b79-11e7-919a-1e14ce4af89b

10   Martin Bentham and Justin Davenport, 'Anti-terror police to have
     new £50m HQ and training centre in London', *Evening Standard*, 11
     September 2017, https://www.standard.co.uk/news/london/antiterror-

police-to-have-new-50m-hq-and-training-centre-in-london-a3631741. html

11   BBC News, 'Met Police to get 600 more armed police to boost terror response', 14 January 2016, http://www.bbc.co.uk/news/uk-35308467

12   *Economist*, 'Jihad at the heart of Europe', 21 November 2015, https:// www.economist.com/news/briefing/2015/11/21/jihad-at-the-heart-of-europe

13   *Guardian*, 'UK police given extra £50m to fund fight against terrorism', 17 December 2017, https://www.theguardian.com/uk-news/2017/ dec/17/uk-police-given-extra-50m-to-fund-fight-against-terrorism

14   Aaron Mehta, 'Here's how much the US has spent fighting terrorism since 9/11', *DefenseNews*, 16 May 2018, https://www.defensenews.com/ pentagon/2018/05/16/heres-how-much-the-us-has-spent-fighting-terrorism-since-911/

15   Todd R. Miller, 'The Freakonomics Of Extreme Extreme Vetting', *Huffington Post*, 6 December 2017, https://www.huffingtonpost.com/ todd-r-miller/the-freakonomics-of-extre_b_11821634.html

16   John Yoo, *War by Other Means: An Insider's Account of the War on Terror* (iBooks, 2007), 174. John Yoo is former Justice Department deputy assistant attorney general.

17   James H. Jackson, *The Counter-Terrorist Handbook* (iBooks, 2013), 263.

18   Rachel Obordo, '"It would change the power dynamic": police officers on carrying guns', *Guardian*, 28 July 2017, https://www.theguardian. com/uk-news/2017/jul/28/it-would-change-the-power-dynamic-police-officers-on-carrying-guns

19   Radley Balko, 'Shedding light on the use of SWAT teams', *Washington Post*, 17 February 2014, https://www.washingtonpost.com/news/ the-watch/wp/2014/02/17/shedding-light-on-the-use-of-swat-teams/?noredirect=on&utm_term=.2cb9c35e25a7

20   *Washington Post*, 'Police shootings 2017 database', https://www. washingtonpost.com/graphics/national/police-shootings-2017/

21   Mark Honigsbaum, 'Brazilian did not wear bulky jacket', *Guardian*, 28 July 2005, https://www.theguardian.com/uk/2005/jul/28/politics.july7

22   *Daily Telegraph*, 'De Menezes "shot 11 times during 30 seconds"', 27 August 2005.

23   BBC News, 'Will police now shoot to kill?', 22 July 2005, http://news. bbc.co.uk/1/hi/uk/4707781.stm

24   John Steele, 'Shoot-to-kill tactic still viable, say police chiefs', *Daily Telegraph*, 8 March 2006, https://www.telegraph.co.uk/news/ uknews/1512406/Shoot-to-kill-tactic-still-viable-say-police-chiefs.html

25   Vikram Dodd and Ewen MacAskill, 'Shoot to kill: what is the UK's

policy?' *Guardian*, 17 November 2015, https://www.theguardian.com/
uk-news/2015/nov/17/shoot-to-kill-what-is-the-uks-policy

26   Jude McCulloch and Vicki Sentas, 'The Killing of Jean Charles De
Menezes: Hyper Militarism in the Neoliberal Economic Free Hire
Zone', *Social Justice* Vol. 33, No. 4 (2007): 92–106, 106.

27   Kevin Blowe, 'The rise of militarised policing', *Red Pepper*, 20 January
2016, https://www.redpepper.org.uk/the-rise-of-militarised-policing/

28   Quoted in David Cole, 'Are We Safer?', *New York Review of Books*, 9
March 2006.

29   Mohamedou Ould Slahi, *Guantánamo Diary* (Edinburgh: Canongate,
2015), 285.

30   *New York Times*, 'The Detainees, The Guantanamo Docket', accessed
11 May 2018, https://www.nytimes.com/interactive/projects/
guantanamo/detainees

31   Human Rights Watch, 'Guantanamo: Facts and Figures', 30 March
2017, https://www.hrw.org/video-photos/interactive/2017/03/30/
guantanamo-facts-and-figures

32   El Gharani v Bush, 593 F. Supp. 2d 144 (D.C. 2009).

33   Reprieve, '7 things you didn't know about Guantanamo Bay', accessed
11 May 2018, https://reprieve.org.uk/update/7-facts-guantanmao-bay/

34   BBC News, 'Guantanamo man tells of "torture"', 3 March 2006, http://
news.bbc.co.uk/1/hi/world/americas/4769604.stm

35   HRW, 'Guantanamo: Facts and Figures'.

36   US Department of Defense, 'Detainee Biographies', accessed 13 June
2018, http://archive.defense.gov/pdf/detaineebiographies1.pdf

37   Murtaza Hussain, 'Obama promised to close Guantánamo. Instead, he's
made it worse', *Guardian*, 6 March 2013, https://www.theguardian.com/
commentisfree/2013/mar/06/obama-promise-close-guantanamo-worse

38   US Department of Defense, 'Detainee Transfer Announced', Release
No: NR-135-18, 2 May 2018, https://www.defense.gov/News/
News-Releases/News-Release-View/Article/1510878/detainee-transfer-
announced/source/GovDelivery/

39   Jonathan Horowitz and Stacy Cammarano, '20 Extraordinary
Facts about CIA Extraordinary Rendition and Secret Detention',
Open Society Foundations, 5 February 2013, https://www.
opensocietyfoundations.org/voices/20-extraordinary-facts-about-cia-
extraordinary-rendition-and-secret-detention

40   Emily Shugerman, 'Trump defends "tough on terror" CIA director
nominee who oversaw prison where detainees were "tortured"',
Independent, 8 May 2018, https://www.independent.co.uk/news/world/
americas/us-politics/donald-trump-gina-haspel-cia-director-terrorists-
waterboarding-torture-911-a8340191.html#commentsDiv

41   El-Masri v. The Former Yugoslav Republic of Macedonia, Application No. 39630/09, Grand Chamber Judgment of 13 December 2012, European Court of Human Rights.

42   BBC News, 'Belhaj rendition: UK apology over Libyan dissident treatment', 10 May 2018, http://www.bbc.co.uk/news/uk-44070304

43   Horowitz and Cammarano, '20 Extraordinary Facts'.

44   Annabelle Timsit, 'What Happened at the Thailand "Black Site" Run by Trump's CIA Pick', *Atlantic*, 14 March 2018, https://www. theatlantic.com/international/archive/2018/03/gina-haspel-black-site-torture-cia/555539/

45   Human Rights First, '"Enhanced Interrogation" Explained', Fact Sheet, February 2016, http://www.humanrightsfirst.org/sites/default/files/Enhanced-Interrogation-Fact-Sheet.pdf

46   Andrew Sullivan, 'Trump Isn't Merely Tolerating Torture – He's Celebrating It', *New York Magazine*, 6 April 2018, http://nymag.com/daily/intelligencer/2018/04/trump-isnt-merely-tolerating-torture-hes-celebrating-it.html

47   Human Rights Watch, 'What Happens When the Gloves Come Off', 8 April 2008, https://www.hrw.org/news/2008/04/08/what-happens-when-gloves-come

48   BBC News, 'Donald Trump says he believes waterboarding works', 26 January 2017, http://www.bbc.co.uk/news/world-us-canada-38753000

49   Andrew Sullivan, 'Trump Isn't Merely Tolerating Torture – He's Celebrating It'.

50   Mark Fallon, *Unjustifiable Means: The Inside Story of How the CIA, Pentagon, and US Government Conspired to Torture* (New York: Reagan Arts, 2017), Google Scholar, 70.

51   Human Rights Watch, United States 2017 report, 'https://www.hrw.org/world-report/2018/country-chapters/united-states#9120f2

52   David Leigh, 'UK forces taught torture methods', *Guardian*, 8 May 2004, https://www.theguardian.com/uk/2004/may/08/iraq.iraq

53   Lara Whyte, '"Britain Taught the World How to Torture": Northern Ireland's Hooded Men Take New Evidence Back to Court', *Vice News*, 24 December 2014, https://news.vice.com/article/britain-taught-the-world-how-to-torture-northern-irelands-hooded-men-take-new-evidence-back-to-court

54   Liberty, 'Detention Without Charge', accessed 11 May 2018, https://www.libertyhumanrights.org.uk/human-rights/countering-terrorism/detention-without-charge

55   Clare Dyer, Michael White and Alan Travis, 'Judges' verdict on terror laws provokes constitutional crisis', *Guardian*, 17 December 2004, https://www.theguardian.com/uk/2004/dec/17/terrorism.humanrights3

56   Liberty, 'Terrorism Pre-Charge Detention Comparative Law Study',
      July 2010, https://www.libertyhumanrights.org.uk/sites/default/files/
      comparative-law-study-2010-pre-charge-detention.pdf

57   BBC News, 'Blair defeated over terror laws', 9 November 2005, http://
      news.bbc.co.uk/1/hi/uk_politics/4422086.stm

58   Liberty, 'Extended pre-charge detention', accessed 11 May 2018,
      https://www.libertyhumanrights.org.uk/human-rights/countering-
      terrorism/extended-pre-charge-detention

59   Human Rights Watch, 'Briefing Paper on U.S. Military Commissions',
      23 June 2006, http://pantheon.hrw.org/legacy/backgrounder/usa/
      gitmo0606/gitmo0606.pdf

60   Reprieve, 'UK renditions case pushed into secret court', 7 March 2017,
      https://reprieve.org.uk/press/uk-renditions-case-pushed-secret-court/

61   Christopher Hope, 'Control orders breach human rights, lords rule',
      Telegraph, 31 October 2007, https://www.telegraph.co.uk/news/
      uknews/1567882/Control-orders-breach-human-rights-lords-rule.html

62   Liberty, 'TPIMs', accessed 11 May 2018, https://www.
      libertyhumanrights.org.uk/human-rights/countering-terrorism/tpims

63   Kevin Rawlinson, 'Photographer held after taking pictures of Hove
      town hall', Guardian, 4 May 2017, https://www.theguardian.com/
      uk-news/2017/may/04/photographer-held-under-anti-terror-law-for-
      taking-hove-town-hall-pictures

64   Alexander Martin, 'Brit cops accused of abusing anti-terror laws to
      hunt colleague', Register, 17 November 2015, https://www.theregister.
      co.uk/2015/11/17/ipcc_ripa_whistleblower_cleveland

65   John Humphreys, 'Terrorism laws: Are they being abused?', YouGov.
      UK, 21 August 2013, https://yougov.co.uk/news/2013/08/21/terrorism-
      laws-are-they-being-abused/

66   FIDH, 'France International fact finding mission report. Counter-
      terrorism measures and human rights: when the exception becomes
      the norm', 8 November 2016, https://www.fidh.org/IMG/pdf/report_
      counter_terrorism_measures_human_rights.pdf, 7

67   DW News, 'Macron anti-terror law replaces French state of emergency',
      1 November 2017, http://www.dw.com/en/macron-anti-terror-law-
      replaces-french-state-of-emergency/a-41191947

68   Amnesty International, 'Upturned Lives: The disproportionate impact
      of France's State of Emergency', 4 February 2016, https://www.amnesty.
      org/download/Documents/EUR2133642016ENGLISH.pdf, 10.

69   Human Rights Watch, 'France: Abuses Under State of Emergency', 3
      February 2016, https://www.hrw.org/news/2016/02/03/france-abuses-
      under-state-emergency

70   HRW, 'Abuses Under State of Emergency'.

71 Eliza Manningham-Buller, *Securing Freedom* (London: Profile Books, 2012), 77.

72 Richard Norton-Taylor, 'Public need answers in "shocking" MI6 rendition scandal, says senior Tory', *Guardian*, 1 June 2016, https://www.theguardian.com/uk-news/2016/jun/01/mi5-chief-right-to-be-disgusted-over-mi6-role-rendition-blair

73 William Jordan, 'People in Britain divided over use of torture', YouGov UK, 11 December 2014, https://yougov.co.uk/news/2014/12/11/people-in-Britain-divided-over-use-of-torture/

74 Andrew Fowler, 'Shooting the messenger: the "chilling effect" of criminalising journalism', *Guardian*, 23 June 2018, https://www.theguardian.com/media/2018/jun/24/shooting-the-messenger-the-chilling-effect-of-criminalising-journalism?CMP=share_btn_tw

75 US Department of State, 'Patterns of Global Terrorism 2003', 68, https://www.state.gov/j/ct/rls/crt/2003/index.htm

76 US Department of State, 'Country Reports on Terrorism 2008', 13, https://www.state.gov/j/ct/rls/crt/2008/index.htm

77 R.A. Neefjes, 'Counterterrorism Policy in Morocco', (Master thesis, Utrecht University, 2017), 21, https://dspace.library.uu.nl/handle/1874/353663

78 Human Rights Watch, 'Morocco: End Abuses in Counterterrorism Arrests', 25 October 2010, https://www.hrw.org/news/2010/10/25/morocco-end-abuses-counterterrorism-arrests

79 *International Convention on Civil and Political Rights.* Article 17. http://www.ohchr.org/EN/ProfessionalInterest/Pages/CCPR.aspx

80 *Information and Communication Technology Act 2006.* Chapter VIII, Section 57. http://www.icnl.org/research/library/files/Bangladesh/comm2006.pdf

81 Mohammad Badruzzaman, 'Controversial Issues of Section-57 of the ICT Act, 2006: A Critical Analysis and Evaluation', *IOSR Journal of Humanities and Social Sciences.* Vol. 21, Issue 1 (2016): 62–71. http://www.iosrjournals.org/iosr-jhss/papers/Vol.%2021%20Issue1/Version-2/L021126271.pdf

82 FIDH, 'Amendment to Anti-Terrorism Act Further Undermines Compliance with International Human Rights Standards', 23 February 2012, https://www.fidh.org/en/region/asia/bangladesh/Amendment-to-Anti-Terrorism-Act

83 Federal Law No. 374 of 6 July 2016, 'Amending the Federal Counter-Terrorism Act and Certain Legislative Acts of the Russian Federation Regarding the Establishment of Additional Measures to Counter Terrorism and Ensure Public Safety', and Federal Law No. 375 of 6 July 2016, 'Amending the Criminal Code of the Russian Federation and the

Code of Criminal Procedure of the Russian Federation with Regard to the Establishment of Additional Measures to Counter Terrorism and Ensure Public Safety'.

84   Monica D. Blumenthal et al., *More About Justifying Violence: Methodological Studies of Attitudes and Behavior* (Ann Arbor: Survey Research Center, Institute for Social Research, University of Michigan, 1975), 182.

85   https://www.counterterrorexpo.com

86   http://www.atom-training.com

87   Asqella, 'Argon', accessed 13 June 2018, https://asqella.com/argon/

88   Sanjay Sharma and Jasbinder Nijjar, 'The racialized surveillant assemblage: Islam and the fear of terrorism', *Popular Communication* 16.1 (2018): 72–85.

89   Jason Zengerle, 'Homeland Security: Big threats, bigger government.' *New York Magazine*, 27 August 2011, http://nymag.com/news/9-11/10th-anniversary/homeland-security/

90   Kimberly Kindy, 'Ex-Homeland Security chief head said to abuse public trust by touting body scanners', *Washington Post*, 1 January 2010, http://www.washingtonpost.com/wp-dyn/content/article/2009/12/31/AR2009123102821.html

91   James Ridgeway, 'The Airport Scanner Scam', *Mother Jones*, 4 January 2010, https://www.motherjones.com/politics/2010/01/airport-scanner-scam/

92   Dana Priest and William M. Arkin, 'Top Secret America', *Washington Post,* 19 July 2010.

93   European Commission, 'Security Union: Protecting Public Spaces', EU Mayors' Conference: 'Building Urban Defences Against Terrorism', 8 March 2018, https://ec.europa.eu/home-affairs/sites/homeaffairs/files/what-we-do/policies/european-agenda-security/20180308_security-union-protecting-public-spaces_en.pdf

94   European Commission, 'Security Union: Commission presents new measures to better protect EU citizens', 18 October 2017, http://europa.eu/rapid/press-release_IP-17-3947_en.htm

95   https://www.youtube.com/watch?time_continue=79&v=G7_OIkwLnwo

96   Royal Institute of British Architects, 'RIBA guidance on designing for counter-terrorism', 2016, https://web.archive.org/web/20160914071117/http://www.frontierpitts.com/fileadmin/user_upload/downloads/nactso/RIBAguidanceoncounterterrorism.pdf

97   BBC News, 'New York to install 1,500 security barriers after vehicle attacks', 3 January 2018, http://www.bbc.co.uk/news/world-us-canada-42553057

98   Patrick Sawer, 'Wimbledon ring of steel: Security barriers to prevent
      London Bridge-style attack', *Daily Telegraph*, 29 June 2017, https://
      www.telegraph.co.uk/news/2017/06/29/wimbledon-ring-steel-security-
      barriers-prevent-london-bridge/

99   Judith Evans, 'Anti-terror architecture easy on the eye', *Financial Times*,
      15 May 2017, https://www.ft.com/content/4b90465a-1f99-11e7-b7d3-
      163f5a7f229c

100   UK Parliament, 'Churchill and the Commons Chamber', accessed 13
      June 2018, http://www.parliament.uk/about/living-heritage/building/
      palace/architecture/palacestructure/churchill/

101   Robert Bevan, *The Destruction of Memory* (London: Reaktion Books,
      2006), 87.

102   NDTV, 'New York Police Poised To Thwart New Year's Eve Suicide
      Bombers', 29 December 2017, https://www.ndtv.com/world-news/
      new-york-police-poised-to-thwart-new-years-eve-suicide-
      bombers-1793347

103   Stephen Johnson, '"It's just evil": Church overlooking Sydney Harbour
      forced to cancel their popular New Year's Eve fireworks party over
      TERROR fears – because they can't afford the $10,000 bill for security
      and bollards to stop an attack', *Daily Mail Australia*, 28 December
      2017, http://www.dailymail.co.uk/news/article-5216855/Sydney-
      Harbour-church-forced-New-Years-Eve-party.html

104   Maximiliano E. Korstanje and Anthony Clayton, 'Tourism and
      terrorism: conflicts and commonalities', *Worldwide Hospitality and
      Tourism Themes* 4.1 (2012): 8–25.

105   Channel News Asia, 'Suicide belts found after attack at Jordan tourist
      spot', 19 December 2016, https://www.channelnewsasia.com/news/
      world/suicide-belts-found-after-attack-at-jordan-tourist-spot-7664294

106   *Hürriyet*, 'Turkey sees steepest decline in monthly foreign arrivals
      since May 1999', 27 May 2016, http://www.hurriyetdailynews.
      com/turkey-sees-steepest-decline-in-monthly-foreign-arrivals-
      since-may-1999-99740

107   Ayla Jean Yackley, 'Suicide bomber kills 10 people, mainly Germans,
      in Istanbul', Reuters, 13 January 2016, https://www.reuters.com/article/
      us-turkey-blast/suicide-bomber-kills-10-people-mainly-germans-in-
      istanbul-idUSKCN0UQ0UJ20160113

108   *CNN Travel*, '18 best places to visit in 2018', 10 March 2018, https://
      edition.cnn.com/travel/article/places-to-visit-2018/index.html

109   Paul Theroux, 'Paul Theroux – 9/11 ten years on', *Daily Telegraph*,
      11 September 2011, http://www.telegraph.co.uk/news/worldnews/
      september-11-attacks/8722089/Paul-Theroux-911-ten-years-on.html

110   Airline Industry Information, 'Pilot arrested at Philadelphia
      airport', 14 January 2002, https://www.thefreelibrary.com/
      Pilot+arrested+at+Philadelphia+airport.-a081765053

111   Barbara Peterson, 'How Airport Security Has Changed Since 9/11',
      Condé Nast Traveler, 10 September 2016, https://www.cntraveler.com/
      story/how-airport-security-has-changed-since-september-11

112   Melanie Zanona, 'How airport security lines got so bad', *The Hill*,
      28 May 2016, http://thehill.com/policy/transportation/281574-how-
      airport-security-lines-got-so-bad

113   Barbara Peterson, 'TSA Scanners Removed From Airports: What
      Fliers Need to Know', *Condé Nast Traveler*, 22 January 2013, https://
      www.cntraveler.com/stories/2013-01-22/tsa-scanners-removed-from-
      airports-what-fliers-need-to-know-012213

114   Barbara Peterson, 'Airport security scandal', *Popular Mechanics*, 1
      December 2012, http://www.popularmechanics.co.za/tech/airport-
      security-scandal/

115   Spencer Ackerman, 'TSA screening program risks racial profiling
      amid shaky science – study', *Guardian*, 8 February 2017, https://www.
      theguardian.com/us-news/2017/feb/08/tsa-screening-racial-religious-
      profiling-aclu-study

116   Stefano Bonino, 'How discrimination against Muslims at airports
      actually hurts the fight against terrorism', *Washington Post*, 26
      August 2016, https://www.washingtonpost.com/news/monkey-cage/
      wp/2016/08/26/how-discrimination-against-muslims-at-airports-
      actually-hurts-the-fight-against-terrorism/?utm_term=.c681cfd94dde

117   Joseph Pugliese, 'Biotypologies of terrorism', *Cultural Studies Review*
      14, no. 2 (2008): 49.

118   US Department of Homeland Security, 'Implementing 9/11
      Commission Recommendations', 14 July 2017, https://www.dhs.gov/
      implementing-911-commission-recommendations

119   *Security Today*, 'Minneapolis Airport TSA Fails 95 Per cent of Security
      Tests', 11 July 2017, https://securitytoday.com/articles/2017/07/11/
      minneapolis-airport-tsa-fails-95-per cent-of-security-tests.aspx

120   Sam Rega, 'If you think the TSA is bad, this is how much worse
      airport security is around the world', *Business Insider UK*, 4 August
      2016, http://uk.businessinsider.com/airport-security-world-countries-
      international-travel-tsa-2016-8

121   Ruth Sherlock, 'Poor airport security in Egypt is a "cultural problem",
      says Philip Hammond', *Daily Telegraph*, 10 November 2015, http://
      www.telegraph.co.uk/news/worldnews/africaandindianocean/
      egypt/11987303/Poor-airport-security-in-Egypt-is-a-cultural-problem-
      says-Philip-Hammond.html

122   Simon Tomlinson and Martin Robinson, 'British passengers
       reveal Sharm airport staff are STILL taking cash to help them
       skip busy security queues despite bomb threat', *Daily Mail*, 5
       November 2015, http://www.dailymail.co.uk/news/article-3305011/
       Security-staff-played-Candy-Crush-smoked-cigarettes-SLEPT-duty-
       British-tourists-reveal-shock-lax-airport-safety-Sharm.html

123   Nicole Arce, 'TSA full-body scanner may not detect guns, bombs
       and knives', *Tech Times*, 22 August 2014, http://www.techtimes.com/
       articles/13617/20140822/tsa-full-body-scanner-may-not-detect-guns-
       bombs-and-knives.htm

124   Siobhan Morrissey, 'Eyewitness: "I Never Heard the Word 'Bomb'"',
       Time, 8 December 2005, http://content.time.com/time/nation/
       article/0,8599,1138965,00.html

125   *Economist*, 'An air marshal leaves her loaded gun in a plane toilet',
       24 April 2017, https://www.economist.com/blogs/gulliver/2017/04/
       hidden-plane-sight

126   Jason Edward Harrington, 'TSA's failures start long before screeners
       fail to detect bombs in security tests', *Guardian*, 7 June 2015, https://
       www.theguardian.com/commentisfree/2015/jun/07/tsa-failures-
       bombs-tests

127   Stratfor, 'AQAP and the Secrets of the Innovative Bomb', 24 February
       2010, https://www.stratfor.com/sample/analysis/aqap-and-secrets-
       innovative-bomb

128   Associated Press, 'Moscow faces 130 fake bomb calls, forcing removal
       of 100,000 people', 6 October 2017, http://www.cbc.ca/beta/news/
       world/moscow-fake-bomb-calls-1.4344236

129   Barbara Ellen, 'No terrorists, but Oxford St panic was still terrifying',
       Guardian, 26 November 2017, https://www.theguardian.com/
       commentisfree/2017/nov/26/no-terrorists-but-oxford-street-panic-
       was-still-terrifying

130   Bill Gertz, '5,000 in U.S. Suspected of Ties to al Qaeda; Groups
       Nationwide Under Surveillance', *Washington Times*, 11 July 2002;
       and Richard Sale, 'US al Qaida Cells Attacked', *UPI*, 31 October
       2002, https://www.upi.com/UPI-Special-US-al-Qaida-cells-
       attacked/75381036108294/

131   Director Mueller's testimony can be found at http://www.fbi.gov/
       congress/congress.htm

132   Rupert Cornwell, 'CIA attacked for "gross exaggeration" of Saddam's
       WMD threat in official US report', *Independent*, 8 July 2004, https://
       www.independent.co.uk/news/world/americas/cia-attacked-for-gross-
       exaggeration-of-saddams-wmd-threat-in-official-us-report-552427.
       html

133   David Bamber, Olga Craig and Francis Elliott, 'Blair sent in tanks after "chilling" threat', *Daily Telegraph*, 16 February 2003, https://www.telegraph.co.uk/news/uknews/1422243/Blair-sent-in-tanks-after-chilling-threat.html

15. Generation Terror

1   Marco Margaritoff, 'Senate Bill Could Grant Homeland Security Power to Seize and Destroy Your Personal Drone', *Drive*, 11 June 2018, http://www.thedrive.com/tech/21453/senate-bill-could-grant-homeland-security-power-to-seize-and-destroy-your-personal-drone

2   Daniel Howden, 'By rejecting a migrant ship, Italian populists are simply following the EU's lead', *Guardian*, 11 June 2018, https://www.theguardian.com/commentisfree/2018/jun/11/italy-migrant-rescue-ship-standoff-aquarius

3   *Moneycontrol News*, 'Mouse movements to storage space — All the data that Facebook sucks up to track users', 13 June 2018, https://www.moneycontrol.com/news/technology/mouse-movements-to-storage-space-here-are-surprising-data-which-facebook-sucks-up-2589141.html

4   Liam Denning, 'Trump's latest "national security" plan for energy is about insecurity', *Business Times*, 5 June 2018, https://www.businesstimes.com.sg/energy-commodities/trumps-latest-national-security-plan-for-energy-is-about-insecurity

5   Eric Wang, 'Maryland lawmakers voted to criminalize online speech in the name of security', *Washington Examiner*, 17 May 2018, https://www.washingtonexaminer.com/opinion/op-eds/maryland-lawmakers-voted-to-criminalize-online-speech-in-the-name-of-security

6   Human Rights Watch, 'Burkina Faso: Killings, Abuse in Sahel Conflict', 21 May 2018, https://www.hrw.org/news/2018/05/21/burkina-faso-killings-abuse-sahel-conflict

7   *Independent*, 'We should all be concerned about our images being stored by the Government, even if it is in the name of security', 21 January 2018, https://www.independent.co.uk/voices/editorials/cctv-surveillance-facial-recognition-storing-images-a8171131.html

8   *Daily Mail*, 'The Daily Mail, the most influential paper in Britain', 2 December 2010, http://www.dailymail.co.uk/news/article-1334894/The-Daily-Mail-influential-paper-Britain.html

9   See: *Daily Mail*, 'When "human rights" are an insult to us all', 21 August 2007, http://www.dailymail.co.uk/news/article-476633/When-human-rights-insult-all.html; *Daily Mail*, 'A nation imperilled by

the Human Rights Act', 1 August 2015, http://www.dailymail.co.uk/
debate/article-3181945/DAILY-MAIL-COMMENT-nation-imperilled-
Human-Rights-Act.html; *Daily Mail*, 'DAILY MAIL COMMENT:
Sorry, human rights DO shield terrorists', 8 June 2017, http://www.
dailymail.co.uk/debate/article-4583006/DAILY-MAIL-COMMENT-
Human-rights-shield-terrorists.html; and *Daily Mail*, 'Now Theresa
May's human rights pledge is axed: Anger as the PM is forced to keep
law that helps terrorists to avoid justice', 14 June 2017, http://www.
dailymail.co.uk/news/article-4601660/Anger-Theresa-forced-axe-
human-rights-pledge.html

10   Sam Greenhill, 'Fighting fund for jailed Marine tops £750,000: More
than 30,000 generous readers help his battle for justice', *Daily Mail*,
5 October 2015, http://www.dailymail.co.uk/news/article-3259939/
Fighting-fund-jailed-Marine-tops-750-000-30-000-generous-readers-
help-battle-justice.html

11   Alseran and Others v. Ministry of Defence, EWHC 3289 (QB),
14 December 2017, http://www.bailii.org/ew/cases/EWHC/
QB/2017/3289.html#para538

12   Tim Shipman and Arthur Martin, 'Human right to make a
killing: Damning dossier reveals taxpayers' bill for European
court payouts to murderers, terrorists and traitors', *Daily Mail*, 7
October 2013, http://www.dailymail.co.uk/news/article-2449256/
Human-right-make-killing-Damning-dossier-reveals-taxpayers-
European-court-payouts-murderers-terrorists-traitors.html

13   *Daily Mail*, 'Clarifications and corrections', 10 November 2013, http://
www.dailymail.co.uk/home/article-2498733/Clarifications-corrections-
European-Court-Human-Rights.html

14   Ryan Grenoble, 'This Daily Mail Anti-Refugee Cartoon Is Straight
Out Of Nazi Germany', *Huffington Post*, 17 November 2015, https://
www.huffingtonpost.com/entry/daily-mail-nazi-refugee-rat-cartoon_
us_564b526ee4b06037734ae115

15   Katie Hopkins, 'Welcome to London: We can say we're not afraid, light
candles and make hearts of our hands but the truth is that we can't
go on like this, says KATIE HOPKINS', *Daily Mail*, 22 March 2017,
http://www.dailymail.co.uk/debate/article-4340290/Truth-t-like-says-
KATIE-HOPKINS.html#ixzz5ERoz6VUk

16   Katie Hopkins, 'Don't let the new politically correct language of
slaughter fool you. Terrorism by any other name is still as terrifying',
Daily Mail, 25 July 2016, http://www.dailymail.co.uk/debate/
article-3706857/KATIE-HOPKINS-Don-t-let-new-politically-correct-
language-slaughter-fool-Terrorism-terrifying.html

17   Douglas Patient, 'REVEALED: SAS commandos packed with

firepower to take out terrorists', *Daily Star*, 25 May 2017, https://www.dailystar.co.uk/news/latest-news/617351/Manchester-bombing-SAS-commandos-soldiers-Brit-streets-terrorists

18 Tom Pettifor, 'Armed troops patrol streets as security services hunt mastermind bomb maker behind Manchester Arena terror attack', *Daily Mirror*, 24 May 2017, https://www.mirror.co.uk/news/uk-news/armed-troops-patrol-streets-security-10493625

19 Ben Farmer, '1,000 troops on the streets after Manchester bombing attack', *Daily Telegraph*, 24 May 2017, https://www.telegraph.co.uk/news/2017/05/24/1000-troops-streets-manchester-bombing-attack/

20 Laura Mowat, 'TERROR WATCH: SAS troops "posing as homeless beggars across UK streets" to foil attacks', *Daily Express*, 14 June 2017, https://www.express.co.uk/news/uk/817190/SAS-troops-pose-homeless-beggars-terror-attacks

21 Harry Cole and Lynn Davidson, 'CORBINEXCUSABLE Theresa May lashes out at Jeremy Corbyn for speech linking Manchester bombing to government's war on terror just four days after atrocity left 22 dead', *Sun*, 26 May 2017, https://www.thesun.co.uk/news/3655714/theresa-may-jeremy-corbyn-manchester-bombing-speech-war-on-terror-uk-general-election-2017/

22 Hassan Morajea et al., 'Manchester Bomber Believed Muslims Were Mistreated, Sought Revenge', *Wall Street Journal*, 25 May 2017, https://www.wsj.com/articles/manchester-bomber-fought-in-libya-1495662073

23 JIC Assessment, 'INTERNATIONAL TERRORISM: WAR WITH IRAQ', 10 February 2003, http://webarchive.nationalarchives.gov.uk/20171123123130/http://www.iraqinquiry.org.uk/media/230918/2003-02-10-jic-assessment-international-terrorism-war-with-iraq.pdf

24 Tom McTague and Jennifer Smith, 'Miliband MUST condemn "apologist for terror" John Prescott after he said BRITAIN is to blame for ISIS fanatics, MPs demand', *Daily Mail*, 22 March 2015, http://www.dailymail.co.uk/news/article-3006583/John-Prescott-accused-apologist-terror-claiming-BRITAIN-blame-fanatics-joining-ISIS.html

25 *Daily Mail*, 'Labour's apologists for terror: The Mail accuses Corbyn troika of befriending Britain's enemies and scorning the institutions that keep us safe', 6 June 2017, http://www.dailymail.co.uk/news/article-4578716/Apologists-terror-Corbyn-McDonnell-Abbott.html

26 Daily Mail, 'DAILY MAIL COMMENT: The bloody price paid for liberal weakness', 24 May 2017, http://www.dailymail.co.uk/debate/article-4535892/DAILY-MAIL-COMMENT-Bloody-price-paid-liberal-weakness.html

27 Mia Bloom, *Dying to Kill: The Allure of Suicide Terror* (New York: Columbia University Press, 2005).

28 Nathan Woolley, 'Opinion: Are explosive weapons more newsworthy?' Action on Armed Violence, 4 November 2015, https://aoav.org. uk/2015/opinion-are-explosive-weapons-more-newsworthy/. Not all things, though, are equal in the world of news. A suicide bombing in the heart of Europe will garner significantly more coverage, and sympathetic headlines, than an attack in the Middle East or North Africa.

29 https://vimeo.com/108682934

30 https://www.youtube.com/watch?v=r02x8gd2v-M

31 https://www.youtube.com/watch?v=nSHQRG-SJkM

32 https://www.youtube.com/watch?v=aHjRQJZsUGg

33 https://www.youtube.com/watch?v=zMSO5mHqFLM

34 https://www.youtube.com/watch?v=vQWmd8REdaE

35 https://www.youtube.com/watch?v=-7LsxKkhozg

36 https://www.youtube.com/watch?v=6Kfqy-8C30o

37 https://www.youtube.com/watch?v=fOhAlProx4U

38 https://www.youtube.com/watch?v=N7JGgdFRero

39 https://www.youtube.com/watch?v=C2tVryPy1uw

40 https://www.youtube.com/watch?v=smQuGbcwNps

41 Krista De Castella, Craig McGarty, and Luke Musgrove, 'Fear appeals in political rhetoric about terrorism: An analysis of speeches by Australian Prime Minister Howard', *Political Psychology* 30.1 (2009): 1–26.

42 Simon Tisdall and Richard Norton-Taylor, 'Barack Obama accused of exaggerating terror threat for political gain', *Guardian*, 7 October 2010, https://www.theguardian.com/world/2010/oct/07/barack-obama-terror-threat-claims

43 Simon Jenkins, 'Enough of Theresa May's outrage. We need a tough response to terror', *Guardian*, 24 May 2017, https://www.theguardian.com/commentisfree/2017/may/24/manchester-theresa-may-outrage-tough-response-terror

44 Anna Getmansky and Thomas Zeitzoff, 'Terrorism and voting: The effect of rocket threat on voting in Israeli elections', *American Political Science Review* 108.3 (2014): 588–604.

45 Jose G. Montalvo, 'Voting after the bombings: A natural experiment on the effect of terrorist attacks on democratic elections', *Review of Economics and Statistics* 93.4 (2011): 1146–54.

46 Robert Pape, 'The Strategic Logic of Suicide Terrorism', *American Political Science Review* 97 (2003): 343–61.

47 Pamela Engel, 'DONALD TRUMP: "I would bomb the s---

out of" ISIS', *Business Insider UK*, 13 November 2015, http://
uk.businessinsider.com/donald-trump-bomb-isis-2015-11

48   *Business Insider Australia*, 'TONY ABBOTT: "Islamophobia hasn't
killed anyone"', 4 June 2017, http://www.businessinsider.com/tony-
abbott-islamophobia-hasnt-killed-anyone-2017-6?IR=T

49   https://www.youtube.com/watch?v=C-ZjotfZY6o

50   Ray Marcano, 'Donald Trump said this about racial profiling, and it's
sure to spark debate', *Palm Beach Post*, 20 June 2016, https://www.
palmbeachpost.com/news/national/donald-trump-said-this-about-
racial-profiling-and-sure-spark-debate/fm56R9VlKYsryXiarlc1kL/

51   Tal Kopan, 'Donald Trump: I meant that Obama founded ISIS,
literally', CNN, 12 August 2016, http://edition.cnn.com/2016/08/11/
politics/donald-trump-hugh-hewitt-obama-founder-isis/index.html

52   Felicia Schwartz and Ben Kesling, 'Countries Under U.S. Entry Ban
Aren't Main Sources of Terror Attacks', *Wall Street Journal*, 29 January
2017, https://www.wsj.com/articles/countries-under-u-s-entry-ban-
arent-main-sources-of-terror-attacks-1485708300

53   Emile Nakhleh, 'I worked in the CIA under Bush. Obama is right to
not say "radical Islam"', *Vox*, 21 September 2016, https://www.vox.
com/2016/6/28/12046626/phrase-islamic-radicalism-meaningless-
counterproductive

54   Reuters, 'Most American voters support limited travel ban: poll', 5 July
2017, https://www.reuters.com/article/us-usa-immigration-poll/most-
american-voters-support-limited-travel-ban-poll-idUSKBN19Q2FW

55   Miranda Green, 'Homeland secretary: People would "never leave the
house" if they knew what I knew', CNN, 26 May 2017, https://amp.
cnn.com/cnn/2017/05/26/politics/john-kelly-terror-threat-people-
wouldnt-leave-the-house/index.html

56   *New America*, 'Terrorism in America After 9/11: Part IV. What is the
Threat to the United States Today?', accessed 15 June 2018, https://
www.newamerica.org/in-depth/terrorism-in-america/what-threat-
united-states-today/#americas-layered-defenses

57   Linda Qiu, 'Fact-checking a comparison of gun deaths and terrorism
deaths', *Politifact*, 5 October 2015, http://www.politifact.com/
truth-o-meter/statements/2015/oct/05/viral-image/fact-checking-
comparison-gun-deaths-and-terrorism-/

58   Human Rights Watch, 'In the Name of Security: Counterterrorism
Laws Worldwide since September 11', June 2012, https://www.hrw.org/
sites/default/files/reports/global0612ForUploadFinal.pdf

59   Kim Ghattas, 'The United States of Islamophobia', Foreign Policy, 5
July 2016, https://foreignpolicy.com/2016/07/05/the-united-states-of-
islamophobia/

60 Shibley Telhami, 'What Americans really think about Muslims and Islam', *Brookings*, 9 December 2015, https://www.brookings.edu/blog/markaz/2015/12/09/what-americans-really-think-about-muslims-and-islam/

61 Joel Rogers de Waal, 'The majority of voters doubt that Islam is compatible with British values', YouGov, 30 March 2015, https://yougov.co.uk/news/2015/03/30/majority-voters-doubt-islam-compatible-british-val/

62 Jim Mann, 'Britain Uncovered survey results: the attitudes and beliefs of Britons in 2015', *Guardian*, 19 April 2015, https://www.theguardian.com/society/2015/apr/19/britain-uncovered-survey-attitudes-beliefs-britons-2015

63 See: Pew Research Center, 'Unfavourable Views of Jews and Muslims on the Increase in Europe', 17 September 2008, http://www.pewglobal.org/2008/09/17/unfavorable-views-of-jews-and-muslims-on-the-increase-in-europe; Change Institute, *Summary Report: Understanding Muslim Ethnic Communities* (London: Crown Copyright, April 2009), http://webarchive.nationalarchives.gov.uk/20120919132719/http://www.communities.gov.uk/documents/communities/pdf/1203896.pdf; Department for Communities and Local Government, *Race, Religion and Equalities: AR on the 2009–10 Citizenship Survey* (London: Crown Copyright, 2011), http://www.tedcantle.co.uk/publications/067%20Citizen%20Survey%202011%20race%20religion%20equalities.pdf

64 Bertrand Russell, 'An outline of intellectual rubbish', in *Unpopular Essays* (New York: Simon and Schuster, 1950), 71–111.

65 European Monitoring Centre on Racism and Xenophobia, 'The Impact of 7 July 2005 London Bomb Attacks on Muslim Communities in the EU', November 2005, http://fra.europa.eu/en/publication/2005/impact-7-july-2005-london-bomb-attacks-muslim-communities-eu

66 Pew Research Center, 'U.S. Muslims Concerned About Their Place in Society, but Continue to Believe in the American Dream', 26 July 2017, http://www.pewforum.org/2017/07/26/findings-from-pew-research-centers-2017-survey-of-us-muslims/

67 Crimes of Britain, Twitter post, 23 January 2018, 5:02 a.m., https://twitter.com/crimesofbrits/status/955787771695763461

68 BBC News, 'Mosque bomber Pavlo Lapshyn given life for murder', 25 October 2013, https://www.bbc.co.uk/news/uk-england-birmingham-24675040

69 Julia Ebner, *The Rage: The Vicious Circle of Islamist and Far-Right Extremism* (London and New York: I.B. Tauris, 2017), 153.

70 Pressreader, 'What the editorials said', 23 September 2017, https://www.pressreader.com/uk/the-week/20170923/281535111172434

71 Lizzie Dearden, 'Damning report condemns rising "racist violence and hate speech" by politicians and press in post-Brexit UK', *Independent*, 4 October 2016, https://www.independent.co.uk/news/uk/home-news/brexit-david-cameron-nigel-farage-council-of-europe-report-racist-violence-intolerance-hate-speech-a7345166.html#commentsDiv

72 Jacob Poushter, 'European opinions of the refugee crisis in 5 charts', Pew Research Center, 16 September 2016, http://www.pewresearch.org/fact-tank/2016/09/16/european-opinions-of-the-refugee-crisis-in-5-charts/

73 Kathy Frankovic, 'A nation divided over immigration, terrorism, and the courts', YouGov, 16 February 2017, https://today.yougov.com/topics/politics/articles-reports/2017/02/16/immigration-terrorism-courts-nation-divided

74 Jan Velinger, 'Terrorism, Migration, Weakening of Christian Values Top Concerns for Czechs in 2018', *Radio Praha*, 2 January 2018, http://www.radio.cz/en/section/curraffrs/terrorism-migration-weakening-of-christian-values-top-concerns-for-czechs-in-2018

75 Andrew Russell and Ryan Rocca, 'Canadians are concerned refugees pose a terror threat. Should they be worried?' *Global News*, 6 July 2017, https://globalnews.ca/news/3568629/canadians-are-concerned-refugees-pose-a-terror-threat-should-they-be-worried/

76 Action on Armed Violence, '85 per cent of refugees in Europe are fleeing explosive violence, AOAV study finds', 2 April 2017, https://aoav.org.uk/2017/press-release-85-refugees-europe-fleeing-explosive-violence-new-research-finds/

77 Megan McArdle, 'Europe's Wave of Migration Brought Too Many Men', *Bloomberg*, 9 August 2016, https://www.bloomberg.com/view/articles/2016-08-09/europe-s-wave-of-migration-brought-too-many-men

78 Ruchi Kumar, 'Europe sends Afghans back to danger', *IRIN*, 4 January 2018, http://www.irinnews.org/news/2018/01/04/europe-sends-afghans-back-danger

79 BBC News, 'EU to sue Poland, Hungary and Czechs for refusing refugee quotas', 7 December 2017, https://www.bbc.co.uk/news/world-europe-42270239

80 Action on Armed Violence, 'The Refugee Explosion – Case study: the UK', 2 April 2017, https://aoav.org.uk/2017/refugee-explosion-case-study-uk/

81 Louise Casey, 'Executive Summary to The Casey Review: A review into opportunity and integration', December 2016, https://assets.publishing.service.gov.uk/government/uploads/system/uploads/attachment_data/file/575975/The_Casey_Review_Executive_Summary.pdf

82   Pew Research Center, 'Being Christian in Western Europe', 29 May
      2018, http://www.pewforum.org/2018/05/29/being-christian-in-
      western-europe/

83   Chloe Farand, 'Marine Le Pen launches presidential
      campaign with hardline speech', *Independent*, 5 February
      2017, https://www.independent.co.uk/news/world/europe/
      marine-le-pen-front-national-speech-campaign-launch-islamic-
      fundamentalism-french-elections-a7564051.html

84   BBC News, 'German election: Merkel vows to win back right-wing
      voters', 25 September 2017, http://www.bbc.co.uk/news/world-
      europe-41384550

85   Dominic Cummings, 'Dominic Cummings: how the Brexit
      referendum was won', *Spectator*, 9 January 2017, https://blogs.spectator.
      co.uk/2017/01/dominic-cummings-brexit-referendum-won/

86   Mikey Smith, 'This Brexit campaign was forced to correct its racist
      tweet about "Londonistan" – and every statistic is still false', *Daily
      Mirror*, 5 April 2018, https://www.mirror.co.uk/news/politics/brexit-
      campaign-forced-correct-its-12312548

87   BBC News, 'Boris Johnson compares Chequers deal to "suicide vest"', 9
      September 2018, https://www.bbc.co.uk/news/uk-politics-45462900

88   Ben Collins, Kevin Poulsen and Spencer Ackerman, 'Exclusive:
      Russians Impersonated Real American Muslims to Stir Chaos on
      Facebook and Instagram', *Daily Beast*, 27 September 2017, https://
      www.thedailybeast.com/exclusive-russians-impersonated-real-
      american-muslims-to-stir-chaos-on-facebook-and-instagram

89   Tim Lister and Clare Sebastian, 'Stoking Islamophobia and secession
      in Texas – from an office in Russia', CNN, 6 October 2017, https://
      edition.cnn.com/2017/10/05/politics/heart-of-texas-russia-event/
      index.html

90   Robert Booth et al., 'Russia used hundreds of fake accounts to tweet
      about Brexit, data shows', *Guardian*, 14 November 2017, https://
      www.theguardian.com/world/2017/nov/14/how-400-russia-run-fake-
      accounts-posted-bogus-brexit-tweets

91   Guy Verhofstadt, Twitter post, 13 June 2018, 2:06 a.m., https://twitter.
      com/guyverhofstadt/status/1006825171888623618

92   Amanda Taub and Max Fisher, 'Facebook Fueled Anti-Refugee Attacks
      in Germany, New Research Suggests', *New York Times*, 21 August 2018,
      https://www.nytimes.com/2018/08/21/world/europe/facebook-refugee-
      attacks-germany.html

93   Jennifer Dathan, 'Explosive Truths: Monitoring explosive violence
      in 2016', Action on Armed Violence, April 2017, https://aoav.org.uk/
      wp-content/uploads/2017/05/AOAV-Explosive-Monitor-2017v9.pdf

94   Mary Wareham, 'It's Time For a Binding, Absolute Ban on Fully
      Autonomous Weapons', Human Rights Watch, 9 November 2017,
      https://www.hrw.org/news/2017/11/09/its-time-binding-absolute-ban-
      fully-autonomous-weapons

95   These are the: Convention on Certain Conventional Weapons
      (Amended Protocol II (2008–2016)): Open-ended informal Group of
      Experts on Improvised Explosive Devices under Amended Protocol II;
      UN Security Council sanctions regimes pursuant to resolutions 1267
      (1999), 1989 (2011), and 2253 (2015) concerning ISIS, Al-Qaeda and
      associated groups; Preventing Terrorists from Acquiring Weapons (S/
      RES/2370), Resolution on Mine Action (S/RES/2365); A/RES/70/46
      (2015): Countering the threat posed by improvised explosive devices;
      and A/71/187 (2016) Report of the Secretary-General: Countering the
      threat posed by improvised explosive devices (drafted pursuant to A/
      RES/70/46(2015) paragraph 16.).

96   International Campaign to Ban Landmines – Cluster Munition
      Coalition, 'Landmine Monitor 2017', December 2017, http://www.the-
      monitor.org/media/2615219/Landmine-Monitor-2017_final.pdf

97   Dathan, 'Explosive Truths: Monitoring explosive violence in 2016'.
      The 2017 Landmine Monitor Report says there were 8,605 reported
      casualties of landmines and explosive remnants of war in 2016, 78
      per cent of them civilians, but such a monitor does not record suicide
      attacks. The Chicago Suicide Database stopped running in 2016. So
      the only monitor that records both landmine harm and suicide bomb
      harm is Action on Armed Violence's.

98   Chris Loughran, 'MAG Policy Brief Humanitarian Response,
      Improvised Landmines and IEDs Policy issues for principled
      mine action', November 2016, https://www.maginternational.org/
      download/58380ceb366ff

99   This is one of the four key humanitarian principles. OCHA on
      Message: Humanitarian Principles, June 2012, https://docs.unocha.
      org/sites/dms/Documents/OOM-humanitarianprinciples_eng_June12.
      pdf

100   Armida van Rij, Hannah Bryce, Benedict Wilkinson and Maxine
      Vining, 'Defining the device: The need for international humanitarian
      standards for improvised explosive device disposal', King's College
      London Policy Institute, April 2017, http://www.kcl.ac.uk/sspp/policy-
      institute/publications/Defining-the-device.pdf

101   Interpol, 'International Counter-Improvised Explosive
      Device (IEDs) Leaders' Forum', 2 – 4 September
      2015, Canberra, Australia, https://www.interpol.int/
      News-and-media/Events/2015/International-Counter-

Improvised-Explosive-Device-IEDs-Leaders%E2%80%99-Forum/
International-Counter-Improvised-Explosive-Device-IEDs-
Leaders%E2%80%99-Forum

102 The Universal Declaration of Human Rights, http://www.un.org/en/
universal-declaration-human-rights/

103 Al Jazeera, 'Al-Shabab storms beachside restaurant in Somali capital',
22 January 2016, http://www.aljazeera.com/news/2016/01/explosions-
hit-beach-restaurant-mogadishu-160121171649971.html

104 Médecins Sans Frontières, 'Nigeria: At least 24,000 displaced people
in dire health situation in Bama', 22 June 2016, https://web.archive.
org/web/20160623170020/http://www.msf.org/en/article/20160622-
nigeria-least-24000-displaced-people-dire-health-situation-bama

105 Frank Furedi, 'Heroes of the Hour', New Scientist, 8 May 2004, 19,
http://www.frankfuredi.com/pdf/NewScientist1.pdf

106 Anne Speckhard, 'Civil Society's Response to Mass Terrorism: Building
Resilience' in Combating Terrorism – Military and Non Military
Strategies, ed. Rohan Gunaratna (Singapore: Eastern Universities Press,
2005).

107 Arkady Ostrovsky, 'Russian Authorities Blame Chechens as Moscow
Subway Train Blast Kills 39', Financial Times, 7 February 2004, 6.

108 Anatoly Medetsky, 'Tbilisi: Russia was Warned of Attack', Moscow
Times, 10 February 2004.

109 Primo Levi, The Drowned and the Saved (New York: Simon and
Schuster, 2017), 25.

110 Martin Evans, 'Parents angered after pupils shoot "terrorist" targets
during visit to police firing range', Daily Telegraph, 26 June 2017,
https://www.telegraph.co.uk/news/2017/06/26/parents-angered-pupils-
shoot-terrorist-targets-visit-police/

111 AFP, 'British trio released after easyJet terror scare', 12 June 2017,
http://www.news.com.au/travel/travel-updates/incidents/british-trio-
released-after-easyjet-terror-scare/news-story/2c944ea4a8294c0b1e85
c45d52707022

112 Phoebe Cooke, 'RACE ATTACK Muslim student battered by three
strangers who called him a "suicide bomber" when he wished them
Merry Christmas', Sun, 28 December 2017, https://www.thesun.co.uk/
news/5223438/muslim-student-battered-strangers-suicide-bomber-
merry-christmas/

113 Guardian, 'The NSA files', accessed 15 June 2018, https://www.
theguardian.com/us-news/the-nsa-files

114 Ben Beaumont-Thomas, 'Ariana Grande: I had PTSD following
Manchester attack', Guardian, 5 June 2018, https://www.theguardian.
com/music/2018/jun/05/ariana-grande-ptsd-manchester-attack

115   Eyal Press, 'The Wounds of the Drone Warrior', *New York Times Magazine*, 13 June 2018, https://www.nytimes.com/2018/06/13/magazine/veterans-ptsd-drone-warrior-wounds.html

116   Netflix Origin, 'November 13 Attack on Paris', Series 1, Episode 2, 2018, https://www.netflix.com/gb/title/80190097

117   Richard Pendlebury, 'In one year at the height of the Afghan war, more British soldiers took their own lives than were killed by the Taliban. RICHARD PENDLEBURY, who spent weeks on the frontline, investigates why ARE so many of our heroes committing suicide?' *Daily Mail*, 9 February 2018, http://www.dailymail.co.uk/news/article-5373801/Why-British-soldiers-committing-suicide.html

118   Citizens Commission on Human Rights, 'The Hidden Enemy: Inside Psychiatry's Covert Agenda', accessed 15 June 2018, http://www.cchr.org/documentaries/the-hidden-enemy.html

16. Paradise Lost

1   https://www.bellingcat.com/news/mena/2017/05/24/types-islamic-state-drone-bombs-find/

2   http://www.koreatimes.co.kr/www/news/nation/2016/12/485_212627.html

3   Marc Sageman, (2008) *Leaderless Jihad – Terror Networks in the Twenty-First Century* (Philadelphia: University of Pennsylvania Press, 2008).

4   Unlike the remains of Shehzad Tanweer, one of the 7/7 London bombers, who was interred in a religious ceremony in Pakistan, or Salman Abedi who was buried in Libya.

5   http://www.muslimphilosophy.com/michot/ITA-Mardin-Conference.pdf

6   https://www.rferl.org/a/pakistan-clerics-fatwa-suicide-bombings-unislamic/28978125.html

7   Nic Robertson and Paul Cruickshank, 'New Jihad Code Threatens al Qaeda', CNN.com, 10 November 2009, http://www.cnn.com/2009/WORLD/africa/11/09/libya.jihadi.code/index.html

Acknowledgements

I am profoundly grateful to all those who shared their stories, their pain and their time with me. This book would not have been possible without your generosity.

While I have not intended this to be a purely academic book, I have tried to offer sources wherever possible. I hope that I interpreted such findings accurately and that it is accepted that a footnote is indicative of thanks and admiration for your work and insight. Where figures on suicide bombings are used without reference, the source is either the University of Chicago's Suicide Attack Database or Action on Armed Violence's Explosive Violence Monitor.

In particular, I am indebted to the following books: Robert Anthony Pape's *Dying to Win: The Strategic Logic of Suicide Terrorism*; Christoph Reuter's *My Life Is a Weapon: A Modern History of Suicide Bombing*; Diego Gambetta's *Making Sense of Suicide Missions*; and Jeffrey William Lewis's excellent *The Business of Martyrdom: A History of Suicide Bombing*. Without such guides, this book would have lost its way. Thank you.

More specifically, a small army of people has helped me in researching and writing the words contained herein. This includes Adam Lankford, Ahmet Dogan, Alex Lemons, Alexander Thurston, Aman Bezreh, Amy O'Brien, Anna Menon, Arthur de Liedekerke, Arun Arokianathan, Bailey Reed, Bhavita Rajguru, Chloé Benoist, Chris Hitchcock, Chris Woods, Christopher Carlin, Ekaterina Derbilova, Emily Mayhew, Franceska Azizi, Gil Kleiman, Grace Lavender, Guy Rhodes, Hugo Dobson, Hugo

Kaaman, Ian Rotsey, James Kearney, Jerome Joseph, Kamelia Kemileva, Katie Burness, Khalil Dewan, Kosyo Ivanov, Krishan Kuruppu, Leyla Slama, Liam Timmons, Lisa Shukov, Louise Ferreira, Maral Quttieneh, Matia Leite, Michael Cardash, Michael Hart, Mikey Nation, Millie Dessent, Muna Abdi, Muttukrishna Sarvananthan, Nadia Al Faour, Nathalie Versavel, Nic Marsh, Nicolas Coussiere, Nicole Yung Au, Noel Trew, Roberts Alhimionoks, Roger Davies, Samantha Pakor, Samuel Brownsword, Seaghan Di Bartolo, Shaza Alsalmoni, Shehryar Ali, Silvia Fiore, Sophie Akram, Susanna Kalaris, Tim Hulse, Tom Sayner, Tom Shore, Venesa Turjaku and Yiming 'Woody' Yu.

In particular, I would like to name Jacob Berntson, Hauke Waskewitz, Jennifer Dathan, Hannah Wallace and Beatrice Blythe for their specific help and assistance in the writing of this book. You have all gone far beyond the call of duty.

I would like to extend my thanks, too, to the board members of Action on Armed Violence – Olivia Dix, Professor Mike Spagat, Dr Marina Brilman, Colonel Steve Smith and Malcolm Rodgers – for their help and support in running the charity. I hope this book furthers our mission.

Thank you, too, Dr Paul Skinner and Professor Gavin Giovannoni, and all his team at the Barts and Royal London Hospital. I cannot stress my thanks enough.

Without Katy Follain at Quercus (who was also my editor on *Gun Baby Gun* at Canongate) or my agent Antony Topping at Greene & Heaton, this book would never have seen the light of day. Thank you both – and all those that support you – for putting your trust in me again and for being such friends. I am forever grateful for your presence in my life.

Finally, I want to thank those who know I love them more than words will ever do justice. Thank you for walking this road with me, for being there when there was darkness and when there was light. I know that I let this book come before anything else at times, but you always have my heart.